READING WRITING AND RHETORIC

REVISED EDITION

James Burl Hogins
Robert E. Yarber

San Diego Mesa College

SCIENCE RESEARCH ASSOCIATES, INC.

Chicago, Palo Alto, Toronto, Henley-on-Thames, Sydney

S R A

A Subsidiary of IBM

Acknowledgments

Reform or Revolution: Copyright 1970, John W. Gardner. Reprinted by permission of the author.

The Sexual Revolution: From an article by Arnold Toynbee in *Réalités,* February 1971. Reprinted by permission.

What Students Can Do for Peace: Reprinted by permission from *The Progressive,* June 1970. Copyright 1970, The Progressive, Inc.

A Modest Proposal: Reprinted by permission from *High Fidelity Magazine,* June 1970. Copyright 1970.

Good Usage, Bad Usage, and Usage: From *The American Heritage Dictionary of the English Language.* © Copyright 1969, 1970, 1971 by American Heritage Publishing Co., Inc. Reprinted by permission.

How to Say Nothing in Five Hundred Words: From UNDERSTANDING ENGLISH by Paul Roberts. Copyright © 1958 by Paul Roberts. Reprinted by permission of Harper and Row, Publishers, Inc.

The Freshman and His Dictionary: From an article by Mitford Mathews in *College Composition Communication,* December 1955. Copyright 1955 by the National Council of Teachers of English. Reprinted by permission of the publisher and Mitford M. Mathews.

But What's a Dictionary For?: Reprinted by permission of the author from *The Atlantic Monthly,* May 1962. Copyright © 1962, The Atlantic Monthly Company, Boston.

Logic and Logical Fallacies: Reprinted by permission of the author from *Handbook for English A.* Copyright © 1941 by the President and Fellows of Harvard University.

Are All Generalizations False?: From *The Art of Making Sense* by Lionel Ruby. Reprinted by permission of the publisher, J. B. Lippincott Company. Copyright 1968.

The Language of White Racism: From an article by Haig Bosmajian in *College English,* December 1969. Copyright © 1969 by the National Council of Teachers of English. Reprinted by permission of the publisher and Haig Bosmajian.

Nix: A Review of *Nixon Agonistes.* Reprinted with permission from *The New York Review of Books.* Copyright © 1971 NY REV, Inc.

To Branch Manager of Bank of America: From *Additional Dialogue, Letters of Dalton Trumbo, 1942–1962.* Copyright 1970 by Dalton Trumbo. Reprinted by permission.

A Visit to America: From *Quite Early One Morning* by Dylan Thomas. Copyright 1954 by New Directions Publishing Corporation. Reprinted by permission of New Directions Publishing Corporation and J. M. Dent and Sons Ltd.

Sharing the Wealth: Originally appeared in PLAYBOY magazine; copyright © 1969 by Playboy. Reprinted by permission of the author and publisher.

Americanism: Reprinted by permission of the author from *A Piece of My Mind* by Edmund Wilson (Farrar, Straus, and Cudahy Company). Copyright © 1956 by Edmund Wilson.

I'd Rather Be Black Than Female: Reprinted by permission of the author from *McCall's,* August 1970. Copyright 1970 by Shirley Chisholm.

Unliberated, but Born Free: Copyright 1970, *Los Angeles Times.* Reprinted by permission.

A Generation in Search of a Future: Reprinted by permission of the author from the *Boston Globe,* March 8, 1969. Copyright 1969 by George Wald.

What to Listen for in Music: Reprinted by permission of McGraw-Hill Book Company from *What to Listen for in Music*, revised edition, by Aaron Copland. Copyright © 1957, McGraw-Hill, Inc.

Conjurer's Art: From *Four Screenplays of Ingmar Bergman*, published by Simon and Schuster, Inc., and Janus Films. Copyright 1960 by Ingmar Bergman. Reprinted by permission of Simon and Schuster, Inc., and Lorrimer Publishing Ltd.

Story and Script: Reprinted by permission of Grove Press, Inc., from *Last Year at Marienbad* by Alain Robbe-Grillet, translated by Richard Howard. Copyright © 1962 by Grove Press, Inc. Published in Great Britain and the British Commonwealth by Calder and Boyars Ltd., London.

Image: From *The World of Film: Michelangelo Antonioni* by Pierre Leprohon. English translation © 1963 by Simon and Schuster, Inc. Reprinted by permission of Simon and Schuster, Inc., and Editions Seghers.

How to Tell Good Guys from Bad Guys: Copyright 1955 by John Steinbeck. Reprinted by permission of McIntosh and Otis, Inc., from *The Reporter*, March 10, 1955.

What Do We Do About Television?: From an article by Nicholas Johnson in *The Saturday Review*, July 11, 1970. Copyright 1970, Saturday Review, Inc. Reprinted by permission of the author and publisher.

Student Illiteracy: Reprinted by permission of the author from *Library Journal*, February 1970. Copyright 1970 by Karl Shapiro.

The Private World of the Man with the Book: Reprinted by permission of the author from *The Saturday Review*, January 7, 1961. Copyright © 1961, Saturday Review, Inc.

. . . an ulcer, gentlemen, is an unwritten poem: First published in *Canadian Business*, 1956. Reprinted by permission of the author.

Why Do We Read Fiction?: Reprinted by permission of the William Morris Agency, Inc., from *The Saturday Evening Post*, October 20, 1962. Copyright 1962 by Robert Penn Warren.

The Polynesian: Reprinted by permission of Houghton Mifflin Company and Victor Gollancz Ltd. from *The Blue of Capricorn* by Eugene Burdick. Copyright 1961 by Eugene L. Burdick.

Once More to the Lake: From *One Man's Meat* by E. B. White. Copyright 1941 by E. B. White. Reprinted by permission of Harper and Row, Publishers, Inc.

Market Day: From MORNINGS IN MEXICO, by D. H. Lawrence. Copyright 1927 and renewed 1955 by Frieda Lawrence Ravagli. Reprinted by permission of Alfred A. Knopf, Inc., Laurence Pollinger Ltd., and the estate of the late Mrs. Frieda Lawrence.

That Day at Hiroshima: Reprinted by permission of Russell & Volkening, Inc., from *Human Relations In A Changing World* by Alexander H. Leighton. Copyright 1949 by Alexander Leighton.

Contents

INTRODUCTION   THE SEVENTIES: REFORM OR REVOLUTION?

Peace, unrest, credibility gaps, demonstrations, alternative life-styles, hard hats, love, welfare, politics, war, law and order, technology, pollution, ecology, modules, rivers, roads, cars, railroads, values, youth, language, news management, surveillance, foreign relations, human rights, drug abuse, controls, plight of cities, taxation, unemployment, genetic management — and the list goes on. That's what the Seventies are about.

1 THE FRESHMAN AND HIS LANGUAGE

Pity the poor student; he is expected to possess a comprehensive knowledge of all aspects of his native tongue — from the language of racism to the criteria for good usage — before he comes to school. When he arrives, clothed in ignorance, he finds his teachers far from unified on how they regard the field of English. Should courses be altered to fit various backgrounds? Is a scholarly approach to writing the only appropriate one? Will transformational grammar save our schools? Since English is a required course, the student must face the challenge. The selections in the following section may do something to help.

Advice to the Freshman

The Freshman and His Dictionary

Language and Logic

Popular Forms

2 THE AMERICAN SCENE

The American Scene is 200 million different views with some common denominators: some things make us proud, some things make us ashamed. Inevitably, there is no unanimity about what events fall into which categories. There are astronauts on the moon and rats in slum beds. We have little respect for people without a job but a national policy that regards an unemployment rate of at least four percent as "acceptable." College students are demanding, and sometimes receiving, new freedoms—at the cost of administrative ulcers and taxpayer unrest.

Sometimes the problems seem so insurmountable—or insupportable—that the possible opportunities are in danger of being overlooked. We have a land with a ready reserve of raw materials, surrounded by two beautiful oceans and nourished by still salvageable rivers. Add to these factors an ingenious people who often can be both generous and loving. With these ingredients and a common purpose, how can we fail to build a greater nation?

Modern Times and People

The Feminist Movement: Two Views

Youth

The Hero

The Racial Revolution

3 PERSONAL VALUES

Personal values are always being aired (or at least exposed in public), which may be what makes them so difficult to hang on to. There seems to be a resurgence of emphasis on the value system of the individual these days—even when it conflicts with the value system represented by authority. One supposes that Thoreau would be pleased. A single question though: if your conscience and my conscience say different things, who decides which is right?

4 THE VOICES OF SCIENCE

Science was once considered the major hope for the salvation of the human race. Science, with its offspring technology, would give us comforts, health, knowledge, control of the universe. That hope has been dissipating for some time, but only recently have we begun to be aware of the dangerous side effects of our naïve faith. What can possibly save us from our present dilemmas? Is more science our only hope?

Overview

Speculations

5 THE ANTIC MUSE

Ogden Nash once said that it is hard to do anything of significance if you realize how funny you may look doing it. The Greeks considered comedy a lower form than tragedy. On the other hand, a well-worn adage calls laughter the best medicine. And recent research indicates that humor—judiciously applied—is the best therapy for suicidal depression.

Among man's distinguishing characteristics is the fact that he is the only animal that laughs. Is what makes him laugh these days so much different from days past? And why has the youth movement of the last several years been so peculiarly devoid of humor?

Some Examples of Humor

Some Analyses of Humor

6 RELIGION AND PHILOSOPHY: DIVERSE VIEWS

When personal values are organized and institutionalized as an expression of group values, they become philosophy and religion. Obviously, then, our philosophy and religion have changed over the years to accommodate changes in our circumstances. Whether these changes have been for the better is often hotly debated. Those who hold that this country is in a state of moral collapse may take comfort in the fact that some observers of the current scene believe things

have gone full circle. In their own instinctive groping for something
to hang on to, young people are rediscovering faith.

The Philosopher Speaks

Man and God

7 THE LIVELY ARTS

What is entertainment for some is a business for others, and it's hard to
know which group takes it more seriously. Some of the selections in
this section are written by people who are in communications and entertainment, telling you—the audience—about the problems and
pleasures of their work. Other selections deal with audience response.

You have doubtlessly had difficulty in enjoying music before being
told how to enjoy it. And you've probably refrained from expressing
opinions on films or television programs before you learned the proper
criteria for judging them. Now, with the aid of several selections presented here, you can forge ahead! (If, on the other hand, you have
been guilty of the solecism of striking out on your own, you may have
fun checking your scoring system against the experts'.)

Critical Awareness

Painting and Music

Film and Television

Literature

8 OTHER PEOPLES, OTHER PLACES

We are all "other people" to someone else. Where we live is "another place" to them. Since an ultimate objective of all people is self-enlightenment, we pursue knowledge of other peoples and other places, hoping to discover ourselves. Whether we share the horror experienced by an entire city or the childhood memories of one man, seek an island paradise or walk in the confusion of the city, we are in a profound way looking not at others, but in a mirror, at ourselves.

Preface

Our basic aims for the revised edition of *Reading, Writing, and Rhetoric* have not changed from those for the original edition published in 1967: to provide, for the instructor, teachable essays that can be used as the basis for classroom discussion and writing assignments; and to provide, for the student, all the help we can to make learning easier and more rewarding.

The text is divided into nine parts — an Introduction and eight sections — each dealing with one of the major concerns of the early 1970s. (In this edition, we purposefully avoided an abundance of journalistic selections in favor of more substantive ones.) Each essay is preceded by a brief headnote and is followed by questions on theme, questions on rhetoric, writing assignments, library-exploration suggestions, and definitions of difficult words. In the back of the book, we have provided a Glossary of Rhetorical Terms and a Guide to Rhetoric. The Guide cites several paragraphs in which a given principle is illustrated.

The Instructor's Guide contains a Rhetorical Table of Contents, additional questions and suggested writing assignments for each essay, and a series of objective tests written by professional test writers. The items in the tests cover both theme and rhetoric. Answers are provided at the back of the guide.

Our greatest thanks is to the tens of thousands of students who have used our materials and the many hundreds of instructors who have taught them. But special thanks must also be given to the staff of SRA, especially Mike Crisp, Dick Carter, Judy Olson, Jim Budd, and Sara Boyd.

James Burl Hogins
Robert E. Yarber

THE SEVENTIES: REFORM OR REVOLUTION?

INTRODUCTION

John Gardner (1912–) was Secretary of Health, Education and Welfare in the administration of President Lyndon B. Johnson, and past chairman of The Urban Coalition. He is presently chairman of Common Cause, a "people's lobby." He was born in Los Angeles, and received his bachelor's and master's degrees from Stanford University and his doctorate from the University of California. Among his many publications are "No Easy Victories" (1968) and "To Turn the Tide" (1968).

In the following article Gardner says that everyone must share the blame for the conflicts currently rending our society. Expressing particular concern for the universities, he probes the nature of the threat to their survival and suggests ways we can help them remain viable.

JOHN W. GARDNER

Reform or Revolution?

1 In these times it is hard to keep renewing hope, to keep saying you are confident in our system and our institutions. I *do* have hope and I think there are grounds for it. But I would not be honest with you if I did not admit that these are days of anxiety and conflict for our nation at large and for our institutions of higher learning.

2 And I want to begin with the simplest possible question: "Where have we failed?"

3 We are great blamers, great villain hunters — indeed villain-inventors — and each of us has some special group on whom we place the blame

for our troubles. But the blame must be widely distributed. All of us are somehow implicated. Let me remind you of some who must share the burden of guilt.

4   There are the chiselers, big time and small, who spread the disease of corruption through every level of this society. They cheat on their taxes, they engage in questionable business practices, they make a mockery of professional ethics, they lie to the consumer, they deliver a sloppy job and overcharge for it.

5   There are the men and women who do not really believe in the values that we as Americans have committed ourselves to, the men and women who do not believe in equality of opportunity, who do not believe in the dignity of the individual, who do not believe in liberty for all.

6   There are the extremists, right wing and left wing, with their promise of salvation through violence and coercion. They disguise themselves as saviors, but there is a satanic gleam in their eyes. They believe that hatred will cure and that violence will pave the way to a better world. They do not understand that in her hour of agony, America needs physicians, not executioners.

7   There are the people of power and influence who could play a significant role in redesigning our institutions but will not do so. Congressional reform is consistently blocked by the powerful committee chairmen. Effective pollution control legislation is skillfully emasculated by powerful industrial polluters. University reform has for years been blocked by the most influential faculty members. Tax reform has died a thousand deaths at the hands of vested interests. Union leaders have often slowed the progress of equal job opportunity.

8   Last but, believe me, not least, I would list the "average citizens" who fatten on the yield of this prosperous society but will not turn a hand or make a sacrifice or risk discomfort to help solve its problems. They are earning higher wages or salaries than ever before, buying more consumer goods, enjoying longer and more elaborate vacations —yet they vote down school bond issues, neglect elementary civic duties, allow their local government to fall into disrepair, nurse their prejudices, and complain. And grow fatter. They are angry at the way things are going, but they will not help to make them go better. Their apathy is the heaviest burden that this free society must carry.

9   So the nation moves through a time of supreme danger, her passage made more hazardous by chiselers, by bigots, by extremists, by vested interest, and by the paralyzing lassitude of well-fed citizens.

10   Edmund Burke said, "The effect of liberty to individuals is that they may do what they please. We ought to see what it will please them to do before we risk congratulations."

11   What will it please free America to do now? Is there a reservoir of devoted citizens yet unheard from, ready to do their duty when they see the path of duty? It remains to be seen.

12   I find many Americans sincerely confused as to where duty lies. Some are confused, I'm bound to say, because they're too lazy to think hard about the problem. Others are confused by the swirl and clash of emotion. And many are confused by the storm of words, slogans, and battle cries.

13   I would remind such Americans that there is a well-tested way out of the dizzying atmosphere of talk and emotion, and that is to put one foot doggedly after another in some concrete, practical activity. And the concrete, practical tasks are there. There *is* an agenda.

14   That agenda begins with peace. The agenda calls for an end to discrimination. It calls for a relentless attack on poverty. It calls for major reforms in taxation and allocation of resources among federal, state, and local levels. It calls for an end to our shameful tolerance of corruption and decay in state and local government. It calls for new solutions in housing, employment, education, health, law enforcement, and the administration of justice.

15   If your proposed solutions are not the same as mine, that is understandable. But if you think that these are someone else's problems, not yours, or if you think they will be solved with the methods of 50 years ago, or if you think that rhetoric will advance them toward solution, then we part company. And if you complain about the state of the world, but aren't at work on some piece of the agenda, then you are part of the problem.

16   But serious Americans who are working night and day on that agenda have a new fear. It is the fear that before we have time to make much further progress, we will tear each other apart—and in the process tear our society apart.

17   If we are to prevent that outcome, we shall have to think hard about some trends of the moment.

18   First, the swift rise of violence and coercion as instruments of social action. I know all the subtle defenses of violence. But I know even better the stark consequences. Violence evokes—I would even say *seeks*—a violent answer. Coercion invites countercoercion. The student with an inclination toward violent or coercive action and the policeman with a taste for brutality are waiting for each other. The politician with a fondness for repressive measures and the ghetto leader with a leaning toward violence are waiting for each other—and eventually they find each other. Each reacting to the other, they escalate first the tensions and then the overt acts, and draw increasing numbers of moderates into the deadly interplay. Thus do they weave their own shrouds and ours too.

19   The consequences run deeper than momentary disorder, and there is no better place to observe those deeper consequences than the campuses of this country. The drop in the quality of discourse has been catastrophic. For the first time in my experience there is fear on the campuses. And on those campuses most seriously afflicted, the community is riven by deep internal lines of conflict. There is an intolerance and a shortening of tempers. Old enmities burn more brightly. Sowers of discord find the soil incomparably fertile. As Malcolm Cowley said of another time and place: "Friendships were broken off. People could no longer endure the little hypocrisies that kept their relations stable; they had to set everything straight, like a man preparing for death."

20   A man preparing for death—or a community preparing for dissolution. A year ago a young acquaintance of mine confidently said, "The universities can be destroyed," and I laughed at him. I laugh no longer.

21   But if the universities are to be saved, they will have to do it themselves. Interventions by the Federal government or state governments are counter-productive and potentially dangerous.

22   It is not just internal conflict that is shaking every great university to the center of its being. There is an erosion of authority in all institutions throughout the world. And this poses exceedingly difficult questions for a free society. A free people, having thrown off the tyranny of raw power, must create and honor its own structure of authority. If it ceases to do so then it moves back toward the only alternative — government by force.

23   Those who derive their authority from the institutions of a free society — professors, for example — have seen their position seriously undermined in recent years. In a time when authority, even the consensual and custom-based authority of a free society is scorned, the teacher-student and master-apprentice relationships are weakened at the core. The role of learner becomes one of distasteful subordination.

24   But when we reject apprenticeship, when we scorn the learner's role, we demolish the path that leads on to craftsmanship and mastery. And then we discover that the most intransigent tyrant of all is hard reality. You can't vote yourself into the company of great heart surgeons or concert pianists.

25   Any society, even a primitive one, is a complex pattern of interlocking roles. To wash out the differentiation of roles makes the total performance impossible. The male dancer who catches the ballerina must not demand that she in turn catch him.

26   Professors should strive to understand the needs of students, but they should not forsake their own role nor for one moment doubt its validity. With respect to the subject at hand, there is an inequality that can only be altered through the hard process of learning.

27   When prolonged and savage attacks are made on those who derive their authority from the institutions of a free society, they begin to doubt their own legitimacy — and they show it. But as they increase their permissiveness, their opponents become increasingly restive and sensitive, so that even the permissiveness seems arrogant.

28   All of which moves inexorably toward the "freedom" of the alley brawl, not toward the confident self-discipline of a free people engaged in the hard, serious business of self-government.

29   The truth is that we have been so busy making each generation of Americans more free that we haven't reminded ourselves of the requirements of freedom. Every step toward the removal of arbitrary constraints on individual behavior must be accompanied by increments in self-imposed discipline. Self-discipline is the free man's yoke.

30   The universities have not, on the whole, been receiving the loving nurture that they need very much at this perilous moment in their history, and I count myself as guilty as others on that score. Faculty members have too often regarded the universities as little more than convenient stepping stones or bases in an active career. Students have too often treated the university as a scapegoat for the problems of the society, as an available target for the anger that is in them. People

interested in solving social problems, such as myself, have urged the universities to run in all directions at once to cope with the issues of the day.

31   I think it is time for all of us to rededicate ourselves to the preservation of our great universities. They are vital embodiments of our civilization and vital resources for our future. And like all human institutions, they will not remain vital without loving nurture.

32   Loving nurture includes criticism. The universities must look forward to a decade of vigorous internal reform. But both the criticism and the reform can be accomplished without the savage and destructive conflict that is raging in our best institutions today.

Discussion of Theme

1. Who are the five groups Gardner blames for our nation's present troubles? Do you belong to any of them? What specific organizations or individuals can you name as members of these groups?
2. According to the author, what is "the heaviest burden this free society must carry"? What is the place of the Silent Majority in this relationship?
3. Why are most people reluctant to "get involved" in solving our nation's problems, according to Gardner? Can you think of specific events and conditions in our society that have contributed to this indifference?
4. What does Gardner recommend as an alternative to inaction and indifference? List the items that he has placed on his "agenda." Has he omitted any that you would like to include?

Discussion of Rhetoric

1. Find instances within this essay in which the author uses classification as an organizational device. Note, for example, paragraphs 4–8.
2. Another technique Gardner employs to give his thoughts and paragraphs coherence is the skillful use of transitional phrases and connectives: words like *however, and, first,* and *so.* Find several such examples and show how each helps the reader follow the thought more easily.
3. What is the function of the anecdote in paragraph 20? Why is the paragraph so brief?
4. Explain the reference to the dancers in paragraph 25. How does it contribute to his overall thesis?
5. In general, how would you describe the tone of Gardner's essay? For example, is he hysterical, wry, ironic, or calmly objective?

Writing Assignments

1. Select one of the items on Gardner's "agenda" and present a practical program for achieving it.

2. Gardner presents, in paragraphs 4-8, "some who must share the burden of guilt" for our nation's troubles. Select one of these groups and show, using specific facts and evidence, how it has contributed to the difficulties our society faces. Be careful to avoid vague charges and platitudes.
3. Gardner suggests that the universities need internal reform. In a theme, present your own proposals for the reform of higher education in our country. Be specific—and offer criticism and suggestions based on solid evidence and reasoning.
4. What has contributed to the erosion of authority throughout the world? Present your views in terms of specific institutions and issues.

Library Exploration

1. Gardner's Common Cause is a new sort of lobby: a "people's lobby," according to its members. Find out what you can about it and determine whether or not it represents you.
2. Many social critics claim that in some ways German society in the days immediately preceding Hitler's rise to power resembles society in the United States today. Investigate this claim and determine its accuracy.
3. Find out how "effective pollution-control legislation is skillfully emasculated by powerful industrial polluters." If possible, determine how this applies to your own state.

Vocabulary

(7) EMASCULATED weakened

(9) LASSITUDE weariness

(18) OVERT open; unconcealed

(24) INTRANSIGENT uncompromising; stubborn

(26) VALIDITY soundness (as of arguments, conclusions)

(28) INEXORABLY inevitably

(29) INCREMENTS additions or increases

(31) EMBODIMENTS concrete examples of certain traits

(31) NURTURE nourishment

Arnold Toynbee (1889–   ), the English historian, is best known for his monumental "A Study of History." The author of works on Greek history and civilization, he has had a varied career: delegate to the Paris Peace Conference in 1919; professor of modern Greek language, literature, and history at the University of London; and professor of international history at the same institution for many years until his retirement.

Taking his evidence from the pages of history, Toynbee argues that the present movement toward greater sexual freedom in this country carries with it serious potential problems. The answer, he suggests, is to codify relations between the sexes—to impose certain regulations on our sexual lives.

ARNOLD TOYNBEE

The Sexual Revolution

1   It is nothing new for sexuality to be one of our central preoccupations. Throughout the history of humanity, the very ambiguity of human nature has made the problem of sexuality extremely difficult to solve. On the one hand we are subject to sexual impulses and drives like all animals, and on the other, our life has a certain spiritual side to it and the requirements of this are incompatible with a pure and simple abandonment to our instincts. The tension created by these two aspects of our nature is all the greater because our sexual life is not regulated naturally, as it is with the majority of mammals. In their case, the female is sexually active only during certain definite periods, while the human female is constantly active. This is another reason

why human beings will always be obliged to regulate their sexual life as well as they can.

2   It seems to me that experience has shown that both man and woman suffer unhappiness where relationships between the sexes are not regulated. This regulation can take very different forms, such as monogamous, polygamous or polyandrous marriage. The essential element in all cases is that there should be some regulation — necessary not only for adults but also and especially for children. It is well-known that one of the causes of the disorderly behavior of a large section of the young of today is the atmosphere of insecurity in which they have grown up because of discord between their parents. Psychologically speaking, this can have devastating repercussions and children run the risk of feeling its traumatic effects throughout their lives. This is why all human societies have felt the necessity to codify relations between the sexes. Since our instincts are very strong, however, the rules have never been very closely followed, and a great deal of hypocrisy has been the result. It is never possible to judge the real circumstances of sexual relations on the basis of official standards of behaviour; one must always try to see what happens in reality.

3   In the 19th century, for instance, official sexual morality was very strict in Anglo-Saxon countries and in France, though to a lesser degree. In practice, however, the official code was frequently flouted and the contradiction between theory and practice finally became very demoralizing. From this point of view, I believe that the present movement in favour of a greater liberty in sexual behaviour is, at least partly, a healthy reaction against Victorian hypocrisy. What the young people of today are saying, in effect, is this: "Our predecessors were no better than us, but pretended to be so. We don't pretend anything; we do openly what they did secretly."

4   But there is a negative side to this revolt. It isn't only hypocrisy which is rejected but, ultimately, all regulation of our sexual life. I even think that the revolt against hypocrisy can become the excuse for a revolt against any type of regulation demanding self-control. And if we abandon all regulation, to all intents and purposes we cease to be human beings, without, however, becoming innocent animals again. Instead, we become monsters, neither totally man nor beast. Another deplorable effect is that any excess in one direction inevitably ends by sparking off a reaction in the other. Thinking of historical precedents to the present situation, two in British history spring immediately to mind: the Restoration of Charles II, when the extreme moral freedom of the time was a reaction against the Puritan dictatorship of Cromwell; and the moral laxity of the Regency period (George IV) which explains the Victorian reaction that followed.

5   If we look outside English history, it is difficult to avoid a comparison with the time of the Roman Empire. One only has to read the Epistles of St. Paul and to see the difficulties he had with people newly converted to the Jewish faith, notably at Corinth, to gain some idea of the sexual liberty which existed in the Greco-Roman world at the beginning of the Christian era. St. Paul had before him the Jewish ideal of stability in marriage and, on this point, I admire the Jews greatly. I think that their very strong sense of family, their concern for their

children, almost sacrificial in spirit, is one of the reasons for their success, not only under the Roman Empire but also more recently.

6   Christianity, however, has gone much further than Judaism towards an essentially unnatural asceticism. Because of the sexual license which was current among the early converts to Christianity, purity in sexual morality has been heavily emphasized, causing Christianity to confuse morality with sexual morality. Consequently, there was a tendency to think that if sexual behaviour conformed to accepted norms everything was well, although it was possible to act very badly in other matters. There are many aspects of good and evil which are not connected with sexuality.

7   The comparison with the Roman Empire also holds good in that great sexual freedom is a sign of decadence in any society or civilization. The Romans of the 3rd century B.C. and the Greeks of the 5th century B.C. were much more virtuous than the contemporaries of St. Paul. The Christian reaction went together with the breaking up of the proletariat within the Empire, which fostered the barbarian invasions. In fact, these invasions were the most visible signs of the fall of the Roman Empire but not the most important. The essential phenomenon was, if I dare say it, the invasion "from below," by which the upper classes were submerged by new social strata. The barbarian invasions were facilitated by this phenomenon, and at the same time made the phenomenon itself more possible. There was a coming together of an internal proletariat and an external proletariat.

8   Similarily, the Victorian reaction against the profligacy of the Regency goes together with the acquisition of political and economic power by a new middle class, industrious, acutely businesslike, and very much attached to the Puritan traditions as far as its private life was concerned. When that class became rich and powerful, it retained its Puritan facade but secretly began to betray the severe ideals which it professed.

9   I feel that the present movement towards greater sexual freedom marks the end of bourgeois liberal society, though it is difficult to see who stands to gain from this. In this context, the case of the United States is instructive. The hippies, whose sexual freedom is well known, are for the most part from families who have been well-off for more than one generation. And the people who detest them more than anyone are the blue-collar workers, the upper class of industrial workers who have just acquired a certain degree of comfort in life. In fact, the American working class is now divided into two quite distinct categories: a stratum of very poor people, like the blacks and the poor whites of the South, and a stratum of workers who have reached the level of the lower middle class. This latter is reasonably comfortable and has no wish at all to see "the American way of life" called into question when it has only just started to enjoy its benefits. Vice-President Agnew, the son of a poor Greek immigrant, seems to me to be very representative of this new rising class. It seems to me, too, that the wish for "law and order" could lead to a fascist-type reaction, very tough and very intolerant, which would concern itself as much with morals and private life as with politics.

10   In Great Britain, the success of Enoch Powell, the racialist leader

who is campaigning against the immigration of coloured people, is explicable by a similar phenomenon. A whole section of the working class does not want to see threatened the comforts and privileges which work and the struggles of the unions have allowed it to acquire.

11   The situation in France is comparable but hard to judge, because of the importance of the Communist Party. From the events of 1968, however, it would seem as though there, too, the workers reject coop- eration with hippie protesters or left-wing students. Whether in its communist or fascist version, the reaction of the new lower middle class against the "permissive society" has a good chance of being in- tolerant and anti-intellectual. Indeed, insofar as one can discern the lower middle class of the future in a section of today's working class, I think that fascism presents more of a threat than communism. The Nazi movement in Germany, after all, was the expression of a sort of social revolution. It brought to power people whose existence had been largely ignored by the ruling classes.

12   If the present increase in sexual freedom marks the decadence of a certain period of bourgeois liberal society, it also marks the beginning of a post-Christian era. Christian dogma and belief have ceased to be real for a majority of our contemporaries. This is really a revolution, since Christian dogma and the moral code which goes with it have constituted the framework of our lives since the 4th century in the West and since the 11th in Russia. I should also add that this frame- work was obscurantist, too rigid and badly balanced; it placed exces- sive importance on sexual repression which consequently led to hypocrisy. It is impossible, however, to reject this framework with impunity, without leaving the impression of a void. I feel this myself, because I do not share the Christian belief and yet I do not know how to replace it.

13   Plutarch tells us that, in the 1st century A.D., whenever a boat anchored at a port in Greece, the sailors heard the spirits of the gods cry: "Great Pan is dead!" It seems that great Pan has been revived today . . . for a short while, at least. But that is not the end of the story. I can see in this provisional resurrection of Pan, and also of Dionysius, a revolt, a protest against a daily life which is increasingly regulated by the demands of technology. This movement is similar to the wildcat strikes in industry, which are a more or less unconscious protest against the monotony of a mechanized and standardized job. This same standardization is spreading throughout our daily life at present. But at this point we find ourselves caught in a cleft stick: on the one hand, we complain about becoming slaves to technology; on the other, we can no longer conceive of a life without the comfort which technology allows us to enjoy.

14   Even in antiquity, the worship of Dionysius, with its orgies and sexual excesses, was an outlet for the surplus vital energy of the human being. Today sex has become a symbol of freedom, of a return to nature in an industrial society. While self-awareness separates man from the rest of the world, sex, which is beyond the control of his will, reunites him with the universe. It is now used as the excuse for pan- theist outpourings or as a way of returning to nature: man thus feels

united with the whole of the animal world and all the unknown life forces of the universe.

15   This is probably the best place to make a distinction between eroticism and pornography. Eroticism is the effort to reach, by way of sex, something which lies beyond sex: nature, beauty, or communion with the universe. Pornography is concerned entirely with sex and inflates its importance, thus making it a simple trick to stimulate orgasm. While eroticism retains a certain element of spontaneity, pornography is calculated stimulation. I feel it remains an open question, however, whether it is to eroticism, as I understand it, that we are returning today. As soon as one completely divorces the sexual act from procreation, is it really possible to speak of a return to nature? Does the sexual act, complete in itself and cut off from everything else, including procreation, amount to anything more, finally, than drinking a good wine or eating caviar?

16   It is clear, too, that scientific progress encourages this dissociation between the sexual act and procreation which is linked to the emancipation of women. The pill, for example, allows women to make love with the same impunity as men, and the results of this transformation can be read on the faces of girls today. They have become much tougher in their relations with men, and their behaviour reminds one of that of young men in the past with women. If a concept like virginity has lost its value today, it is because women have now become the equals of men. Virginity has been glorified by Christianity, because women were freely considered as superior beings in the Greco-Roman world. The Christian virgin, however, was considered the equal of man and not just as the instrument of his pleasure. But it was only when a woman remained unmarried that this equality was possible, and this situation lasted for a long time. At the end of the last century, when the movement for the emancipation of women got under way in Great Britain, the principals of the women's colleges of English universities were currently heard to say of their pupils, "She had a lot of promise and she could have been an outstanding doctor . . . and then she went and got married." It was as if they had said, "And then she died young." Today neither marriage, nor — with or without marriage — the sexual act means that the woman loses her position of equality with the man.

17   Scientifically speaking, it is not at all impossible that pregnancies will soon be extrauterine and that children will grow in test tubes. We shall thus have reached Aldous Huxley's *Brave New World*. It is even conceivable that scientific and social evolution will be such that it will no longer be economically or socially acceptable for a woman to become pregnant. Midwives will disappear like a species which has become extinct. If we add the possibilities of artificial insemination, it should ultimately be possible to manufacture children at will, without recognized parents, under the pretext of improving the human species.

18   But what will such children be? Will they not be worse off than an orphan, because an orphan does at least know that he has had parents? There are already problems with adopted children, when they have to be told the truth. But I think that if there were no parents at

all, the effect would be terrifying: no roots, no personal ancestry, no successors. Even now, in the United States, the blacks suffer from not knowing from which region in Africa they have come, from feeling cut off from a historical background, and from the fact that many of them, because of their extreme promiscuity, have no real father, since their mother has had children by several men. The psychological results are disastrous.

19 Without going to the extreme of the test-tube baby, there is a risk that women's emancipation will go together with a certain masculinization. This will be to the detriment of the children, since the maternal instinct may atrophy or be repressed. I know the case of two women who have brilliant careers, get on very well with their husbands and apparently give their children a lot of attention. Yet the children have suffered because their mother has not been sufficiently available psychologically and they have not remained at the centre of her preoccupations. However, I do not believe that the maternal instinct can be suppressed completely by any scientific progress. I do, however, think that it can be twisted or repressed and that this could cause considerable frustration in women, because it is, after all, a very deeply-felt instinct.

20 In man there are certain innate feelings which progress cannot suppress. Take, for example, the sense of sin and the feeling of guilt. Today's sexual freedom does not do away with the sense of sin altogether, but causes it rather to turn in another direction. The hippies, for example, have a guilt complex about the war in Vietnam, the colour problem and the pollution of nature. In the same way, I think asceticism is perhaps reappearing in America, with regard not to sex but to money: students are deliberately refusing to go into business, rejecting the attractive propositions of the biggest firms, and opting for more humanitarian careers, such as medicine.

21 There were still people who poked fun at the ascetic tendencies of Christianity in the 2nd century A.D. Two centuries later, however, the anchorites in the desert had become famous and their names were as well-known as those of the great courtesans and the champions of the chariot races. In Syria, Simeon Stylites and his followers, who remained perched on their columns for years, attracted crowds of pilgrims and caused a whole tourist industry to come into being. We have not reached this point. We have our stars in films, in pop music, and in sport; the champions of asceticism have yet to come. But come they will. The late Padre Pio, the priest of the village of San Giovanni Rotondo in southern Italy, was perhaps their precursor. And since history is made so much more quickly in our time because of rapid communications, I do not think we will have to wait two centuries for this reversal in morality.

Discussion of Theme

1. According to Toynbee, why is the regulation of human sexual life difficult? Is it a desirable goal? Do you agree?

2. It has often been remarked that our society is hypocritical in its attitude toward sex and morals. If you agree, what explanation can you give? What examples can you cite to support such a view?
3. What does Toynbee regard as the positive aspects of today's sexual revolt? What are its negative effects?
4. The author states that today's young people have a "sense of sin and . . . feeling of guilt" about sexual matters. Do you agree?

Discussion of Rhetoric

1. What is the underlying organization pattern to this essay? Why is it effective?
2. Comment on the author's diction. Is it appropriate?
3. Toynbee uses transitional devices to hold his essay together. Note, for example, *for instance* (paragraph 3), *But* (paragraph 4), *however* (paragraph 6), *Similarly* (paragraph 8). Find several other such examples. How does using these terms make the reader's task easier?

Writing Assignments

1. Do you think the moral standards of today's college students are lower than those of the previous generation? Present your views in a theme.
2. What is your attitude toward the women's liberation movement?
3. Defend (or attack) monogamy as a desirable practice or custom.
4. Can a woman successfully combine motherhood with a career? Will her children suffer?

Library Exploration

1. For a light-hearted treatment of contemporary morals, read Morton Hunt's *The Affair*.
2. In what ways has the Puritan legacy survived in this country?

Vocabulary

(1) AMBIGUITY   confusion; doubt; two or more possible meanings

(2) MONOGAMOUS   being married to one person at a time

(2) POLYGAMOUS   having more than one wife at a time

(2) POLYANDROUS   having more than one husband at a time

(2) TRAUMATIC   physically or behaviorally disordered because of shock

(7) DECADENCE   decline; decay

(8) PROFLIGACY   corruption, particularly moral

(10) EXPLICABLE   capable of explanation

A United States senator from Arkansas since 1945, William Fulbright (1905–   ) has become an eloquent spokesman for those Americans – particularly the young – who clamor for a reordering of our national priorities. Chairman of the Senate Committee on Foreign Relations, Fulbright has earned degrees from the University of Arkansas, Oxford University, and George Washington University.

Addressing himself to youthful protesters, Senator Fulbright advocates dissent based not on violence but on strategy. He warns that repressive countermeasures directed against violent demonstrations can only endanger democracy.

SENATOR J. W. FULBRIGHT

What Students Can Do for Peace

1 It takes extraordinary restraint to contain anger and prevent violence at a time when so many young people are angry and disillusioned with a Government which appears to have turned its back on them, a Government in which prominent figures have shown themselves coldly unresponsive to the wishes and convictions of the young. It is difficult indeed to contain anger at such a time, but it is also essential – vitally essential – if the protests are to be effective in arousing public sentiment against the war, and not against dissent.

2   The point can hardly be overstressed. The only people whose purposes are served by student violence are those who are ready and waiting for an excuse to suppress dissent by force. Some of our young people have said they are willing to pay the price of martyrdom, but there is more at stake than that. The violent oppression which violent

dissent invites would not end with the martyrdom of a few university students; it might well culminate in nothing less than the destruction of American democracy.

3 Who wants to be a martyr anyway? Who wants to go down to glorious defeat, or create a gallant legend — while the war goes on and the Philistines take over our country? Who wants to go down fighting when, with strategy and organization, you just might possibly win; you just might possibly succeed in changing some of the things that need to be changed in our society and saving the things that are worth saving. Dissent against this squalid war is more than an expression of democracy; it is also a reaffirmation of democracy, of youth's commitment to it, and of the desire of people of all ages to save American democracy from becoming another casualty of war.

4 I hope and urge that the young people of America continue their protests against the war. I hope and urge that they sustain their protests until the last American soldier has been withdrawn from Indochina. But I also stress the importance of strategy in dissent.

5 Instead of confining their expressions to mass demonstrations, the thousands of students who have come to the capital to protest the war are beginning to employ the technique that businessmen and farmers and labor unions have found so rewarding over the years. The students seem to be in the process of becoming lobbyists for peace, making their views known, in a concerted, persistent, but peaceful and orderly way, to their elected representatives.

6 In so doing they are acting in the best tradition of representative democracy. They are also acting as *patriots* — not in the jingoist sense in which the term "patriotism" is commonly misused but in the sense defined by Albert Camus, who said that the true patriot is one who gives his highest loyalty not to his country as it *is* but to his own best conception of what it can and *ought* to be, and also in the sense defined by Adlai Stevenson, who used to point out that the true patriot was not only willing to fight for principles but also willing to live up to them.

7 For what cold comfort it may have, students may be interested in knowing that the feeling of an unresponsive Administration is not confined to the nation's campuses. Some of us in the Senate get the feeling now and then that our message is not getting through to people on the other side of town. Some months ago the Vice President paid me the compliment of saying that he had been "trying very hard for five or six years" to understand my positions but, unfortunately, "without any success." I appreciate his effort, and I have noted his lack of success, and I do indeed regret the inability of some of us in the Senate to get our meaning across.

8 For my own part, I have taken every opportunity I could find to bring authoritative and persuasive witnesses to the Foreign Relations Committee to discuss the war. Much of the potential political impact of what these witnesses have had to say has unfortunately been lost, because the media have not seen fit to transmit some extremely interesting testimony beyond the Committee chamber, except in limited and fragmentary form. In this respect — if not in some others — I am inclined to agree with Vice President Agnew that ". . . perhaps it is

time that the networks were made more responsive to the people they serve."

9   The problem for some of us in the Senate, as well as for people in the academic community, is how to get through to the country and to the President so as to bring an end to a stupid and indecent war. I am of the opinion that, at this stage of events, something more than rational argument is required—which is not to make a case for irrational argument, still less for violence and disorderly protest, which do far more to damage the cause of peace than to advance it. The problem is essentially one of political strategy, of campaigns, elections, and lobbying—of the bringing to bear of political pressures through the various channels open to us within the American political system.

10   Discouraging though it has seemed at times, I believe that the years of dissent have had important, though insufficient, effect. It is always difficult to speculate on what might have been, but I strongly suspect that things would be even worse today if it had not been for the determination of students and other citizens who opposed the policies of the previous Administration. I think particularly of those who became involved in practical political activities such as the New Hampshire primary.

11   Active, organized dissent is the only reliable restraint we have on a leadership which seems bent upon a disastrous course in Indochina. Cynical though it may sound, I have always suspected that Mr. Nixon did not put a stop to the Johnson escalation policy for purely philosophical reasons. He had a political incentive too, and I would hate to see that incentive taken away from him—all the more now when the Administration appears to have forgotten the fate of its predecessor, or else persuaded itself that it can pursue the same policies and still come out on top politically. Boring, repetitious, and simple-minded though it may seem, it is up to all those of us who oppose this war to keep on boring, badgering, and lobbying our leaders until they make peace. If they find this annoying, as they sometimes have in the past, we can always recall for them President Nixon's words of last December 8, that "the people of the United States are entitled to know everything that they possibly can with regard to any involvement of the United States abroad."

12   Turning now to the means by which students can most effectively influence our Vietnam policy, I stress again reliance on the conventional, institutional procedures. Some of us in the Senate are trying to build support for the Cooper-Church amendment to the Foreign Military Sales Act, which would prohibit the expenditure of any further funds for the conduct of hostilities in Cambodia. Some of us are also engaged in an effort to repeal the notorious Gulf of Tonkin resolution. Students who wish to lobby for peace—and, for that matter, non-students who wish to lobby for peace—might find it worthwhile to commend this legislation to their representatives in Congress.

13   Perhaps, to cite another example, a student campaign might be organized to build public and Congressional support for a negotiated, compromise peace based on the principles of a sharing of power among the various South Vietnamese factions and the prompt, phased withdrawal of all American forces from Indochina. Whatever the exact

approach, organization and planning are required. Dissent, no less than war, requires a strategy if it is to succeed.

14   I am not much alarmed by the "revolutionary" activities of our young revolutionaries. They do not appear to have the numbers, the resources, the skill — or, most important of all, the opportunity — to make a radical revolution, but they might succeed in bringing on something resembling a counterrevolution from the right, inflated by support from great numbers of honest and decent but frightened citizens.

15   If there is any bias in our history and in the character of our society, it is not toward the Left but toward the Right. The "Red scares" of our past, from Sacco-Vanzetti to Alger Hiss to the "effete snobs" and "rotten apples" of more recent vintage, have never amounted to much as far as threatening our society is concerned, but the anti-Red reactions have amounted to a great deal. Taken together, the right wing bias of our past, the intense, obsessive fear of Communism, the disruption wrought by thirty years of chronic war, the power of the military-industrial-labor-academic complex which chronic war has spawned, and our failure to come to grips with urgent problems at home — all these collectively have posed a great strain on American democracy.

16   Confronted with so great a concentration of forces on the other side, the extremists of the Left can have little hope of working their will on our society, but they could bring down on themselves a counterrevolution from the Right which would surely destroy their movements and possibly destroy democracy as well. I venture to predict that, if American democracy is overthrown in our generation, it will not be by radicals flying the Vietcong flag but by right-wing radicals flying the American flag.

17   Even if it were possible, and desirable, to overthrow the existing system, history suggests that what we would get would not be something better but chaos and disaster — as was the case with the French and Russian Revolutions, at least in their immediate aftermaths. I think our system is a good one, given the nature of our society, but even if one does not think so, there is an excellent case to be made for preserving it. That case, quite simply, is that destruction of the system would almost certainly lead to something worse — and somethng quite different from the dreams of the revolutionaries.

18   Radically different in motive and purpose though they are, the humanitarians of the New Left who would remake our society through social revolution share one common trait with the social scientists who think they can manipulate society with their computers, with the strategists who write about the "responsibilities of power," and with the theologians who construct ponderous theories of the "just war." That common trait is a supreme confidence in their own capacity for moral choice.

19   I am unattracted by that excess of conscience which leads individuals to invoke a "higher moral law." I mistrust too much conscience because it places too heavy a burden on human judgment, which we all know — or ought to know — is susceptible to distortions ranging from rationalization to total obsession. In broad terms, and for most pur-

poses, I would rather be ruled by law than by conscience, because law, imperfect though it is, is the only means we have of protecting ourselves from the arbitrariness, capriciousness, and susceptibility of our own human nature. A reliable, undeluded, objective morality would be preferable to law if it were attainable, but I do not think that it is.

20   In any matter of justice or morality, the critical question is always: *Who* is to make the distinction between right and wrong, between progress and regression? Professor Herbert Marcuse suggests that the man qualified to make this distinction for society as a whole is "everyone in the maturity of his faculties as a human being, everyone who has learned to think rationally and autonomously." With all respect for Professor Marcuse's significant insights into the nature of our society, I think that he begs the question of moral choice. How are we to select those special individuals whose maturity and capacity to think rationally and autonomously qualify them to make important decisions for society as a whole? Can they really select themselves? Would any of us volunteer to disqualify ourselves?

21   To be in a position to make moral judgments for society as a whole, one must possess power, and nothing distorts human judgment more certainly than the possession of great power. If history has taught us anything about power, it has taught us that the corrupting effects of power are not confined to bad men; good men are corrupted too, and the evil which they do in good causes is no less evil than the evil done by bad men in bad causes.

22   It is not just *what* one thinks but *how* one thinks that makes a person dangerous and destructive. It was not just the moral and strategic opinions of our leaders and their intellectual supporters that got us into Vietnam; it was their arrogant certainty of the rightness of their own predictions and opinions. Like it or not, there is one thing that even the most committed of social reformers share with the strategists and the moral crusaders: human nature and its susceptibilities. We cannot escape them, much as we might like to, and, because we cannot, we do well to remember Judge Learned Hand's warning that "the spirit of liberty is the spirit that is not too sure that it is right."

23   I am aware of the skepticism young people may feel when they are called upon to respect their country's institutions. They have seen these institutions misused and even corrupted in too many instances in recent years. Some of us in the Senate have shared that experience. We were deceived about the Gulf of Tonkin in 1964; we were deceived about the Dominican Republic in 1965; and, as the special subcommittee headed by Senator Stuart Symington has shown, we have been deliberately and systematically deceived over the past several years about the extent of American military involvement in Laos. The term "credibility gap" is a tame euphemism for the practices to which it refers.

24   If many of our young people feel contempt for their country's institutions, it must be admitted that an example was set for them on the highest level. No one, however, is under any obligation to follow that example. We can, if we wish, undertake to restore the integrity of American democracy rather than compound the problem, as some

liberals have done, by bestowing their benedictions on violence and disorder. To my mind it makes no sense at all, when we see our democratic institutions misused, to decide that we might as well go on to finish the job by destroying the institutions altogether.

25   There are ample possibilities for a strategy of dissent through the processes of American democracy. In addition to lobbying for peace through the legislative process, there is an obvious and promising strategy in this election year: to take to the political hustings and to work in an efficient and organized way for candidates who favor peace. In many if not most of the contests for the Senate and House of Representatives this year, the outcome might be significantly affected by, say, fifty or 100 efficient precinct workers seeking support for their candidates on the weekends preceding either primaries or the general election. It was not, I remind you, a purely intellectual process that led President Johnson to reverse his escalation policy in Vietnam.

26   The election of 1968 did not resolve the issue of Vietnam as we had hoped it would, and as it should have. That is a disappointment, but there is no use crying about it now when our efforts can be put to more productive use in elections still to come. Ringing doorbells and passing out handbills are neither as dramatic nor as cathartic as a march on Washington or a student strike, but they speak the language that politicians understand: the language of votes.

27   Discouraging though it may seem at times, peaceful political dissent at home is the most powerful incentive our policymakers have for bringing the war in Indochina to an end. The real impact of orderly, democratic dissent in America is not on the policymakers in Hanoi, as people who support the present course are fond of asserting, but on the policymakers in Washington. That, no doubt, is why they object to dissent, and that is why those of us who oppose this war must sustain it.

Discussion of Theme

1. What can students do for peace, according to Senator Fulbright? Can you add to his list of suggestions?
2. What are the two kinds of dissent described by the author? Which one does he regard as dangerous?
3. A common defense of revolution today is that our country was founded on a revolution. Is this a valid defense of today's revolutionaries?
4. What are the conditions referred to by Senator Fulbright as having imposed a great strain on American democracy?
5. Many people believe that demonstrations in this country against the war in Vietnam actually aid the enemy. Do you agree?

Discussion of Rhetoric

1. What rhetorical device does the author employ at the outset? Does it effectively attract your attention?

2. How does Fulbright attempt to establish his credibility with his audience?
3. One of Fulbright's weapons is irony. Find several instances of this device, showing how it is effective.
4. Find the sentence in this essay that would serve as the central idea or thesis statement. How does Fulbright develop it?

Writing Assignments

1. Present your views on the actions of the Ohio National Guard on the campus of Kent State University.
2. What part can students play in effecting change in this country? What would be the most effective political strategy, for example?
3. React to the following statement: "You can't trust anyone over thirty."
4. Write a letter to your congressman or senator expressing your views on a particular piece of controversial legislation.

Library Exploration

1. Investigate the events behind the Gulf of Tonkin resolution. In particular, investigate the controversy engendered by the resolution.
2. Read newspaper accounts of some of the peace marches, such as the march on Washington in 1970. What effect have they had on our foreign policy?
3. Senator Fulbright has written a number of articles and books elaborating his views. You might enjoy *The Arrogance of Power,* in which he expands several ideas found in this essay.
4. What were the "chaos and disaster which followed the French and Russian revolutions"? Compare these events with those following the American Revolution.

Vocabulary

(3) PHILISTINES persons lacking culture

(6) JINGOIST excessively patriotic or nationalistic

(15) EFFETE decadent; no longer productive

(19) ARBITRARINESS unreasonableness

(19) CAPRICIOUSNESS fickleness; unpredictability

(20) AUTONOMOUSLY independently

Gene Lees (1928–   ) was born in Ontario, Canada. He has been a reporter for Canadian newspapers, as well as classical-music critic and film and drama editor for the Louisville "Times." Later he became editor of "Down Beat" magazine and a contributing editor to "Hi Fi/ Stereo Review." Since 1965, Lees has been the popular-music editor of "High Fidelity." He has also written the words and music for numerous popular songs.

The following article gives his brutally frank and sometimes startling proposal for handling the problem of drug addiction. Whether or not he's serious about his "modest proposal" is for you to decide.

GENE LEES

A Modest Proposal

1 Jonathan Swift once made what he called a Modest Proposal: since the Irish could not grow enough food to feed themselves but had no trouble producing babies, he suggested that babies should be made the prime Irish export (perhaps served as a table delicacy in England). There were those who thought he meant it. Perhaps, in a bitter and angry way, he did.

2   I wish to make a Modest Proposal myself. It relates to two serious contemporary problems: narcotics addiction and overpopulation. I feel that it is incumbent upon me as a man who makes his living from the record industry to offer this proposal. For the record industry is as responsible as any sector of our society for the growing number of deaths from the use of heroin and other drugs.

3   Now don't be hasty in condemning them. They've done no more than other industries have. Detroit finds 40,000 deaths a year in crash-worthy cars an acceptable price for profits. Why shouldn't the record industry too be allowed to kill its quota of people for profit?

4   Ten years ago I devoted an issue of *Down Beat* to the drug problem. At the time only a few music-business people thought addiction was an important issue. A Negro singer I know said to me recently, "No-body gave a damn about it when only black kids were dying in the doorways of Harlem. Nobody gave a damn until the well-to-do middle-class white kids started dying." *Touché*.

5   There is a great deal of criminal money invested in the music busi-ness, both in groups and in some record labels. Rock groups began pushing drug use. The kids bought it. The kids are dying. The under-world is making money on it. This is all coincidence, right? Oh sure.

6   Drug education in the schools is only going to make the problem worse, I am convinced. It will increase fascination, or even cause it, among youngsters who had never even thought much about using drugs. Watch it happen in the next two years.

7   And so I have come around to another view of the matter. I modestly propose that to all our other welfare programs we add free narcotics for the kids, including heroin. If you're a parent, this may shock you. But it shouldn't. You have been permitting your kids to take dope intellectually for years—from Bob Dylan, the Jefferson Airplane, the Lovin' Spoonful, the Beatles. When your five-year-old was wandering around the house singing, "I get by with a little help from my friends, I get high with a little help from my friends," didn't you say, "Isn't that cute? He's singing a Beatles song." All right, so now he's a few years older, and you're startled at the circulation of drugs in his school, and fearful that he'll start using them. (Maybe he's already started.) Why? You permitted it.

8   Now the main thing wrong with junkies is that they steal. Sometimes they go farther than that: in desperation for money, they *kill* and steal. This is a great social inconvenience, tying up the time of all kinds of policemen whom we need for such things as messing up traffic.

9   If I get my way, and the government subsidizes addiction the way it now subsidizes lethargy, all this will stop. It is useless to tell young people that the Beatles and heroin are bad for them. It simply is not so: the kids have told us this. And they are the wisest and most honest and idealistic and decent and loving and unprejudiced and well-informed generation of Americans in history. We know it because they have told us this too. And the advertising industry and Marshall Mc-Luhan have confirmed it. Who in his right mind would doubt the com-bined wisdom of Marshall McLuhan, the advertising industry, and our wonderful young people?

10   Now, if we supply them with all the heroin they can use—and I am talking about the pure, uncut stuff, not the powdered sugar that's floating around in many places these days—it will have immediate and far-reaching social benefits.

11   First, they'll stop rioting. Heroin makes you terribly passive. They'll start nodding out all over the place, and this will permit the police to catch up on *their* sleep in parked cruisers.

12   Then a lot of them will start dropping out of school. This will reduce the overload on our schools and universities. It will stop the building program, thus braking the felling of trees which give us our oxygen. Our air will improve.

13   Third, it will increase the food supply, since junkies don't eat much even when they can get it.

14   Fourth (and here is the real genius of my plan), ultimately the program will end the population explosion. One junkie I know told me that he and his strung-out wife hadn't had sexual relations in two years. Heroin produces profound sexual indifference, and impotence. But that isn't the end of it. Junkies die. In the late 1940s and early 1950s, a great many jazz musicians were on heroin. None of them are now. They are either in their graves or they are off drugs. There is no middle road, apparently.

15   Kids consitute nearly fifty percent of the population. The population explosion, then, is them. Now since anyone forty years old is going to be around only for another thirty years or so tops, they're not going to be much of a problem. They're starting to die off now, from working too hard to make enough money for their kids to buy the Doors' records and acid and junk. But that eighteen-year-old over there — man, he's going to be around breathing air, using up food, making garbage for another forty or fifty years. Even a kid can grasp that he himself is the real enemy.

16   Now when we begin the widespread free distribution of drugs, this group will start dying like flies. And still more benefits will accrue to society as a whole.

17   Junk music will fade from the radio. There won't be so many cars on the highway, and those that are there won't be in such steady use. Air pollution will be further reduced. Since we won't need so many highways, the grass and trees will grow again, making more oxygen. Drug use, incidentally, including acid, is becoming as common a cause of traffic deaths as alcohol. So we get a bonus here too.

18   I know there are those out there in Readerland who will write me letters telling me I've got it all wrong — like the people who wrote me letters telling me New York is not dying. They'll say my proposal is heartless and cruel. But it isn't, I assure you. We have given the young what they want until now. Why should we draw the line at death?

19   To young people I would say this: don't believe old squares when they tell you that drugs, even grass, are damn dangerous. Don't believe the growing reports that the grass available now is often spiked with heroin to hook you on hard narcotics. Don't believe those who tell you that heroin is evil stuff. You know all those people are just trying to keep you from having a hip kind of good time.

20   And don't think about death. Think instead how you will be reducing the pressures of population on the rest of us. Think what a noble deed you'll be doing. Think Zen thoughts about eternity and the continuum of consciousness and about astrology and how mortal existence is a mere passing cloud. Think not of going into a valley of blackness. Think instead how you are going to join the great All-Consciousness and rest forever in nirvana. As you sit there, listening to John and Yoko with a needle in your arm, reflect not on the dying

you're about to do. Just think how high you're going to be as you go.
21   And to the record industry I would say: keep up the good work,
gentlemen. You've done a hell of a job thus far.

Discussion of Theme

1. Do you agree with the statement made by the singer in paragraph
   4? Is this society's attitude?
2. In paragraph 7, Lees makes a familiar accusation against well-
   known pop groups. Is he justified in his assessment of their songs?
   How have these musicians responded to such criticism?
3. What is the author's purpose in writing this article? How do you
   know? Is his approach effective?
4. Is the author serious in his proposals? Explain your reasoning.

Discussion of Rhetoric

1. What is the dominant tone of the article? Where is it especially
   strong? What devices does the author use to support his tone?
2. Is this article aimed at young people or their parents? What clues
   are responsible for your opinion? How effective do you consider it
   for each class of readers?
3. In paragraphs 14 and 17, Lees makes positive statements to the
   effect that (a) none of the older jazz musicians is currently using
   heroin, and (b) drug use causes as many traffic deaths as alcohol.
   How might he have increased the effectiveness of these statements?
4. The impact of paragraphs 19 and 20 is due to a particular rhetorical
   device. What is it?

Writing Assignments

1. "Schools Should (Should Not) Preach About the Dangers of Drug
   Abuse." Support your belief with reasons and evidence.
2. Analyze the content of at least two popular songs that you consider
   obviously drug-oriented.
3. If you were in the record industry, how would you respond to Lees?

Library Exploration

1. For a moving autobiography of a young black who kicked the habit,
   read Piri Thomas's *Down These Mean Streets*.
2. Check out current periodical literature to determine the present
   dimensions of drug abuse among young people.
3. Find out what other writers have to say about the influence of
   popular music on drug use.

Vocabulary

(2) INCUMBENT required as a duty

(4) TOUCHÉ a word used to tell one's opponent that he has successfully made his point

(9) LETHARGY sluggish indifference

(16) ACCRUE to come to as a gain

THE
FRESHMAN
AND HIS
LANGUAGE

1

Morris Bishop (1893–   ), professor of romance languages at Cornell University until his retirement in 1960, is the author of several books on language and intellectual history, including "Horizon Book of the Middle Ages" (1968) and "The Exotics" (1969). A native of New York, he received his A.B., A.M., and Ph.D. from Cornell.

Who–and what–should determine "correct" usage? This question has been debated, often with more heat than light, for more than two hundred years. The following selection, taken from "The American Heritage Dictionary of the English Language," gives the background on this debate, and suggests a tentative answer.

MORRIS BISHOP

Good Usage, Bad Usage, and Usage

1 The words of a living language are like creatures: they are alive. Each word has a physical character, a look and a personality, an ancestry, an expectation of life and death, a hope of posterity. Some words strike us as beautiful, some ugly, some evil. The word *glory* seems to shine; the common word for excrement seems to smell. There are holy words, like the proper name of God, pronounced only once a year in the innermost court of Jerusalem's Temple. There are magic words, spells to open gates and safes, summon spirits, put an end to the world. What are magic spells but magic spellings? Words sing to us, frighten us, impel us to self-immolation and murder. They belong

to us; they couple at our order, to make what have well been called the aureate words of poets and the inkhorn words of pedants. We can keep our words alive, or at our caprice we can kill them—though some escape and prosper in our despite.

2   Thought makes the word; also the word makes thought. Some psychologists allege that explicit thought does not exist without verbalization. Thought, they say, emerges from our silent secret speech, from tiny quivers of the speech organs, from the interior monologue we all carry on endlessly. Let us pause a moment and reflect on our thought; we reflect in words, on a surge of hurrying words.

3   Much of our formless, secret thought is, to be sure, idiotic. "We find it hard to believe that other people's thoughts are as silly as our own, but they probably are," said the American scholar James Harvey Robinson. Before we permit silent speech to emerge as spoken language, we must make choices and arrange words in patterns of sense and form, accessible to other people. These choices and patterns are usage. And usage is the ruler, the governor, the judge of language. Horace said it nearly two thousand years ago in his *Ars Poetica: "usus, Quem penes arbitrium est, et jus, et norma loquendi."* Or, in an old translation of the passage:

> Yes, words long faded may again revive;
> And words may fade now blooming and alive,
> If USAGE wills it so, to whom belongs
> The rule and law, the government of tongues.

4   Deferring to the rule and law of usage, we may yet order our words well or ill, thus creating Good Usage and Bad Usage.

5   Now the trouble begins. Whose usage is good, whose bad? Is not my usage good for me? May I not tell my own words what to do? Do you have authority over my usage? Does anyone have authority? And if authority exists, is it helpful or hurtful to usage?

6   We tend to demand freedom for our own usage, authority for others'. Yet we are not above seeking comfort and support from authority. One of our commonest phrases is "look it up in the dictionary." (Not any particular dictionary; just "the dictionary.") Every court of law has its big dictionary; the law settles cases, awards millions, rates crimes and misdemeanors, by quoting the definitions of some poor attic lexicographer, "a harmless drudge," as defined by lexicographer Samuel Johnson. We acclaim freedom, but we love the word *freedom* more than the fact. Most people most of the time would rather be secure than free; they cry for law and order. In the matter of usage, we suspect that complete freedom might outbabble Babel; without common agreement on the meaning of most words, communication would cease.

7   Who, then, shall wield authority? The King, perhaps? The phrase *the King's English* came in, we are told, with Henry VIII, who ruled from 1509 to 1547. He was a poet and a man of letters when he had the time. The King's English remained standard, even under George I, who could not speak English. Recent Kings and Queens of England have not been noteworthy for an exemplary style. In America the President's English has never ruled the citizenry. The one notorious

Presidential venture into lexicography was Harding's use of *normalcy.* But he said that he had looked it up in the dictionary.

8   The King's English was naturally identified with the spoken style of gentlemen and ladies of the English court. Similarly in France, the grammarian Vaugelas defined (in 1647) good usage as the speech habits of the sounder members of the court, in conformity with the practice in writing of the sounder contemporary authors. Good usage, then, would represent the practice of an elite of breeding, station, and intellect.

9   The idea of an elite with authority over language clearly needed delimitation. In France, Cardinal Richelieu, who piqued himself on his style in verse and prose, authorized in 1635 the formation of an *Académie française,* composed of writers, bookish nobles and magistrates, and amateurs of letters. The *Académie,* the supreme court of the French literary world, set itself the task of preparing a dictionary. It has been working at its dictionary, off and on, for over three hundred years. But England and America have always refused to constitute government-sponsored academies with power to regulate citizens' words.

10   Lacking an academy, Englishmen appealed to the practice of good writers to preserve or "fix" general usage. Thence more trouble. Who are the good writers? Shakespeare, no doubt. But Shakespeare, with his wild and carefree coinages, his cheery disregard for grammatical agreements, demands our admiration more than our imitation. In Latin, a fossilized tongue, the rule is simple: if a locution is in Cicero, it is correct. In English we have no Cicero. The only writers whom all critics would accept as "best" have been so long dead that their works are uncertain models for the living language of our times.

11   We should, perhaps, make the authority of the best writers defer to that of professional judges of language, the critics and grammarians. Quintilian, rhetorician of the first century A.D., appealed to the consensus of the *eruditi,* the scholarly, the well-informed. Ben Jonson said: "Custom is the most certain mistress of language, as the public stamp makes the current money . . . That I call custom of speech, which is the consent of the learned; as custom of life, which is the consent of the good." In the 17th and 18th centuries, the English grammarians appeared, devoting themselves to "refining, ascertaining, and fixing" the language. They were scholars. Aware of linguistic history, they conceived of English usage as a development from primitive barbarism to the harmonious perfection of their own times. They regarded the past as a preparation, the present as a glorious achievement, the future as a threatening decadence. Jonathan Swift was terrified of the coming corruption and invoked governmental authority to "fix" the language; else, he feared, within two centuries the literary works of his time, including his own, would be unreadable.

12   The grammarians justified their judgments by appealing not only to history but to reason. They strengthened the concepts of Good and Bad to become Right and Wrong. They regarded language as something existing mysteriously apart from man, governed by a universal grammar waiting to be discovered by intrepid scholars. No doubt they were sympathetically fascinated by the story Herodotus tells of the

king who isolated two small children with a deaf-and-dumb shepherd to find out what language they would learn to speak, thus to identify the original speech of mankind. (It was Phrygian.) Rightness was to be achieved by logical analysis of form and meaning, with much use of analogy. Popular usage was scouted, as of its nature corrupt. The grammarians made great play with Purity and Impurity. Pure English lived in perpetual danger of defloration by the impure.

13   The grammarians did some useful work in rationalizing the language. However, their precepts were often overlogical or based on faulty logic. From them, derive many of the distinctions that have ever since tortured scholars young and old. The *shall/will, should/would* rules are said to be an invention of the 17th-century John Wallis. John Lowth, in 1762, first laid it down that two negatives are equivalent to an affirmative. It was Lowth who banned the use of the superlative to indicate one of two, as in Jane Austen's "the youngest of the two daughters of a most affectionate, indulgent father."

14   Samuel Johnson, whose epoch-making *A Dictionary of the English Language* appeared in 1755, shared many of the convictions of the grammarians. He was concerned to fix the language against lowering corruption, for, he said in his Preface, "Tongues, like governments, have a natural tendency to degeneration; we have long preserved our constitution, let us make some struggle for our language." He foresaw linguistic calamity. "The tropes of poetry will make hourly encroachments, and the metaphorical will become the current sense; pronunciation will be varied by levity or ignorance, and the pen must at length comply with the tongue; illiterate writers will at one time or other, by publick infatuation, rise into renown, who, not knowing the original import of words, will use them with colloquial licentiousness, confound distinction, and forget propriety." Those who knew better must fight on in the hopeless war: "we retard what we cannot repel, we palliate what we cannot cure."

15   One will have noticed, amid the funeral music of Dr. Johnson's Preface, the startling phrase: "the pen must at length comply with the tongue." This was a view already accepted more cheerfully by some other distinguished writers. Malherbe, 17th-century scholar-poet-critic and "legislator of Parnassus," said that he learned proper French listening to the porters at the haymarket. Though Dr. Johnson deplored the fact, he recognized that speech, not writing, not grammatical logic, must in the end command usage. This idea took shape and found fuller expression in the work of Noah Webster (1758–1843).

16   Webster was a Connecticut farm boy with a Yale education, in a day when colleges did not teach English as a course. His series of spelling books and dictionaries actually went far toward "fixing" the American language. His standard of correctness, however, was the usage of the enlightened members of each community, not just that of the "polite part" of city society, which he believed consisted largely of coxcombs. "General custom must be the rule of speaking," he said; and "it is always better to be *vulgarly* right than *politely* wrong." He was astonishingly liberal, even radical, in his acceptance of popular usage, giving his approval to *It is me, Who is she married to?* and *Them horses are mine.*

17   Thus, common usage began to assume dominance at the expense of formal grammar. The scholarly Irish archbishop Richard C. Trench in 1857 defined a dictionary as an inventory of the language: "It is no task of the maker of it to select the *good* words of a language . . . He is an historian of it, not a critic."

18   This view of language and its use has prevailed in the 20th century and seems unlikely to fade. A school of linguistic scientists constituted itself, and in time found a place on most college faculties, ousting the old-fashioned philologists of the English and foreign-language departments. The descriptive or structural linguists, as they called themselves, would no more criticize a locution than a physicist would criticize an atom or an entomologist a cockroach.

19   The principles of descriptive linguistics have thus been simply put: (1) Language changes constantly; (2) Change is normal; (3) Spoken language is *the* language; (4) Correctness rests upon usage; (5) All usage is relative. This creed arouses indignation if not wrath in many people, including highly educated ones. But with the exception of number 3, which has been felt even by some linguists to be an over-statement on the part of gentlemen whose livelihood requires the writ-ten word, dispute about these principles seems to be nearly over among those who profess the study of English. The underlying as-sumption is that language, by its very nature, is a growing, evolving thing; and that whereas it may be cultivated, it cannot be "fixed" without killing it. Like any other fundamental social activity, it will undergo vicissitudes that to the older generation often seem regret-table; and indeed, some changes in language turn out to be empty fads that are soon forgotten, like some changes in women's fashions. Others are found to be enduringly useful, so that a generation later it becomes hard to imagine how we got along without them.

20   A descriptive linguist's lexicon can be expected to refrain from value judgments, from imposed pronunciations and spellings. It may classify usages as standard or nonstandard, formal, informal, or slang; but not right or wrong. It describes usage; it piously avoids prescribing it. Yet surely there is the possibility of self-deception here, of an objectivity more imaginary than real. By the very act of leaving *alrite* out of a dictionary, the lexicographer implies that that spelling—which does, after all, exist—is not all right. On the other hand, if he exhibits his scientific disinterest by reporting that "*ain't* is used orally in most parts of the United States by many cultivated speakers," the truth is that he is being inadequately descriptive with respect to contexts of usage. A reader who takes that description seriously is likely to lay an egg (*slang*) at his next cocktail party unless he has the charm of Eliza Doolittle.

21   The makers of *The American Heritage Dictionary of the English Language* accept usage as the authority for correctness, but they have eschewed the "scientific" delusion that a dictionary should contain no value judgments. Some, to be sure, they have made merely im-plicit: the arrant solecisms of the ignoramus are here often omitted entirely, "irregardless" of how he may feel about this neglect. What is desirable is that when value judgments are explicit, they should be clearly attributed. Thus good usage can usually be distinguished from

bad usage, even as good books can be distinguished from bad books. The present editors maintain that those best fitted to make such distinctions are, as Noah Webster said, the enlightened members of the community; not the scholarly theoreticians, not the instinctive verbalizers of the unlettered mass. The best authorities, at least for cultivated usage, are those professional speakers and writers who have demonstrated their sensitiveness to the language and their power to wield it effectively and beautifully.

22 The lexicographers of this Dictionary therefore commissioned a Usage Panel of about a hundred members — novelists, essayists, poets, journalists, writers on science and sports, public officials, professors. (Their names and credentials are to be found in a list preceding this section of special articles.) The panelists have in common only a recognized ability to speak and write good English. They accepted their task and turned to it with gusto. They revealed, often with passion, their likes and dislikes, their principles, and also their whims and crotchets. "We all get self-righteous in our judgments on language." Malcolm Cowley observes. As a matter of fact, many of them revealed, on particular questions, an attitude more reminiscent of Dr. Johnson than of the modern linguistic view: they tend to feel that the English language is going to hell if "we" don't do something to stop it, and they tend to feel that their own usage preferences are clearly *right*.

23 This does not mean for a moment that their preferences are invalid or negligible. Where this Dictionary differs notably from those that have preceded it, with regard to usage, is in exposing the lexical opinions of a larger group of recognized leaders than has heretofore been consulted, so that the ordinary user, looking up an expression whose social status is uncertain, can discover just how and to what extent his presumed betters agree on what he ought to say or write. Thus, he is not turned away uncounseled and uncomforted: he has before him an authoritative statement on a disputed issue; yet, he is left one of the most valuable of human freedoms, the freedom to say what he pleases.

24 It is significant that on specific questions, the Usage Panel disagreed more than they agreed, revealing a fact often conveniently ignored — that among those best qualified to know, there is a very considerable diversity of usage. Anyone surveying the panelists' various opinions is likely to conclude that good usage is indeed an elusive nymph, well worth pursuing but inconstant in shape and dress, and rather hard to back into a corner. In only one case did they agree 100 per cent — in disfavor of *simultaneous* as an adverb ("the referendum was conducted *simultaneous* with the election"). Some other scores approached unanimity, as in the following:

EXPRESSION	APPROVED BY	DISAPPROVED BY
ain't I? in writing		99%
between you and I in writing		99%
dropout used as a noun	97%	
thusly		97%

EXPRESSION	APPROVED BY	DISAPPROVED BY
debut as a verb ("the company will debut its new models")		97%
slow as an adverb ("Drive Slow")	96%	
medias as a plural (instead of *media*)		95%
their own referring to the singular ("nobody thinks the criticism applies to their own work")		95%
but what ("There is no doubt but what he will try")		95%
myself instead of *me* in compound objects, in writing ("He invited Mary and myself to dinner")		95%
anxious in the sense of *eager*	94%	
type for *type of* ("that type shrub")		94%
rather unique; most unique		94%

25   While the panelists tend toward conservatism, they try to avoid overniceness, prissiness. (*Was graduated,* says John Bainbridge contemptuously, is preferred "by all who write with a quill pen.") Sixty-one per cent of them feel bad about the expression *I feel badly* when they see it in writing; only 45 per cent object when they hear it in speech. More than most people, they know the history of words and have tested the value of idioms. More than most, they have grown tired of overused vogue words. They dislike *senior citizen* ("I'd as soon use *underprivileged* for *poor*—or any other social science Choctaw"—Berton Roueché). They are not concerned that senior citizens themselves seem to rejoice in the term and recoil at *old folks* and even at *old. Enthuse* finds little favor, and stirs preservative zeal in some: "By God, let's hold the line on this one!" cries Dwight Mac-donald. *Finalize,* says Isaac Asimov, "is nothing more than bureaucratic illiteracy." But for the consensus, the reader is referred to the entries *enthuse* and *finalize,* each of which, like many other neologisms, is discussed in a Usage note.

26   The panelists are by no means opposed to all coinages. "I have great admiration," says Gilbert Highet, "for the American genius for creating short vivid words (often disyllabic) to express complex ideas, for example, a collision between a vehicle and another object which is not direct but lateral or oblique, *sideswipe.*" In general, the jurymen are more cordial toward popular, low-level inventions than toward the pomposities of professional jargons. John K. Sherman welcomes *rambunctious* as a "tangy Americanism." Forty per cent of the Panel are ready to accept the expression *not about,* used to express determination not to do something; but the other 60 per cent are not about

to do so. None of them, however, likes Business English; and they betray a particular spite against the language of Madison Avenue, once a very respectable street, now an avenue of ill fame. Yet the advertisers are, after all, fecund creators languagewise.

27   It would seem that the panelists are often more attentive to the practice of their own social group than to grammatical logic or etymological precision. They are antipedantic, scornful of the grammarians' effort to ban *it's me*. Some, like Theodore C. Sorenson, would throw away the rule that the relative *that* must introduce restrictive clauses, *which* nonrestrictive. One or two would drop *whom* altogether, as a needless refinement. Ninety-one per cent of the panelists accept the use of *internecine* to mean "pertaining to civil war or to a struggle within a family, group, organization, nation, or the like." They know, of course, that the Latin *internecinus* just means mutually deadly, but they do not seem to care.

28   The Usage Panel has given us the enlightened judgments of a cultivated elite on a great many interesting and troublesome expressions. The very diversity of their response attests that language is alive and well in the United States, and that even the most descriptive of dictionaries could not succeed in reporting all of its shifting nuances.

29   Within their field — the determination of good current usage — the counselors found, as we have observed, no absolute standard of rightness. Though naturally believing in their own superiority, they do not presume to dictate. They seem to conclude, without explicit statement, that usage is our own affair, with due regard to the usage of other good writers and speakers. Let that be our conclusion. The duty of determination falls upon us all. By our choices we make usage, good or bad. Let us then try to make good choices, and guard and praise our lovely language and try to be worthy of her.

Discussion of Theme

1. How does Bishop define good usage? Bad usage?
2. What were Samuel Johnson's fears about the English language when he undertook his dictionary? How had his attitude changed when he completed it?
3. What are the basic ideas held by descriptive linguists? What determines "correctness" for them? What is Bishop's attitude toward them? Do you agree?
4. What was the basis for the linguistic determinations adopted by the publisher of *The American Heritage Dictionary?* How reliable do you regard this method? What are its drawbacks?
5. Are the "rules" for spoken language different from those for written language? Explain your answer.

Discussion of Rhetoric

1. This selection is divided into main sections. What is the purpose of each? Where does the second section begin?

2. Explain the phrase *social science Choctaw* (paragraph 25). What connotative values is Bishop suggesting when he employs *ill fame* (paragraph 26) in discussing advertising? *Languagewise* (also in paragraph 26)?
3. Why are quotation marks placed around "irregardless" (paragraph 21) and "we" (paragraph 22)? What is the author's intent?
4. Bishop admits that his stand on usage is somewhat arbitrary. What argumentative techniques does he use to support it?

Writing Assignments

1. In a theme, define "correct" English.
2. What suggestions would you have for improving the teaching of English in high school?
3. Give your reasons for the establishment of an academy of "correctness" in this country. Who would serve on it? How would it determine "correct" usage? How would violators be punished?
4. In a theme, explain why educated people are more permissive in linguistic matters than uneducated people are. Relate your answer to Bishop's remark that most people would rather be secure than free.

Library Exploration

1. Investigate the furor over the publication of *Webster's Third New International Dictionary*.
2. What is transformational grammar? For an interesting look into the revolution taking place in linguistics, investigate some of the research being done in this area.
3. The history of the English language is fascinating. Several good studies are available; you might enjoy writing a report on one of them.

Vocabulary

(1) IMMOLATION sacrificial killing
(2) VERBALIZATION putting into words
(6) LEXICOGRAPHER dictionary maker
(10) LOCUTION expression
(14) TROPES figures of speech
(14) ENCROACHMENT intrusion
(14) COLLOQUIAL informal or conversational in style or expression
(14) LEVITY lightness of speech or manner
(14) LICENTIOUSNESS lack of moral (now, especially sexual) restraint
(14) PROPRIETY state or quality of being proper
(14) PALLIATE cover by excuses or apologies
(19) VICISSITUDES changes of fortune

(21) ESCHEWED   avoided;
shunned

(21) ARRANT   thoroughgoing;
out-and-out

(21) SOLECISMS   nonstandard
usages or expressions

(22) CROTCHETS   odd notions

(26) POMPOSITIES   instances of
exaggerated or excessively
ornate language or behavior

(26) FECUND   fruitful; productive

(28) NUANCES   subtle variations

Paul Roberts (1917–66) was a specialist in structural linguistics and a member of the faculty of Cornell University. Roberts is the author of "Understanding Grammar" (1954); "Patterns of English" (1956); "Understanding English" (1958); and "Cornflakes and Beaujolais" (1958), written after a sojourn in Europe.

This clever essay points out the major pitfalls that snare many freshman theme writers. Roberts then gives some advice: avoid the obvious, be unusual, watch for abstractions, avoid padding, don't hedge, use clear words.

PAUL ROBERTS

How to Say Nothing in Five Hundred Words

1   It's Friday afternoon, and you have almost survived another week of classes. You are just looking forward dreamily to the weekend when the English instructor says: "For Monday you will turn in a five-hundred-word composition on college football."

2   Well, that puts a good big hole in the weekend. You don't have any strong views on college football one way or the other. You get rather excited during the season and go to all the home games and find it rather more fun than not. On the other hand, the class has been reading Robert Hutchins in the anthology and perhaps Shaw's "Eighty-Yard Run," and from the class discussion you have got the idea that the instructor thinks college football is for the birds. You are no fool. You can figure out what side to take.

3   After dinner you get out the portable typewriter that you got for high school graduation. You might as well get it over with and enjoy

Saturday and Sunday. Five hundred words is about two double-spaced pages with normal margins. You put in a sheet of paper, think up a title, and you're off:

Why College Football Should Be Abolished

4   College football should be abolished because it's bad for the school and also bad for the players. The players are so busy practicing that they don't have any time for their studies.

This, you feel, is a mighty good start. The only trouble is that it's only thirty-two words. You still have four hundred and sixty-eight to go, and you've pretty well exhausted the subject. It comes to you that you do your best thinking in the morning, so you put away the typewriter and go to the movies. But the next morning you have to do your washing and some math problems, and in the afternoon you go to the game. The English instructor turns up too, and you wonder if you've taken the right side after all. Saturday night you have a date, and Sunday morning you have to go to church. (You can't let English assignments interfere with your religion.) What with one thing and another, it's ten o'clock Sunday night before you get out the typewriter again. You make a pot of coffee and start to fill out your views on college football. Put a little meat on the bones.

Why College Football Should Be Abolished

5   In my opinion, it seems to me that college football should be abolished. The reason why I think this to be true is because I feel that football is bad for the colleges in nearly every respect. As Robert Hutchins says in his article in our anthology in which he discusses college football, it would be better if the colleges had race horses and had races with one another, because then the horses would not have to attend classes. I firmly agree with Mr. Hutchins on this point, and I am sure that many other students would agree too.

6   One reason why it seems to me that college football is bad is that it has become too commercial. In the olden times when people played football just for the fun of it, maybe college football was all right, but they do not play football just for the fun of it now as they used to in the old days. Nowadays college football is what you might call a big business. Maybe this is not true at all schools, and I don't think it is especially true here at State, but certainly this is the case at most colleges and universities in America nowadays, as Mr. Hutchins points out in his very interesting article. Actually the coaches and alumni go around to the high schools and offer the high school stars large salaries to come to their colleges and play football for them. There was one case where a high school star was offered a convertible if he would play football for a certain college.

7   Another reason for abolishing college football is that it is bad for the players. They do not have time to get a college education, because they are so busy playing football. A football player has to practice every afternoon from three to six and then he is so tired that he can't concentrate on his studies. He just feels like dropping off to sleep after dinner, and then the next day he goes to his classes without having studied and maybe he fails the test.

(Good ripe stuff so far, but you're still a hundred and fifty-one words from home. One more push.)

8   Also I think college football is bad for the colleges and the universities because not very many students get to participate in it. Out of a college of ten thousand students only seventy-five or a hundred play football, if that many. Football is what you might call a spectator sport. That means that most people go to watch it but do not play it themselves.

(Four hundred and fifteen, Well, you still have the conclusion, and when you retype it, you can make the margins a little wider.)

9   These are the reasons why I agree with Mr. Hutchins that college football should be abolished in American colleges and universities.

10   On Monday you turn it in, moderately hopeful, and on Friday it comes back marked "weak in content" and sporting a big "D."

11   This essay is exaggerated a little, not much. The English instructor will recognize it as reasonably typical of what an assignment on college football will bring in. He knows that nearly half of the class will contrive in five hundred words to say that college football is too commercial and bad for the players. Most of the other half will inform him that college football builds character and prepares one for life and brings prestige to the school. As he reads paper after paper all saying the same thing in almost the same words, all bloodless, five hundred words dripping out of nothing, he wonders how he allowed himself to get trapped into teaching English when he might have had a happy and interesting life as an electrician or a confidence man.

12   Well, you may ask, what can you do about it? The subject is one on which you have few convictions and little information. Can you be expected to make a dull subject interesting? As a matter of fact, this is precisely what you are expected to do. This is the writer's essential task. All subjects, except sex, are dull until somebody makes them interesting. The writer's job is to find the argument, the approach, the angle, the wording that will take the reader with him. This is seldom easy, and it is particularly hard in subjects that have been much discussed: College Football, Fraternities, Popular Music, Is Chivalry Dead?, and the like. You will feel that there is nothing you can do with such subjects except repeat the old bromides. But there are some things you can do which will make your papers, if not throbbingly alive, at least less insufferably tedious than they might otherwise be.

AVOID THE OBVIOUS CONTENT

13 Say the assignment is college football. Say that you've decided to be against it. Begin by putting down the arguments that come to your mind: it is too commercial, it takes the students' minds off their studies, it is hard on the players, it makes the university a kind of circus instead of an intellectual center, for most schools it is financially ruinous. Can you think of any more arguments, just off hand? All right. Now when you write your paper, *make sure that you don't use any of the material on this list.* If these are the points that leap to your mind, they will leap to everyone else's too, and whether you get a "C" or a "D" may depend on whether the instructor reads your paper early when he is fresh and tolerant or late, when the sentence "In my opin-

ion, college football has become too commercial," inexorably repeated, has brought him to the brink of lunacy.

14   Be against college football for some reason or reasons of your own. If they are keen and perceptive ones, that's splendid. But even if they are trivial or foolish or indefensible, you are still ahead so long as they are not everybody else's reasons too. Be against it because the colleges don't spend enough money on it to make it worthwhile, because it is bad for the characters of the spectators, because the players are forced to attend classes, because the football stars hog all the beautiful women, because it competes with baseball and is therefore un-American and possibly Communist inspired. There are lots of more or less unused reasons for being against college football.

15   Sometimes it is a good idea to sum up and dispose of the trite and conventional points before going on to your own. This has the advantage of indicating to the reader that you are going to be neither trite nor conventional. Something like this:

16   We are often told that college football should be abolished because it has become too commercial or because it is bad for the players. These arguments are no doubt very cogent, but they don't really go to the heart of the matter.

Then you go to the heart of the matter.

TAKE THE LESS USUAL SIDE

17 One rather simple way of getting into your paper is to take the side of the argument that most of the citizens will want to avoid. If the assignment is an essay on dogs, you can, if you choose, explain that dogs are faithful and lovable companions, intelligent, useful as guardians of the house and protectors of children, indispensable in police work — in short, when all is said and done, man's best friends. Or you can suggest that those big brown eyes conceal, more often than not, a vacuity of mind and an inconstancy of purpose; that the dogs you have known most intimately have been mangy, ill-tempered brutes, incapable of instruction; and that only your nobility of mind and fear of arrest prevent you from kicking the flea-ridden animals when you pass them on the street.

18   Naturally personal convictions will sometimes dictate your approach. If the assigned subject is "Is Methodism Rewarding to the Individual?" and you are a pious Methodist, you have really no choice. But few assigned subjects, if any, will fall in this category. Most of them will lie in broad areas of discussion with much to be said on both sides. They are intellectual exercises, and it is legitimate to argue now one way and now another, as debaters do in similar circumstances. Always take the side that looks to you hardest, least defensible. It will almost always turn out to be easier to write interestingly on that side.

19   This general advice applies where you have a choice of subjects. If you are to choose among "The Value of Fraternities" and "My Favorite High School Teacher" and "What I Think About Beetles,"

by all means plump for the beetles. By the time the instructor gets to your paper, he will be up to his ears in tedious tales about the French teacher at Bloombury High and assertions about how fraternities build character and prepare one for life. Your views on beetles, whatever they are, are bound to be a refreshing change.

20   Don't worry too much about figuring out what the instructor thinks about the subject so that you can cuddle up with him. Chances are his views are no stronger than yours. If he does have convictions and you oppose him, his problem is to keep from grading you higher than you deserve in order to show he is not biased. This doesn't mean that you should always cantankerously dissent from what the instructor says; that gets tiresome too. And if the subject assigned is "My Pet Peeve," do not begin, "My pet peeve is the English instructor who assigns papers on 'my pet peeve.'" This was still funny during the War of 1812, but it has sort of lost its edge since then. It is in general good manners to avoid personalities.

SLIP OUT OF ABSTRACTION

21 If you will study the essay on college football [near the beginning of this essay], you will perceive that one reason for its appalling dullness is that it never gets down to particulars. It is just a series of not very glittering generalities: "football is bad for the colleges," "it has become too commercial," "football is a big business," "it is bad for the players," and so on. Such round phrases thudding against the reader's brain are unlikely to convince him, though they may well render him unconscious.

22   If you want the reader to believe that college football is bad for the players, you have to do more than say so. You have to display the evil. Take your roommate, Alfred Simkins, the second-string center. Picture poor old Alfy coming home from football practice every evening, bruised and aching, agonizingly tired, scarcely able to shovel the mashed potatoes into his mouth. Let us see him staggering up to the room, getting out his econ textbook, peering desperately at it with his good eye, falling asleep and failing the test in the morning. Let us share his unbearable tension as Saturday draws near. Will he fail, be demoted, lose his monthly allowance, be forced to return to the coal mines? And if he succeeds, what will be his reward? Perhaps a slight ripple of applause when the third-string center replaces him, a moment of elation in the locker room if the team wins, of despair if it loses. What will he look back on when he graduates from college? Toil and torn ligaments. And what will be his future? He is not good enough for pro football, and he is too obscure and weak in econ to succeed in stocks and bonds. College football is tearing the heart from Alfy Simkins and, when it finishes with him, will callously toss aside the shattered hulk.

23   This is no doubt a weak enough argument for the abolition of college football, but it is a sight better than saying, in three or four variations, that college football (in your opinion) is bad for the players.

24   Look at the work of any professional writer and notice how constantly he is moving from the generality, the abstract statement, to the concrete example, the facts and figures, the illustration. If he is writing on juvenile delinquency, he does not just tell you that juveniles are (it seems to him) delinquent and that (in his opinion) something should be done about it. He shows you juveniles being delinquent, tearing up movie theatres in Buffalo, stabbing high school principals in Dallas, smoking marijuana in Palo Alto. And more than likely he is moving toward some specific remedy, not just a general wringing of the hands.

25   It is no doubt possible to be *too* concrete, too illustrative or anecdotal, but few inexperienced writers err this way. For most the soundest advice is to be seeking always for the picture, to be always turning general remarks into seeable examples. Don't say, "Sororities teach girls the social graces." Say, "Sorority life teaches a girl how to carry on a conversation while pouring tea, without sloshing the tea into the saucer." Don't say, "I like certain kinds of popular music very much." Say, "Whenever I hear Gerber Sprinklittle play 'Mississippi Man' on the trombone, my socks creep up my ankles."

GET RID OF OBVIOUS PADDING

26 The student toiling away at his weekly English theme is too often tormented by a figure: five hundred words. How, he asks himself, is he to achieve this staggering total? Obviously by never using one word when he can somehow work in ten.

27   He is therefore seldom content with a plain statement like "Fast driving is dangerous." This has only four words in it. He takes thought, and the sentence becomes:

> In my opinion, fast driving is dangerous.

Better, but he can do better still:

> In my opinion, fast driving would seem to be rather dangerous.

If he is really adept, it may come out:

> In my humble opinion, though I do not claim to be an expert on this complicated subject, fast driving, in most circumstances, would seem to be rather dangerous in many respects, or at least so it would seem to me.

Thus four words have been turned into forty, and not an iota of content has been added.

28   Now this is a way to go about reaching five hundred words, and if you are content with a "D" grade, it is as good a way as any. But if you aim higher, you must work differently. Instead of stuffing your sentences with straw, you must try steadily to get rid of the padding, to make your sentences lean and tough. If you are really working at it, your first draft will greatly exceed the required total, and then you will work it down, thus:

29   It is thought in some quarters that fraternities do not contribute as much as might be expected to campus life.

30   Some people think that fraternities contribute little to campus life.
        The average doctor who practices in small towns or in the country must
        toil night and day to heal the sick.
31   Most country doctors work long hours.
        When I was a little girl, I suffered from shyness and embarrassment in the
        presence of others.
32   I was a shy little girl.
        It is absolutely necessary for the person employed as a marine fireman to
        give the matter of steam pressure his undivided attention at all times.
        The fireman has to keep his eye on the steam gauge.

33   You may ask how you can arrive at five hundred words at this rate.
        Simple. You dig up more real content. Instead of taking a couple of
        obvious points off the surface of the topic and then circling warily
        around them for six paragraphs, you work in and explore, figure out
        the details. You illustrate. You say that fast driving is dangerous, and
        then you prove it. How long does it take to stop a car at forty and at
        eighty? How far can you see at night? What happens when a tire
        blows? What happens in a head-on collision at fifty miles an hour?
        Pretty soon your paper will be full of broken glass and blood and head-
        less torsos, and reaching five hundred words will not really be a
        problem.

CALL A FOOL A FOOL

34 Some of the padding in freshman themes is to be blamed not on
    anxiety about the word minimum but on excessive timidity. The stu-
    dent writes, "In my opinion, the principal of my high school acted in
    ways that I believe every unbiased person would have to call foolish."
    This isn't exactly what he means. What he means is, "My high school
    principal was a fool." If he was a fool, call him a fool. Hedging the thing
    about with "in-my-opinion's" and "it-seems-to-me's" and "as-I-see-
    it's" and "at-least-from-my-point-of-view's" gains you nothing. Delete
    these phrases whenever they creep into your paper.
35   The student's tendency to hedge stems from a modesty that in other
    circumstances would be commendable. He is, he realizes, young and
    inexperienced, and he half suspects that he is dopey and fuzzy-
    minded beyond the average. Probably only too true. But it doesn't
    help to announce your incompetence six times in every paragraph.
    Decide what you want to say and say it as vigorously as possible, with-
    out apology and in plain words.
36   Linguistic diffidence can take various forms. One is what we call
    euphemism. This is the tendency to call a spade "a certain garden
    implement" or women's underwear "unmentionables." It is stronger
    in some eras than others and in some people than others but it always
    operates more or less in subjects that are touchy or taboo: death, sex,
    madness, and so on. Thus we shrink from saying "He died last night"
    but say instead "passed away," "left us," "joined his Maker," "went
    to his reward." Or we try to take off the tension with a lighter cliché:
    "kicked the bucket," "cashed in his chips," "handed in his dinner

pail." We have found all sorts of ways to avoid saying *mad:* "mentally ill," "touched," "not quite right upstairs," "feeble-minded," "innocent," "simple," "off his trolley," "not in his right mind." Even such a now plain word as *insane* began as a euphemism with the meaning "not healthy."

37   Modern science, particularly psychology, contributes many polysyllables in which we can wrap our thoughts and blunt their force. To many writers there is no such thing as a bad schoolboy. Schoolboys are maladjusted or unoriented or misunderstood or in the need of guidance or lacking in continued success toward satisfactory integration of the personality as a social unit, but they are never bad. Psychology no doubt makes us better men and women, more sympathetic and tolerant, but it doesn't make writing any easier. Had Shakespeare been confronted with psychology, "To be or not to be" might have come out, "To continue as a social unit or not to do so. That is the personality problem. Whether 'tis a better sign of integration at the conscious level to display a psychic tolerance toward the maladjustments and repressions induced by one's lack of orientation in one's environment or—" But Hamlet would never have finished the soliloquy.

38   Writing in the modern world, you cannot altogether avoid modern jargon. Nor, in an effort to get away from euphemism, should you salt your paper with four-letter words. But you can do much if you will mount guard against those roundabout phrases, those echoing polysyllables that tend to slip into your writing to rob it of its crispness and force.

BEWARE OF PAT EXPRESSIONS

39 Other things being equal, avoid phrases like "other things being equal." Those sentences that come to you whole, or in two or three doughy lumps, are sure to be bad sentences. They are no creation of yours but pieces of common thought floating in the community soup.

40   Pat expressions are hard, often impossible, to avoid, because they come too easily to be noticed and seem too necessary to be dispensed with. No writer avoids them altogether, but good writers avoid them more often than poor writers.

41   By "pat expressions" we mean such tags as "to all practical intents and purposes," "the pure and simple truth," "from where I sit," "the time of his life," "to the ends of the earth," "in the twinkling of an eye," "as sure as you're born," "over my dead body," "under cover of darkness," "took the easy way out," "when all is said and done," "told him time and time again," "parted the best of friends," "stand up and be counted," "gave him the best years of her life," "worked her fingers to the bone." Like other clichés, these expressions were once forceful. Now we should use them only when we can't possibly think of anything else.

42   Some pat expressions stand like a wall between the writer and thought. Such a one is "the American way of life." Many student writers feel that when they have said that something accords with the American way of life or does not they have exhausted the subject.

Actually, they have stopped at the highest level of abstraction. The American way of life is the complicated set of bonds between a hundred and eighty million ways. All of us know this when we think about it, but the tag phrase too often keeps us from thinking about it.

43   So with many another phrase dear to the politician: "this great land of ours," "the man in the street," "our national heritage." These may prove our patriotism or give a clue to our political beliefs, but otherwise they add nothing to the paper except words.

COLORFUL WORDS

44 The writer builds with words, and no builder uses a raw material more slippery and elusive and treacherous. A writer's work is a constant struggle to get the right word in the right place, to find that particular word that will convey his meaning exactly, that will persuade the reader or soothe him or startle or amuse him. He never succeeds altogether — sometimes he feels that he scarcely succeeds at all — but such successes as he has are what make the thing worth doing.

45   There is no book of rules for this game. One progresses through everlasting experiment on the basis of ever-widening experience. There are few useful generalizations that one can make about words as words, but there are perhaps a few.

46   Some words are what we call "colorful." By this we mean that they are calculated to produce a picture or induce an emotion. They are dressy instead of plain, specific instead of general, loud instead of soft. Thus, in place of "Her heart beat," we may write, "Her heart *pounded, throbbed, fluttered, danced.*" Instead of "He sat in his chair," we may say, "He *lounged, sprawled, coiled.*" Instead of "It was hot," we may say, "It was *blistering, sultry, muggy, suffocating, steamy, wilting.*"

47   However, it should not be supposed that the fancy word is always better. Often it is as well to write "Her heart beat" or "It was hot" if that is all it did or all it was. Ages differ in how they like their prose. The nineteenth century liked it rich and smoky. The twentieth has usually preferred it lean and cool. The twentieth century writer, like all writers, is forever seeking the exact word, but he is wary of sounding feverish. He tends to pitch it low, to understate it, to throw it away. He knows that if he gets too colorful, the audience is likely to giggle.

48   See how this strikes you: "As the rich, golden glow of the sunset died away along the eternal western hills, Angela's limpid blue eyes looked softly and trustingly into Montague's flashing brown ones, and her heart pounded like a drum in time with the joyous song surging in her soul." Some people like that sort of thing, but most modern readers would say, "Good grief," and turn on the television.

COLORED WORDS

49 Some words we would call not so much colorful as colored — that is, loaded with associations, good or bad. All words — except perhaps structure words — have associations of some sort. We have said that

the meaning of a word is the sum of the contexts in which it occurs. When we hear a word, we hear with it an echo of all the situations in which we have heard it before.

50   In some words, these echoes are obvious and discussable. The word *mother,* for example, has, for most people, agreeable associations. When you hear *mother* you probably think of home, safety, love, food, and various other pleasant things. If one writes, "She was like a mother to me," he gets an effect which he would not get in "She was like an aunt to me." The advertiser makes use of the associations of *mother* by working it in when he talks about his product. The politician works it in when he talks about himself.

51   So also with such words as *home, liberty, fireside, contentment, patriot, tenderness, sacrifice, childlike, manly, bluff, limpid.* All of these words are loaded with associations that would be rather hard to indicate in a straightforward definition. There is more than a literal difference between "They sat around the fireside" and "They sat around the stove." They might have been equally warm and happy around the stove, but *fireside* suggests leisure, grace, quiet tradition, congenial company, and *stove* does not.

52   Conversely, some words have bad associations. *Mother* suggests pleasant things, but *mother-in-law* does not. Many mothers-in-law are heroically lovable and some mothers drink gin all day and beat their children insensible, but these facts of life are beside the point. The point is that *mother* sounds good and *mother-in-law* does not.

53   Or consider the word *intellectual.* This would seem to be a complimentary term, but in point of fact it is not, for it has picked up associations of impracticality and ineffectuality and general dopiness. So also such words as *liberal, reactionary, Communist, socialist, capitalist, radical, schoolteacher, truck driver, undertaker, operator, salesman, huckster, speculator.* These convey meaning on the literal level, but beyond that — sometimes, in some places — they convey contempt on the part of the speaker.

54   The question of whether to use loaded words or not depends on what is being written. The scientist, the scholar, try to avoid them; for the poet, the advertising writer, the public speaker, they are standard equipment. But every writer should take care that they do not substitute for thought. If you write, "Anyone who thinks that is nothing but a Socialist (or Communist or capitalist)" you have said nothing except that you don't like people who think that, and such remarks are effective only with the most naive readers. It is always a bad mistake to think your readers more naïve than they really are.

COLORLESS WORDS

55   But probably most student writers come to grief not with words that are colorful or those that are colored but with those that have no color at all. A pet example is *nice,* a word we would find it hard to dispense with in casual conversation but which is no longer capable of adding much to a description. Colorless words are those of such general

meaning that in a particular sentence they mean nothing. Slang adjectives like *cool* ("That's real cool") tend to explode all over the language. They are applied to everything, lose their original force, and quickly die.

56   Beware also of nouns of very general meaning, like *circumstances, cases, instances, aspects, factors, relationships, attitudes, eventualities,* etc. In most circumstances you will find that those cases of writing which contain too many instances of words like these will in this and other aspects have factors leading to unsatisfactory relationships with the reader resulting in unfavorable attitudes on his part and perhaps other eventualities, like a grade of "D." Notice also what "etc." means. It means "I'd like to make this list longer, but I can't think of any more examples."

Discussion of Theme

1. Would students write more interesting themes if they could choose their own subjects? Should an instructor ever assign writing subjects? Explain.
2. Why is it difficult to make a college theme interesting?
3. How can you improve your writing if you use the advice here?
4. What do you think of the advice that a student should "always take the side that looks to you the hardest, least defensible. It will almost always turn out to be easier to write interestingly on that side." Why might this be true?
5. Roberts says that most assigned subjects will not require discussion on a personal basis but will, instead, "lie in broad areas of discussion." Would it be more appropriate to assign personal, intimate topics? Would this perhaps be a good way for instructors to become acquainted with their students as individuals?

Discussion of Rhetoric

1. Is Roberts's essay an example of the kind of good writing he asks for? If you wrote this essay, would you change anything—the use of examples or analogies, for instance?
2. In paragraph 11 Roberts suggests that a teacher might have had a happier life as "an electrician or a confidence man." Why does this combination produce a humorous effect? Would it be just as amusing if he had said "an electrician or house painter"?
3. Analyze the humor of Roberts's analogy in paragraph 39. Can you suggest others that would be amusing for the same reason?
4. Does the author's use of examples of poor writing help clarify his discussion?

Writing Assignments

1. How do politicians and advertisers use generalities to win people over to their point of view? What is the advantage in avoiding specifics?
2. Write to a high school senior, telling him how to succeed as a writer in college. Make sure that you follow your own advice.
3. Using Roberts's ideas, analyze a paper you have recently written.
4. Do you believe that "because an instructor is only human, after all," he is bound to grade papers at least partially on the basis of prejudice — personal, political, or social?

Library Exploration

Check out a book that explains — in the words of the writers themselves — how successful and highly regarded authors go about getting words down on paper.

Vocabulary

(2) ANTHOLOGY   a collection of literary works

(3) ABOLISHED   done away with

(11) CONTRIVE   manage by devious methods or with difficulty

(12) BROMIDES   clichés

(12) TEDIOUS   tiresome

(13) INEXORABLY   relentlessly

(15) TRITE   stale; hackneyed

(16) COGENT   well reasoned

(17) VACUITY   emptiness; lack of intelligence

(20) BIASED   prejudiced

(20) CANTANKEROUSLY   in an ill-natured or quarrelsome manner

(22) CALLOUSLY   unfeelingly

(25) ANECDOTAL   containing stories

(27) ADEPT   skillful

(33) WARILY   carefully; cautiously

(36) DIFFIDENCE   timidity; unassertiveness

(37) POLYSYLLABLES   words of several syllables

(37) INDUCED   brought on

(38) JARGON   lingo; specialized vocabulary

(44) ELUSIVE   hard to pin down

(51) CONGENIAL   friendly

(53) INEFFECTUALITY   inability to produce the proper or usual effect

(54) NAÏVE   innocent; unsophisticated

(56) EVENTUALITIES   outcomes

Mitford M. Mathews (1891–), editor and author of several books on language, was born in Alabama and educated at Southern University (Baton Rouge), the University of Alabama, and Harvard. He taught English and linguistics at the University of Chicago, and served on the editorial staff for the "Webster's New World Dictionary." Among his works are "The Beginnings of American English" (1931), "A Dictionary of Americanisms" (1951), and "American Words" (1959).

As every English teacher knows, too many students believe that a dictionary contains little more than the spelling and meaning of words. Here Mathews suggests that it has riches and resources beyond mere definitions.

MITFORD M. MATHEWS

The Freshman and His Dictionary

1   When I was a small boy a carpenter once said in my presence that few workmen, even among master mechanics, knew more than a fraction of the uses of an ordinary steel square. The remark amazed me, as at that early age I thought a carpenter's square was a very simple tool. It certainly appeared so to me—nothing more than two flat pieces of metal forming a right angle, and useful in marking a plank that one wished to saw in two in something like a workmanlike manner. True, the instrument has numerous markings and numbers on it, but I had never seen anyone making the slightest use of these, so I had concluded they might be ignored.

2   When I became older and found that large books have been written on the uses of the steel square, I changed my mind about the simplicity of the tool and the limited range of its usefulness. For many years as I have observed the use made of dictionaries by even good students, I have been reminded of that remark by the carpenter about steel squares.

3   Dictionaries are tools, and they are much more complicated, and capable of many more uses than students suspect. All of us know students need encouragement and guidance in the use of dictionaries, and perhaps there are few teachers of freshman composition but that devote a part of their program to an effort to help students form the habit of consulting dictionaries. Composition books for freshmen point out the need for instruction of this kind.

4   Despite what is being done, however, the fact is easily observable that few students are able to use their dictionaries with anything like efficiency. Certainly there must be very few of those who come up through the grades these days who are not familiar with the details of looking up words in dictionaries, but it is one thing to find a word in a dictionary and quite another to understand fully the information there given about it. It seems to me that college freshmen are fully prepared for and could profit by a well-planned introduction to the larger English dictionaries, and an acquaintance with what they contain. Such a program might well include material of the following kinds.

5   1. Students should know something about the large, unabridged dictionaries to which they have ready access in college. They might well be given brief sketches of the *Oxford English Dictionary,* the *English Dialect Dictionary,* by Joseph Wright, the old *Century Dictionary* (12 volumes), and the modern unabridged *Webster.* These may be called the "Big Four" in the dictionary field, and while it is certainly not anticipated that the freshman will ever provide himself with all of them, it is a cultural experience for him to become acquainted with the circumstances under which each of them was produced, and with the special excellencies each exhibits.

6   An acquaintance with these larger works will not only make the student aware of what kind of information about words is available in them, but it will leave him much better prepared to make efficient use of the desk-size dictionary with which he has some familiarity.

7   Many years ago a graduate student inconvenienced himself greatly to come a long distance to see me to ask if I could help him secure some information about the term "poll tax." He was preparing a doctor's thesis, he told me, and needed to know how long this term had been in the language, what its basic meaning was, and what other meanings it may have had in the course of its use in English. He was most surprised when I opened the *OED* to the appropriate place and showed him that all he needed to know about this term had been available within a few feet of his desk in the school where he was studying. It is not at all likely that any but the exceptional student will ever need all the information about words that the larger dictionaries afford, but it is well worth the while of every student to become acquainted with the fact that such information is available for those who at any time need to make use of it.

8   It is to be hoped that in such general instruction as may be given about the different dictionaries, some emphasis will be placed on the fact that modern dictionaries do their utmost to *record* usage, not to *prescribe* it. The tendency to regard the lexicographer as a linguistic legislator is so deep-seated that it will probably never be entirely overcome. The habit of thought that is back of such expressions as "the dictionary now permits us to pronounce it thus," has been with us for a long time, and will continue. But every student should have the wholesome experience of being taught that dictionaries attempt to give commonly accepted usage, and that correctness in the use of language varies sometimes according to time and place.

9   2. Along with some information about the origin and scope of the large dictionaries mentioned, there should be given some elementary information about the history of the English language and the place it occupies with reference to the others of the Indo-European group. I am certainly not foolish enough to suggest that all teachers of freshman composition become instructors in Germanic philology. What I have in mind is nothing more detailed than could be easily covered in one, or at most two, class sessions, the over-all relationships of the languages being presented briefly, with a few well chosen examples to indicate the relationship of a few of them.

10   The desirability of this elementary acquaintance with the linguistic position occupied by English is brought out quite clearly by Professor Pei in his *Story of Language:*

> Many years ago I was requested to tutor in French a young girl who had to take College Entrance Examinations. Knowing that she had had four years of Latin as well as three years of French, I spared no occasion in the course of the tutoring to remind her that certain French words which she had difficulty in remembering came from Latin words she knew. For a time she took it patiently, though with a somewhat bewildered air. But one day she finally blurted out: "Do you mean to tell me that there is a *connection* between Latin and French?" In the course of four years of one language and three of the other, it had never occurred to any of her Latin teachers to inform her that Latin had descendants, or to her French teacher to tell her that French has a progenitor!

11   3. The attention usually devoted to instruction in the use of the dictionary apparently stresses spellings, meanings, and pronunciations somewhat in the order here given. Certainly these are conspicuous features of any dictionary, and it is altogether desirable for students to be encouraged to turn to these works when they are confronted with a problem of the kind indicated.

12   The impression, however, inevitably conveyed by instruction restricted altogether to employing the dictionary as a problem-solver, is that such a book is of no particular use unless there is a problem requiring immediate attention. Students are sorely tempted to so manipulate things as to avoid encountering problems that drive them to a dictionary. It is to be feared that, for many of them, the dictionary is a form of medicine to be resorted to only in time of unavoidable need. They associate it perhaps with castor oil or some other undesirable, dynamic type of cathartic. It is a most helpful thing for the student to learn that dictionaries are filled with interesting information from

which one can derive much pleasure and instruction, even though he may not be confronted with an urgent problem of any kind.

13   Students should be encouraged to develop a wholesome curiosity about words that present no particular problem in spelling, pronunciation, or meaning. As a rule, the words we know well do not rise to the surface of our consciousness. It is only rarely that some common, everyday term forces itself upon our attention so urgently that for the first time we turn to the dictionary to see what lies back of it.

14   This use of the dictionary when there is no immediate, pressing need to do so, this giving attention to words we have known for a long time but have never grown curious about, is most rewarding. This kind of use of the dictionary we may think of as the labor of free men; the forced use is more properly likened to that of slaves.

15   On every hand there are words of fascinating backgrounds about which the dictionary has much to teach us. Certainly the name *Jesus,* that of the founder of Christianity, is well known to all those with whom you and I come in contact. Perhaps few of us have ever felt impelled to look the word up in a dictionary, or even realized that dictionaries contain it. An examination of the dictionary, however, reveals that the name his parents gave the Savior was Joshua, and it was by this thoroughly Jewish name that He was known by those He lived among.

16   The first accounts of His life were written in Greek, and in these writings *Joshua* was transliterated into *Jesus,* a name that is certainly not Jewish in its present dress and at the same time appears odd as a Greek name.

17   Not even a grade-school pupil is likely to be baffled by *ostrich,* but one who is allergic to words may well become curious about it. Allow it to become the focus of your attention for a moment and see how odd the word appears. Make a guess as to where you think it might have come from, and then check up on yourself by turning to the dictionary. You might be surprised, as I was, to find the word is made up of two, one from Latin and one from Greek, which have so blended as to obscure altogether the fact that the expression signifies "bird-bird" or "bird-sparrow." It is a good term to bear in mind and use upon those of our brethren who insist that only "pure English" should be used, and profess to be pained by such obvious hybrids as *cablegram* and *electrocute.*

18   There may be few teachers who have discovered how rewarding it is to look curiously at the scientific terms used in dictionaries in the definitions of plants and animals. These expressions are usually hurried over by most of us as being the exclusive property of scientists and of very little interest for others.

19   It is surprisingly interesting to linger over such terms. It is a gratifying experience to discover one that yields its significance somewhat readily. Our common mocking bird, for instance, is *Mimus polyglottos.* The ingenuity needed for deciphering this expression is possessed by all of us. *Mimic* and *polyglot* are all we need to see that our expression means "the many-tongued mimic," a fitting description of the bird in question.

20   In the spring when the snow has melted, and the earth is warming

up from its long cold sleep, the cheerful piping notes of a very small frog begin to be heard in the woods and marshes. People call this little creature a *spring peeper* because of the season when his little peeping notes are first heard, but scientists dub him *Hyla crucifer.* As we puzzle over this name we are likely to give up on *Hyla* for there is no other word in the English language with which we can, perhaps, associate it properly. It has descendants among us, but we are not likely to be acquainted with them.

21 *Crucifer* though is easier. Even if we do not know that a *crucifer* is one who carries a cross, especially in a church procession, we can reason out the two elements in the word and see that it must have the meaning of one who carries a cross. Our ability to reason out this much of the scientific expression may increase our curiosity about the first element *Hyla.* Here is a helpful hint. As we all know, these scientific genus names are often from Greek. So we are reasoning sensibly when we suppose *Hyla* is Greek.

22 The fact is elementary that when we are confronted with a Greek word which begins with an *h,* i.e. with a rough breathing, it behooves us as cautious scouts to cast about in our minds for a possible Latin cognate beginning with an *s.* Substituting an *s* in *hyla* we come up with *syla.* Let us study *syla* a bit. It is almost a word. If we might be so bold as to insert a -v- and make it *sylva* we have a word that is in our dictionary, and one we met in a slightly different form, *silva,* when we studied first-year Latin.

23 The little detail of why this -v- is necessary need not bother us in the slightest at this point, because we are just having fun with no idea of becoming linguisticians. And this is it. *Hyla* and *sylva* go together and they both mean wood or forest. Now we can interpret this *Hyla crucifer* "the (little) fellow who lives in the woods and carries a cross," and when we find that this spring peeper has a dark marking on his back shaped like a cross, we are indeed gratified that now light is shining where previously all was darkness.

24 A teacher who is fortunate enough to have an assiduously cultivated curiosity about words will over and over again bring to a class gleanings of unexpected sorts from dictionaries. Such sharing of treasures will do more than anything else to bring home to students the fact that dictionaries are not dull, enlarged spelling books. They are filled with such a number of things that we can never exhaust their treasures but we can all be as happy as kings as we come time after time upon interesting nuggets of the kind just mentioned.

Discussion of Theme

1. How accurate is Mathews's description of the attitude most students have toward the dictionary?
2. Does the practice of making students look up words in dictionaries and write down definitions make them dislike using a dictionary? How helpful are spelling and vocabulary tests in learning new words?

3. Why do many people tend to equate the authority of the dictionary with that of the Bible? Does Mathews attack or share this point of view?
4. Do we judge others by the way they speak? How significant are accent, vocabulary, and diction in the formation of our impressions of strangers?
5. If you had absolutely no access to a dictionary, how much effect would it have on your writing? On your speaking?

Discussion of Rhetoric

1. Although this article was originally a speech to a convention of English teachers, Mathews occasionally expresses himself as one might to a young person. Where do such phrases and sentences occur? Is this effective?
2. What is the function of the opening anecdote? What analogy is established by Mathews? Would you classify this as an effective opening?
3. What is the level of Mathews's language? Formal, informal? Give examples to illustrate your answer.
4. If you have been taught that *each* is always singular, look up its treatment in your dictionary and in a grammar handbook. Are there any inconsistencies?

Writing Assignments

1. Give your suggestions for improving your present desk dictionary so that it would better serve your needs.
2. When the *Dictionary of American Slang* appeared in 1960, it created a furor because it contained so-called obscene words. Give your opinion of this adverse reaction.
3. Explain why you do or do not enjoy consulting a dictionary.
4. The author begins his essay with an analogy: he compares a steel square to a dictionary. Using analogy, compare a familiar object to a technical or unfamiliar subject.

Library Exploration

1. Examine the dictionaries mentioned by Mathews, in particular the *Oxford English Dictionary* and *Webster's Third New International Dictionary*.
2. A new unabridged dictionary has been published by Random House. Choose a few words from the vocabulary and compare their definitions in this dictionary with those in *Webster's Third*.
3. There was considerable controversy about *Webster's Third*. Look at a book like *Dictionaries and That Dictionary*, by James Sledd and Wilma R. Ebbitt, and summarize the major criticisms.

4. Linguistic experts have tried to clarify the problem of usage in American English. Make a brief report on the positions of Theodore Bernstein, E. B. White, and Bergen Evans.

Vocabulary

(5) UNABRIDGED complete; uncut

(8) PRESCRIBE dictate; authorize

(8) LEXICOGRAPHER compiler of a dictionary

(8) LINGUISTIC of or relating to language

(9) PHILOLOGY study of human speech as an index of cultural history

(10) PROGENITOR forefather

(11) CONSPICUOUS obvious

(12) MANIPULATE operate; manage artfully

(12) CATHARTIC cleansing or purifying agent; laxative

(12) DERIVE take; receive

(15) IMPELLED driven by strong force

(16) TRANSLITERATED rendered in the letters of a different alphabet

(19) INGENUITY skill; cleverness

(19) DECIPHERING converting into understandable forms; decoding

(21) GENUS group with common characteristics

(22) COGNATE word related by derivation or descent

(24) ASSIDUOUSLY attentively; diligently

Bergen Evans (1904–), well known to the American public as the writer of a daily syndicated feature, "The Last Word," and former moderator of several television programs, is the author of popular works on language. He received his degrees from Miami University, Harvard, and Oxford and is now professor of English at Northwestern University. Among his works are "Natural History of Nonsense" (1946), "Boswell's Life of Johnson" (1952), and "Comfortable Words" (1962). He often contributes articles to leading magazines, including the "Atlantic" and "New Republic."

This essay is a defense of "Webster's Third New International Dictionary" against the criticism that greeted its publication. Evans points out that "a dictionary is good only insofar as it is a comprehensive and accurate description of current usage."

BERGEN EVANS

But What's a Dictionary For?

1 The storm of abuse in the popular press that greeted the appearance of *Webster's Third New International Dictionary* is a curious phenomenon. Never has a scholarly work of this stature been attacked with such unbridled fury and contempt. An article in the *Atlantic* viewed it as a "disappointment," a "shock," a "calamity," "a scandal and a disaster." The New York *Times,* in a special editorial, felt that

the work would "accelerate the deterioration" of the language and sternly accused editors of betraying a public trust. The *Journal* of the American Bar Association saw the publication as "deplorable," "a flagrant example of lexicographic irresponsibility," "a serious blow to the cause of good English." *Life* called it "a non-word deluge," "monstrous," "abominable," and "a cause for dismay." They doubted that "Lincoln could have modelled his Gettysburg Address" on it—a concept of how things get written that throws very little light on Lincoln but a great deal on *Life*.

2   What underlies all this sound and fury? Is the claim of the G. & C. Merriam Company, probably the world's greatest dictionary maker, that the preparation of the work cost $3.5 million, that it required the efforts of three hundred over a period of twenty-seven years, working on the largest collection of citations ever assembled in any language — is all this a fraud, a hoax?

3   So monstrous a discrepancy in evaluation requires us to examine basic principles. Just what's a dictionary for? What does it propose to do? What does the common reader go to a dictionary to find? What has the purchaser of a dictionary a right to expect for his money?

4   Before we look at basic principles, it is necessary to interpose two brief statements. The first of these is that a dictionary is concerned with words. Some dictionaries give various kinds of other useful information. Some have tables of weights and measures on the flyleaves. Some list historical events, and some, home remedies. And there's nothing wrong with their so doing. But the great increase in our vocabulary in the past three decades compels all dictionaries to make more efficient use of their space. And if something must be eliminated, it is sensible to throw out these extraneous things and stick to words.

5   Yet wild wails arose. The *Saturday Review* lamented that one can no longer find the goddess Astarte under a separate heading—though they point out that a genus of mollusks named after the goddess is included! They seemed to feel that out of sheer perversity the editors of the dictionary stooped to mollusks while ignoring goddesses and that, in some way, this typifies modern lexicography. Mr. Wilson Follett, folletizing (his mental processes demand some special designation) in the *Atlantic,* cried out in horror that one is not even able to learn from the Third International "that the Virgin was Mary the mother of Jesus"!

6   The second brief statement is that there has been even more progress in the making of dictionaries in the past thirty years than there has been in the making of automobiles. The difference, for example, between the much-touted Second International (1934) and the much-clouted Third International (1961) is not like the difference between yearly models but like the difference between the horse and buggy and the automobile. Between the appearance of these two editions a whole new science related to the making of dictionaries, the science of descriptive linguistics, has come into being.

7   Modern linguistics gets its character from Leonard Bloomfield's *Language* (1933). Bloomfield, for thirteen years professor of Germanic philology at the University of Chicago and for nine years professor

of linguistics at Yale, was one of those inseminating scholars who can't be relegated to any department and don't dream of accepting established categories and procedures just because they're established. He was as much an anthropologist as a linguist and his concepts of language were shaped not by Strunk's *Elements of Style* but by his knowledge of Cree Indian dialects.

8   The broad general findings of the new science are:

1. All languages are systems of human conventions, not systems of natural laws. The first—and essential—step in the study of any language is observing and setting down precisely what happens when native speakers speak it.

2. Each language is unique in its pronunciation, grammar, and vocabulary. It cannot be described in terms of logic or of some theoretical, ideal language. It cannot be described in terms of any other language, or even in terms of its own past.

3. All languages are dynamic rather than static, and hence a "rule" in any language can only be a statement of contemporary practice. Change is constant—and normal.

4. "Correctness" can only rest upon usage, for the simple reason that there is nothing else for it to rest on. And all usage is relative.

9   From these propositions it follows that a dictionary is good only insofar as it is a comprehensive and accurate description of current usage. And to be comprehensive it must include some indication of social and regional associations.

10   New dictionaries are needed because English has changed more in the past two generations than any other time in its history. It has had to adapt to extraordinary cultural and technical changes, two world wars, unparalleled changes in transportation and communication, and unprecedented movements of populations.

11   More subtly, but pervasively, it has changed under the influence of mass education and the growth of democracy. As written English is used by increasing millions and for more reasons than ever before, the language has become more utilitarian and more informal. Every publication in America today includes pages that would appear, to the purist of forty years ago, unbuttoned gibberish. Not that they are; they simply show that you can't hold the language of one generation up as a model for the next.

12   It's not that you mustn't. You *can't*. For example, in the issue in which *Life* stated editorially that it would follow the Second International, there were over forty words, constructions, and meanings which are in the Third International but not in the Second. The issue of the New York *Times* which hailed the Second International as the authority to which it would adhere and the Third International as a scandal and a betrayal which it would reject used one hundred and fifty-three separate words, phrases, and constructions which are listed in the Third International but not in the Second and nineteen others which are condemned in the Second. Many of them are used many times, more than three hundred such uses in all. The Washington *Post,* in an editorial captioned "Keep Your Old Webster's," says, in the first sentence, "don't throw it away," and in the second, "hang on to

it." But the old Webster's labels *don't* "colloquial" and doesn't include "hang on to," in this sense, at all.

13   In short, all of these publications are written in the language that the Third International describes, even the very editorials which scorn it. And this is no coincidence, because the Third International isn't setting up any new standards at all; it is simply describing what *Life,* the Washington *Post,* and the New York *Times* are doing. Much of the dictionary's material comes from these very publications, the *Times* in particular, furnishing more of its illustrative quotations than any other newspaper.

14   And the papers have no choice. No journal or periodical could sell a single issue today if it restricted itself to the American language of twenty-eight years ago. It couldn't discuss half the things we are interested in, and its style would seem stiff and cumbrous. If the editorials were serious, the public—and the stockholders—have reason to be grateful that the writers on these publications are more literate than the editors.

15   And so back to our questions: what's a dictionary for, and how, in 1962, can it best do what it ought to do? The demands are simple. The common reader turns to a dictionary for information about the spelling, pronunciation, meaning, and proper use of words. He wants to know what is current and respectable. But he wants—and has a right to—the truth, the full truth. And the full truth about any language, and especially about American English today, is that there are many areas in which certainty is impossible and simplification is misleading.

16   Even in so settled a matter as spelling, a dictionary cannot always be absolute. *Theater* is correct, but so is *theatre.* And so are *traveled* and *travelled, plow* and *plough, catalog* and *catalogue,* and scores of other variants. The reader may want a single certainty. He may have taken an unyielding position in an argument, he may have wagered in support of his conviction and may demand that the dictionary "settle" the matter. But neither his vanity nor his purse is any concern of the dictionary's; it must record the facts. And the fact here is that there are many words in our language which may be spelled, with equal correctness, in either of two ways.

17   So with pronunciation. A citizen listening to his radio might notice that James B. Conant, Bernard Baruch, and Dwight D. Eisenhower pronounce *economics* as ECKuhnomiks, while A. Whitney Griswold, Adlai Stevenson, and Herbert Hoover pronounce it EEKuhnomiks. He turns to the dictionary to see which of the two pronunciations is "right" and finds that they are both acceptable.

18   Has he been betrayed? Has the dictionary abdicated its responsibility? Should it say that one *must* speak like the president of Harvard or like the president of Yale, like the thirty-first President of the United States or like the thirty-fourth? Surely it's none of its business to make a choice. Not because of the distinction of these particular speakers; lexicography, like God, is no respecter of persons. But because so widespread and conspicuous a use of two pronunciations among people of this elevation shows that there *are* two pronunciations. Their speaking establishes the fact which the dictionary must record.

19   Among the "enormities" with which *Life* taxes the Third International is its listing of "the common mispronunciation" *heighth*. That it is labeled a "dialectal variant" seems, somehow, to compound the felony. But one hears the word so pronounced, and if one professes to give a full account of American English in the 1960s, one has to take some cognizance of it. All people do not possess *Life's* intuitive perception that the word is so "monstrous" that even to list it as a dialect variation is to merit scorn. Among these, by the way, was John Milton, who, in one of the greatest passages in all literature, besought the Holy Spirit to raise him to the "highth" of his great argument. And even the *Oxford English Dictionary* is so benighted as to list it, in full boldface, right alongside of *Height* as a variant that has been in the language since at least 1290.

20   Now there are still, apparently, millions of Americans who retain, in this as in much else, some of the speech of Milton. This particular pronunciation seems to be receding, but the *American Dialect Dictionary* still records instances of it from almost every state on the Eastern seaboard and notes that it is heard from older people and "occasionally in educated speech," "common with good speakers," "general," "widespread."

21   Under these circumstances, what is a dictionary to do? Since millions speak the word this way, the pronunciation can't be ignored. Since it has been in use as long as we have any record of English and since it has been used by the greatest writers, it can't be described as substandard or slang. But it is heard now only in certain localities. That makes it a dialectal pronunciation, and an honest dictionary will list it as such. What else can it do? Should it do?

22   The average purchaser of a dictionary uses it most often, probably, to find out what a word "means." As a reader, he wants to know what an author intended to convey. As a speaker or writer, he wants to know what a word will convey to his auditors. And this, too, is complex, subtle, and forever changing.

23   An illustration is furnished by an editorial in the Washington *Post* (January 17, 1962). After a ringing appeal to those who "love truth and accuracy" and the usual bombinations about "abdication of authority" and "barbarism," the editorial charges the Third International with "pretentious and obscure verbosity" and specifically instances its definition of "so simple an object as a door."

24   The definition reads:

> a movable piece of firm material or a structure supported usu. along one side and swinging on pivots or hinges, sliding along a groove, rolling up and down, revolving as one of four leaves, or folding like an accordion by means of which an opening may be closed or kept open for passage into or out of a building, room, or other covered enclosure or a car, airplane, elevator, or other vehicle.

Then follows a series of special meanings, each particularly defined and, where necessary, illustrated by a quotation.

25   Since, aside from roaring and admonishing the "gentlemen from Springfield" that "accuracy and brevity are virtues," the *Post's* editorial fails to explain what is wrong with the definition, we can only

infer from "so simple" a thing that the writer takes the plain, down-right, man-in-the-street attitude that a door is a door and any damn fool knows that.

26   But if so, he has walked into one of lexicography's biggest booby traps: the belief that the obvious is easy to define. Whereas the opposite is true. Anyone can give a fair description of the strange, the new, or the unique. It's the commonplace, the habitual, that challenges definition, for its very commonness compels us to define it in uncommon terms. Dr. Johnson was ridiculed on just this score when his dictionary appeared in 1755. For two hundred years his definition of a network as "any thing reticulated or decussated, at equal distances, with interstices between the intersections" has been good for a laugh. But in the merriment one thing is always overlooked: no one has yet come up with a better definition! Subsequent dictionaries defined it as a mesh and then defined a mesh as a network. That's simple, all right.

27   Anyone who attempts sincerely to state what the word *door* means in the United States of America today can't take refuge in a log cabin. There has been an enormous proliferation of closing and demarking devices and structures in the past twenty years, and anyone who tries to thread his way through the many meanings now included under *door* may have to sacrifice brevity to accuracy and even have to employ words that a limited vocabulary may find obscure.

28   Is the entrance to a tent a door, for instance? And what of the thing that seals the exit of an airplane? Is this a door? Or what of those sheets and jets of air that are now being used, in place of old-fashioned oak and hinges, to screen entrances and exits. Are they doors? And what of those accordion-like things that set off various sections of many modern apartments? The fine print in the lease takes it for granted that they are doors and that spaces demarked by them are rooms — and the rent is computed on the number of rooms.

29   Was I gypped by the landlord when he called the folding contraption that shuts off my kitchen a door? I go to the Second International, which the editor of the *Post* urges me to use in preference to the Third International. Here I find that a door is

> The movable frame or barrier of boards, or other material, usually turning on hinges or pivots or sliding, by which an entranceway into a house or apartment is closed and opened; also, a similar part of a piece of furniture, as in a cabinet or bookcase.

This is only forty-six words, but though it includes the cellar door, it excludes the barn door and the accordion-like thing.

30   So I go on to the Third International. I see at once that the new definition is longer. But I'm looking for accuracy, and if I must sacrifice brevity to get it, then I must. And, sure enough, in the definition which raised the *Post*'s blood pressure, I find the words "folding like an accordion." The thing *is* a door, and my landlord is using the word in one of its currently accepted meanings.

31   We don't turn to a work of reference merely for confirmation. We all have words in our vocabularies which we have misunderstood, and to come on the true meaning of one of these words is quite a shock. All our complacency and self-esteem rise to oppose the discovery. But

eventually we must accept the humiliation and laugh it off as best we can.

32   Some, often those who have set themselves up as authorities, stick to their error and charge the dictionary with being in a conspiracy against them. They are sure that their meaning is the only "right" one. And when the dictionary doesn't bear them out they complain about "permissive" attitudes instead of correcting their mistake.

33   The New York *Times* and the *Saturday Review* both regarded as contemptibly "permissive" the fact that one meaning of one word was illustrated by a quotation from Polly Adler. But a rudimentary knowledge of the development of any language would have told them that the underworld has been a far more active force in shaping and enriching speech than all the synods that have ever convened. Their attitude is like that of the patriot who canceled his subscription to the *Dictionary of American Biography* when he discovered that the very first volume included Benedict Arnold!

34   The ultimate of "permissiveness," singled out by almost every critic for special scorn, was the inclusion in the Third International of *finalize*. It was this, more than any other one thing, that was given as the reason for sticking to the good old Second International—that "peerless authority on American English," as the *Times* called it. But if it was such an authority, why didn't they look into it? They could have found *finalize* if they had.

35   And why shouldn't it be there? It exists. It's been recorded for two generations. Millions employ it every day. Two Presidents of the United States—men of widely differing cultural backgrounds—have used it in formal statements. And so has the Secretary-General of the United Nations, a man of unusual linguistic attainments. It isn't permitting the word but omitting it that would break faith with the reader. Because it is exactly the sort of word we want information about.

36   To list it as substandard would be to imply that it is used solely by the ignorant and the illiterate. But this would be a misrepresentation: President Kennedy and U Thant are highly educated men, and both are articulate and literate. It isn't even a freak form. On the contrary, it is a classic example of a regular process of development in English, a process which has given us such thoroughly accepted words as *generalize, minimize, formalize,* and *verbalize.* Nor can it be dismissed on logical grounds or on the ground that it is a mere duplication of *complete.* It says something that *complete* doesn't say and says it in a way that is significant in the modern bureaucratic world: one usually *completes* something which he has initiated but *finalizes* the work of others.

37   One is free to dislike the word. I don't like it. But the editor of a dictionary has to examine the evidence for a word's existence and seek it in context to get, as clearly and closely as he can, the exact meaning that it conveys to those who use it. And if it is widely used by well-educated, literate, reputable people, he must list it as a standard word. He is not compiling a volume of his own prejudices.

38   An individual's use of his native tongue is the surest index to his position within his community. And those who turn to a dictionary

expect from it some statement of the current status of a word or a grammatical construction. And it is with the failure to assume this function that modern lexicography has been most fiercely charged. The charge is based on a naïve assumption that simple labels can be attached in all instances. But they can't. Some words are standard in some construction and not in others. There may be as many shades of status as of meaning, and modern lexicography instead of abdicating this function has fulfilled it to a degree utterly unknown to earlier dictionaries.

39 Consider the word *fetch,* meaning to "go and bring to." Until recently a standard word of full dignity ("Fetch me, I pray thee, a little water in a vessel" — I Kings 17:10), it has become slightly tainted. Perhaps the command latent in it is resented as undemocratic. Or maybe its use in training dogs to retrieve has made some people feel that it is an undignified word to apply to human beings. But, whatever the reason, there is a growing uncertainty about its status, and hence it is the sort of word that conscientious people look up in a dictionary.

40 Will they find it labeled "good" or "bad"? Neither, of course, because either applied indiscriminately would be untrue. The Third International lists nineteen different meanings of the verb *to fetch.* Of these some are labeled "dialectal," some "chiefly dialectal," some "obsolete," one "chiefly Scottish," and two "not in formal use." The primary meaning — "to go after and bring back" — is not labeled and hence can be accepted as standard, accepted with the more assurance because the many shades of labeling show us that the word's status has been carefully considered.

41 On grammatical questions the Third International tries to be equally exact and thorough. Sometimes a construction is listed without comment, meaning that in the opinion of the editors it is unquestionably respectable. Sometimes a construction carries the comment "used by speakers and writers on all educational levels though disapproved by some grammarians." Or the comment may be "used in substandard speech and formerly also by reputable writers." Or "less often in standard speech." Or simply "dial."

42 And this very accurate reporting is based on evidence which is presented for our examination. One may feel that the evidence is inadequate or that the evaluation is erroneous. But surely, in the face of classification so much more elaborate than any known heretofore, one cannot fly into a rage and insist that the dictionary is "out to destroy . . . every vestige of linguistic punctilio . . . every criterion for distinguishing between better usages and worse."

43 Words, as we have said, are continually shifting their meanings and connotations and hence their status. A word which has dignity, say, in the vocabulary of an older person may go down in other people's estimation. Like *fetch.* The older speaker is not likely to be aware of this and will probably be inclined to ascribe the snickers of the young at his speech to that degeneration of manners which every generation has deplored in its juniors. But a word which is coming up in the scale — like *jazz,* say, or more recently, *crap* — will strike his ear at once. We are much more aware of the offenses given us than of those we give.

And if he turns to a dictionary and finds the offending word listed as standard — or even listed, apparently — his response is likely to be an outburst of indignation.

44   But the dictionary can neither snicker nor fulminate. It records. It will offend many, no doubt, to find the expression *wise up*, meaning to inform or to become informed, listed in the Third International with no restricting label. To my aging ears it still sounds like slang. But the evidence — quotations from the *Kiplinger Washington Letter* and the *Wall Street Journal* — convinces me that it is I who am out of step, lagging behind. If such publications have taken to using *wise up* in serious contexts, with no punctuational indication of irregularity, then it is obviously respectable. And finding it so listed and supported, I only say that it's nice to be informed and sigh to realize that I am becoming an old fogy. But, of course, I don't have to use it (and I'll be damned if I will! "Let them smile, as I do now, At the old forsaken bough Where I cling").

45   In part, the trouble is due to the fact that there is no standard for standard. Ideas of what is proper to use in serious, dignified speech and writing are changing — and with breathtaking rapidity. This is one of the major facts of contemporary American English. But it is no more the dictionary's business to oppose this process than to speed it up.

46   Even in our standard speech some words are more dignified and some more informal than others, and dictionaries have tried to guide us through these uncertainties by marking certain words and constructions as "colloquial," meaning "inappropriate in a formal situation." But this distinction, in the opinion of most scholars, has done more harm than good. It has created the notion that these particular words are inferior, when actually they might be the best possible words in an informal statement. And so — to the rage of many reviewers — the Third International has dropped this label. Not all labels, as angrily charged, but only this one out of a score. And the doing so may have been an error, but it certainly didn't constitute "betrayal" or "abandoning of all distinctions." It was intended to end a certain confusion.

47   In all the finer shades of meaning, of which the status of a word is only one, the user is on his own, whether he likes it or not. Despite *Life*'s artless assumption about the Gettysburg Address, nothing worth writing is written *from* a dictionary. The dictionary, rather, comes along afterwards and describes what *has been* written.

48   Words in themselves are not dignified, or silly, or wise, or malicious. But they can be used in dignified, silly, wise, or malicious ways by dignified, silly, wise, or malicious people. *Egghead,* for example, is a perfectly legitimate word, as legitimate as *highbrow* or *long-haired*. But there is something very wrong and very undignified, by civilized standards, in a belligerent dislike for intelligence and education. *Yak* is an amusing word for persistent chatter. Anyone could say, "We were just yakking over a cup of coffee," with no harm to his dignity. But to call a Supreme Court decision *yakking* is to be vulgarly insulting and so, undignified. Again, there's nothing wrong with *confab* when it's appropriate. But when the work of a great research project, employing hundreds of distinguished scholars over several decades and in-

volving the honor of the greatest publishing houses in the world, is described as *confabbing* (as the New York *Times* editorially described the preparation of the Third International), the use of this particular word asserts that the lexicographers had merely sat around and talked idly. And the statement becomes undignified — if not, indeed, slanderous.

49   The lack of dignity in such statements is not in the words, nor in the dictionaries that list them, but in the hostility that deliberately seeks this tone of expression. And in expressing itself the hostility frequently shows that those who are expressing it don't know how to use a dictionary. Most of the reviewers seem unable to read the Third International and unwilling to read the Second.

50   The *American Bar Association Journal,* for instance, in a typical outburst ("a deplorable abdication of responsibility"), picked out for special scorn the inclusion in the Third International of the word *irregardless.* "As far as the new Webster's is concerned," said the *Journal,* "this meaningless verbal bastard is just as legitimate as any other word in the dictionary." Thirty seconds spent in examining the book they were so roundly condemning would have shown them that in it *irregardless* is labeled "nonstand" — which means "nonstandard," which means "not conforming to the usage generally characteristic of educated native speakers of the language." Is that "just as legitimate as any other word in the dictionary"?

51   The most disturbing fact of all is that the editors of a dozen of the most influential publications in America are under the impression that *authoritative* must mean *authoritarian.* Even the "permissive" Third International doesn't recognize this identification — editors' attitudes being not yet, fortunately, those of the American people. But the Fourth International may have to.

52   The new dictionary may have many faults. Nothing that tries to meet an everchanging situation over a terrain as vast as contemporary English can hope to be free of them. And much in it is open to honest, and informed, disagreement. There can be linguistic objection to the eradication of proper names. The removal of guides to pronunciation from the foot of every page may not have been worth the valuable space it saved. The new method of defining words of many meanings has disadvantages as well as advantages. And of the half million or more definitions, hundreds, possibly thousands, may seem inadequate or imprecise. To some (of whom I am one) the omission of the label "colloquial" will seem meritorious; to others it will seem a loss.

53   But one thing is certain: anyone who solemnly announces in the year 1962 that he will be guided in matters of English usage by a dictionary published in 1934 is talking ignorant and pretentious nonsense.

Discussion of Theme

1. Discuss the points of inconsistency in the positions taken by the *New York Times, Washington Post,* and *Life.* (See paragraphs 11–13.)
2. What is a thesaurus? How does it differ from a dictionary?

3. Can a dictionary tell one what one *should* say and what a word *should* mean? Explain.
4. How have social changes in the past fifty years increased the need for new dictionaries?
5. Speculate about why it is frequently difficult for us to explain the meaning of a word in spite of "knowing" what it means and being able to use it correctly.

Discussion of Rhetoric

1. This essay makes excellent use of illustration, example, and evidence. Cite several examples of these rhetorical devices.
2. What is Evans's best evidence favoring his own viewpoint?
3. In paragraphs 5 and 6 what examples do you find of Evans's pleasure in playing with words? What relation — if any — does the example in paragraph 5 have to the topic he introduces in paragraph 34?
4. In the latter portion of the second sentence, paragraph 51, which word bears the full weight of what Evans wishes to imply? How would its absence alter his meaning?

Writing Assignments

1. Many adults object to the language used by many young persons on the grounds that it is obscene or drug-oriented. Argue for or against this attitude toward language.
2. State clearly what you believe is the purpose of a dictionary.
3. Examine the reasons why "an individual's use of his native tongue is the surest index to his position within his community." Illustrate your response with examples of the sort of language used by various kinds of individuals.
4. Using paragraph 48 as a guide, examine similar words, showing how their connotations shift in varying situations.

Library Exploration

1. Learn the identity of Polly Adler to clarify Evans's point in paragraph 33.
2. Find out what *phonemes* means.

Vocabulary

(1) PHENOMENON extraordinary or significant fact or event

(1) UNBRIDLED unrestrained

(1) LEXICOGRAPHIC relating to the making of a dictionary

(3) DISCREPANCY variation; lack of agreement

(4) EXTRANEOUS nonessential

(5) LAMENTED mourned

(5) PERVERSITY contrariness; obstinacy in opposing what is right or reasonable

(7) PHILOLOGY study of human speech as it relates to cultural history

(7) INSEMINATING idea-planting

(7) RELEGATED consigned by way of classification

(10) UNPRECEDENTED without example; novel

(11) UTILITARIAN useful

(11) GIBBERISH meaningless chatter

(14) CUMBROUS unwieldy; heavy

(18) ABDICATED renounced; abandoned

(18) CONSPICUOUS obvious

(19) ENORMITIES serious offenses

(19) COGNIZANCE recognition

(19) INTUITIVE based on insight

(19) BENIGHTED unenlightened

(23) BOMBINATIONS buzzings; dronings

(23) PRETENTIOUS showy; inflated

(23) VERBOSITY wordiness

(25) INFER guess; conclude

(26) RETICULATED divided

(26) DECUSSATED intersected into units

(26) INTERSTICES intervals; spaces

(27) PROLIFERATION rapid reproduction

(31) COMPLACENCY smugness; self-assurance

(33) RUDIMENTARY undeveloped; beginning

(33) SYNODS (church) councils

(36) ARTICULATE capable of precise expression

(37) REPUTABLE respectable; said to be good

(39) LATENT hidden

(39) CONSCIENTIOUS scrupulous; careful

(42) ERRONEOUS mistaken

(42) PUNCTILIO careful observance

(43) ASCRIBE attribute; credit

(43) DEGENERATION decline; deterioration

(44) FULMINATE rage vociferously

(48) MALICIOUS deliberately mean

(52) ERADICATION elimination

(52) MERITORIOUS deserving of honor

Robert Gorham Davis (1908–
), professor of English at
Columbia University, was born
in Massachusetts and educated
at Harvard University. He has
lectured abroad and participated in the Salzburg Seminar
in American Studies. Among his
special interests are the history
of prose fiction and contemporary literature.

This essay, originally written for
freshman English students at
Harvard University, defines and
illustrates the major kinds of
logical fallacies. As you read it,
relate what Davis says to your
own thinking and writing.

ROBERT GORHAM DAVIS

Logic and Logical Fallacies

UNDEFINED TERMS

1 The first requirement for logical discourse is knowing what the words
you use actually mean. Words are not like paper money or counters
in a game. Except for technical terms in some of the sciences, they do
not have a fixed face value. Their meanings are fluid and changing,
influenced by many considerations of context and reference, circumstances and association. This is just as true of common words such as
fast as it is of literary terms such as *romantic*. Moreover, if there is to
be communication, words must have approximately the same meaning for the reader that they have for the writer. A speech in an unknown language means nothing to the hearer. When an adult speaks
to a small child or an expert to a layman, communication may be seriously limited by lack of a mature vocabulary or ignorance of technical terms. Many arguments are meaningless because the speakers are
using important words in quite different senses.

2 Because we learn most words—or guess at them—from the contexts in which we first encounter them, our sense of them is often in-

complete or wrong. Readers sometimes visualize the Assyrian who comes down like the wolf on the fold as an enormous man dressed in cohorts (some kind of fancy armor, possibly) gleaming in purple and gold. "A rift in the lute" suggests vaguely a cracked mandolin. Failure to ascertain the literal meaning of figurative language is a frequent reason for mixed metaphors. We are surprised to find that the "devil" in "the devil to pay" and "the devil and the deep blue sea" is not Old Nick, but part of a ship. Unless terms mean the same thing to both writer and reader, proper understanding is impossible.

ABSTRACTIONS

3 The most serious logical difficulties occur with abstract terms. An abstraction is a word which stands for a quality found in a number of different objects or events from which it has been "abstracted" or taken away. We may, for instance, talk of the "whiteness" of paper or cotton or snow without considering qualities of cold or inflammability or usefulness which these materials happen also to possess. Usually, however, our minds carry over other qualities by association. See, for instance, the chapter called "the Whiteness of the Whale" in *Moby-Dick*.

4 In much theoretic discussion the process of abstraction is carried so far that although vague associations and connotations persist, the original objects or events from which the qualities have been abstracted are lost sight of completely. Instead of thinking of words like *sincerity* and *Americanism* as symbols standing for qualities that have to be abstracted with great care from examples and test cases, we come to think of them as real things in themselves. We assume that Americanism is Americanism just as a bicycle is a bicycle, and that everyone knows what it means. We forget that before the question "Is Arthur Godfrey sincere?" can mean anything, we have to agree on the criteria of sincerity.

5 When we try to define such words and find examples, we discover that almost no one agrees to their meaning. The word *church* may refer to anything from a building on the corner of Spring Street to the whole tradition of institutionalized Christianity. *Germany* may mean a geographical section of Europe, a people, a governing group, a cultural tradition, or a military power. Abstractions such as *freedom, courage, race, beauty, truth, justice, nature, honor, humanism, democracy,* should never be used in a theme unless their meaning is defined or indicated clearly by the context. Freedom for whom? To do what? Under what circumstances? Abstract terms have merely emotional value unless they are strictly defined by asking questions of this kind. The study of a word such as *nature* in a good unabridged dictionary will show that even the dictionary, indispensable though it is, cannot determine for us the sense in which a word is being used in any given sentence. Once the student understands the importance of definition, he will no longer be betrayed into fruitless arguments over such questions as whether free verse is "poetry" or whether you can change "human nature."

NAME-CALLING

6 It is a common unfairness in controversy to place what the writer dislikes or opposes in a generally odious category. The humanist dismisses what he dislikes by calling it *romantic;* the liberal, by calling it *fascist;* the conservative, by calling it *communistic.* These terms tell the reader nothing. What is *piety* to some will be *bigotry* to others. *Non-Catholics* would rather be called *Protestants* than *heretics.* What is *right-thinking* except a designation for those who agree with the writer? Social security measures become *creeping socialism;* industrial organizations, *forces of reaction;* investigation into communism, *witch hunts;* prison reforms, *coddling;* progressive education, *fads and frills.* Such terms are intended to block thought by an appeal to prejudice and associative habits. Three steps are necessary before such epithets have real meaning. First, they must be defined; second, it must be shown that the object to which they are applied actually possesses these qualities; third, it must be shown that the possession of such qualities in this particular situation is necessarily undesirable. Unless a person is alert and critical both in choosing and in interpreting words, he may be alienated from ideas with which he would be in sympathy if he had not been frightened by a mere name.

GENERALIZATION

7 Similar to the abuse of abstract terms and epithets is the habit of presenting personal opinions in the guise of universal laws. The student often seems to feel that the broader the terms in which he states an opinion, the more effective he will be. Ordinarily the reverse is true. An enthusiasm for Thomas Wolfe should lead to a specific critical analysis of Wolfe's novels that will enable the writer to explain his enthusiasm to others; it should not be turned into the argument that Wolfe is "the greatest American novelist," particularly if the writer's knowledge of American novelists is somewhat limited. The same questions of *who* and *when* and *why* and under what *circumstances* which are used to check abstract terms should be applied to generalizations. Consider how contradictory proverbial wisdom is when detached from particular circumstances. "Look before you leap," but "he who hesitates is lost."

8 Superlatives and the words *right* and *wrong, true* and *untrue, never* and *always* must be used with caution in matters of opinion. When a student says flatly that X is true, he often is really saying that he or his family or the author of a book he has just been reading, persons of certain tastes and background and experience, *think* that X is true. If his statement is based not on logic and examination of evidence, but merely reproduces other people's opinions, it can have little value or relevance unless these people are identified and their reasons for thinking so explained. Because many freshmen are taking survey courses in which they read a single work by an author or see an historical event through the eyes of a single historian whose bias they may not be able to measure, they must guard against this error.

SAMPLING

9 Assertions of a general nature are frequently open to question because they are based on insufficient evidence. Some persons are quite ready, after meeting one Armenian or reading one medieval romance, to generalize about Armenians and medieval romances. One ought, of course, to examine objectively as many examples as possible before making a generalization, but the number is less important than the representativeness of the example chosen. The Literary Digest Presidential Poll, sent to hundreds of thousands of people selected from telephone directories, was far less accurate than the Gallup Poll which questioned far fewer voters, but selected them carefully and proportionately from all different social groups. The "typical" college student, as portrayed by moving pictures and cartoons, is very different from the "average" college student as determined statistically. We cannot let uncontrolled experience do our sampling for us; instances and examples which impress themselves upon our minds do so usually because they are exceptional. In propaganda and arguments extreme cases are customarily treated as if they were characteristic.

10 If one is permitted arbitrarily to select some examples and ignore others, it is possible to find convincing evidence for almost any theory, no matter how fantastic. The fact that the mind tends naturally to remember those instances which confirm its opinions imposes a duty upon the writer, unless he wishes to encourage prejudice and superstition, to look carefully for exceptions to all generalizations which he is tempted to make, We forget the premonitions which are not followed by disaster and the time when our hunches failed to select the winner in a race. Patent medicine advertisements print the letters of those who survived their cure, and not of those who died during it. All Americans did not gamble on the stock exchange in the twenties, or become Marxists in the thirties, and all Vermonters are not thin-lipped and shrewd. Of course the search for negative examples can be carried too far. Outside of mathematics or the laboratory, few generalizations can be made airtight, and most are not intended to be. But quibbling is so easy that resort to it is very common, and the knowledge that people can and will quibble over generalizations is another reason for making assertions as limited and explicitly conditional as possible.

FALSE ANALOGY

11 Illustration, comparison, analogy are most valuable in making an essay clear and interesting. It must not be supposed, however, that they prove anything or have much argumentative weight. The rule that what is true of one thing in one set of circumstances is not necessarily true of another thing in another set of circumstances seems almost too obvious to need stating. Yet constantly nations and businesses are discussed as if they were human beings with human habits and feelings; human bodies are discussed as if they were machines; the universe, as if it were a clock. It is assumed that what held true for seventeenth century New England or the thirteen Atlantic colonies

also holds true for an industrial nation of 150,000,000 people. Carlyle dismissed the arguments for representative democracy by saying that if a captain had to take a vote among his crew every time he wanted to do something, he would never get around Cape Horn. This analogy calmly ignores the distinction between the lawmaking and the executive branches of constitutional democracies. Moreover, voters may be considered much more like the stockholders of a merchant line than its hired sailors. Such arguments introduce assumptions in a metaphorical guise in which they are not readily detected or easily criticized. In place of analysis they attempt to identify their position with some familiar symbol which will evoke a predictable, emotional response in the reader. The revival during the 1932 presidential campaign of Lincoln's remark, "Don't swap horses in the middle of the stream," was not merely a picturesque way of saying keep Hoover in the White House. It made a number of assumptions about the nature of depressions and the function of government. This propagandist technique can be seen most clearly in political cartoons.

DEGREE

12 Often differences in degree are more important than differences in kind. By legal and social standards there is more difference between an habitual drunkard and a man who drinks temperately, than between a temperate drinker and a total abstainer. In fact differences of degree produce what are regarded as differences of kind. At known temperatures ice turns to water and water boils. At an indeterminate point affection becomes love and a man who needs a shave becomes a man with a beard. The fact that no men or systems are perfect makes rejoinders and counteraccusations very easy if differences in degree are ignored. Newspapers in totalitarian states, answering American accusations of brutality and suppression, refer to lynchings and gangsterism here. Before a disinterested judge could evaluate these mutual accusations, he would have to settle the question of the degree to which violent suppression and lynching are respectively prevalent in the countries under consideration. On the other hand, differences in degree may be merely apparent. Lincoln Steffens pointed out that newspapers can create a "crime wave" any time they wish, simply by emphasizing all the minor assaults and thefts commonly ignored or given an inch or two on a back page. The great reported increases in insanity may be due to the fact that in a more urban and institutionalized society cases of insanity more frequently come to the attention of authorities and hence are recorded in statistics.

CAUSATION

13 The most common way of deciding that one thing causes another thing is the simple principle: *post hoc, ergo propter hoc,* "After this, therefore because of this." Rome fell after the introduction of Christianity; therefore Christianity was responsible for the fall of Rome. Such rea-

soning illustrates another kind of faulty generalization. But even if one could find ten cases in which a nation "fell" after the introduction of Christianity, it still would not be at all certain that Christianity caused the fall. Day, it has frequently been pointed out, follows night in every observable instance, and yet night cannot be called the cause of day. Usually a combination of causes produces a result. Sitting in a draught may cause a cold, but only given a certain physical condition in the person sitting there. In such instances one may distinguish between necessary and sufficient conditions. Air is a necessary condition for the maintenance of plant life, but air alone is not sufficient to produce plant life. And often different causes at different times may produce the same result. This relation is known as plurality of causes. If, after sitting in a stuffy theatre on Monday, and then again after eating in a stuffy restaurant on Thursday, a man suffered from headaches, he might say, generalizing, that bad air gave him headaches. But actually the headache on Monday may have been caused by eyestrain and on Thursday by indigestion. To isolate the causative factor it is necessary that all other conditions be precisely the same. Such isolation is possible, except in very simple instances, only in the laboratory or with scientific methods. If a picture falls from the wall every time a truck passes, we can quite certainly say that the truck's passing is the proximate or immediate cause. But with anything as complex and conditional as a nation's economy or human character, the determination of cause is not easy or certain. A psychiatrist often sees a patient for an hour daily for a year or more before he feels that he understands his neurosis.

14   Ordinarily when we speak of cause we mean the proximate or immediate cause. The plants were killed by frost; we had indigestion from eating lobster salad. But any single cause is one in an unbroken series. When a man is murdered, is his death caused by the loss of blood from the wound, or by the firing of the pistol, or by the malice aforethought of the murderer? Was the World War "caused" by the assassination at Sarajevo? Were the Navigation Acts or the ideas of John Locke more important in "causing" the American Revolution? A complete statement of cause would comprise the sum total of the conditions which preceded an event, conditions stretching back indefinitely into the past. Historical events are so interrelated that the isolation of a causative sequence is dependent chiefly on the particular preoccupations of the historian. An economic determinist can "explain" history entirely in terms of economic development; an idealist, entirely in terms of the development of ideas.

SYLLOGISTIC REASONING

15 The formal syllogism of the type,

> All men are mortal
> John is a man
> Therefore John is mortal,

is not so highly regarded today as in some earlier periods. It merely fixes an individual as a members of a class, and then assumes that the individual has the given characteristics of the class. Once we have decided who John is, and what "man" and "mortal" mean, and have canvassed all men, including John, to make sure that they are mortal, the conclusion naturally follows. It can be seen that the chief difficulties arise in trying to establish acceptable premises. Faults in the premises are known as "material" fallacies, and are usually more serious than the "formal" fallacies, which are logical defects in drawing a conclusion from the premises. But although directly syllogistic reasoning is not much practiced, buried syllogism can be found in all argument, and it is often a useful clarification to outline your own or another writer's essay in syllogistic form. The two most frequent defects in the syllogism itself are the undistributed and the ambiguous middle. The middle term is the one that appears in each of the premises and not in the conclusion. In the syllogism,

> All good citizens vote
> John votes
> Therefore John is a good citizen,

the middle term is not "good citizens," but "votes." Even though it were true that all good citizens vote, nothing prevents bad citizens from voting also, and John may be one of the bad citizens. To distribute the middle term "votes" one might say (but only if that is what one meant),

> All voters are good citizens
> John is a voter
> Therefore John is a good citizen.

16   The ambiguous middle term is even more common. It represents a problem in definition, while the undistributed middle is a problem in generalization. All acts which benefit others are virtuous, losing money at poker benefits others, therefore losing at poker is a virtuous act. Here the middle term "act which benefits others" is obviously used very loosely and ambiguously.

NON-SEQUITUR

17 This phrase, meaning "it does not follow," is used to characterize the kind of humor found in pictures in which the Marx Brothers perform. It is an amusing illogicality because it usually expresses, beneath its apparent incongruity, an imaginative, associative, or personal truth. "My ancestors came over on the Mayflower; therefore I am naturally opposed to labor unions." It is not logically necessary that those whose ancestors came over on the Mayflower should be opposed to unions; but it may happen to be true as a personal fact in a given case. It is usually a strong personal conviction which keeps people from realizing that their arguments are non-sequiturs, that they do not follow the given premises with logical necessity. Contemporary psychologists have effectively shown us that there is often such a wide difference between the true and the purported reasons for an attitude that, in rationalizing our behavior, we are often quite unconscious of the mo-

tives that actually influence us. A fanatical antivivisectionist, for instance may have temperamental impulses toward cruelty which he is suppressing and compensating for by a reasoned opposition of any kind of permitted suffering. We may expect, then, to come upon many conclusions which are psychologically interesting in themselves, but have nothing to do with the given premises.

IGNORATIO ELENCHI

18 This means, in idiomatic English, "arguing off the point," or ignoring the question at issue. A man trying to show that monarchy is the best form of government for the British Empire may devote most of his attention to the charm of Elizabeth II and the affection her people feel for her. In ordinary conversational argument it is almost impossible for disputants to keep to the point. Constantly turning up are tempting side-issues through which one can discomfit an opponent or force him to irrelevant admissions that seem to weaken his case.

BEGGING THE QUESTION; ARGUING IN A CIRCLE

19 The first of these terms means to assume in the premises what you are pretending to prove in the course of your argument. The function of logic is to demonstrate that because one thing or group of things is true, another must be true as a consequence. But in begging the question you simply say in varying language that what is assumed to be true is assumed to be true. An argument which asserts that we shall enjoy immortality because we have souls which are immaterial and indestructible establishes nothing, because the idea of immortality is already contained in the assumption about the soul. It is the premise which needs to be demonstrated, not the conclusion. Arguing in a circle is another form of this fallacy. It proves the premise by the conclusion and the conclusion by the premise. The conscience forbids an act because it is wrong; the act is wrong because the conscience forbids it.

ARGUMENTS AD HOMINEM AND AD POPULUM

20 It is very difficult for men to be persuaded by reason when their interest or prestige is at stake. If one wishes to preach the significance of physiognomy, it is well to choose a hearer with a high forehead and a determined jaw. The arguments in favor of repealing the protective tariff on corn or wheat in England were more readily entertained by manufacturers than by landowners. The cotton manufacturers in New England who were doing a profitable trade with the South were the last to be moved by descriptions of the evils of slavery. Because interest and desire are so deeply seated in human nature, arguments are frequently mingled with attempts to appeal to emotion, arouse fear, play upon pride, attack the characters of proponents of an opposite

view, show that their practice is inconsistent with their principles; all matters which have, strictly speaking, nothing to do with the truth or falsity, the general desirability or undesirability, of some particular measure. If men are desperate enough they will listen to arguments proper only to an insane asylum but which seem to promise them relief.

21   After reading these suggestions, which are largely negative, the student may feel that any original assertion he can make will probably contain one or several logical faults. This assumption is not true. Even if it were, we know from reading newspapers and magazines that worldly fame is not dimmed by the constant and, one suspects, conscious practice of illogicality. But generalizations are not made only by charlatans and sophists. Intelligent and scrupulous writers also have a great many fresh and provocative observations and conclusions to express and are expressing them influentially. What is intelligence but the ability to see the connection between things, to discern causes, to relate the particular to the general, to define and discriminate and compare? Any man who thinks and feels and observes closely will not want for something to express.

22   And in his expression a proponent will find that a due regard for logic does not limit but rather increases the force of his argument. When statements are not trite, they are usually controversial. Men arrive at truth dialectically; error is weeded out in the course of discussion, argument, attack, and counterattack. Not only can a writer who understands logic show the weaknesses of arguments he disagrees with, but also, by anticipating the kind of attack likely to be made on his own ideas, he can so arrange them, properly modified with qualifications and exceptions, that the anticipated attack is made much less effective. Thus, fortunately, we do not have to depend on the spirit of fairness and love of truth to lead men to logic; it has the strong support of argumentative necessity and of the universal desire to make ideas prevail.

(Since this selection is concerned with logic and language, the exercises do not follow the usual pattern. Discussion of the theme, of rhetoric, and of vocabulary will automatically be a part of your answers to these questions.)

Identify the errors in logic in each of the following:

1. The United States became involved in two major wars during the terms of Democratic presidents. The Democratic party therefore is rightly known as the war party.
2. I have no doubt that Coach Smith will make an excellent principal. After all, he could really handle those gym classes!
3. This is the best movie I have seen all year; it should win an Oscar.
4. Mr. Walters, a Lutheran, is an alcoholic. I guess it's true what they say about Lutherans.
5. Sue will do well in college; she received good grades in high school.

6. Last month's atomic bomb testing was followed by earthquakes in Chile and Turkey. Obviously there is a relation between earthquakes and explosions in the atmosphere.
7. My party has always stood for equal opportunity.
8. Common sense is needed in public office today.
9. The human body is like a machine, so of course it can work without sleep.
10. Chairman Edwards and his henchmen are responsible for our high taxes.
11. It is reported that he subscribes to left-wing magazines. How can you respect his judgment?
12. Forty-three percent of the women who were asked said that Bubble-O soap got their clothes cleaner.
13. If you allow a high school student to drive a car, you are guaranteeing his academic failure.
14. Mr. Webster is from the South; obviously, he is for the right-to-work law.
15. His morals are made of steel, but we know steel will rust and fail.
16. A Catholic tried to kill the Pope; another one tried to kill his wife just last week. What should we do about the Catholics?
17. All teachers are too removed from real life.
    Mr. Thompson is my English teacher.
    Therefore, Mr. Thompson doesn't know what's going on.
18. Why would anyone vote for Mr. Clane? Just look at his private life.
19. Anyone with good taste will like "My Sister's Mistake," now showing at the Plaza.
20. How could I agree with you? Our families came from different countries.

Lionel Ruby (1889–   ) was educated at Harvard University
and at the University of Chicago, where he received his
Ph.D. He has taught at Indiana,
Northwestern, and Roosevelt
universities. He is the author of
"Logic: An Introduction" (1950)
and "The Art of Making Sense"
(1954).

This is a clear explanation of
one kind of inductive reasoning
– generalization. The essay also
discusses the adequacy of generalizations and points out that
"some generalizations are true,
others are false, and still others
are uncertain or doubtful."

LIONEL RUBY

Are All Generalizations False?

1 We begin with a generalization: human beings are great generalizers.
Every race has its proverbs, and proverbs are generalizations. "It
never rains but it pours." "Faint heart never won fair lady." "Familiarity breeds contempt." Sometimes, of course, these proverbs are incompatible with each other, as in "Absence makes the heart grow
fonder," and "Out of sight, out of mind."[1]

2   Listen attentively to those around you, and note the generalizations
that float into every conversation: Europeans are lazy and shiftless.
European girls make good wives. American girls are selfish. Politicians are crooks. Gentlemen prefer blondes. On a somewhat more
"intellectual" level, we find: Liberals never think a matter through.
Intellectuals always show a lack of practical judgment. Americans are

---
[1] Once translated by a foreign student as "invisible idiot."

idealists. Americans are materialists. All American men suffer from "momism." Economics is bunk. Modern art is trash. Psychiatrists never bring up their own children properly. In the middle ages everyone was religious. And so on. After more of the same we may be tempted to agree with Justice Holmes that "the chief end of man is to frame general propositions, and no general proposition is worth a damn."

3   Our awareness of the inadequacy of "sweeping generalizations" may lead us to say that all generalizations are false. But this is truly a sweeping generalization! And worse: if it is true, then the witticism that "all generalizations are false, *including this one*" would appear to be justified. But this will not do either, for this generalization asserts that it itself is false, from which it follows that it is not the case that all generalizations are false. Or perhaps we should say that "all generalizations are half-truths — including this one"? But this is not much better. The fact of the matter is that some generalizations are true, others are false, and still others are uncertain or doubtful. The deadliness of this platitude may be forgiven because of its truth.

4   By a "generalization" is meant a general law or principle which is inferred from particular facts. As a sample of the way in which we arrive at such generalizations consider the following: Some years ago I visited France, and ate at a number of Parisian restaurants that had been recommended to me. The food was excellent in each. Then one day I was unable to get to any of my customary eating places. I ate in a small restaurant in an outlying district of Paris. The food was excellent. I then tried other restaurants always with the same results. I ate in large restaurants, small restaurants, on ships and trains, and in railway station restaurants. I generalized: All French restaurants serve excellent meals.

5   A generalization is a statement that *goes beyond* what is actually observed, to a rule or law covering both the observed cases and those that have not as yet been observed. This going-beyond is called the "inductive leap." An inductive leap is a "leap in the dark," for the *generalization may not be true,* even though the *observations* on which it is based *are* true. Thus, somewhere in France there may be a poor French restaurant — happily I am ignorant of its location — but if so, then I should not say that *all* are good.

6   A generalization involves an "inductive leap." The word *induction,* from Latin roots meaning "to lead in," means that we examine particular cases (French restaurants), and "lead in" to a generalization. Induction is the method we use when we learn lessons from our experience: we generalize from particular cases. *Deduction,* on the other hand, refers to the process of "drawing out" the logical consequences of what we already know (or assume) to be true. By induction we learn that French cooking is delectable. If a friend tells us that he had tasteless meals while in Europe, then by deduction we know that he did not eat in French restaurants. Both induction and deduction are essential characteristics of rational thinking.

7   A generalization is a statement of the form: "All A's are B's." "All" means exactly what it says: *all* without exception. A single exception overthrows a generalization of this kind. Before we proceed further

we must first dispose of a popular confusion concerning the expression: "The exception proves the rule." This is a sensible statement when properly interpreted, but it is sometimes understood in a manner that makes it nonsense. If I say that "all A's are B's," a single exception will make my statement false. Now, suppose that someone says: "The fact that there is a poor French restaurant proves that *all* are good because *it* is an exception, and the exception proves the rule!" Does a wicked woman prove that all women are saints? The sensible interpretation of the expression, "The exception proves the rule" is this: When we *say* that a certain case *is* an "exception," we imply that there is a rule which is generally true. When a mother tells her daughter, "Have a good time at the prom, and, for tonight, you have my permission to stay out until 3 A.M.," she implies that this is an exception to the rule which requires earlier reporting. A statement that *creates* an exception implies a rule for all non-exceptional cases; but a generalization that is stated as a rule without exceptions (all A's are B's) would be overthrown by a single exception.

8   All too often "general propositions are not worth a damn," as Holmes remarked. This is because we generalize too hastily on the basis of insufficient evidence. The fallacy called the "hasty generalization" simply refers to the fact that we jump too quickly to conclusions concerning "all." For example, we see a woman driving carelessly, and generalize: "All women are poor drivers." We see a car weaving in and out of traffic, and note that it has a California license: "Wouldn't you know," we say. "A California driver. That's the way they all drive out there." Anita Loos' gay heroine thought that gentlemen preferred blondes because she was a blonde and men were attracted to her.

9   We learn that Napoleon got along on five hours of sleep. From this we may conclude that "five hours of sleep is all that anybody really needs." Our assumption is that what Napoleon could do, anybody can do, until we learn that we are not Napoleons. (If we don't learn this eventually, we aren't permitted to circulate freely.) The next example is undoubtedly the worst example of generalizing ever committed: A man declared that all Indians walk single file. When challenged for his evidence, he replied, "How do I know that? I once saw an Indian walk that way."

10   Hasty generalizing is perhaps the most important of popular vices in thinking. It is interesting to speculate on some of the reasons for this kind of bad thinking. One important factor is prejudice. If we are already prejudiced against unions, or businessmen, or lawyers, or doctors, or Jews, or Negroes, then one or two instances of bad conduct by members of these groups will give us the unshakable conviction that "they're all like that." It is very difficult for a prejudiced person to say, "Some are, and some aren't." A prejudice is a judgment formed *before* examining the evidence.

11   A psychological reason for asserting "wild" generalizations is exhibitionism: The exhibitionist desires to attract attention to himself. No one pays much attention to such undramatic statements as "Some women are fickle," or that some are liars, or "Some politicians are no better than they ought to be." But when one says that "all women are

liars" this immediately attracts notice. Goethe once said that it is easy to appear brilliant if one respects nothing, not even the truth.

12   Let us avoid careless and hasty generalizing. The proverb warns us that one swallow does not make a summer. Unfortunately, we usually forget proverbs on the occasions when we ought to remember them. We ought to emulate "the Reverend" in Faulkner's novel, *The Hamlet*. He was discussing the efficacy of a rural society. "Do you know it will work, Reverend?" his friend asked. "I know it worked once," the Reverend answered. "Oh, then you have knowed it to fail?" "I never knowed it to be tried but once." The fault of bad generalizing, however, need not make us take refuge in the opposite error: the refusal to generalize. This error is illustrated in the anecdote concerning the student who wrote an essay on labor relations, in which he argued for equal pay for women. Women, he wrote, work hard, they need the money, they are the foundation of the family, and, most important, they are the mothers of most of the human race! There is another old anecdote about the cautious man whose friend pointed to a flock of sheep with the remark, "Those sheep seem to have been sheared recently." "Yes," said the cautious man, "at least on this side."

13   Generalizations are dangerous, but we must generalize. To quote Justice Holmes once more: he said that he welcomed "anything that will discourage men from believing general propositions." But, he added, he welcomed that "only less than he welcomed anything that would encourage men to make such propositions"! For generalizations are indispensable guides. One of the values of knowledge lies in its predictive power—its power to predict the future. Such knowledge is stated in generalizations. It is of little help to me to know that water froze at 32° F. yesterday unless this information serves as a warning to put anti-freeze in my car radiator before winter comes. History, in the "pure" sense of this term, merely tells us what has happened in the past, but science furnishes us with general laws, and general laws tell us what *always* happens under certain specified conditions.

14   Science is interested in the general, rather than in the particular or individual. When Newton saw an apple fall from a tree in his orchard— even if this story is a fable, and therefore false in a literal sense, it is true in its insight—he was not interested in the size and shape of the apple. Its fall suggested an abstract law to him, the law of gravity. He framed this law in general terms: Every particle of matter attracts every other particle of matter with a force directly proportional to the product of their masses and inversely proportional to the square of their distances. Chemists seek general laws concerning the behavior of matter. The physician wants to know the general characteristics of the disease called myxedema, so that when he has a case he will recognize it and know exactly how to treat it. The finding of general laws, then, is the aim of all science—including history insofar as it is a science.

15   The problem of the scientist is one of achieving sound generalizations. The scientist is careful not to make assertions which outrun his evidence, and he refuses to outtalk his information. He generalizes, but recognizes that no generalization can be more than probable, for

we can never be certain that *all* the evidence is in, nor can the future be guaranteed absolutely—not even future eclipses of the sun and moon. But the scientist knows that certain laws have a very high degree of probability.

16 Let us look at the logic involved in forming sound generalizations. The number of cases investigated in the course of formulating a scientific law is a factor in establishing the truth of the law, but it is by no means the most important one. Obviously, if we observed one hundred swans, all of which are white, our generalization that "all swans are white" does not have the same probability it would have if we observed one thousand swans. But no matter how great the number of specimens involved in this type of observation, no more than a high degree of probability is ever established. Countless numbers of white swans were observed throughout the ages (without any exceptions) and then in the nineteenth century black swans were observed in Australia.

17 The weakness of the method of "induction by simple enumeration of cases" is amusingly illustrated by Bertrand Russell's parable in his *A History of Western Philosophy:*

> There was once upon a time a census officer who had to record the names of all householders in a certain Welsh village. The first that he questioned was called William Williams; so were the second, third, fourth. . . . At last he said to himself: "This is tedious; evidently they are all called William Williams. I shall put them down so and take a holiday." But he was wrong; there was just one whose name was John Jones.

18 Scientific generalizations based on other types of evidence than simple enumeration often acquire a much higher degree of probability after only a few observations. When a chemist finds that pure sulphur melts at 125° C., in an experiment in which every factor is accurately analyzed and controlled, the law concerning the melting point of sulphur achieves as great a degree of certainty as is humanly attainable. Accurate control of every element of one case, then, is more important in establishing probabilities than is *mere enumeration* of many cases.

19 A single carefully controlled experiment, such as the sulphur experiment, can give us a much higher degree of probability than the mere observation of thousands of swans. The reason is that we also know that no chemical element thus far observed has a variable melting point under conditions of constant pressure. The chemical law is thus consistent with and is borne out by the rest of chemical knowledge, whereas the "law" holding that all swans are white was based on an "accidental" factor. Or consider the generalization concerning the mortality of mankind. This law is based not merely on the fact that countless numbers of human beings have died in the past, but also on the fact that all living beings must, by reason of physiological limitations, die; and that all matter wears out in time. So the harmony of a particular generalization with the rest of our knowledge is also a factor in giving it a high degree of probability.

20 So much for the logical analysis of generalizations. Thus far, we have been concerned with "uniform" generalizations, which take the

form: "all A's are B's." A generalization, we have seen, is a statement that says something about "all" of a group, the evidence consisting of items in which we always find a single characteristic. The observed cases are taken as a *sample* of the whole group or population with which we are concerned. We observe a number of swans, and take these as a sample of all swans, past, present, and future. We find that all are white, and make the inductive leap: Swans are always white, everywhere.

21 We shall now examine "statistical" statements. Statistical statements give us information not about characteristics possessed by *all* of a group or population, but by a definite proportion (or most) of the group or population, as when we say, "Most A's are B's" or "Sixty-five per cent of all A's are B's." The first thing to note here is that statistical statements may in fact be *generalizations,* and thus involve the notions of "all." This point involves very important (and common) misunderstandings.

22 In order to make this point clear, let us re-interpret our "uniform" generalizations. We say: "The sample is so-and-so (all observed swans are uniformly white)—*therefore,* the whole population of swans are uniformly white." Now, we do the same sort of thing in statistical generalizations. We say: "In the sample of red-heads we examined, fifty-three per cent were hot-tempered—therefore, fifty-three per cent of *all* red-heads are hot-tempered." (Or: fifty-three per cent of the whole population of red-heads is hot-tempered.) Logically, both examples, uniform and statistical, are of the same type, for in each we make the inductive leap from the sample to the whole population. The only difference between them is that in the one case we assert a *uniform* character in the whole population; in the other we assert that a characteristic holds in a certain *proportion* in the whole population.

23 This fundamental point will help us to evaluate the degree of probability of a statistical generalization. We saw earlier that uniform generalizations can never be absolutely certain—though for practical purposes we often consider them so, especially in the physical sciences. The probability of a generalization depends especially on the *quality* and also on the *quantity* of the cases that constitute the sample. The same holds for statistical generalizations, which may have a high probability, depending on the character of the evidence. Though the inductive leap is involved in all generalizations, in some cases the leap is justified. Let us examine the criteria of justification for the leap.

24 Before we proceed we shall discuss an important distinction: that between the sample and the inference we draw from it. It is one thing to describe a sample accurately; quite another to draw an accurate inference. If I say, "I have observed ten swans [the sample] and all were white," we may assume that the sample is accurately described. But if I now go on to generalize (that is, draw the inference) concerning *all* swans, my inference may not be a good one. A generalization always involves a "leap in the dark," sometimes justified and sometimes not. Similarly, if I say, "I have talked to ten friends concerning their income, and six [sixty per cent] told me that they earned more than $10,000 a year," the description of the sample may be accepted as true. But suppose I now go on to make the following inference:

"Therefore, sixty per cent of all Americans earn more than $10,000 a year." This would be a hasty generalization indeed.

25   We distinguish, then, between the sample and the inference. A statistical statement concerning the sample is purely descriptive. The book *They Went to College* is a statistical study, as of 1947, of 9,064 college graduates. Averages are given. Fifty-three per cent were in business, sixteen per cent were doctors, lawyers or dentists, sixteen per cent were teachers. The doctors earned the most: over half making more than $7,500 a year. Teachers and preachers earned the least: median income $3,584. Now, these averages involve no inferences. They simply describe the actual facts *in the sample.* We draw an inference, on the other hand, when we assume that the whole population of six million college graduates will show the same kinds of averages as the sample. In our discussion, henceforth, we shall be concerned only with the logical problems in statistical inferences.

26   Suppose that a public opinion poll was taken recently. The polling organization tells us that fifty-eight per cent of the American people approve of the record of the present administration in Washington. How do they know this? Let us examine the evidence on which this finding is based. Obviously not everyone was consulted. A sample was taken. There were three thousand interviews. Since there are seventy-five million adults in the United States, each individual in this sample is taken as representative of twenty-five thousand adults. Further, in the sample, one thousand persons said that they had "no opinion." Eleven hundred and sixty said that they "approved," and eight hundred and forty said they did not. Thus fifty-eight per cent of those with opinions approved, and this means, we are told, that forty-three and one-half million Americans approve. The pollsters assume that the undecided individuals will probably divide in the same proportion as the others when they make up their minds.

27   Now, we are not raising any questions concerning the truth of the report made of the sample. But is the inductive leap from the sample to the generalization concerning seventy-five million people justified? It may be. It all depends upon the reliability of the sample. What makes a sample reliable? It must be *fair, unbiased,* and *representative* of the whole. But what determines whether it has these characteristics? This is the crucial question.

28   The size of the sample is obviously important. A sample of one hundred would not be so reliable as one of one thousand, and one thousand would not be so reliable as one of a million. But numbers in themselves are not the most important factor in establishing the reliability of generalizations or inferences.

29   The unimportance of large numbers as such is best illustrated by the ill-fated *Literary Digest* presidential election poll in 1936. The magazine sent pre-election ballots to ten million persons, and received over two million responses. The responses showed Landon running ahead of Roosevelt. In the election in November, however, Roosevelt got about twenty-eight million votes; Landon around eighteen million.

30   The reason for this colossal failure was the unrepresentative character of the sample. The *Digest* took names "at random" from telephone directories and lists of registered owners of automobiles. These

were relatively well-to-do folk. The lower income groups, however, were completely, or almost completely, unrepresented.

31 An ideal sample is one taken "at random" from the entire population, and not from a selected portion of the population being studied. The Gallup, Roper, and Crossley polls have proved more successful — barring a spectacular failure in 1948 — than the *Literary Digest* poll. Let us see how the Gallup poll operates. A sample of three thousand individuals is taken, but with great care to make the sample representative. The population is classified into sub-groups by geographic regions, by rural or urban residence, economic status, age, education, and declared politics. In 1948, for example, Gallup estimated that twenty-eight per cent of the American people live in the Middle Atlantic states, ten per cent on the West Coast; that thirty-four per cent live in cities of over 100,000 population; that twenty-three per cent are of an "average" economic station; that forty-three per cent are between the ages of thirty and forty-nine; that forty-two per cent have gone to high schools; and that thirty-eight per cent call themselves Democrats, thirty-six per cent Republicans, and twenty-six per cent independents or members of smaller parties. The three thousand interviews in the sample are distributed so that each geographic area, each economic group, etc., will be represented in its appropriate numerical strength.

32 Individuals are then chosen "at random," rather than by selection, from within each sub-group, and the resulting sample is highly representative of the whole population. The Gallup poll enjoys a successful record, on the whole, except for 1948. In other words, the method works, and one must respect its findings. But no poll can ever eliminate the possibility of error, or guarantee accuracy except within a margin of error of several percentage points. And in a presidential election forecast the pollster is either completely right or completely wrong in predicting who will win. Odds of 10 to 1 against a candidate of one of the major parties are probably not justified even if all the polls are unanimous as to the final results. These were the odds against Harry Truman in 1948!

33 An election prediction can be judged by the election results, and a long series of successful predictions gives us confidence in the methods of the pollsters. This check cannot be made on polls which tabulate public opinion on issues of the day, for the whole population is never counted. Similarly for polls which rate television shows, for the whole audience is not counted. Such polls, of course, also generalize on the basis of samples. To illustrate the logical problems in assessing the reliability of a statistical study of the "public opinion poll" type we shall comment on *Sexual Behavior in the Human Female* by Alfred C. Kinsey and his staff.

34 Kinsey's study tabulates and classifies data concerning 5,940 white American females, ages two to ninety. He does not claim that his averages necessarily apply to all human females, despite the title of his book, nor even to all American women, of whom there are approximately seventy millions. It is inevitable, however, that such inferences will be drawn, and our question is: Are such inferences justified? This depends entirely on the representativeness of Kinsey's sample.

35   Critics of Kinsey's report have emphasized the unrepresentative-ness of his sample. His subjects are not distributed proportionately in geographic areas: most are from Illinois, Florida, and California. They are more highly educated than a representative cross-section of the population: seventy-five per cent of his subjects went to college, as compared with a national average of thirteen per cent. Three per cent of his women did not go beyond grade school as compared with the national average of thirty-seven per cent. A larger than average proportion are from middle and upper economic groups. Very few of the women were Roman Catholics or orthodox Jews.

36   Critics have also argued that the very nature of the study involves a kind of bias, for many women will refuse to discuss matters of such "delicate privacy" with interviewers, so that his volunteers must be unrepresentative of women in general. And there is also the problem of credibility. Critics have said that people who like to talk about such things tend to understate or overstate, and even to fabricate a little.

37   Kinsey, of course, recognizes the limitations and incompleteness of his sample, and, as noted, does not claim that it is representative of the whole population. But it will be interpreted in this way, and if Kinsey wished to avoid such interpretations, he should have called his study "Sexual Behavior of 5,940 Women." Inferences would probably be drawn, however, even if he had so titled his study.

38   The elements of distortion in Kinsey's sample detract from its reli-ability as a basis for generalizing. On the other hand, as a review of the book in *Life* put it, though the statistics are not perfect they are at any rate "the only statistics in town." His study is by no means worthless as an index of sexual behavior. We must not use an "all or nothing" approach here. The reliability of his sample with respect to university women as a single group, for example, is certainly much higher than that for the female population as a whole. But we cannot conclude that the whole female population resembles the sample since the sample is not a representative one.

39   Generalizations in statistics, then, are judged by the same logical criteria we use in judging any generalizations. Fallacies, however, are more common in statistical than they are in uniform generalizations. For it is easier to check on the reliability of a uniform generalization: one exception overthrows the general rule or "law." In statistics, how-ever, since nothing is said about any specific individual, an "excep-tion" is a meaningless term. An exceptional individual does not disprove an "average." But there is, as we have already noted, a method for checking the reliability of a statistical generalization con-cerning a population, and that is to count the whole "voting" popula-tion. But even a test of this kind is not conclusive, for many of the voters do not vote on election day, because of laziness, overconfi-dence, or some other reason.

40   Errors of inference in statistics are frequently overlooked because of the mathematical language in which statistics are presented. The spell which numbers weave often prevents us from seeing errors in arguments—errors which would be obvious were they not clothed in mathematical garb. And many dishonest reasoners take advantage of this fact and present highly selected data for purposes of propa-

ganda rather than information. Misuses of the science of statistics have resulted in such jibes as, "Figures don't lie, but liars figure," and "There are three kinds of lies: ordinary lies, damnable lies, and statistics." But these cynical remarks should not be taken as criticisms of statistics. The fault never lies with the figures, or with the science, but with their careless use. It is simply not the case that "you can prove anything with figures" (or statistics), just as it is never the case that "you can prove anything by logic." To the uninitiated, it just *seems* that you can.

Discussion of Theme

1. What is the answer to the question asked in the title?
2. What is the main hazard in generalizing?
3. What is the difference between inductive and deductive reasoning?
4. With reference to polls, what makes a sample reliable? What determines whether it has these characteristics?
5. Discuss the statement, "The exception proves the rule."
6. Why do people generalize so much?

Discussion of Rhetoric

1. How does the author's use of several common generalizations serve to invoke interest in his subject?
2. The first sentence in both paragraph 4 and paragraph 7 makes a statement about generalizations. Is either a definition in itself, and if so, which?
3. Why does the author discuss the two most famous failures of polls rather than some spectacular successes?
4. On the basis of the information the article supplies about the Kinsey report, as well as the criticism of it, what title would the study have to have in order to avoid all false inferences?
5. Although the title of the article concerns all generalizations, the conclusion makes no mention of them. Would it have been better if the author had done so?
6. The author consistently uses "we" and "us," rather than "you." What is his probable purpose?

Writing Assignments

1. What hasty generalizations do you encounter most frequently? Why do you consider them hasty?
2. Evaluate several proverbs like "He who hesitates is lost" or "Look before you leap."
3. The author says that "generalizations are indispensable guides." What generalizations do you rely on to guide you?
4. Account for the fact that politicians use polls in their campaigns.

5. What does the habit of hasty generalization have to do with race prejudice?
6. Pure research, which is an expression of science's "interest in the general rather than the particular or individual," is often criticized by laymen because it seems aimless and time-consuming. Write a defense of the necessity for allocating time, money, and manpower to pure research.

Library Exploration

1. Virtually the same proverbs exist in all languages. Look up proverbs that have been translated from various languages and compare them with similar proverbs in our own language.
2. Report on the Gallup poll of 1948 which failed to predict Harry S Truman's election.

Vocabulary

(1) INCOMPATIBLE   incapable of existing together in harmony

(3) PLATITUDE   dull or insipid remark

(4) INFERRED   concluded; indicated

(8) FALLACY   a type of erroneous reasoning (in logic)

(12) EMULATE   imitate; try to equal or excel

(12) EFFICACY   effectiveness

(12) ANECDOTE   an interesting or amusing tale

(13) INDISPENSABLE   necessary; essential

(14) INVERSELY   in opposite order

(15) ASSERTIONS   declarations

(18) ENUMERATION   counting; listing

(33) TABULATE   summarize

(33) ASSESSING   estimating; evaluating

(36) CREDIBILITY   believability

(36) FABRICATE   invent; create

(40) CYNICAL   distrustful; pessimistic

Haig A. Bosmajian (1928–) is a speech professor at the University of Washington. He has published essays and books on dissent, freedom of speech, and nonverbal communication.

The language of white racism is not always blatant or even deliberate. The following essay cites ample evidence to show that the English language contains built-in racial slurs.

HAIG A. BOSMAJIAN

The Language of White Racism

1   The attempts to eradicate racism in the United States have been focused notably on the blacks of America, not the whites. What is striking is that while we are inundated with TV programs portraying the plight of black Americans, and with panel discussions focusing on black Americans, we very seldom hear or see any extensive public discussion, literature or programs directly related to the source of the racism, the white American. We continually see on our TV sets and in our periodicals pictures and descriptions of undernourished black children, but we seldom see pictures or get analyses of the millions of schoolage white suburban children being taught racism in their white classrooms; we see pictures of unemployed blacks aimlessly walking the streets in their black communities, but seldom do we ever see the whites who have been largely responsible, directly or indirectly, for this unemployment and segregation; we continually hear panelists discussing and diagnosing the blacks in America, but seldom do we hear panelists diagnosing the whites and their subtle and not so subtle racism.

2   Gunnar Myrdal, in the Introduction to his classic *An American Dilemma,* wrote that as he "proceeded in his studies into the Negro problem [an unfortunate phrase], it became increasingly evident that little, if anything, could be scientifically explained in terms of the peculiarities of the Negroes themselves." It is the white majority group, said Myrdal, "that naturally determines the Negro's 'place.' All our attempts to reach scientific explanations of why the Negroes are what

they are and why they live as they do have regularly led to determinants on the white side of the race line." As the July 1966 editorial in *Ebony* put it, "for too long now, we have focused on the symptoms of the disease rather than the disease itself. It is time now for us to face the fact that Negroes are oppressed in America not by 'the pathology of the ghetto,' as some experts contend, but by the pathology of the white community." In calling for a White House Conference on Whites, the *Ebony* editorial made the important point that "we need to know more about the pathology of the white community. We need conferences in which white leaders will talk not about us [Negroes] but about themselves."

3   White Americans, through the mass media and individually, must begin to focus their attention not on the condition of the victimized, but on the victimizer. Whitey must begin to take the advice of various black spokesmen who suggest that white Americans start solving the racial strife in this country by eradicating white racism in white communities, instead of going into black communities or joining black organizations or working for legislation to "give" the blacks political and social rights. This suggestion has come from Floyd McKissick, Malcolm X, and Stokely Carmichael. McKissick, when asked what the role of the white man was in the black man's struggle, answered: "If there are whites who are not racists, and I believe there are a few, a *very* few, let them go to their own communities and teach; teach white people the truth about the black man." Malcolm X wrote in his autobiography: "The Negroes aren't the racists. Where the really sincere white people have to do their 'proving' of themselves is not among the black *victims,* but on the battle lines of where America's racism really *is*—and that's in their own home communities; America's racism is among their own fellow whites. That's where the sincere whites who really mean to accomplish something have to work." Stokely Carmichael, writing in the September 22, 1966, issue of *The New York Review of Books,* said: "One of the most distrubing things about almost all white supporters of the movement has been that they are afraid to go into their own communities—which is where the racism exists—and work to get rid of it."

4   A step in that direction which most whites can take is to clean up their language to rid it of words and phrases which connote racism to the blacks. Whereas many blacks have demonstrated an increased sensitivity to language and an awareness of the impact of words and phrases upon both black and white listeners, the whites of this nation have demonstrated little sensitivity to the language of racial strife. Whitey has been for too long speaking and writing in terminology which, often being offensive to the blacks, creates hostility and suspicions and breaks down communication.

5   The increased awareness and sensitivity of the black American to the impact of language is being reflected in various ways. Within the past two years, there have been an increasing number of references by Negro writers and speakers to the *Through the Looking Glass* episode where Humpty Dumpty says: "When I use a word it means just what I choose it to mean—neither more nor less." "The question is," said Alice, "whether you can make words mean so many different

things." "The question is," said Humpty Dumpty, "which is to be master—that's all." The *Through the Looking Glass* episode was used by Lerone Bennett, Jr., in the November 1967 issue of *Ebony* to introduce his article dealing with whether black Americans should call themselves "Negroes," "Blacks," or "Afro-Americans." In a speech delivered January 16, 1967, to the students at Morgan State College, Stokely Carmichael prefaced a retelling of the above Lewis Carroll tale with: "It [definition] is very, very important because I believe that people who can define are masters." Carmichael went on to say: "So I say 'black power' and someone says 'you mean violence.' And they expect me to say, 'No, no. I don't mean violence, I don't mean that.' . . . I am master of my own terms. If black power means violence to you, that is your problem. . . . I know what it means in my mind. I will stand clear and you must understand that because the first need of a free people is to be able to define their own terms and have those terms recognized by their oppressors. . . . Camus says that when a slave says 'no' he begins to exist."

6   This concern for words and their implications in race relations was voiced also by Martin Luther King who pointed out that "even semantics have conspired to make that which is black seem ugly and degrading." Writing in his last book before his death, *Where Do We Go from Here: Chaos or Community?*, King said: "In Roget's Thesaurus there are some 120 synonyms for 'blackness' and at least 60 of them are offensive—such words as 'blot,' 'soot,' 'grime,' 'devil,' and 'foul.' There are some 134 synonyms for 'whiteness,' and all are favorable, expressed in such words as 'purity,' 'cleanliness,' 'chastity,' and 'innocence.' A white lie is better than a black lie. The most degenerate member of the family is the 'black sheep,' not the 'white sheep.'"

7   In March 1962, *The Negro History Bulletin* published an article by L. Eldridge Cleaver, then imprisoned in San Quentin, who devoted several pages to a discussion of the black American's acceptance of a white society's standards for beauty and to an analysis of the negative connotations of the term "black" and the positive connotations of the term "white." Cleaver tells black Americans that "what we must do is stop associating the Caucasian with these exalted connotations of the word *white* when we think or speak of him. At the same time, we must cease associating ourselves with the unsavory connotations of the word black." Cleaver makes an interesting point when he brings to our attention the term "non-white." He writes: "The very words that we use indicate that we have set a premium on the Caucasian ideal of beauty. When discussing inter-racial relations, we speak of 'white people' and 'non-white people.' Notice that that particular choice of words gives precedence to 'white people' by making them a center—a standard—to which 'non-white' bears a negative relation. Notice the different connotations when we turn around and say 'colored' and 'non-colored,' or 'black' or 'non-black.'"

8   Simon Podair, writing in the Fourth Quarter issue, 1956, of *Phylon*, examines the connotations of such words as "blackmail," "blacklist," "blackbook," "blacksheep," and "blackball." The assertion made by Podair that it has been white civilization which has attributed to the word "black" things undesirable and evil warrants brief examination.

He is correct when he asserts that "language as a potent force in our society goes beyond being merely a communicative device. Language not only expresses ideas and concepts but it may actually shape them. Often the process is completely unconscious, with the individual concerned unaware of the influence of the spoken or written expressions upon his thought processes. Language can thus become an instrument of both propaganda and indoctrination for a given idea." Further, Podair is correct in saying that "so powerful is the role of language in its imprint upon the human mind that even the minority group may begin to accept the very expressions that aid in its stereotyping. Thus, even Negroes may develop speech patterns filled with expressions leading to the strengthening of stereotypes." Podair's point is illustrated by the comments made by a Negro state official in Washington upon hearing of the shooting of Robert Kennedy. The Director of the Washington State Board Against Discrimination said: "This is a black day in our country's history." Immediately after uttering this statement with the negative connotation of "black," he declared that Robert Kennedy "is a hero in the eyes of black people — a champion of the oppressed — and we all pray for his complete recovery."

9   Although King, Cleaver, and Podair, and others who are concerned with the negative connotations of "black" in the white society are partially correct in their analysis, they have omitted in their discussions two points which by their omission effect an incomplete analysis. First, it is not quite accurate to say, as Podair has asserted, that the concepts of black as hostile, foreboding, wicked, and gloomy "cannot be considered accidental and undoubtedly would not exist in a society wherein whites were a minority. Historically, these concepts have evolved as a result of the need of the dominant group to maintain social and economic relationships on the basis of inequality if its hegemony was to survive." This is inaccurate because the terms "blackball," "blacklist," "blackbook," and "blackmail" did not evolve as "a result of the need of the dominant group to maintain social and economic relationships on the basis of inequality if its hegemony was to survive." The origins of these terms are to be found in the sixteenth and seventeenth centuries in England where the terms were mostly based on the color of the book cover, the color of printing, or the color of the object from which the word got its meaning, as for instance the term "to blackball" coming from "the black ball" which centuries ago was a small black ball used as a vote against a person or thing. A "black-letter day" had its origin in the eighteenth century to designate an inauspicious day, as distinguished from a "red-letter day," The reference being to the old custom of marking the saint's days in the calendar with red letters.

10   More important, the assertion that the negative connotations of "black" and the positive connotations of "white" would not exist in a society wherein whites were a minority is not accurate. Centuries ago, before black societies ever saw white men, "black" often had negative connotations and "white" positive in those societies. T. O. Beidelman has made quite clear in his article "Swazi Royal Ritual," which appeared in the October 1966 issue of *Africa,* that black societies in southeast Africa, while attributing to black positive qualities,

can at the same time attribute to black negative qualities; the same applies to the color white. Beidelman writes that for the Swazi "darkness, as the 'covered' moon, is an ambiguous quality. Black symbolizes 'impenetrability of the future,' but also the 'sins and evils of the past year. . . .'" Black beads may symbolize marriage and wealth in cattle, but at the same time they can symbolize evil, disappointment, and misfortune. "The word *mnyama* means black and dark, but also means deep, profound, unfathomable, and even confused, dizzy, angry." To the Swazi, "that which is dark is unknown and ambiguous and dangerous, but it is also profound, latent with unknown meanings and possibilities." As for "white," *mhlophe* means to the Swazi "white, pale, pure, innocent, perfect, but this may also mean destitute and empty. The whiteness of the full moon, *inyanga isidindile,* relates to fullness; but this term *dinda* can also mean to be useless, simply because it refers to that which is fully exposed and having no further unknown potentialities."

11   What King, Cleaver, and Podair have failed to do in their discussions of the negative connotations of "black" and the positive connotations of "white" is to point out that in black societies "black" often connotes that which is hostile, foreboding, and gloomy; and "white" has symbolized purity and divinity. Furthermore, in white societies, "white" has numerous negative connotations: white livered (cowardly), white flag (surrender), white elephant (useless), white plague (tuberculosis), white wash (conceal), white feather (cowardice), *et cetera.* The ugliness and terror associated with the color white are portrayed by Melville in the chapter "the Whiteness of the Whale" in *Moby Dick.* At the beginning of the chapter, Melville says: "It was the whiteness of the whale that above all things appalled me."

12   What I am suggesting here is that the Negro writers, while legitimately concerned with the words and phrases which perpetuate racism in the United States have, at least in their analysis of the term "black," presented a partial analysis. This is not to say, however, that most of the analysis is not valid as far as it goes. Podair is entirely correct when he writes: "In modern American life language has become a fulcrum of prejudice as regards Negro-white relationships. Its effect has been equally potent upon the overt bigot as well as the confused member of the public who is struggling to overcome conscious or unconscious hostility towards minority groups. In the case of the Negro, language concepts have supported misconceptions and disoriented the thinking of many on the question of race and culture." Not only has the Negro become trapped by these "language concepts," but so too have the whites who, unlike the blacks, have demonstrated very little insight into the language of white racism and whose "language concepts" have "supported misconceptions and disoriented the thinking of many on the question of race and culture."

13   The Negroes' increased understanding and sensitivity to language as it is related to them demands that white Americans follow suit with a similar understanding and sensitivity which they have not yet demonstrated too well. During the 1960's, at a time when black Americans have been attempting more than ever to communicate with whites, through speeches, marches, sit-ins, demonstrations, through violence

and nonviolence, the barriers of communication between blacks and whites seem to be almost as divisive as they have been in the past one hundred years, no thanks to the whites. One has only to watch the TV panelists, blacks and whites, discussing the black American's protest and his aspirations, to see the facial expressions of the black panelists when a white on the panel speaks of "our colored boys in Vietnam." The black panelists knowingly smile at the racist phrasing and it is not difficult to understand the skepticism and suspicion which the blacks henceforth will maintain toward the white panelist who offends with "our colored boys in Vietnam." "Our colored boys in Vietnam" is a close relation to "our colored people" and "our colored," phrases which communicate more to the black American listener than intended by the white speaker. John Howard Griffin has pointed out something that applies not only to Southern whites, but to white Americans generally: "A great many of us Southern whites have grown up using an expression that Negroes can hardly bear to hear and yet tragically enough we use it because we believe it. It's an expression that we use when we say how much we love, what we patronizingly call 'our Negroes.'" The white American who talks of "our colored boys in Vietnam" offends the Negro triply; first, by referring to the black American men as "our" which is, as Griffin points out, patronizing; second, by using the nineteenth century term "colored"; third, by referring to the black American men as "boys."

14   Most whites, if not all, know that "nigger" and "boy" are offensive to the Negro; in fact, such language could be classified as "fighting words." But the insensitive and offensive whites continue today to indulge in expressing their overt and covert prejudices by using these obviously derogatory terms. Running a series of articles on racism in athletics, *Sports Illustrated* quoted a Negro football player as saying: "The word was never given bluntly; usually it took the form of a friendly, oblique talk with one of the assistant coaches. I remember one time one of the coaches came to me and said, '[Head Coach] Jim Owens loves you boys. We know you get a lot of publicity, but don't let it go to your head.' Hell, when he said 'Jim Owens loves you boys,' I just shut him off. That did it. I knew what he was talking about." An athletic director at one of the larger Southwestern Universities, discussing how much sports have done for the Negro, declared: "In general, the nigger athlete is a little hungrier and we have been blessed with having some real outstanding ones. We think they've done a lot for us, and we think we've done a lot for them" (*Sports Illustrated,* July 1, 1968). One of the Negro athletes said of the coaching personnel at the same university: "They can pronounce Negro if they want to. *They can pronounce it.* But I think it seems like such a little thing to them. The trouble with them is they're not thinking of the Negro and how he feels. Wouldn't you suppose that if there was one word these guys that live off Negroes would get rid of, one single word in the whole vocabulary, it would be *nigger*?" (*Sports Illustrated,* July 15, 1968). When a newspaperman tried to get the attention of Elvin Hayes, star basketball player at the University of Houston, the reporter shouted, "Hey, boy!" Hayes turned to the reporter and said: "Boy's on *Tarzan.* Boy plays on *Tarzan.* I'm no boy. I'm 22 years old.

I worked hard to become a man. I don't call you boy." The reporter apologized and said: "I didn't mean anything by it" (*Sports Illustrated,* July 1, 1968).

15   Whites who would never think of referring to Negroes as "boy" or "nigger" do, however, reveal themselves through less obviously racist language. A day does not go by without one hearing, from people who should know better, about "the Negro problem," a phrase which carries with it the implication that the Negro is a problem. One is reminded of the Nazis talking about "the Jewish problem." There was no Jewish problem! Yet the phrase carried the implication that the Jews were a problem in Germany and hence being a problem invited a solution and the solution Hitler proposed and carried out was the "final solution." Even the most competent writers fall into the "Negro problem" trap; James Reston of the *New York Times* wrote on April 7, 1968: "When Gunnar Myrdal, the Swedish social philosopher who has followed the Negro problem in American for forty years, came back recently, he felt that a great deal had changed for the better, but concluded that we have greatly underestimated the scope of the Negro problem." Myrdal himself titled his 1944 classic work *The American Dilemma: The Negro Problem and Modern Democracy.* A book published in 1967, *The Negro in 20th Century America,* by John Hope Franklin and Isidore Starr, starts off in the Table of Contents with "Book One: *The Negro Problem*"; the foreword begins, "The Negro problem was selected because it is one of the great case studies in man's never-ending fight for equal rights." One of the selections in the book, a debate in which James Baldwin participates, has Baldwin's debate opponent saying that "the Negro problem is a very complicated one." There are several indications that from here on out the black American is no longer going to accept the phrase "the Negro problem." As Lerone Bennett, Jr., said in the August 1965 issue of *Ebony,* "there is no Negro problem in America. The problem of race in America, insofar as that problem is related to packets of melanin in men's skins, is a white problem." In 1966, the editors of *Ebony* published a book of essays dealing with American black-white relations entitled *The WHITE Problem in America.* It is difficult to imagine Negroes sitting around during the next decade talking about "the Negro problem," just as it is difficult to imagine Jews in 1939 referring to themselves as "the Jewish problem."

16   The racial brainwashing of whites in the United States leads them to utter such statements as "You don't sound like a Negro" or "Well, he didn't sound like a Negro to me." John Howard Griffin, who changed the color of his skin from white to black to find out what it meant to be black in America, was ashamed to admit that he thought he could not pass for a Negro because he "didn't know how to speak Negro." "There is an illusion in this land," said Griffin, "that unless you sound as though you are reading Uncle Remus you couldn't possibly have an authentic Negro dialect. But I don't know what we've been using for ears because you don't have to be in the Negro community five minutes before the truth strikes, and the truth is that there are just as many speech patterns in the Negro community as there are in any other, particularly in areas of rigid segregation where your right

shoulder may be touching the shoulder of a Negro PhD and your left shoulder the shoulder of the disadvantaged." A black American, when told that he does not "sound like a Negro," legitimately can ask his white conversationalist, "What does a Negro sound like?" This will probably place the white in a dilemma for he will either have to admit that sounding like a Negro means sounding like Prissy in *Gone With the Wind* ("Who dat say who dat when you say dat?") or that perhaps there is no such thing as "sounding like a Negro." Goodman Ace, writing in the July 27, 1968, issue of the *Saturday Review*, points out that years ago radio program planners attempted to write Negroes into the radio scripts, portraying the Negro as something else besides janitors, household maids, and train porters. Someone suggested that in the comedy radio show *Henry Aldrich* Henry might have among his friends a young Negro boy, without belaboring the point that the boy was Negro. As Mr. Ace observes, "just how it would be indicated on radio that the boy is black was not mentioned. Unless he was to be named Rufus or Rastus." Unless, it might be added, he was to be made to "sound like a Negro."

17   Psychiatrist Frantz Fanon, who begins his *Black Skin, White Masks* with a chapter titled "The Negro and Language," explains the manner of many whites when talking to Negroes and the effects of this manner. Although he is writing about white Europeans, what Fanon says applies equally to white Americans. He points out that most whites "talk down" to the Negro, and this "talking down" is, in effect, telling the Negro, "You'd better keep your place." Fanon writes: "A white man addressing a Negro behaves exactly like an adult with a child and starts smirking, whispering, patronizing, cozening." The effect of the whites' manner of speaking to the Negro "makes him angry, because he himself is a pidgin-nigger-talker." "But I will be told," says Fanon, "there is no wish, no intention to anger him. I grant this; but it is just this absence of wish, this lack of interest, this indifference, this automatic manner of classifying him, imprisoning him, primitivizing him, decivilizing him, that makes him angry." If a doctor greets his Negro patient with "You not feel good, no?" or "G'morning pal. Where's it hurt? Huh? Lemme see—belly ache? Heart pain?" the doctor feels perfectly justified in speaking that way, writes Fanon, when in return the patient answers in the same fashion; the doctor can then say to himself, "You see? I wasn't kidding you. That's just the way they are." To make the Negro talk pidgin, as Fanon observes, "is to fasten him to the effigy of him, to snare him, to imprison him, the eternal victim of an essence, of an *appearance* for which he is not responsible. And naturally, just as a Jew who spends money without thinking about it is suspect, a black man who quotes Montesquieu had better be watched." The whites, in effect, encourage the stereotype of the Negro; they perpetuate the stereotype through the manner in which they speak about and speak to Negroes. And if Fanon is correct, the whites by "talking down" to the Negro are telling that black American citizen to "remember where you come from!"

18   Another facet of the racism of the whites' language is reflected in their habit of referring to talented and great writers, athletes, enter-

tainers, and clergymen as "a great Negro singer" or "a great black poet" or "a great Negro ball player." What need is there for whites to designate the color or race of the person who has excelled? Paul Robeson and Marian Anderson are great and talented singers. James Baldwin and LeRoi Jones are talented writers. Why must the whites qualify the greatness of these individuals with "black" or "colored" or "Negro"? Fanon briefly refers to this predilection of whites to speak with this qualification:

> . . . Charles-André Julien introducing Aimé Césaire as "a Negro poet with a university degree," or again, quite simply, the expression, "a great black poet."
>
> These ready-made phrases, which seem in a common-sense way to fill a need—for Aimé Césaire is really black and a poet—have a hidden subtlety, a permanent rub. I know nothing of Jean Paulhan except that he writes very interesting books; I have no idea how old Roger Caillois is, since the only evidence I have of his existence are the books of his that streak across my horizon. And let no one accuse me of affective allergies; what I am trying to say is that there is no reason why André Breton should say of Césaire, "Here is a black man who handles the French language as no white man today can."

19   The tendency to designate and identify a person as a Negro when the designation is not necessary carries over into newspaper and magazine reporting of crimes. There was no need for *Time* magazine (July 19, 1968) to designate the race of the individual concerned in the following *Time* report: "In New York City, slum dwellers were sent skidding for cover when Bobby Rogers, 31, Negro superintendent of a grubby South Bronx tenement, sprayed the street with bullets from a sawed-off .30 cal. semiautomatic carbine, killing three men and wounding a fourth." *Time,* for whatever reason, designated the race of the person involved in this instance, but the reports on other criminal offences cited by *Time,* on the same page, did not indicate the race of the "suspects." As a label of primary potency, "Negro" stands out over "superintendent." The assumption that whites can understand and sympathize with the Negro's dismay when black "suspects" are identified by race and white "suspects" are not, is apparently an unwarranted assumption; or it may be possible that the whites *do* understand the dismay and precisely for that reason continue to designate the race of the black criminal suspect. To argue that if the race is not designated in the news story then the reader can assume that the suspected criminal is white, is not acceptable for it makes all the difference if the suspect is identified as "a Negro superintendent," "a white superintendent," or "a superintendent." If we were told, day in and day out, that "a *white* bank clerk embezzled" or "a *white* service station operator stole" or "a *white* unemployed laborer attacked," it would make a difference in the same sense that it makes a difference to identify the criminal suspect as "Negro" or "black."

20   If many Negroes find it hard to understand why whites have to designate a great writer or a great artist or a common criminal as "colored" or "Negro," so too do many Negroes find it difficult to

understand why whites must designate a Negro woman as a "Negress." Offensive as "Negress" is to most blacks, many whites still insist on using the term. In a July 28, 1968, *New York Times Magazine* article, the writer, discussing the 1968 campaigning of Rockefeller and Nixon, wrote: "A fat Negress on the street says, passionately, 'Rocky! Rocky!'" As Gordon Allport has written in *The Nature of Prejudice,* "members of minority groups are often understandably sensitive to names given them. Not only do they object to deliberately insulting epithets, but sometimes see evil intent where none exists." Allport gives two examples to make his point: one example is the spelling of the word "Negro" with a small "n" and the other example is the word "Negress." "Sex differentiations are objectionable," writes Allport, "since they seem doubly to emphasize ethnic differences: why speak of Jewess and not of Protestantess, or of Negress, and not of whitess?" Just as "Jewess" is offensive to the Jews, so too is "Negress" offensive to the Negroes. "A Negro woman" does not carry the same connotations as "Negress," the latter conveying an emotional emphasis on both the color and sex of the individual. *Webster's New World Dictionary of the American Language* says of "Negress": "A Negro woman or girl: often a patronizing or contemptuous term."

21   When the newspaper reporter tried to get the attention of twenty-two-year-old basketball star Elvin Hayes by shouting, "Hey, boy!" and Hayes vigorously objected to being called "boy," the reporter apologized and said: "I didn't mean anything by it." In a few cases, a very few cases, white Americans indeed "didn't mean anything by it." That excuse, however, will no longer do. The whites must make a serious conscious effort to discard the racist clichés of the past, the overt and covert language of racism. "Free, white, and 21" or "That's white of you" are phrases whites can no longer indulge in. Asking white Americans to change their language, to give up some of their clichés, is disturbing enough, since the request implies a deficiency in the past use of that language; asking that they discard the language of racism is also disturbing, because the people being asked to make the change, in effect, are being told that they have been the perpetrators and perpetuators of racism. Finally, and most important, calling the Negro "nigger" or "boy," or "speaking down" to the Negro, gives Whitey a linguistic power over the victimized black American, a power most whites are unwilling or afraid to give up. A person's language is an extension of himself and to attack his use of language is to attack him. With the language of racism, this is exactly the point, for the language of white racism and the racism of the whites are almost one and the same. Difficult and painful as it may be for whites to discard their racist terms, phrases, and clichés, it must be done before blacks and whites can discuss seriously the eradication of white racism.

Discussion of Theme

1. Why does Bosmajian object to the phrase "the Negro problem"? Why is it inappropriate?

2. What examples from your own speech can you cite that suggest, even subtly, racial overtones?
3. If, following the author's suggestion, a group of white leaders met to talk not about Negroes but about themselves, what topics might they discuss to alleviate racial tension?
4. According to this essay, what changes in language would occur if whites were a minority?
5. Have black demands, demonstrations, and marches failed as instruments of communication with whites? If so, why?

Discussion of Rhetoric

1. Why does the author repeatedly use the term "whitey"? Is he trying to offend his white readers? Or is there another purpose?
2. What audience does Bosmajian have in mind for this article: white or black, prejudiced or nonprejudiced? What evidence can you cite to support your answer?
3. How would you describe the tone of the author's language? Is he dispassionate or emotional in his argument?
4. Why are there so many quotations in this article? Do they detract from, or add to, the central thesis?
5. What are the connotations of the following terms: "colored"; "black"; "noncolored." Are there parallel terms referring to whites?

Writing Assignments

1. Develop the following title into an effective theme: "The White Problem in America."
2. Write a theme illustrating and developing the following quotation, taken from this selection (paragraph 21): "A person's language is an extension of himself and to attack his use of language is to attack him."
3. Should every college student be required to take courses in black studies? Present your views in a theme.

Vocabulary

(1) ERADICATE pull up by the roots; destroy completely

(1) INUNDATED flooded; overwhelmed by

(2) PATHOLOGY abnormality; disease

(12) FULCRUM prop; support

(12) OVERT open; visible

(14) DEROGATORY degrading

(15) MELANIN dark pigment

(17) COZENING deceiving; beguiling

(17) PIDGIN a dialect or jargon

Nicholas von Hoffman (1929–
), a native New Yorker, is a
columnist for the "Washington
Post," as well as author of several books, including "Mississippi Notebook" (1964) and "We
Are the People Our Parents
Warned Us Against" (1968).

Von Hoffman's review of Garry
Wills's book "Nixon Agonistes"
presents his opinion not only of
the book but of its subject matter as well.

NICHOLAS VON HOFFMAN

Nix: A Review of Nixon Agonistes

1 Garry Wills has got Nixon's number and it adds up to less than one. Keeping count of Nixon is so exasperatingly dull that you'd think only Nixon could do it.

2   Wills's tally reveals that even the early Nixon possessed a meticulous determination to assemble large amounts of useless information in an orderly way . . . as lawyers and accountants do. As a boy he used his cast-iron ass to outstudy his fellow students and graduate with distinction in order to apply for a job as a G-man. He was turned down.

3   Nixon still collects information, assembling data on his own Presidency as the small boy Nixon probably once assembled his grammar school batting and fielding averages. There are people who can give you from memory the earned run averages of the 1938 Pittsburgh Pirates. Surely Nixon is one.

4   The studious Nixon has recently released a report on his first two years in the White House. It tells us that during that time the President has

> met or talked by phone with leaders — both individually and in groups —
> from every area of American life: from labor more than 30 such contacts,
> racial minorities, almost 30 such contacts, campus representatives, more
> than 50 such contacts, businessmen, more than 150 such contacts . . .
> worship services in the East Room of the White House, more than 8,000

guests attended . . .. More than 13,000 guests enjoyed the Nixons' hospitality at 132 dinners . . . and more than 40,000 additional guests enjoyed an ongoing series of breakfasts, luncheons, teas, coffees and receptions.

It is also estimated in this publication, subtitled "Balance, Direction and Forward Thrust," that he shook 200,000 hands in that space of time.

5   Only a man who can't stand to be around people would allow such a figure to be compiled about himself. Garry Wills has caught that quality in *Nixon Agonistes,* which must be the best book so far about the man, the best written, the best thought out.

6   Many of us who live in Washington get so annoyed with Nixon, so bored by him that we fail to exercise the charity that's needed to understand another person, even a President. Wills doesn't do that. While his verdict is a depressing, but probably correct, condemnation of the man as an obsolete exemplar of old and morbidly weakened ideas, he's never cruel, and he never loses the sympathy necessary for insight.

7   The only objection you can make to the book is that it's about Nixon. Wills has such a good mind you wish he'd chosen a subject that could keep it occupied. There's so little of Nixon to grab onto, so unlike his yeasty, chesty, feisty predecessor. This wafer thin, nearly tasteless personality is hard for a writer to nourish his words with. Wills is constantly forced to write about all the qualities the man doesn't have:

Nixon's background haunts him, yet does not show—not, at least, in helpful ways. Eisenhower, a virtual exile to exotic places most of his active life . . . could still make his grin hazily fulgurant with Kansas, with the dust-prismed sun of his childhood afternoons. All recent Presidents have had the stamp of place on them—patrician Roosevelt of upper New York, raffish Harry Truman from Missouri, Boston-Irish Kennedy thinly veneered at Harvard, and Johnson out of Texas like a walking tall tale . . . . Nixon alone, though deeply shaped by Whittier, has no attractive color of place to him.

8   If Wills's Nixon lacks grain and texture, he's also not the man a lot of detractors take him to be. Less vicious, more intelligent, and not so unprincipled, a portrait that serves to explain the dreary person we see on TV.

9   America is a bother to the President, a pain in the neck. The Presidency is a foreign policy job, so much so that Nixon gives the impression that domestic cares are an intrusion on his real work. He'd like to strike a deal with us—you run the country and I'll run the world. Wills has caught this part of the man perfectly:

He feels—mistakenly—that the country can run itself through local and congressional machinery, but only a President can make and carry out policy toward other nations. Nixon cannot admit the importance of presidential style and presence in easing domestic fears . . . arousing confidence in the young . . . assuaging racial bitterness . . . . To admit this would be to recognize his own incapacities. Better to insist that the President is on hand to steer the ship of state . . . . This is not a matter of charisma, but for detailed work and study—just what Nixon excels at.

10   You don't have to reveal much of yourself if you live in the White House—the power of the Presidential role obviates that, but least of

all do you have to permit people a peep at who lives behind your eyes if you're doing foreign policy. It's so formal, and, as Wills says, Nixon loves hierarchy, form, and uniform, not because he's a militarist or a fascist, but because he's scared to let anyone get too close:

> His rigid wall of decorum, in dress and manner, is one of the means he uses to fend off the world, avoid participation in it . . . . Nixon restored the white-tie ceremony to the White House. Some, it is true, took the toy hats and tunics added to White House police as a sign of Nixon's imagination . . . . Quite the opposite. Each added symbol of uniform, function, office makes man's role in the social chess game clearer, his place marked, moves limited. Clothes structure a situation . . . .

11   Still Wills penetrates the distance and the formalism to find a man who does believe in something, who's other than a shady operator. That's easy to forget when you're watching the day-to-day Nixon, the bring-us-all-together Nixon of two and a half years ago; the Southern Strategy Nixon, the Phoenix tough guy Nixon, and now this new character, the recently arrived reconciler of youth and age, the Nixon who turned up to make the University of Nebraska speech and now talks of "ecology" and "revolution."

12   The substances of all these seemingly disparate Nixons are pretty much the same. For Wills this coherent and ultimately consistent Nixon is the last free-market, laissez-faire liberal, the sort who finds justification for the soul in the justification of fetching a high price on an open, competitive market. "Nixon's victory," he writes,

> was the nation's concession of defeat, an admission that we have no politics left but the old individualism, a web of myths that have lost their magic. We cannot convincingly proclaim that where we stand is a "vital center." Our "mainstream" is a sludge.

13   This is our Nixon, an anemic descendant of Teddy Roosevelt, a hemophiliac child of Woodrow Wilson, trying with deficient strength to restore localism and competition at home and to bestow our peculiar American self-determination abroad. "Nixon is emphatic about the traditional moral assumptions of our foreign policy because he believes in them . . . . He does not woo the Forgotten American cynically: he *agrees* with the silent majority. Those who misunderstand him, trusted him or what he says." (Wills's italics.)

14   It's hard to know exactly what people mean when they use hypothetical notions like the silent majority, but Wills is certainly right in not regarding Nixon as the anything-goes used car salesman, the Tricky Dick of liberal execration. Sure, he's tricky—politics is tricky—but not any shiftier than many another recent occupant of his office. What Wills knows is that Nixon believes; he believes in opposing communists, believes in Teddy Roosevelt's interventionist America, in the Wilsonian God-given and global responsibility to put down Bolshevism.

15   When he came into office, the Washington know-it-alls explained that "Dick Nixon is too smart a politician not to end this war. He knows he's got to do it if he's going to win the off-year Congressional elections and be re-elected in '72." They forgot they'd said the same of Lyndon.

16   Well, Nixon's been in office twenty-six months now, two years and two months, and it isn't ended. It isn't ended because he's not going to end it except on his terms: a staunchly implanted anticommunist government in Saigon.

17   You're not going to pick up many votes anywhere in America by continuing this war. Even the hawks are sick of it; but Nixon isn't and that's why we're not out. He shares Johnson's obsessional desire to win, as well as his tactics. Johnson started out thinking he could win with bombings; Nixon the same, except that he's more dangerous because he's more rational. It's doubtful Johnson knew why he ought to stay out of Cambodia and Laos; he must have just had a feeling. Nixon doesn't operate on feelings. He thinks that he thinks. So he reasons that if you smash 'em good, stun 'em, then Thieu and that whole mob of armed houseboys and currency-swapping madams will have the chance they need to dig in deep enough to stay. The same goes for Laos. They're even saying in Washington that one of the reasons for this latest violation of the neutrality of the Belgium of the Far East is to ensure Thieu's re-election.

18   For Nixon, America has the license to smash in anywhere, the right of hot pursuit after the Red Peril. We are the twentieth century's freedom fighters. As he reads the Constitution, it is he, the President, who alone determines the national interest and foreign policy because, outside the twelve-mile limit, he is the United States of America. Very dangerous, but very Wilsonian as Wills shows.

19   Since Hoover, Ike has probably been the only American President not infected with an overblown definition of the job. The Elective Kaiser. The Embodiment of the National Will. The Supreme War Lord and Commander-in-Chief. The Pontiff of Patriotic Self-Sacrifice. There was John Kennedy daring to say — and Nixon must have been applauding — Ask not what your country can do for you, but what you can do for your country!

20   The people at the service of the state. Monstrously antithetical to the popular idea of what the government is for, but it's a job description that seems to go with whoever has the office.

21   Yet while the Embodiment of the National Will presses forward, the nation leaves him. His armies are beginning to break up with sliding discipline, race riots, slot machines, corruption, alcohol, and dope. A full chicken colonel in the Air Force is cashiered for smoking pot.

22   In civilian life everyone rushes to get his. Nixon's appointees are compromised before they take office — Haynesworth and Carswell. Stans is involved in the Penn Central affair, but more unnerving is the general attitude to screw it, screw the job, grab and get it, cops, teachers, electric utilities, doctors, oil companies, trash collectors. The virtues and probities which Nixon honors the most are more despised in his reign than in Johnson's, when this drift in our behavior first accelerated into visibility.

23   In the face of this endemic conviction that if nobody else cares why should I, the National War Lord, Priest Embodiment calls us to a collective purpose which is meant to raise us above our increasingly destructive individualism, but who's listening? We don't want a foreign policy and that's what he's got most to give.

24   Although Wills has an accurate sense of the President's values, he perhaps makes a mistake in underestimating the Keynes-New Deal influence on Nixon. In addition to being a very old liberal (TR-Wilson), he's a new old liberal, a New Dealer in so many ways. Thirty-five years ago the New Deal hadn't failed yet; it was the best thing anybody could think of, a program a reasonable man could put hope in. Not that Nixon's that far back. He's at the end of the New Deal, the ADA circa 1957, same platform at home and abroad. Negotiate disarmament with appropriate safeguards, national health insurance, desegregate the schools, deficit spending, all that. If he'd been President in 1957 with his 1971 program, Hubert Humphrey would worship him.

25   In 1971 it's a gloppy, unworkable mess, like Nixon and the railroads, a stop-gap saga of semipublic corporations, loans, leasebacks, rentals, here a strike, there an emergency, neither private nor public nor a partnership, a programmatic mish-mash, not muddling through, just muddling. And Nixon's stockbroker insurance law, so characteristic of the New Deal, allows these guys to stay in business by letting them gamble with other people's money while government promises to make good the losses. This isn't the reconstitution of the free market — Wall Street is a monopoly in restraint of trade anyhow — it's the maintenance of an unreasonable, free market illusion, this gluey blend of old, wilting values and virile statism.

26   Nixon is all the time trying, looking for ways to create the free market which Wills points out never existed in this country, except as men like Nixon recall their own competitive experience; it endowed them with a price and for them a man without a price is worthless. It's this that explains why he doesn't want to use the Presidential power to jawbone prices and profits into line, and why, finally, he'll most likely have to use wage and price control, saying, as a good New Dealer does, that the Nixon NRA will restore price competition.

27   Since that January two years ago when he returned to Washington and killed Camp by giving us too much of it, he's been tenacious against price control, but the unseen hand of the market has arthritis. The hardhats are biting the pampering hand that pins the medals on their chests; his adored cops, all his forgotten Americans, are making a run on the treasury, the doctors won't stop reaching for the extra dollar, and inch by inch he's forced back to the methods that the liberal Keynesians prepared for him. He knows no other way.

28   He also knows and says out loud that the country wants Washington off its neck, so he's bringing government to the people with flying visits to the mayors and metropolitans and, dearest of all, revenue sharing. Give the money back to the people and let them decide. True decentralization. But it isn't. True decentralization, something more than an administrative reshufflement, would mean returning the taxing power to the states, or some significant proportion of it. Let the people of the states and localities tax themselves or not, let them make their own mistakes and achieve their own solutions.

29   But in the New Deal system, the control of taxation, the sluicing and channeling of moneys is how the economy is run. There can't be local

autonomy without a new and different kind of planning, and there can't be planning because the Nixon New Deal rests on the premise that you plan a free market economy without admitting it, even to yourself.

30   Instead, let's have revenue sharing which, if it ever comes to pass, means government will be made even more complex. For at the center of the revenue sharing proposal is an elaborate mechanism to disguise categorical grants in aid and make it look like the people down below want the money spent the same old way of their free will and choice. Failing that, let's reorganize the government. Make all the departments that don't work now, because they're too big and too demoralized, bigger and cry out, "Accountability!"

31   Fewer and fewer people in Washington think it will work because fewer and fewer people in the capital think anything will work. As it used to be said that New York's ungovernable, it's coming to be said that the whole country is, and as that conviction grows, Nixon appears more and more acceptable. Not in the infuriated manner of two years ago when there was all the foot-stomping and yelling he and Humphrey were alike.

32   This is the resignation that comes from a loss of energy and knowing what probably needs to be done requires too much effort and will cause too much strife. Maybe Nader can keep going, and Proxmire can talk himself hoarse opposing the SST, but so many more accommodate to Nixon on the supposition that the time's not right for anything better, and what *would* be better?

33   He's President Not-So-Bad, not so vindictive, not so stupid, not so repressive, not so dangerous except when he goes off on his tears — Cambodia and San Jose. So he savaged Cambodia, so he trashed Laos. It might have been (and may yet be) worse but it's so far not so bad as it could have been. There are still some people left alive. Unless he accidentally destroys the world playing *macho* across a line drawn on the ground, with some other insecure leader, he's not going to do much, except kill thousands of Asians and make more homeless. We know that about him now. If he's in there two more years or six, it's going to be pretty much the same. He's shown us what he really is and it's not quite so bad as was feared.

34   But still bad enough. Wills knows this:

> It is only a calm realization that our main myths are dead or dying that can make us, as a nation, live on. We are shaped by those beliefs, but we are something more than they ever were, we can outlive them . . . it is comforting — needed comfort — to reflect that this is so, that we can survive our creed dissolution; for Nixon, by embodying that creed, by trying to bring it back to life, has at last reduced it to absurdity.

Discussion of Theme

1. Why does Von Hoffman regard Richard Nixon as a liberal, rather than a conservative, as most people would label him? How would you characterize Nixon's political philosophy?

2. In general, do you think that von Hoffman is too irreverent in his criticism of Nixon? Or is he merely exercising his right of free speech? How fair is he in his criticisms?
3. Both von Hoffman and Wills believe that at the time of Nixon's election this country was dwelling in the political past and operating on the basis of outmoded myths. What were some of those myths? How have the times changed since 1968?
4. What is the Silent Majority? Is Nixon a member of this group? Are you? In general, what are its identifying characteristics?

Discussion of Rhetoric

1. Is the tone of this review one of reason and objectivity, or is it personal and emotional? Is the tone appropriate? Would it convince a reader who had no opinion before reading it?
2. Von Hoffman employs irony throughout his review; find several examples and show why each is (or is not) appropriate. Note, for example, paragraph 30.
3. Explain the significance of *Agonistes* in Wills's title.
4. Does von Hoffman supply evidence to support his statements about Nixon? Or does he use them merely to shock and annoy the reader?

Writing Assignments

1. If you disagree with von Hoffman and Wills's estimate of Richard Nixon, write a rebuttal.
2. Should the electoral-college system be abandoned? Give your views in a theme.
3. Present your reaction to Kennedy's famous quotation "Ask not what your country can do for you, but what you can do for your country." Do you agree with it, or does it really demand compliance with the wishes of the state, as von Hoffman suggests?
4. Write an estimate of Nixon's administration, from 1968 to 1972, as you think history will record it.

Library Exploration

1. There are several books available on Richard Nixon: attempts to assess his Presidency, analyses of his personality, and studies of his political philosophy. You might be interested in reading and reporting on one of these. For a statement by Nixon himself, read *My Six Crises*.
2. Much has been said and written about Nixon's "Southern strategy." Write a report on this plan, and include your estimate of its effectiveness.
3. Investigate the role of Henry Kissinger or John Mitchell in the Nixon administration.

Vocabulary

(6) EXAMPLAR   a model or pattern to be imitated

(7) FULGURANT   dazzling; flashing like lightning

(7) RAFFISH   devil-may-care; rakish

(9) ASSUAGING   making milder or less severe

(9) CHARISMA   personal qualities that give certain individuals influence over large numbers of followers

(10) OBVIATES   makes unnecessary

(12) DISPARATE   distinct; separate

(22) PROBITIES   moral virtues

Dalton Trumbo (1905–   ), play-wright, magazine writer, novel-ist, and screenwriter, was born in Colorado and educated at the University of Colorado and UCLA. In 1948 he was fined $1000 and sentenced to a year in prison for refusing to tell the House Un-American Activities Committee whether or not he was a Communist. Among his novels are "Eclipse" (1935) and "Johnny Got His Gun" (1939).

Most of us have had experi-ences dealing with huge corpor-ations. In the following letter to the manager of his bank, Dalton Trumbo recounts some of his difficulties.

DALTON TRUMBO

To Branch Manager of Bank of America, La Canada Branch

Los Angeles, California
November 23, 1957

My dear sir:

1   Attached to this letter please find notice of a $20 overdraft against the account of Cleo and/or Dalton Trumbo, together with your custom-ary $1.50 charge for such service. Permit me to suggest that you would have been a wiser man and a better banker had you paid the check instead of returning it and charged me under the category of "Paid against insufficient funds." . . .

2   In passing, I may add this isn't the first time I have received similar intimations of your disesteem. I am a writer, and a bad mathematician, and a poor bookkeeper, and I may upon occasion be briefly and minutely overdrawn. But most of the expense to which I have been put by your idiotic charges, and most of the embarrassment I have suffered by returned checks, have been the result of your own inefficiency, rather than mine.

3   Example: I have deposited checks drawn against the Sunset and Clark Branch of the Bank of America in my account in the La Canada Branch, and drawn against the deposit, and had my checks returned because my deposit had not been cleared between your branches. No telephone call was made to the Sunset and Clark Branch—which is, after all, the same bank—to see whether my deposit was backed by sufficient funds in that bank. (It always was, for the signature to the Sunset and Clark Branch checks was the Paul Kohner Agency, which is one of the wealthiest talent agencies in Hollywood.) Nor was any call made to me. The checks I'd drawn were simply returned. You have grown so enormously as a system of banks that you are no longer one bank. You don't trust your own accounts and apparently you have no way of verifying them. You don't just shoot first and think later: you shoot and never think at all.

4   Example: Upon a certain Friday afternoon I was so stupid as to deposit by mail a check drawn on the Sunset and Clark Branch in the sum of $2,700 in your La Canada Branch for my account. On the following Tuesday a businessman telephoned me that he was holding my returned check for $80 odd. I told him to run it through again, since I had made a substantial deposit. He differed with me. He had just talked with your branch, and had been informed my account did not have sufficient funds to redeem my check.

5   I telephoned your bookkeeper. True enough, my account held less than $80.00 and there was no record of any $2,700 deposit. I told her of my Friday mail deposit which certainly should have arrived in La Canada in Monday's (the previous day's) mail. She bestirred herself. She reported back that the check had, indeed, arrived the preceding (Monday) morning before the opening of the bank. I then asked why the check hadn't been posted to my account, and why, some thirty hours later, you were giving out information over the telephone that was not only hundreds of dollars wrong, but thousands. She then tried to explain to me a new and dazzling system of posting checks by which you penalize depositors by delays of up to two days in placing his own funds at his disposal.

6   I then asked the young lady to telephone the aggrieved businessman to whom she had given her misinformation. I requested this small favor so that the gentleman in question would cease thinking me a liar, so he would understand that it was the bank that had erred and not I. She promised effusively to do so. At five o'clock that afternoon I telephoned the businessman. She had not called him. She clearly had no intention of doing so. You will briskly advertise a man's small accounting errors to all his associates, and charge him for it to boot, but you will not make the slightest effort to rectify your own by the same route.

7   Example: During the spring a thousand-dollar deposit in my account was erroneously entered twice by your teller in my bank book. My wife quite naturally entered both deposits in our check book. About six weeks later we were rewarded with a blizzard of returned checks, to each of which an appropriate charge was attached. Again I got on the telephone, and again I ran down the error, and again it lay at your door. One ten-cent telephone call, one decent little business courtesy, would have stopped the whole sequence at the outset. But you don't do business that way. The only recognition of error I got out of you was a series of charges against my account which placed me in the happy — from your point of view — position of standing the bill for a typical banker's blunder.

8   I am not a rich man, and I am not a bookkeeper, but neither am I a pauper or a hot-check artist. I have a $26,000 equity in a house which you yourself approved for a $10,000 loan. I carry $60,000 of insurance on my own life, and $34,000 more on the lives of my family, plus two family health policies. I own four insured automobiles, a great deal of furniture and household and office equipment, a large library, certain valuable copyrights, blocked sums of money in various foreign countries, and other real estate. My income is all earned personal income, and most of it, although not all of it, has been deposited in your branch. My present deposit book accounts only for the past twenty-three months. I find that I have deposited in that period some $76,630.46, for a rough average of $3,330 per month. It's not a large account nor a large income, but I am informed by your extensive advertisements that you are eager to accommodate such small accounts as mine. What the ads don't say is that you are inefficient, unaccommodating, as inclined toward error as you are toward delay, and eager at all times to destroy the good names of your depositors.

9   I have selected my new bank very carefully. I have gone over these figures and examples with them in order to make certain I shall not be subjected at their hands to the same stupidity I have encountered at yours. They assure me that they handle such matters with intelligence, good faith, efficiency and reasonable celerity. I ask for nothing more.

10   I shall allow a week for present checks to clear, and then close my account. I have an escrow pending with you. Cancel it and return whatever funds remain in it to my account. I recently ordered two new checkbooks printed up. Cancel the order. If I am too late for cancellation I shall, as usual, pay the bill and leave them with you as my last gift to the Bank of America.

Very truly,
DALTON TRUMBO

Discussion of Theme

1. In your opinion, who was to blame for the mishandling of Trumbo's bank account? Is a mistake like this inevitable when dealing with a large organization — is this the price one pays?

2. What effect does a letter of this sort have on the policies of an organization? Is it merely a futile gesture?
3. Has the computer made banking and other business activities more accurate and better organized, or has it merely served to compound the confusion?

Discussion of Rhetoric

1. How does Trumbo emerge, as a result of his tone and diction: sane, rational, and patient, or irrational, hysterical, and just plain cranky?
2. Find examples of exaggerated courtesy directed to the manager of the bank. What is their purpose?
3. Locate the sudden shifts from humor and irony to sarcasm and icy rage.

Writing Assignments

1. Write a letter to the manager of a company with which you have had a similar experience.
2. Imagine that you are the manager of the Bank of America branch; reply to Trumbo's letter.
3. Describe the image that banks have traditionally had in this country; show how they have perhaps contributed to that image.

Library Exploration

1. What steps has the Bank of America taken to change its image among young people?
2. Dalton Trumbo was a member of the "Hollywood Ten," a group of screen writers singled out for investigation by the House Un-American Activities Committee. Why were these men investigated? What happened to them? Were they Communists, as was alleged?

Vocabulary

(2) INTIMATIONS   hints
(2) DISESTEEM   lack of approval or esteem
(5) BESTIRRED   moved with life or vigor
(6) AGGRIEVED   offended; injured

(6) EFFUSIVELY   with unrestrained emotion; in a gushing manner
(6) RECTIFY   correct; amend
(9) CELERITY   speed

THE
AMERICAN
SCENE

Cesar Chavez (1927–   ) has been active in the unionization of migrant workers in the West and Southwest for the last several years. An official in the United Farm Workers Organizing Committee, he has frequently been arrested for his participation in strikes and demonstrations.

As its title suggests, the following essay contains proposals for the redistribution of wealth in this country, as well as for the granting of political power to the dispossessed.

CESAR CHAVEZ

Sharing the Wealth

1 How can we narrow the gap between the wealthy and the poor in this country? What concrete steps can be taken *now* to abolish poverty in America? There are a number of things that President Nixon could do immediately, if he wanted to. In terms of our own grape pickers' strike, he could tell the Pentagon to stop shipping extraordinary amounts of grapes to Vietnam — the Government's most obvious tool in its attempt to break our strike. And he could improve the lot of *all* the farmworkers in the Southwest — easily, under existing legislation — by putting an end to the importing and exploitation of cheap foreign labor. The Immigration Service has allowed almost 500,000 poor Mexicans to flood across the border since 1965. Absorbing this number of resident aliens would not be detrimental if they actually became residents, but most of these workers return to Mexico after each harvest season, since their American wages go much farther there than they would in this country. They have no stake in either economic or political advances here; it is the domestic farmworker who wants our union, who wants better schools, who wants to participate in the political system. Our poor Mexican brothers who are allowed to come across the border for

the harvest are tools in the Government's and the growers' attempts to break our strike.

2   In the still larger framework of all the country's poor, President Nixon should acknowledge that the War on Poverty programs of the Sixties have failed. The Office of Economic Opportunity pumped out propaganda about "community action programs" through which the poor were supposedly going to have a say in the solution of their own problems. Then, just as the communities were organizing for meaningful change through these programs, the money was suddenly yanked away. Washington seemed to realize that if it lived up to its rhetoric, it would actually be encouraging real political participation and building real economic power among the poor, and got cold feet. The Government and the power class will never allow their money to be used to build another power class — especially if they are convinced, however wrongly, that their own economic security and self-interest would be jeopardized.

3   It might be expected for me to propose that the anti-poverty programs be continued — but with better financing and with complete control over them given to representatives of the communities and the people involved. I could also plead for the money that has been spent in the past few years on anti-poverty programs to be simply distributed among the poor. But neither of these sensible alternatives is going to come to pass under an Administration that made it perfectly clear last fall that it intended to channel all Federal funds through local governments, no matter how corrupt.

4   Nothing is going to happen until we, the poor, can generate our own political and economic power. Such a statement sounds radical to many middle-class Americans, but it should not. Though many of the poor have come to see the affluent middle class as its enemy, that class actually stands between the poor and the real powers in this society — the administrative octopus with its head in Washington, the conglomerates, the military complex. It's like a camel train: The herder, way up in front, leads one camel and all the other camels follow. We happen to be the last camel, trudging along through the leavings of the whole train. We see only the camel in front of us and make him the target of our anger, but that solves nothing. The lower reaches of the middle class, in turn, are convinced that blacks, Mexican Americans, Puerto Ricans, Indians, and poor whites want to steal their jobs — a conviction that the power class cheerfully perpetuates. The truth of the matter is that, even with automation, there can still be enough good-paying jobs for *everyone* in this country. If all of us were working for decent wages, there would be a greater demand for goods and services, thus creating even more jobs and increasing the gross national product. Full and fair employment would also mean that taxes traceable to welfare and all the other hidden costs of poverty — presently borne most heavily by middle-income whites — would inevitably go down.

5   At one time, we would have searched for ways to bring about a direct change in the course of the camel driver. That was the situation in the Thirties, when President Roosevelt initiated such massive programs as the Works Progress Administration and the Civilian Con-

servation Corps. At that time, *most* Americans were poor, white and nonwhite alike; but most were white. The union movement was fighting to win gains for its members, then an underclass. (Now it feels it has to fight to protect the economic independence it has since achieved.) And there was only a relatively small upper class trying to frustrate change. But today the majority of Americans—most of them still white—are relatively well off financially. The country's policies naturally respond to the desires of the majority, and that majority—having joined the comfortable middle class—is no longer motivated to eliminate poverty.

6   The forces in control today at the top, furthermore, are so immense, powerful, and interlocked that it would be absurd to expect dramatic change from them. The Pentagon, for example, has a hand-in-glove relationship with the same industrialists who manufacture tractors, reapers, and mechanical grape harvesters. How can we expect the Defense Department to do anything *but* undermine our battle with the growers? The poor today, finally, are not only impoverished; most of them are also members of minority races. Thus, as a class, we are racially as well as economically alienated from the mainstream.

7   Despite this alienation, however, and despite the magnitude of the forces opposing us, the poor have tremendous potential economic power, as unlikely as that may seem. That power can derive from two facts of life: First, even though our numbers are much smaller than they were in the Thirties, we are still a sizable group—some 30,000,000. Perhaps even more important, we have a strong sense of common indignation; the poor always identify with one another more than do the rich. What instruments can we use to win this power? Perhaps the most effective technique is the boycott. Most Americans realize that the black civil rights revolution of the late Fifties and early Sixties effectively began with Dr. Martin Luther King's successful bus boycott in Montgomery, Alabama. This tool is being perfected, for blacks, by the Reverend Jesse Jackson in Chicago. Our own nationwide grape boycott is hurting corporate agriculture so much that the growers are eventually going to have to deal with us, no matter how hard the power class tries to weaken the boycott's effectiveness.

8   Another powerful tool is the strike. Attacking the unions is fashionable today, but the labor movement, for all its faults, is one of the few institutions in the country that I see even trying to reach down to us. The universities, thanks to some student organizations, and the churches, thanks to a few radical groups, are the only other institutions making a real attempt to alleviate our plight. With their help, we farmworkers are now trying to build our own union, a new kind of union that will actively include people rather than exclude them. A man is a man and needs an organization even when—in fact, especially when—a machine displaces him. The poor are also beginning to experiment with cooperatives of all kinds and with their own credit unions—that is, with the creation of our own institutions, the profits from which can go to us rather than to the wealthy. And, at least in the Southwest, we are looking at ways to give the farmworkers plots of land they can call their own, because we know that power always comes with landownership.

9   We need greater control of important noneconomic institutions, too.
We have very little to say, for example, about the attitude of our
churches to economic and political problems. We are looking for ways
to get the church involved in the struggle, to make it relevant to our
needs. The poor also need control of their schools and medical facilities and legal defenses; but these advances are all subsidiary, in my
opinion, to the need for developing strictly economic power. Economic
power has to precede political power. Gandhi understood this when,
in 1930, he and his followers resolved to defy the British government's
salt monopoly by making their own salt from the sea; this boycott was
one of the crucial steps in the Indian fight for independence. We, the
poor of the United States, have not yet hit upon the specific issue
around which we can bring all of our boycotting and striking capabil-
ities to bear. But we will.

10   The poor are badly prepared to participate in the political arena.
Entire nations of us, such as the American Indians, have never had
more than token representation in Federal, state, county or city government. Migratory farmworkers are almost always disenfranchised
by voter-registration residency requirements. Minority immigrants
face long waits for citizenship papers and the additional barrier of
literacy tests. And even if they qualify, it is prohibitively expensive for
many of the poor to vote. A farmworker putting in long hours simply
can't afford to take half or all of a weekday off to travel to the polls.

11   In a society that truly desired full participation, all 18-year-olds and
convicts would be given the franchise; the whole practice of voter
registration would be scrapped; immigrants would automatically be
given a citizenship certificate at the end of one year if their record was
clean, whether or not they were literate in English or in their own language; elections would last up to 72 hours and would include Satur-
days and Sundays.

12   These are some of the simpler things that could be done to increase
participation. But they aren't being done and they won't be done unless the poor can change the political *status quo*. Our vote simply
doesn't matter that much today. Once we give it away, we lose it because we can't control the men we elect. We help elect liberals and
then they pass civil rights bills that defuse our boycotts and strikes,
taking the steam out of our protest but leaving the basic problems of
injustice and inequality unsolved. Or, worse, we elect a candidate who
says he will represent us and then discover that he has sold out to
some special interest.

13   I propose two reforms that would go a long way toward a cure. First,
the whole system of campaign financing should make it as easy for a
poor man as for a millionaire to put his case before the people. Second,
the various minority groups — as well as such pockets of poor whites as
the Appalachians, who make up a distinct economic subculture —
should be given a proportionate number of seats in every governing
body affecting them. Black people should have 43 or 44 seats in the
House of Representatives and 10 or 11 seats in the Senate. In California, where ten percent of the population is Mexican American, eight
seats in the state assembly should be set aside for us; there is now

only one Mexican American assemblyman. This same procedure should be followed all the way down the line, through the county level down to the school and water districts. In each case, the electorate would be allowed to vote for whomever they pleased—even if he weren't of the same race as the majority of voters—but the representative would clearly be an advocate of their needs. Though this system may seem alien to many Americans, something like it already works in the cities, where tickets are often drawn up to reflect the racial balance of the community. And the idea of special representation for minority political groups is common in foreign countries. Once the minority group or the economic subculture is completely assimilated, of course, the need for special representation will wither away.

14   These are the kinds of reforms we will work for once we have an economic base established; they certainly aren't going to come about as long as we remain powerless. But we will remain powerless until we help ourselves. I know that there are men of good conscience in the affluent society who are trying to help. Many of them are middle-class people who remember the Depression, or unionists who wear scars of the battle to liberate workingmen. They are like a large army of guerrillas within the establishment. We are depending on them to hear our cry, to respect our picket lines, and to support our grape boycott, the Reverend Ralph Abernathy's Poor People's Campaign, and the Reverend Jesse Jackson's Operation Breadbasket. And we hope that they will understand how crucial it is that the vote become truly universal. As long as democracy exists mainly as a catchword in politicians' speeches, the hopes for *real* democracy will be mocked.

15   In the final analysis, however, it doesn't really matter what the political system is; ultimately, the results are the same, whether you have a general, a king, a dictator, or a civilian president running the country. We don't need perfect political systems; we need perfect participation. If you don't participate in the planning, you just don't count. Until the chance for political participation is there, we who are poor will continue to attack the soft part of the American system—its economic structure. We will build power through boycotts, strikes, new unions— whatever techniques we can develop. These attacks on the *status quo* will come not because we hate but because we know America *can* construct a humane society for all of its citizens—and that if it does not, there will be chaos.

16   But it must be understood that once we have substantial economic power—and the political power that follows in its wake—our work will not be done. We will then move on to effect even more fundamental changes in this society. The quality of compassion seems to have vanished from the American spirit. The power class and the middle class haven't done anything that one can truly be proud of, aside from machines and rockets. It's amazing how people can get so excited about a rocket to the moon and not give a damn about smog, oil leaks, the devastation of the environment with pesticides, hunger, disease. When the poor share some of the power that the affluent now monopolize, we *will* give a damn.

Discussion of Theme

1. What "tools" does Chavez accuse the government and the growers of using as strike-breaking techniques? How do these accomplish their purpose?
2. According to Chavez, what caused the failure of the various poverty programs in the 1960s? Why does he doubt that similar programs can succeed today?
3. Why do the blue-collar workers fear racial minorities and poor whites? Is their fear based purely on economics? What does Chavez propose as a remedy for this fear?
4. What factors give the poor "tremendous potential economic power"? What instruments can they use to gain it?
5. What must the poor do to bring about the necessary changes in our society, according to Chavez? Are his proposals practical?

Discussion of Rhetoric

1. What device does Chavez use at the outset to capture the reader's attention?
2. Where does he state his thesis? Where is his solution to the problem stated?
3. This article advances controversial proposals, yet does not support them with facts, data, and other "hard" information. What, then, is his argument based on? Is it convincing?
4. Describe the diction in this selection. What does it say about the writer?

Writing Assignments

1. Develop the following statement taken from this article into a theme: "The quality of compassion seems to have vanished from the American spirit."
2. What are the arguments for (or against) community control of schools, the police, medical facilities, and legal defense?
3. Chavez would like to change campaign procedures to make it possible for poor persons to run for public office. Do you agree? What changes do you recommend in our current system of selecting public officials?

Library Exploration

1. Cesar Chavez has been the subject of many magazine articles and books. Prepare a report on one of these.
2. Chavez singled out Mahatma Ghandi as having had an influence on him. Investigate the teachings of this great Indian advocate of nonviolence.

3. Read about the activities of Reverend Ralph Abernathy and his Poor People's Campaign, and Reverend Jesse Jackson and his Operation Breadbasket.
4. Learn what you can about the laws in your state regarding migrant workers: wages, living conditions, and child labor.
5. The following books deal with the subject of this essay: *The Other America*, by Michael Harrington; *Poverty, America's Enduring Paradox*, by Sidney Lens; *They Harvest Despair*, by Dale Wright.

Vocabulary

(9) SUBSIDIARY secondary; subordinate to

(11) FRANCHISE the right to vote

Dylan Thomas (1914–53), widely regarded as the greatest lyric poet of his generation, was born in Wales and virtually self-educated. He was a successful short-story writer, novelist, poet, and radio scriptwriter. "Collected Poems" (1953) and two posthumous prose works, "Quite Early One Morning" (1954) and "Adventures in the Skin Trade" (1955), are among his most significant works. Recordings of the last two works in Thomas's own voice are still available.

The following is one of the lectures given by Thomas in 1953 on his last tour of the United States. It reflects his growing distaste for such performances and for the "lecture tour" in its peculiarly American form.

DYLAN THOMAS

A Visit to America

1 Across the United States of America, from New York to California and back, glazed, again, for many months of the year, there streams and sings for its heady supper a dazed and prejudiced procession of European lecturers, scholars, sociologists, economists, writers, authorities on this and that and even, in theory, on the United States of America. And, breathlessly between addresses and receptions, in 'planes and trains and boiling hotel bedroom ovens, many of these attempt to keep journals and diaries.

2 At first, confused and shocked by shameless profusion and almost shamed by generosity, unaccustomed to such importance as they are assumed, by their hosts, to possess, and up against the barrier of a common language, they write in their notebooks like demons, general-

ising away, on character and culture and the American political scene. But, towards the middle of their middle-aged whisk through middle-western clubs and universities, the fury of the writing flags; their spirits are lowered by the spirit with which they are everywhere strongly greeted and which, in everincreasing doses, they themselves lower; and they begin to mistrust themselves, and their reputations — for they have found, too often, that an audience will receive a lantern-lecture on, say, Ceramics, with the same uninhibited enthusiasm that it accorded the very week before to a paper on the Modern Turkish Novel. And, in their diaries, more and more do such entries appear as, "No way of escape!" or "Buffalo!" or "I am beaten," until at last they cannot write a word. And, twittering all over, old before their time, with eyes like rissoles in the sand, they are helped up the gangway of the homebound liner by kind bosom friends (of all kinds and bosoms) who boister them on the back, pick them up again, thrust bottles, sonnets, cigars, addresses, into their pockets, have a farewell party in their cabin, pick them up again, and, snickering and yelping, are gone: to wait at the dockside for another boat from Europe and another batch of fresh, green lecturers.

3   There they go, every spring, from New York to Los Angeles: exhibitionists, polemicists, histrionic publicists, theological rhetoricians, historical hoddy-doddies, balletomanes, ulterior decorators, windbags and bigwigs and humbugs, men in love with stamps, men in love with steaks, men after millionaires' widows, men with elephantiasis of the reputation (huge trunks and teeny minds), authorities on gas, bishops, best-sellers, editors looking for writers, writers looking for publishers, publishers looking for dollars, existentialists, serious physicists with nuclear missions, men from the B.B.C. who speak as though they had the Elgin marbles in their mouths, potboiling philosophers, professional Irishmen (very lepri-corny), and, I am afraid, fat poets with slim volumes.

4   And see, too, in that linguaceous stream, the tall monocled men, smelling of saddle soap and club armchairs, their breath a nice blending of whisky and fox's blood, with big protruding upper-class tusks and county moustaches, presumably invented in England and sent abroad to advertise *Punch,* who lecture to women's clubs on such unlikely subjects as "The History of Etching in the Shetland Islands"; and the brassy-bossy men-women, with corrugated-iron perms, and hippo hides, who come, self-announced, as "ordinary British housewives," to talk to rich minked chunks of American matronhood about the iniquity of the Health Services, the criminal sloth of the miners, the *visible* tail and horns of Mr. Aneurin Bevan, and the fear of everyone in England to go out alone at night because of the organised legions of coshboys against whom the police are powerless owing to the refusal of those in power to equip them with revolvers and to flog to ribbons every adolescent offender on any charge at all.

5   And there shiver and teeter also, meek and driven, those British authors unfortunate enough to have written, after years of unadventurous forgotten work, one bad novel which became enormously popular on both sides of the Atlantic. At home, when success first hit them,

they were mildly delighted; a couple of literary luncheons went sugar-tipsy to their heads, like the washing sherry served before those luncheons; and perhaps, as the lovely money rolled lushly in, they began to dream, in their moony writers' way, of being able to retire to the country, keep wasps (or was it bees?) and never write another lousy word. But in come the literary agent's triggermen and the publisher's armed narks: "You must go to the States and make a Personal Appearance. Your novel is *killing* them over there, and we're not surprised either. You must go round the States lecturing to women." And the inoffensive writers, who have never dared lecture anyone, let alone women — they are frightened of women, they do not understand women, they write about women as creatures that never existed, and the women lap it up — these sensitive plants cry out, "But what shall we lecture about?" "The English Novel." "I don't read novels." "Great Women in Fiction." "I don't like fiction *or* women." But off they are wafted, firstclass, in the plush bowels of the *Queen Victoria,* with a list of engagements long as a New York menu or a half-hour with a book by Charles Morgan, and soon they are losing their little cold-as-goldfish paw in the great general glutinous handshake of a clutch of enveloping hostesses.

6   I think, by the way, that it was Ernest Raymond, the author of *Tell England,* who once made a journey round the American women's clubs, being housed and entertained at each small town he stopped at, by the richest and largest and furriest lady available. On one occasion he stopped at some little station and was met, as usual, by an enormous motor-car full of a large horn-rimmed business-man — looking exactly like a large horn-rimmed business-man on the films — and his roly-poly pearly wife. Mr. Raymond sat with her in the back of the car, and off they went, the husband driving. At once, she began to say how utterly delighted she and her husband and the committee were to have him at their Women's Literary and Social Guild, and to compliment him on his books. "I don't think I've ever, in all my life, enjoyed a book so much as *Sorrel and Son,*" she said. "What you don't know about human nature! I think Sorrel is one of the most beautiful characters ever portrayed."

7   Ernest Raymond let her talk on, while he stared, embarrassed, in front of him. All he could see were the three double chins that her husband wore at the back of his neck. On and on she gushed in praise of *Sorrel and Son* until he could stand it no longer. "I quite agree with you," he said. "A beautiful book indeed. But I'm afraid I didn't write *Sorrel and Son.* It was written by an old friend of mine, Mr. Warwick Deeping." And the large horn-rimmed double-chinned husband at the wheel said without turning: "Caught again, Emily."

8   See the garrulous others, also, gabbing and garlanded from one nest of culture-vultures to another: people selling the English way of life and condemning the American way as they swig and guzzle through it; people resurrecting the theories of surrealism for the benefit of remote parochial female audiences who did not know it was dead, not having ever known it had been alive; people talking about Etruscan pots and pans to a bunch of dead pans and wealthy pots in Boston.

And there, too, in the sticky thick of lecturers moving across the continent black with clubs, go the foreign poets, catarrhal troubadours, lyrical one-night-standers, dollar-mad nightingales, remittance-bards from at home, myself among them booming with the worst.

9   Did we pass one another, *en route,* all unknowing, I wonder; one of us spry-eyed, with clean, white lectures and a soul he could call his own, going bouyantly west to his remunerative doom in the great State University factories; another returning dog-eared as his clutch of poems and his carefully-typed impromptu asides? I ache for us both. There one goes, unsullied as yet, in his pullman pride, toying — oh boy! — with a blunderbuss bourbon, being smoked by a large cigar, riding out to the wide open spaces of the faces of his waiting audience. He carries, besides his literary baggage, a new, dynamic razor, just on the market, bought in New York, which operates at the flick of a thumb but cuts the thumb to the bone; a tin of new shaving-lather which is worked with the other, unbleeding, thumb, and covers not only the face but the whole bathroom and, instantly freezing, makes an arctic, icicled cave from which it takes two sneering bellboys to extract him; and, of course, a nylon shirt. This, he dearly believes from the advertisements, he can himself wash in his hotel, hang to dry overnight, and put on, without ironing, in the morning. (In my case, no ironing was needed, for, as someone cruelly pointed out in print, I looked anyway like an unmade bed.)

10   He is vigorously welcomed at the station by an earnest crew-cut platoon of giant collegiates, all chasing the butterfly culture with net, notebook, poison-bottle, pin and label, each with at least thirty-six terribly white teeth, and nursed away, as heavily gently as though he were an imbecile rich aunt with a short prospect of life, into a motor-car in which, for a mere fifty miles or so travelled at poet-breaking speed, he assures them of the correctness of their assumption that he is half-witted by stammering inconsequential answers in an over-British accent to the genial questions about what international conference Stephen Spender might be attending at the moment, or the reactions of British poets to the work of a famous American whose name he did not know or catch. He is then taken to a small party of only a few hundred people all of whom hold the belief that what a visiting lecturer needs before he trips on to the platform is just enough martinis so that he can trip off the platform as well. And, clutching his explosive glass, he is soon contemptuously dismissing, in a flush of ignorance and fluency, the poetry of those androgynous literary ladies with three names who produce a kind of verbal ectoplasm to order as a waiter dishes up spaghetti — only to find that the fiercest of these, a wealthy huntress of small, seedy lions (such as himself), who stalks the middle-western bush with ears and rifle cocked, is his hostess for the evening. Of the lecture, he remembers little but the applause and maybe two questions: "Is it true that the young English intellectuals are *really* psychological?" or, "I always carry Kierkegaard in my pocket. What do you carry?"

11   Late at night, in his room, he fills a page of his journal with a confused, but scathing, account of his first engagement, summarises

American advanced education in a paragraph that will be meaningless tomorrow, and falls to sleep where he is immediately chased through long, dark thickets by a Mrs. Mabel Frankincense Mehaffey, with a tray of martinis and lyrics.

12   And there goes the other happy poet bedraggledly back to New York which struck him all of a sheepish never-sleeping heap at first but which seems to him now, after the ulcerous rigours of a lecturer's spring, a haven cosy as toast, cool as an icebox, and safe as skyscrapers.

Discussion of Theme

1. On the basis of their brief exposure to America, are most "European . . . authorities on this and that" ill-equipped to pronounce judgment on America and Americans?
2. Is Thomas fair in his description of the kinds of people who attend lectures? How accurate is his portrayal of American audiences?
3. Is it true that American audiences—female especially—are not critical enough of lectures given by persons who have been introduced as authorities?
4. Do you find evidence that the author does not take himself too seriously?
5. Is there a deeper criticism of America implied here? Or should we read the essay merely as a humorous account of his experiences on the lecture circuit?
6. Is there an apparent contradiction between the author's commitment to filling lecture engagements and his apparent distaste for the experience?

Discussion of Rhetoric

1. Thomas wants his reader to share the same blurred, scrambled, and disjointed series of images that he experienced on a coast-to-coast lecture tour. How successful is he?
2. Much of Thomas's humor is tongue-in-cheek or unexpected. Find several examples of such humor.
3. What does Thomas imply in paragraph 10 about his college hosts?
4. What rhetorical clues identify Thomas as British rather than American?
5. A characteristic of Thomas's style in all of his prose is his fondness for listing series of items. Where is this used, and how is contrast utilized?

Writing Assignments

1. If you feel that you have sufficiently grasped the elements of Thomas's style, write a parody of it on some subject of your own choosing.

2. In a humorous way, describe a tour of England by an American lecturing on some subject alien to British audiences.
3. Imagine that you are a member of an audience that has heard a series of lectures presented by any of the persons mentioned in Thomas's essay. Describe your experience and your reactions.
4. Thomas was, of course, first and foremost a serious writer — a fine, innovative poet who because of personal difficulties was unable to concentrate on that facet of his career. Discuss the financial and family problems that might be involved in the life of a serious artist.

Library Exploration

1. Dylan Thomas was a brilliant reader of poetry. His rich Welsh voice can be heard reading his poetry and short stories on several long-playing albums. Three are issued by Caedmon Records.
2. Thomas's views of America should be compared with those of other Europeans. Read Charles Dickens's *American Notes* (1842) and Alexis de Tocqueville's *Democracy in America* (1835).
3. If you enjoyed this selection, read some of Thomas's other works: *Portrait of the Artist as a Young Dog, Under Milk Wood, Quite Early One Morning,* and *Collected Poems.*
4. Many of the unfamiliar words are purely British and may or may not have counterparts in American English. Look up these words and write a commentary on their use:
         coshboys   publicist   nark   humbug
5. Look up Kierkegaard and see if you can discover why Thomas chose his name to typify the kind of writer that would appeal to the American intellectual.

Vocabulary

(2) PROFUSION   abundance
(2) RISSOLES   small meatballs fried in deep fat
(3) EXHIBITIONISTS   show-offs; attention getters
(3) POLEMICISTS   those who engage in controversial discussion or argument
(3) HISTRIONIC PUBLICISTS   affected press agents
(3) RHETORICIANS   eloquent writers or speakers
(3) BALLETOMANES   devotees of the ballet
(3) HUMBUGS   phonies
(3) ELEPHANTIASIS   enormous enlargement (a disease)

(3) POTBOILING   shoddy; inferior
(4) LINGUACEOUS   many-tongued
(4) SLOTH   laziness
(4) COSHBOYS   young hoodlums
(5) NARKS   spies; stool pigeons
(5) GLUTINOUS   gummy; sticky
(8) GARRULOUS   excessively talkative
(8) SURREALISM   fantastic or incongruous imagery
(8) CATARRHAL   affected by catarrh (chronic nose and throat inflammation)
(9) BUOYANTLY   joyfully

(9) BLUNDERBUSS having an explosive impact

(10) IMBECILE feebleminded person

(10) INCONSEQUENTIAL unimportant

(10) CONTEMPTUOUSLY disrespectfully

(10) ANDROGYNOUS having the characteristics of both sexes

(10) ECTOPLASM emanation from a spiritualistic medium

When John F. Kennedy (1917–63) was assassinated, the world (particularly the youth of the United States) was left in a state of shock. He was the youngest man and the first Roman Catholic to be elected President. His tremendous personal appeal and his energy won over millions, and he fired their imagination with his wit and intelligence. His administration took as its slogan "The New Frontier," an accurate description of his approach to the Presidency.

The typical inaugural address, surrounded with pomp and circumstance, is usually little noted and soon forgotten. There are exceptions: Washington's First, Lincoln's First and Second, Franklin D. Roosevelt's Third. Kennedy's is in this class; it has a timeless quality, yet bears directly on the style of his short administration.

JOHN F. KENNEDY

Inaugural Address January 10, 1961

1 We observe today not a victory of party but a celebration of freedom, symbolizing an end as well as a beginning, signifying renewal as well as change. For I have sworn before you and Almighty God the same solemn oath our forebears prescribed nearly a century and three-quarters ago.

2 The world is very different now. For man holds in his mortal hands the power to abolish all forms of human poverty and all forms of

human life. And yet the same revolutionary belief for which our forebears fought is still at issue around the globe, the belief that the rights
of man come not from the generosity of the state but from the hand of
God.

3   We dare not forget today that we are the heirs of this first revolution.
Let the word go forth from this time and place, to friend and foe alike,
that the torch has been passed to a new generation of Americans, born
in this century, tempered by war, disciplined by a hard and bitter
peace, proud of our ancient heritage, and unwilling to witness or permit the slow undoing of those human rights to which this nation has
always been committed, and to which we are committed today at
home and around the world.

4   Let every nation know, whether it wishes us well or ill, that we shall
pay any price, bear any burden, meet any hardship, support any
friend, oppose any foe to assure the survival and the success of liberty.

5   This much we pledge—and more.

6   To those old allies whose cultural and spiritual origins we share, we
pledge the loyalty of faithful friends. United, there is little we cannot
do in a host of co-operative ventures. Divided, there is little we can
do, for we dare not meet a powerful challenge at odds and split as-
sunder.

7   To those new states whom we welcome to the ranks of the free, we
pledge our word that one form of colonial control shall not have passed
away merely to be replaced by a far more iron tyranny. We shall not
always expect to find them supporting our view. But we shall always
hope to find them strongly supporting their own freedom, and to remember that, in the past, those who foolishly sought power by riding
the back of the tiger ended up inside.

8   To those peoples in the huts and villages of half the globe struggling
to break the bonds of mass misery, we pledge our best efforts to help
them help themselves, for whatever period is required, not because
the Communists may be doing it, not because we seek their votes, but
because it is right. If a free society cannot help the many who are poor,
it cannot save the few who are rich.

9   To our sister republics south of our border, we offer a special pledge:
to convert our good words into good deeds, in a new alliance for progress, to assist free men and free governments in casting off the chains
of poverty. But this peaceful revolution of hope cannot become the
prey of hostile powers. Let all our neighbors know that we shall join
with them to oppose aggression or subversion anywhere in the Amer-
icas. And let every other power know that this hemisphere intends to
remain the master of its own house.

10   To that world assembly of sovereign states, the United Nations, our
last best hope in an age where the instruments of war have far out-
paced the instruments of peace, we renew our pledge of support: to
prevent it from becoming merely a forum for invective, to strengthen
its shield of the new and the weak, and to enlarge the area in which its
writ may run.

11   Finally, to those nations who would make themselves our adversary, we offer not a pledge but a request: that both sides begin anew
the quest for peace, before the dark powers of destruction unleashed

by science engulf all humanity in planned or accidental self-destruction.

12   We dare not tempt them with weakness. For only when our arms are sufficient beyond doubt can we be certain beyond doubt that they will never be employed.

13   But neither can two great and powerful groups of nations take comfort from our present course — both sides overburdened by the cost of modern weapons, both rightly alarmed by the steady spread of the deadly atom, yet both racing to alter that uncertain balance of terror that stays the hand of mankind's final war.

14   So let us begin anew, remembering on both sides that civility is not a sign of weakness, and sincerity is always subject to proof. Let us never negotiate out of fear, but let us never fear to negotiate.

15   Let both sides explore what problems unite us instead of belaboring those problems which divide us.

16   Let both sides, for the first time, formulate serious and precise proposals for the inspection and control of arms, and bring the absolute power to destroy other nations under the absolute control of all nations.

17   Let both sides seek to invoke the wonders of science instead of its terrors. Together let us explore the stars, conquer the deserts, eradicate disease, tap the ocean depths and encourage the arts and commerce.

18   Let both sides unite to heed in all corners of the earth the command of Isaiah to "undo the heavy burden . . . [and] let the oppressed go free."

19   And if a beachhead of co-operation may push back the jungle of suspicion, let both sides join in creating a new endeavor, not a new balance of power, but a new world of law, where the strong are just and the weak secure and the peace preserved.

20   All this will not be finished in the first one hundred days. Nor will it be finished in the first one thousand days, nor in the life of this Administration, nor even perhaps in our lifetime on this planet. But let us begin.

21   In your hands, my fellow citizens, more than mine, will rest the final success or failure of our course. Since this country was founded, each generation of Americans has been summoned to give testimony to its national loyalty. The graves of young Americans who answered the call to service surround the globe.

22   Now the trumpet summons us again — not as a call to bear arms, though arms we need; not as a call to battle, though embattled we are; but a call to bear the burden of a long twilight struggle, year in and year out, "rejoicing in hope, patient in tribulation," a struggle against the common enemies of man: tyranny, poverty, disease and war itself.

23   Can we forge against these enemies a grand and global alliance, North and South, East and West, that can assure a more fruitful life for all mankind? Will you join in that historic effort?

24   In the long history of the world, only a few generations have been granted the role of defending freedom in its hour of maximum danger. I do not shrink from this responsibility; I welcome it. I do not believe that any of us would exchange places with any other people or any other generation. The energy, the faith, the devotion which we bring

to this endeavor will light our country and all who serve it, and the glow from that fire can truly light the world.

25   And so, my fellow Americans, ask not what your country can do for you; ask what you can do for your country.

26   My fellow citizens of the world, ask not what America will do for you, but what together we can do for the freedom of man.

27   Finally, whether you are citizens of America or citizens of the world, ask of us here the same high standards of strength and sacrifice which we ask of you. With a good conscience our only sure reward, with history the final judge of our deeds, let us go forth to lead the land we love, asking His blessing and His help, but knowing that here on earth God's work must truly be our own.

Discussion of Theme

1. Do you agree that "the rights of man come not from the generosity of the state but from the hand of God"? Is a state displaying "generosity" when it provides man with his "rights"?
2. What is the purpose of Kennedy's reference to America's revolutionary background? How does he develop this theme?
3. For what new struggle does he ask his listeners' help? In what way is it a *new* struggle?
4. What does Kennedy believe should be the emphasis of science? To what extent have his hopes been realized?
5. Does paragraph 4 express your willingness to do what you think is necessary for the survival and success of liberty?

Discussion of Rhetoric

1. Would the address have been as effective if Kennedy had said in his opening paragraph "nearly 175 years ago" instead of "nearly a century and three-quarters ago"? What is special about his phrasing?
2. Find and alanyze several examples of parallelism of words, of phrases, and of sentences in this address. In general, what are the benefits of parallel structure?
3. Find the metaphors and other figures of speech in paragraphs 7, 9, 11, 19, and 24.
4. Would the sentence in paragraph 22 have been as effective if Kennedy had said "though we need arms" and "though we're embattled" instead of the phrases he did use? Why? Do people speak this way in ordinary conservation?
5. What is there about the word choice and sentence rhythm of this address that suggests it was meant to be heard rather than read?

Writing Assignments

1. Discuss your concept of the rights of man.

2. What is your reaction to the quotation, "Undo the heavy burden [and] let the oppressed go free."?
3. Define *politician*.
4. What were some of the novel characteristics of the New Frontier?
5. In paragraph 3 Kennedy speaks of "the slow undoing of those human rights to which the nation has always been committed, . . ." Which of these rights do you believe are being undone—or are in danger of being undone—at the present time?

Library Exploration

1. Compare Kennedy's address with the inaugural speeches of some other famous men—Washington, Lincoln, Roosevelt.
2. Read *The Making of the President 1960,* by Theodore H. White.
3. Read *The Kennedy Wit,* edited by Bill Adler.

Vocabulary

(10) INVECTIVE   abusive insult
(10) WRIT   a written order
(11) ADVERSARY   enemy; opponent
(14) CIVILITY   courtesy; polite act or expression

(17) ERADICATE   pull up by the roots; erase
(22) TRIBULATION   trouble; trial

Edmund Wilson (1895–   ) has achieved distinction as one of the most formidable U.S. literary critics. He was graduated from Princeton in 1916, and has written poetry, drama, novels, history, literary criticism, and trenchant commentary on American political and cultural life. Among his outstanding volumes are "Axel's Castle" (1931), "The Shock of Recognition" (1943), "Patriotic Gore: Studies in the Literature of the Civil War" (1962), and "The Bit Between My Teeth" (1966).

Our language is so full of superlatives that most of them have lost their force. There are also hazards in using all kinds of highly charged words. Here Wilson reminds us that terms like "Americanism," which are often used not for their meaning but for the effect they have on an audience, shift their meaning from one age to another—even within the vocabulary of one man.

EDMUND WILSON

Americanism

It is curious to trace the vicissitudes of the term *Americanism*. The first quotation given in the *Dictionary of Americanisms* published by Chicago University is from a letter of Jefferson's of 1797: "The parties here in debate continually charged each other . . . with being governed by an attachment to this or that of the belligerent nations, rather than the dictates of reason and pure Americanism." This is Americanism in the sense defined by Webster (1906) as "a love of America and preference of her interest." In Jefferson's time, of course, it meant the interests of the revolted colonists. But by the fifties of the following century, the word *Americanism* was to take on a new political meaning. It was used by the American or Know Nothing party to designate its own policy—already mentioned above—of combating the Roman Catholicism of German and Irish immigrants and of debarring persons of foreign birth from exercising political rights till they had lived here twenty-one years. It is in this sense that Lincoln uses it when, in a letter of May 15, 1858, he speaks of the chances of the Republican party: "I think our prospects gradually, and steadily, grow better; though we are not clear out of the woods by a great deal. There is still some effort to make trouble out of 'Americanism.'" This meaning was soon to lapse with the demise of the Know Nothing party. But the word was to be revived, with quite different implications, by Theodore Roosevelt in the nineties. The first use of it in Roosevelt's correspondence is in a letter of December 8, 1888, to Thomas R. Lounsbury, congratulating him on his *Life of Cooper:* "As a very sincere American myself, I feel like thanking you for the genuine Americanism of your book; which is quite as much displayed in its criticisms as in its praises." Here he is speaking merely of an American point of view; but by the time he writes to William Archer in 1899 (August 31), he is giving the word a meaning of his own: "I have exactly the feeling about Americanism you describe. Most important of all is it for this country to treat an American on his worth as a man, and to disregard absolutely whether he be of Catholic or Protestant faith." . . . This is Roosevelt at his best. He has changed the Know Nothings' emphasis: instead of wanting to exclude the immigrant, he wishes to take him in and to propose a common ideal of disinterested public service. He is to talk, from the nineties on, a good deal about Americanism, and to give the word a general currency. He is eventually to make it stand for the whole of his political philosophy. Here is his definition in a letter to S. Stanwood Menken of January 10, 1917: "Americanism means many things. It means equality of rights and therefore equality of duty and of obligation. It means service to our common country. It means loyalty to one flag, to our flag, the flag of all of us. It means on the part of each of us respect for the rights of the rest of us. It means that all of us guarantee the rights of each of us. It means free education, genuinely representative government, freedom of speech and thought, equality before the law for all men, genuine political and religious freedom, and the democratizing of industry so as to give at least a measurable quality of opportunity for all, and so as to place before us, as our ideal in all industries where this ideal is possible of attainment, the system of cooperative ownership and management, in order that the tool-users may, so far as possible, become the tool-owners. Everything is un-American that tends either to government by a plutocracy or government by a mob. To divide along the lines of section or caste or creed is un-American. All privileges based on wealth, and all enmity to honest men merely because they are wealthy, are un-American—both of them equally so. Americanism means the virtues of courage, honor, justice, truth, sincerity, and hardihood—the virtues that made America." The last letter included in his published correspondence—written on January 3, 1919, three days before his death, to be read at a benefit concert of the American Defense Society — has, however, an emphasis that is somewhat different. This was written at the end of the first world war, in the era — referred to above — of the mass deportation of radicals. The old chief in retirement had by this time passed into an apoplectic phase in which he was convinced, for example, that the International Workers of the World were necessarily a criminal organization and that labor leaders were guilty, as a matter of course, of the crimes of which, in that moment of hysteria, they were lavishly being accused. "There must be no sagging back," writes Roosevelt, "in the fight for Americanism merely because the war is over. . . . There can be no divided allegiance here. . . . Any man who says he is an American, but something else also, isn't an American at all. We have room for but one flag, the American flag, and this excludes the red flag which symbolizes all wars against liberty and civilization just as much as it excludes any foreign flag of a nation to which we are hostile." This is the fear of the foreigner again. It was rampant after Roosevelt's death, and anyone with a non-Anglo-Saxon name who ventured to complain about anything or to propose a social reform was likely to be told at once that if he didn't like it here in the United States, he ought to go back where he came from. By this time, the very term "Americanism" had become a black-mailing menace. One remembers reading in the New York *Tribune* of March 3, 1920, that the younger Theodore Roosevelt, chairman of the American Legion's "Americanism Commission," had called a meeting "at which it was decided to thoroughly Americanize all war veterans, then to utilize them in the work of making good citizens of the foreign-born of the State." It may not be true that "Americanism" — like Dr. Johnson's "patriotism" — is invariably "the last refuge of a scoundrel"; but it has been made to serve some very bad causes, and is now a word to avoid.

Discussion of Theme

1. Does any one group today believe that it has a monopoly on Americanism? Characterize the behavior of such people.
2. What is the irony of the fact that this particular term has acquired disagreeable connotations for some people? What does it connote to so-called liberals?
3. The American Legion has always emphasized its own brand of Americanism. Why might war veterans be obsessed with Americanism?
4. Speaking of Theodore Roosevelt, Wilson says that "instead of excluding the immigrant, he wishes to take him in . . ." The immigrant was "taken in" by political parties. How did the parties use immigrants to gain votes?
5. What is Wilson's own idea of Americanism? Do you agree that Americanism is a word to avoid?
6. What are some other words that have undergone changes in meaning? How have they changed? Do such changes tell you anything about how society has changed?

Discussion of Rhetoric

1. Although Americanism has become a word fraught with emotional significance, Wilson's tone is dispassionate. Why?
2. In his final sentence, is Wilson implying that Americanism is, in fact, "the last refuge of a scoundrel"?
3. How does Wilson arrange his material in this essay?
4. What is the meaning of *curious* in the first sentence? Is this a common use of the word?
5. What is the significance of quoting Jefferson, Lincoln, and Theodore Roosevelt, rather than lesser-known figures?

Writing Assignments

1. State your reaction to the bumper sticker "America — Love it or Leave It."
2. Which definition of Americanism — or portions thereof — most nearly expresses your own? Elaborate on it.
3. Should we de-emphasize nationalism and stress instead our role as world citizens? What benefits might that have for mankind?
4. Are some groups today attempting to achieve "government by a mob," and others trying to develop "government by plutocracy"? Who are they and what are their methods?
5. Do you think that the word *Americanism* will eventually lose the unpleasant connotations it has for the less conservative elements of our society? What could bring about the change?

Library Exploration

1. Wilson refers to the Know Nothing party. Find out more about this organization. You might consult a U.S. history text, a book on the development of political parties, or an encyclopedia.
2. Examine the concept of Americanism as espoused by various organizations. Do their definitions differ from yours? How?
3. Wilson refers to the *Dictionary of Americanisms*. If the library has this reference work, consult it for the history of other common terms. The title says "on Historical Principles." What does this mean? How does the book differ from your regular dictionary?

Vocabulary

VICISSITUDES ups and downs; chance variations

BELLIGERENT warring

DEBARRING preventing; excluding

DEMISE death

DISINTERESTED unbiased

CURRENCY prevalence; widespread use

PLUTOCRACY rule by the wealthy

CREED belief

HARDIHOOD resoluteness; vigor

APOPLECTIC having fits

LAVISHLY abundantly; even excessively

RAMPANT flourishing unchecked

Shirley Chisholm (1924–   ) is a political activist: she is a congresswoman (from Brooklyn), a supporter of various peace causes, and a staunch advocate of rights for the poor, for racial minorities, and for women.

In the following article, Mrs. Chisholm tells what it is like to be both black and female.

SHIRLEY CHISHOLM

I'd Rather Be Black than Female

1 Being the first black woman elected to Congress has made me some kind of phenomenon. There are nine other blacks in Congress; there are ten other women. I was the first to overcome both handicaps at once. Of the two handicaps, being black is much less of a drawback than being female.

2   If I said that being black is a greater handicap than being a woman, probably no one would question me. Why? Because "we all know" there is prejudice against black people in America. That there is prejudice against women is an idea that still strikes nearly all men—and, I am afraid, most women—as bizarre.

3   Prejudice against blacks was invisible to most white Americans for many years. When blacks finally started to "mention" it, with sit-ins, boycotts, and freedom rides, Americans were incredulous. "Who, us?" they asked in injured tones. "We're prejudiced?" It was the start of a long, painful reeducation for white America. It will take years for whites—including those who think of themselves as liberals—to discover and eliminate the racist attitudes they all actually have.

4   How much harder will it be to eliminate the prejudice against women? I am sure it will be a longer struggle. Part of the problem is that women in America are much more brainwashed and content with their roles as second-class citizens than blacks ever were.

5   Let me explain. I have been active in politics for more than twenty years. For all but the last six, I have done the work—all the tedious details that make the difference between victory and defeat on election day—while men reaped the rewards, which is almost invariably the lot of women in politics.

6   It is still women—about three million volunteers—who do most of this work in the American political world. The best any of them can hope for is the honor of being district or county vice-chairman, a kind of separate-but-equal position with which a woman is rewarded for years of faithful envelope stuffing and card-party organizing. In such a job, she gets a number of free trips to state and sometimes national meetings and conventions, where her role is supposed to be to vote the way her male chairman votes.

7   When I tried to break out of that role in 1963 and run for the New York State Assembly seat from Brooklyn's Bedford-Stuyvesant, the resistance was bitter. From the start of that campaign, I faced undisguised hostility because of my sex.

8   But it was four years later, when I ran for Congress, that the question of my sex became a major issue. Among members of my own party, closed meetings were held to discuss ways of stopping me.

9   My opponent, the famous civil-rights leader James Farmer, tried to project a black, masculine image; he toured the neighborhood with sound trucks filled with young men wearing Afro haircuts, dashikis, and beards. While the television crews ignored me, they were not aware of a very important statistic, which both I and my campaign manager, Wesley MacD. Holder, knew. In my district there are 2.5 women for every man registered to vote. And those women are organized—in PTAs, church societies, card clubs, and other social and service groups. I went to them and asked their help. Mr. Farmer still doesn't quite know what hit him.

10   When a bright young woman graduate starts looking for a job, why is the first question always: "Can you type?" A history of prejudice lies behind that question. Why are women thought of as secretaries, not administrators? Librarians and teachers, but not doctors and lawyers? Because they are thought of as different and inferior. The happy homemaker and the contented darky are both stereotypes produced by prejudice.

11   Women have not even reached the level of tokenism that blacks are reaching. No women sit on the Supreme Court. Only two have held Cabinet rank, and none do at present. Only two women hold ambassadorial rank. But women predominate in the lower-paying, menial, unrewarding, dead-end jobs, and when they do reach better positions, they are invariably paid less than a man gets for the same job.

12   If that is not prejudice, what would you call it?

13   A few years ago, I was talking with a political leader about a promising young woman as a candidate. "Why invest time and effort to build the girl up?" he asked me. "You know she'll only drop out of the game to have a couple of kids just about the time we're ready to run her for mayor."

14   Plenty of people have said similar things about me. Plenty of others have advised me, every time I tried to take another upward step, that I should go back to teaching, a woman's vocation, and leave politics to the men. I love teaching, and I am ready to go back to it as soon as I am convinced that this country no longer needs a woman's contribution.

15   When there are no children going to bed hungry in this rich nation, I may be ready to go back to teaching. When there is a good school

for every child, I may be ready. When we do not spend our wealth on hardware to murder people, when we no longer tolerate prejudice against minorities, and when the laws against unfair housing and unfair employment practices are enforced instead of evaded, then there may be nothing more for me to do in politics.

16   But until that happens—and we all know it will not be this year or next—what we need is more women in politics, because we have a very special contribution to make. I hope that the example of my success will convince other women to get into politics—and not just to stuff envelopes, but to run for office.

17   It is women who can bring empathy, tolerance, insight, patience, and persistence to government—the qualities we naturally have or have had to develop because of our suppression by men. The women of a nation mold its morals, its religion, and its politics by the lives they live. At present, our country needs women's idealism and determination, perhaps more in politics than anywhere else.

Discussion of Theme

1. "If I said that being black is a greater handicap than being a woman, probably no one would question me." Do you agree with the author's statement? Do people acknowledge prejudice against women as readily as they acknowledge prejudice against blacks?
2. Is the author guilty of stereotyping when she talks about men and women?
3. What are some of the bases for the prejudice that makes young girls "automatically" aspire to become typists, secretaries, and nurses?
4. What is the solution to problems like the one referred to in paragraph 13?
5. Are there any advantages for men if the women's liberation movement is successful?

Discussion of Rhetoric

1. How does the author support her thesis? What kinds of evidence and techniques does she use?
2. What is the function of the question raised in paragraph 12: "If that is not prejudice, what would you call it?"
3. Look at paragraph 15. What structural device has the author used to convey her thoughts. Is it effective?
4. In what way is the last paragraph related to the rest of the essay?
5. Describe the tone of the language in this essay.

Writing Assignments

1. Write an essay entitled "I'd Rather Be _____ than Female." (Insert any word in the blank.)

2. Write a paper presenting your views of the goals of the women's liberation movement.
3. Describe an experience in which you encountered sex prejudice.
4. Develop a paper reacting to the following statement: "I believe that there are (are not) basic differences (other than anatomical) between the sexes."

Library Exploration

1. Read and report on one of the following books: Ashley Montague's *The Natural Superiority of Women*; Germaine Greer's *The Female Eunuch*; Kate Millet's *Sexual Politics*; or Norman Mailer's *The Prisoner of Sex*.
2. Read something about the major figures in the current women's movement: Betty Friedan, Ti-Grace Atkinson, Aileen Hernandez, Gloria Steinem.
3. Trace the history of the women's suffrage movement in England and the United States. Compare the current legal position of women in these countries with that of women in Switzerland and in Sweden.

Vocabulary

(1) PHENOMENON extraordinary or remarkable person, thing, or occurrence
(3) INCREDULOUS unbelieving
(5) TEDIOUS dull and tiring
(9) DASHIKIS loose-fitting African shirts
(10) STEREOTYPES standardized, oversimplified images (of members of a certain group)

(11) MENIAL low; humble
(17) EMPATHY imaginative identification with the feelings or thoughts of another

A native Californian, Jack Smith (1916–) has been with the "Los Angeles Times" since 1953. He is also the author of "Three Coins in the Birdbath" (1965).

This selection, originally presented as a talk at a women's organization, defends the "unliberated" female of the 1940s and 1950s against her modern-day detractors. Among her many accomplishments, he suggests, was giving birth to today's young rebels and idealists.

JACK SMITH

Unliberated, but Born Free

1 I picture myself as that notorious sexist, Sir Galahad, come to the rescue of a lady we might call the woman nobody knows.

2 Actually, she happens to be the woman I know best. But she's not one particular woman; she's collective. She's all the unliberated housewives of my generation, give or take a few years. She came of age just before or during or right after the war. She got married and had children and raised them. She belonged to the PTA, even though it didn't always swing.

3 She did housework and yardwork and sometimes she marched, for Dimes or Community Chest. She never heard of Women's Liberation, or if she did she thought it had something to do with that musical comedy, "Bloomer Girl."

4 Then one day her children were grown up and gone and her budget was balanced. Her work was done. She had come through. And only then did she find out what a mess she'd made of it.

5 How did she find out? Everybody told her. The sociologists. The psychologists. The new feminists. Her own children. Even the *Ladies' Home Journal* was a little mean.

6   What were her sins—besides obsolescence?

7   The indictment was long. She had turned our meadows into slums called suburbs. She had filled our homes with gadgets and junk. Her taste had created the desert of television. Her tyranny had turned her offspring into hairy anarchists. Her lust—quite unrequited, as far as we know—had turned our nice deadend streets into Peyton Place.

8   And all this time, remember, she was unliberated—in chains, a prisoner. Think what she might have done if she'd got loose.

9   It wasn't enough that she'd botched everything. What hurt even more was to be told she hadn't really lived. She hadn't been fulfilled, or to use the new vogue word—she hadn't been potentialized.

10   She was a prisoner of the male-dominated society, of her conditioning, of folkways, of fate. She wasn't even a woman, really, much less a free human being.

11   Who was this creature anyway? How did she get started in this sorry path?

12   Not long ago I inherited a batch of old Bill Mauldin cartoons, from 1954—the last year of the war. One shows Joe and Willie, talking to a new recruit in a dugout. The recruit is wearing a helmet. And Willie says, "Take off yer hat when ya mention dames here. They're a revrint subjict."

13   So you see, this woman was in a sense created, overseas, in the minds of sexists like Joe and Willie, and the other young men of my generation.

14   We had priorities. We wanted a car and a girl and a job and a house and some children, not necessarily in that order, but sort of whichever came first, after the girl. We wanted a good life for ourselves and our children, the best life ever, and we wanted peace.

15   We got the girl. That was easy, because they wanted the same things. We got the children. That was easy, too. But there weren't any houses, and the schools were too old and too few. There wasn't enough of anything but energy.

16   So we built the houses. We built schools and highways and aquaducts. It was the most fantastic outpouring of energy—for peaceful purposes—in the history of man—and woman. I don't know if that's a fact, but I'll vouch for it.

17   We built tract houses because that was the only way to build a million houses overnight. We moved into tract houses because they were there. No down payment. Today's experts call them instant slums. Instant experts.

18   But for one generation, at least, they were homes. They had heat and light and laughter—and not all of it came out of the boob tube in the living room.

19   Willie lived here. Another old Mauldin cartoon shows Willie's buddy Joe standing in front of a pool hall in his uniform. He's re-enlisted. He's a master sergeant now. And Willie walks by. His arms are full of groceries and he's pushing a baby buggy.

20   And Joe is saying, "How's it feel to be a free man, Willie?"

21   I like that one. It's full of irony, because Willie is a free man, by his lights. He's doing exactly what he had in mind back there in the dugout, when he told that rookie to speak revrint of dames.

22   As I say, the women who lived in these homes—maybe I should say the women who were kept in these homes—were unliberated. They cooked and scrubbed and painted. They got clothes whiter than white. Sometimes, as the psychologists say, the sex roles got blurred, and they mowed the lawn and mixed concrete. Some of them did the plumbing.

23   They threw batting practice in Little League. They planted flowers and trees. Has it ever occurred to you that we'd all be dead of air pollution except for the oxygen these women released with their prodigious plantings? They got into politics and rang doorbells and they voted. In fact, a hell of a lot of them voted the wrong way.

24   They suffered through the golden age of KFWB, when every morning the house jumped with Purple People Eaters and Little Blue Men. They suffered never knowing it was going to get worse—that Elvis Presley was just around the corner, and the Beatles right behind him.

25   But then, even though there wasn't always enough money, and never enough time, they reached out for something more. They bought encyclopedias on the installment plan—at the supermarket or at the front door. They got "Carmen" and "Swan Lake" into the house on KFAC. They learned which was the proper Gallo wine to serve with frozen halibut. They set their tables with candles and flowers. They bought Van Gogh prints from the May Co. and temple bells from the Akron.

26   It wasn't a high culture, but in the 1950s it was all we had.

27   I guess some of the new feminists would feel what they call "rage" if they heard me eulogizing this generation of women, as if they'd had a good life. They'd say he's only a sexist in disguise. I hope I'm not. I'm absolutely for them when they say they want women to be treated as equal human beings.

28   That's exactly why I hate to see a whole generation of women swept under the rug, as if they were less than human—an embarrassment to their sex. I think most of them were equal as hell. They had a lot of fun, and dignity, too, if any human being has. They made a contribution. What's more they were relevant, meaningful, and viable. Even if they weren't potentialized.

29   The woman of my generation had her eyes on the best of all possible worlds. She didn't quite get her hands on it. And now she's told she blew it. Her young are rebels. They use bad words and flout authority and turn their backs on good old values.

30   She could have done worse. She could have raised a generation of young who *weren't* rebels, who *didn't* prefer peace to war, who *didn't* want to search and inquire, and change the world.

31   Maybe this woman's role is obsolete. I don't know. But it was absolutely essential for her time. There was no other way—in the 1950s and 60s—that we could have given the world the hope of the world, which is our youth.

32   If these women were unliberated, I hope history will at least honor them for the services they performed in captivity.

33   I hope this hasn't sounded like an obituary. It isn't. It's a bouquet. These women are still with us—liberated now, of course, but still

reaching. Some of them, I believe, will be called up here to the stage in a moment, as soon as I have the grace to sit down.

Discussion of Theme

1. Why does Smith call the subject of his article "the woman nobody knows"? Could she also be "the woman I know best"?
2. For what qualities does Smith praise the women of his own generation? Is his praise excessive?
3. Smith describes the role that women played some years ago. Is that role now obsolete — was it "essential for the time," but now outmoded?
4. Is there any substance to the theory that today's rebellious youth are reacting against the compliance of their parents?
5. What is Smith's real attitude toward the women's liberation movement?

Discussion of Rhetoric

1. Do you consider Smith's article overly sentimental, or is his view based solely on reason?
2. Note the frequent use of short, staccato sentences and sentence fragments in this article. How do they affect the tone of the article?
3. Irony is often used by writers to convey subtle meanings and to express humor. Find examples of both uses in this selection. Note, for instance, the first sentence.
4. Is Smith fair in his "indictment" of the "unliberated housewife" (paragraphs 7–10)? Has he stated the "charges" in the same way a supporter of women's liberation would?

Writing Assignments

1. Write a rebuttal to Smith's article if you disagree with his point of view.
2. What changes in the family do you foresee as a result of the changing roles of women, the "sexual revolution," and the many other upheavals taking place today? Is the traditional family unit approaching obsolescence?

Library Exploration

1. For a rebuttal to the viewpoint expressed by this article, read one of the many books currently available on the women's liberation movement. Of particular interest is *Sexual Politics*, by Kate Millett.

Vocabulary

(1) SEXIST   one who believes in distinct roles for male and female

(6) OBSOLESCENCE   state of being out of date; outmoded

(7) INDICTMENT   accusation

(7) UNREQUITED   unreturned

(23) PRODIGIOUS   extraordinary in size, amount, etc.

(27) EULOGIZE   praise highly

(28) VIABLE   capable of growing or developing

(29) FLOUT   mock; ridicule

George Wald (1906–   ), professor of biology at Harvard and
co-recipient of the Nobel Prize
for Medicine in 1967, received
his education at New York University and Columbia. The author of many scientific articles
and books on physiology and vision, he is particularly interested in the responsibility of the
scientist to society.

The following article was originally delivered as a speech at
the Massachusetts Institute of
Technology in 1969. Probing
the reasons for worldwide student unrest, Dr. Wald analyzes
America's powerful military establishment and its effects on
the values of the young.

GEORGE WALD

A Generation in Search of a Future

1   All of you know that in the last couple of years there has been student
unrest breaking at times into violence in many parts of the world: in
England, Germany, Italy, Spain, Mexico, and, needless to say, in many
parts of this country.

2   There has been a great deal of discussion as to what it all means.
Perfectly clearly it means something different in Mexico from what it
does in France, and something different in France from what it does
in Tokyo, and something different in Tokyo from what it does in this
country. Yet unless we are to assume that students have gone crazy
all over the world, or that they have just decided it's the thing to do,
there must be some common meaning.

3   I don't need to go so far afield to look for that meaning. I am a teacher, and at Harvard, I have a class of about 350 students — men and women — most of them freshmen and sophomores. Over the past few years I have felt increasingly that something is terribly wrong — and this year ever so much more than last. Something has gone sour, in teaching and in learning. It's almost as though there were a wide-spread feeling that education has become irrelevant.

4   A lecture is much more of a dialogue than many of you probably appreciate. As you lecture, you keep watching the faces; and information keeps coming back to you all the time. I began to feel, particularly this year, that I was missing much of what was coming back. I tried asking the students, but they didn't or couldn't help me very much.

5   But I think I know what's the matter even a little better than they do. I think that this whole generation of students is beset with a profound uneasiness. I don't think that they have yet quite defined its source. I think I understand the reasons for their uneasiness even better than they do. What is more, I share their uneasiness.

6   What's bothering those students? Some of them tell you it's the Vietnam War. I think the Vietnam War is the most shameful episode in the whole of American history. The concept of War Crimes is an American invention. We've committed many War Crimes in Vietnam, but I'll tell you something interesting about that. We were committing War Crimes in World War II, even before the Nuremburg trials were held and the principle of war crimes started. The saturation bombing of German cities was a War Crime and if we had lost the war, some of our leaders might have had to answer for it.

7   I've gone through all of that history lately, and I find that there's a gimmick in it. It isn't written out, but I think we established it by precedent. That gimmick is that if one can allege that one is repelling or retaliating for an aggression — after that everything goes. And you see we are living in a world in which all wars are wars of defense. All War Departments are now Defense Departments. This is all part of the doubletalk of our time. The aggressor is always on the other side. And I suppose this is why our ex-Secretary of State, Dean Rusk — a man in whom repetition takes the place of reason, and stubbornness takes the place of character — went to such pains to insist, as he still insists, that in Vietnam we are repelling an agression. And if that's what we are doing — so runs the doctrine — anything goes. If the concept of war crimes is ever to mean anything, they will have to be defined as categories of acts, regardless of provocation. But that isn't so now.

8   I think we've lost that war, as a lot of other people think, too. The Vietnamese have a secret weapon. It's their willingness to die, beyond our willingness to kill. In effect they've been saying, you can kill us, but you'll have to kill a lot of us, you may have to kill all of us. And thank heavens, we are not yet ready to do that.

9   Yet we have come a long way — far enough to sicken many Americans, far enough even to sicken our fighting men. Far enough so that our national symbols have gone sour. How many of you can sing about "the rockets' red glare, bombs bursting in air" without thinking, those are our bombs and our rockets burning over South Vietnamese vil-

lages? When those words were written, we were a people struggling for freedom against oppression. Now we are supporting real or thinly disguised military dictatorships all over the world, helping them to control and repress peoples all over the world, helping them to control and repress peoples struggling for their freedom.

10   But that Vietnam War, shameful and terrible as it is, seems to me only an immediate incident in a much larger and more stubborn situation. Part of my trouble with students is that almost all the students I teach were born since World War II. Just after World War II, a series of new and abnormal procedures came into American life. We regarded them at the time as temporary aberrations. We thought we would get back to normal American life some day. But those procedures have stayed with us now for more than 20 years, and those students of mine have never known anything else. They think those things are normal. They think we've always had a Pentagon, that we have always had a big army, and that we always had a draft. But those are all new things in American life; and I think that they are incompatible with what American meant before.

11   How many of you realize that just before World War II the entire American army including the Air Force numbered 130,000 men? Then World War II started, but we weren't in it yet; and seeing that there was great trouble in the world, we doubled this army to 268,000 men. Then in World War II it got to be 8 million. And then World War II came to an end, and we prepared to go back to a peacetime army somewhat as the American army had always been before. And indeed in 1950 — you think about 1950, our international commitments, the Cold War, the Truman Doctrine, and all the rest of it — in 1950 we got down to 600,000 men.

12   Now we have 3.5 million men under arms — about 800,000 in Vietnam, about 300,000 more in support areas elsewhere in the Pacific, about 250,000 in Germany. And there are a lot at home. Some months ago we were told that 300,000 National Guardsmen and 200,000 reservists had been specially trained for riot duty in the cities.

13   I say the Vietnam War is just an immediate incident, because so long as we keep that big army, it will always find things to do. If the Vietnam War stopped tomorrow, with that big a military establishment, the chances are that we would be in another such adventure abroad or at home before you knew it.

14   As for the draft: Don't reform the draft. Get rid of it.

15   A peacetime draft is the most unAmerican thing I know. All the time I was growing up I was told about oppressive Central European countries and Russia, where young men were forced into the army, and I was told what they did about it. They chopped off a finger or shot off a couple of toes, or better still, if they could manage it, they came to this country. And we understood that, and sympathized, and were glad to welcome them.

16   Now by present estimates four to six thousand Americans of draft age have left this country for Canada, another two or three thousand have gone to Europe, and it looks as though many more are preparing to emigrate.

17   A few months ago I received a letter from the Harvard Alumni Bulletin posing a series of questions that students might ask a professor involving what to do about the draft. I was asked to write what I would tell those students. All I had to say to those students was this: If any of them had decided to evade the draft, and asked my help, I would help him in any way I could. I would feel as I suppose members of the underground railway felt in pre–Civil War days, helping runaway slaves get into Canada. It wasn't altogether a popular position then; but what do you think of it now?

18   A bill to stop the draft was recently introduced in the Senate (s.503), sponsored by a group of senators that ran the gamut from McGovern and Hatfield to Barry Goldwater. I hope it goes through, but any time I find that Barry Goldwater and I are in agreement, that makes one take another look.

19   And indeed there are choices in getting rid of the draft. I think that when we get rid of the draft we must also cut back the size of the armed forces. It seems to me that in peacetime a total of one million men is surely enough. If there is an argument for American military forces of more than one million men in peacetime, I should like to hear the argument debated.

20   There is another thing being said closely connected with this: that to keep an adequate volunteer army, one would have to raise the pay considerably. That's said so positively and often that people believe it. I don't think it is true.

21   The great bulk of our present armed forces are genuine volunteers. Among first-term enlistments, 49 percent are true volunteers. Another 30 percent are so-called "reluctant volunteers" — persons who volunteer under pressure of the draft. Only 21 percent are draftees. All re-enlistments, of course, are true volunteers.

22   So the great majority of our present armed forces are true volunteers. Whole services are comprised entirely of volunteers: the Air Force, for example, the Submarine Service, the Marines. That seems like proof to me that present pay rates are adequate. One must add that an Act of Congress in 1967 raised the base pay throughout the services in three installments, the third installment still to come, on April 1, 1969. So it is hard to understand why we are being told that to maintain adequate armed services on a volunteer basis will require large increases in pay; they will cost an extra $17 billion per year. It seems plain to me that we can get all the armed forces we need as volunteers, and at present rates of pay.

23   But there is something ever so much bigger and more important than the draft. The bigger thing, of course, is what ex-President Eisenhower warned us of, calling it the military-industrial complex. I am sad to say that we must begin to think of it now as the military-industrial-labor union complex. What happened under the plea of the Cold War was not alone that we built up the first big peacetime army in our history, but we institutionalized it. We built, I suppose, the biggest government building in history to run it, and we institutionalized it.

24   I don't think we can live with the present military establishment and its $80–100 billion a year budget, and keep America anything like we have known it in the past. It is corrupting the life of the whole country.

It is buying up everything in sight; industries, banks, investors, universities; and lately it seems also to have bought up the labor unions.

25   The Defense Department is always broke; but some of the things they do with that $80 billion a year would make Buck Rogers envious. For example, the Rocky Mountain Arsenal on the outskirts of Denver was manufacturing a deadly nerve poison on such a scale that there was a problem of waste disposal. Nothing daunted, they dug a tunnel two miles deep under Denver, into which they have injected so much poisoned water that beginning a couple of years ago Denver began to experience a series of earth tremors of increasing severity. Now there is a grave fear of major earthquake. An interesting debate is in progress as to whether Denver will be safer if that lake of poisoned water is removed or left in place. (*N.Y. Times,* July 4, 1968; *Science,* Sept. 17, 1968)

26   Perhaps you have read also of those 6000 sheep that suddenly died in Skull Valley, Utah, killed by another nerve poison — a strange and, I believe, still unexplained accident, since the nearest testing seems to have been 30 miles away.

27   As for Vietnam, the expenditure of fire power has been frightening. Some of you may still remember Khe Sanh, a hamlet just south of the Demilitarized Zone, where a force of U.S. Marines was beleaguered for a time. During that period we dropped on the perimeter of Khe Sanh more explosives than fell on Japan throughout World War II, and more than fell on the whole of Europe during the years 1942 and 1943.

28   One of the officers there was quoted as having said afterward, "It looks like the world caught smallpox and died." (*N.Y. Times,* Mar. 28, 1968)

29   The only point of government is to lifeguard and foster life. Our government has become preoccupied with death, with the business of killing and being killed. So-called Defense now absorbs 60 percent of the national budget and about 12 percent of the Gross National Product.

30   A lively debate is beginning again on whether or not we should deploy antiballistic missiles, the ABM. I don't have to talk about them, everyone else here is doing that, but I should like to mention a curious circumstance. In September 1967, or about 1½ years ago, we had a meeting of M.I.T. and Harvard people, including experts on these matters, to talk about whether anything could be done to block the Sentinel system, the deployment of ABM's. Everyone present thought them undesirable; but a few of the most knowledgeable persons took what seemed to be the practical view. "Why fight about a dead issue? It has been decided, the funds have been appropriated. Let's go on from there."

31   Well, fortunately, it's not a dead issue. An ABM is a nuclear weapon. It takes a nuclear weapon to stop a nuclear weapon. And our concern must be with the whole issue of nuclear weapons.

32   There is an entire semantics ready to deal with the sort of thing I am about to say. It involves such phrases as "those are the facts of life." No — these are the facts of death. I don't accept them, and I advise you not to accept them. We are under repeated pressures to accept things that are presented to us as settled — decisions that have

been made. Always there is the thought: let's go on from there! But this time we don't see how to go on. We will have to stick with those issues.

33   We are told that the United States and Russia, between them, have by now stockpiles in nuclear weapons approximately the explosive power of 15 tons of TNT for every man, woman and child on earth. And now it is suggested that we must make more. All very regrettable, of course: but those are "the facts of life." We really would like to disarm, but our new Secretary of Defense has made the ingenious proposal that one must be practical. Now is the time to greatly increase our nuclear armaments so that we can disarm from a position of strength.

34   I think all of you know there is no adequate defense against massive nuclear attack. It is both easier and cheaper to circumvent any known nuclear defense system than to provide it. It's all pretty crazy. At the very moment we talk of deploying ABM's, we are also building the MIRV, the weapon to circumvent ABM's.

35   So far as I know, with everything working as well as can be hoped and all foreseeable precautions taken, the most conservative estimates of Americans killed in a major nuclear attack run to about 50 millions. We have become callous to gruesome statistics, and this seems at first to be only another gruesome statistic. You think, Bang! —and next morning, if you're still there, you read in the newspapers that 50 million people were killed.

36   But that isn't the way it happens. When we killed close to 200,000 people with those first little, old-fashioned uranium bombs that we dropped on Hiroshima and Nagasaki, about the same number of persons were maimed, blinded, burned, poisoned, and otherwise doomed. A lot of them took a long time to die.

37   That's the way it should be. Not a bang, and a certain number of corpses to bury; but a nation filled with millions of helpless, maimed, tortured, and doomed survivors huddled with their families in shelters, with guns ready to fight off their neighbors, trying to get some uncontaminated food and water.

38   A few months ago, Sen. Richard Russell of Georgia ended a speech in the Senate with the words: "If we have to start over again with another Adam and Eve, I want them to be Americans; and I want them on this continent and not in Europe." That was a United States Senator holding a patriotic speech. Well, here is a Nobel Laureate who thinks that those words are criminally insane. (Prolonged applause.)

39   How real is the threat of a full-scale nuclear war? I have my own very inexpert idea, but realizing how little I know and fearful that I may be a little paranoid on this subject, I take every opportunity to ask reputed experts. I asked that question of a very distinguished professor of government at Harvard about a month ago. I asked him what sort of odds he would lay on the possibility of full-scale nuclear war within the foreseeable future. "Oh," he said comfortably, "I think I can give you a pretty good answer to that question. I estimate the probability of a full-scale nuclear war, provided that the situation remains about as it is now, at 2 percent per year." Anybody can do the simple calculation that shows that 2 percent per year means that the chance of

having that full-scale nuclear war by 1990 is about one in three, and by 2000 it is about 50-50.

40   I think I know what is bothering the students. I think that what we are up against is a generation that is by no means sure that it has a future.

41   I am growing old, and my future so to speak is already behind me. But there are those students of mine who are in my mind always; there are my children, two of them now 7 and 9, whose future is infinitely more precious to me than my own. So it isn't just their generation; it's mine too. We're all in it together.

42   Are we to have a chance to live? We don't ask for prosperity, or security; only for a reasonable chance to live, to work out our destiny in peace and decency. Not to go down in history as the apocalyptic generation.

43   And it isn't only nuclear war. Another overwhelming threat is in the population explosion. That has not yet even begun to come under control. There is every indication that the world population will double before the year 2000; and there is a widespread expectation of famine on an unprecedented scale in many parts of the world. The experts tend to differ only in their estimates of when those famines will begin. Some think by 1980, others think they can be staved off until 1990, very few expect that they will not occur by the year 2000.

44   That is the problem. Unless we can be surer than we are now that this generation has a future, nothing else matters. It's not good enough to give it tender loving care, to supply it with breakfast foods, to buy it expensive educations. Those things don't mean anything unless this generation has a future. And we're not sure it does.

45   I don't think that there are problems of youth, or student problems. All the real problems I know are grown-up problems.

46   Perhaps you will think me altogether absurd, or "academic," or hopelessly innocent—that is, until you think of the alternatives—if I say to you as I do now: we have to get rid of those nuclear weapons. There is nothing worth having that can be obtained by nuclear war; nothing material or ideological, no tradition that it can defend. It is utterly self-defeating. Those atom bombs represent an unusable weapon. The only use for an atom bomb is to keep somebody else from using it. It can give us no protection, but only the doubtful satisfaction of retaliation. Nuclear weapons offer us nothing but a balance of terror; and a balance of terror is still terror.

47   We have to get rid of those atomic weapons, here and everywhere. We cannot live with them.

48   I think we've reached a point of great decision, not just for our nation, not only for all humanity, but for life upon the Earth. I tell my students, with a feeling of pride that I hope they will share, that the carbon, nitrogen, and oxygen that make up 99 percent of our living substance were cooked in the deep interiors of earlier generations of dying stars. Gathered up from the ends of the universe, over billions of years, eventually they came to form in part the substance of our sun, its planets, and ourselves. Three billion years ago life arose upon the Earth. It seems to be the only life in the solar system. Many a star has since been born and died.

49   About two million years ago, man appeared. He has become the dominant species on the Earth. All other living things, animal and plant, live by his sufferance. He is the custodian of life on Earth and in the solar system. It's a big responsibility. The thought that we're in competition with Russians or with Chinese is all a mistake, and trivial. We are one species, with a world to win. There's life all over this universe, but the only life in the solar system is on Earth; and in the whole universe, we are the only men.

50   Our business is with life, not death. Our challenge is to give what account we can of what becomes of life in the solar system, this corner of the universe that is our home and, most of all, what becomes of men —all men of all nations, colors, and creeds. It has become one world, a world for all men. It is only such a world that now can offer us life and the chance to go on.

Discussion of Theme

1. What is Wald's explanation for the student unrest that he says has spread throughout the world? Is it confined solely to the young?
2. What is the "gimmick" the author finds in our history? When was it introduced? How has it been used in Vietnam?
3. Why is the nuclear bomb unusable, according to Wald? What alternative does he suggest? What actions does he recommend that the young take?
4. How do you suppose this nation got its priorities confused? Was it inevitable? Can the trend be reversed?
5. According to Wald, the Second World War introduced certain "abnormal procedures" into the American scene. What were they? Are they still present? In what sense is Vietnam "only an immediate incident"?

Discussion of Rhetoric

1. How does Wald establish his credibility with his audience? Does he talk down to them?
2. What evidence is there that this was delivered as a speech, rather than prepared as an essay? Consider, for example, diction and sentence length and variety.
3. Wald is taking a controversial position, particularly with respect to the use of nuclear weapons. What sort of evidence or proof does he offer his audience? Is his argument solely emotional?
4. Comment on the sentence structure in paragraph 13. Why is it effective? Find other examples of this technique.

Writing Assignments

1. Does the "military-industrial-labor union complex" govern the decisions made by our government and determine the direction of our country as Wald suggests? Present your views in a theme.

2. Should the draft be abolished? Give your views.
3. Were the sentences handed down at Nuremberg appropriate? Should military leaders be held morally and legally responsible in time of war? What about the political leaders — the President and various cabinet officers?

Library Exploration

1. What were the Nuremberg War Trials? Who participated? What was the outcome? If they were held today, based on the same principles, would the United States be found guilty of war crimes?
2. Read about student demonstrations and riots in other parts of the world, particularly in Paris, Mexico City, and Tokyo. What issues were involved? How did the governments react?

Vocabulary

(10) ABERRATIONS deviations
(18) GAMUT an entire range or scale

(39) REPUTED supposed; alleged
(49) SUFFERANCE tolerance

Dixon Wecter (1906–50), a Texas-born historian and author, received degrees from Baylor University, Yale, and Oxford. He taught at the Universities of Colorado, Denver, and California at Berkeley and Los Angeles. In addition to three volumes on Mark Twain, Wecter wrote several books of social history. Among them are "Saga of American Society" (1937), "The Hero in America" (1941), and "The Age of the Great Depression" (1948).

As its title suggests, the following article analyzes the qualities that Americans seek in their heroes.

DIXON WECTER

How Americans Choose Their Heroes

1 The sort of man whom Americans admire, trust, and are willing to follow can be sketched with a few lines. East and west, north and south, his portrait is familiar. At the basic level he must be self-respecting, decent, honorable, with a sense of fair play; no Machiavelli nor Mussolini need apply. He must be firm and self-confident in leadership: Davy Crockett's "Be always sure you're right, then go ahead!" is approved American doctrine, whether in the headstrong and cocksure types we sometimes follow, like Old Hickory and Theodore Roosevelt, or in the great characters of our imagination, like Paul Bunyan and Huckleberry Finn. Mother wit and resourcefulness we love. But a reputation for "genius" is unnecessary and may do the hero harm. Brilliantly clever men like Alexander Hamilton and John

Randolph of Roanoke, and pure intellectuals like John Quincy Adams (by the guess of educators given the highest I.Q., 165, of all Americans in the Hall of Fame), are not major idols. An able man must not glory in his cleverness. By our standards one is sometimes allowed to "put over a fast one"—Benjamin Franklin and Abraham Lincoln did, repeatedly—but he must not appear to relish the coup for its own sake. Art must conceal art. A clodhopper Politician like Huey Long, boasting "There are not many people in the United States who are smarter than I am, and none in Louisiana," did not understand this restraint. Long's scornful assertion that he could buy votes in his Legislature "like sacks of potatoes," to the country at large was equally bad politics. Uncle Sam allows his favorites to be shrewd in a good cause, but there must be no avowal of cynicism in principle. (In modern movies, the hero may pull a fast one for the sake of his mother, or his girl friend, or some worthy ideal, but not for himself.) The backwoods always has a certain admiration for rustic rascality, and the metropolis loves a flippant wisecrack—but in America at large there is pretty strong prejudice against the wise guy.

2   Vanity or personal arrogance in any form is taboo. The dandy in public life—accepted more tolerantly in the England of Disraeli and Lord Curzon—is disliked by Americans. Meriwether Lewis, a great explorer of the West, was handicapped by the nickname of "The Sublime Dandy" and his manners of a Beau Nash. William Pinkney, one of the most brilliant lawyers of a century ago, was ridiculed because of his fawn-colored gloves and corsets, and the vanity that led him to begin a speech all over again when he saw ladies enter the visitors' gallery of the Supreme Court.

3   Effeminacy is fatal. Martin Van Buren failed of re-election in 1840 after the public had grown tired of his lace-tipped cravats and morocco shoes, and a ribald Whig politician had exposed his use of a lotion called "Essence of Victoria." In the West the dude was a traditional villain. (Ironically, in 1860 Lincoln's campaign manager worked hard to get him photographed in a boiled shirt with pearl studs, to make a better impression in the East.)

4   The arrogance of caste is equally deadly in American hero-worship. Hancock, Jay, Gouverneur Morris were snobs who never won the sway, with even a seasoning of popular admiration, that some Tory statesmen have enjoyed in England. The public can never forget that Hamilton once exclaimed, "Your people, sir, is a great beast!" (These words, quoted in the second decade of this century in school texts on American history by William B. Guitteau, McLaughlin and Van Tyne, and Albert Bushnell Hart, were omitted after protests from school boards and patrons, from subsequent editions in the 1920s when the Hamiltonian philosophy was in favor during the era of Republican prosperity.) Harding paid Hamilton the dubious compliment of saying, in 1921, "No man's life ever gave me greater inspiration than Hamilton's"; and bankers have often praised the first Secretary of the Treasury. But the people at large have repaid his scorn with neglect.

5   Even Daniel Webster—for all his adoration in New England and among the propertied classes—has failed, for like reasons, to make the

upper rungs of hero worship. All else favored him: a head so noble that it was often said "no man could be as great as Webster looked," a record of success from barefoot boy on a New Hampshire farm to the United States Senate and Cabinet, a superb voice that made the blood pound in men's temples. But he was known as "the pensioner of Wall Street," who spent his days so exclusively around mahogany tables in clubs and directors' rooms—where the smoke of Havana cigars hung blue, and "mountain dew" Scotch regaled his fine palate —that in the end he became not the idol of the People, but of the Best People. There are apparent exceptions. The rich man's friend is sometimes elected President—as in the days of McKinley, Harding, and Coolidge—when the voters look upon themselves as potential rich men, but his popularity strikes no roots in the substratum of affection and legend.

6   Within limits, the mores of the hero may vary with his times. Emerson, living in the day of Old Hickory, Clay, and Webster, remarked that to the great man, "doing for the people what they wish done and cannot do, of course, everything will be permitted and pardoned—gaming, drinking, fighting, luxury . . . everything short of infamous crime will pass." Hadn't Jackson run off with another man's wife? Didn't he and Clay fight duels and bet on racehorses? Weren't Clay and Webster notoriously heavy drinkers—even though Webster was said to concede enough to appearances on the platform to refresh himself with white brandy out of a water-glass? Emerson's conclusion was probably too sweeping: in the first place he forgot that the capital of Puritanism had already moved from New England into insular America, and secondly he failed to reckon with the merely regional popularity of Clay and Webster which even then was fading. Only Jackson endured, a greater democrat as well as a man of higher personal integrity. The hero of a democracy—unlike the Stuarts, Bourbons, and Napoleons of the Old World—cannot invite public opinion to go to hell. He must pay tribute to conformity.

7   Through most of our cultural history, for the average man sex and religion have been life's two most serious subjects, and irregularity, even in the mighty leader, must not go too far. Aaron Burr's "one hundred bastards" belong to the legend of villainy, along with Thaddeus Stevens' alleged mistresses white and black; while Tom Paine's agnostic mockery made him, in spite of his great patriotic services, an object of folk hate. As for the hero, debunkery by sensational writers has usually addressed itself to secret nips at the bottle, failure to attend church, or flirtation with a neighbor's wife—rather than to matters of rightful public concern, like soundness of military strategy, foresight, or statemanly wisdom.

8   The great man who wins acceptance as a hero will find his vagaries and skepticisms trimmed down by convention. Nevertheless, it is surprising how few of the American great, in comparison with those of the Old World, have cultivated lush private lives, though their individual views on religion have often shown more independence than orthodoxy. To a man's man, the sturdy profanity of Washington and Old Hickory, like the earthy jokes of Franklin and Lincoln, will be for-

given and, in the main, forgotten. Fundamentally, the hero is required to be chaste, loyal, honest, humble before duty and before God. He is apt to have a dash of Puritan conscience, but the beauty of holiness is no more expected than is a sense of poetry.

9   The people's choice of heroes for America has been prevailingly sound; our major favorites are those any nation might be proud of. They go far toward vindicating the whole democratic theory of careers open to talent. We believe that character is more important than brains. Hard work, tenacity, enterprise, and firmness in the face of odds are the qualities that Americans most admire, rather than originality or eloquence of tongue and pen.

10   The hero must be a man of good will and also a good neighbor, preferably something of a joiner. Of the solitudes and lonely isolations of a great man like Lincoln the public has little conception. It likes to think of its idol as simple in greatness. Manliness, forthright manners, and salty speech are approved. Love of the soil, of dogs and horses and manual hobbies and fishing, is better understood than absorption in art, literature, and music. (The public distrusts Presidents who are photographed fishing in their store clothes.) The hero must not lose touch with his birthplace and origins, however humble; the atmosphere of small towns and front-porch campaigns, cultivated by so many candidates for President, pays tribute to this demand. "I really believe there are more attempts at flattering the farmers than any other class," Lincoln as candidate for President remarked at the Wisconsin State Fair, "the reason for which I cannot perceive, unless it be that they cast more votes than any other."

11   Also, the touch of versatility and homely skill is applauded in a hero. Thomas Jefferson is remembered less as the eighteenth-century virtuoso than as an inventor of gadgets from which he plainly got a great deal of fun. "Tinkering" is American. European lads—like Henrich Steffens growing up in Denmark, and Michael Pupin in a Serbian village—have testified to the fascination that Franklin, "wiser than all the wise men of Idvor," held for them. The hero must do things better than the common folk, but his achievements (unlike those of the artist, philosopher, and pure scientist) must lie open to everyman's comprehension. It is well, too, that the labels of the hero conform to those of the group, so that identification between him and the majority can more easily be made: for example, all of our major idols have been both Anglo-Saxon and Protestant.

12   Bravery, honesty, strength of character are the stuff for hero-worship. At the boy's level, this worship gravitates toward the doer of spectacular deeds; on the average adult level, toward the wielder of power; and in the eyes of a more critical judgment, toward idealism and moral qualities. The most universal hero is he who can fill all these specifications. This, by the many shapes of their courage, integrity, and strength, Washington and Lincoln and Lee are able to do. When the dust of partisanship has settled, another leader in two great crises, economic and military—Franklin D. Roosevelt—will probably join their august company. But Jefferson the sedentary man, Ben Franklin the opportunist, and Andrew Jackson the rough-hewn soldier fail

to satisfy everybody. Upon a still lower rank, men like Daniel Boone and Crockett and Buffalo Bill and Edison remain almost juvenile heroes. They do not have all the dimensions of our few supreme symbols. Was it not Emerson who suggested that we Americans were the shattered pieces of a great mould?

13   Our most powerful hero epics center about our leaders. What then, in the final analysis do Washington, Franklin, Jefferson, Jackson, Lincoln, and in a provisional verdict Wilson and the Roosevelts have in common? Among them lie many differences. In heredity, economic origins, training, skill, temperament, party affiliations, and attachment to specific policies they may seem as diverse as we could find by sifting the nation from Atlantic to Pacific. All save perhaps Washington were "liberals" by the gauge of their times — and Washington, one must not forget, was an arch political rebel, who even in old age sought to balance his conservatism by an honest effort to be nonpartisan. (And even Washington has slowly waned before the warmer humanity of Lincoln.) What is their common denominator?

14   All of them, the people believe, loved America more deeply than any selfish consideration. The hero as made in America is a man who has the power and yet does not abuse it. He is the practical demonstration of romantic democracy. Washington is most sublime because, after winning our freedom, he refused a crown, military dictatorship, and every personal reward. Lee is grandest because he did what he thought was his duty, failed under heartbreaking odds, and then with gentleness did his best to repair all hate and malice. Lincoln is most appealing because, in the conduct of that same desperate war which gave him the power of a czar, he never forgot his love for the common people of North and South.

15   More clearly than the great heroes of Europe, military and political, ours stand for a progress concept. They spring from stock that has bred schemes both wise and foolish — with its talk about the pursuit of happiness, the more abundant life, and the American Dream. None of these epic leaders left the Republic as he found it — although to avoid disturbing a single stick or stone seems to have been the policy of men like James Buchanan, Chester A. Arthur, William McKinley, and Calvin Coolidge. At times, to be sure, the people themselves have wanted no change, felt no urge to take on fresh responsibility in the national sphere. In eras like theirs, nothing is added to the stature of American ideals — such as civil liberty, equality of opportunity, faith in the average man, social justice, respect for the rights of weaker nations and for the good estate of democracy throughout the earth. A Chief Executive may then be called to office who rules as a minor Augustus over a gilded age, or serves as the genial host at a great barbecue. But ten years hence he is not likely to be remembered as a great man, or even as a symbol worth keeping.

16   Our heroes, we believe, are cast in a different mould. Their ruling passion, as we see it, is a sense of duty, alert to the best among the stirring impulses of their time, and able to make the impulse effective. They translate the dream into act. The supreme leader is he who can hitch the great bandwagon to the star of American idealism.

Discussion of Theme

1. In paragraph 1, Wecter states that the following phrase is approved American doctrine: "Be always sure you're right, then go ahead." Is this doctrine always a wise one to follow? Is there such a thing as being *sure* one is *right*?
2. In the final sentence, Wecter speaks of "the star of American idealism." Have public events of recent years made Americans too cynical to retain their ideals?
3. How do we know when a man has attained hero's status? Who decides that he is a hero, and what proportion of the population must regard him as such before he is considered a hero?
4. Why do you think Wecter doesn't name any women?

Discussion of Rhetoric

1. Does the author use a great deal of figurative language? Do you consider it appropriate to his subject matter? Identify the figure of speech used in the final sentence. Is it effective? On what quotation is it based?
2. Wecter follows a pattern in organizing his paragraphs. What is the pattern? To what extent does it contribute to the clarity of his writing?
3. How important is Wecter's overall organization of his material? Could the paragraphs be rearranged without detracting from either the sense or the impact of what the author has to say?
4. Find the sentence in paragraph 8 that serves as the pivot, or turning point, of the essay. What has Wecter accomplished in the first seven paragraphs?

Writing Assignments

1. Using the qualities described as unsuitable for heroes as a guide, explain why various contemporary American leaders could not be accepted as heroes by the general public.
2. Three articles in this anthology discuss heroes. What about villains? Write a paper in which you examine the characteristics of the kind of individual who would be the opposite of a hero.
3. Select a modern American hero—not necessarily your own—and analyze his appeal.
4. Is hero worship harmful to society, or is it a healthy phenomenon?

Library Exploration

1. Some current literature is concerned with what critics call the "anti-hero." Define this paradoxical term.

2. Read Max Eastman's *Heroes I Have Known; Twelve Who Have Lived Great Lives.*
3. Read John F. Kennedy's *Profiles in Courage.*

Vocabulary

(1) AVOWAL   declaration; acknowledgment

(1) RUSTIC   rural; countrified

(3) EFFEMINACY   womanish characteristics in a man

(3) RIBALD   coarse; indelicate

(5) PENSIONER   dependent; someone receiving money (pension)

(5) SUBSTRATUM   underlying layer; foundation

(6) MORES   habits; customs

(6) INFAMOUS   notorious; disgraceful

(7) AGNOSTIC   unbelieving

(7) DEBUNKERY   attempts to expose sham or explode myths

(8) VAGARIES   peculiarities; oddities

(9) VINDICATING   justifying; supporting

(9) TENACITY   persistency; stick-to-it-iveness

(11) VIRTUOSO   scholar; star performer

(12) GRAVITATES   moves toward something as if attracted

(12) AUGUST   grand; imposing

(12) SEDENTARY   relatively inactive

Arthur M. Schlesinger, Jr.
(1917–) is the Albert
Schweitzer professor of human-
ities at the City University of
New York and former special
assistant to Presidents John F.
Kennedy and Lyndon B. Johnson. Educated at Harvard,
where he later taught history,
Schlesinger received the Pulitzer Prize for History in 1945
for "The Age of Jackson." He
has written "The Coming of the
New Deal" (1958), "The Politics
of Upheaval" (1960), and an account of the Kennedy administration, "A Thousand Days"
(1965).

The argument here is that "ours
is an age without heroes" and
that we need great men in a
democracy because they enable us "to rise to our own highest potentialities."

ARTHUR M. SCHLESINGER, JR.

The Decline
of Heroes

1   Ours is an age without heroes—and, when we say this, we suddenly
realize how spectacularly the world has changed in a generation. Most
of us grew up in a time of towering personalities. For better or for
worse, great men seemed to dominate our lives and shape our destiny. In the United States we had Theodore Roosevelt, Woodrow Wilson, Franklin Roosevelt. In Great Britain, there were Lloyd George
and Winston Churchill. In other lands, there were Lenin, Stalin, Hitler, Mussolini, Clemenceau, Gandhi, Kemal, Sun Yat-sen. Outside of
politics there were Einstein, Freud, Keynes. Some of these great men
influenced the world for good, others for evil; but, whether for good or
for evil, the fact that each had not died at birth made a difference, one
believed, to everyone who lived after them.

2   Today no one bestrides our narrow world like a colossus; we have no giants who play roles which one can imagine no one else playing in their stead. There are a few figures on the margin of uniqueness, perhaps: Adenauer, Nehru, Tito, De Gaulle, Chiang Kai-shek, Mao Tse-tung. But there seem to be none in the epic style of those mighty figures of our recent past who seized history with both hands and gave it an imprint, even a direction, which it otherwise might not have had. As De Gaulle himself remarked on hearing of Stalin's death, "The age of giants is over." Whatever one thought, whether one admired or detested Roosevelt or Churchill, Stalin or Hitler, one nevertheless felt the sheer weight of such personalities on one's own existence. We feel no comparable pressures today. Our own President, with all his pleasant qualities, has more or less explicitly renounced any desire to impress his own views on history. The Macmillans, Khrushchevs, and Gronchis have measurably less specific gravity than their predecessors. Other men could be in their places as leaders of America or Britain or Russia or Italy without any change in the course of history. Why ours should thus be an age without heroes, and whether this condition is good or bad for us and for civilization, are topics worthy of investigation.

3   Why have giants vanished from our midst? One must never neglect the role of accident in history; and accident no doubt plays a part here. But too many accidents of the same sort cease to be wholly accidental. One must inquire further. Why should our age not only be without great men but even seem actively hostile to them? Surely one reason we have so few heroes now is precisely that we had so many a generation ago. Greatness is hard for common humanity to bear. As Emerson said, "Heroism means difficulty, postponement of praise, postponement of ease, introduction of the world into the private apartment, introduction of eternity into the hours measured by the sitting-room clock." A world of heroes keeps people from living their own private lives.

4   Moreover, great men live dangerously. They introduce extremes into existence — extremes of good, extremes of evil — and ordinary men after a time flinch from the ultimates and yearn for undemanding security. The Second World War was the climax of an epoch of living dangerously. It is no surprise that it precipitated a universal revulsion against greatness. The war itself destroyed Hitler and Mussolini. And the architects of victory were hardly longer-lived. After the war, the British repudiated Churchill, and the Americans (with the adoption of the 22nd Amendment), Roosevelt. In due course, the French repudiated De Gaulle (they later repented, but it took the threat of civil war to bring him back); the Chinese, Chiang Kai-shek; and the Russians, Stalin. Khrushchev, in toppling Stalin from his pedestal, pronounced the general verdict against the uncommon man: the modern world, he said, had no use for the "cult of the individual." And, indeed, carried to the excesses to which the worshipers of Hitler and Stalin carried it, even to the much milder degree to which admirers of Roosevelt and Churchill sometimes carried it, the cult of the individual was dangerous. No man is infallible, and every man needs to be reminded of this on occasion. Still, our age has gone further than this — it objects not

just to hero worship but to heroes. The century of the common man has come into its own.

5   This term, "common man," suggests the deeper problem. There is more involved than simply a dismissal of those colossi whom the world identified with a season of blood and agony. The common man has always regarded the great man with mixed feelings — resentment as well as admiration, hatred as well as love. The Athenian who refused to vote for Aristides because he was so tired of hearing him called "the Just" expressed a natural reaction. Great men make small men aware of their smallness. Rancor is one of the unavowed but potent emotions in politics; and one must never forget that the envy of the have-nots can be quite as consuming when the haves have character or intelligence as it is when they have merely material possessions.

6   Modern democracy inadvertently gave envy new scope. While the purpose of democracy was to give everyone a fair chance to rise, its method enabled rancorous men to invoke "equality" as an excuse for keeping all down to their own level. "I attribute the small number of distinguished men in political life," wrote Alexis de Tocqueville after visiting the United States in the 1830s, "to the ever-increasing despotism of the majority. . . . The power of the majority is so absolute and irresistible that one must give up one's rights as a citizen and almost abjure one's qualities as a human being, if one intends to stray from the track which it prescribes." James Bryce even titled a chapter in his *American Commonwealth,* Why Great Men Are Not Chosen President.

7   History has shown these prophets unduly pessimistic. Distinguished men do enter American politics; great men have been chosen President. Democracy demonstrates a capability for heroic leadership quite as much as it does a tendency toward mediocrity. Yet Tocqueville and the others were correct enough in detecting the dislike of great men as a permanent potentiality in a democracy. And the evolution of industrial society appears to have given this sentiment new force. More and more of us live and work within great organizations; an influential book has already singled out the organization man as the American of the future. The bureaucratization of American life, the decline of the working class, the growth of the white-collar class, the rise of suburbia — all this has meant the increasing homogeneity of American society. Though we continue to speak of ourselves as rugged individualists, our actual life has grown more and more collective and anonymous. As a Monsanto Chemical film put it, showing a group of technicians at work in a laboratory: "No geniuses here; just a bunch of average Americans working together." Our ideal is increasingly smooth absorption into the group rather than self-realization in the old-fashioned, strong-minded, don't-give-a-damn sense. Where does the great man fit into our homogenized society?

8   "The greatness of England is now all collective," John Stuart Mill wrote a century ago: "individually small, we only appear capable of anything great by our habit of combining." He might have been writing about contemporary America; but where we Americans are inclined to rejoice over the superiority of the "team," Mill added somberly, "It was men of another stamp than this that made England

what is has been; and men of another stamp will be needed to prevent its decline."

9   But was Mill right? Do individuals really have impact on history? A powerful school of philosophers has denied any importance at all to great men. Such thinkers reject heroes as a childish hangover from the days when men ascribed everything to the action of gods. History, they assert, is not made by men, but by inexorable forces or irrevocable laws: if these forces or laws do not manifest themselves through one individual, they will do so through another. What has happened already has comprehensively and absolutely decided what will happen in the future. "If there is a single human action due to free will," wrote Tolstoi, "no historical law exists, and no conception of historical events can be formed." If all this is so, obviously the presence or absence of any particular "hero" at any particular time cannot make the slightest difference.

10   This view of history is a form of fatalistic determinism; and Tolstoi's *War and Peace* offers one of its most eloquent statements. Why, Tolstoi asked, did millions of men in the time of Napoleon, repudiating their common sense and their human feeling, move from west to east, slaughtering their fellows? The answers provided by historians seemed to him hopelessly superficial. His own answer was: "The war was bound to happen simply because it was bound to happen"; all previous history predetermined it. Where did this leave the great men? In Tolstoi's view, they were the most deluded figures of all. Great men, he said, "are but the labels that serve to give a name to an event and, like labels, they have the least possible connection with the event itself." The greater the man, "the more conspicuous is the inevitability and predestination of every act he commits." The hero, said Tolstoi, "is the slave of history."

11   There are many forms of historical fatalism. Toynbee and Spengler, with their theory of the inexorable growth and decay of civilizations, represent one form. The Marxists, with their theory that changes in the modes of production control the course of history, represent another. When Khrushchev denounced the practice of making "a hero" out of "a particular leader" and condemned the cult of the individual as "alien to the spirit of Marxism-Leninism," he was speaking the true spirit of his faith. And Marxism is not the only form of economic determinism; there are also, for example, economic determinists of the laissez-faire school who believe that all civilization is dependent on rigid adherence to a certain theory of the sacredness of private property.

12   Fatalists differ greatly among themselves. But, however much they differ, they unite in the conclusion that the individual plays no role of his own in history. If they are right, then nothing else could matter less whether or not this is an age without heroes.

13   But they are not right. The philosophy of historical fatalism rests on serious fallacies. For one thing, it supposes that, because a thing happens, it had to happen. But causation is one matter; predestination another. The construction of a causal explanation after an event merely renders that event in some sense intelligible. It does not in the least show that this particular event, and no other, had to take place;

that nothing else could possibly have occurred in its stead. The serious test of the fatalist case must be applied before the event. The only conclusive proof of fatalism would lie in the accurate prediction of events that have not yet happened. And to say, with Tolstoi, that all prior history predetermines everything that follows is to say nothing at all. It is to produce an explanation which applies equally to everything — and thus becomes so vague and limitless as to explain nothing.

14   Fatalism raises other difficulties. Thus it imputes reality to mythical historical "forces" — class, race, nation, the will of the people, the spirit of the times, history itself. But there are no such forces. They are merely abstractions or metaphors with no existence except in the mind of the beholder. The only evidence for them is deduction from the behavior of individuals. It is therefore the individual who constitutes the basic unit of history. And, while no individual can be wholly free — and, indeed, recent discoveries of the manifold ways in which we are unconsciously conditioned should constitute a salutary check on human vanity — one must assume the reality of an area of free choice until that assumption is challenged, not by metaphysical affirmation, but by verifiable proof — that is, consistently accurate prediction of the future.

15   Fatalism, moreover, is incompatible with human psychology and human morality. Anyone who rigorously accepted a deterministic view of life, for example, would have to abandon all notions of human responsibility, since it is manifestly unfair to praise or punish people for acts which are by definition beyond their control. But such fatalism is belied by the assumption of free choice which underlies every move we make, every word we utter, every thought we think. As Sir Isaiah Berlin observes of determinism, "If we begin to take it seriously, then, indeed, the changes in our language, our moral notions, our attitudes toward one another, our views of history, of society, and of everything else will be too profound to be even adumbrated." We can no more imagine what the universe of the consistent determinist would be like than we can imagine what it would be like to live in a world without time or one with seventeen-dimensional space.

16   For the historian concerned with concrete interpretation of actual events, he can easily demonstrate the futility of fatalism by trying to apply it to specific historical episodes. According to the extreme determinist view, no particular individual can make the slightest difference. As slaves of history, all individuals are, so to speak, interchangeable parts. If Napoleon had not led his armies across Europe, Tolstoi implies, someone else would have. William James, combating this philosophic fatalism, once asked the determinists whether they really believed "the convergence of sociological pressures to have so impinged on Stratford on Avon about April 23, 1564, that a W. Shakespeare, with all his mental peculiarities, had to be born there." And did they further believe, James continued, that "if the aforesaid W. Shakespeare had died of cholera infantum, another mother at Stratford on Avon would needs have engendered a duplicate of him to restore the sociological equilibrium?" Who could believe such stuff? Yet, if the determinists do not mean exactly this, how can they read the individual out of history?

17   In December, 1931, a British politician, crossing Fifth Avenue in

New York between 76th and 77th streets around ten-thirty at night, was knocked down and gravely injured by an automobile. Fourteen months later an American politician, sitting in an open car in Miami, Florida, was fired on by an assassin; a man standing beside him was killed. Would the next two decades of history have been the same had Contasini's car killed Winston Churchill in 1931 and Zangara's bullets killed Franklin Roosevelt in 1933? Suppose, in addition, that Adolf Hitler had been killed in the street fighting during the Munich *Putsch* of 1923, and that Lenin and Mussolini had died at birth. Where would our century be now?

18   Individuals, of course, must operate within limits. They cannot do everything. They cannot, for example, propel history into directions for which the environment and the human material are not prepared: no genius, however heroic, could have brought television to ancient Troy. Yet, as Sidney Hook has convincingly argued in his thoughtful book, *The Hero in History,* great men can count decisively "where the historical situation permits of major alternative paths of development."

19   This argument between fatalism and heroism is not one on which there is a lot to be said on both sides. The issue is far too sharp to be straddled. Either history is rigidly determined and foreordained, in which case individual striving does not matter; or it is not, in which case there is an essential role for the hero. Analysis of concrete episodes suggests that history is, within limits, open and unfinished; that men have lived who did what no substitute could ever have done; that their intervention set history on one path rather than another. If this is so, the old maxim, "There are no indispensable men," would seem another amiable fallacy. There is, then, a case for heroes.

20   To say that there is a case for heroes is not to say that there is a case for hero worship. The surrender of decision, the unquestioning submission to leadership, the prostration of the average man before the Great Man—these are the diseases of heroism, and they are fatal to human dignity. But, if carried too far, hero worship generates its own antidote. "Every hero," said Emerson, "becomes a bore at last." And we need not go too far. History amply shows that it is possible to have heroes without turning them into gods.

21   And history shows, too, that when a society, in flight from hero worship, decides to do without great men at all, it gets into troubles of its own. Our contemporary American society, for example, has little use for the individualist. Individualism implies dissent from the group; dissent implies conflict; and conflict suddenly seems divisive, un-American and generally unbearable. Our greatest new industry is evidently the production of techniques to eliminate conflict, from positive thoughts through public relations to psychoanalysis, applied everywhere from the couch to the pulpit. Our national aspiration has become peace of mind, peace of soul. The symptomatic drug of our age is the tranquilizer. "Togetherness" is the banner under which we march into the brave new world.

22   Obviously society has had to evolve collective institutions to cope with problems that have grown increasingly complex and concentrated. But the collective approach can be overdone. If Khrushchev worried because his collectivist society developed a cult of the indi-

vidual, maybe we Americans should start worrying as our so-called individualist society develops a cult of the group. We instinctively suppose that the tough questions will be solved by an interfaith conference or an interdisciplinary research team or an interdepartmental committee or an assembly of wise men meeting at Arden House. But are not these group tactics essentially means by which individuals hedge their bets and distribute the responsibilities? And do they not nearly always result in the dilution of insight and the triumph of mishmash? If we are to survive, we must have ideas, vision, courage. These are rarely produced by committees. Everything that matters in our intellectual and moral life begins with an individual confronting his own mind and conscience in a room by himself.

23   A bland society will never be creative. "The amount of eccentricity in a society," said John Stuart Mill, "has generally been proportional to the amount of genius, mental vigor and moral courage it contained. That so few now dare to be eccentric marks the chief danger of the time." If this condition frightened Mill in Victorian England, it should frighten us much more. For our national apotheosis of the group means that we systematically lop off the eccentrics, the originals, the proud, imaginative lonely people from whom new ideas come. What began as a recoil from hero worship ends as a conspiracy against creativity. If worship of great men brings us to perdition by one path, flight from great men brings us there just as surely by another. When we do not admire great men, then our instinct for admiration is likely to end by settling on ourselves. The one thing worse for democracy than hero worship is self-worship.

24   A free society cannot get along without heroes, because they are the most vivid means of exhibiting the power of free men. The hero exposes to all mankind unsuspected possibilities of conception, unimagined resources of strength. "The appearance of a great man," wrote Emerson, "draws a new circle outside of our largest orbit and surprises and commands us." Carlyle likened ordinary, lethargic times, with their unbelief and perplexity, to dry, dead fuel, waiting for the lightning out of heaven to kindle it. "The great man, with his free force direct out of God's own hand, is the lightning. . . . The rest of men waited for him like fuel, and then they too would flame."

25   Great men enable us to rise to our own highest potentialities. They nerve lesser men to disregard the world and trust to their own deepest instinct. "In picking out from history our heroes," said William James, "each one of us may best fortify and inspire what creative energy may lie in his own soul. This is the last justification of hero worship." Which one of us has not gained fortitude and faith from the incarnation of ideals in men, from the wisdom of Socrates, from the wondrous creativity of Shakespeare, from the strength of Washington, from the compassion of Lincoln, and above all, perhaps, from the life and the death of Jesus? "We feed on genius," said Emerson. "Great men exist that there may be greater men."

26   Yet this may be only the smaller part of their service. Great men have another and larger role — to affirm human freedom against the supposed inevitabilities of history. The first hero was Prometheus, who defied the gods and thus asserted the independence and autonomy of

man against all determinism. Zeus punished Prometheus, chaining
him to a rock and encouraging a vulture to pluck at his vitals.

27   Ever since, man, like Prometheus, has warred against history. It
has always been a bitter and remorseless fight; for the heavy weight
of human inertia lies with fatalism. It takes a man of exceptional vision
and strength and will — it takes, in short, a hero — to try to wrench history from what lesser men consider its preconceived path. And often
history tortures the hero in the process, chains him to a rock and exposes him to the vulture. Yet, in the model of Prometheus, man can
still hold his own against the gods. Brave men earn the right to shape
their own destiny.

28   An age without great men is one which acquiesces in the drift of
history. Such acquiescence is easy and seductive; the great appeal of
fatalism, indeed, is as a refuge from the terror of responsibility. Where
a belief in great men insistently reminds us that individuals can make
a difference, fatalism reassures us that they can't. It thereby blesses
our weakness and extenuates our failure. Fatalism, in Berlin's phrase,
is "one of the great alibis" of history.

29   Let us not be complacent about our supposed capacity to get along
without great men. If our society has lost its wish for heroes and its
ability to produce them, it may well turn out to have lost everything
else as well.

Discussion of Theme

1. Are heroic qualities absolute, or do they vary from one era to the
   next and from one society to another? What is the hero's relation to
   his culture? Have certain so-called "heroic qualities" endured
   throughout America's history?
2. Are heroes individualists, or are they, rather, conventional people
   who epitomize the qualities valued most highly by their own society?
3. Is a martyr always a hero?
4. Does our age have heroes?
5. Was President Kennedy a hero? Is his legend making him one?
6. Must a society have great heroes to remain great and to give identity to each individual?

Discussion of Rhetoric

1. What is an "amiable fallacy" (paragraph 19)?
2. Look again at paragraph 17. Is such speculation merely an entertaining mental exercise, or can it serve as the basis for serious argument?
3. Why does Schlesinger avoid defining a hero?
4. Schlesinger's essay is built around two questions and a fallacy.
   What are these crucial ideas?
5. Comment on the author's use of quotation marks to give emphasis
   to words.

Writing Assignments

1. Whom do you regard as America's—or the world's—greatest *unsung* hero? Describe his or her qualities.
2. Schlesinger says that "A free society cannot get along without heroes, because they are the most vivid means of exhibiting the power of free men." With this in mind, consider whether a closed society also has its heroes and what they represent to "unfree men." Are such heroes officially selected or are they spontaneously acclaimed by the populace?
3. Write a paper that examines evidence to support Schlesinger's claim that this is the age of "the common man." Be sure to define the highly connotative phrase "common man."
4. Choose a man who is considered a hero and describe the characteristics that account for his reputation.

Library Exploration

1. Read Sidney Hook's *The Hero in History.*
2. What is the 22nd Amendment? Why does the author say that it repudiated Roosevelt? Do you approve of the 22nd Amendment?
3. For a treatment of a man regarded by many as a modern-day hero, read Schlesinger's *A Thousand Days* (1965).

Vocabulary

(2) COLOSSUS   gigantic statue; person of great power or influence

(2) UNIQUENESS   being one of a kind

(2) EPIC   heroic in scale

(2) EXPLICITLY   distinctly stated

(4) EPOCH   period of time

(4) PRECIPITATED   brought about; caused

(4) REPUDIATED   rejected

(4) INFALLIBLE   without error

(5) RANCOR   intense spite or ill-will

(5) UNAVOWED   not admitted

(5) POTENT   powerful

(5) CONSUMING   engrossing; absorbing

(6) INADVERTENTLY   not intentionally

(6) DESPOTISM   tyranny

(6) ABJURE   renounce; deny

(7) MEDIOCRITY   the ordinary; commonness

(7) HOMOGENEITY   similarity in nature or character

(7) ANONYMOUS   without personality or individuality

(9) INEXORABLE   relentless; unyielding

(9) IRREVOCABLE   unalterable

(9) MANIFEST   show; demonstrate

(9) COMPREHENSIVELY   completely

(9) CONCEPTION   idea; theory

(10) FATALISTIC   believing that events are determined by fate

(10) DELUDED   misled; deceived

(10) INEVITABILITY   inescapability; unavoidability

(10) PREDESTINATION determining beforehand

(11) LAISSEZ-FAIRE noninter-
ference

(13) FALLACIES mistakes in
logical reasoning

(14) IMPUTES ascribes; assigns

(14) METAPHORS literary devices using images for
comparison

(14) MANIFOLD many

(14) SALUTARY healthy

(14) METAPHYSICAL based on
abstract reasoning on the
nature of reality

(14) VERIFIABLE provable

(15) INCOMPATIBLE irreconcil-
able; not in keeping

(15) ADUMBRATED fore-
shadowed

(16) CONVERGENCE coming
together

(16) IMPINGED touched; made
contact

(16) CHOLERA INFANTUM a
usually fatal child's disease

(16) ENGENDERED given birth
to

(16) EQUILIBRIUM balance

(19) FOREORDAINED decreed in
advance of the event

(19) INDISPENSABLE essential

(19) AMIABLE agreeable;
obliging

(20) PROSTRATION lying prone;
hence, submission

(20) ANTIDOTE remedy

(21) DIVISIVE causing disagreement or dissension

(21) SYMPTOMATIC characteristic

(22) INTERDISCIPLINARY from
many intellectual dis-
ciplines, or fields of knowledge

(22) DILUTION watering down;
weakening

(23) BLAND mild; insipid

(23) ECCENTRICITY abnormal
or unconventional behavior

(23) APOTHEOSIS glorification;
deification

(23) PERDITION ruin; damnation

(24) LETHARGIC slow-moving;
dull

(25) FORTITUDE firm courage;
patient endurance

(25) INCARNATION incorpora-
tion into human form

(27) REMORSELESS merciless;
ruthless

(27) INERTIA difficulty in getting started

(28) ACQUIESCES accepts
without protest

(28) EXTENUATES excuses;
lessens the seriousness of

(29) COMPLACENT self-satisfied;
smug

Sir C. M. Bowra (1898–1971) was warden of Wadham College, Oxford, and a leading authority on Greek and Latin literature. An honors graduate of Oxford, he served as professor of poetry and vice-chancellor at Wadham College. Among his many scholarly books and articles are "Tradition and Design in the Illiad" (1930), "From Virgil to Milton" (1945), and "The Greek Experience" (1957).

After analyzing the appeal and qualities of Aeneas, the hero of "The Aeneid," Bowra suggests that through him Virgil recast the heroic ideal into a new mold and by so doing set an example for later poets.

C. M. BOWRA

Aeneas: The Roman Hero

1 Virgil was not the first to write the epic of Rome. In the third century B.C. Naevius had used the old Saturnian measure for his *Punic War* and in the next century Ennius' *Annals* traced the Roman story from Romulus to his own day. The first of these poems must have had many similarities to oral epic or even to ballad; the second, despite its use of the hexameter and many effective adaptations of the Homeric manner, was built on the annalistic plan which is always liable to appear when poetry annexes history. Virgil knew both works, and his own poem must have been meant to supersede them and to give in a more satisfactory form the truth about Rome as it had been revealed to his own generation. To do this he adopted a remarkable method. He abandoned the annalistic scheme and instead of versifying history presented the Roman character and destiny through a poem about a legendary and largely imaginary past. His concern was less with historical events than with their meaning, less with Rome at this or that

time than as it was from the beginning and forever, less with individual Romans than with a single, symbolical hero who stands for the qualities and the experiences which are typically Roman. By skillful literary devices, such as prophecies spoken by gods or visions seen in Elysium or scenes depicted on works of art, Virgil links up the mythical past with recorded history and his own time. But such excursions are exceptional and take up less than 300 lines in a total of nearly 10,000. The main action of the *Aeneid* takes place some three hundred years before the foundation of Rome; the leading hero and his followers are not Romans or even Italians but Trojans whose ancestral connection with Italy is dim and remote; much of the action takes place outside Italy, and when it moves there, is confined to a small area around the Tiber; Aeneas himself is a homeless wanderer who asks for no more than a few acres for himself and his company. This remote past is connected with the present by many ingenious ties. The Trojan heroes are the ancestors of famous Roman families and bear names honoured in Roman history; their ceremonies, their habits, their games, forecast what are later to be characteristic of Rome; they touch at places familiar to every Roman; into their story local legends and traditions are woven; the gods who support and sustain them are those whose cults formed the official religion of the Roman people. And more significant than these external connections are the Roman spirit, virtues and outlook which the Trojans display. The difficulties encountered by these first ancestors, their relations to the gods, their emotions and their ideals, their family loyalties, their behaviour in peace and war, their attitude to the divine task laid upon them, are somehow typical and representative of the Romans as they were believed to have always been. Virgil is less concerned with origins than with a permanent reality as it was displayed from the first and is still being displayed in his own time.

2   Such a plan and such a purpose demanded a new kind of poetry, and when we turn from the *Iliad* to the *Aeneid,* it is clear that the whole outlook is different and that Virgil has a new vision of human nature and of heroic virtue. Homer concentrates on individuals and their destinies. The dooms of Achilles and Hector dominate his design; their characters determine the action. But from the start Virgil shows that his special concern is the destiny not of a man but of a nation, not of Aeneas but of Rome. Though he opens with "Arms and the man" and suggests that his hero is another Achilles or Odysseus, he has, before his first paragraph is finished, shown that he reaches beyond Aeneas to the long history that followed from him:

> whence came the Latin race,
> The Alban sires and lofty walls of Rome.

Soon afterwards, when he has noted the obstacles which the Trojans meet in their wanderings, he again ends a period on a similar note:

> So vast a task to found the Roman race.

Then, when Venus complains that her son, Aeneas, is unjustly treated, Jupiter replies not only by promising that all will be well with Aeneas but by giving a prophetic sketch of Roman history to Julius Caesar.

The reward which the ancestor of the Roman race is to receive is much more than his own success or glory, more even than his settlement in Italy; it is the assurance of Rome's destiny, of universal and unending dominion:

> To them I give no bounds in space or time
> But empire without end.

At the outset Virgil shows what kind of destiny is the subject of his poem. The wanderings and sufferings and ultimate success of Aeneas and his followers are but a preliminary and a preparation for a much vaster theme. It was with reason that Petronius, like Tennyson, called the poet "Roman Virgil."

3   The fundamental theme of the *Aeneid* is the destiny of Rome as it was revealed in this mythical dawn of history before Rome itself existed. This destiny is presented in the person of Aeneas who not only struggles and suffers for the Rome that is to be but is already a typical Roman. If his individual fortune is subordinate to the fortune of Rome, his character shows what Romans are. He is Virgil's hero in a new kind of heroic poem, and in him we see how different Virgil's epic vision is from Homer's. Aeneas is Virgil's own creation, conceived with the special purpose of showing what a Roman hero is. Unlike Homer, Virgil owes little in his hero's character to tradition. Whereas Homer has to conform to established notions and make his Achilles "swift of foot," his Agamemnon "king of men" and his Odysseus "of many wiles," Virgil was bound by no such obligations. He could find his characters where he chose and shape them to suit his own purpose. His Aeneas owes something to Homeric precedent in being a great warrior and a devout servant of the gods, but he has taken on a new personality and is the true child of Virgil's brooding meditation and imaginative vision. The persons of the *Aeneid* are created and fashioned for a special purpose. They contribute to the main design, and everything that they say or do may be considered in the light of Rome's destiny. For this reason it is wrong to treat them as if they were dramatic characters like Homer's. They are more, and they are less. They are more, because they stand for something outside themselves, for something typically and essentially Roman; they are types, examples, symbols. And they are less, because any typical character will lack the lineaments and idiosyncrasies, the personal appeal and the intimate claims, of a character who is created for his own sake and for the poet's pleasure in him. . . .

4   Against the imperfect types of Turnus and Dido Virgil had to set his own reformed and Roman ideal of manhood. His task was indeed difficult. He had to create a man who should on the one hand be comparable to the noblest Homeric heroes in such universally honoured qualities as courage and endurance and on the other hand should present in himself the qualities which the Augustan age admired beyond all others but which had meant nothing to Homer. Virgil's treatment of Dido and Turnus shows that his new hero could not be ruled by the self-assertive spirit and cult of honour which inspired the heroic outlook; he must be based on some other principle more suited to an age of peace and order. But if he was to rival Achilles and Odysseus,

he must be a great man and a ruler of men. Virgil had to present a hero who appealed both by his greatness and by his goodness, by his superior gifts and by his Roman *virtus*.[1] On the one hand he must be a fitting member of the heroic age to which legend assigned him, and on the other he must represent in its fullness and variety the new idea of manhood which Augustus advocated and proclaimed as characteristically Roman. The result was Aeneas, a character so compounded of different elements that he has often been derided even by those who love Virgil. Yet to him Virgil gave his deepest meditations and some of his finest poetry. To understand him we must try to recapture some of the ideas and sentiments of the Augustan age.

5   Aeneas comes from Homer, and in the *Aeneid* he is presented as a great warrior who is almost the equal of Hector. To him Hector appears after death, as to his legitimate successor in the defense of Troy. Andromache associates him with Hector when she asks if the boy Ascanius has the courage and spirit of his father Aeneas and his uncle Hector. Aeneas' fame has spread through the whole world, and Dido knows all about him before she sees him, while in Italy Pallas is amazed that so renowned a man should appear before him on the Tiber. He has the heroic qualities of divine blood, prowess in war, personal beauty, and power to command men. But he has something more than this. His essential quality, as his distinguishing epithet of *pius* shows, in his *pietas,* his devotion to the gods and to all their demands. When Iloneus speaks of him to Dido, he shows the combination of qualities in Aeneas:

> A king we had, Aeneas: none more just,
> More righteous, more renowned in war and arms.

Aeneas is not only a great soldier; he is a good man. So to some degree, Homer had made him when he told of his many sacrifices to Poseidon, but Virgil enlarges the concept of this goodness until it covers much more than the performance of religious rites. Aeneas' *pietas*[2] is shown in his devotion to his country, to his father, to his wife, to his child, to his followers and above all to the many duties and the special task which the gods lay on him. He is *pius* because he does what a good man should. The epithet which Virgil gives him is unlike the epithets which Homer gives to his heroes. For while these denote physical characteristics or qualities useful in war, *pius* indicates a spiritual quality which has nothing to do with war and is specially concerned with the relations between Aeneas and the gods. Thus at the start Virgil's hero is set in a different order of things and claims a different kind of attention. In this unprecedented epithet for an epic hero and in all that it implies is the clue to Virgil's conception of Aeneas.

6   Aeneas is *pius,* but he is not a perfect and ideal man throughout the poem. The indignation which he has excited in more than one critic for his obvious faults shows not that Virgil's idea of goodness was singularly unlike our own but that he chose to show a good man in the

---

[1] Virtue or power.
[2] Piety or fidelity.

making and the means by which he is made. To understand Aeneas we must understand the scheme by which Virgil presents him, a scheme based on the moral views of the Augustan age but modified by Virgil's own beliefs and admirations. The clue to Aeneas is that he is built on a Stoic plan. St. Augustine hints at this when he touches on Aeneas' treatment of Dido and treats it as being typically Stoic because while he sheds tears for her, his purpose is not shaken by her sufferings:

> His mind unmoved, his tears fall down in vain.

It is not certain that St. Augustine interprets the line correctly, but his main conclusion is right. Aeneas has undeniably something Stoic about him which accounts for the alleged paradoxes and contradictions of his character. There is nothing strange in this. In the moral reforms which Augustus preached and planned a revived Stoicism took a prominent place. It breathes through the patriotic odes of Horace, and it survived through the first two centuries A.D. Originally Stoicism was a creed to meet the horrors of an age in which there was no political or personal security. Against this disorder it set the citadel of a man's soul in which he could live at peace with himself and with the universe and by subduing his emotions be undismayed at whatever might happen. The Augustan Romans took over this creed and gave it a new reference. It suited them because it disapproved of self-assertion and ambition and laid great emphasis on social duties. It was well suited to an age which hoped to recover from the excesses of unfettered individualism. The quiet, self-denying, self-sacrificing citizen who was prepared to do what he was told was a type dear to Augustus. Virgil knew the theory and the doctrine, and though in his youth he had leaned toward Epicurus, he was deeply affected by them. . . .

7   In his relations with Dido Aeneas fails though not quite in the way that modern critics find so deplorable. What is wrong is not his desertion of her, which is ordered by the gods and necessary for the fulfilment of his task in Italy, but his surrender in the first place to her love and his subsequent neglect of his real duty which lies away from Carthage. Virgil does not show clearly what Aeneas' motives are; they seem at least not to be love for Dido, for whom he shows little more than grateful affection. But of his fault there is no question; it is neglect and forgetfulness of duty. Mercury, sent by Jupiter, makes it quite clear:

> Forgetful of thy realm and fate!

This forgetfulness, due to sloth and love of ease, is a kind of intemperance, a failure in moderation, a state of false pleasure in which a temporary advantage is mistaken for a real good. Aeneas' duty, as Mercury tells him, is owed to his son, and he must do it. This is precisely what he tells Dido, and though her furious reception of his defense makes it look feeble, it is all that he can say, and it is right. Nor would it perhaps have seemed so weak to a Roman. For his duty is concerned with the foundation of Rome, and it cannot be right to set a woman's feelings before that destiny. Aeneas is fond of Dido and he feels pity for her, but his conscience is stronger than his emotions and wins in the end. When he leaves her, he acts as a Stoic should, and undoes, so far as he can, the evil which he has committed by allowing himself to forget his task in her company.

8   In Book V Aeneas is faced with another crisis. During the Funeral Games of his father, the women of his company, stirred up by Juno's agent, begin to burn his ships with the purpose of keeping him in Sicily. Aeneas sees the havoc that they have started and prays to Jupiter to stop it. Jupiter sends rain and the fire is quenched. But even after this display of divine help, Aeneas is full of misgivings:

> But prince Aeneas, by that sad mischance
> Sore stricken, rolls the burden of his thoughts
> This way and that. There should he make his home,
> Heedless of fate, or grasp Italian shores?

It seems almost incredible that Aeneas should at this juncture think of abandoning his quest. Yet he does, and it shows how deeply his emotions still rule him. The catastrophe of the burned ships has filled him with such despair that for the moment he ceases to believe in his destiny. Fortunately he is saved by the old sailor Nautes, who not only gives him sensible advice about leaving the women in Sicily and sailing with the rest of his company, but sums up the situation in a way that must have appealed to every Roman conscience:

> Go, goddess' son, where fate drives — back or on.
> Endurance conquers fortune, come what may.

The fate which Aeneas should follow is the destiny which the gods have given him, and he should be master enough of himself to know this. Nautes brings him to his senses, and when this advice is fortified by words from the spirit of Anchises, Aeneas recovers his confidence and sets sail for Italy. He never again allows his feelings to *obscure* his knowledge of his duty.

9   Once he lands in Italy Aeneas is a new man. He makes no more mistakes, and always does what is right in the circumstances. He is never again assailed by doubt or despair; his only hesitations are about the right means to the known end, and these after due consideration he finds. . . . When Aeneas touches the fated soil of Italy, he has learned his lessons and found that self-control and wisdom which the Stoics regarded as the mark of a good man. His earlier adventures and mistakes have not been in vain. For they have made him surer of himself and more confident of the divine destiny which leads him.

10   The Stoic ideas which inform Virgil's conception of Aeneas' ordeal and development persist to some degree in the later books of the *Aeneid,* but with a different purpose. Aeneas is the just and wise prince, and he must not act unjustly, particularly in such important matters as peace and war, about which the Augustan age had been taught by bitter experience to hold strong views. Aeneas is very like an invader, and he lives in a heroic past, but he must not be allowed to make war as Homer's heroes make it, simply to indulge his own desire for glory. For this reason Virgil makes Aeneas face war with a con-

sciousness of grave responsibilities and of nice distinctions between moral issues. Just as Cicero says that the only right reason for declaring war is that "life may be lived in peace without wrong," so Virgil is careful to put Aeneas in the right when war is forced upon him by the Latins. Earlier versions of the story said that the Trojans began the attack and were resisted by the Latins; Virgil reverses the situation and makes Aeneas do everything to secure his aims by peaceful negotiations. His envoy makes the most modest demands of King Latinus, and the king is perfectly willing to accede to them. When war is begun by the Latins, Aeneas conducts it in the spirit which Cicero advocates, "that nothing should be sought but peace." Even after the aggression of the Latins, Aeneas tells their envoys, who ask for leave to bury the dead, that he is willing to grant much more than that:

> Peace for the dead and slain in war you ask.
> I'd grant it gladly to the living too.

When the truce is broken, his chief thought is to have it restored. He tries to avert a general slaughter and offers to settle the issue by a single combat between himself and Turnus. He cries out to the excited armies:

> Oh stay your wrath! The pact is made, and all
> The rules are fixt. My right to fight alone!

In this we hear the spirit of the Augustan age as its master proclaimed it when he said that he himself had never made war "without just and necessary reasons" and that he always pardoned his enemies when the general safety allowed. Such an attitude toward war bears no resemblance to anything heroic or Homeric. War had become an evil which may be undertaken only when there is no alternative, and it must be conducted in a spirit of chivalry and clemency.

11   Though Aeneas is built largely on a Stoic plan and conforms in some important respects to the Stoic ideal of the wise man, he is not only this. He has other qualities which lie outside the Stoic purview and are even hostile to it. This is not hard to understand. The Stoic ideal, interesting though it is as an attempt to set a man above his troubles and his failings and to provide him with a feeling of security in a disordered society, failed to conquer mankind because it denied the worth of much that the human heart thinks holy and will not willingly forgo. St. Augustine was not alone in feeling that the Stoics were inhuman in their attempt to suppress all emotions, no matter how reputable. Many other men felt that such an exaltation of reason is wrong insofar as it dries up the natural springs of many excellent actions. Though Virgil used Stoic conceptions for the development of Aeneas' character, his warm-hearted, compassionate temperament was not satisfied with an ordeal so cold and so remote. If Stoicism provides a scheme by which Aeneas is tested and matured, it does not explain much else in him. Aeneas, with all his faults and contradictions, is essentially a creature of emotions. It is true that at first these are the cause of his failures and may be condemned, but Virgil did not believe that his ideal Roman should lack emotions altogether. His confident Aeneas of the latter books is still highly emotional, but his emotions

are now in harmony with his appointed purpose and help in his pursuit of it.

12   The most important of these divagations from the Stoic norm is the part played by pity on the character of Aeneas. For many readers this is the most Virgilian of all qualities, the most typical and most essential feature of the *Aeneid*. When Aeneas sees the episodes of the Trojan War depicted in stone at Carthage, he utters the famous words which have so often been quoted as the centre of Virgil's outlook and message:

> Here praise has its rewards,
> Fortune its tears, and man's fate stirs the heart.

The words do not mean all that is sometimes claimed for them; they are certainly not a declaration that human life is nothing but tears. But they show that Aeneas on arriving in a strange land feels that here too is not only the glory but the pathos of life. In his mind the two are equally important, and such a view is far removed from Stoic detachment. The same quality comes out when Aeneas sees the ghosts of the unburied dead wandering in the underworld and halts his steps:

> With thought and pity for their unjust lot.

He allows his compassion here to assert itself at the expense of a divine ordinance and to criticize the government of the universe. No correct Stoic would dream of doing such a thing, and it shows how strong pity is in Aeneas and what importance Virgil attaches to it. . . .

13   More surprising than Aeneas' outbursts of pity are his outbursts of anger and fury, which continue after he has arrived in Italy and are evidently essential to his mature personality. The Stoics would have disapproved of them without qualification. They defined anger as the desire for revenge and thought it odious because it makes deliberate and considered action impossible. Seneca says that it is the result not of goodness but of weakness, often frivolous or flippant, and that any good it may do in the way of punishment or correction can be better done from a sense of duty. Even Marcus Aurelius, who in many ways resembles Aeneas and seems to embody the ideal Roman in his historical self, condemns anger with majestic austerity. In anger, he says, the soul wrongs itself; it is senseless against wrongdoers because they act unwillingly through ignorance, and it is not a proper function of man. Yet Virgil made anger part of Aeneas' character and a potent force in his warlike doings. It rises at the death of Pallas and takes the form of a violent desire to punish Turnus, though for a time it is exercised at the expense of others like Magus, Tarquitus and Lucagus, who do not share Turnus' responsibility for killing Pallas. In the second part of Book X Aeneas is driven by wild fury against all his opponents. He takes the four sons of Sulmo to be a human sacrifice at Pallas' pyre, and not all the admiration of Donatus — "how great Aeneas' virtue is shown to be, how great his devotion in honouring the memory of the dead" — can make us feel that he is acting humanly or even rationally. When Magus makes a pitiful appeal for mercy, Aeneas refuses with heartless irony and tells him that his death is demanded

by the dead Anchises and the boy Iulus. He throws Tarquitus to the fishes and denies him the decencies of burial with the derisive taunt that his mother will not bury him nor lay his limbs in the ancestral tomb. . . .

14   The combination of such qualities in a single hero demands some explanation. It is sometimes said that in it Virgil modelled Aeneas on Achilles and did not reconcile the obvious discords. It is true that these episodes have their parallels in the furious revenge which Achilles exacts for the death of Patroclus. But if so, Virgil has failed to make his hero convincing or consistent. These outbursts of heroic fury ill suit the exponent of Roman virtues with his strong distaste for war. But another explanation is possible. Virgil liked and admired Augustus, and at the same time knew that Augustus' dominion was based on force. In his youth he had risen to power by a series of violent acts, which he justified as the vengeance for the death of Julius. Legends had gathered round this vengeance and portrayed Augustus as moved by violent and angry feelings. They may not be true, but they were circulated and known and had become part of Augustus' myth. After Philippi Augustus was said to have behaved much as Aeneas behaves after the death of Pallas. Aeneas refuses burial to Tarquitus and tells him that the birds and fishes will lick his wounds; when a dying man asked Augustus for burial, he said that the birds would soon settle that question. Aeneas is so angry that no appeal to the names of his father and his son moves him to spare Lucagus; Augustus is said to have made a father play a game with his sons to decide which should live and then looked on while both were killed. Aeneas sacrifices the sons of Sulmo at Pallas' pyre; Augustus was said to have sacrificed three hundred prisoners of war after Perusia on the Ides of March at the altar of Julius. Whether these tales are true or not, Augustus un-doubtedly took a fierce revenge for the murder of his adopted father, and it is possible that Virgil modelled Aeneas' revenge for Pallas on it. He seems to have felt that there are times when it is right even for a compassionate man like Aeneas to lose control of himself and to be carried away by anger. This anger is thought to be good not only in its results. It helps Aeneas to secure his destiny and to overcome those who resist it. Normally considerate and compassionate, he is slow to anger, but some things so shock him that they awake it, and, when it comes, it is terrible. At the back of his mind Virgil seems to have had a conception of a great man whose natural instincts are all for reason and agreement, but who, when he finds that these are useless, shows how powerful his passions can be. Aeneas, who has to subdue so much of himself, has also at times to subdue his gentler feelings and to allow full liberty to more primitive elements which are normally alien to him.

15   Virgil has put so much into Aeneas that he has hardly made him a living man. But though he lacks human solidity, he is important as an ideal and a symbol. So far from acting for his own pleasure or glory, he does what the gods demand of him. In the performance of this duty he finds little happiness. He would rather at times give up his task, and he envies the Trojans who have settled in Sicily and have no such labours as his. His stay in Carthage shows how easily his natural in-

stincts can conquer his sense of duty, and there is a pathetic sincerity in his words to Dido:

> I seek not Italy by choice.

He takes no pride in his adventures, no satisfaction in their successful conclusion. His whole life is dictated by the gods. They tell him what to do and make him do it, and he obeys in an uncomplaining but certainly not a joyful spirit of acceptance. He is aptly symbolized by Virgil's picture of him shouldering the great shield on which Vulcan has depicted the deeds of his descendants:

> His shoulder bears his grandson's fame and fate.

On Aeneas the whole burden of Rome seems to lie, and it is not surprising that he lacks the instinctive vigour and vitality of Homer's heroes. The new world which Virgil sought to interpret needed men like this, not heroes like Turnus whose individual ambitions lead to destruction. . . .

16   In the *Aeneid* Virgil presented a new ideal of heroism and showed in what fields it could be exercised. The essence of his conception is that a man's *virtus* is shown less in battle and physical danger than in the defeat of his own weaknesses. The chief obstacles which Aeneas finds are in himself, and his greatest victories are when he triumphs over them. Even in battle his highest moments are when he sees past the fury of the fight to some higher end of unity and harmony. Conversely, Dido and Turnus fail because, despite their innate nobility and strength of will, they give in to their passions and desires. Virgil's idea of heroism is quite different from Homer's because it depends much less on physical gifts than on moral strength and is displayed not merely in battle but in many departments of life. Moreover, Homer's heroes never question the worth of the glory which they seek, but Aeneas, hampered by doubts and misgivings, is unsure not only about his glory but about his whole destiny. This uncertainty is one of his greatest trials, and he shows his worth by pursuing his task despite all his doubts about it. His success is all the greater because it is won largely in spite of his own human feelings. In him Virgil displays what man really is, a creature uncertain of his place in the universe and of the goal to which he moves. To the distrustful and uncertain Augustan age this conception came with the urgency of truth, and Virgil's immediate and lasting success was due to his having found an answer to the spiritual needs of his time. In the vision of Rome he presented an ideal strong enough to win the devotion of his contemporaries, and in his belief in sacrifice and suffering he prepared the way across the centuries to those like Marcus Aurelius and St. Augustine who asked that men should live and die for an ideal city greater and more truly universal than Rome. Once Virgil had opened up a new vision of human worth and recast the heroic ideal in a new mould, he set an example which later poets could not but follow. They might not accept his interpretation of human destiny in all its details, but they felt that he had marked out the main lines for epic poetry and that any new heroic ideal must take account of what he said.

Discussion of Theme

1. Why has the word *hero* acquired overtones of derision? Does this mean that we look down on heroic qualities?
2. What is a Stoic? Is there anything to be said in favor of Stoic philosophy? How did Aeneas differ from the Stoics in his behavior?
3. In literature, what is the difference between an anti-hero and any ordinary character?
4. According to Bowra, what was Virgil's purpose in writing the *Aeneid?* What is its fundamental theme?
5. What is *pietas?* Is it still regarded as a heroic virtue today?

Discussion of Rhetoric

1. Look at the last sentence of paragraph 8. Why did Bowra put *obscure* in italics?
2. In paragraph 9, as well as in other portions of the essay, a series of dots (an ellipsis) is used to end a sentence. What does this indicate?
3. In paragraph 2 Bowra says that "such a purpose demanded a new kind of poetry," and in paragraph 3 he refers to "a new kind of heroic poem." How do the two paragraphs differ in focus?
4. In paragraph 10 Bowra refers to "nice" distinctions between moral issues. Look up *nice* in your dictionary. What does it mean in Bowra's sentence? Is this the usual definition of the word?
5. What relation does paragraph 16 have to the rest of the essay, particularly to the opening paragraphs?
6. Select a passage containing several allusions and — by explaining their meaning — show how the passage is enriched.

Writing Assignments

1. Just as Virgil introduced a new sort of hero in the person of Aeneas, modern writers have introduced a new concept in the anti-hero. Give your opinion on why the anti-hero appeared and why he is so popular in films and novels.
2. Respond to Cicero's statement that the only right reason for declaring war is that "life may be lived in peace without wrong."
3. Does Aeneas emerge from Bowra's essay as a real-life human being? Give your reasons for reacting as you do.
4. Bowra lays a good deal of stress on Virgil's imbuing Aeneas with anger. In what ways is anger useful; in what ways harmful? Relate it to your own reactions to anger.

Library Exploration

1. One of the first and funniest of the modern anti-hero novels was *Lucky Jim,* by Kingsley Amis.

2. If you have not read the *Aeneid,* you will find several good trans-
lations available in inexpensive paperback editions. To understand
the ancient Greek's concept of a hero, read the *Illiad* and the
Odyssey, by Homer.

Vocabulary

(1) HEXAMETER   line of verse
containing six metrical feet or
measures

(1) ANNALISTIC   pertaining to
year-by-year report of events

(1) INGENIOUS   clever; inventive

(3) LINEAMENTS   features;
characteristics

(3) IDIOSYNCRASIES   peculiarities or mannerisms

(5) PROWESS   bravery; skill

(5) EPITHET   a word describing
a characteristic quality

(6) ALLEGED   supposed

(6) PARADOXES   inconsis-
tencies

(6) UNFETTERED   unrestrained;
free

(7) DEPLORABLE   regrettable;
unfortunate

(10) CLEMENCY   mercy

(12) DIVAGATIONS   digressions;
wandering away from

(13) ODIOUS   hateful; offensive

A Sioux Indian from South Dakota and the son of an Episcopal missionary, Vine Deloria (1934–) has a Bachelor of Divinity degree from Augustana Lutheran Seminary and a law degree from the University of Colorado. He has served as executive director of the National Congress of American Indians and has worked for the United Scholarship Service.

From the time of Christopher Columbus to the present, the white man has misunderstood the Indian. In this article an articulate spokesman for his people puts to rest some of the erroneous notions cherished by the white man, and interprets the Indian's values and culture.

VINE DELORIA, JR.

Custer Died for Your Sins

1   Indians are like the weather. Everyone knows all about the weather, but none can change it. When storms are predicted, the sun shines. When picnic weather is announced, the rain begins. Likewise, if you count on the unpredictability of Indian people, you will never be sorry.

2   One of the finest things about being an Indian is that people are always interested in you and your "plight." Other groups have difficulties, predicaments, quandaries, problems, or troubles. Traditionally we Indians have had a "plight."

3   Our foremost plight is our transparency. People can tell just by looking at us what we want, what should be done to help us, how we feel, and what a "real" Indian is really like. Indian life, as it relates to the real world, is a continuous attempt not to disappoint people who know us. Unfulfilled expectations cause grief, and we have already had our share.

4   Because people can see right through us, it becomes impossible to tell truth from fiction or fact from mythology. Experts paint us as they would like us to be. Often we paint ourselves as we wish we were or as we might have been.

5   The more we try to be ourselves the more we are forced to defend what we have never been. The American public feels most comfortable with the mythical Indians of stereotype-land who were always THERE. These Indians are fierce, they wear feathers and grunt. Most of us don't fit this idealized figure since we grunt only when overeating, which is seldom.

6   To be an Indian in modern American society is in a very real sense to be unreal and ahistorical. In this book we will discuss the other side—the unrealities that face *us* as Indian people. It is this unreal feeling that has been welling up inside us and threatens to make this decade the most decisive in history for Indian people. In so many ways, Indian people are re-examining themselves in an effort to redefine a new social structure for their people. Tribes are reordering their priorities to account for the obvious discrepancies between their goals and the goals whites have defined for them.

7   Indian reactions are sudden and surprising. One day at a conference we were singing "My Country 'Tis of Thee" and we came across the part that goes:

> *Land where our fathers died*
> *Land of the Pilgrims' pride . . .*

Some of us broke out laughing when we realized that our fathers undoubtedly died trying to keep those Pilgrims from stealing our land. In fact, many of our fathers died because the Pilgrims killed them as witches. We didn't feel much kinship with those Pilgrims, regardless of who they did in.

8   We often hear "give it back to the Indians" when a gadget fails to work. It's a terrible thing for a people to realize that society has set aside all nonworking gadgets for their exclusive use.

9   During my three years as Executive Director of the National Congress of American Indians, it was a rare day when some white didn't visit my office and proudly proclaim that he or she was of Indian descent.

10   Cherokee was the most popular tribe of their choice and many people placed the Cherokees anywhere from Maine to Washington State. Mohawk, Sioux, and Chippewa were next in popularity. Occasionally I would be told about some mythical tribe, from lower Pennsylvania, Virginia, or Massachusetts, which had spawned the white standing before me.

11   At times I became quite defensive about being a Sioux when these white people had a pedigree that was so much more respectable than mine. But eventually I came to understand their need to identify as partially Indian and did not resent them. I would confirm their wildest stories about their Indian ancestry and would add a few tales of my own hoping that they would be able to accept themselves someday and leave us alone.

12   Whites claiming Indian blood generally tend to reinforce mythical beliefs about Indians. All but one person I met who claimed Indian blood claimed it on their grandmother's side. I once did a projection backward and discovered that evidently most tribes were entirely female for the first three hundred years of white occupation. No one, it seemed, wanted to claim a male Indian as a forebear.

13   It doesn't take much insight into racial attitudes to understand the real meaning of the Indian-grandmother complex that plagues certain whites. A male ancestor has too much of the aura of the savage warrior, the unknown primitive, the instinctive animal, to make him a respectable member of the family tree. But a young Indian princess? Ah, there was royalty for the taking. Somehow the white was linked with a noble house of gentility and culture if his grandmother was an Indian princess who ran away with an intrepid pioneer. And royalty has always been an unconscious but all-consuming goal of the European immigrant.

14   The early colonists, accustomed to life under benevolent despots, projected their understanding of the European political structure onto the Indian tribe in trying to explain its political and social structure. European royal houses were closed to ex-convicts and indentured servants, so the colonists made all Indian maidens princesses, then proceeded to climb a social ladder of their own creation. Within the next generation, if the trend continues, a large portion of the American population will eventually be related to Powhattan.

15   While a real Indian grandmother is probably the nicest thing that could happen to a child, why is a remote Indian princess grandmother so necessary for many whites? Is it because they are afraid of being classed as foreigners? Do they need some blood tie with the frontier and its dangers in order to experience what it means to be an American? Or is it an attempt to avoid facing the guilt they bear for the treatment of the Indian?

16   The phenomenon seems to be universal. Only among the Jewish community, which has a long tribal-religious tradition of its own, does the mysterious Indian grandmother, the primeval princess, fail to dominate the family tree. Otherwise, there's not much to be gained by claiming Indian blood or publicly identifying as an Indian. The white believes that there is a great danger the lazy Indian will eventually corrupt God's hard-working people. He is still suspicious that the Indian way of life is dreadfully wrong. There is, in fact, something *un-American* about Indians for most whites.

17   I ran across a classic statement of this attitude one day in a history book which was published shortly after the turn of the century. Often have I wondered how many Senators, Congressmen, and clergymen of the day accepted the attitudes of that book as a basic fact of life in America. In no uncertain terms did the book praise God that the Indian had not yet been able to corrupt North America as he had South America:

It was perhaps fortunate for the future of America that the Indians of the North rejected civilization. Had they accepted it the whites and Indians might have intermarried to some extent as they did in Mexico. That would have given us a population made up in a measure of shiftless half-breeds.

I never dared to show this passage to my white friends who had claimed Indian blood, but I often wondered why they were so energetic if they did have some of the bad seed in them.

18 Those whites who dare not claim Indian blood have an asset of their own. They *understand* Indians.

19 Understanding Indians is not an esoteric art. All it takes is a trip through Arizona or New Mexico, watching a documentary on TV, having known *one* in the service, or having read a popular book on *them.*

20 There appears to be some secret osmosis about Indian people by which they can magically and instantaneously communicate complete knowledge about themselves to these interested whites. Rarely is physical contact required. Anyone and everyone who knows an Indian or who is *interested,* immediately and thoroughly understands them.

21 You can verify this great truth at your next party. Mention Indians and you will find a person who saw some in a gas station in Utah, or who attended the Gallup ceremonial celebration, or whose Uncle Jim hired one to cut logs in Oregon, or whose church had a missionary come to speak last Sunday on the plight of Indians and the mission of the church.

22 There is no subject on earth so easily understood as that of the American Indian. Each summer, work camps disgorge teenagers on various reservations. Within one month's time the youngsters acquire a knowledge of Indians that would astound a college professor.

23 Easy knowledge about Indians is a historical tradition. After Columbus "discovered" America he brought back news of a great new world which he assumed to be India and, therefore, filled with Indians. Almost at once European folklore devised a complete explanation of the Seven Cities of Gold, and other exotic attractions. The absence of elephants apparently did not tip off the explorers that they weren't in India. By the time they realized their mistake, instant knowledge of Indians was a cherished tradition.

24 Missionaries, after learning some of the religious myths of tribes they encountered, solemnly declared that the inhabitants of the new continent were the Ten Lost Tribes of Israel. Indians thus received a religious-historical identity far greater than they wanted or deserved. But it was an impossible identity. Their failure to measure up to Old Testament standards doomed them to a fall from grace and they were soon relegated to the status of a picturesque species of wildlife.

25 Like the deer and the antelope, Indians seemed to play rather than get down to the serious business of piling up treasures upon the earth where thieves break through and steal. Scalping, introduced prior to the French and Indian War by the English,* confirmed the suspicion

*Notice, for example the following proclamation:
Given at the Council Chamber in Boston this third day of November 1755 in the twenty-ninth year of the Reign of our Sovereign Lord George the

Second by the Grace of God of Great Britain, France, and Ireland, King Defender of the Faith.

By His Honour's command
J. Willard, Secry.
God Save the King

Whereas the tribe of Penobscot Indians have repeatedly in a perfidious manner acted contrary to their solemn submission unto his Magesty long since made and frequently renewed.

I have, therefore, at the desire of the House of Representatives . . . thought fit to issue this Proclamation and to declare the Penobscot Tribe of Indians to be enemies, rebels and traitors to his Majesty. . . . And I do hereby require his Majesty's subjects of the Province to embrace all opportunities of pursuing, captivating, killing and destroy-all and every of the aforesaid Indians.

And whereas the General Court of this Province have voted that a bounty . . . be granted and allowed to be paid out of the Province Treasury . . . the premiums of bounty following viz:

For every scalp of a male Indian brought in as evidence of their being killed as aforesaid, forty pounds.

For every scalp of such female Indian or male Indian under the age of twelve years that shall be killed and brought in as evidence of their being killed as aforesaid, twenty pounds.

that Indians were wild animals to be hunted and skinned. Bounties were set and an Indian scalp became more valuable than beaver, otter, marten, and other animal pelts.

26   American blacks had become recognized as a species of human being by amendments to the Constitution shortly after the Civil War. Prior to emancipation they had been counted as three-fifths of a person in determining population for representation in the House of Representatives. Early Civil Rights bills nebulously state that other people shall have the same rights as "white people," indicating there *were* "other people." But Civil Rights bills passed during and after the Civil War systematically excluded Indian people. For a long time an Indian was not presumed capable of initiating an action in a court of law, of owning property, or of giving testimony against whites in court. Nor could an Indian vote or leave his reservation. Indians were America's captive people without any defined rights whatsoever.

27   Then one day the white man discovered that the Indian tribes still owned some 135 million acres of land. To his horror he learned that much of it was very valuable. Some was good grazing land, some was farm land, some mining land, and some covered with timber.

28   Animals could be herded together on a piece of land, but they could not sell it. Therefore it took no time at all to discover that Indians were really people and should have the right to sell their lands. Land was the means of recognizing the Indian as a human being. It was the method whereby land could be stolen legally and not blatantly.

29   Once the Indian was thus acknowledged, it was fairly simple to determine what his goals were. If, thinking went, the Indian was just like the white, he must have the same outlook as the white. So the

future was planned for the Indian people in public and private life. First in order was allotting them reservations so that they could sell their lands. God's foreordained plan to repopulate the continent fit exactly with the goals of the tribes as they were defined by their white friends.

30   It is fortunate that we were never slaves. We gave up land instead of life and labor. Because the Negro labored, he was considered a draft animal. Because the Indian occupied large areas of land, he was considered a wild animal. Had we given up anything else, or had anything else to give up, it is certain that we would have been considered some other thing.

31   Whites have had different attitudes toward the Indians and the blacks since the Republic was founded. Whites have always refused to give nonwhites the respect which they have been found to legally possess. Instead there has always been a contemptuous attitude that although the law says one thing, "we all know better."

32   Thus whites steadfastly refused to allow blacks to enjoy the fruits of full citizenship. They systematically closed schools, churches, stores, restaurants, and public places to blacks or made insulting provisions for them. For one hundred years every program of public and private white America was devoted to the exclusion of the black. It was, perhaps, embarrassing to be rubbing shoulders with one who had not so long before been defined as a field animal.

33   The Indian suffered the reverse treatment. Law after law was passed requiring him to conform to white institutions. Indian children were kidnapped and forced into boarding schools thousands of miles from their homes to learn the white man's ways. Reservations were turned over to different Christian denominations for governing. Reservations were for a long time church operated. Everything possible was done to ensure that Indians were forced into American life. The wild animal was made into a household pet whether or not he wanted to be one.

34   Policies for both black and Indian failed completely. Blacks eventually began the Civil Rights movement. In doing so they assured themselves some rights in white society. Indians continued to withdraw from the overtures of white society and tried to maintain their own communities and activities.

35   Actually both groups had little choice. Blacks, trapped in a world of white symbols, retreated into themselves. And people thought comparable Indian withdrawal unnatural because they expected Indians to behave like whites.

36   The white world of abstract symbols became a nightmare for Indian people. The words of the treaties, clearly stating that Indians should have "free and undisturbed" use of their lands under the protection of the federal government, were cast aside by the whites as if they didn't exist. The Sioux once had a treaty plainly stating that it would take the signatures or marks of three-fourths of the adult males to amend it. Yet through force the government obtained only 10 percent of the required signatures and declared the new agreement valid.

37   Indian solutions to problems which had been defined by the white society were rejected out of hand and obvious solutions discarded when they called for courses of action that were not proper in white society. When Crow Dog assassinated Spotted Tail the matter was solved under traditional Sioux customs. Yet an outraged public, furious because Crow Dog had not been executed, pressured for the Seven Major Crimes Act for the federal government to assume nearly total criminal jurisdiction over the reservations. Thus foreign laws and customs using the basic concepts of justice came to dominate Indian life. If, Indians reasoned, justice is for society's benefit, why isn't our justice accepted? Indians became convinced they were the world's stupidest people.

38   Words and situations never seemed to fit together. Always, it seemed, the white man chose a course of action that did not work. The white man preached that it was good to help the poor, yet he did nothing to assist the poor in his society. Instead he put constant pressure on the Indian people to hoard their worldly goods, and when they failed to accumulate capital but freely gave to the poor, the white man reacted violently.

39   The failure of communication created a void into which poured the white do-gooder, the missionary, the promoter, the scholar, and every conceivable type of person who believed he could help. White society failed to understand the situation because this conglomerate of assistance blurred the real issues beyond recognition.

40   The legend of the Indian was embellished or tarnished according to the need of the intermediates to gain leverage in their struggle to solve problems that never existed outside of their own minds. The classic example, of course, is the old-time missionary box. People were horrified that Indians continued to dress in their traditional garb. Since whites did not wear buckskin and beads, they equated such dress with savagery. So do-gooders in the East held fantastic clothing drives to supply the Indians with civilized clothes. Soon boxes of discarded evening gowns, tuxedos, tennis shoes, and uniforms flooded the reservations. Indians were made to dress in these remnants so they could be civilized. Then, realizing the ridiculous picture presented by the reservation people, neighboring whites made fun of the Indian people for having the presumption to dress like whites.

41   But in the East, whites were making great reputations as "Indian experts," as people who devoted their lives to helping the savages. Whenever Indian land was needed, the whites pictured the tribes as wasteful people who refused to develop their natural resources. Because the Indians did not "use" their lands, argued many land promoters, the lands should be taken away and given to people who knew what to do with them.

42   White society concentrated on the individual Indian to the exclusion of his group, forgetting that any society is merely a composite of individuals. Generalizations by experts universalized "Indianness" to the detriment of unique Indian values. Indians with a common cultural base shared behavior patterns. But they were expected to behave like a similar group of whites and rarely did. Whites, on the other

hand, generally came from a multitude of backgrounds and shared only the need for economic subsistence. There was no way, therefore, to combine white values and Indian behavior into a workable program or intelligible subject of discussion.

43   One of the foremost differences separating white and Indian was simply one of origin. Whites derived predominantly from western Europe. The earliest settlers on the Atlantic seaboard came from England and the low countries. For the most part they shared the common experiences of their peoples and dwelt within the world view which had dominated western Europe for over a millenium.

44   Conversely Indians had always been in the western hemisphere. Life on this continent and views concerning it were not shaped in a post-Roman atmosphere. The entire outlook of the people was one of simplicity and mystery, not scientific or abstract. The western hemisphere produced wisdom, western Europe produced knowledge.

45   Perhaps this distinction seems too simple to mention. It is not. Many is the time I have sat in Congressional hearings and heard the chairman of the committee crow about "our" great Anglo-Saxon heritage of law and order. Looking about the hearing room I saw row after row of full-blood Indians with blank expressions on their faces. As far as they were concerned, Sir Walter Raleigh was a brand of pipe tobacco that you got at the trading post.

46   When we talk about European background, we are talking about feudalism, kings, queens, their divine right to rule their subjects, the Reformation, Christianity, the Magna Charta and all of the events that went to make up European history.

47   American Indians do not share that heritage. They do not look wistfully back across the seas to the old country. The Apache were not at Runymede to make King John sign the Magna Charta. The Cherokee did not create English common law. The Pima had no experience with the rise of capitalism and industrialism. The Blackfeet had no monasteries. No tribe has an emotional, historical, or political relationship to events of another continent and age.

48   Indians have had their own political history which has shaped the outlook of the tribes. There were great confederacies throughout the country before the time of the white invader. The eastern Iroquois formed a strong league because as single tribes they had been weak and powerless against larger tribes. The Deep South was controlled by three confederacies: the Creeks with their town system, the Natchez, and the Powhattan confederation which extended into tidelands Virginia. The Pequots and their cousins the Mohicans controlled the area of Connecticut, Massachusetts, Rhode Island, and Long Island.

49   True democracy was more prevalent among Indian tribes in pre-Columbian days than it has been since. Despotic power was abhorred by tribes that were loose combinations of hunting parties rather than political entities.

50   Conforming their absolute freedom to fit rigid European political forms has been very difficult for most tribes, but on the whole they have managed extremely well. Under the Indian Reorganization Act, Indian people have generally created a modern version of the old tribal political sturcture and yet have been able to develop compre-

hensive reservation programs which compare favorably with governmental structures anywhere.

51   The deep impression made upon American minds by the Indian
struggle against the white man in the last century has made the contemporary Indian somewhat invisible compared with his ancestors.
Today Indians are not conspicuous by their absence from view. Yet
they should be.

52   In *The Other America,* the classic study of poverty by Michael
Harrington, the thesis is developed that the poor are conspicuous by
their invisibility. There is no mention of Indians in the book. A century
ago, Indians would have dominated such a work.

53   Indians are probably invisible because of the tremendous amount
of misinformation about them. Most books about Indians cover some
abstract and esoteric topic of the last century. Contemporary books
are predominantly by whites trying to solve the "Indian problem."
Between the two extremes lives a dynamic people in a social structure
of their own, asking only to be freed from cultural oppression. The
future does not look bright for the attainment of such freedom, because the white does not understand the Indian and the Indian does
not wish to understand the white.

54   Understanding Indians means understanding so-called Indian
Affairs. Indian Affairs, like Gaul, is divided into three parts: the government, the private organizations, and the tribes themselves. Myth-
ological theories about the three sectors are as follows: paternalism
exists in the governmental area, assistance is always available in the
private sector, and the tribes dwell in primitive splendor. All three
myths are false.

55   The government has responsibility for the Indian estate because
of treaty commitments and voluntary assumption of such responsibility. It allegedly cares for Indian lands and resources. Education, health
services, and technical assistance are provided to the major tribes by
the Bureau of Indian Affairs, which is in the Department of the Interior.

56   But the smaller tribes get little or nothing from the Interior Department. Since there are some 315 distinct tribal communities and only
about 30 get any kind of federal services, there is always a Crisis in
Indian Affairs. Interior could solve the problems of 250 small tribes in
one year if it wanted to. It doesn't want to.

57   The name of the game in the government sector is TASK FORCE
REPORT. Every two years some reporter causes a great uproar about
how Indians are treated by the Bureau of Indian Affairs. This, in turn,
causes great consternation among Senators and Congressmen who
have to answer mail from citizens concerned about Indians. So a TASK
FORCE REPORT is demanded on Indian problems.

58   The conclusion of every TASK FORCE REPORT is that Congress is not
appropriating enough money to do an adequate job of helping Indians. Additionally, these reports find that while Indians are making
some progress, the fluctuating policy of Congress is stifling Indian
progress. The reports advise that a consistent policy of self-help with
adequate loan funds for reservation development be initiated.

59   Since Congress is not about to appropriate any more money than

possible for Indian Affairs, the TASK FORCE REPORT is filed away for future reference. Rumor has it that there is a large government building set aside as a storage bin for TASK FORCE REPORTS.

60   This last year saw the results of a number of TASK FORCE REPORTS. In 1960, when the New Frontier burst upon the scene, a TASK FORCE REPORT was prepared. It made the recommendations listed above. In 1966 two additional TASK FORCES went abroad in search of the solution to the "Indian problem." One was a secret Presidential TASK FORCE. One was a semi-secret Interior TASK FORCE. In March of 1968 the President asked for a 10 percent increase in funds for Indian programs and after eight years of Democratic rule, a TASK FORCE recommendation was actually carried out.

61   Government agencies always believe that their TASK FORCES are secret. They believe that anonymous experts can ferret out the esoteric answers to an otherwise insoluble problem. Hence they generally keep secret the names of people serving on their TASK FORCES until after the report is issued. Only they make one mistake. They always have the same people on the TASK FORCE. So when Indians learn there is a TASK FORCE abroad they automatically know who are on it and what they are thinking.

62   Paternalism is always a favorite subject of the TASK FORCES. They make it one of the basic statements of their preambles. It has therefore become an accepted tenet that paternalism dominates government-Indian relationships.

63   Congress always wants to do away with paternalism. So it has a policy designed to do away with Indians. If there are no Indians, there cannot be any paternalism.

64   But governmental paternalism is not a very serious problem. If an employee of the Bureau of Indian Affairs gives any tribe any static, the problem is quickly resolved. The tribal chairman gets on the next plane to Washington. The next morning he walks into the Secretary of the Interior's office and raises hell. Soon a number of bureaucrats are working on the problem. The tribal chairman has a good dinner, goes to a movie, and takes the late plane back to his reservation. Paternalism by field men is not very popular in the Department of the Interior in Washington. Consequently, there is very little paternalism in the governmental sector if the tribe knows what it is doing. And most tribes know what they are doing.

65   In the private sector, however, paternalism is a fact of life. Nay, it is the standard operating procedure. Churches, white interest organizations, universities, and private firms come out to the reservations asking only to be of service IN THEIR OWN INIMITABLE WAY. No one asks them to come out. It is very difficult, therefore, to get them to leave.

66   Because no chairman has the time to fly into New York weekly and ask the national churches to stop the paternalistic programs of their missionaries, the field is ripe for paternalism. Most of them are not doing much anyway.

67   But, people in the private area are working very hard to keep Indians happy. When Indians get unhappy they begin to think about

kicking out the white do-gooders, paternalism or not. And if the private organizations were kicked out of a reservation, where would they work? What would they claim as their accomplishments at fund-raising time?

68   Churches, for example, invest great amounts to train white men for Indian missions. If there were ever too great a number of Indian missionaries, Indians might think they should have their own churches. Then there would be no opportunity to convert the pagans. Where, then, would clergy misfits go if not to Indian missions?

69   So paternalism is very sophisticated in the private sector. It is disguised by a board of "Indian advisors," selected from among the Indians themselves on the reservation. These "advisors" are put to use to make it appear as if all is well. Pronouncements by Indian advisory boards generally commend the private organization for its work. They ask it to do even more work, for only in that way, they declare, can justice be done to their people.

70   To hear some people talk, Indians are simultaneously rich from oil royalties and poor as church mice. To hear others, Indians have none of the pleasures of the mainstream, like riots, air pollution, snipers, ulcers, and traffic. Consequently, they class Indians among the "underprivileged" in our society.

71   Primitive purity is sometimes attributed to tribes. Some tribes keep their rituals and others don't. The best characterization of tribes is that they stubbornly hold on to what they feel is important to them and discard what they feel is irrelevant to their current needs. Traditions die hard and innovation comes hard. Indians have survived for thousands of years in all kinds of conditions. They do not fly from fad to fad seeking novelty. That is what makes them Indian.

Discussion of Theme

1. What are some of the common myths about Indians? How would you account for the origin of these myths?
2. In what ways have Indians and blacks been treated differently by the white man? How has this affected life on the reservations?
3. According to Deloria, what special qualities do the Indians possess? Does he regard the Indian as superior to the white man?
4. What is the Indian's primary goal today, according to the author? What has been the white man's goal for the Indian?

Discussion of Rhetoric

1. What is the organizational pattern of this selection? Where does each section begin and end? What is its central thesis?
2. Describe Deloria's tone: for example, is he irate, jesting? What suggests the tone in the article?
3. Deloria often uses bitter humor to mask his thesis. For example, he states, "Other groups have difficulties, predicaments, quandaries,

problems, or troubles. Traditionally we Indians have had a 'plight.'"
Find other instances of this technique.

Writing Assignments

1. Describe the Indian as he has been portrayed in American literature and in the movies, particularly in Westerns.
2. What should be the goal of the Indian: to merge with the white man
and be absorbed into his culture, or to retain the Indian culture and
live in a distinct manner, different from the white man?
3. What are the values of the Indian culture that the white man can
profit from by imitating?
4. What actions should our government take with respect to the
Indian?

Library Exploration

1. If you enjoy reading about American Indians, you might want to
read one of the following books: *Stay Away, Joe,* by Dan Cushman;
Little Big Man, by Thomas Berger; *House Made of Dawn,* by N.
Scott Momaday; and *When the Legends Die,* by Hal Borland.
2. Investigate the role and activities of the Bureau of Indian Affairs.
3. From among the many tribes mentioned by Deloria, select one and
learn what you can about it.

Vocabulary

(2) QUANDARIES   states of uncertainty or doubt
(13) AURA   a distinctive air or
character
(14) BENEVOLENT   kind
(14) DESPOT   tyrant or oppressor
(16) PRIMEVAL   original; associated with the first stages

(40) EQUATED   regarded as
equivalent
(61) ESOTERIC   understood by
or meant for only a select
few

William Faulkner (1897–1962), generally regarded as one of this country's great novelists, created a classic saga of the fictional Yoknapatawpha county of northern Mississippi with its now famous characters and customs. Among his novels are "The Sound and the Fury" (1929), "Absalom! Absalom!" (1936), "The Hamlet" (1940), and "The Mansion" (1959). He received the Nobel Prize in Literature in 1950.

Faulkner wrote this statement in 1956, one of the very few times he ever commented on public problems. In this article, which was not well received at the time, Faulkner says that he is against compulsory segregation as well as compulsory integration. His advice to both Northerners and Southerners is to go slow.

WILLIAM FAULKNER

Letter to the North

1 My family has lived for generations in one small section of north Mississippi. My great-grandfather held slaves and went to Virginia in command of a Mississippi infantry regiment in 1861. I state this simply as credentials for the sincerity and factualness of what I will try to say.

2 From the beginning of this present phase of the race problem in the South, I have been on record as opposing the forces in my native country which would keep the condition out of which the present evil and trouble has grown. Now I must go on record as opposing the forces outside the South which would use legal or police compulsion to eradicate the evil overnight. I was against compulsory segregation. I am

just as strongly against compulsory integration. Firstly of course from principle. Secondly because I don't believe compulsion will work.

3   There are more Southerners than I who believe as I do and have taken the same stand I have taken, at the same price of contumely and insult and threat from other Southerners which we foresaw and were willing to accept because we believed we were helping our native land which we love, to accept a new condition which it must accept whether it wants to or not. That is, by still being Southerners, yet not being a part of the general majority Southern point of view; by being present yet detached, committed and attainted neither by Citizens' Council nor NAACP; by being in the middle, being in a position to say to any incipient irrevocability: "Wait, wait now, stop and consider first."

4   But where will we go, if that middle becomes untenable? If we have to vacate it in order to keep from being trampled? Apart from the legal aspect, apart even from the simple incontrovertible immorality of discrimination by race, there was another simply human quantity which drew us to the Negro's side: the simple human instinct to champion the underdog.

5   But if we, the (comparative) handful of Southerners I have tried to postulate, are compelled by the simple threat of being trampled if we don't get out of the way, to vacate that middle where we could have worked to help the Negro improve his condition — compelled to move for the reason that no middle any longer exists — we will have to make a new choice. And this time the underdog will not be the Negro, since he, the Negro, will now be a segment of the topdog, and so the underdog will be that white embattled minority who are our blood and kin. These non-Southern forces will now say, "Go then. We don't want you because we won't need you again." My reply to that is, "Are you sure you won't?"

6   So I would say to the NAACP and all the organizations who would compel immediate and unconditional integration: "Go slow now. Stop now for a time, a moment. You have the power now; you can afford to withhold for a moment the use of it as a force. You have done a good job, you have jolted your opponent off-balance and he is now vulnerable. But stop there for a moment; don't give him the advantage of a chance to cloud the issue by that purely automatic sentimental appeal to that same universal human instinct for automatic sympathy for the underdog simply because he is under."

7   And I would say this too. The rest of the United States knows next to nothing about the South. The present idea and picture which they hold of a people decadent and even obsolete through inbreeding and illiteracy — the inbreeding a result of the illiteracy and the isolation — as to be a kind of species of juvenile delinquents with a folklore of blood and violence, yet who, like juvenile delinquents, can be controlled by firmness once they are brought to believe that the police mean business, is as baseless and illusory as that one a generation ago of (oh yes, we subscribed to it too) columned porticoes and magnolias. The rest of the United States assumes that this condition in the South is so simple and so uncomplex that it can be changed tomorrow

by the simple will of the national majority backed by legal edict. In fact, the North does not even recognize what it has seen in its own newspapers.

8   I have at hand an editorial from the New York *Times* of February 10th on the rioting at the University of Alabama because of the admission of Miss Lucy, a Negro. The editorial said: "This is the first time that force and violence have become part of the question." That is not correct. To all Southerners, no matter which side of the question of racial equality they supported, the first implication, and — to the Southerner — even promise, of force and violence was the Supreme Court decision itself. After that, by any standards at all and following as inevitably as night and day, was the case of the three white teenagers, members of a field trip group from a Mississippi high school (and, as teen-agers do, probably wearing the bright parti-colored blazers or jackets blazoned across the back with the name of the school) who were stabbed in passing on a Washington street by Negroes they had never seen before and who apparently had never seen them before either; and that of the Till boy and the two Mississippi juries which freed the defendants from both charges; and of the Mississippi garage attendant killed by a white man because, according to the white man, the Negro filled the tank of the white man's car full of gasoline when all the white man wanted was two dollars' worth.

9   This problem is far beyond a mere legal one. It is even far beyond the moral one it is and still was a hundred years ago in 1860, when many Southerners, including Robert Lee, recognized it as a moral one at the very instant when they in turn elected to champion the underdog because that underdog was blood and kin and home. The Northerner is not even aware yet of what that war really proved. He assumes that it merely proved to the Southerner that he was wrong. It didn't do that because the Southerner already knew he was wrong and accepted that gambit even when he knew it was the fatal one. What the war should have done, but failed to do, was to prove to the North that the South will go to any length, even that fatal and already doomed one, before it will accept alteration of its racial condition by mere force of law or economic threat.

10   Since I went on record as being opposed to compulsory racial inequality, I have received many letters. A few of them approved. But most of them were in opposition. And a few of these were from Southern Negroes, the only difference being that they were polite and courteous instead of being threats and insults, saying in effect: "Please, Mr. Faulkner, stop talking and be quiet. You are a good man and you think you are helping us. But you are not helping us. You are doing us harm. You are playing into the hands of the NAACP so that they are using you to make trouble for our race that we don't want. Please hush, you look after your white folks' trouble and let us take care of ours." This one in particular was a long one, from a woman who was writing for and in the name of the pastor and the entire congregation of her church. It went on to say that the Till boy got exactly what he asked for, coming down there with his Chicago ideas, and that all his mother wanted was to make money out of the role of her

bereavement. Which sounds exactly like the white people in the South who justified and even defended the crime by declining to find that it was one.

11   We have had many violent inexcusable personal crimes of race against race in the South, but since 1919 the major examples of communal race tension have been more prevalent in the North, like the Negro family who were refused acceptance in the white residential district in Chicago, and the Korean-American who suffered for the same reason in Anaheim, California. Maybe it is because our solidarity is not racial, but instead is the majority of white segregationist plus the Negro minority like my correspondent above, who prefer peace to equality. But suppose the line of demarcation should become one of the race; the white minority like myself compelled to join the white segregation majority no matter how much we oppose the principle of inequality; the Negro minority who want peace compelled to join the Negro majority who advocate force, no matter how much that minority wanted only peace?

12   So the Northerner, the liberal, does not know the South. He can't know it from his distance. He assumes that he is dealing with a simple legal theory and a simple moral idea. He is not. He is dealing with a fact: the fact of an emotional condition of such fierce unanimity as to scorn the fact that it is a minority and which will go to any length and against any odds at this moment to justify and, if necessary, defend that condition and its right to it.

13   So I would say to all the organizations and groups which would force integration on the South by legal process: "Stop now for a moment. You have shown the Southerner what you can do and what you will do if necessary; give him a space in which to get his breath and assimilate that knowledge; to look about and see that (1) Nobody is going to force integration on him from the outside; (2) That he himself faces an obsolescence in his own land which only he can cure; a moral condition which not only must be cured but a physical condition which has got to be cured if he, the white Southerner, is to have any peace, is not to be faced with another legal process or maneuver every year, year after year, for the rest of his life."

Discussion of Theme

1. Does Faulkner claim to be against integration, or only forced integration? Are all southern whites opposed to integration?
2. Faulkner says that segregation is based on "an emotional condition," and that for this reason it cannot be dealt with on the basis of laws or morals. How else could emotional bias be dealt with? Does violence work?
3. Faulkner insists that the South must handle integration in its own way. What is the South's "own way"?
4. Should the black southerner have to choose — as Faulkner implies — between peace and equality? Or could he have both?

5. Do Faulkner's credentials make him an authority on solutions to race-relations problems?
6. Faulkner concedes the moral wrongness of the southern position, but does he show any specific evidence of change?

Discussion of Rhetoric

1. Find examples of rationalization in Faulkner's letter.
2. Faulkner's literary style is characterized by frequent use of long rambling sentences. Locate some in the letter. Do they make for effective contrast with shorter sentences?
3. Faulkner probably did not believe that he had a patronizing attitude toward blacks. What passages in his letter reveal this attitude?
4. Is Faulkner's purpose in listing his credentials in paragraph 1 merely to inform, or is it to serve a more personal reason?
5. Does Faulkner make effective use of examples? Explain.
6. Why does the author use the word *but* to begin paragraphs 4 and 5?

Writing Assignments

1. Write a paper attacking some commonly accepted myths about black people.
2. Analyze the South's spoken and unspoken reasons for opposing racial integration.
3. Have television and newspapers presented a distorted picture of the South? Describe the South as you know it (whether you're a northerner or a southerner).
4. Give your opinion of the oft-repeated statement: "The southern Negro doesn't want integration any more than the white man does! He's happier sticking with his own people!"
5. Is busing a good way to achieve racial balance in schools?
6. Has the South made significant progress toward integration since 1956, the date of Faulkner's letter? Give your opinion.

Library Exploration

1. What is the latest Supreme Court decision on the legality of school districts' busing children to school?
2. *Native Son*, by Richard Wright.
3. *The Blacks*, by Jean Genêt.
4. *Blues for Mister Charley*, by James Baldwin.
5. Chapter 7 of James Baldwin's *Nobody Knows My Name* (1961) is an answer to Faulkner. You might be interested in a famous black writer's reaction to Faulkner.
6. Read some reviews of Faulkner's books and see how the critics treat his attitude toward integration.

Vocabulary

(2) ERADICATE   pull up by the roots; destroy completely

(3) CONTUMELY   abuse; rudeness

(3) INCIPIENT   beginning

(4) UNTENABLE   impossible to maintain; indefensible

(4) INCONTROVERTIBLE   undeniable

(5) POSTULATE   give as a premise for reasoning

(6) VULNERABLE   open to injury, attack, or assault

(7) DECADENT   in a state of decay

(7) ILLUSORY   unreal

(7) PORTICOES   colonnades

(7) EDICT   official pronouncement

(8) INEVITABLY   unavoidably

(8) BLAZONED   exhibited conspicuously

(9) GAMBIT   maneuver for advantage

(11) DEMARCATION   separation

(12) UNANIMITY   complete agreement

(13) ASSIMILATE   take in; absorb

(13) OBSOLESCENCE   the process of going out of style or use

Born in Omaha, Nebraska, Malcolm (1925–65) took the name Al Hajj Malik Shabazz when he joined the Black Muslims. His strong views on black separatism became more moderate after a pilgrimage to Mecca in 1964. A year later he was shot to death by a discontented follower while speaking at a rally in New York City.

This article, delivered as a speech before a group of his followers, is a call for independence—a demand that the American Negro cease his reliance on the white politician and determine his own end through political action. The alternative, Malcolm suggests, is violence.

MALCOLM X

The Ballot or the Bullet

1   Mr. Moderator, Brother Lomax, brothers and sisters, friends and enemies: I just can't believe everyone in here is a friend and I don't want to leave anybody out. The question tonight, as I understand it, is "The Negro Revolt, and Where Do We Go From Here?" or "What Next?" In my little humble way of understanding it, it points toward either the ballot or the bullet.

2   Before we try and explain what is meant by the ballot or the bullet, I would like to clarify something concerning myself. I'm still a Muslim, my religion is still Islam. That's my personal belief. Just as Adam Clayton Powell is a Christian minister who heads the Abyssinian Baptist Church in New York, but at the same time takes part in the political struggles to try and bring about rights to the black people in the country; and Dr. Martin Luther King is a Christian minister down in Atlanta, Georgia, who heads another organization fighting for the civil rights of black people in this country; and Rev. Galamison, I

guess you've heard of him, is another Christian minister in New York who has been deeply involved in the school boycotts to eliminate segregated education; well, I myself am a minister, not a Christian minister, but a Muslim minister; and I believe in action on all fronts by whatever means necessary.

3   Although I'm still a Muslim, I'm not here tonight to discuss my religion. I'm not here to try and change your religion. I'm not here to argue or discuss anything that we differ about, because it's time for us to submerge our differences and realize that it is best for us to first see that we have the same problem, a common problem — a problem that will make you catch hell whether you're a Baptist, or a Methodist, or a Muslim, or a nationalist. Whether you're educated or illiterate, whether you live on the boulevard or in the alley, you're going to catch hell just like I am. We're all in the same boat and we all are going to catch the same hell from the same man. He just happens to be a white man. All of us have suffered here, in this country, political oppression at the hands of the white man, economic exploitation at the hands of the white man, and social degradation at the hands of the white man.

4   Now in speaking like this, it doesn't mean that we're anti-white, but it does mean we're anti-exploitation, we're anti-degradation, we're anti-oppression. And if the white man doesn't want us to be anti-him, let him stop oppressing and exploiting and degrading us. Whether we are Christians or Muslims or nationalists or agnostics or atheists, we must first learn to forget our differences. If we have differences, let us differ in the closet; when we come out in front, let us not have anything to argue about until we get finished arguing with the man. If the late President Kennedy could get together with Khrushchev and exchange some wheat, we certainly have more in common with each other than Kennedy and Khrushchev had with each other.

5   If we don't do something real soon, I think you'll have to agree that we're going to be forced either to use the ballot or the bullet. It's one or the other in 1964. It isn't that time is running out — time has run out! 1964 threatens to be the most explosive year America has ever witnessed. The most explosive year. Why? It's also a political year. It's the year when all of the white politicians will be back in the so-called Negro community jiving you and me for some votes. The year when all of the white political crooks will be right back in your and my community with their false promises, building up our hopes for a letdown, with their trickery and their treachery, with their false promises which they don't intend to keep. As they nourish these dissatisfactions, it can only lead to one thing, an explosion; and now we have the type of black man on the scene in America today — I'm sorry, Brother Lomax — who just doesn't intend to turn the other cheek any longer.

6   Don't let anybody tell you anything about the odds are against you. If they draft you, they send you to Korea and make you face 800 million Chinese. If you can be brave over there, you can be brave right here. These odds aren't as great as those odds. And if you fight here, you will at least know what you're fighting for.

7   I'm not a politician, not even a student of politics; in fact, I'm not a student of much of anything. I'm not a Democrat, I'm not a Republican, and I don't even consider myself an American. If you and I were Americans, there'd be no problem. Those Hunkies that just got off the boat, they're already Americans; Polacks are already Americans; the Italian refugees are already Americans. Everything that came out of Europe, every blue-eyed thing, is already an American. And as long as you and I have been over here, we aren't Americans yet.

8   Well, I am one who doesn't believe in deluding myself. I'm not going to sit at your table and watch you eat, with nothing on my plate, and call myself a diner. Sitting at the table doesn't make you a diner, unless you eat some of what's on that plate. Being here in America doesn't make you an American. Being born here in America doesn't make you an American. Why, if birth made you American, you wouldn't need any legislation, you wouldn't need any amendments to the Constitution, you wouldn't be faced with civil-rights filibustering in Washington, D.C., right now. They don't have to pass civil-rights legislation to make a Polack an American.

9   No, I'm not an American. I'm one of the 22 million black people who are the victims of Americanism. One of the 22 million black people who are the victims of democracy, nothing but disguised hypocrisy. So, I'm not standing here speaking to you as an American, or a patriot, or a flag-saluter, or a flag-waver—no, not I. I'm speaking as a victim of this American system. And I see America through the eyes of the victim. I don't see any American dream; I see an American nightmare.

10   These 22 million victims are waking up. Their eyes are coming open. They're beginning to see what they used to only look at. They're becoming politically mature. They are realizing that there are new political trends from coast to coast. As they see these new political trends, it's possible for them to see that every time there's an election the races are so close that they have to have a recount. They had to recount in Massachusetts to see who was going to be governor, it was so close. It was the same way in Rhode Island, in Minnesota, and in many other parts of the country. And the same with Kennedy and Nixon when they ran for president. It was so close they had to count all over again. Well, what does this mean? It means that when white people are evenly divided, and black people have a bloc of votes of their own, it is left up to them to determine who's going to sit in the White House and who's going to be in the dog house.

11   It was the black man's vote that put the present administration in Washington, D.C. Your vote, your dumb vote, your ignorant vote, your wasted vote put in an administration in Washington, D.C., that has seen fit to pass every kind of legislation imaginable, saving you until last, then filibustering on top of that. And your and my leaders have the audacity to run around clapping their hands and talk about how much progress we're making. And what a good president we have. If he wasn't good in Texas, he sure can't be good in Washington, D.C. Because Texas is a lynch state. It is in the same breath as Mississippi, no different; only they lynch you in Texas with a Texas accent and lynch you in Mississippi with a Mississippi accent. And

these Negro leaders have the audacity to go and have some coffee in the White House with a Texan, a Southern cracker—that's all he is—and then come out and tell you and me that he's going to be better for us because, since he's from the South, he knows how to deal with the Southerners. What kind of logic is that? Let Eastland be president, he's from the South too. He should be better able to deal with them than Johnson.

12   In this present administration they have in the House of Representatives 257 Democrats to only 177 Republicans. They control two-thirds of the House vote. Why can't they pass something that will help you and me? In the Senate, there are 67 senators who are of the Democratic Party. Only 33 of them are Republicans. Why, the Democrats have got the government sewed up, and you're the one who sewed it up for them. And what have they given you for it? Four years in office, and just now getting around to some civil-rights legislation. Just now, after everything else is gone, out of the way, they're going to sit down now and play with you all summer long—the same old giant con game that they call filibuster. All those are in cahoots together. Don't you ever think they're not in cahoots together, for the man that is heading the civil-rights filibuster is a man from Georgia named Richard Russell. When Johnson became president, the first man he asked for when he got back to Washington, D.C., was "Dicky"—that's how tight they are. That's his boy, that's his pal, that's his buddy. But they're playing that old con game. One of them makes believe he's for you, and he's got it fixed where the other one is so tight against you, he never has to keep his promise.

13   So it's time in 1964 to wake up. And when you see them coming up with that kind of conspiracy, let them know your eyes are open. And let them know you got something else that's wide open too. It's got to be the ballot or the bullet. The ballot or the bullet. If you're afraid to use an expression like that, you should get on out of the country, you should get back in the cotton patch, you should get back in the alley. They get all the Negro vote, and after they get it, the Negro gets nothing in return. All they did when they got to Washington was give a few big Negroes big jobs. Those big Negroes didn't need big jobs, they already had jobs. That's camouflage, that's trickery, that's treachery, window-dressing. I'm not trying to knock out the Democrats for the Republicans, we'll get to them in a minute. But it's true—you put the Democrats first and the Democrats put you last.

14   Look at it the way it is. What alibis do they use, since they control Congress and the Senate? What alibi do they use when you and I ask, "Well, when are you going to keep your promise?" They blame the Dixiecrats. What is a Dixiecrat? A Democrat. A Dixiecrat is nothing but a Democrat in disguise. The titular head of the Democrats is also the head of the Dixiecrats, because the Dixiecrats are a part of the Democratic Party. The Democrats have never kicked the Dixiecrats out of the party. The Dixiecrats bolted themselves once, but the Democrats didn't put them out. Imagine, these lowdown Southern segregationists put the Northern Democrats down. But the Northern Democrats have never put the Dixiecrats down. No, look at that thing the way it is. They have got a con game going on, a political con game,

and you and I are in the middle. It's time for you and me to wake up and start looking at it like it is, and trying to understand it like it is; and then we can deal with it like it is.

15   The Dixiecrats in Washington, D.C., control the key committees that run the government. The only reason the Dixiecrats control these committees is because they have seniority. The only reason they have seniority is because they come from states where Negroes can't vote. This is not even a government that's based on democracy. It is not a government that is made up of representatives of the people. Half of the people in the South can't even vote. Eastland is not even supposed to be in Washington. Half of the senators and congressmen who occupy these key positions in Washington, D.C., are there illegally, are there unconstitutionally.

16   I was in Washington, D.C., a week ago Thursday, when they were debating whether or not they should let the bill come onto the floor. And in the back of the room where the Senate meets, there's a huge map of the United States, and on that map it shows the location of Negroes throughout the country. And it shows that the Southern section of the country, the states that are most heavily concentrated with Negroes, are the ones that have senators and congressmen standing up filibustering and doing all other kinds of trickery to keep the Negro from being able to vote. This is pitiful. But it's not pitiful for us any longer; its actually pitiful for the white man, because soon now, as the Negro awakens a little more and sees the vise that he's in, sees the bag that he's in, sees the real game that he's in, then the Negro's going to develop a new tactic.

17   These senators and congressmen actually violate the constitutional amendments that guarantee the people of that particular state or county the right to vote. And the Constitution itself has within it the machinery to expel any representative from a state where the voting rights of the people are violated. You don't even need new legislation. Any person in Congress right now, who is there from a state or a district where the voting rights of the people are violated, that particular person should be expelled from Congress. And when you expel him, you've removed one of the obstacles in the path of any real meaningful legislation in this country. In fact, when you expel them, you don't need new legislation, because they will be replaced by black representatives from counties and districts where the black man is in the majority, not in the minority.

18   If the black man in these Southern states had his full voting rights, the key Dixiecrats in Washington, D.C., which means the key Democrats in Washington, D.C., would lose their seats. The Democratic Party itself would lose its power. It would cease to be powerful as a party. When you see the amount of power that would be lost by the Democratic Party if it were to lose the Dixiecrat wing, or branch, or element, you can see where it's against the interests of the Democrats to give voting rights to Negroes in states where the Democrats have been in complete power and authority ever since the Civil War. You just can't belong to that party without analyzing it.

19   I say again, I'm not anti-Democrat, I'm not anti-Republican, I'm not anti-anything. I'm just questioning their sincerity, and some of

the strategy that they've been using on our people by promising them promises that they don't intend to keep. When you keep the Democrats in power, you're keeping the Dixiecrats in power. I doubt that my good Brother Lomax will deny that. A vote for a Democrat is a vote for a Dixiecrat. That's why, in 1964, it's time for you and me to become more politically mature and realize what the ballot is for; what we're supposed to get when we cast a ballot; and that if we don't cast a ballot, it's going to end up in a situation where we're going to have to cast a bullet. It's either a ballot or a bullet.

20   In the North, they do it a different way. They have a system that's known as gerrymandering, whatever that means. It means when Negroes become too heavily concentrated in a certain area, and begin to gain too much political power, the white man comes along and changes the district lines. You may say, "Why do you keep saying white man?" Because it's the white man who does it. I haven't ever seen any Negro changing any lines. They don't let him get near the line. It's the white man who does this. And usually, it's the white man who grins at you the most, and pats you on the back, and is supposed to be your friend. He may be friendly, but he's not your friend.

21   So, what I'm trying to impress upon you, in essence, is this: You and I in America are faced not with a segregationist conspiracy, we're faced with a government conspiracy. Everyone who's filibustering is a senator—that's the government. Everyone who's finagling in Washington, D.C., is a congressman—that's the government. You don't have anybody putting blocks in your path but people who are a part of the government. The same government that you go abroad to fight for and die for is the government that is in a conspiracy to deprive you of your voting rights, deprive you of your economic opportunities, deprive you of decent housing, deprive you of decent education. You don't need to go to the employer alone, it is the government itself, the government of America, that is responsible for the oppression and exploitation and degradation of black people in this country. And you should drop it in their lap. This government has failed the Negro. This so-called democracy has failed the Negro. And all these white liberals have definitely failed the Negro.

22   So, where do we go from here? First, we need some friends. We need some new allies. The entire civil-rights struggle needs a new interpretation, a broader interpretation. We need to look at this civil-rights thing from another angle—from the inside as well as from the outside. To those of us whose philosophy is black nationalism, the only way you can get involved in the civil-rights struggle is give it a new interpretation. That old interpretation excluded us. It kept us out. So, we're giving a new interpretation to the civil-rights struggle, an interpretation that will enable us to come into it, take part in it. And these handkerchief-heads who have been dillydallying and pussyfooting and compromising—we don't intend to let them pussyfoot and dillydally and compromise any longer.

23   How can you thank a man for giving you what's already yours? How then can you thank him for giving you only part of what's already yours? You haven't even made progress, if what's being given to you, you should have had already. That's not progress. And I love my

Brother Lomax, the way he pointed out we're right back where we were in 1954. We're not even as far up as we were in 1954. We're behind where we were in 1954. There's more segregation now than there was in 1954. There's more racial animosity, more racial hatred, more racial violence today in 1964, than there was in 1954. Where is the progress?

24 And now you're facing a situation where the young Negro's coming up. They don't want to hear that "turn-the-other-cheek" stuff, no. In Jacksonville, those were teenagers, they were throwing Molotov cocktails. Negroes have never done that before. But it shows you there's a new deal coming in. There's new thinking coming in. There's new strategy coming in. It'll be Molotov cocktails this month, hand grenades next month, and something else next month. It'll be ballots, or it'll be bullets. It'll be liberty, or it will be death. The only difference about this kind of death—it'll be reciprocal. You know what is meant by "reciprocal"? That's one of Brother Lomax's words, I stole it from him. I don't usually deal with those big words because I don't usually deal with big people. I deal with small people. I find you can get a whole lot of small people and whip hell out of a whole lot of big people. They haven't got anything to lose, and they've got everything to gain. And they'll let you know in a minute: "It takes two to tango; when I go, you go."

25 The black nationalists, those whose philosophy is black nationalism, in bringing about this new interpretation of the entire meaning of civil rights, look upon it as meaning, as Brother Lomax has pointed out, equality of opportunity. Well, we're justified in seeking civil rights, if it means equality of opportunity, because all we're doing there is trying to collect for our investment. Our mothers and fathers invested sweat and blood. Three hundred and ten years we worked in this country without a dime in return—I mean without a *dime* in return. You let the white man walk around here talking about how rich this country is, but you never stop to think how it got rich so quick. It got rich because you made it rich.

26 You take the people who are in this audience right now. They're poor, we're all poor as individuals. Our weekly salary individually amounts to hardly anything. But if you take the salary of everyone in here collectively it'll fill up a whole lot of baskets. It's a lot of wealth. If you can collect the wages of just these people right here for a year, you'll be rich—richer than rich. When you look at it like that, think how rich Uncle Sam had to become, not with this handful, but millions of black people. Your and my mother and father, who didn't work an eight-hour shift, but worked from "can't see" in the morning until "can't see" at night, and worked for nothing, making the white man rich, making Uncle Sam rich.

27 This is our investment. This is our contribution—our blood. Not only did we give of our free labor, we gave of our blood. Every time he had a call to arms, we were the first ones in uniform. We died on every battlefield the white man had. We have made a greater sacrifice than anybody who's standing up in America today. We have made a greater contribution and have collected less. Civil rights, for those of us whose philosophy is black nationalism, means: "Give it to us now.

Don't wait for next year. Give it to us yesterday, and that's not fast enough."

28   I might stop right here to point out one thing. Whenever you're going after something that belongs to you, anyone who's depriving you of the right to have it is a criminal. Understand that. Whenever you are going after something that is yours, you are within your legal rights to lay claim to it. And anyone who puts forth any effort to deprive you of that which is yours, is breaking the law, is a criminal. And this was pointed out by the Supreme Court decision. It outlawed segregation. Which means segregation is against the law. Which means a segregationist is breaking the law. A segregationist is a criminal. You can't label him as anything other than that. And when you demonstrate against segregation, the law is on your side. The Supreme Court is on your side.

29   Now, who is it that opposes you in carrying out the law? The police department itself. With police dogs and clubs. Whenever you demonstrate against segregation, whether it is segregated education, segregated housing, or anything else, the law is on your side, and anyone who stands in the way is not the law any longer. They are breaking the law, they are not representatives of the law. Any time you demonstrate against segregation and a man has the audacity to put a police dog on you, kill that dog, kill him, I'm telling you, kill that dog. I say it, if they put me in jail tomorrow, kill—that—dog. Then you'll put a stop to it. Now, if these white people in here don't want to see that kind of action, get down and tell the mayor to tell the police department to pull the dogs in. That's all you have to do. If you don't do it, someone else will.

30   If you don't take this kind of stand, your little children will grow up and look at you and think "shame." If you don't take an uncompromising stand—I don't mean go out and get violent; but at the same time you should never be nonviolent unless you run into some nonviolence. I'm nonviolent with those who are nonviolent with me. But when you drop that violence on me, then you've made me go insane, and I'm not responsible for what I do. And that's the way every Negro should get. Any time you know you're within the law, within your legal rights, within your moral rights, in accord with justice, then die for what you believe in. But don't die alone. Let your dying be reciprocal. This is what is meant by equality. What's good for the goose is good for the gander.

31   When we begin to get in this area, we need new friends, we need allies. We need to expand the civil-rights struggle to a higher level— to the level of human rights. Whenever you are in a civil-rights struggle, whether you know it or not, you are confining yourself to the jurisdiction of Uncle Sam. No one from the outside world can speak out in your behalf as long as your struggle is a civil-rights struggle. Civil rights comes within the domestic affairs of this country. All of our African brothers and our Asian brothers and our Latin-American brothers cannot open their mouths and interfere in the domestic affairs of the United States. And as long as it's civil rights, this comes under the jurisdiction of Uncle Sam.

32   But the United Nations has what's known as the charter of human rights, it has a committee that deals in human rights. You may wonder why all of the atrocities that have been committed in Africa and in Hungary and in Asia and in Latin America are brought before the UN, and the Negro problem is never brought before the UN. This is part of the conspiracy. This old, tricky, blue-eyed liberal who is supposed to be your and my friend, supposed to be in our corner, supposed to be subsidizing our struggle, and supposed to be acting in the capacity of an adviser, never tells you anything about human rights. They keep you wrapped up in civil rights. And you spend so much time barking up the civil-rights tree, you don't even know there's a human-rights tree on the same floor.

33   When you expand the civil-rights struggle to the level of human rights, you can then take the case of the black man in this country before the nations in the UN. You can take it before the General Assembly. You can take Uncle Sam before a world court. But the only level you can do it on is the level of human rights. Civil rights keeps you under his restrictions, under his jurisdiction. Civil rights keeps you in his pocket. Civil rights means you're asking Uncle Sam to treat you right. Human rights are something you were born with. Human rights are your God-given rights. Human rights are the rights that are recognized by all nations of this earth. And any time any one violates your human rights, you can take them to the world court. Uncle Sam's hands are dripping with blood, dripping with the blood of the black man in this country. He's the earth's number-one hypocrite. He has the audacity—yes, he has—imagine him posing as the leader of the free world. The free world!—and you over here singing "We Shall Overcome." Expand the civil-rights struggle to the level of human rights, take it into the United Nations, where our African brothers can throw their weight on our side, where our Asian brothers can throw their weight on our side, where our Latin-American brothers can throw their weight on our side, and where 800 million Chinamen are sitting there waiting to throw their weight on our side.

34   Let the world know how bloody his hands are. Let the world know the hypocrisy that's practiced over here. Let it be the ballot or the bullet. Let him know that it must be the ballot or the bullet.

35   When you take your case to Washington, D.C., you're taking it to the criminal who's responsible; it's like running from the wolf to the fox. They're all in cahoots together. They all work political chicanery and make you look like a chump before the eyes of the world. Here you are walking around in America, getting ready to be drafted and sent abroad, like a tin soldier, and when you get over there, people ask you what you are fighting for, and you have to stick your tongue in your cheek. No, take Uncle Sam to court, take him before the world.

36   By ballot I only mean freedom. Don't you know—I disagree with Lomax on this issue—that the ballot is more important than the dollar? Can I prove it? Yes. Look in the UN. There are poor nations in the UN; yet those poor nations can get together with their voting power and keep the rich nations from making a move. They have one nation —one vote, everyone has an equal vote. And when those brothers

from Asia, and Africa and the darker parts of this earth get together, their voting power is sufficient to hold Sam in check. Or Russia in check. Or some other section of the earth in check. So, the ballot is most important.

37   Right now, in this country, if you and I, 22 million African-Americans — that's what we are — Africans who are in America. You're nothing but Africans. Nothing but Africans. In fact, you'd get farther calling yourself African instead of Negro. Africans don't catch hell. You're the only one catching hell. They don't have to pass civil-rights bills for Africans. An African can go anywhere he wants right now. All you've got to do is tie your head up. That's right, go anywhere you want. Just stop being a Negro. Change your name to Hoogagagooba. That'll show you how silly the white man is. You're dealing with a silly man. A friend of mine who's very dark put a turban on his head and went into a restaurant in Atlanta before they called themselves desegregated. He went into a white restaurant, he sat down, they served him, and he said, "What would happen if a Negro came in here?" And there he's sitting, black as night, but because he had his head wrapped up the waitress looked back at him and says, "Why, there wouldn't no nigger dare come in here."

38   So, you're dealing with a man whose bias and prejudice are making him lose his mind, his intelligence, every day. He's frightened. He looks around and sees what's taking place on this earth, and he sees that the pendulum of time is swinging in your direction. The dark people are waking up. They're losing their fear of the white man. No place where he's fighting right now is he winning. Everywhere he's fighting, he's fighting someone your and my complexion. And they're beating him. He can't win any more. He's won his last battle. He failed to win the Korean War. He couldn't win it. He had to sign a truce. That's a loss. Any time Uncle Sam, with all his machinery for warfare, is held to a draw by some rice-eaters, he's lost the battle. He had to sign a truce. America's not supposed to sign a truce. She's supposed to be bad. But she's not bad any more. She's bad as long as she can use her hydrogen bomb, but she can't use hers for fear Russia might use hers. Russia can't use hers, for fear that Sam might use his. So, both of them are weaponless. They can't use the weapon because each's weapon nullifies the other's. So the only place where action can take place is on the ground. And the white man can't win another war fighting on the ground. Those days are over. The black man knows it, the brown man knows it, the red man knows it, and the yellow man knows it. So they engage him in guerrilla warfare. That's not his style. You've got to have heart to be a guerrila warrior, and he hasn't got any heart. I'm telling you now.

39   I just want to give you a little briefing on guerrilla warfare because, before you know it, before you know it — It takes heart to be a guerrilla warrior because you're on your own. In conventional warfare you have tanks and a whole lot of other people with you to back you up, planes over your head and all that kind of stuff. But a guerrilla is on his own. All you have is a rifle, some sneakers and a bowl of rice, and that's all you need — and a lot of heart. The Japanese on some of those islands in the Pacific, when the American soldiers landed, one Japanese

sometimes could hold the whole army off. He'd just wait until the sun went down, and when the sun went down they were all equal. He would take his little blade and slip from bush to bush, and from American to American. The white soldiers couldn't cope with that. Whenever you see a white soldier that fought in the Pacific, he has the shakes, he has a nervous condition, because they scared him to death.

40   The same thing happened to the French up in French Indochina. People who just a few years previously were rice farmers got together and ran the heavily-mechanized French army out of Indochina. You don't need it — modern warfare today won't work. This is the day of the guerrilla. They did the same thing in Algeria. Algerians, who were nothing but Bedouins, took a rifle and sneaked off to the hills, and de Gaulle and all of his highfalutin' war machinery couldn't defeat those guerrillas. Nowhere on this earth does the white man win in a guerrilla warfare. It's not his speed. Just as guerrilla warfare is prevailing in Asia and in parts of Africa and in parts of Latin America, you've got to be mighty naïve, or you've got to play the black man cheap, if you don't think some day he's going to wake up and find that it's got to be the ballot or the bullet.

41   I would like to say, in closing, a few things concerning the Muslim Mosque, Inc., which we established recently in New York City. It's true we're Muslims and our religion is Islam, but we don't mix our religion with our politics and our economics and our social and civil activities — not any more. We keep our religion in our mosque. After our religious services are over, then as Muslims we become involved in political action, economic action, and social and civic action. We become involved with anybody, anywhere, any time, and in any manner that's designed to eliminate the evils, the political, economic, and social evils that are afflicting the people of our community.

42   The political philosophy of black nationalism means that the black man should control the politics and the politicians in his own community; no more. The black man in the black community has to be re-educated into the science of politics so he will know what politics is supposed to bring him in return. Don't be throwing out any ballots. A ballot is like a bullet. You don't throw your ballots until you see a target, and if that target is not within your reach, keep your ballot in your pocket. The political philosophy of black nationalism is being taught in the Christian church. It's being taught in the NAACP. It's being taught in CORE meetings. It's being taught in SNCC [Student Nonviolent Coordinating Committee] meetings. It's being taught in Muslim meetings. It's being taught where nothing but atheists and agnostics come together. It's being taught everywhere. Black people are fed up with the dillydallying, pussyfooting, compromising approach that we've been using toward getting our freedom. We want freedom *now*, but we're not going to get it saying "We Shall Overcome." We've got to fight until we overcome.

43   The economic philosophy of black nationalism is pure and simple. It only means that we should control the economy of our community. Why should white people be running all the stores in our community? Why should white people be running the banks of our community? Why should the economy of our community be in the hands of the

white man? Why? If a black man can't move his store into a white community, you tell me why a white man should move his store into a black community. The philosophy of black nationalism involves a re-education program in the black community in regards to economics. Our people have to be made to see that any time you take your dollar out of your community and spend it in a community where you don't live, the community where you live will get poorer and poorer, and the community where you spend your money will get richer and richer. Then you wonder why where you live is always a ghetto or a slum area. And where you and I are concerned, not only do we lose it when we spend it out of the community, but the white man has got all our stores in the community tied up; so that though we spend it in the community, at sundown the man who runs the store takes it over across town somewhere. He's got us in a vise.

44   So the economic philosophy of black nationalism means in every church, in every civic organization, in every fraternal order, it's time now for our people to become conscious of the importance of controlling the economy of our community. If we own the stores, if we operate the businesses, if we try and establish some industry in our own community, then we're developing to the position where we are creating employment for our own kind. Once you gain control of the economy of your own community, then you don't have to picket and boycott and beg some cracker downtown for a job in his business.

45   The social philosophy of black nationalism only means that we have to get together and remove the evils, the vices, alcoholism, drug addiction, and other evils that are destroying the moral fiber of our community. We ourselves have to lift the level of our community, the standard of our community to a higer level, make our own society beautiful so that we will be satisfied in our own social circles and won't be running around here trying to knock our way into a social circle where we're not wanted.

46   So I say, in spreading a gospel such as black nationalism, it is not designed to make the black man re-evaluate the white man—you know him already—but to make the black man re-evaluate himself. Don't change the white man's mind—you can't change his mind, and that whole thing about appealing to the moral conscience of America —America's conscience is bankrupt. She lost all conscience a long time ago. Uncle Sam has no conscience. They don't know what morals are. They don't try and eliminate an evil because it's evil, or because it's illegal, or because it's immoral; they eliminate it only when it threatens their existence. So you're wasting your time appealing to the moral conscience of a bankrupt man like Uncle Sam. If he had a conscience, he'd straighten this thing out with no more pressure being put upon him. So it is not necessary to change the white man's mind. We have to change our own mind. You can't change his mind about us. We've got to change our own minds about each other. We have to see each other with new eyes. We have to see each other as brothers and sisters. We have to come together with warmth so we can develop unity and harmony that's necessary to get this problem solved ourselves. How can we do this? How can we avoid jealousy? How can we

avoid the suspicion and the divisions that exist in the community? I'll tell you how.

47   I have watched how Billy Graham comes into a city, spreading what he calls the gospel of Christ, which is only white nationalism. That's what he is. Billy Graham is a white nationalist; I'm a black nationalist. But since it's the natural tendency for leaders to be jealous and look upon a powerful figure like Graham with suspicion and envy, how is it possible for him to come into a city and get all the cooperation of the church leaders? Don't think because they're church leaders that they don't have weaknesses that make them envious and jealous — no, everybody's got it. It's not an accident that when they want to choose a cardinal [as Pope] over there in Rome, they get in a closet so you can't hear them cussing and fighting and carrying on.

48   Billy Graham comes in preaching the gospel of Christ, he evangelizes the gospel, he stirs everybody up, but he never tries to start a church. If he came in trying to start a church, all the churches would be against him. So, he just comes in talking about Christ and tells everybody who gets Christ to go to any church where Christ is; and in this way the church cooperates with him. So we're going to take a page from his book.

49   Our gospel is black nationalism. We're not trying to threaten the existence of any organization, but we're spreading the gospel of black nationalism. Anywhere there's a church that is also preaching and practicing the gospel of black nationalism, join that church. If the NAACP is preaching and practicing the gospel of black nationalism, join the NAACP. If CORE is spreading and practicing the gospel of black nationalism, join CORE. Join any organization that has a gospel that's for the uplift of the black man. And when you get into it and see them pussyfooting or compromising, pull out of it because that's not black nationalism. We'll find another one.

50   And in this manner, the organizations will increase in number and in quantity and in quality, and by August, it is then our intention to have a black nationalist convention which will consist of delegates from all over the country who are interested in the political, economic and social philosophy of black nationalism. After these delegates convene, we will hold a seminar, we will hold discussions, we will listen to everyone. We want to hear new ideas and new solutions and new answers. And at that time, if we see fit then to form a black nationalist party, we'll form a black nationalist party. If it's necessary to form a black nationalist army, we'll form a black nationalist army. It'll be the ballot or the bullet. It'll be liberty or it'll be death.

51   It's time for you and me to stop sitting in this country, letting some cracker senators, Northern crackers and Southern crackers, sit there in Washington, D.C., and come to a conclusion in their mind that you and I are supposed to have civil rights. There's no white man going to tell me anything about *my* rights. Brothers and sisters, always remember, if it doesn't take senators and congressmen and presidential proclamations to give freedom to the white man, it is not necessary for legislation or proclamation or Supreme Court decisions to give freedom to the black man. You let that white man know, if this is a

country of freedom, let it be a country of freedom; and if it's not a country of freedom, change it.

52   We will work with anybody, anywhere, at any time, who is genuinely interested in tackling the problem head-on, nonviolently as long as the enemy is nonviolent, but violent when the enemy gets violent. We'll work with you on the voter-registration drive, we'll work with you on rent strikes, we'll work with you on school boycotts—I don't believe in any kind of integration; I'm not even worried about it because I know you're not going to get it anyway; you're not going to get it because you're afraid to die; you've got to be ready to die if you try and force yourself on the white man, because he'll get just as violent as those crackers in Mississippi, right here in Cleveland. But we will still work with you on the school boycotts because we're against a segregated school system. A segregated school system produces children who, when they graduate, graduate with crippled minds. But this does not mean that a school is segregated because it's all black. A segregated school means a school that is controlled by people who have no real interest in it whatsoever.

53   Let me explain what I mean. A segregated district or community is a community in which people live, but outsiders control the politics and the economy of that community. They never refer to the white section as a segregated community. It's the all-Negro section that's a segregated community. Why? The white man controls his own school, his own bank, his own economy, his own politics, his own everything, his own community—but he also controls yours. When you're under someone else's control, you're segregated. They'll always give you the lowest or the worst that there is to offer, but it doesn't mean you're segregated just because you have your own. You've got to *control* your own. Just like the white man has control of his, you need to control yours.

54   You know the best way to get rid of segregation? The white man is more afraid of separation than he is of integration. Segregation means that he puts you away from him, but not far enough for you to be out of his jurisdiction; separation means you're gone. And the white man will integrate faster than he'll let you separate. So we will work with you against the segregated school system because it's criminal, because it is absolutely destructive, in every way imaginable, to the minds of the children who have to be exposed to that type of crippling education.

55   Last but not least, I must say this concerning the great controversy over rifles and shotguns. The only thing that I've ever said is that in areas where the government has proven itself either unwilling or unable to defend the lives and the property of Negroes, it's time for Negroes to defend themselves. Article number two of the constitutional amendments provides you and me the right to own a rifle or a shotgun. It is constitutionally legal to own a shotgun or a rifle. This doesn't mean you're going to get a rifle and form battalions and go out looking for white folks, although you'd be within your rights—I mean, you'd be justified; but that would be illegal and we don't do anything illegal. If the white man doesn't want the black man buying rifles and

shotguns, then let the government do its job. That's all. And don't let the white man come to you and ask you what you think about what Malcolm says — why, you old Uncle Tom. He would never ask you if he thought you were going to say, "Amen!" No, he is making a Tom out of you.

56   So, this doesn't mean forming rifle clubs and going out looking for people, but it is time, in 1964, if you are a man, to let that man know. If he's not going to do his job in running the government and providing you and me with the protection that our taxes are supposed to be for, since he spends all those billions for his defense budget, he certainly can't begrudge you and me spending $12 or $15 for a single-shot, or double-action. I hope you understand. Don't go out shooting people, but any time, brothers and sisters, and especially the men in this audience — some of you wearing Congressional Medals of Honor, with shoulders this wide, chests this big, muscles that big — any time you and I sit around and read where they bomb a church and murder in cold blood, not some grownups, but four little girls while they were praying to the same god the white man taught them to pray to, and you and I see the government go down and can't find who did it.

57   Why, this man — he can find Eichmann hiding down in Argentina somewhere. Let two or three American soldiers, who are minding somebody else's business way over in South Vietnam, get killed, and he'll send battleships, sticking his nose in their business. He wanted to send troops down to Cuba and make them have what he calls free elections — this old cracker who doesn't have free elections in his own country. No, if you never see me another time in your life, if I die in the morning, I'll die saying one thing: the ballot or the bullet, the ballot or the bullet.

58   If a Negro in 1964 has to sit around and wait for some cracker senator to filibuster when it comes to the rights of black people, why, you and I should hang our heads in shame. You talk about a march on Washington in 1963, you haven't seen anything. There's some more going down in '64. And this time they're not going like they went last year. They're not going singing "We Shall Overcome." They're not going with white friends. They're not going with placards already painted for them. They're not going with round-trip tickets. They're going with one-way tickets.

59   And if they don't want that non-nonviolent army going down there, tell them to bring the filibuster to a halt. The black nationalists aren't going to wait. Lyndon B. Johnson is the head of the Democratic Party. If he's for civil rights, let him go into the Senate next week and declare himself. Let him go in there right now and declare himself. Let him go in there and denounce the Southern branch of his party. Let him go in there right now and take a moral stand — right now, not later. Tell him, don't wait until election time. If he waits too long, brothers and sisters, he will be responsible for letting a condition develop in this country which will create a climate that will bring seeds up out of the ground with vegetation on the end of them looking like something these people never dreamed of. In 1964, it's the ballot or the bullet. Thank you.

Discussion of Theme

1. Is this speech really racist—is Malcolm X encouraging anti-white feelings on the part of his listeners?
2. Explain his statement that "being born in America doesn't make you an American." Is he speaking only of blacks? Could his remark apply to other groups?
3. How does racial discrimination in the North differ from that in the South? Which is more harmful?
4. What is it that Malcolm X wants his listeners to do? Is he encouraging them to adopt violence as a tactic?

Discussion of Rhetoric

1. Notice the repetition of the phrase "the ballot or the bullet." Why is it effective? Find several other examples of repetition; explain why they help to convey the author's message.
2. How would you know that this originally was a speech?
3. In several parts of his speech Malcolm uses inflammatory phrases; what is their purpose?
4. What level of language is used throughout this speech? Is it appropriate?

Writing Assignments

1. Define Black Power.
2. Which course of action has been more effective for blacks: violence or peaceful demonstrations? Explain your choice.
3. Should blacks have community control over the schools and police force in those areas where they are in the majority?

Library Exploration

Read other selections from *Malcolm X Speaks.*

Claude Brown (1937–) was born in New York City, and attended Howard University. He is the author of several plays performed by the American Afro-Negro Theater Guild. In 1965 he published the autobiographical novel "Manchild in the Promised Land."

Because the language of soul is unique, not everyone can use it meaningfully. Claude Brown, himself a black, shows the meaning of soul to blacks.

CLAUDE BROWN

The Language of Soul

1   Perhaps the most soulful word in the world is "nigger." Despite its very definite fundamental meaning (the Negro man), and disregarding the deprecatory connotation of the term, "nigger" has a multiplicity of nuances when used by soul people. Dictionaries define the term as being synonymous with Negro, and they generally point out that it is regarded as a vulgar expression. Nevertheless, to those of chitlins-and-neck-bones background the word nigger is neither a synonym for Negro nor an obscene expression.

2   "Nigger" has virtually as many shades of meaning in Colored English as the demonstrative pronoun "that," prior to application to a noun. To some Americans of African ancestry (I avoid using the term Negro whenever feasible, for fear of offending the Brothers X, a pressure group to be reckoned with), nigger seems preferable to Negro and has a unique kind of sentiment attached to it. This is exemplified in the frequent—and perhaps even excessive—usage of the term to denote either fondness or hostility.

3   It is probable that numerous transitional niggers and even established ex-soul brothers can—with pangs of nostalgia—reflect upon a day in the lollipop epoch of lives when an adorable lady named Mama bemoaned her spouse's fastidiousness with the strictly secular utterance: "Lord, how can one nigger be so hard to please?" Others are

likely to recall a time when that drastically lovable colored woman, who was forever wiping our noses and darning our clothing, bellowed in a moment of exasperation: "Nigger, you gonna be the death o' me." And some of the brethren who have had the precarious fortune to be raised up, wised up, thrown up, or simply left alone to get up as best they could, on one of the nation's South Streets or Lenox Avenues, might remember having affectionately referred to a best friend as "My nigger."

4   The vast majority of "back-door Americans" are apt to agree with Webster—a nigger is simply a Negro or black man. But the really profound contemporary thinkers of this distinguished ethnic group—Dick Gregory, Redd Foxx, Moms Mabley, Slappy White, etc.—are likely to differ with Mr. Webster and define nigger as "something else"—a soulful "something else." The major difference between the nigger and the Negro, who have many traits in common, is that the nigger is the more soulful.

5   Certain foods, customs, and artistic expressions are associated almost solely with the nigger: collard greens, neck bones, hog maws, black-eyed peas, pigs' feet, etc. A nigger has no desire to conceal or disavow any of these favorite dishes or restrain other behavioral practices such as bobbing his head, patting his feet to funky jazz, and shouting and jumping in church. This is not to be construed that all niggers eat chitlins and shout in church, nor that only niggers eat the aforementioned dishes and exhibit this type of behavior. It is to say, however, that the soulful usage of the term nigger implies all of the foregoing and considerably more.

6   The Language of Soul—or, as it might also be called, Spoken Soul or Colored English—is simply an honest vocal portrayal of black America. The roots of it are more than three hundred years old.

7   Before the Civil War there were numerous restrictions placed on the speech of slaves. The newly arrived Africans had the problem of learning to speak a new language, but also there were inhibitions placed on the topics of the slaves' conversation by slave masters and overseers. The slaves made up songs to inform one another of, say, the underground railroads' activity. When they sang *Steal Away* they were planning to steal away to the North, not to heaven. Slaves who dared to speak of rebellion or even freedom usually were severely punished. Consequently, Negro slaves were compelled to create a semi-clandestine vernacular in the way that the criminal underworld had historically created words to confound law-enforcement agents. It is said that numerous Negro spirituals were inspired by the hardships of slavery, and that what later became songs were initially moanings and coded cotton-field lyrics. To hear these songs sung today by a talented soul brother or sister or by a group is to be reminded of an historical spiritual bond that cannot be satisfactorily described by the mere spoken word.

8   The American Negro, for virtually all of his history, has constituted a vastly disproportionate number of the country's illiterates. Illiteracy has a way of showing itself in all attempts at vocal expression by the uneducated. With the aid of colloquialisms, malapropisms, battered

and fractured grammar, and a considerable amount of creativity, Colored English, the sound of soul, evolved.

9   The progress has been cyclical. Often terms that have been discarded from the soul people's vocabulary for one reason or another are reaccepted years later, but usually with completely different meaning. In the Thirties and Forties "stuff" was used to mean vagina. In the middle Fifties it was revived and used to refer to heroin. Why certain expressions are thus reactivated is practically an indeterminable question. But it is not difficult to see why certain terms are dropped from the soul language. Whenever a soul term becomes popular with whites it is common practice for the soul folks to relinquish it. The reasoning is that "if white people can use it, it isn't hip enough for me." To many soul brothers there is just no such creature as a genuinely hip white person. And there is nothing more detrimental to anything hip than to have it fall into the square hands of the hopelessly unhip.

10   White Americans wrecked the expression "something else." It was bad enough that they couldn't say "sump'n else," but they weren't even able to get out "somethin' else." They had to go around saying *something else* with perfect or nearly perfect enunciation. The white folks invariably fail to perceive the soul sound in soulful terms. They get hung up in diction and grammar, and when they vocalize the expression it's no longer a soulful thing. In fact, it can be asserted that spoken soul is more of a sound than a language. It generally possesses a pronounced lyrical quality which is frequently incompatible to any music other than that ceaseless and relentlessly driving rhythm that flows from poignantly spent lives. Spoken soul has a way of coming out metered without the intention of the speaker to invoke it. There are specific phonetic traits. To the soulless ear the vast majority of these sounds are dismissed as incorrect usage of the English language and, not infrequently, as speech impediments. To those so blessed as to have had bestowed upon them at birth the lifetime gift of soul, these are the most communicative and meaningful sounds ever to fall upon human ears: the familiar "mah" instead of "my," "gonna" for "going to," "yo" for "your." "Ain't" is pronounced "ain'"; "bread" and "bed," "bray-ud" and "bay-ud"; "baby" is never "bay-bee" but "bay-buh"; Sammy Davis, Jr., is not "Samme" but a kind of "Sam-eh"; the same goes for "Eddeh" Jefferson. No matter how many "man's" you put into your talk, it isn't soulful unless the word has the proper plaintive, nasal "maee-yun."

11   Spoken soul is distinguished from slang primarily by the fact that the former lends itself easily to conventional English, and the latter is diametrically opposed to adaptations within the realm of conventional English. Police (pronounced pō´lice) is a soul term, whereas "The Man" is merely slang for the same thing. Negroes seldom adopt slang terms from the white world and when they do the terms are usually given a different meaning. Such was the case with the term "bag." White racketeers used it in the Thirties to refer to the graft that was paid to the police. For the past five years soul people have used it when referring to a person's vocation, hobby, fancy, etc. And once the

appropriate term is given the treatment (soul vocalization) it becomes soulful.

12   However, borrowings from spoken soul by white men's slang—particularly teen-age slang—are plentiful. Perhaps because soul is probably the most graphic language of modern times, everybody who is excluded from Soulville wants to usurp it, ignoring the formidable fettering to the soul folks that has brought the language about. Consider "uptight," "strung-out," "cop," "boss," "kill 'em," all now widely used outside Soulville. Soul people never question the origin of a slang term; they either dig it and make it a part of their vocabulary or don't and forget it. The expression "uptight," which meant being in financial straits, appeared on the soul scene in the general vicinity of 1953. Junkies were very fond of the word and used it literally to describe what was a perpetual condition with them. The word was pictorial and pointed; therefore it caught on quickly in Soulville across the country. In the early Sixties when "uptight" was on the move, a younger generation of soul people in the black urban communities along the Eastern Seaboard regenerated it with a new meaning: "everything is cool, under control, going my way." At present the term has the former meaning for the older generation and the latter construction for those under thirty years of age.

13   It is difficult to ascertain if the term "strung-out" was coined by junkies or just applied to them and accepted without protest. Like the term "uptight" in its initial interpretation, "strung-out" aptly described the constant plight of the junkie. "Strung-out" had a connotation of hopeless finality about it. "Uptight" implied a temporary situation and lacked the overwhelming despair of "strung-out."

14   The term "cop" (meaning "to get") is an abbreviation of the word "copulation." "Cop," as originally used by soulful teen-agers in the early Fifties, was deciphered to mean sexual coition, nothing more. By 1955 "cop" was being uttered throughout national Soulville as a synonym for the verb "to get," especially in reference to illegal purchases, drugs, pot, hot goods, pistols, etc. ("Man, where can I cop now?") But by 1955 the meaning was all-encompassing. Anything that could be obtained could be "copped."

15   The word "boss," denoting something extraordinarily good or great, was a redefined term that had been popular in Soulville during the Forties and Fifties as a complimentary remark from one soul brother to another. Later it was replaced by several terms such as "groovy," "tough," "beautiful," and, most recently, "out of sight." This last expression is an outgrowth of the former term "way out," the meaning of which was equivocal. "Way out" had an ad hoc hickish ring to it which made it intolerably unsoulful and consequently it was soon replaced by "out of sight," which is also likely to experience a relatively brief period of popular usage. "Out of sight" is better than "way out," but it has some of the same negative, childish taint of its predecessor.

16   The expression, "kill 'em," has neither a violent nor a malicious interpretation. It means "good luck," "give 'em hell," or "I'm pulling for you," and originated in Harlem from six to nine years ago.

17   There are certain classic soul terms which, no matter how often

borrowed, remain in the canon and are reactivated every so often, just as standard jazz tunes are continuously experiencing renaissances. Among the classical expressions are: "solid," "cool," "jive" (generally as a noun), "stuff," "thing," "swing" (or "swinging"), "pimp," "dirt," "freak," "heat," "larceny," "busted," "okee doke," "piece," "sheet" (a jail record), "squat," "square," "stash," "lay," "sting," "mire," "gone," "smooth," "joint," "blow," "play," "shot," and there are many more.

18 Soul language can be heard in practically all communities throughout the country, but for pure, undiluted spoken soul one must go to Soul Street. There are several. Soul is located at Seventh and "T" in Washington, D.C., on One Two Five Street in New York City; on Springfield Avenue in Newark; on South Street in Philadelphia; on Tremont Street in Boston; on Forty-seventh Street in Chicago, on Fillmore in San Francisco, and dozens of similar locations in dozens of other cities.

19 As increasingly more Negroes desert Soulville for honorary membership in the Establishment clique, they experience a metamorphosis, the repercussions of which have a marked influence on the young and impressionable citizens of Soulville. The expatriates of Soulville are often greatly admired by the youth of Soulville, who emulate the behavior of such expatriates as Nancy Wilson, Ella Fitzgerald, Eartha Kitt, Lena Horne, Diahann Carroll, Billy Daniels, or Leslie Uggams. The result—more often than not—is a trend away from spoken soul among the young soul folks. This abandonment of the soul language is facilitated by the fact that more Negro youngsters than ever are acquiring college educations (which, incidentally, is not the best treatment for the continued good health and growth of soul); integration and television, too, are contributing significantly to the gradual demise of spoken soul.

20 Perhaps colleges in America should commence to teach a course in spoken soul. It could be entitled the Vocal History of Black America, or simply Spoken Soul. Undoubtedly there would be no difficulty finding teachers. There are literally thousands of these experts throughout the country whose talents lie idle while they await the call to duty.

21 Meanwhile the picture looks dark for soul. The two extremities in the Negro spectrum—the conservative and the militant—are both trying diligently to relinquish and repudiate whatever vestige they may still possess of soul. The semi-Negro—the soul brother intent on gaining admission to the Establishment even on an honorary basis—is anxiously embracing and assuming conventional English. The other extremity, the Ultra-Blacks, are frantically adopting everything from a Western version of Islam that would shock the Caliph right out of his snugly fitting shintiyan to anything that vaguely hints of that big, beautiful, bountiful black bitch lying in the arms of the Indian and Atlantic Oceans and crowned by the majestic Mediterranean Sea. Whatever the Ultra-Black is after, it's anything but soulful.

Discussion of Theme

1. Describe the conditions that gave rise to Colored English. What did the language have in common with the language of criminals?
2. Brown says that there is a difference between spoken soul and slang. What is it, and what examples does he offer as illustration?
3. What causes black people to drop certain terms from spoken soul? What unique qualities does the language have that make it difficult for outsiders to speak it?
4. Do you consider the article an affront to black people? Why or why not? Does the fact that the author is black help form your opinion? Explain.

Discussion of Rhetoric

1. With what sentence does Brown arouse his readers' interest? How does it do this?
2. What key word does Brown repeat in the first five paragraphs? What is its function?
3. Find the sentence that illustrates a particularly striking use of personification. To what is the author referring in this sentence? Why or in what ways is the sentence effective?
4. From time to time the author uses alliteration for special effect. Where does he do so? In what sentence is it especially noticeable?

Writing Assignments

1. If you are familiar with soul talk, write a critique of the article, using this special language wherever possible.
2. Does your town have a Soul Street? Describe it.
3. Discuss the advantages of using the language of soul.
4. Offer your own definition of "soul."

Library Exploration

1. What was the Underground Railroad? What individuals and groups were particularly active in it?
2. Read a biography of one of the persons—black or white—involved in the Underground Railroad. (Sojourner Truth had a particularly interesting life story.)
3. What was the slave's early relationship to the Christian Church?

Vocabulary

(1) DEPRECATORY expressing disapproval or condemnation

(7) CLANDESTINE concealed, usually for some secret or illicit purpose

(7) VERNACULAR a language or dialect native to a particular region (as opposed to literary, cultured, or foreign language)

(8) COLLOQUIALISMS   informal expressions

(19) EMULATE   try to equal or excel

(21) REPUDIATE   disown; refuse to accept

(21) VESTIGE   trace; remnant

Alan Westin (1929–   ) a native of New York, holds degrees from the University of Florida and Harvard. He is professor of public law and government at Columbia University and is on the board of directors of the American Civil Liberties Union. An expert witness for constitutional rights at Senate hearings on wiretapping, Westin has written books on constitutional law and the Supreme Court.

What should be the proper balance between the citizen's right to privacy and the government's need for information to help it operate in an increasingly complex society? The author of the following essays suggests answers to this problem, which touches each of us.

ALAN F. WESTIN

Privacy

1 Are Americans worried today about invasion of their privacy? If so, just what intrusions do they fear, by whom, and are these worries real or imaginary? In August 1970, Louis Harris and Associates, Inc., a leading public opinion survey organization, published the results of a national poll of American attitudes toward invasion of privacy. The survey asked each respondent whether he felt that people are trying to find out things about him that "are not any of their business." Sixty-two percent of those queried said they did not feel that their privacy was being invaded in this way, 34 percent said that they felt it was, and 4 percent said they were "not sure."

2   One can interpret these findings in two opposite ways. On the one hand, almost two-thirds of those polled reported that they did not feel that they were being subjected to intrusive and prying practices. On the other hand, one in every three persons felt that his privacy was being invaded, and that represents a lot of people in the United States.

3   What kinds of intrusions are one in three Americans worried about? When the Harris poll asked respondents to check off specific viola- tions of privacy that concerned them, part of the list reflected issues of neighborhood and personal life, such as "people looking in your win- dows"; "people overhearing your conversations with other people"; "neighbors who gossip about your family"; "hotel and motel phone operators"; and even "public opinion poll-takers."

4   But the main fears — those which 10 to 19 percent of the respondents identified as their particular worries — were intrusions with a more political and institutional basis, issues that have been primary topics of public debate during the past decade. Specifically, one in every five respondents listed "computers which collect a lot of information about you" and "business which sells you things on credit" as intrusive practices. Other "violations" respondents checked off were "the gov- ernment when it collects tax returns"; "people listening in to your tele- phone conversations"; "the government when it takes a census"; and, finally, "employment interviewing."

5   The Harris poll tends to confirm what much other evidence also suggests: concern over intrusive practices by government agencies and private organizations represents a growing issue in contemporary American political and cultural life. This concern has been heightened by the development of advanced surveillance technology, from micro- miniaturized listening and watching devices and new eye-blink emo- tion-reading sensors to giant computerized data banks. For many Americans, George Orwell's *1984* seems to be rushing in ahead of schedule with its portrait of the ultimate loss of privacy.

6   To sort out facts from nightmare fiction in this area, some basic definitions, concepts, history, and social analysis must be sketched in as background. First, the norms of privacy in any society will be set at three basic levels — political, sociocultural, and personal.

7   At the political level, every society sets a distinctive balance be- tween the private sphere and the public order, based on the political philosophy of the state. In authoritarian societies, where public life is celebrated as the highest good and the fulfillment of man's purpose on earth, the concept of legally or socially protected privacy for the indi- vidual, family, social group, and private association is rejected as he- donistic and immoral. It is also politically dangerous to the regime. Such governments keep extensive records on people to watch for "deviationist" behavior and use a wide range of physical surveillance techniques to watch and listen secretly to elite groups. In contrast, constitutional democracies, with a strong commitment to individualism and freedom of association, regard the private sector as a major force for social progress and morality. The public order, government, is seen as a useful and necessary mechanism for providing services and pro- tection, but one that is expressly barred by bills of rights and other guarantees of civil liberty from interfering with the citizen's private beliefs, associations, and acts, except in extraordinary situations and then only through tightly controlled procedures.

8   This political balance is the framework for a second level of privacy — the sociocultural level. Environmental factors, such as crowded cities, and class factors of wealth and race shape the real opportunities

people have to claim freedom from the observation of others. In this sense, privacy is frequently determined by the individual's power and status. The rich can withdraw from society when they wish; the lower classes cannot.

9   Finally, within the political and sociocultural limits just described there are levels of privacy set by each individual as he seeks an "intrapsychic balance" between his needs for privacy and his needs for disclosure and communication. This balance is generally a function of one's family life, education, and psychological makeup and reflects each individual's particular needs and desires.

10   The extent of personal privacy varies, but there are four degrees that can be identified. Sometimes the individual wants to be completely out of the sight and hearing of anyone else, in solitude; alone, he is in the most relaxed state of privacy. In a second situation the individual seeks the intimacy of his confidants—his family, friends, or trusted associates with whom he chooses to share his ideas and emotions. But there are still some things that he does not want to disclose, whether he is with intimates or in public. Either by personal explanation or by social convention, the individual may indicate that he does not wish certain aspects of himself discussed or noticed, at least at that particular moment. When his claim is respected by those around him, he achieves a third degree of privacy, the state of reserve. Finally, an individual sometimes goes out in public to seek privacy, for by joining groups of people who do not recognize him, he achieves anonymity, being seen but not known. Such relaxation on the street, in bars or movies or in the park constitutes still another dimension of the individual's quest for privacy.

11   In all these states of privacy the individual's needs usually change from time to time. At one moment, he may desperately want to be alone. At another, aloneness can be so frightening that he desperately seeks the companionship either of an intimate friend or of a complete stranger, a one-time acquaintance who will listen to his problems but who will not be encountered again.

12   The fundamental element of choice involved in personal privacy is embodied in every definition of privacy used today in law, social science, or common understanding. With some variation in terminology, these definitions all agree that privacy is the claim of an individual to determine for himself whether and how he will communicate with others—what he will reveal, when, and to whom.

13   The importance of the right to choose, both to the individual's self-development and to the exercise of responsible citizenship, makes the claim to privacy a fundamental part of civil liberty in a constitutional society. Without the power to decide when to remain private, we cannot exercise many other basic freedoms. If we are switched "on" without our knowledge or consent, we have lost our constitutional rights to decide when and with whom we speak, publish, worship, and associate. We have been made glass men.

14   So far, we have stressed the importance of privacy to the individual in a democracy. But every society must also provide for the disclosure of information necessary to the rational conduct of public affairs and must engage in some surveillance of individual and group activity in

order to control illegal or antisocial acts. From the earliest periods of Western society, these disclosure-surveillance functions have been vested in five authorities: the employer-landlord, the church, the heads of other associations to which the individual belongs, local governmental officials, and the national regime. In every historical era, as conflicts for primacy raged between church and state, town and guild, or king and baron, the individual's immunity from unwanted surveillance or disclosure has been a part of these basic power struggles.

15   In fact, looking back over 2,000 years of Western political history, we can identify two basic patterns of privacy and disclosure-surveillance. In the authoritarian tradition — exemplified by Sparta, the Roman Empire, early France, and modern totalitarian regimes — unlimited or very extensive powers to compel disclosure and carry on surveillance have been an essential part of the system. In the libertarian tradition — typified by Periclean Athens, the Roman Republic, the English constitutional state, the American republic, and modern democratic nations — basic limits have been placed on the powers of the authorities to put individuals or groups under surveillance or to compel their disclosure of information considered private or privileged. While the issue of privacy is complicated historically — it has often been enmeshed in rival claims to power by the contesting authorities — it is fair to say that no political system with a reputation for liberty in its time failed to provide important legal and social limits on surveillance by authorities.

16   This is the broad background for the issue of privacy in the 1970's. Until the post–World War II era, American law and social norms provided an effective libertarian balance of privacy. Because the presence of walls and doors provided people with a shelter within which to speak and act in private, American society forbade physical entry into the "constitutional castle" by uninvited private persons or by government officials unless the latter met the requirements of probable cause and specificity in warrants provided for in state and federal constitutions. Because torture and compulsory test oaths were the only ways to penetrate the thoughts and mind of an individual, such practices were forbidden. And because daily life in a mobile, frontier society was beyond the monitoring capacity of record-keepers, the federal government concentrated on forbidding or minimizing the practice of spying, the maintenance of dossiers by police, and the use of internal passport systems that marked the autocratic regimes of royal Europe, to all of which the American republic was fundamentally opposed.

17   In the past two decades, however, a combination of new technology and sociopolitical changes has overturned the classic balance of privacy in the United States. On the technological front, microminiaturized bugs, television monitors, and devices capable of penetrating solid surfaces to listen or photograph have dissolved the physical barriers of walls and doors. Polygraph devices to measure emotional states have been improved as a result of space research, and increased use has been made of personality tests for personnel selection. The development of electronic computers and long-distance communication networks has made it possible to collect, store, and process far

more information about an individual's life and transactions than was practical in the era of typewriter and file cabinet.

18   These dramatic advances in technology — revolutionizing the means of conducting physical, psychological, and data surveillance over the citizenry — were accompanied by equally critical changes in American society. As the industrial economy became more complex and interconnected; as government took on giant programs in social welfare; as the social sciences moved toward behavioral, data-dependent theories of social explanation; and as both criminal and revolutionary groups made use of modern technology, a whole new framework for data collection and use by authorities had to be defined, and a new balance of privacy had to be worked into American law and social practice.

19   Just how this new balance should be set for the 1970's is the heart of the privacy issue today. Whether the specific concern is government power to eavesdrop on conversations, compulsory questions on the decennial census, or computerized data banks, what is really at issue is how to have both effective government and organizational life *and* protected zones of individual and group privacy. If the United States must choose between these equally compelling aspects of civilized social life, the nation will have failed in the art of democracy.

20   With this perspective, we can identify three important suggestions that have been made for setting a new balance of privacy in the electronic age. The first suggestion, a total ban approach, calls for the use of legislation, judicial decisions, and organizational rules to forbid the use of new technological measures which intrude too deeply into personal privacy. A second approach, administrative discretion, favors letting the authorities use new methods under their own regulations and safeguards until a clear case is made that the intervention of law is needed to set standards and control abuses. The third approach calls for a variety of policy responses — bans, regulations, and nonintervention — according to the particular state of the technological art, the need for information collection, the impact on the individuals concerned, and the effect on society as a whole.

21   In my view, neither a total ban or administrative discretion is the answer, since each misunderstands both the nature of sociotechnological development and the essence of constitutional government. Let me illustrate with some current controversies. Why shouldn't we simply outlaw intrusive public opinion polling, electronic eavesdropping, and computerized data banks? The answer lies in a careful assessment of what is really at stake in each situation.

22   As long as the individual is free to refuse to answer private and government opinion surveys, to close the door with a firm "I do not want to reply," it is the height of legalized puritanism to forbid Americans to speak out voluntarily and make their individual wishes, needs, and fears known to leaders of government and private institutions. Indeed, some critical changes in mores and laws have come about as a result of facts learned by such opinion surveys as the Kinsey reports, in which people willingly revealed their intimate sexual behavior. Because what is told to a legitimate opinion surveyor is kept confidential — identities are not revealed and the respondent's disclosure does not

result in his being regulated—total bans on such polling are unwarranted and dangerous. On the other hand, some regulation may well be needed to forbid salesmen from posing as pollsters to push their wares, voluntary government questionnaires from being presented as though responses were legally required, or governmental agencies from violating the confidential nature of survey research data for investigative or regulatory purposes or from selling lists or information to private business firms.

23   The issue of electronic eavesdropping is harder to resolve, since the specter of federal or local law enforcement agents overhearing conversations and building transcript files is not one to reassure citizens of a democratic nation. But the bedrock facts brought out by many legislative hearings and legal studies reveal that there are criminal and revolutionary conspiracies which do engage in violence, theft, and murder and that these groups are shrewd enough so that traditional methods of investigation are inadequate. In an era of rapid communication and mobility, no government in the world refrains from all use of electronic eavesdropping. And if any nation were to enact a total ban, it is almost certain that police working on kidnapping, bombing, and similar cases would use such techniques covertly and that the public would approve.

24   But if total bans are unrealistic, so are counsels for administrative discretion. Law enforcement agencies cannot be left to decide within executive department ranks when to eavesdrop, for how long, and what uses to make of the material they obtain. For this, a constitutional system requires legislative definition of a highly limited set of crimes for which this intrusive technique is to be permitted, judicial procedures to assess the need for eavesdropping in each case, and extensive controls over the process and products of eavesdropping. While this was the basic policy adopted by the federal Omnibus Crime Control and Safe Streets Act of 1968 and by many state legislatures under the guidelines of that act, there are still serious issues arising from that legislation. Broad powers are given the attorney general to eavesdrop without court authorization on organizations that he decides pose a threat to internal security. It was under this provision that wiretaps and bugs were used to get information on new left groups involved in the 1968 demonstrations in Chicago and on such organizations as the Black Panthers. Similarly, under the 1968 federal law, state police powers were broadened to allow electronic eavesdropping in any crime punishable under state law by more than a year's imprisonment; in some states this would allow eavesdropping for such offenses as defacing a cemetery. Either judicial interpretation or legislative amendment of such provisions seems necessary to prevent abuse.

25   A final example involves computerized data banks, one of the two issues with which the Harris poll found one-third of the population to be most concerned. At every level of government today—in city, county, state, and federal agencies—written records are gradually being converted into computer-stored material. The same is true in business, universities, hospitals, churches, and voluntary associations. As such organizations consolidate their records about each client,

patient, parishioner, customer, or member and as it becomes possible to exchange data files among organizations by machine-to-machine communication, the possibility of a complete record on every citizen arises. His educational, medical, military, employment, governmental, and civic activities could be so assembled and circulated that he would confront an "official" portrait of himself everywhere he turned, at critical stage of his life. Not only would this close off escapes from past mistakes or failures and give unprecedented powers to the authorities who compiled and used such dossiers, but it also would raise fundamental issues as to what information should be collected at all, how errors could be caught and subjective evaluations challenged, and how such files could be prevented from suffocating free expression and political dissent.

26   Confronted with these technological possibilities for the future, some critics have called for a total ban, urging that the creation of all such data banks be outlawed. Others say that no public intervention is needed at this time; aware that any total consolidation of information within agencies is unrealistic today and aware that the assembling of life dossiers using data from many organizations is even more remote, they believe that existing regulations about the confidential nature of information are enough to protect rights to privacy or to individual review of file contents.

27   Again, I believe it is the variety of responses that are most effective in dealing with the real social dilemmas. We need extensive information to manage a rational and humane society—to make judgments about individuals, programs, and policies. The computer cannot be stuffed back in the bottle of undiscovered technology, nor should we have to do so to preserve civil liberties. What is needed is a ban by law on any computerized data banks that are so dangerous per se that they should not be allowed (such as a proposal that the California national guard compile a data bank on political protesters). Among other possible responses, we might convene hearings before legislatures and regulatory commissions so that government agencies and interstate organizations may present their plans for computerized systems and demonstrate necessary safeguards before they are allowed to computerize sensitive files containing personal information. Within the computerized systems, we can reexamine existing rules, such as those which pertain to the confidential nature of data, and then formulate rules that are fully responsible to norms of privacy and due process.

28   As these examples of policy choices suggest, what confronts us is the age-old problem of how man uses the tools that nature or science make available to him. If we mean to preserve and update the right of privacy in the electronic age, there are ways to do so intelligently.

29   What may well be the underlying question for the 1970's is whether American society as a whole is able to provide the racial and economic justice and able to provide the paths to world peace which will allow the nation to become unified again, pursuing the goals of a humane democracy. If we move along those paths, we can work out the problems of balancing privacy, disclosure, and surveillance. If we do not, if the internal struggles of American society deepen, then those who oppose the structure of the society will challenge any measures that

would make elected government or private institutions more effective; the claim to privacy will then become open defiance and a withdrawal from organized society. At the same time, authorities facing such challenges are likely to seek greater surveillance powers to cope with the sharpening conflict. What this tells us is that privacy is not an end in itself, for either the individual or society. It is a means for helping to achieve a healthy personality in a healthy social system. As in the time of Athens, Rome, and the early European nation-states, the enjoyment of privacy will, in the United States, depend for its vitality on the state of the nation.

Discussion of Theme

1. What evidence does Westin cite to show that Americans are concerned about the increasing invasion of their privacy? Do you agree with his interpretation of the findings?
2. Is our society moving toward an authoritarian society with respect to the privacy of the individual? If you think so, what evidence can you cite?
3. What technological developments have contributed to the loss of privacy? Sould wiretapping be banned completely? Should it ever be allowed?
4. How much surveillance and investigation are necessary for the government to function properly? Is the collection of information by the government an activity that should be halted?

Discussion of Rhetoric

1. Note the use of questions in the opening paragraph. What is their purpose? How do they help the reader? Why does he repeat one of the questions?
2. Locate several instances of the use of comparison and contrast in this selection.
3. From time to time Westin summarizes the preceding paragraph in a single sentence. Locate several instances of this. Is this a good device?
4. What statistical (or other) evidence does Westin cite to support his thesis? Where is the central idea stated?

Writing Assignments

1. In a theme, present your reactions to one of the following statements:
   If a person doesn't have anything to hide, he shouldn't object to being investigated or having a file kept on him.
   Our national security requires that the government invade its citizens' privacy from time to time.

2. Write a paper using the following title: "A Man's Home Is His Castle."
3. Should the FBI or the local law-enforcement agencies allow agents to impersonate college students on campuses in an effort to control crime? Present your views in a theme.

Library Exploration

1. Learn what you can about the House of Representatives' Committee on Internal Security.
2. What are the landmark Supreme Court decisions on cases involving privacy? What has the tendency of the Court been in recent years with respect to wiretapping and electronic surveillance?

Vocabulary

(7) HEDONISTIC   devoted to pleasure

(7) DEVIATIONIST   in Communist ideology, one who departs from accepted ideas

(16) DOSSIERS   files

John East (1931–) received degrees from Earlham College, the University of Illinois, and the University of Florida. He is professor of political science at East Carolina University.

Why are there so few conservatives teaching on the campuses of American colleges and universities? The author gives reasons for this paucity and suggests remedies.

JOHN P. EAST

Why So Few Conservatives on Campus?

1 Today in American colleges and universities political "liberalism" is the established *Weltanschauung*. This is hardly a new or startling finding, and in fact it is so commonly known that, in the words of the lawyer, we need not "prove" it, we may simply take "judicial notice" that it is so. The noted sociologist Seymour Lipset has written recently, "Intellectuals, academics . . . in the United States tend as a group to be disproportionately on the left. They are either liberal Democrats or supporters of left-wing minor parties."

2 In those academic disciplines where the discussion of politics is central, political science and history, the liberal-left dominance is greater than it is in the whole of academe. In my discipline of political science, and to a lesser extent it is true of history departments, conservatism, either of traditional or libertarian strains, is represented by an exceedingly small group of professors.

3 The most crucial effect of faculty liberalism is upon the students. There are studies indicating that colleges and universities have a liberalizing effect on young people. As Seymour Lipset puts it, "Universities clearly do have a liberalizing effect, so that there is a gradual shift to the left." It is hardly surprising that liberal faculties would produce liberal students.

4   Liberal dominance of the faculties means a shutting out of conservative thought and ideas. Students are likely to know who Arthur Schlesinger, Jr., and John Kenneth Galbraith are, and they are almost certain to know of Che, Fidel, Ho, Malcolm X, Goodman, Sarte, Cleaver and Marcuse. Their teachers have prepared them well. On the other hand ask them about Kirk, Burnham, Voegelin, Strauss, Hazlitt, Tonsar, Molnar, Herberg, Possony, Kinter, or any figure affiliated with contemporary conservative thought, and the likelihood is great they will have never heard of them. At best they may know of Buckley (who doesn't?), but the image they will have of him is usually unfavorable.

CONSERVATIVE THOUGHT MANHANDLED

5 One of the most appalling manhandlings of conservative thought I have encountered of late is the statement by Professor Thomas Greer in his widely used paperback text, "A Brief History of Western Man." Greer informs his student readers, "Drawing upon the political tradition of Edmund Burke, the Fascists asserted that the state is a living entity, transcending the individuals who compose it." One could weep silently at philosophical illiterates who cannot distinguish between Burke and Mussolini, but we must cry out with anguish that they should write our textbooks.

6   A further effect of liberal dominance and the absence of conservative voices on the campus is to frame the discussion of political issues for the students in terms of liberal versus radical. No conservative alternative is offered.

7   A profound effect of faculty liberalism has been, in the words of Russell Kirk, the growth of "Behemoth University" in America with all of its ugly side effects. With liberal faith in mass education the emphasis in higher education has too often been on size rather than quality with the resulting impersonality and IBM syndrome of the modern campus. This has been a contributing factor to student radicalism, for it fosters rootlessness and alienation. Conservative guidance would have stressed quality over quantity, the personal over the impersonal, it would have kept research and teaching in proper balance, and because of this emphasis it is doubtful that anomie and alienation would have blossomed so extensively on the modern campus.

8   Under liberal guidance "Behemoth University" has tended, in its lust for quantity over quality, to emphasize "things," whereas under conservative influence the emphasis would more likely have been on ideas and "the life of the mind." Where the campus liberal has encouraged direct political "action and involvement," the conservative, if present, would have encouraged thought, contemplation and reflection, and he would have resisted the politicizing of the campus for any point of view.

WHY THE IMBALANCE?

9 One is still plagued, however, with the nagging question of why liberal dominance is so utterly disproportionate in academe compared with

American thought and life in general. We have conservatives in journalism, the professions, business, practical politics and throughout American culture generally. Indeed, a broadly defined conservatism may well be the dominant theme of American life. Certainly it is clear that the liberal-left professoriate is hardly representative of "mainstream" America. Why is the imbalance so great and so pronounced?

10   The problem is more fruitfully approached not by concentrating on why liberals move into academic work (why shouldn't they? It is an honorable and challenging profession), but rather by focusing on why conservatives shy away from college and university teaching.

11   To begin with, the graduate schools, which train our future faculties, are overwhelmingly liberal and they attract and reproduce their own kind. This vicious circle is difficult to break. At best the graduate school environment for the conservative is usually a neutral one, and sometimes it can be hostile. Too often liberal academe equates liberalism with intelligence, and conservatism with lack of same. The end result is to discourage conservative students from entering graduate work in such crucial disciplines as political science and history where this formula is more likely to be honored.

12   Furthermore, the academic world is heavily bureaucratized and socialized, and unappealing to the conservative. It may be questionable whether college and university organizations are any more bureaucratized than the modern business corporations, but it is true that they can be highly socialized in terms of economic rewards. The difference between "top" and "bottom" salaries at a given institution is often not great, and salaries overall are held at levels lower than comparable jobs in private industry. If college and university salaries were based upon a "free market," they would increase dramatically, for clearly today a college education is a "service" or "commodity" in great demand. But the libertarian spirit of the free market is anathema to the liberal professoriate, and it would prefer lower salaries to a breach of faith regarding its sacred economic theories. This is not an economic setting sufficiently challenging to many conservatives.

13   Part of the blame for conservative absence on the campus must be placed upon American conservatism itself, which is heavily rooted in the narrow confines of economic conservatism or laissez-faire capitalism, and its growth beyond those roots has been qualitatively but not quantitatively impressive. Many of our most talented conservatives in America have been caught up in either creating or servicing the great industrial-technological revolution that has preoccupied America over the past century. This point was personally brought home to me by a close and brilliant conservative friend who is now a partner in one of America's leading law firms. He was a Phi Beta Kappa undergraduate in history, and graduated first in his law school class. He told me, "I would rather be a third-rate lawyer than a first-rate history professor."

A FRENZIED LIFE STYLE

14 I find my non-teaching conservative friends in their frenzied lives of maintaining and servicing the great American industrial-technological

apparatus (I agree that someone must do it, but why not make the liberals do some of this dirty work?) live almost wholly in a world of "action" in which "the life of the mind" is at best a remote dream. In this regard their life style is not much different from the liberal world where action takes priority over thought, contemplation and reflection. There can even be a subtle anti-intellectualism in which books and "ideas" are considered hallmarks of the effete to the "dynamic" young executive "on the go."

15   In short, too much of American conservatism is an intuitive, narrowly based economic conservatism with at best an additional exposure to popular conservative editorial writers. But when it comes to the cultural conservatives of the stature of Kirk, et al., American conservatives know little. "Getting and spending" exacts a heavy toll. Because it lacks cultural breadth and depth, American conservatism itself is partially to blame for the dearth of conservative teachers on our campuses. Unfortunately to a considerable extent it lacks the intellectual content to nurture potential young teachers.

16   We need to encourage our talented undergraduate conservatives to enter college teaching. Why not? It is an honorable profession, the financial rewards in it have improved significantly in recent years and, above all, opportunity for service to the country and conservative principles in general is unexcelled.

17   Unfortunately there is evidence that some leading conservatives no longer feel the struggle on the campus is worth the effort. Russell Kirk has recently written, ". . . wild horses couldn't drag me back to permanent residence on the typical campus." Similarly, prior to his recent entry into the partisan political arena, former Professor Philip M. Crane wrote, "If there were a genuine hope of reforming the university from within, conservative professors could take the lack of promotions, minimal pay raises, cramped offices, paper work, committee overloads, suppression in the journals, prejudice in the reviews as a small price to pay to achieve the restoration of the academy. But the prospect of internal reform appears remote."

18   Is American conservatism willing to concede the loss of higher education to the liberals and radicals? If so, a great and tragic watershed in the history of this Republic has been passed. The struggle today on our campuses for the minds of the young is spirited and vital. If you will, this is where the action is. If conservatives are willing to concede this crucial battle, I fear they will ultimately lose the war.

Discussion of Theme

1. According to East, why do liberals dominate the faculties of most colleges? Whose fault is it?
2. Is there another reason—besides the fact that the faculty is predominantly liberal—that students become progressively more liberal during their college years.
3. What is Behemoth University? What is it a symbol of?
4. Should more conservatives be hired to offset the dominance of

liberals on college faculties? In this case is the argument for hiring more blacks also valid?

5. What has been your own experience with respect to this subject? Have most of your own instructors been more liberal than conservative in their political views?

Discussion of Rhetoric

1. Would East's article have been strengthened if he had defined "liberal" and "conservative"?
2. The author restates his central question in paragraph 9; where does he answer it? How does he neutralize his answer? Could he have made his argument stronger?
3. The author often uses "loaded" language and words with emotional connotations. Is this fair? Does it strengthen or detract from his argument? Find several examples of this technique.

Writing Assignments

1. Develop the following title into a theme: "Why I Am a Conservative (or Liberal)."
2. If you were in a position to make major changes in higher education, what would you do? Be specific.
3. Define the following term: "The Educated Man."

Library Exploration

1. In paragraph 4 East mentions several conservative writers and thinkers. If you would like to know more about what conservatives think, investigate the writings of one of these men.
2. Seymour Lipset (mentioned in paragraphs 1 and 3) has written two interesting studies of today's student: *Student Politics* and *Students in Revolt.*

Vocabulary

(7) SYNDROME   a group of symptoms that characterize a particular abnormal condition

(7) ANOMIE   a condition marked by disorientation, isolation, and anxiety

(7) ALIENATION   psychological withdrawal or separation

(12) ANATHEMA   a person or thing detested or loathed

(13) LAISSEZ-FAIRE   the theory that government should interfere as little as possible in economic affairs

Lewis M. Magill (1913–), educated at Illinois Wesleyan University and the University of
Illinois, is a professor of English
at Washington State University.
He has served as a member of
the admissions committee at
Washington State, and is the
editor of an edition of Shakespeare's plays.

The value of a college education
can scarcely be overempha-
sized today. Yet it must be remembered, as Magill points out,
that not everyone will be a financial or social failure if he fails
to graduate from college.

LEWIS M. MAGILL

Get Off Johnny's Back!

1 I shall never forget the shock I received when at the age of fifteen
or sixteen I first read *The Way of All Flesh*. Because I had been
raised in the tradition of honoring one's father and one's mother,
exposure to neither Henry Miller nor Mary McCarthy could at that
time have lacerated my sensibilities so roughly as did this paragraph:

> Why should the generations overlap one another at all? Why cannot we
> be buried as eggs in neat little cells with ten or twenty thousand pounds
> each wrapped round us in Bank of England notes, and wake up, as the
> sphex wasp does, to find that its papa and mamma have not only left
> ample provision at its elbow, but have been eaten by sparrows some weeks
> before it began to live consciously on its own account. . . . The ants and the
> bees, who far outnumber men, sting their fathers to death, . . . yet where
> shall we find communities more universally respected?

G. B. Shaw insists that in passages like this, Old Samuel Butler was
symbolically "committing parricide"; yet the older I get and the more
I work with and counsel parents and their children, the less inclined I
become to write off these assertions as purely symbolic.

2   How does a college official answer a young man who, after flunking out of college, writes "My father insisted that if I were to make anything of my life I must major in physics. I had no interest in this field but since my father was paying for my education I felt I should do what he wanted."? Or how answer a mother who, when begging the college to readmit her son, confesses, "We had too much influence with his choice of a major. It wasn't his choosing. He went along only because of an 'I can't let my parents down' attitude."?

3   What does one say to an attractive coed who sits crying in one's office, inarticulately trying to explain that she didn't want to go to college — that she wanted instead to go to business school but that her mother wanted her to join a good sorority? Or how does one even communicate with the sullen son of an M.D. who has no aptitude or desire to become a doctor and who is deliberately flunking himself out of school to spite a martinet father?

4   If the road to perdition is paved with "I-meant-wells," these parents have at least spread the rock for the road bed. This is the fugitive thought that flits through the official's mind while he searches for something, *anything*, to say.

5   All these parents, I am sure, are eminently respected citizens of their communities. Their actions have nothing to do with that old cliché of the social scientists to the effect that "there are no delinquent children, only delinquent parents." In fact, I believe that these college students would be more fortunate if their parents had intentionally indulged in certain mild delinquencies, such as refusing to continue to train the child in the way he should go after he reaches seventeen or eighteen.

6   My vantage point, while not unique in major universities, gives me an unusually complete view of many parents' relationships with their college-age children. Although I know through many conversations that some of my experiences are duplicated by admissions officers of state colleges and universities, I have the double advantage of sitting as a member of an Admissions Committee and at the same time chairing a seventeen-member committee of faculty members that handles all requests made by academic delinquents for reinstatement at Washington State University.

7   As the front man for the Committee, I meet with and talk or write to parents and students in similar situations every day in the year. I have communicated with hundreds of them. In general, a number of parents err in two directions.

8   First, some insist that come flood, fire, devastation, or death their children must become college graduates; and second, they and others are just as sure they know exactly the course of study Johnny or Susie should pursue, despite the best efforts of high school counselors, college counseling centers, and their own common sense.

9   The first of these errors generally stems from the publicity given to the nonsensical supposition that a youngster will be a financial failure or a social failure or both if he fails to graduate from college. I am not at this point quarreling with statistics compiled by social scientists to establish the lifetime earnings of college-bred men or of the husbands

trapped by college-bred women; nor do I have any serious objection to those solemn studies, beloved by some sociologists, that compile and tabulate the prestige value of occupations. The unfortunate truth is, however, that many parents, like their children, do not read carefully — especially when the stories appear in Sunday supplements on sleepy Sunday mornings. And saddest of all, many of these parents are themselves certified as educated.

10   Anyone who reads carefully knows that not a single reputable educator believes or asserts that *all* high school seniors should eventually graduate from a four-year college. The prime interest of conscientious educators lies in trying to make as sure as humanly possible that every student who can profit from a college education receives the opportunity to do so. Their exhortations have, however, lodged themselves in the minds of a considerable segment of the American public as a blanket endorsement of an A.B. for everyone. Naturally, public institutions are the particular target of this group of parents. "We pay taxes, don't we?"

11   Most administrators are willing, if not overly anxious, to put up with such nonsense as part of the price of being administrators. If, however, parents were the only people hurt when a student flunks out at state university, their motivations would not require dissection. But in spite of rumors floating around every college campus, most administrators are humane people who hate to see people used as sacrificial lambs for parental pride or emotionalism.

12   The boy who is too immature to meet his academic responsibilities and who subconsciously knows that he should go to work for at least a few years, serve his hitch in the armed forces, or even knock around Route 66 for a time is often nagged or cajoled into becoming a reluctant member of the freshman class at a major university. Sometimes he is even convinced through repeated brain washings that he really wants to attend college. He promptly flunks out. Three years later his younger brother may know deep within himself that he cannot meet the competition at the "right school," but he is forced into the same pattern, even though he should attend a trade school or otherwise try his wings in a less rarefied atmosphere.

13   The highly-motivated, conscientious, mature girl who has consistently overachieved in high school and who often can estimate her chances of success at State U. more accurately than a set of doting parents is also far too often asked to immolate herself on the altar of parental standing in the community.

14   Let no one question that the experiences described above are traumatic to the student, as well as detrimental to the best interests of our society. Sometime in the future, I am convinced, the girl who comes into my office crying her heart out will pay a heavy price for her parents' indiscretions. And the future seems as dour for the youngster who steals a car and flees from the campus after failing to meet the challenge of final examinations and who is impelled to say to the arresting officer that he ran away because he cannot face his parents or his parents' friends. I am afraid that all society will suffer with and through both of them.

15   If the parents who commit this kind of error may be termed un-feeling, what is one to call those who commit the second error by insisting that a boy or girl follow a specific course of study, without regard for the youngster's abilities and interests? Every September, thousands of high school seniors are packed off to college to major in a field in which they have not the slightest interest or for which they have not the slightest aptitude. For example, I remember with dis-quiet a freshman's almost unbelievable statement made to me not long ago. I had called him in to suggest that he should seek vocational guidance. His immediate answer was that his parents had sent him to college to become a mechanical engineer and that nothing I or anyone else could say would shake that determination. His mathematics grade and scores in themselves were evidence that he had no real bent for engineering. Thereupon, I asked him what he wanted to do when he graduated.

16   He exclaimed, "Well, I know I don't want to sit at a drafting board all my life. I want to work directly with machinery." When I then asked him what kinds of work mechanical engineers do, he had not the foggiest notion. "But my parents sent me to college to be a mechanical engineer." I had to give up at that point.

17   I recall talking to a young pre-med major just last spring. He had failed both his zoology and his chemistry. After I glanced at his grades, I asked him why he wanted to become a doctor. His unusually frank and disarming answer was simply, "to make money."

18   "Why do you want to make this much money?" was my next question.

19   "My father believes that money is the only reason why a boy should go to college."

20   "Is there another possible reason that a young man might like to become a doctor?" I asked.

21   "None that I can think of!" was his clincher.

22   I give myself credit for keeping my temper and not shouting, "I'd hate to call you in an emergency." But then I was sure as it is humanly possible to be that he would never become a college graduate, much less an M.D.

23   Then there was the coed who could not pass a chemistry course. Yet she was in pre-nursing because her mother is a frustrated nurse. She probably would have done well in business college or perhaps even in an elementary teaching curriculum, so long as she did not have to use chemistry.

24   Because we have a large and rigorous engineering program at W.S.U., I see more pre-engineering students than perhaps any other group. As the young man sits across from me, my invariable first question is simply, "Why do you want to be an engineer?"

25   A tremendous segment of this group of students will answer just as simply, "Because my father told me that engineers make a lot of money."

26   I can still remember how amazed and disgusted at parental pres-sures I became when I first began to counsel students at a state university larger than W.S.U. I was attempting to interpret a profile

to a high school senior who planned to enroll at the university the following September. Although his scores in mathematics and science were very low, the tests showed high interest in music. He intended, however, to become an engineer.

27   I asked a few pointed questions calculated to probe the motives behind his intention. Finally, he blurted out, "My dad teaches engineering on this campus, and he wants me to become an engineer."

28   I excused myself for a moment, found a telephone outside my office, and called his high school band director to discover whether the interest test reflected an aptitude for music. The director assured me that the boy could do excellent work in music school. But when I returned and suggested that perhaps he should consider majoring in music, he seemed so thoroughly brainwashed that he became almost inarticulate.

29   Finally, when he left my office, I added as a parting question, "Do you really want to be an engineer?"

30   He gulped out a muffled, "No."

31   Within an hour I received a telephone call from an indignant *mother*, who asked me what right I had to interfere in family matters. She screamed into the phone for fifteen or twenty minutes and then fairly shrieked, "Well, if it's any satisfaction to you, he's going to major in music."

32   Enduring her shouting was, I felt, a small price to pay for the salvation of a human soul.

33   Any counselor on a college campus can multiply my examples by infinity. And yet for some reason many parents cannot rid themselves of the notion that they can totally direct their children's lives and selfishly seek vicarious satisfaction in launching their children into careers that presumably will bring prestige to the family or that will salve an old frustration.

34   One more point must be made. Most of the parents about whom I have written are not uneducated or illiterate. In fact, professional people are the worst with whom we have to deal. I make no claim to be a sociologist, but I believe sincerely that the more prestigious the occupation, the more unreasonable parents tend to be. Certainly M.D.s are the most stubborn group we encounter in knowing what is *right* for their children. Whether they are subconsciously impressed by the great prestige now attached to being a doctor or whether they are far too used to having their slightest orders carried out and their prescriptions followed to the letter, I have reluctantly come to the conclusion that it is a wise doctor who knows his own child.

35   And those in my profession — college professors — are in some ways almost as bad. Perhaps we get intoxicated by our captive audience, or perhaps we just have faith in the delusion that it is impossible for us to have "dim" children (to use that wonderful British expression). Without attempting to delineate a hierarchy, I would list engineers, dentists, lawyers, officers in the armed forces, and pharmacists as following close behind. The working man, on the other hand, is generally so happy that his children have a chance to go to college that he keeps his hands off, although I can cite some obvious exceptions.

36   I can think of no better way of emphasizing the points I have been trying to make than to quote in full (with some modifications to protect the innocent) a letter I received several years ago.

> To whom it may concern:
> To get to the point. I do not want to be reinstated! Today my mother is mailing the application for re-enrollment and the application for reinstatement. It is none of my doing, because I do not want to return to W.S.U. I would rather attend . . . (here he names a trade-school). There has been a great deal of trouble in our home because of this.
> I do not want my parents to know about this letter, so please do not acknowledge this, or return an answer. Just simply do not reinstate me! Please do what I am asking, as it is very important to me.
> If this letter is disregarded, I will not meet the requirements of reinstatement if I am reinstated. Whether I am qualified to be reinstated or not, I do not know. But, I do know that I do not want to be reinstated!
> I hope I have made myself clear to you.
> If you think that you must return an answer to this letter, please mail your answer to . . . (an address other than the one on the application).
> I hope you will please do as I ask. I do not want my parents to know about this letter to you. It is very important to all concerned.
> Please, please do as I ask you.
>
> Thank you.

37   We obliged the young man. Does anyone want to emulate the sphex wasp?

Discussion of Theme

1. Do too many people settle on a career prematurely, with the result that, after working for several years, they discover that they would have been happier in a different field?
2. The author says that he wouldn't like to be treated by a doctor who had gone into medicine chiefly to make money. Are there a great many doctors—or, for that matter, lawyers, engineers, and others—who go into a field almost solely to make money? Is this as good a reason as any for choosing one's lifework? What should motivate people in choosing a profession?
3. Should young people work or, as Magill says, "knock around" for a year or two before enrolling in college? In what ways might such experiences help them later on in college?
4. Is there any room for the idea that "father knows best" in answer to Magill's argument?
5. In paragraph 14 Magill refers to a girl who "will pay a heavy price for her parents' indiscretions." What does he mean?

Discussion of Rhetoric

1. Is the article addressed to parents, young people, or both?

2. In what way does the author's diction reveal his status as an English professor?
3. Comment on the contrast between the language level in Magill's title and in the essay. Suggest a title that would be more in keeping with the author's style.
4. What is the meaning of the phrase (paragraph 13) "to immolate herself on the altar of parental standing"? What is the effect of the image?
5. How does Magill use the two kinds of parental errors as an organizational device for his essay?
6. Why does Magill start out with the quotation from Butler? How is it related to the last sentence in the essay?

Writing Assignments

1. Is college necessary, or can young people learn as much on their own? What are some of the advantages and disadvantages of self-education?
2. State your opinion of a pass-fail grading system. Can it work, or do students need the competition of striving for letter grades?
3. Because of the overcrowding in colleges today, some people have suggested that too much emphasis is placed on the desirability of "a college education for everyone." Discuss the wisdom of this point of view. Would many college students be better off learning a trade instead of a profession?

Library Exploration

1. Read about some well-known aptitude and ability tests; find out what kinds of abilities or aptitudes these tests measure. Answer the questions in some of the Kuder Occupational Interest surveys.
2. See if you can uncover any support for Magill's argument from other sources.
3. What is the advice of current experts — educational and business — about acquiring a college degree?

Vocabulary

(1) LACERATED torn; mangled
(1) PARRICIDE murder of a parent or close relative
(3) MARTINET strict disciplinarian
(4) PERDITION ruin
(5) EMINENTLY conspicuously
(10) EXHORTATIONS strong admonitions
(12) CAJOLED coaxed; wheedled
(13) DOTING foolishly fond
(13) IMMOLATE sacrifice
(14) TRAUMATIC severely shocking
(14) DOUR gloomy; forbidding
(28) INARTICULATE unable to speak clearly

(33) VICARIOUS   by way of another's experience

(34) PRESTIGIOUS   honored; esteemed

(35) DELINEATE   outline; depict

(35) HIERARCHY   system of graded ranks

(36) REINSTATED   restored to a former position

(37) EMULATE   try to equal or excel

PERSONAL VALUES

Warren Schmidt (1920–) is assistant dean of the UCLA Graduate School of Management and senior lecturer in behavioral science. He is also the author of "Organizational Frontiers and Human Values" (1970) and the Academy-Award-winning animated film "Is It Always Right to Be Right?."

Not all frontiers are geographical, as the following article makes clear.

WARREN H. SCHMIDT

View at the Frontier

1   What does it mean to live at the frontier?

2   The frontier where we live now cannot be a single place — for we are from many places.

3   It cannot be the conquering of a single problem — for each is a part of a continuing process.

4   It cannot be a moment in time — for this day is not that different from yesterday. Like a birthday in the life of a man, a day or a year or a decade is but a convenient occasion for marking growth and age and achievement.

5   Far out on the western ocean man has drawn an invisible date-line where instantaneously today becomes yesterday and the westward voyager crosses into what the world behind him calls "tomorrow." Whether he crosses that line in calm seas or raging storm makes no difference. For him it is still tomorrow — for he journeys with the sun.

6   But there is something different about a frontier. To live at the frontier is to live with a sense of significance and high adventure.

To believe that tomorrow can be different from today.
To make a commitment to shape some portion of that tomorrow rather than to drift on the commitments of others.
To feel that sense of personal worth reserved for those who risk the new and unexperienced.

7   Action on the frontier need not always be dramatic or heroic—for the pattern of progress is made of many pieces, some bold, some subdued. In a moment of impatience we may call to another who complains, "If you can't stand the heat, stay out of the kitchen." But in a moment of reflection, we may also ask, "Does the kitchen really need to be so hot?"

8   For there is a time to confront but also a time to reduce tension:

> *A time to use power but also a time to use persuasion.*
> *A time to act but also a time to diagnose.*
> *A time to accelerate change but also a time to slow it down.*
> *A time to intervene but also a time to refrain from intervening.*

9   But whether we confront or collaborate, intervene or analyze, let it flow from understanding and courage and love and not from ignorance and cowardice and fear—for these cannot long survive on any frontier.

10   To live on a frontier is to live with loneliness at one time and the deepest love at another—for bonds between men are strongest in moments of crisis and common quest.

11   Those who would live creatively and usefully at the frontier need now and then to pause and ask themselves:

> *Am I prepared to live with uncertainty—to move before all the facts are in (they never are) or arranged in clear patterns (they seldom are)?*
> *Am I willing to risk a failure from acting now on the basis of my best judgment rather than waiting for others to take the first chance?*
> *Can I stay open to new learning from every experience—my own and others'?*
> *Can I continue, even in crisis, to remember the humanness of those whose lives I touch—whether they view things my way or not?*

12   And having paused to answer, let us together cross another frontier and journey with the sun.

Discussion of Theme

1. Define, as specifically as possible, "frontier" as it is used in this selection. What is "another frontier" alluded to in paragraph 15?
2. What are some of the traditional beliefs being questioned today that suggest we are on the threshold of radical social (or other) change?
3. In paragraph 7 the author makes some general statements about action. Can you think of any current problems to which his words might apply?
4. This article is written on a rather abstract level. In your own words, what is the author for or against?

Discussion of Rhetoric

1. For what kind of audience did the author write this selection? What assumptions about his readers does he make?

2. Would this selection have been strengthened by the inclusion of specific examples? Or is it more effective the way it stands?
3. The author uses parallel structure throughout this selection. Find several examples of this technique and discuss the intended effect.
4. What is the purpose of the reference to the dateline in paragraph 5? The question at the conclusion of paragraph 7? Does it match the tone and style of the rest of the article?
5. Who or what is "it" in paragraph 9?

Writing Assignments

1. In what ways is the frontier facing Americans today just as challenging as the one encountered by the pioneers of a hundred years ago? Cite specific instances.
2. Henry David Thoreau made a famous observation about being "out of step" with society. Find the statement and explain what he meant by it; then show how it can be applied today.

Library Exploration

For an interesting study of the impact of the frontier on the American mind, read *The Frontier in American History*, by Frederick Jackson Turner.

Henry David Thoreau (1817–62) is probably best known for "Walden" (1854), an account of the two years he lived alone beside a New England lake with practically no money. He is also famous as the author of "Civil Disobedience" (1849). An associate of Ralph Waldo Emerson, he was an American transcendentalist philosopher, essayist, and naturalist.

Thoreau reflects on the pace of life and concludes that its tempo should be slow and deliberate.

HENRY DAVID THOREAU

Where I Lived and What I Lived For

1 We must learn to reawaken and keep ourselves awake, not by mechanical aids, but by an infinite expectation of the dawn, which does not forsake us in our soundest sleep. I know of no more encouraging fact than the unquestionable ability of man to elevate his life by a conscious endeavor. It is something to be able to paint a particular picture, or to carve a statue, and so to make a few objects beautiful; but it is far more glorious to carve and paint the very atmosphere and medium through which we look, which morally we can do. To affect the quality of the day, that is the highest of arts. Every man is tasked to make his life, even in its details, worthy of the contemplation of his most elevated and critical hour. If we refused, or rather used up, such paltry information as we get, the oracles would distinctly inform us how this might be done.

2 I went to the woods because I wished to live deliberately, to front only the essential facts of life, and see if I could not learn what it had to teach, and not, when I came to die, discover that I had not lived. I did not wish to live what was not life, living is so dear; nor did I wish to practice resignation, unless it was quite necessary. I wanted to live deep and suck out all the marrow of life, to live so sturdily and Spartanlike as to put to rout all that was not life, to cut a broad swath and shave

close, to drive life into a corner, and reduce it to its lowest terms, and, if it proved to be mean, why then to get the whole and genuine meanness of it, and publish its meanness to the world; or if it were sublime, to know it by experience, and be able to give a true account of it in my next excursion. For most men, it appears to me, are in a strange uncertainty about it, whether it is of the devil or of God, and have *somewhat hastily* concluded that it is the chief end of man here to "glorify God and enjoy him forever."

3   Still we live meanly, like ants; though the fable tells us that we were long ago changed into men; like pygmies we fight with cranes; it is error upon error, and clout upon clout, and our best virtue has for its occasion a superfluous and evitable wretchedness. Our life is frittered away by detail. An honest man has hardly need to count more than his ten fingers, or in extreme cases he may add his ten toes, and lump the rest. Simplicity, simplicity, simplicity! I say, let your affairs be as two or three, and not a hundred or a thousand; instead of a million count half a dozen, and keep your accounts on your thumb nail. In the midst of this chopping sea of civilized life, such are the clouds and storms and quicksands and thousand-and-one items to be allowed for, that a man has to live, if he would not founder and go to the bottom and not make his port at all, by dead reckoning, and he must be a great calculator indeed who succeeds. Simplify, simplify. Instead of three meals a day, if it be necessary eat but one; instead of a hundred dishes, five; and reduce other things in proportion. Our life is a German Confederacy, made up of petty states, with its boundary forever fluctuating, so that even a German cannot tell you how it is bounded at any moment. The nation itself, with all its so-called internal improvements, which, by the way, are all external and superficial, is just such an unwieldy and overgrown establishment, cluttered with furniture and tripped up by its own traps, ruined by luxury and heedless expense, by want of calculation and a worthy aim, as the million households in the land; and the only cure for it as for them is in a rigid economy, a stern and more than Spartan simplicity of life and elevation of purpose. It lives too fast. Men think that it is essential that the *Nation* have commerce, and export ice, and talk through a telegraph, and ride thirty miles an hour, without a doubt, whether *they* do or not; but whether we should live like baboons or like men, is a little uncertain. If we do not get our sleepers, and forge rails, and devote days and nights to the work, but go to tinkering upon our *lives* to improve *them*, who will build railroads? And if railroads are not built, how shall we get to heaven in season? But if we stay at home and mind our business, who will want railroads? We do not ride on the railroad; it rides upon us. Did you ever think what those sleepers are that underlie the railroad? Each one is a man, an Irishman, or a Yankee man. The rails are laid on them, and they are covered with sand, and the cars run smoothly over them. They are sound sleepers, I assure you. And every few years a new lot is laid down and run over; so that, if some have the pleasure of riding on a rail, others have the misfortune to be ridden upon. And when they run over a man that is walking in his sleep, a supernumerary sleeper in the wrong position, and wake him up, they suddenly stop the cars, and make a hue and cry about it, as if this were an exception.

I am glad to know that it takes a gang of men for every five miles to keep the sleepers down and level in their beds as it is, for this is a sign that they may sometime get up again.

4   Why should we live with such hurry and waste of life? We are determined to be starved before we are hungry. Men say that a stitch in time saves nine, and so they take a thousand stitches today to save nine tomorrow. As for *work*, we haven't any of any consequence. We have the Saint Vitus' dance, and cannot possibly keep our heads still. If I should only give a few pulls at the parish bell-rope, as for a fire, that is, without setting the bell, there is hardly a man on his farm in the outskirts of Concord, notwithstanding that press of engagements which was his excuse so many times this morning, nor a boy, nor a woman, I might almost say, but would forsake all and follow that sound, not mainly to save property from the flames, but, if we will confess the truth, much more to see it burn, since burn it must, and we, be it known, did not set it on fire, — or to see it put out, and have a hand in it, if that is done as handsomely; yes, even if it were the parish church itself. Hardly a man takes a half hour's nap after dinner, but when he wakes he holds up his head and asks, "What's the news?" as if the rest of mankind had stood his sentinels. Some give directions to be waked every half hour, doubtless for no other purpose; and then, to pay for it, they tell what they have dreamed. After a night's sleep, the news is as indispensable as the breakfast. "Pray tell me any thing new that has happened to a man anywhere on this globe," — and he reads it over his coffee and rolls, that a man has had his eyes gouged out this morning on the Wachito River; never dreaming the while that he lives in the dark unfathomed mammoth cave of this world, and has but the rudiment of an eye himself.

5   For my part, I could easily do without the post-office. I think that there are very few important communications made through it. To speak critically, I never received more than one or two letters in my life — I wrote this some years ago — that were worth the postage. The penny-post is, commonly, an institution through which you seriously offer a man that penny for his thoughts which is so often safely offered in jest. And I am sure that I never read any memorable news in a newspaper. If we read of one man robbed, or murdered, or killed by accident, or one house burned, or one vessel wrecked, or one steamboat blown up, or one cow run over on the Western Railroad, or one mad dog killed, or one lot of grasshoppers in the winter, — we never need read of another. One is enough. If you are acquainted with the principle, what do you care for a myriad instances and applications? To a philosopher all *news*, as it is called, is gossip, and they who edit and read it are old women over their tea. Yet not a few are greedy after this gossip. There was such a rush, as I hear, the other day at one of the offices to learn the foreign news by the last arrival, that several large squares of plate glass belonging to the establishment were broken by the pressure, — news which I seriously think a ready wit might write a twelve-month or twelve years beforehand with sufficient accuracy. As for Spain, for instance, if you know how to throw in Don Carlos and the Infanta, and Don Pedro and Seville and Granada, from time to time in the right proportions — they may have

changed the names a little since I saw the papers, — and serve up a bull-fight when other entertainments fall, it will be true to the letter, and give us as good an idea of the exact state or ruin of things in Spain as the most succinct and lucid reports under this head in the newspapers: and as for England, almost the last insignificant scrap of news from that quarter was the revolution of 1649; and if you have learned the history of her crops for an average year, you never need attend to that thing again, unless your speculations are of a merely pecuniary character. If one may judge who rarely looks into the newspapers, nothing new does ever happen in foreign parts, a French revolution not excepted.

6   What news! how much more important to know what that is which was never old! "Kieou-he-yu (great dignitary of the state of Wei) sent a man to Khoung-tseu to know his news. Khoung-tseu caused the messenger to be seated near him, and questioned him in these terms: What is your master doing? The messenger answered with respect: My master desires to diminish the number of his faults, but he cannot come to the end of them. The messenger being gone, the philosopher remarked: What a worthy messenger! What a worthy messenger!" The preacher, instead of vexing the ears of drowsy farmers on their day of rest at the end of the week, — for Sunday is the fit conclusion of an ill-spent week, and not the fresh and brave beginning of a new one, — with this one other draggle-tail of a sermon, should shout with thundering voice, — "Pause! Avast! Why so seeming fast, but deadly slow?"

7   Shams and delusions are esteemed for soundest truths, while reality is fabulous. If men would steadily observe realities only, and not allow themselves to be deluded, life, to compare it with such things as we know, would be like a fairy tale and the Arabian Nights' Entertainments. If we respected only what is inevitable and has a right to be, music and poetry would resound along the streets. When we are unhurried and wise, we perceive that only great and worthy things have any permanent and absolute existence, — that petty fears and petty pleasures are but the shadow of the reality. This is always exhilarating and sublime. By closing the eyes and slumbering, and consenting to be deceived by shows, men establish and confirm their daily life of routine and habit everywhere, which still is built on purely illusory foundations. Children, who play life, discern its true law and relations more clearly than men, who fail to live it worthily, but who think that they are wiser by experience, that is, by failure. I have read in a Hindoo book, that "there was a king's son, who, being expelled in infancy from his native city, was brought up by a forester, and, growing up to maturity in that state, imagined himself to belong to the barbarous race with which he lived. One of his father's ministers having discovered him, revealed to him what he was, and the misconception of his character was removed, and he knew himself to be a prince. So soul," continues the Hindoo philosopher, "from the circumstances in which it is placed, mistakes its own character, until the truth is revealed to it by some holy teacher, and then it knows itself to be *Brahme*." I perceive that we inhabitants of New England live this mean life that we do because our vision does not penetrate the

surface of things. We think that *is* which *appears* to be. If a man should walk through this town and see only the reality, where, think you, would the "Mill-dam" go to? If he should give us an account of the realities he beheld there, we should not recognize the place in his description. Look at a meeting-house, or a court-house, or a jail, or a shop, or a dwelling-house, and say what that thing really is before a true gaze, and they would all go to pieces in your account of them. Men esteem truth remote, in the outskirts of the system, behind the farthest star, before Adam and after the last man. In eternity there is indeed something true and sublime. But all these times and places and occasions are now and here. God himself culminates in the present moment, and will never be more divine in the lapse of all the ages. And we are enabled to apprehend at all what is sublime and noble only by the perpetual instilling and drenching of the reality that surrounds us. The universe constantly and obediently answers to our conceptions; whether we travel fast or slow, the track is laid for us. Let us spend our lives in conceiving then. The poet or the artist never yet had so fair and noble a design but some of his posterity at least could accomplish it.

8   Let us spend one day as deliberately as Nature, and not be thrown off the track by every nutshell and mosquito's wing that falls on the rails. Let us rise early and fast, or break fast, gently and without perturbation; let company come and let company go, let the bells ring and the children cry, — determined to make a day of it. Why should we knock under and go with the stream? Let us not be upset and overwhelmed in that terrible rapid and whirlpool called a dinner, situated in the meridian shallows. Weather this danger and you are safe, for the rest of the way is down hill. With unrelaxed nerves, with morning vigor, sail by it, looking another way, tied to the mast like Ulysses. If the engine whistles, let it whistle till it is hoarse for its pains. If the bell rings, why should we run? We will consider what kind of music they are like. Let us settle ourselves, and work and wedge our feet downward through the mud and slush of opinion, and prejudice, and tradition, and delusion, and appearance, that alluvion which covers the globe, through Paris and London, through New York and Boston and Concord, through church and state, through poetry and philosophy and religion, till we come to a hard bottom and rocks in place, which we can call *reality*, and say, This is, and no mistake; and then begin, having a *point d'appui*, below freshet and frost and fire, a place where you might found a wall or a state, or set a lamp-post safely, or perhaps a gauge, not a Nilometer, but a Realometer, that future ages might know how deep a freshet of shams and appearances had gathered from time to time. If you stand right fronting and face to face to a fact, you will see the sun glimmer on both its surfaces, as if it were a cimeter, and feel its sweet edge dividing you through the heart and marrow, and so you will happily conclude your moral career. Be it life or death, we crave only reality. If we are really dying, let us hear the rattle in our throats and feel cold in the extremities; if we are alive, let us go about our business.

9   Time is but the stream I go a-fishing in. I drink at it; but while I drink I see the sandy bottom and detect how shallow it is. Its thin current

slides away, but eternity remains. I would think deeper; fish in the sky, whose bottom is pebbly with stars. I cannot count one. I know not the first letter of the alphabet. I have always been regretting that I was not as wise as the day I was born. The intellect is a cleaver; it discerns and rifts its way into the secret of things. I do not wish to be any more busy with my hands than is necessary. My head is hands and feet. I feel all my best faculties concentrated in it. My instinct tells me that my head is an organ for burrowing, as some creatures use their snout and fore-paws, and with it I would mine and burrow my way through these hills. I think that the richest vein is somewhere hereabouts; so by the divining rod and thin rising vapors I judge; and here I will begin to mine.

Discussion of Theme

1. In recent years there has been an upsurge of interest in Thoreau's life-style. What do you believe is responsible for this?
2. What practical difficulties might we encounter today if we attempted to live as Thoreau did?
3. Thoreau was considered an individualist in his own day. What would most people think of him today? What would he, in turn, think of modern society?
4. What is the theme of this essay? Can you point to one sentence that states it?
5. Is it true that we live our lives too fast? Why do people consider it necessary to lead such fast-paced lives?

Discussion of Rhetoric

1. What rhetorical clues indicate that this essay was written in an earlier era?
2. What does Thoreau convey when he suggests that you "keep accounts on your thumb nail"? Does this express the concept better than more literal language?
3. Which passages do you consider especially poetic in this selection? What gives them their poetic quality?
4. The final sentence of paragraph 4 contains an allusion to classical mythology. What is it?
5. This essay was based on Thoreau's personal experience. Does this make for good writing? Why?
6. Is Thoreau's advice on how to live persuasive? Why?

Writing Assignments

1. Mentally review the details of your daily life; then discuss those that you would like to eliminate as either unnecessary or undesirable. How would you go about it?

2. Thoreau defended the right of an individual to be out of step with the rest of society ("perhaps it is because he hears a different drummer"). In what ways do you consider yourself in this category? What are the pleasures and pains associated with it?
3. Thoreau suggested that people "stay at home and mind [their] business." What are the drawbacks to following his advice?
4. Thoreau said: "We do not ride on the railroad; it rides upon us." What supposedly helpful mechanical conveniences exert tyranny over men's lives today?
5. What do you consider the essentials of life?

Library Exploration

1. Read either a full-length biography of Thoreau or an entry in an encyclopedia.
2. *The Night Thoreau Spent in Jail* is a play written about a little-known incident in the writer-naturalist's life.
3. Summarize the two years Thoreau spent at Walden Pond.
4. Read *Civil Disobedience* and report on it.

Vocabulary

(1) PALTRY   trifling; practically worthless

(1) ORACLES   persons who give wise or authoritative opinions

(3) SUPERFLUOUS   excessive; unnecessary

(3) EVITABLE   avoidable

(3) FLUCTUATING   continually changing

(3) SLEEPERS   railroad ties

(3) SUPERNUMERARY   an extra person or thing

(4) SAINT VITUS' DANCE   muscular twitch

(4) RUDIMENT   beginning; undeveloped form

(5) MYRIAD   countless

(5) SUCCINCT   terse; concise

(5) LUCID   clear

(5) PECUNIARY   financial

(6) VEXING   annoying; disturbing

(7) DELUDED   deceived

(7) PETTY   trivial; insignificant

(7) BARBAROUS   uncivilized

(7) CULMINATES   reaches the highest point

(7) APPREHEND   understand

(7) POSTERITY   all future generations

(8) PERTURBATION   disturbance

(8) MERIDIAN   midday

(8) ALLUVION   matter deposited on land by a flood

(8) POINT D'APPUI   foundation; base

(8) FRESHET   freshwater stream

(8) CIMETER   (scimitar) sword; saber

(9) DIVINING ROD   forked stick used to locate water

Albert Schweitzer (1875–1965) was a surgeon, organist, missionary, writer, composer, and humanitarian. He was born in Alsace and educated at the universities of Strasbourg, Paris, and Berlin, receiving degrees in philosophy, theology, and medicine. His fame rests on his self-sacrificing work at the hospital he founded at Lambaréné, in West Africa. He wrote dozens of books on religion, music, and world peace, among which are "The Quest of the Historical Jesus" (1910), "From My African Notebook" (1939), and "Peace or Atomic War?" (1958). He was awarded the Nobel Peace Prize in 1953.

In this selection Schweitzer examines the feelings of pessimism and optimism he had about the present and future condition of man.

ALBERT SCHWEITZER

Pessimism and Optimism

1   To the question whether I am a pessimist or an optimist, I answer that my knowledge is pessimistic, but my willing and hoping are optimistic.

2   I am pessimistic in that I experience in its full weight what we conceive to be the absence of purpose in the course of world happenings. Only at quite rare moments have I felt really glad to be alive. I could not but feel with a sympathy full of regret all the pain that I saw around me, not only that of men but that of the whole creation. From this community of suffering I have never tried to withdraw myself. It seemed to me a matter of course that we should take our share of the burden of pain which lies upon the world. Even while I was a boy at school it

was clear to me that no explanation of the evil in the world could ever satisfy me; all explanations, I felt, ended in sophistries, and at bottom had no other object than to make it possible for men to share in the misery around them, with less keen feelings. That a thinker like Leibnitz could reach the miserable conclusion that though this world is, indeed, not good, it is the best that was possible, I have never been able to understand.

3   But however much concerned I was at the problem of the misery in the world, I never let myself get lost in broodings over it; I always held firmly to the thought that each one of us can do a little to bring some portion of it to an end. Thus I came gradually to rest content in the knowledge that there is only one thing we can understand about the problem, and that is that each of us has to go his own way, but as one who means to help to bring about deliverance.

4   In my judgment, too, of the situation in which mankind finds itself at the present time I am pessimistic. I cannot make myself believe that that situation is not so bad as it seems to be, but I am inwardly conscious that we are on a road which, if we continue to tread it, will bring us into "Middle Ages" of a new character. The spiritual and material misery to which mankind of today is delivering itself through its renunciation of thinking and of the ideals which spring therefrom, I picture to myself in its utmost compass. And yet I remain optimistic. One belief of my childhood I have preserved with the certainty that I can never lose it: belief in truth. I am confident that the spirit generated by truth is stronger than the force of circumstances. In my view no other destiny awaits mankind than that which, through its mental and spiritual disposition, it prepares for itself. Therefore I do not believe that it will have to tread the road to ruin right to the end.

5   If men can be found who revolt against the spirit of thoughtlessness, and who are personalities sound enough and profound enough to let the ideals of ethical progress radiate from them as a force, there will start an activity of the spirit which will be strong enough to evoke a new mental and spiritual disposition in mankind.

6   Because I have confidence in the power of truth and of the spirit, I believe in the future of mankind. Ethical acceptance of the world contains within itself an optimistic willing and hoping which can never be lost. It is, therefore, never afraid to face the dismal reality, and to see it as it really is.

7   In my own life anxiety, trouble, and sorrow have been allotted to me at times in such abundant measure that had my nerves not been so strong, I must have broken down under the weight. Heavy is the burden of fatigue and responsibility which has lain upon me without a break for years. I have not much of my life for myself, not even the hours I should like to devote to my wife and child.

8   But I have had blessings too: that I am allowed to work in the service of mercy; that my work has been successful; that I receive from other people affection and kindness in abundance; that I have loyal helpers, who identify themselves with my activity; that I enjoy a health which allows me to undertake most exhausting work; that I have a well-balanced temperament which varies little, and an energy which exerts itself with calmness and deliberation; and, finally, that I

can recognize as such whatever happiness falls to my lot, accepting it also as a thing for which some thank offering is due from me.

9   I feel it deeply that I can work as a free man at a time when an oppressive lack of freedom is the lot of so many, as also that though my immediate work is material, yet I have at the same time opportunities of occupying myself in the sphere of the spiritual and intellectual.

10   That the circumstances of my life provide in such varied ways favorable conditions for my work, I accept as something of which I would fain prove myself worthy.

11   How much of the work which I have planned and have in mind shall I be able to complete?

12   My hair is beginning to turn. My body is beginning to show traces of the exertions I have demanded of it, and of the passage of the years.

13   I look back with thankfulness to the time when, without needing to husband my strength, I could get through an uninterrupted course of bodily and mental work. With calmness and humility I look forward to the future, so that I may not be unprepared for renunciation if it be required of me. Whether we be workers or sufferers, it is assuredly our duty to conserve our powers, as being men who have won their way through to the peace which passeth all understanding.

Discussion of Theme

1. What makes Schweitzer feel pessimistic? What makes him feel optimistic? Do you react as he does?
2. Have the sort of men Schweitzer describes in paragraph 5 been found? If so, who are or were they? Have they had the effect on mankind that the author predicted they would? Was he such a man?
3. Did Schweitzer expect to have a wide influence on mankind, or was he content to improve conditions in his own small corner of the world?
4. Are you optimistic or pessimistic about the future of mankind? Why?
5. How would you classify Schweitzer as a person?
6. Do you agree with Schweitzer that each of us should feel the misery of all those who suffer, and do something about it?

Discussion of Rhetoric

1. In paragraphs 4 and 6 does Schweitzer express himself on too abstract a level to make communication effective?
2. What is his purpose in paragraph 7? Is he looking for sympathy, or is he trying to inspire other people who may have had "anxiety, trouble, and sorrow"?
3. Occasionally Schweitzer produces an unwieldy sentence. How might each of these be changed for the sake of clarity?
4. To what source does the author allude in his final sentence? Why is this an appropriate conclusion for his essay?

5. How does Schweitzer use the words *pessimism* and *optimism* to organize his essay?

Writing Assignments

1. Instead of discussing our society from the point of view of an optimist or a pessimist, write a paper based on your view of it as a realist. What do you see? What do you conclude about the future of America?
2. What is your "explanation of the evil of the world"?
3. What are the drawbacks to concluding that "this is the best of all possible worlds"?
4. Discuss: "I am confident that the spirit generated by truth is stronger than the force of circumstances."
5. Who among the world's leaders fits the description in paragraph 5? Explain.

Library Exploration

1. Dr. Thomas Dooley also devoted his life to the service of others. Read about his work and the dedication he inspired in others.
2. Why did Schweitzer go to Lambaréné? What did he do there?
3. Report on the lesser known aspects of Schweitzer's life—his work as a musician, composer, or philosopher.
4. What was the effect of Schweitzer's work from the African's viewpoint?

Vocabulary

(2) PESSIMISTIC expecting the worst

(2) SOPHISTRIES clever but misleading arguments

(4) RENUNCIATION giving up voluntarily

(4) COMPASS scope; range

(5) ETHICAL conforming to standards of right behavior

(8) DELIBERATION careful consideration

(10) FAIN eagerly; gladly

One of this country's best known modern poets, Carl Sandburg (1878–1967) was the son of poor immigrant parents. His works have been anthologized in many collections of American literature. Among his books are "Abraham Lincoln: The War Years" (1939), "Remembrance Rock" (1948), and "Wind Song" (1960). In addition to his writing, he was a collector (and singer) of American folk songs.

This short selection is a parable that has a meaning for all of us.

CARL SANDBURG

Elephants Are Different to Different People

1 Wilson and Pilcer and Snack stood before the zoo elephant.

2 Wilson said, "What is its name? Is it from Asia or Africa? Who feeds it? Is it a he or a she? How old is it? Do they have twins? How much does it cost to feed? How much does it weigh? If it dies how much will another one cost? If it dies what will they use the bones, the fat, and the hide for? What use is it besides to look at?"

3 Pilcer didn't have any questions; he was murmuring to himself, "It's a house by itself, walls and windows, the ears came from tall cornfields, by God; the architect of those legs was a workman, by God; he stands like a bridge out across deep water; the face is sad and the eyes are kind; I know elephants are good to babies."

4 Snack looked up and down and at last said to himself, "He's a tough son-of-a-gun outside and I'll bet he's got a strong heart, I'll bet he's as strong as a copper-riveted boiler inside."

5 They didn't put up any arguments.

6 They didn't throw anything in each other's faces.

7 Three men saw the elephant three ways

8   And let it go at that.

9   They didn't spoil a sunny afternoon;

10   "Sunday comes only once a week," they told each other.

Discussion of Theme

1. What do Wilson, Pilcer, and Snack all have in common? In what ways are they different from one another? What does this imply?
2. How do we know that each man is sure of his identity? What are some of the obstacles in today's society that prevent many men from possessing this certainty?
3. What point is Sandburg making when he remarks that "they didn't put up any argument. They didn't throw anything"?
4. This piece was written in 1943. What message does it have for us today?
5. In view of the three men's behavior, what might be the implication of the observation that "Sunday comes only once a week"?

Discussion of Rhetoric

1. On a symbolic level, what might the zoo represent? What does "Sunday" symbolize?
2. How does Sandburg show the distinctive traits of the three men? How does their language relate to their respective personalities?
3. Find examples of parallelism in this selection. What is its purpose?
4. Which of Sandburg's metaphors or similes do you find particularly effective?

Writing Assignments

1. On the basis of each man's response to the elephant, write a brief character sketch of Wilson, Pilcer, and Snack.
2. Write your own reaction to the elephant. What would *you* say?
3. For "elephant" substitute a word designating someone identifiable in our society (a hippy, student, black, or professor). Then write a set of comments illustrating the differing reactions of three persons.

Library Exploration

If you enjoyed this selection, you will also enjoy Sandburg's poetry and prose. He has written novels, children's verse, poems, and biographies.

John Donne (1573–1631) was an Elizabethan poet and later a preacher. He wrote copiously, his works ranging from some of the world's most evocative love poems to involved theological "Devotions" and "Sermons." Eventually he became dean of St. Paul's Cathedral in London. He was concerned with the affairs of men in a world of turmoil not unlike our own.

This short dissertation will reveal the source of familiar quotations, the title of a famous book, and a succinct statement of Donne's basic beliefs.

JOHN DONNE

Devotion XVII

Nunc lento sonitur dicunt, Morieris.

Now, this Bell tolling softly for another, saies to me, Thou must die.

Perchance he for whom this bell tolls may be so ill, as that he knows not it tolls for him; and perchance I may think myself so much better than I am, as that they who are about me, and see my state, may have caused it to toll for me, and I know not that. The church is catholic, universal, so are all her actions; all that she does belongs to all. When she baptizes a child, that action concerns me; for that child is thereby connected to that head which is my head too, and ingrafted into that body whereof I am a member. And when she buries a man, that action concerns me: all mankind is of one author, and is one volume; when one man dies, one chapter is not torn out of the book, but translated into a better language; and every chapter must be so translated; God employs several translators; some pieces are translated by age, some by sickness, some by war, some by justice; but God's hand is in every translation, and his hand shall bind up all our scattered leaves again for that library where every book shall lie open to one another. As therefore the bell that rings to a sermon calls not upon the preacher only, but upon the congregation to come, so this bell calls us all; but how much more me, who am brought so near the door by this sickness. There was a contention as far as a suit (in which both piety and dignity, religion and estimation, were mingled), which of the religious orders should ring to prayers first in the morning; and it was determined, that they should ring first that rose earliest. If we understand aright the dignity of this bell that tolls for our evening prayer, we would be glad to make it ours by rising early, in that application, that it might be ours as well as his, whose indeed it is. The bell doth toll for him that thinks it doth; and though it intermit again, yet from that minute that that occasion wrought upon him, he is united to God. Who casts not up his eye to the sun when it rises? but who takes off his eye from a comet when that breaks out? Who bends not his ear to any bell which upon any occasion rings? but who can remove it from that bell which is passing a piece of himself out of this world? No man is an island, entire of itself; every man is a piece of the continent, a part of the main. If a clod be washed away by the sea, Europe is the less, as well as if a promontory were, as well as if a manor of thy friend's or of thine own were: any man's death diminishes me, because I am involved in mankind, and therefore never send to know for whom the bell tolls; it tolls for thee. Neither can we call this a begging of misery, or a borrowing of misery, as though we were not miserable enough of ourselves, but must fetch in more from the next house, intaking upon us the misery of our neighbors. Truly it were an excusable covetousness if we did, for affliction is a treasure, and scarce any man hath enough of it. No man hath affliction enough that is not matured and ripened by it, and made fit for God by that affliction. If a man carry treasure in bullion, or in a wedge of gold, and have none coined into current money, his treasure will not defray him as he travels. Tribulation is a treasure in the nature of it, but it is not current money in the use of it, except we get nearer and nearer our home, Heaven, by it. Another man may be sick too, and sick to death, and this affliction may lie in his bowels, as gold in a mine, and be of no use to him; but this bell, that tells me of his affliction, digs out and applies that gold to me: if by this consideration of another's danger I take mine own into contemplation, and so secure myself, by making my recourse to my God, who is our only security.

Discussion of Theme

1. How are Donne's well-known, widely quoted lines that begin with "No man is an island" usually interpreted? Is it possible that they might actually have a narrower—perhaps strictly religious— meaning?
2. Is it acceptable to interpret a writer's meaning in your own way, whether or not you think he would have shared your view?
3. Why did Donne believe that "affliction is a treasure, and scarce any man hath enough of it"? Does it make sense to you?
4. What is the picture of his own era which Donne gives you in this selection?
5. Donne says God is man's only real security. Is this idea still valid today?

Discussion of Rhetoric

1. How appropriate do you consider the comparison of "this affliction . . . in his bowels" with "gold in a mine"? Is it farfetched or suitable? Does it meet the chief requirements of a good analogy?
2. What is the mood of this essay? What contributes to it?
3. How does the tolling of the bell unify the entire selection?
4. Why is the part of the selection beginning "No man is an island" so famous?
5. Notice the unusual construction of some of the sentences. How does this kind of writing affect today's readers?

Writing Assignments

1. Do you think that people in Donne's day were more religious than those of today? Why? Support your opinion with thoughtful reasons.
2. Does religion serve a valuable purpose in people's lives? What is its effect on yours?
3. If you have no formal religion, discuss the code of ethics that guides your behavior.
4. Do you believe every man's death diminishes you? Why?
5. Do ethics vary from one generation to the next? Are yours the same as your parents'?

Library Exploration

1. What was the political situation in England during Donne's time?
2. How have T. S. Eliot, Ezra Pound, and other modern writers been influenced by Donne and other metaphysical poets?
3. Why did Hemingway call his book on the Spanish civil war *For Whom the Bell Tolls?* What has it to do with Donne's thesis?

Vocabulary

INGRAFTED   grafted onto; established firmly on

CONTENTION   controversy; argument

INTERMIT   stop for a time

WROUGHT   formed

PROMONTORY   land that juts out over water

MANOR   main residence or estate

COVETOUSNESS   desire for another's property

BULLION   bulk gold or silver

DEFRAY   pay the way; pay the costs

TRIBULATION   trial; deep sorrow

William Faulkner (1897–1962), generally regarded as one of this country's great novelists, was awarded the Nobel Prize in Literature in 1949. Among his novels are "The Sound and the Fury" (1929), "Absalom! Absalom!" (1936), "The Hamlet" (1940), "The Town" (1957), and "The Mansion" (1959). Probably his greatest creation was the saga of the fictional Yoknapatawpha county of northern Mississippi with its now famous characters and customs.

In this speech, delivered in Stockholm, Faulkner states his belief that writers have a responsibility to help society remember the "old verities."

WILLIAM FAULKNER

Nobel Prize Acceptance Speech

1   I feel that this award was not made to me as a man, but to my work — a life's work in the agony and sweat of the human spirit, not for glory and least of all for profit, but to create out of the materials of the human spirit something which did not exist before. So this award is only mine in trust. It will not be difficult to find a dedication for the money part of it commensurate with the purpose and significance of its origin. But I would like to do the same with the acclaim too, by using this moment as a pinnacle from which I might be listened to by the young men and women already dedicated to the same anguish and travail, among whom is already that one who will some day stand here where I am standing.

2   Our tragedy today is a general and universal physical fear so long sustained by now that we can even bear it. There are no longer problems of the spirit. There is only the question: When will I be blown up? Because of this, the young man or woman writing today has forgotten the problems of the human heart in conflict with itself which alone can

make good writing because only that is worth writing about, worth the agony and the sweat.

3   He must learn them again. He must teach himself that the basest of all things is to be afraid; and, teaching himself that, forget it forever, leaving no room in his workshop for anything but the old verities and truths of the heart, the old universal truths lacking which any story is ephemeral and doomed — love and honor and pity and pride and compassion and sacrifice. Until he does so, he labors under a curse. He writes not of love but of lust, of defeats in which nobody loses anything of value, of victories without hope and, worst of all, without pity or compassion. His griefs grieve on no universal bones, leaving no scars. He writes not of the heart but of the glands.

4   Until he relearns these things, he will write as though he stood among and watched the end of man. I decline to accept the end of man. It is easy enough to say that man is immortal simply because he will endure: that when the last ding-dong of doom has clanged and faded from the last worthless rock hanging tideless in the last red and dying evening, that even then there will be one more sound: that of his puny inexhaustible voice, still talking. I refuse to accept this. I believe that man will not merely endure: he will prevail. He is immortal, not because he alone among creatures has an inexhaustible voice, but because he has a soul, a spirit capable of compassion and sacrifice and endurance. The poet's, the writer's, duty is to write about these things. It is his privilege to help man endure by lifting his heart, by reminding him of the courage and honor and hope and pride and compassion and pity and sacrifice which have been the glory of his past. The poet's voice need not merely be the record of man, it can be one of the props, the pillars to help him endure and prevail.

Discussion of Theme

1. Faulkner delivered this speech in 1949. Are we still preoccupied with the question: When will I be blown up? Have we dismissed this as a possibility, or have we simply learned to live with it?
2. Faulkner says that "the young man or woman writing today has forgotten the problems of the human heart in conflict with itself." What have you read recently that would contradict this statement?
3. What are some of the old "universal truths"? Why might they make the best stories? Do they recur in the world's enduring literature?
4. Is Faulkner's advice as useful for a college student as it is for a young novelist? Can you apply it in your own writing?
5. Does Faulkner overestimate the writer's ability to "help man endure"? How can the writer accomplish this?

Discussion of Rhetoric

1. Faulkner's writing is stylistically strong and distinctive. What are the qualities of the style in this speech?

2. Is it possible to distinguish a man from his work, as Faulkner apparently does in the opening sentence? What distinction is he attempting to make?
3. What is the significance of the rock's "hanging tideless" in the description in paragraph 4?
4. Is Faulkner's argument for his view of man effective? Why?
5. How would you characterize the diction of this essay? Is it formal, abstract, or poetic?

Writing Assignments

1. What question do you think is today's version of 1949's "When will I be blown up"?
2. Select a theme that you consider one of the "old verities." Explain how it was handled in at least four novels, short stories, poems, or plays. Use any one form or combination of forms that you wish.
3. State your own views about the decline (or endurance) of man.

Library Exploration

1. Read one of Faulkner's novels and compare his style with Hemingway's (or with that of another modern American author).
2. Faulkner says he will use the prize money for something "commensurate with the purpose and significance of its origin." What was its origin?

Vocabulary

(1) COMMENSURATE corresponding; equal
(1) PINNACLE peak
(1) TRAVAIL toil

(3) EPHEMERAL fleeting; temporary
(4) PREVAIL overcome

Robert Lindner (1914–56), a Baltimore psychologist educated at Cornell University, was a rare combination of imaginative scientist and compelling writer. As a practicing analyst he was particularly interested in studying young people and their problems. He was also consulting psychologist to Maryland's state prisons. When he died at the age of forty-two he left a small but vital legacy of his acute perception in his books "Rebel Without a Cause" (1944), "The Fifty-Minute Hour" (1955), and "Must You Conform?" (1956).

In this selection Lindner probes the nature of man to examine his will either to conform or to rebel.

ROBERT LINDNER

Must You Conform?

1 And now . . . *must* you conform, *must* we conform? This is the question that confronts every man today, the question that must be answered before silence descends and the voice of humanity fades to a whimper. It is a question only a few fortunate ones can still ask, a question that cannot even be raised behind the barbed wire where half of humanity lives.

2 Must we conform? Must we fit ourselves into the pattern that molds Mass Man? Must we bend, submit, adjust, give in? Must we, finally, cease to be men?

3 The forces of Society tell us that we must. Aligned already with the emergent dominant class, they and the institutions they represent have put individuality and liberty on the sacrificial altar. For a brief moment of respite, and in the vain hope that they will in this way themselves escape a destiny just over the horizon, they have become its

heralds. In chorus, these forces proclaim the myth that smooths the way of the conqueror and robs their fellow of the will to resist tyranny.

4   Abroad in the world today is a monstrous falsehood, a consummate fabrication, to which all social agencies have loaned themselves and into which most men, women and children have been seduced. In previous writings I have called this forgery "the Eleventh commandment"; for such, indeed, has become the injunction: You Must Adjust!

5   Adjustment, that synonym for conformity that comes more easily to the modern tongue, is the theme of our swan song, the piper's tune to which we dance on the brink of the abyss, the siren's melody that destroys our senses and paralyzes our wills. But this is something known only to the few who have penetrated its disguises and glimpsed the death's head beneath: for the many, adjustment is the only way of life they know, the only way of life permitted to them by the powers that govern their existence from cradle to grave.

6   *You must adjust* . . . This is the motto inscribed on the walls of every nursery, and the processes that break the spirit are initiated there. In birth begins conformity. Slowly and subtly, the infant is shaped to the prevailing pattern, his needs for love and care turned against him as weapons to enforce submission. Uniqueness, individuality, difference—these are viewed with horror, even shame; at the very least, they are treated like diseases, and a regiment of specialists are available today to "cure" the child who will not or cannot conform. Does he violate the timetable of Gesell?—Call the pediatrician, quickly! Does he contradict Spock?—Get the telephone number of the nearest child analyst! Is he unhappy? maladjusted? lonely? too noisy? too quiet? too slow? too fast?—Let us be thankful for the special schools, the nurseries and, above all, for the magazines on the rack at the corner drugstore!

7   *You must adjust* . . . This is the legend imprinted in every schoolbook, the invisible message on every blackboard. Our schools have become vast factories for the manufacture of robots. We no longer send our young to them primarily to be taught and given the tools of thought, no longer primarily to be informed and acquire knowledge; but to be "socialized"—which in the current semantic means to be regimented and made to conform. The modern report card reflects with horrible precision the preoccupations of our teachers and the philosophy of our educators. Today, in the public schools, grades are given for the "ability" of a child to "adjust" to group activities, for whether he is "liked" by others, for whether he "enjoys" the subjects taught, for whether he "gets along" with his schoolmates. In the private schools, especially in those which designate themselves "progressive," the situation is more frightening, in some cases known to me actually revealing a cynical kind of anti-intellectualism. So the school takes up where the parent leaves off; and the children who emerge from it with a few shreds of individuality clinging to their blue jeans or bobby-socks are rare birds, indeed. But even if they manage to retain some uniqueness after passing through the mill of primary and secondary education, the young who go on to institutions of higher learning are exposed to pressures of conformity that must surely de-

prive them of the pitiful remnants of singularity and independence they still have.

8   In the colleges and universities it is not necessarily the teachers or the system of education that command adjustment, although currently, with academic freedom under attack and access to knowledge blocked, professors live in fear of saying or doing anything unorthodox. Here the Eleventh Commandment is more often enjoined by the young themselves upon themselves. By this time completely enslaved by the myth, they have acquired title to it, and now it comprises almost the whole of their philosophy and the basis of their code of conduct. This phenomenon, moreover, is a recent one, apparently dating from the last war. It has been brought to my attention by teachers in many colleges I have visited during the last few years. The collegian of today, they tell me, is hardly to be compared with the student of, say, twenty years ago. Today's undergraduate is almost a caricature of conformism. Like the new uniform he wears — the uniform of the junior executive that is *de rigueur* on Madison Avenue — his opinions, attitudes, tastes and behavior are ultra-conservative. In the world that is being born he will have little conflict about exchanging his charcoal grays for the deeper black of the élite guard.

9   *You must adjust* . . . This is the command etched above the door of every church, synagogue, cathedral, temple, and chapel. It constitutes a passport to salvation, an armor against sin: it sums the virtues and describes the virtues. For there is no formal religion that does not insist, as its first requirement, on a confession of conformity. Nor is there, any longer, a religion which offers a path to Heaven other than the autobahn of submission. One and all, they have conspired, in the name of the Spirit, against the spirit of man: one and all, they have sold him into slavery. Under threat of damnation, hell-fire, purgatory, eternal non-being or even re-incarnation as some lower form of life, they have ordered him to renounce protest, to forego revolt, to be passive, to surrender. And while most of them were founded upon protest and by rebellion, these are the very things they now uniformly hold in horror. With Caesar and poverty, with war and hate, with disease and violence, with famine, crime and destruction, our priests, ministers, rabbis, imams, yogin, hierophants and lamas have signed a treaty to guarantee human tractability. All they have to sell us subverts the nature of man. Conformity, humility, acceptance — with these coins we are to pay our fares to paradise. Meanwhile, we must adjust, we must accept. And among the things we are to accept, in our time, are the following: riot guns, tear gas, transhydrogen explosives, character assassination, radioactive dust, tanks, nerve gas, guilt by association, atomic submarines, concentration camps, gas masks, guided missiles, censorship over thought and expression, rubber hoses, bacteriological warfare, purges, slave labor, bomb shelters, liquidations, brain-washing, Roy Cohn's opinions and Bishop Sheen's God . . . .

10   *You must adjust* . . . This is the slogan emblazoned on the banners of all political parties, the inscription at the heart of all systems that contend for the loyalties of men. Our lives today, more than ever before, are governed by politics. Some observers, as a matter of fact, insist that modern man be called *homo politicus;* for there is hardly an

area of existence that remains untouched by politics, hardly an act that in some way does not involve the manner in which our social affairs are regulated or the principles by which they are determined. Love, hate, friendship, enmity — these and other emotions have come to have political significance and, to some extent, to involve political choices. But there is no freedom even here, since conformity is of the essence of all the organizations that rule over us. Paradoxically, the systems which most loudly proclaim the right of human liberty and offer themselves as the instruments of change are those systems that oppress most heavily. On the way to power their sole condition is discipline, the severe regulation of mind and act so that the aim of the organization, the seizure somehow of power, can be achieved. At this stage of struggle, the surrender of individuality is urged or forced, but those of whom conformity is exacted are the voluntary adherents, the dedicated, the passionate few who believe truly in the slogans, in the high-sounding words of deliverance from slavery, and give over their selves to the Party. Once in power, however, what has been the dedication of a few is elevated to the religion of the many. In the congealing amber of politics the individual is pressed and imprisoned. The erstwhile revolutionary, no longer rebel but policeman and bureaucrat, becomes an oppressor; and against the revolution he has wrought he now turns — or, becoming a heretic, he dies. Meanwhile, for the masses, what has been an act of faith is now an order to surrender. Simple discipline, obedience and passivity are not enough when the Party becomes the All, for only in the collective orgasm of conformity can power be affirmed. Now is the day of the Committee, the high noon of the Inquisitor, the time of the midnight awakening, the bright lights, the spittle in the faces and the breaking of bones, the long corridor, the Confession, and the merciful bullet in the back of the head.

11 *You must adjust* . . . This is the creed of the sciences that have sold themselves to the status quo, the prescription against perplexity, the placebo for anxiety. For psychiatry, psychology and the medical or social arts that depend from them have become devil's advocates and sorcerers' apprentices of conformity. Joined in the criminal conspiracy against human nature, they have poisoned the last oasis for the relief of man. Of all betrayals, their treachery has been the greatest, for in them we have placed our remaining hope, and in them, sadly, hope has fled. Equating protest with madness and nonconformity with neurosis, in the clinics and hospitals, the consulting rooms and offices, they labor with art and skill to gut the flame that burns eternally at the core of being. Recklessly and with the abandon of some demented sower of noxious seeds, they fling abroad their soporifics, their sedatives, their palliative drugs and their opiate dopes, lulling the restlessness of man, besotting him so that he sleepwalks through his days and does not recognize the doom-writing on the wall. Or with the soft persuasion and counsel that apes wisdom, with pamphlets and tracts and books that flow over the mind and drown it in a rising flood of imbecile recipes for contented existence, they prepare his ankles for chains, his back for the brand, and his head for a crown of thorns. But if these do not "cure" him into conformity, do not level him into the mass, there remain in the arsenals of adjustment the ultimate weapons: the little

black box for shock "therapy" and the swift and silent knife for psychosurgery. From the skies the lightning and the thunder are stolen to be discharged into the brain, the seat of reason, the home of evolution and the treasury of manhood. In the convulsion that follows, resistance ebbs and another sheep is added to the flock. Or the scalpel, quiet and sterile, probes with unerring aim toward the target behind the eyes . . . up, down, to one side, then the other . . . and a walking zombie, the penultimate conformist, stands where a man once stood, "cured" of his humanity.[1]

12   The question remains: must we conform? Or can we, somehow, resist the powers that conspire to domesticate us? Can we woo or win our liberty from an emergent segment devoted to raw power? Can we, in short, recover Society for all humanity? And if so, with what arms are we to redeem our almost-lost manhood? How can we withstand the total onslaught I have hardly begun to describe? Where are we to find the weapons of resistance?

13   I believe that the question of conformity, in the long run, answers itself. I think that if there was a possibility, once, of a yes or no — if at one time humans could decide "we must conform" or "we must not" — that possibility has been lost in the long reaches of evolution, far back along the corridors of Time. The simple truth, stark and severe in its simplicity, is that *we cannot conform;* for it seems there is an ingredient in the composition of our cells, a chemistry in our blood, and a substance in our bones that will not suffer man to submit forever.

14   Built into man, the foundation of his consciousness, the source of his humanity and the vehicle of his evolution up from the muck of a steaming primeval swamp, is an instinct. I have chosen to call it the "instinct of rebellion," since it reveals itself as a drive or urge toward mastery over every obstacle, natural or man-made, that stands as a barrier between man and his distant, perhaps never-to-be-achieved but always-striven-after goals. It is this injustice that underwrites his survival, this instinct from which he derives his nature: a great and powerful dynamic that makes him what he is — restless, seeking, curious, forever unsatisfied, eternally struggling and eventually victorious. Because of the instinct of rebellion man has never been content with limits of his body: it has led him to extend his senses almost infinitely, so that his fingers now probe space, his eyes magnify the nuclei of atoms, and his ears detect whispers from the bottom of seas. Because of the instinct of rebellion man has never been content with the limits of his mind: it has led him to inquire its secrets of the universe, to gather and learn and manipulate the fabulous inventory of the cosmos, to seek the very mysteries of creation. Because of the instinct of

---

[1] There are certain situations wherein the use of shock therapy or psychosurgery is justified by medical necessity, but occasions for resorting to such "heroic" techniques grow fewer as time and research go on. Despite this, the statistical fact is that these drastic measures are applied with increasing frequency amounting almost to abandon. One must therefore suspect that the black box and scalpel are often used to sustain the myth of the medicos' magic powers and to obtain quick and cheap — even if impermanent — "cures." Undeniably, the real if unconscious aim of many psychiatrists and physicians is to subdue the patient by any means, to force him into line, and to stamp out his distressing and stubborn tendency toward non-conformity.

rebellion, man has never been content, finally, with the limits of his life: it has caused him to deny death and to war with mortality.

15   Man is a rebel. He is committed by his biology *not* to conform, and herein lies the paramount reason for the awful tension he experiences today in relation to Society. Unlike other creatures of earth, man cannot submit, cannot surrender his birthright of protest, for rebellion is one of his essential dimensions. He cannot deny it and remain man. In order to live he must rebel. Only total annihilation of humanity as a species can eliminate this in-built necessity. Only with the death of the last man will the revolt that is the essence of his nature also die.

16   But this is cold comfort in the present when the forces of conformity have collected against the spirit of man. It offers us, in the modern world, faced as we are with these forces, little satisfaction to know that the destiny of man is to conquer and that the final victory will be his.

17   What about now? What about today?

18   I suggest that the answer to the all-important question in the here and now lies in the mobilization and implementation of the instinct of rebellion. We must, in short, become acquainted with our protestant nature and learn how to use it in our daily lives, how to express it ourselves, how to infuse it throughout all levels of our culture, and how to nourish it in our young.

19   Today, in the struggle between man and Society over the issue of conformity, Society is winning because man, the rebel, does not yet know how to rebel successfully — positively. His protest is expressed in negative forms, in ways which may discharge somewhat the energy of his rebellious instinct but which yield him little profit; indeed, in ways which are often actually harmful to himself and to the community. Non-conformity, as it is now conceived, is largely exhibited as psychosis, neurosis, crime, and psychosomatic illness; or it appears as pitifully hopeless and vain little defiances of convention and custom in dress, manner, opinion and taste. All of these ways are negative, unproductive, totally inadequate to meet the situation man faces.

20   The productive way toward non-conformity is the way of positive rebellion, of protest that at once affirms the rebellious nature of man *and* the fundamental human values. These values reside in the common treasury of humanity. They form the basic aspirations of all humans everywhere and are expressed most clearly in the great documents and contracts — such as our own Bill of Rights — which men have seen fit to declare from time to time. *Rebellion and protest in their name, and conducted in a fashion which does not in any way violate their spirit, is positive rebellion, authentic rebellion.*

21   Our instruction in the methods of positive rebellion, of affirmative protest, must come from two sources — one inner, one outer. The first of these, the inner source, is the slower and less dependable one. It requires that men themselves awaken to the knowledge, first, that rebellion is native in them and that there exist positive ways of protest which await discovery. The inspiration and example of the all-too-few positive rebels in our culture may assist this admittedly protracted and precarious self-awakening by contagion.

22   The outer source of instruction is more rapid and more sure. It consists of direct tuition in positive rebellion by those to whom we have

always looked, and will always look, for edification: our psychologists, educators, and artists.

23   While it is true, as I have charged, that these guides in human affairs have always identified with — and in some cases sold themselves to — the emerging dominant segment; and while it is true that in the current crisis they have shamefully ranged themselves on the side of conformity, it is no less true that they have done so largely out of desperation and ignorance. They have not known about the instinct at the very navel of man's being, and in their unawareness have been forced into the position they now occupy. But if once they become informed, if once they learn about the existence of such an instinct and its cosmic possibilities, it is unavoidable that the motives which inspired them toward the vocation they practice will fuse with this knowledge and become animated by it. In this manner will the methods of positive rebellion, of life-affirming protest, be explored and spread about.

24   The answer to the question, "Must we conform?" is a resounding No! *No* . . . not only because, in the end, we are creatures who cannot conform and who are destined to triumph over the forces of conformity; but *no* because there is an alternate way of life available to us here and now. It is the way of positive rebellion, the path of creative protest, the road of productive revolt. This is the way natural to man, the way he must and will take to achieve the values he aspires to just because he is human. By taking it, man can find the future of which he dreams, the future in which he will achieve his far, high, and unforeseeable goals . . . .

Discussion of Theme

1. The author says that the infant's "needs for love and care [are] turned against him as weapons to enforce submission." How is this done? Does this process continue throughout a person's lifetime?
2. Is it fair for teachers to use peer pressure to bring a nonconforming student into line?
3. Is Lindner wrong? Must you conform?
4. If an unadjusted man is adjusted to the society that created his maladjustment in the first place, what help has he had?
5. Since all formal religions begin with "a confession of conformity" (paragraph 9), does this weaken religion per se?

Discussion of Rhetoric

1. Does Lindner rely more heavily on denotative or connotative language? Why?
2. In this analysis of conformity the author begins with opposing arguments. What is the effect?
3. What is the allusion to the sirens in paragraph 5?
4. In which paragraph does the author advance his own arguments?
5. Notice how the author reiterates his central question, "Must you conform?" What is the effect of this technique?

Writing Assignments

1. Do you consider yourself a conformist or a nonconformist? Why?
2. Write a character sketch of the most nonconforming person you have ever known.
3. What benefits does society derive from nonconformists? From conformists? Does it benefit more from one than the other?
4. If everyone in our society were nonconforming, would the result be complete anarchy?

Library Exploration

1. Read one of Lindner's books mentioned in the headnote.
2. For a journalistic study of conformity, read Vance Packard's *The Status Seekers*.

Vocabulary

(3) EMERGENT rising
(3) RESPITE interval of rest or relief
(4) CONSUMMATE complete
(4) FABRICATION invention; falsehood
(7) SEMANTIC system of meaning
(8) PHENOMENON observable fact or event
(8) CARICATURE exaggerated image
(8) DE RIGUEUR absolutely required
(9) AUTOBAHN expressway
(9) IMAMS Moslem priests
(9) YOGIN Hindu holy men
(9) HIEROPHANTS high priests (of ancient Greece)
(9) LAMAS Buddhist monks
(9) TRACTABILITY docility
(10) EMBLAZONED inscribed; adorned with heraldic devices
(10) ESSENCE fundamental nature
(10) PARADOXICALLY contradictorily

(10) EXACTED demanded
(10) CONGEALING hardening
(10) ERSTWHILE former
(11) PLACEBO fake medication given to gratify a patient; thus anything that soothes but does not cure
(11) DEMENTED mad
(11) NOXIOUS harmful
(11) SOPORIFICS sleeping powders
(11) PALLIATIVE alleviating
(11) BESOTTING stupefying
(11) PENULTIMATE next to last
(14) INVENTORY list of contents
(15) PARAMOUNT prime
(18) IMPLEMENTATION carrying out; putting into effect
(19) PSYCHOSIS severe psychological disturbance
(19) PSYCHOSOMATIC resulting from emotional stress
(21) PRECARIOUS dangerous
(21) CONTAGION transmission by direct or indirect contact
(22) TUITION instruction
(22) EDIFICATION enlightenment

Franz Kafka (1883–1924) has become, since his death, one of the important writers of this century. He worked for many years as a civil employee of the Austrian government; all his creative energy was channeled into his literary works. "Kafkaesque" has come to mean a kind of gothic, mysterious, and terror-filled writing. Among his works are "The Castle," "The Trial," and "The Penal Colony."

This nightmarish story is an allegory. In it the author describes the foolish behavior of what we think of as the lowest of animals.

FRANZ KAFKA

Jackals and Arabs

1 We were camping in the oasis. My companions were asleep. The tall, white figure of an Arab passed by; he had been seeing to the camels and was on his way to his own sleeping place.

2 I threw myself on my back in the grass; I tried to fall asleep; I could not; a jackal howled in the distance; I sat up again. And what had been so far away was all at once quite near. Jackals were swarming round me, eyes gleaming dull gold and vanishing again, lithe bodies moving nimbly and rhythmically as if at the crack of a whip.

3 One jackal came from behind me, nudging right under my arm, pressing against me, as if he needed my warmth, and then stood before me and spoke to me almost eye to eye.

4 "I am the oldest jackal far and wide. I am delighted to have met you here at last. I had almost given up hope, since we have been waiting endless years for you; my mother waited for you, and her mother, and all our fore-mothers right back to the first mother of all the jackals. It is true, believe me!"

5   "That is surprising," said I, forgetting to kindle the pile of firewood which lay ready to smoke away jackals, "that is very surprising for me to hear. It is by pure chance that I have come here from the far North, and I am making only a short tour of your country. What do you jackals want, then?"

6   As if emboldened by this perhaps too friendly inquiry the ring of jackals closed in on me; all were panting and openmouthed.

7   "We know," began the eldest, "that you have come from the North; that is just what we base our hopes on. You Northerners have the kind of intelligence that is not to be found among Arabs. Not a spark of intelligence, let me tell you, can be struck from their cold arrogance. They kill animals for food, and carrion they despise."

8   "Not so loud," said I, "there are Arabs sleeping near by."

9   "You are indeed a stranger here," said the jackal, "or you would know that never in the history of the world has any jackal been afraid of an Arab. Why should we fear them? Is is not misfortune enough for us to be exiled among such creatures?"

10   "Maybe, maybe," said I, "matters so far outside my province I am not competent to judge; it seems to me a very old quarrel; I suppose it's in the blood, and perhaps will only end with it."

11   "You are very clever," said the old jackal; and they all began to pant more quickly; the air pumped out of their lungs although they were standing still; a rank smell which at times I had to set my teeth to endure streamed from their open jaws, "you are very clever; what you have just said agrees with our old tradition. So we shall draw blood from them and the quarrel will be over."

12   "Oh!" said I, more vehemently than I intended, "they'll defend themselves; they'll shoot you down in dozens with their muskets."

13   "You misunderstand us," said he, "a human failing which persists apparently even in the far North. We're not proposing to kill them. All the water in the Nile couldn't cleanse us of that. Why, the mere sight of their living flesh makes us turn tail and flee into cleaner air, into the desert, which for that very reason is our home."

14   And all the jackals around, including many newcomers from farther away, dropped their muzzles between their forelegs and wiped them with their paws; it was as if they were trying to conceal a disgust so overpowering that I felt like leaping over their heads to get away.

15   "Then what are you proposing to do?" I asked, trying to rise to my feet; but I could not get up; two young beasts behind me had locked their teeth through my coat and shirt; I had to go on sitting. "These are your trainbearers," explained the old jackal, quite seriously, "a mark of honor." "They must let go!" I cried, turning now to the old jackal, now to the youngsters. "They will, of course," said the old one, "if that is your wish. But it will take a little time, for they have got their teeth well in, as is our custom, and must first loosen their jaws bit by bit. Meanwhile, give ear to our petition." "Your conduct hasn't exactly inclined me to grant it," said I. "Don't hold it against us that we are clumsy," said he, and now for the first time had recourse to the natural plaintiveness of his voice, "we are poor creatures, we have nothing but our teeth; whatever we want to do, good or bad, we can

tackle it only with our teeth." "Well, what do you want?" I asked, not much mollified.

16   "Sir," he cried, and all the jackals howled together; very remotely it seemed to resemble a melody. "Sir, we want you to end this quarrel that divides the world. You are exactly the man whom our ancestors foretold as born to do it. We want to be troubled no more by Arabs; room to breathe; a skyline cleansed of them; no more bleating of sheep knifed by an Arab; every beast to die a natural death; no interference till we have drained the carcass empty and picked its bones clean. Cleanliness, nothing but cleanliness is what we want" — and now they were all lamenting and sobbing — "how can you bear to live in such a world, O noble heart and kindly bowels? Filth is their white; filth is their black; their beards are a horror; the very sight of their eye sockets makes one want to spit; and when they lift an arm, the murk of hell yawns in the armpit. And so, sir, and so, dear sir, by means of your all-powerful hands slit their throats through with these scissors!" And in answer to a jerk of his head a jackal came trotting up with a small pair of sewing scissors, covered with ancient rust, dangling from an eyetooth.

17   "Well, here's the scissors at last, and high time to stop!" cried the Arab leader of our caravan who had crept upwind toward us and now cracked his great whip.

18   The jackals fled in haste, but at some little distance rallied in a close huddle, all the brutes so tightly packed and rigid that they looked as if penned in a small fold girt by flickering will-o'-the-wisps.

19   "So you've been treated to this entertainment too, sir," said the Arab, laughing as gaily as the reserve of his race permitted. "You know, then, what the brutes are after?" I asked. "Of course," said he, "it's common knowledge; so long as Arabs exist, that pair of scissors goes wandering through the desert and will wander with us to the end of our days. Every European is offered it for the great work; every European is just the man that Fate has chosen for them. They have the most lunatic hopes, these beasts; they're just fools, utter fools. That's why we like them; they are our dogs; finer dogs than any of yours. Watch this, now, a camel died last night and I have had it brought here."

20   Four men came up with the heavy carcass and threw it down before us. It had hardly touched the ground before the jackals lifted up their voices. As if irresistibly drawn by cords each of them began to waver forward, crawling on his belly. They had forgotten the Arabs, forgotten their hatred, the all-obliterating immediate presence of the stinking carrion bewitched them. One was already at the camel's throat, sinking his teeth straight into an artery. Like a vehement small pump endeavoring with as much determination as hopefulness to extinguish some raging fire, every muscle in his body twitched and labored at the task. In a trice they were all on top of the carcass, laboring in common, piled mountain-high.

21   And now the caravan leader lashed his cutting whip crisscross over their backs. They lifted their heads; half swooning in ecstasy; saw the Arabs standing before them; felt the sting of the whip on their muz-

zles; leaped and ran backward a stretch. But the camel's blood was already lying in pools, reeking to heaven, the carcass was torn wide open in many places. They could not resist it; they were back again; once more the leader lifted his whip; I stayed his arm.

22   "You are right, sir," said he, "we'll leave them to their business; besides, it's time to break camp. Well, you've seen them. Marvelous creatures, aren't they? And how they hate us!"

Discussion of Theme

1. By what other people in what nations might the last two lines have been spoken? Do the words have a familiar ring?
2. What is the significance of the jackals' switch from boldness to servility in paragraph 15? What caused the change in attitude?
3. How much are you able to determine (other than that he is opposed to war) about Kafka's political or social convictions from this allegory?
4. Is it possible to extract more than one meaning from this tale? What?
5. How can we take a story about talking animals seriously as a comment on the affairs of men?

Discussion of Rhetoric

1. Would this story be just as interesting if it were not an allegory? Why or why not?
2. What makes allegories timeless?
3. This story is a narration in the form of an allegory. How effective is this writing technique?
4. What is the effect of the author's use of such phrases as "blood . . . reeking to heaven" and "carcass was torn wide open"?
5. What do the jackals symbolize? The Arabs?

Writing Assignments

1. Write an allegory about the war in Vietnam.
2. Write an animal allegory illustrating one of the Seven Deadly Sins.

Library Exploration

1. Read about the French-Algerian conflict. Does this allegory apply?
2. Make a report on the life of Kafka.
3. If this essay interested you, read and report on one of the books mentioned in the biographical note.

Vocabulary

(2) LITHE   supple
(2) NIMBLY   agilely
(6) EMBOLDENED   given courage
(7) CARRION   decaying flesh
(12) VEHEMENTLY   intensely
(15) PLAINTIVENESS   sorrowfulness

(15) MOLLIFIED   appeased
(18) GIRT   encircled
(18) WILL-O'-THE-WISPS   mysterious flashes of light
(20) OBLITERATING   wiping out

Lewis Mumford (1895–) is famous as a writer and cultural philosopher. He was born in New York and educated at the City College of New York and Columbia University, and has taught at several universities, including Columbia, Dartmouth, and Stanford. As the author of more than twenty books, he has established himself as an authority in many fields, including architecture and city planning.

Mumford traces war to what may be for some a startling beginning and examines the paradox that as civilizations grow, war grows rather than diminishes.

LEWIS MUMFORD

How War Began

1 At the time that the first great civilizations of the ancient world were coming into existence, the human race suffered an injury from which it has not yet recovered. If I interpret the evidence correctly, that injury still plays an active part in our lives, and caps our most hopeful dreams about human improvement with nightmares of destruction and extermination.

2　This injury happened at a moment when primitive man's powers, like ours today, had suddenly expanded; and it was due essentially to an aberration, or a series of aberrations, which put his most beneficent inventions at the command of his neurotic anxieties. So far from disappearing with time and being healed by the growth of law and reason, this original injury has only tightened its hold upon the collective actions of tribes and nations.

3　The aberration I refer to is the institution of war; and my purpose in discussing its origins is to bring into consciousness a group of events and beliefs that have long remained buried, partly through sheer neglect, partly through a repression of painful irrationalities that contradicted civilized man's belief in his own orderly and rational behavior. It is only today, after a century of prodigious research into human origins, that some of these events have come to light and been thrown open to interpretation.

4   That early injury had an effect upon civilized life, somewhat comparable to the kind of childhood injury that psychiatrists characterize as a trauma: an injury whose worst results may not show themselves till far on in adult life. Instead of being buried in the psyche of an individual, it became embedded in the institutional life of every succeeding city, state and empire.

5   In making this analysis, I shall have to start from an assumption that is unprovable; namely, that there is a parallel between the general human situation today and that faced by the individual, unable to cope with the problems of his life, unable to make rational decisions, baffled, depressed, paralyzed, because he is still the prey of infantile fantasies he is unable to escape or control. In the case of individuals, we know that such fantasies, deeply embedded in childhood, may keep on poisoning the whole system, though the wound has seemingly healed and the scar is hardly visible. Childhood misapprehensions, animosities and resentments, childhood misinterpretations of natural events, such as birth, death, separation—all account for the persistence of infantile patterns of conduct. Often, later in life, these patterns overcome the adult and leave him helpless. He still views present realities through the distorting glasses of his childhood fantasy.

6   That something unfortunate once happened to man at the very moment when an immense creativity was released was perhaps recognized in part in the Jewish and Christian myth of the Fall, which was anticipated by even earlier Egyptian lamentations over the perverse wickedness of man in going contrary to the gods. Many other peoples, from China to Greece, looked back to a golden age when war and strife were unknown, and when, as Lao-tse put it, one village might look at the smoke rising from the chimneys of another nearby, without envy or rivalry.

7   There is now enough anthropological and archaeological evidence to show that there is at least a partial basis for these wistful memories of a more peaceful past, when scarcity of food, violence, danger and death were mainly the results of natural disasters, not the deliberate products of man. If civilization's first great achievements awakened new fears and anxieties, we must understand how and why this happened; for these fears and anxieties still press on us. As long as the source of our irrational acts remains hidden, the forces that are still driving us to destruction will seem uncontrollable. The worst part about civilized man's original errors and the most threatening aspect of our present situation are that we regard some of our most self-destructive arts as normal and unavoidable.

8   There is a close parallel between our own age, exalted yet stunned by the seemingly limitless expansion of all its powers, and the epoch that marked the emergence of the earliest civilizations in Egypt and Mesopotamia. In his pride over his present accomplishments, it is

perhaps natural for modern man to think that such a vast release of physical energy and human potentiality had never taken place before. But on examination this proves a too flattering illusion: the two ages of power, modern and ancient, are bound together by many similar characteristics, both good and evil, which set them apart from other phases of human history.

9   Just as the prelude to the nuclear age came with the large-scale introduction of water, wind and steam power, so the first steps toward civilization were taken in the neolithic domestication of plants and animals. This agricultural revolution gave man food, energy, security and surplus manpower on a scale no earlier culture had known. Among the achievements that mark this transformation from barbarism to civilization were the beginnings of astronomy and mathematics, the first astronomical calendar, the sailboat, the plow, the potter's wheel, the loom, the irrigation canal, the man-powered machine. Civilized man's emotional and intellectual potentialities were raised further through the invention of writing, the elaboration of the permanent record in painting, sculpture and monuments, and the building of walled cities.

10   This great leap forward came to a climax about 5000 years ago. A like mobilization and magnification of power did not again take place until our own era. For most of recorded history, mankind has lived on the usufruct of that early advance, making many piecemeal additions and widening the province held by civilization, but never essentially changing the original pattern.

11   There was probably an important religious side to this whole transformation. With the priestly observations that produced the measured months and years, people became conscious, as never before, of human dependence upon the cosmic forces, the sun, the moon, the planets, on whose operation all life depended. Planetary movement of "clockwork" regularity gave man his first glimpse of an orderly, repetitive, impersonal world, utterly reliable, but benignly productive only within the frame of its inflexible laws.

12   With this new cosmic theology there came a sudden fusion of sacred and secular power, in the person of the all-powerful king, standing at the apex of the social pyramid. The king was both a secular ruler and the chief priest or even, in the case of the Egyptians, a living god. He no longer needed to follow village tradition and customs like the village council of elders. His will was law. Kingship by divine right claimed magic powers and evoked magic collective responses.

13   What kingly power could not do solely by intimidation, and what magical rites and orderly astronomical observations could not do alone by successful prediction, the two in combination actually did accomplish. Large assemblages of men moved and acted as if they were one, obedient to the royal command, fulfilling the will of the gods and rulers. People were driven to heroic physical efforts and sacrifices beyond all precedent. Throughout history, the major public works — canals, embankments, roads, walls, "pyramids" in every form — have been built with forced labor, either conscripted for part of the year or permanently enslaved. The enduring symbol of this vast expansion and regimentation of power is, of course, the Great Pyramid of

Cheops, built without wheeled vehicles or iron tools, by relays of 100,000 men working over many years.

14 Should we be surprised that the achievements of our own age of nuclear power appeared first at this period as myths and fantasies associated with the gods? Absolute power, power to create and annihilate, became the attribute of a succession of deities. Out of his own substance the Egyptian sun god, Atum, created the universe. Instantaneous communication, remote control, the collective incineration of whole cities (Sodom and Gomorrah), and germ warfare (one of the plagues of Egypt) were freely practiced by a succession of inhumane deities in order to insure that their commands would be obeyed. Human rulers, who still lacked the facilities to carry out these dreams on a great scale, nevertheless sought to counterfeit them. With the growth of an efficient bureaucracy, a trained army, systematic taxation and forced labor, this early totalitarian system showed all the depressing features that similar governments show in our own day.

15 An overconcentration on power as an end in itself is always suspect to the psychologist. He reads in it attempts to conceal inferiority, anxiety and impotence. Perhaps early civilized man was justifiably frightened by the forces he himself had brought into existence, in the way that many people are frightened now by nuclear power. In neither case was the extension of physical power and political command accompanied by a complementary development of moral direction and humane control.

16 There were further grounds for doubt and fear among men of that early civilization. Though they had achieved a hitherto unattainable security and wealth, the very growth of population and the extension of trade made their whole economy more subject to conditions and forces they could not control.

17 Our age knows how difficult it is to achieve equilibrium and security in an economy of abundance. But the early fabric of civilization was far more precariously balanced, since the welfare of the whole was based on the magical identification of the king and the community in the beliefs and rites of their religion. The king personified the community; he was the indispensable connecting link between ordinary men and the cosmic powers they must propitiate and obey. While the king assumed full responsibility for the life and welfare of his subjects, the community, in turn, waxed and waned with the life of its ruler.

18 The magical identification produced a further occasion for anxiety, far deeper than any threat of actual floods or bad crops, for despite their claims to divine favor and immortality, kings too were subject to mortal accidents and misfortunes. So constant was this anxiety that the Egyptian Pharaoh's name could not be uttered without interjecting the prayer, "Life! Prosperity! Health!" This identification of the king's life with the community's fate produced an even more sinister perversion. To avert the wrath of the gods, indicated by any natural mischance, the king himself must be slain as a sacrifice. At this early stage, dream and fact, myth and hallucination, religion and science formed a confused welter. One lucky change in weather after a ritual sacrifice might give sanction to a long-repeated chain of ritualistic slaughters.

19   To save the king from this discouraging fate, which might lessen the attractions of the office, a further trick of religious magic came into play. A stand-in would be chosen and temporarily treated with all the honors and privileges of a king, in order to perform the final role of sacrificial victim on the altar. As the demand for such victims increased in times of trouble, these substitutes were sought outside the community, by violent capture. And what began as a one-sided raid for captives in time brought about the collective reprisals and counter-raids that became institutionalized as war. Back of war lay this barbarous religious sanction: only by human sacrifice can the community be saved.

20   War, then, was a specific product of civilization—the outcome of an organized effort to obtain captives for a magical blood sacrifice. In time, armed might itself took on a seemingly independent existence, and the extension of power became an end in itself, a manifestation of the "health" of the state. But underneath the heavy overlayers of rationalization, war remained colored by the original infantile misconception that communal life and prosperity could be preserved only by sacrificial expiation. Civilized man's later efforts to impute the origin of war to some primal animal instinct toward murderous aggression against his own kind are empty rationalizing. Here the words of the anthropologist, Bronislaw Malinowski, are decisive: "If we insist that war is a fight between two independent and politically organized groups, war does not occur at a primitive level."

21   What is most remarkable about the spread of war as a permanent institution is that the collective anxiety that originally brought about the ritual of human sacrifice seems to have deepened with material progress. And as anxiety increased, it could no longer be appeased by a mere symbolic sacrifice at the altar, for the ritual itself produced hatred, fear and a natural desire for revenge among the people victimized. In time ever greater numbers, with more effective weapons, were drawn into the brutal ceremony, so that what was at first a preliminary, one-sided raid before the sacrifice became the essential sacrifice itself. The alternative to permitting the mass slaughter of one's own people was the destruction of the enemy's city and temple and the enslavement of the population. These acts periodically eased anxiety and enhanced power. War provided a kind of self-justification in displacing neurotic anticipations by actual dangers—that return to reality seems to restore human equipoise. Psychiatrists observed during the blitz in London that the need for facing real dangers often removed a patient's load of neurotic anxiety. But war performs this service at a ghastly price. Psychologically healthy people have no need to court dismemberment and death.

22   The growth of law and orderly behavior and morals, which improved the relation of men in cities, was not transferred to the collective relations of communities; for the ability to produce disorder, violence and destruction itself remained a symbol of royal power. From the relatively peaceful Egyptians to the bloodthirsty Assyrians and Mongolians, one monument after another boasts of kings humiliated, prisoners killed, cities ruined. The solemn association of kingship, sacred power, human sacrifice and military effectiveness

formed a dominant complex that governed human behavior everywhere. But in time the search for sacrificial captives took on a utilitarian disguise—if spared as slaves, they added to the labor force. So
the secondary products of military effort—slaves, booty, land, tribute—
supplanted and concealed the original anxiety motive. Since a general
expansion of productive power and culture had accompanied kingship and human sacrifice, people were conditioned to accept the evil
as the only way of securing the good. The repeated death of civilizations from internal disintegration and outward assault underscores the
fact that the evil elements in this amalgam largely canceled the goods
and blessings.

23   This perception is not a discovery of modern historians. After the
eighth century B.C. the working principles of a power-centered civilization were boldly challenged by a long series of religious prophets,
from Amos and Isaiah to Lao-tse and Mo Ti. Whatever their differences the exponents of these new ideas scorned the notion of
a mere increase of power and material wealth as the central purpose
of life. In the name of peace and love they rejected irrational human
sacrifice in every form—on the altar or on the battlefield. Christianity
went even further. Alone among the religions, instead of sacrificing
human beings to appease the divine wrath, its God sacrificed himself,
renouncing His power in behalf of love, in order to save mankind by
cleansing the sinner of anxiety and guilt.

24   But the power complex, embedded in the routines of civilization,
was not dislodged by even this challenge. Ironically, Christianity itself
supplanted its pagan rivals by seizing the power of the state under
Constantine (A.D. 313) and utilizing all its engines of compulsion. As
in the times of Moloch and Bel, the bloodiest collective sacrifices in
history were those made in wars to establish the supremacy of a state
religion.

25   How are we to explain the persistence of war, with its victories that
turn out as disastrous as its defeats, its just causes that produce unjust
or contradictory consequences, and its heroic martyrdoms sullied and
betrayed by the base, selfish conduct of the survivors? There seem to
me two general answers. One is that the original pattern of civilization,
as it took form in the walled city and in turn produced the "walled"
state, has remained unaltered until modern times. War was an integral
part of the constellation of civilized institutions, held in tension within
the city, on the basis of a division of classes, slavery and forced labor,
and religious uniformity. To remove any part of this fabric seemed, to
the rulers of men, a threat to every other part. They exalted the
sacrifices of war because they wanted to maintain their own power.

26   There was an additional mitigating factor: until recent times, only a
small part of the world's population accepted the terms of civilized life
and its constant involvement with war; moreover, the amount of damage any army could inflict was limited. In Christian nations the human
cost of war had been further reduced by the acceptance of a military
code that limited violence to armed soldiers and generally exempted
civilians and even their property from capture or deliberate destruction. Finally, the greater part of the world's population, living in rural
communities, immune by their feebleness and poverty from the

rapacious temptations of urbanized power, constituted a reservoir of vitality and sanity.

27   These mitigations and compensations progressively reduced the evils of total war as practiced by the early empires; but neither the needs of commerce, nor the admonitions of religion, nor the bitter experience of bereavement and enslavement altered the basic pattern. By any reasonable standard, war should early have been classed with individual murder, as an unqualified collective crime or an insane act, but those who held power never permitted any subversive judgment on the irrationality of the method, even if applied to rational ends. The fact that war has persisted and now threatens, at the very peak of our advances in science and technology, to become all-enveloping and all-destructive, points to the deep irrationality that first brought it into existence. This irrationality springs not only from the original aberration but from the unconscious depths of man, plagued with repressed guilt and anxiety over the godlike powers he presumptuously has learned to wield.

28   Western culture during the last four centuries has produced an explosive release of human potentialities and powers. Unfortunately the irrationalities of the past have been subjected to a similar projection and magnification.

29   The most formidable threat we confront, perhaps, is the fact that the fantasies that governed the ancient founders of civilization have now become fully realizable. Our most decisive recent inventions, the atom bomb and the planetary rocket, came about through a fusion of secular and "sacred" power, similar to their ancient union. Without the physical resources of an all-powerful state and the intellectual resources of an all-knowing corps of scientists, that sudden command of cosmic energy and interplanetary space would not have been possible. Powers of total destruction that ancient man dared impute only to his gods, any mere Russian or American air-force general can now command. So wide and varied are the means of extermination by blast and radiation burns, by slow contamination from radioactive food and water, to say nothing of lethal bacteria and genetic deformities, that the remotest hamlet is in as great peril as a metropolis. The old factor of safety has vanished.

30   As our agents of destruction have reached cosmic dimensions, both our tangible fears and our neurotic apprehensions have increased until they are so terrifying to live with that they are involuntarily repressed. This repression is particularly notable in America, where it is marked by the virtual absence of any discussion or critical challenge of either our nuclear weapons or our ultimate aims. This is perhaps an indication of the unconscious guilt we feel for developing and actually using the atom bomb. Along with an unwillingness to face our own conduct or search for alternative courses, our behavior presents an even more dangerous symptom — an almost pathological sense of compulsion to pyramid our errors. This drives us to invest ever-increasing quantities of intelligence and energy in the building of ever more dangerous absolute weapons, while devoting but an insignificant fraction of this same energy and intelligence to the development of

indispensable political and moral controls. We are in fact using our new knowledge and our new powers to reinforce ancient errors and prolong the life of obsolete institutions that should long ago have been liquidated.

31   What is more disturbing than our official reversion to the lowest level of barbarism in war is the fact that even after the last war only a minority of our countrymen seems to have reflected on the moral implications of this practice of total extermination as a normal and acceptable means of overcoming an enemy's resistance. There is nothing in our own code now to distinguish us from moral monsters like Genghis Khan. If we are willing to kill 100,000 people with one blow by random genocide, as at Hiroshima, there is nothing to keep us from killing 100,000,000 — except the thought that our own country-men may be massacred in equally large numbers.

32   During the last dozen years every responsible head of government has confessed openly that with our present readiness to use methods of atomic, bacterial and chemical extermination, we might bring an end to civilization and permanently deform, if not destroy, the whole human race. Our failure to act on this warning, as an animal would act in the face of a comparable danger, gives the measure of our neurotic compulsions. So even the prudent thought of our own retributory, collective death offers no guarantee against the misuse of our powers so long as the engines of total annihilation remain available and the neurosis itself persists.

33   The two principal nuclear powers have been acting as if each was all-powerful and could dictate the terms of existence to the rest of the planet. In the name of absolute sovereignty they have actually achieved impotence. What has been called the "stalemate of terror" is in fact a deliberate checkmate of those humane gifts and adroit moves that might save us. This precarious stalemate may be ended at any moment by a careless gesture, which could upset the board itself and sweep away all the pieces. It can be effectively ended only by both sides acknowledging their paralyzing inability to move and agreeing to start a new game.

34   To conceive this new game, which can no longer be played under the old rules with the old pieces, both powers must take their eyes off each other and address themselves to the common task of saving the world from the threatened catastrophe they have impetuously brought within range. Instead, these governments with the connivance of their allies have been seeking to normalize their neurosis and have made participation in their infantile plans and infantile fantasies a test of political sanity. By now, a respected official in charge of Civil Defense finds it easier to envisage a whole nation of 180,000,000 living permanently underground than to conceive of any means of delivering the world of its diabolical hatreds and collective paranoias. Strangely, such a national burial is put forward as an ingenious method for com-bating possible Russian blackmail. This failure to recognize when the remedy is worse than the disease is one of the score of current symp-toms of mental disorder in apparently orderly minds.

35   If no great changes were yet visible in the general pattern of

civilization, this picture would be extremely dismal; for as long as the old institutions remain operative, war will continue an integral expression of the anxieties and tensions they produce. Fortunately, this original structure has undergone a profound change during the past four centuries; and a large part of it is no longer acceptable. The old urban container has in fact exploded, leaving behind only a few citadels of absolute power on the ancient pattern, like the Kremlin and the Pentagon. What is even more important, the invisible walls between classes and castes have been breaking down steadily during the last several decades—more rapidly in the United States perhaps than in Communist countries.

36   What applies to the division of classes also applies to the disparity between nations. Neither knowledge nor power nor material goods can be monopolized by any privileged class or privileged country. Those Americans who fancied we had a permanent monopoly of atomic energy and technical skill recently found this out to their dismay; but the moral is not that we must "catch up with the Russians," but that we must accept the duties and demands of living in an open world among our equals. The real world of modern man has become porous and penetrable: every part of it is more closely interrelated than ever before and therefore more dependent upon the good will and sympathy and self-restraint of the rest of mankind. St. Paul's injunction to the little Christian congregations that everyone should be "members one of another," has now become a practical necessity of survival among the nations.

37   If so many other institutions of civilization, which held together solidly for 6000 years, have been crumbling away and are being replaced, is it likely that war will escape the same fate? The logic of history suggests it will not—if history has a logic. Our own military leaders have wryly admitted that in any large-scale war neither side can hope for a victory; indeed they have not the faintest notion of how such a war, once begun, might be ended, short of total extermination for both sides. Thus we are back at the very point at which civilization started, but at an even lower depth of savagery and irrationality. Instead of a token sacrifice to appease the gods, there would now be a total sacrifice, merely to bring an end to our neurotic anxieties.

38   In short, only the irrational, superstitious, magical function of war remains as a live possibility—the propitiation of gods in whom we do not believe by a sacrifice that would nullify the meaning of human history. In that surviving pocket of festering irrationality lies our chief, if not our only, enemy.

39   What are the possibilities of mankind's acquiring a fresh grip on reality and shedding the compulsive fantasies that are pushing us to destruction? There is little question of what measures must be taken to avoid a general nuclear catastrophe. Every intelligent observer understands the minimum precautions necessary for securing physical safety and for enabling a reconstituted United Nations to operate, not as a feeble hand brake on power politics, but as an active agent of international justice and comity. The only vital problem now is whether we can liberate ourselves from our irrational attitudes and

habits, so that we may firmly take the necessary steps. It is not enough to appeal to human reason alone, as intelligent people often so earnestly do, to avert a general holocaust. We must first bring our long-buried sacrificial fantasies into the open before they erupt once more through internal pressure. Only exposure will counteract their power over us.

40   As with a neurotic patient, one of the conditions for resuming control and making rational decisions, free from pathological deformation, is the continued existence of large areas of conduct that are still orderly, co-operative, harmonious, life-directed. Once the patient has the courage to unburden himself of his disruptive experiences and recognize them for what they are, the sound parts of his personality can be brought into play. Fortunately, much of our life is still conducted on wholly rational and humane terms; furthermore, modern man is closer to confronting his hidden irrationalities than ever before. Scientific curiosity, which led to the discovery of the hidden structure of matter, also led to the exploration of the hidden structure of the human psyche. We now begin to understand the actual meaning of the morbid dreams, fantasies and nightmares that have repeatedly undermined the highest human achievements.

41   With the knowledge that the biologist and the psychologist have furnished us, we must now perceive that both the original premises of civilization and those of our own so-called Nuclear, or Space, Age are humanly obsolete — and were always false. In purely physical terms, we now have possession of absolute power of cosmic dimensions, as in a thermonuclear reaction. But "absolute power" belongs to the same magico-religious scheme as the ritual of human sacrifice itself; living organisms can use only limited amounts of power. "Too much" or "too little" is equally fatal to life. Every organism, indeed, possesses a built-in system of automatic controls which governs its intake of energy, limits its excessive growth, and maintains its equilibrium. When those controls do not operate, life itself comes to an end. When we wield power extravagantly without respect to other human goals, we actually upset the balance of the organism and threaten the pattern of the whole organic environment. Unqualified power diminishes the possibilities for life, growth, development. More than a century ago Emerson wrote, "Do not trust man, great God! with more power until he has learned to use his little power better."

42   The test of maturity, for nations as for individuals, is not the increase of power, but the increase of self-understanding, self-control, self-direction and self-transcendence. For in a mature society, man himself, not his machines, or his organizations, is the chief work of art.

43   The real problem of our age is to search into the depths of the human soul, both in the present generation and in the race's history, in order to bring to light the devious impulses that have deflected man for so long from his fullest development. For the human race has always lived and flourished, not by any one-sided exhibition of power, but by the constant sustenance and co-operation of the entire world of living beings. Not to seize power, but to protect and cherish life is the chief end of man; and the godlike powers that the human race now

commands only add to its responsibilities for self-discipline and make more imperative a post-magical, post-mechanical, post-nuclear ideology which shall be centered, not on power, but on life.

44   Can such a new approach become operative in time to liberate man from war itself, as he was once liberated by his own efforts from incest, cannibalism, the blood feud and slavery? It is too early to answer this question, and it is perhaps almost too late to ask it. Admittedly it may take an all-but-fatal shock treatment, close to catastrophe, to break the hold of civilized man's chronic neurosis. Even such a belated awakening would be a miracle. But with the diagnosis so grave and the prognosis so unfavorable, one must fall back on miracles — above all, the miracle of life itself, that past master of the unexpected, the unpredictable, the all-but-impossible.

Discussion of Theme

1. To what extent is our society based on fear? Fear of what? Do you agree with Mumford that understanding the source of our fear can bring an end to war?
2. Should war be "classed with individual murder, as an unqualified crime or an insane act"? What problems might be entailed in trying and convicting the criminals or madmen? Do you think there would ever be universal agreement that war is "individual murder"?
3. Mumford says that we are "using our new knowledge and our new powers to . . . prolong the life of obsolete institutions that should long ago have been liquidated." What institutions is he referring to? Why should they be abolished?
4. In explaining his theory, Mumford traces a long and complex course from early civilization to the present. What is the relationship, as he sees it, between human sacrifices and modern war?
5. Mumford states that "the physical resources of an all-powerful state and the intellectual resources of an all-knowing corps of scientists" are responsible for developing modern warfare to its present state. Has the government corrupted scientists?
6. Mumford admits that man experienced an injury not unlike a trauma in the beginning, yet he declares the Jewish-Christian explanation of that trauma to be a myth. Do you agree with his reasoning?

Discussion of Rhetoric

1. In what paragraph does the connection between ancient customs and modern warfare become clear to you? Would it have been better if the author had stated it at the outset of the article?
2. Why does Mumford wait until paragraph 3 to state his thesis?
3. Rhetorically speaking, what value is there in comparing and contrasting modern man and ancient man in paragraphs 8, 9, and 10?
4. Did you have trouble in following the argument in this selection? Why? Was it the diction, the organization, or the sentence structure?

Writing Assignments

1. Is the American character basically violent? Give your reasons for agreeing or disagreeing. Support with specific evidence.
2. Defend the competitive spirit, citing the good that it accomplishes in our society.
3. Analyze Mumford's logic.
4. Discuss organized religion's contribution to war, including the position of various churches during recent years.

Library Exploration

1. For further discussion of this topic by Mumford, read *The Transformations of Man* (1956).
2. Probably the most famous contemporary analysis of war is *Study of War*, by Quincy Wright.

Vocabulary

(2) ABERRATION deviation from the normal or right way

(2) BENEFICENT helpful; resulting in good

(3) PRODIGIOUS vast

(5) MISAPPREHENSIONS misunderstandings

(6) LAMENTATIONS expressions of grief

(8) EPOCH era

(9) NEOLITHIC designating the later part of the Stone Age

(10) USUFRUCT use of the fruits of another's labors

(11) BENIGNLY kindly

(13) INTIMIDATION forcing by threats

(13) CONSCRIPTED drafted

(15) COMPLEMENTARY supplying something that is lacking or felt to be needed

(16) HITHERTO before this time

(17) PRECARIOUSLY dangerously; uncertainly

(17) PROPITIATE appease

(17) WAXED AND WANED increased and declined in power, prosperity, etc.

(19) REPRISALS retaliations for injuries received

(20) EXPIATION making amends

(20) IMPUTE attribute

(20) PRIMAL primitive

(21) EQUIPOISE balance

(22) UTILITARIAN practical

(22) AMALGAM combination

(26) MITIGATING moderating

(26) RAPACIOUS voracious; greedy

(27) BEREAVEMENT loss of loved ones by death

(27) PRESUMPTUOUSLY brazenly

(30) TANGIBLE real

(31) GENOCIDE killing an entire race

(32) EXTERMINATION wiping out

(32) PRUDENT cautiously wise

(32) RETRIBUTORY marked by retribution, that is, requital according to merits or deserts, especially for evil

(34) IMPETUOUSLY impulsively

(34) CONNIVANCE implied consent to wrongdoing

(34) DIABOLICAL devilish

(34) PARANOIAS   excessive or abnormal suspiciousness and distrustfulness of others

(34) INGENIOUS   very clever

(35) CITADELS   strongholds

(36) DISPARITY   inequality

(36) POROUS   full of tiny holes; permeable

(37) WRYLY   with slightly bitter humor

(39) COMITY   courteous behavior; mutual consideration

(42) SELF-TRANSCENDENCE rising above oneself

(44) CHRONIC   lasting over time

(44) PROGNOSIS   prediction of the probable course (of a disease)

A paradox of our involvement in Vietnam is that in giving aid to the country and its people, we are destroying both. As this article makes clear, our massive bombings, defoliation, and herbicide programs have been the cause of environmental ruin in that Asian country.

THE SIERRA CLUB BULLETIN

A Fable for Our Times

Once upon a time there was a small, beautiful, green and graceful country called Vietnam. It needed to be saved. (In later years no one could remember exactly what it needed to be saved from, but that is another story.) For many years Vietnam was in the process of being saved by France, but the French eventually tired of their labors and left. Then America took on the job. America was well equipped for country-saving. It was the richest and most powerful nation on earth. It had, for example, nuclear explosives on hand and ready to use equal to six tons of TNT for every man, woman, and child in the world. It had huge and very efficient factories, brilliant and dedicated scientists, and most (but not everybody) would agree, it had good intentions. Sadly, America had one fatal flaw—its inhabitants were in love with technology and thought it could do no wrong. A visitor to America during the time of this story would probably have guessed its outcome after seeing how its inhabitants were treating their own country. The air was mostly foul, the water putrid, and most of the land was either covered with concrete or garbage. But Americans were never much on introspection, and they didn't foresee the result of their loving embrace on the small country. They set out to save Vietnam with the same enthusiasm and determination their forefathers had displayed in conquering the frontier. They bombed. More than 3 million tons of explosives were dropped—50 per cent more than the total bomb tonnage dropped in both theatres of World War II. Technologists looked on in awe and spoke of a ditch 30 feet deep, 45 feet wide, and 30 thousand miles long if all the bomb craters were placed in a row. What the Vietnam peasant spoke of was never recorded. Entire villages were destroyed by bombing, napalm fires, and artillery. After one such mission an American officer made the prophetic explanation that it was necessary to destroy the village in order to save it. Unquestioned, the logic of such a statement became sanctified. They bombed with chemicals as well as explosives, and trees, bushes, plants died by the millions of acres in a program with the Orwellian name of "Operation Ranch Hand," whose macabre motto was "only we can prevent forests." The consequences of such a deliberate and massive ecological attack were unknown and unknowable, but that was no deterrent. Thousands of herbicide and defoliant missions were flown before anyone seriously questioned their long-range effect on humans and animals, as well as on plants. By the time deformed fetuses began appearing and signs of lasting ecological damage were becoming increasingly apparent, success had been achieved. Vietnam had been saved. But the country was dead.

Discussion of Theme

1. What is it that Vietnam "needed to be saved from"? Was this, in your opinion, sufficient cause for American intervention?
2. How do you account for the fact that the North Vietnamese did not waver in the face of increased bombing (over 3 million tons of explosives), and in fact became even more determined?
3. What contradictions do you see between the statements our political leaders have made concerning population control and the environment, and the actions of our government in Vietnam?
4. Some have claimed that our government is guilty of genocide in Vietnam. Do you agree?

Discussion of Rhetoric

1. In what sense is this selection a fable, as its title suggests?
2. What is the meaning of the paradox at the end of the selection?
3. Comment on the tone of this selection. How does the language help to establish the dominant mood?

Writing Assignments

1. Fables usually end with a moral. Write an appropriate moral for this one.
2. Should chemical and biological warfare be outlawed? Give your views in a short theme.
3. What has Vietnam become a symbol of in our society?

Library Exploration

1. The Pentagon Papers released by the *New York Times* and other newspapers in 1971 present many previously unpublished facts

about our country's activities in Vietnam. If copies of these articles are available to you, prepare a report based on several sections of them.

2. What is the Geneva Treaty? Who signed it and what are its terms? Why did the United States refuse to sign it?

Vocabulary

INTROSPECTION   self-examination or self-analysis

SANCTIFIED   made holy

MACABRE   gruesome

DETERRENT   something that prevents or discourages another's actions

FETUS   unborn baby

Henry David Thoreau (1817–62) is probably best known for his "Walden" (1854), an account of the two years he lived alone beside a New England lake on practically no money at all. He is also famous as the author of "Civil Disobedience" (1849). An associate of Ralph Waldo Emerson, he was an American transcendentalist philosopher, essayist, and naturalist.

In this selection taken from "Walden," Thoreau examines two warring groups of ants and draws some conclusions about them.

HENRY DAVID THOREAU

The Battle of the Ants

1 One day when I went out to my wood-pile, or rather my pile of stumps, I observed two large ants, the one red, the other one much larger, nearly half an inch long, and black, fiercely contending with one another. Having once got hold they never let go, but struggled and wrestled and rolled on the chips incessantly. Looking farther, I was surprised to find that the chips were covered with such combatants, that it was not a *duellum,* but a *bellum,* a war between two races of ants, the red always pitted against the black, and frequently two red ones to one black. The legions of these Myrmidons covered all the hills and vales in my wood-yard, and the ground was already strewn with the dead and dying, both red and black. It was the only battle which I have ever witnessed, the only battle-field I ever trod while the battle was raging; internecine war; the red republicans on the one hand, and the black imperialists on the other. On every side they were engaged in deadly combat, yet without any noise that I could hear, and human soldiers never fought so resolutely. I watched a couple that were fast locked in each other's embraces, in a little sunny valley amid the chips, now at noon-day prepared to fight till the sun went

down or life went out. The smaller red champion had fastened himself like a vise to his adversary's front, and through all the tumblings
on that field never for an instant ceased to gnaw at one of his feelers
near the root, having already caused the other to go by the board;
while the stronger black one dashed him from side to side, and, as I
saw on looking nearer, had already divested him of several of his
members. They fought with more pertinacity than bull-dogs. Neither
manifested the least disposition to retreat. It was evident that their
battle-cry was Conquer or die. In the meanwhile there came along a
single red ant on the hill-side of this valley, evidently full of excitement, who either had dispatched his foe, or had not yet taken part in
the battle; probably the latter, for he had lost none of his limbs; whose
mother had charged him to return with his shield or upon it. Or perchance he was some Achilles, who had nourished his wrath apart, and
had now come to avenge or rescue his Patroclus. He saw this unequal
combat from afar,—for the blacks were nearly twice the size of the
red,—he drew near with rapid pace till he stood on his guard within
half an inch of the combatants; then, watching his opportunity, he
sprang upon the black warrior, and commenced his operations near
the root of his right fore-leg, leaving the foe to select among his own
members; and so there were three united for life, as if a new kind of
attraction had been invented which put all other locks and cements to
shame. I should not have wondered by this time to find that they had
their respective musical bands stationed on some eminent chip, and
playing their national airs the while, to excite the slow and cheer the
dying combatants. I was myself excited somewhat even as if they had
been men. The more you think of it, the less the difference. And certainly there is not the fight recorded in Concord history, at least, if in
the history of America, that will bear a moment's comparison with
this, whether for the numbers engaged in it, or for the patriotism and
heroism displayed. For numbers and for carnage it was an Austerlitz
or Dresden. Concord Fight! Two killed on the patriots' side, and Luther Blanchard wounded! Why, here, every ant was a Buttrick,—"Fire!
for God's sake fire!"—and thousands shared the fate of Davis and
Hosmer. There was not one hireling there. I have no doubt that it was
a principle they fought for, as much as our ancestors, and not to avoid
a three-penny tax on their tea; and the results of this battle will be as
important and memorable to those whom it concerns as those of the
battle of Bunker Hill, at least.

2   I took up the chip on which the three I have particularly described
were struggling, carried it into my house, and placed it under a tumbler on my window-sill, in order to see the issue. Holding a microscope to the first-mentioned red ant, I saw that, though he was
assiduously gnawing at the near fore-leg of his enemy, having severed
his remaining feeler, his own breast was all torn away, exposing what
vitals he had there to the jaws of the black warrior, whose breastplate
was apparently too thick for him to pierce; and the dark carbuncles of
the sufferer's eyes shown with ferocity such as war only could excite.
They struggled half an hour longer under the tumbler, and when I
looked again the black soldier had severed the heads of his foes from
their bodies, and the still living heads were hanging on either side of

him like ghastly trophies at his saddle-bow, still apparently as firmly fastened as ever, and he was endeavoring with feeble struggles, being without feelers and with only the remnant of a leg, and I know not much how many other wounds, to divest himself of them; which at length, after half an hour more, he accomplished. I raised the glass, and he went off over the window-sill in that crippled state. Whether he finally survived that combat, and spent the remainder of his days in some Hotel des Invalides, I do not know: but I thought that his industry would not be worth much thereafter. I never learned which party was victorious, nor the cause of the war; but I felt for the rest of that day as if I had had my feelings excited and harrowed by witnessing the struggle, the ferocity and carnage, of a human battle before my door.

Discussion of Theme

1. In the act of lifting up the chip on which the ants were fighting, does Thoreau suggest the helplessness of men in the hands of God?
2. When Thoreau says "The more you think of it, the less the difference," is he saying that men are just as unimportant as ants, or that ants are as important as men?
3. Who were the red republicans? The black imperialists?
4. Is Thoreau showing the stupidity or the necessity of war by comparing ants to men?
5. Why should an ant war fascinate an apparently peaceful man?

Discussion of Rhetoric

1. Thoreau says that "I had had my feelings excited and harrowed." How does he convey his emotion in the body of the essay?
2. Notice that the broad view of the woodpile in the first part of the article narrows to a mere chip under a glass in the last part. Discuss the effectiveness of this technique.
3. Point out at least five examples of parallel structure.
4. Does Thoreau use *loose* or *periodic* sentences? Consult the glossary at the back of this book for a definition of these terms.
5. The sentence in paragraph 1 beginning "I watched a couple that were fast locked" has several poetic images in it. What are they?

Writing Assignments

1. Probably you're familiar with the concept that people look like ants to someone who is gazing down at them from a great height. Viewing humanity from a figurative height, develop your own analogy between people and ants.
2. Thoreau says: "I never learned which party was victorious, nor the cause of the war." In your opinion, is any cause worth fighting for? If so, what?

3. Describe a scene of action in nature that you have seen and what you thought about it.
4. Analyze the organization of this essay.

Library Exploration

1. Report on Thoreau as a naturalist rather than as a writer.
2. Compare the prose styles of Thoreau and Emerson.
3. Read all of *Walden,* from which this selection is taken, and sum up Thoreau's major theses.

Vocabulary

(1) INCESSANTLY   without stopping

(1) INTERNECINE   internal; involving conflict within a group

(1) DIVESTED   stripped

(1) PERTINACITY   persistence

(1) MANIFESTED   showed

(1) PERCHANCE   perhaps

(2) ASSIDUOUSLY   diligently

(2) SEVERED   cut off

(2) CARBUNCLES   formerly, red gems

(2) FEROCITY   fury

Bertrand Russell (1872–1970), one of the most significant mathematicians and philosophers of the twentieth century, was born and educated in England. He collaborated with A. N. Whitehead in 1910 to write "Principia Mathematica," a landmark in the history of symbolic logic. Russell contributed to the founding of the modern philosophy of logical analysis. In recent years he was a leader of anti-war movements. Among his many works are "Mysticism and Logic" (1918), "What I Believe" (1925), "The ABC of Relativity" (1925), and "The History of Western Philosophy" (1940). He was awarded the Nobel Prize in Literature in 1950.

Lord Russell says that East and West face an unprecedented problem in the H-bomb and that the solution will be found either in the extinction of the race or in an agreement not to fight.

BERTRAND RUSSELL

Co-existence or No Existence: The Choice Is Ours

1 The recent changes in the technique of war have produced a situation which is wholly unprecedented. War has existed ever since there were organized states, that is to say for some six thousand years. This ancient institution is now about to end. There are two ways in which the end may come about: the first is the extinction of the human race; the

second is an agreement not to fight. I do not know which of these will be chosen.

2   Neither the general public nor the majority of powerful statesmen have as yet realized that war with modern weapons cannot serve the purposes of any government in the world. It is of the first importance that this should be realized by those who control policy both in the East and in the West. It is generally conceded by those who are in a position to speak with authority that no complete defense against an H-bomb attack is possible. We must, I think, consider it the most likely hypothesis that if a great war broke out tomorrow each side would be successful in attack and unsuccessful in defense. This means that in the first days of such a war all the great centers of population on each side would be obliterated. Those who survived this first disaster would perish slowly or quickly as a result of the fall-out from radioactive cloud. Destruction of life from this cause would not be confined to the belligerent countries. The winds would gradually spread death throughout the world. This, at least, is what is to be feared. It cannot be said that the worst outcome is certain, but it is sufficiently probable to deter any sane man from incurring the risk.

3   Apart from the totality of destruction, there is another new element in the situation. In old days if you had a military advantage over your enemy, you might hope to win in time. But now, if each side has enough H-bombs to wipe out the other, there is no longer any advantage in having twice as many as your adversary.

4   Both in the United States and in Great Britain there has been much talk of civil defense. Russian military journals contain talk of the same kind. All such plans, I am convinced, show either ignorance or hypocrisy in those who advocate them. Deep shelters would enable a portion of the population to survive the first explosion, but sooner or later these people would have to emerge from their shelters into a radioactive world.

5   Although the H-bomb is the center of public attention at the moment, it is only one of the possibilities of destruction which science has put in the hands of irresponsible politicians. Chemical and bacteriological warfare are studied by all powerful states and may have consequences at least as horrifying as those of the H-bomb. There is no visible end to the methods of inflicting death that may be invented. Even if a portion of the human race were to survive a great war now, it cannot be doubted that the next war, if scientific technique survives, would complete what its predecessor had left unfinished.

6   There is therefore no escape from the choice that lies before us: Shall we renounce war, or shall we bring our species to an end?

ESCAPE FROM REALITY

7 If men realized that these are the only alternatives, no one can doubt that they would choose peace. But there are various ways in which people escape the realization of unpleasant facts. I have seen statements by Russians and Chinese that a thermonuclear war would of course destroy the rotten capitalistic civilization of the West but would

not vitally injure the sturdy Communist nations of the East. I have also seen statements by American authorities claiming that the West would be victorious. Both seemed to me, if genuinely believed, to be mere fantasies of wishfulfilment and, if not genuinely believed, to be part of the silly game of bluff which great nations have been allowing themselves. I hope that this is beginning to be understood. Recently there have been hopeful signs that neither side is willing to push issues to the point of war. And with every month that passes there is a better chance that statesmen both in the East and in the West will become aware of some of the important facts by which their policy ought to be guided.

8   Another widespread delusion is that perhaps in a great war H-bombs would not be employed. People point to the fact that gas was not employed in the Second World War. They forget that gas had not proved a decisive weapon even in the First World War and that in the meantime gas-masks had been provided which were a complete protection. Any analogy is therefore entirely misleading.

9   It is thought by many that the first step forward should be an international agreement not to use H-bombs in the event of war. and this is generally coupled with the suggestion that both sides should destroy their existing stock of these weapons. This suggestion has certain merits but also certain drawbacks. Its chief merit is that if the destruction of existing stocks were honestly carried out, the danger of a sudden attack in the style of Pearl Harbor would be lessened. Against this we must set the fact that no system of inspection can now make sure that bombs are not being manufactured. This is a new fact. At the time of the Baruch proposal it was still possible for an inspectorate to gain control of the raw materials, but this is so no longer. Each side would therefore suspect that the other side was manufacturing bombs surreptitiously, and this might make relations worse than if no agreement had been concluded. What is even more important is that, if war did break out, neither side would consider itself bound by the agreement, and after a certain number of months H-bomb warfare would be in full swing. Only by not making war can the danger be avoided. We must therefore turn our thoughts away from war to the methods by which peace can be made secure.

PEACE BY STAGES

10 The transition from the cold war to a condition of secure peace cannot be made in a day. But it can be made, and it must be made. It will have to be made by stages. The first stage will consist in persuading all powerful governments of the world that their aims, whatever they may be, cannot be achieved by war. In this first stage, scientists — not only nuclear physicists but also physiologists, geneticists, and bacteriologists — have a very important part to play. Their discoveries have created the dangers, and it is their obvious duty to arouse the public and the governments to a sense of the risks they are running. They may, in performing this duty, be compelled to take action of which their governments disapprove, but loyalty to mankind should be for them

the paramount consideration. I am convinced that it is within their power to persuade the governments both of the East and of the West to look to negotiation rather than war for a solution of their problems.

11   The next stage must be to create temporary machinery to negotiate settlements of all the questions at present causing conflict between East and West. It will be necessary to refer such questions to a body of negotiators in which East and West have equal representation and the balance of power is in the hands of the neutrals. I do not venture to suggest what solution should be reached on any of the vexed questions of the present. I think that a body constituted as I have suggested would avoid gross unfairness to either side, and subject to this condition almost any settlement would be preferable to a continuation of the present state of tension. A very important part of any settlement should of course be a drastic reduction of armaments. It is hardly to be supposed that the very delicate negotiations which will be required can be conducted successfully in the atmosphere of strained hostility that has existed during recent years. Each side will have to abandon perpetual abuse of the other and learn to practice that degree of toleration which after centuries of warfare was at last achieved between Christians and Moslems and between Catholics and Protestants. We cannot now wait for the slow operation of reason through the discouragements of long indecisive wars. We must learn in advance a manner of thinking and feeling which in the past has been learned slowly and through bitter experience. I will not pretend that this is easy. But if men can be made to realize the dreadful alternative I do not think it will prove impossible.

THE THIRD STEP

12 If the immediate problems that now divide East and West were settled in some such way, we could reach the third stage of progress toward secure peace. The international problems of our day are not the last that will ever arise. There will be new problems, perhaps dividing the world quite differently from the way in which it is now divided between Communist and anti-Communist blocs. So long as there is not an established international authority capable of enforcing peace, the risk of war will remain, and with every advance in science the risk will become more terrible. The international anarchy resulting from a multitude of states with unrestricted sovereignty must be brought to an end. The international authority which is to end it will have to be federal and endowed with only such powers as are necessary for preserving the peace of the world. The most important of these powers, and also the most difficult to secure, will be an obvious preponderance of armed forces over those of any national state or alliance of states. The anarchic liberty at present enjoyed by sovereign states is dear to most people and will not be surrendered easily, but it will have to be surrendered if the human species is to survive. The process required is a continuation of that which occurred in the fifteenth and sixteenth centuries. Before that time powerful barons in their castles could defy national governments, and there was the same sort of anarchy within

a nation as now exists between nations. Gunpowder and artillery put an end to internal anarchy in France, Spain, and England. The hydrogen bomb has the same part to play in ending international anarchy. The loss of liberty, though it may be distasteful, is precisely of the same kind as that which private individuals suffer by being forbidden to commit murder, for after all it is the right to murder which hitherto sovereign states will be asked to surrender.

LEGITIMATE HOPES

13 I have been speaking of dangers and how to avoid them, but there is another thing which it is just as important to emphasize, for while fears are at present unavoidable, hopes are equally legitimate. If we take the measures needed to end our fears, we shall thereby create a world capable of such well-being as has never been known and scarcely even imagined. Throughout the long ages since civilization began, the bulk of mankind have lived lives of misery and toil and bondage. All the long burden of misery that has darkened the slow progress of mankind has now become unnecessary. If we can learn to tolerate each other and to live in amity, poverty can be abolished everywhere more completely than it is now abolished in the most fortunate nations. Fear can be so much diminished that a new buoyancy and a new joy will brighten the daily lives of all. The work of science, which while war survives is largely evil, will become wholly beneficent. Nothing stands in the way but the darkness of atavistic evil passions. New technical possibilities of well-being exist, but the wisdom to make use of them has hitherto been lacking. Shall we collectively continue to turn our back upon the things that each one of us individually desires? We can make a world of light, or we can banish life from our planet. One or other we must do, and do soon. A great duty rests upon those who realize these alternatives, for it is they who must persuade mankind to make the better choice.

Discussion of Theme

1. When Russell says, in his title, that "The Choice Is Ours," is he referring to individual citizens or government leaders?
   How much choice does the individual have? How can he exercise his choice?
2. How, according to Russell, do people avoid accepting the reality of destruction by hydrogen bomb? By what reasoning does he reject these attitudes?
3. Have we made progress toward reaching any of the "three stages" Russell says are necessary for peace?
4. Are there choices for the world to consider that are not offered in this essay?

Discussion of Rhetoric

1. What is the meaning of *cold war*? Is it a war, or isn't it? How would you translate the phrase into more formal and conventional language?
2. Lord Russell makes a startling statement in his opening paragraph. What is it? Does it make you pay close attention to what follows?
3. The purpose of this essay is to persuade. What methods of persuasion does the author use?
4. What analogies does the author disagree with in the essay?

Writing Assignments

1. Should American citizens be permitted to travel anywhere in the world without passport? Wouldn't this help lessen tensions among nations? Give your opinions.
2. How would the elimination of war or the fear of war help abolish poverty?
3. Many people claim that because man is violent and competitive, we'll always have wars. Support or defend this position.
4. From new materials, support or attack Russell's arguments.
5. Cite evidence for believing (or not believing) that the cold war could last forever.

Library Exploration

1. Read *Catch-Twenty-Two,* by Joseph Heller.
2. This statement was written more than 15 years ago. Check on Lord Russell's later pronouncements and activities.
3. Russell says that scientists have created dangers and therefore have a responsibility for helping lessen them. Check through *The Bulletin of the Atomic Scientists* to see how some have taken action.

Vocabulary

(1) UNPRECEDENTED without example

(1) EXTINCTION wiping out

(2) CONCEDED admitted

(2) HYPOTHESIS tentative assumption

(2) OBLITERATED wiped out

(2) BELLIGERENT warring

(2) DETER discourage

(2) INCURRING meeting with; becoming subject to

(4) HYPOCRISY the act of pretending to be something one is not or to believe what one does not

(8) DELUSION a false belief resulting from self-deception

(9) SURREPTITIOUSLY secretly

(11) VEXED troublesome

(11) PERPETUAL continual

(12) ANARCHY absence of government

(12) SOVEREIGNTY supreme power

(12) PREPONDERANCE majority

(13) AMITY friendship; harmony

(13) BUOYANCY exuberance; lightheartedness

(13) ATAVISTIC marked by a reversion to the characteristics of a remote ancestor or primitive type

Paul Jacobs (1918–   ), a social scientist and writer, is a staff member of the Center for the Study of Democratic Institutions at Santa Barbara, California. He was born in New York City and attended City College of New York and the University of Minnesota. He has long had an interest in the labor movement, first as a union organizer and later as publisher of a labor paper. Among his books are "Labor in a Free Society" (1959) and "Is Curley Jewish?" (1965).

The following essay takes an irreverent look at an American institution, Forest Lawn Cemetery, and its creator, Hubert "Digger" Eaton.

PAUL JACOBS

The Most Cheerful Graveyard in the World

1   Along with amassing a comfortable fortune by convincing Los Angelenos that the only fitting way to begin a "happy Eternal Life" is by being laid to rest, in one way or another, at Forest Lawn Memorial Park, the cemetery he founded in 1917, Dr. Hubert Eaton, or "Digger" as he is known in the trade, has also succeeded in almost completely revising the dying industry.

2   The Digger, whose official title of "Doctor" is purely honorary, accomplished this revision by the simple but profound device of converting the hitherto prosaic act of dying into a gloriously exciting, well-advertised event, somehow intimately and patriotically connected with the American way of life.

3   Today, thanks to Eaton, dying in Los Angeles is something to be eagerly anticipated, because it is only after death that one can gain permanent tenure at Forest Lawn. Eaton, in one of his earlier roles — that of "the Builder" — described Forest Lawn as "a place where lovers new and old shall love to stroll and watch the sunset's glow, planning for the future or reminiscing of the past; a place where artists study and sketch; where school teachers bring happy children to see the things they read of in books; where little churches invite, triumphant in the knowledge that from their pulpits only words of Love can can be spoken; where memorialization of loved ones in sculptured marble and pictorial glass shall be encouraged but controlled by acknowledged artists; a place where the sorrowing will be soothed and strengthened because it will be God's garden. A place that shall be protected by an immense Endowment Care Fund, the principal of which can never be expended — only the income therefrom used to care for and perpetuate this Garden of Memory.

4   "This is the Builder's Dream; this is the Builder's Creed."

5   The Builder's Creed is chiseled into a huge, upright stone slab on Forest Lawn's Cathedral Drive, just outside the Great Mausoleum and hard by the Shrine of Love. Viewed, usually in reverent awe, by more than a million visitors each year, Forest Lawn is, along with Disneyland, a favorite tourist attraction in Southern California, far outdrawing the concrete footprints in front of Grauman's Chinese Theatre.

6   A smaller inscription underneath the Creed points out that on New Year's Day, 1917, Eaton stood on a hilltop overlooking the small country cemetery which had just been placed in his charge. An unemployed mining engineer, Eaton had gone into the cemetery business after a vein of gold in his mine had suddenly vanished.

7   "A vision came to the man of what this tiny 'God's Acre' might become; and standing there, he made a promise to The Infinite. When he reached home, he put this promise into words and called it 'The Builder's Creed.' Today, Forest Lawn's almost three hundred acres are eloquent witness that The Builder kept faith with his soul."

8   Indeed, yes. The "almost three hundred acres" also bear eloquent witness to the fact that Eaton, still digging holes in the ground, worked a vein of gold infinitely more reliable than the one that vanished from his mine — the "Science and Art," as he describes it, "of Persuasion." So strongly does Eaton believe the "profession of salesmanship is the greatest of all professions" that he has established The Foundation for the Science and Art of Persuasion at his alma mater, William Jewell College, Liberty, Missouri.

9   Forest Lawn reflects Eaton's skill in the "science." The "country cemetery" with only a "scant dozen acres of developed ground" has grown into Forest Lawn Memorial Park, with a permanent "population" of more than 170,000 increasing at the rate of approximately 6,500 a year.

10   In fact, business has been so good that there are now two additional Forest Lawn "Memorial Parks" in Los Angeles: Forest Lawn-Hollywood Hills, the focus of a bitter political struggle in the city, and ad-

jacent to it Mount Sinai, designed to attract the growing Jewish population of Los Angeles.

11   Forest Lawn offers the largest religious painting in the United States, displayed in a building, the Hall of the Crucifixion, specially designed for it. There, for a voluntary contribution of twenty-five cents, the visitor sits comfortably in a large theatre, in one of a "broad sweep of seats, richly upholstered in burgundy, rising tier above tier, matching the splendor of the architecture," and watches the three-thousand-pound curtain open on Jesus at Calvary, forty-five feet high and 195 feet long. A lecture about the painting, supplemented with a moving arrow, is delivered by a tape recording in the special kind of rich, organ-tone voice used throughout Forest Lawn.

12   There are also hundreds of statues, both originals and reproductions, scattered throughout the three hundred acres. Typical of these is an eighteen-figure group depicting Forest Lawn's solution to the "Mystery of Life." Interpretations of the eighteen figures are supplied: "(17) the atheist, the fool, who grinningly cares not at all; while (18) the stoic sits in silent awe and contemplation of that which he believes he knows but cannot explain with any satisfaction."

13   At the Court of David there is a huge reproduction of Michelangelo's "David"—with a large fig leaf added by Forest Lawn. An exact copy of the sculptor's "Moses" is displayed at the entrance to the Cathedral Corridor in Memorial Terrace, "the only one," according to Forest Lawn, "cast from clay masks placed directly on the original statue in the Church of Saint Peter in Chains at Rome, Italy."

14   So that the masks could be made, the Church of Saint Peter had to be closed for a day, something that had not happened before. "I gave a lot of dinners and I bought a lot of wine and I sent a lot of cables and St. Peter's was closed," Eaton modestly explains.

15   Color photos and post cards of the "Moses" statue can be purchased, along with thousands of other items, at Forest Lawn's souvenir shop. There, browsing visitors can choose from showcases displaying money clips, cocktail napkins, book matches, jigsaw puzzles, and charm bracelets—all decorated with Forest Lawn motifs. Prices range from a modest twenty-nine cents for a key chain to $125 for a glass vase etched with a Forest Lawn scene.

16   There are brown plastic nutshells containing little photos of Forest Lawn, ladies' compacts, cigarette lighters, cufflinks, salt and pepper shakers, picture frames, demitasse spoons, bookmarks, cups and saucers, pen and pencil sets, glass bells, wooden plaques, ashtrays, place mats and doilies, perfume and powder sets, jackknives, and a great variety of other goodies, all with an appropriate Forest Lawn theme. Books like *The Loved One,* Evelyn Waugh's satire of Forest Lawn, are not on sale in the souvenir shop. (Eaton occasionally expresses resentment over the treatment given the cemetery by novelists—especially by one writer to whom he extended free run of the park only to be parodied later. But Eaton also understands that such novels have brought world-wide publicity to Forest Lawn and have not adversely affected his sales, which come not from England but from Los Angeles.)

17   Among the most popular items at the souvenir shop are those showing reproductions of Forest Lawn's three churches, the Church of the
Recessional, The Little Church of the Flowers, and the Wee Kirk o'
the Heather.

18   "Providing a dignified setting for final tribute," the three churches
"serve also for the joyous and memorable ceremonies of christening
and the exchange of marriage vows." Since the churches have opened,
more than 43,000 persons have had "memorable" marriages in them.
But Forest Lawn makes no money directly from marrying people, and
the profits from the souvenir shop are used for the upkeep of the Hall
of the Crucifixion. Forest Lawn's real business is burying people.

19   "The hardest thing in the world to sell," states one of the organization's top officials, "are 'spaces.'" ("Space" is the euphemism used at
Forest Lawn for "grave plot.") The reason for the difficulty is that
Forest Lawn's sales organization, which comprises about 175 people,
concentrates on sales made "Before Need," another phrase in Forest
Lawn's own peculiar language of the flowers. Selling cemetery plots
"Before Need" rather than "At Time of Need" or "Post Need," although difficult, is very profitable, since under California law a cemetery pays taxes only on its unsold plots. Once a "space" has been sold,
it is removed from the tax rolls. Thus it is to the obvious advantage of
Forest Lawn to sell off its land as quickly as possible, without waiting
for "Need."

20   There are approximately fifteen hundred individual "spaces" to the
acre in Forest Lawn. Prices average $300 per space. There are also
rather more elegant neighborhoods at Forest Lawn which are less
crowded and therefore more expensive. In the Gardens of Memory,
entered only with a special key, there are "memorial sanctuaries designed for families who desire the privacy and protection of crypt
interment, but who at the same time long for the open skies and the
natural beauty of a verdant garden bathed in sunlight. Under the
lawns in the Gardens of Memory have been created a number of
monolithically constructed crypts of steel-reinforced concrete."

21   In the area of ground burial, Forest Lawn has contributed a pleasant innovation. No tombstones are permitted, only markers, set flush
with the ground so that there is in fact the pleasant appearance of a
park with sweeping green lawns.

22   But one does not have to be interred to take up permanent residence at Forest Lawn. A number of other arrangements can be made,
including being inurned after cremation in the columbarium for as
little as $145 or entombed in a mausoleum crypt—which can cost as
much as $800,000, as in the case of the Irving Thalberg mausoleum.
One can also be placed in a large wall out in the open air. Families may
be interred, inurned, or entombed as a unit to maintain "togetherness." Should one feel the need for fresh air while spending the
"happy Eternal Life" in a crypt, it is possible, at added cost naturally,
to have a ventilating system installed. In the mausoleum, tape-
recorded music is played as well.

23   Inurnment is not restricted to a single form of urn. The law in California, which has a strong undertakers' lobby, provides that after
cremation ashes must be buried or placed in a columbarium. A wide

variety of urn designs can be seen, ranging from books and loving cups to miniature coffins.

24 The price for the casket or urn sets the approximate amount paid for the funeral itself, but here the range is far greater than for the "space." The least expensive casket, with the metal screw heads showing, is $115; the most expensive goes for $17,500.

25 Forest Lawn's rich, creamy advertising presentations combine the hard and the soft sell. On radio and television, the same institutional approach is as manifest as at the cemetery itself. Programs of church services and organ music are announced in deep, sonorous tones, and practically no mention is made of the company's product. The institutional approach is also used on billboards picturing stained-glass windows or the "Moses" statue. However, many of Forest Lawn's billboards are given over to the hard, competitive sell, featuring what is Hubert Eaton's original contribution to the American way of death: the concept of combining in one place mortuary functions, such as embalming, with funeral services and burial, thus obviating the necessity for outside undertakers, florists, funeral chapels, and long processions to the cemetery. Forest Lawn successfully undertook the elimination of the undertaking middleman.

26 Today, Forest Lawn's hard-sell slogans of "Everything In One Beautiful Place" and "Just One Phone Call" are widely copied, as are the ads which usually feature back or side views, sometimes in color, of two dry-eyed, well-groomed people talking to a distinguished-looking gray-mustached bank-president or diplomat-type man, identified by a discreet sign on his desk as a "Funeral Counselor." Sometimes only the "Counselor" is shown, answering the "Just One Phone Call" with the dedicated air of a statesman. It is clear from the ads that at Forest Lawn, where the concept of death has been abolished, the standards of accepted behavior demand no vulgar signs of outward grief.

27 But even though its competitors copy Forest Lawn today, Eaton faced a bitter battle when he first attempted to bring a mortuary into the cemetery. Forest Lawn's permit to operate a mortuary was given only after a determined struggle waged against him by some of the undertakers who foresaw disaster for themselves in the new trend of combined services. It was during this period that Forest Lawn began to build up its own political operations, which today make it the most powerful spokesman for the industry in the state.

28 There have been a number of occasions when, in its self-interest, Forest Lawn has had to do battle, sometimes in ways that might have been frowned on by the dignified gentlemen in their ads. From the 1930's to the early 1950's Forest Lawn was in a running argument with the county assessor's office over the tax assessments made on its property, with Forest Lawn always claiming that the assessments were too high and almost always getting them reduced, even as much as fifty per cent, by the county board of supervisors. Some supervisors did consistently oppose Forest Lawn's plea for tax reduction and supported the assessor, but when the votes were taken a majority always supported Forest Lawn.

29 In 1938, in one of its early appearances before the board of super-

visors, Forest Lawn requested a tax reduction, claiming that the vacant property in the land it then owned would remain unsold until 1973. At the time, the county assessor pointed out that Forest Lawn had "acquired additional property when they said it was going to take thirty-five years to sell out what they now have, yet they go to work and buy seventy-five acres adjoining at a big price."

30   Ten years later, in 1948, the issue of how long it would take to fill Forest Lawn's vacant "spaces" became one of the central points in a bitter political hassle within the Los Angeles City Council, and the cemetery completely reversed its argument of ten years earlier. At issue was Forest Lawn's request for a zoning change to permit the use, as a cemetery, of 480 acres of land adjoining Griffith Park, a public park and playground in the Hollywood area.

31   Forest Lawn's first request to develop this new cemetery was submitted to and rejected by the city planning commission in 1946. When the request was again rejected in 1948, Forest Lawn appealed, claiming, in contrast to its 1938 plea of unsold land, that "by the year 1965 all of the available grave spaces in existing cemeteries will have been exhausted."

32   The odds against Forest Lawn's gaining approval for its plan to open a new cemetery seemed formidable. The planning commission opposed it, the park department opposed it, the board of health commissioners opposed it, the water and power commission opposed it, the board of public works opposed it, the Hollywood chamber of commerce opposed it, and a variety of community groups opposed it. But "the Builder's Dream" triumphed, and on March 9, 1948, the city council voted 11–3 to permit the opening of the cemetery.

33   Never an organization to leave stones unturned, within a few hours Forest Lawn had hastily dug six holes in the ground and buried six bodies in them; a move which, under state law, immediately qualified the area as a commercial graveyard that could not then be disturbed or moved except under very specific circumstances.

34   "We got the bodies we buried through the county hospital or from their next of kin in advance," states Ugene Blalock, vice-president and general counsel at Forest Lawn, "and we made no charge for our services. If the vote in the council had gone against us, we would have given them a free burial elsewhere."

35   In fact, however, the council vote has rarely gone against Forest Lawn, even when the city fathers were voting on whether to give Beverly Hills the street where Eaton lives, thus providing the Digger with a more distinguished address. Although he hasn't moved, Eaton now lives in Beverly Hills.

36   No one is quite sure about the exact basis for Eaton's influence; or if they are, they're not willing to talk about it for the record. Blalock states that Forest Lawn as an institution has not made, as far as he knows, any campaign contribution in eighteen years, although he adds, "Individuals may make political contributions." But politics aside, it is Hubert Eaton, master salesman, who is chiefly responsible for Forest Lawn's success.

37   It is from Eaton's mind that has come the creation of the Council of Regents of Memorial Court of Honor, twenty-two "outstanding busi-

ness and professional men" who advise "on all matters concerning the growth of the Memorial Park as a cultural center of religion and fine arts."

38   Its members, who include the president of Occidental College and the chancellor of the University of Southern California, wear a handsome, flowing red robe, trimmed with velvet, and an elegant round red hat, also trimmed daintily with velvet, while around their necks hangs a kind of Maltese Cross decoration, perhaps the Order of Forest Lawn.

39   Such touches as these distinguish the imaginative Eaton from his colleagues. Eaton's devotion to salesmanship, as evidenced by his creating special heart-shaped children's sections at Forest Lawn, named Babyland and Lullabyland, began early in life, according to "The Forest Lawn Story," his biography sold at the souvenir shop.

40   The son of a college professor, Eaton, states the biography, "sat in his little cubbyhole behind his father's bookshelves ostensibly studying but actually eavesdropping on his father's conversations with callers. Invariably they came for advice on one thing or another but more often than not, it was advice on matters affecting money. From these conversations he learned the word salesmanship and what it meant."

41   It was Eaton, too, who initiated many Forest Lawn public-service activities — the inspirational speaker made available to service clubs, the thirteen half-hour Bible films, and the giving of the Forest Lawn Awards for Persuasive Writing as a "practical service to students and Christian liberal arts colleges."

42   Long interested in "small, independent, liberal arts colleges" as being "America's last bulwark against the march of Socialism. . . ." Eaton believes that "most" college professors are "semi-socialists at heart" who teach young people that salesmanship "smacks of chicanery, demogoguery, of influencing people against their wills. . . ."

43   But Eaton isn't always so serious. Even when he was at college himself, he always had a "good sense of humor." His biography relates that one of his favorite tricks was to persuade a visitor to allow a funnel to be inserted into the top of his trousers and then to make him balance a penny on his chin and try to drop it into the funnel. While the visitor was in this position, young Hubert "or one of his cronies would pour a cup of cold water into the funnel."

44   Eaton's "good sense of humor changed little in succeeding years," states his biographer, and it certainly hadn't changed much the night when Eaton gave one of his usual huge, lavish parties for a group of friends and guests. It was called "An Enchanged Evening in the South Pacific," of which "Trader" Hubert Eaton was the master of ceremonies. Elaborate Hawaiian acts were presented, and guests received a large, beautifully printed eight-page souvenir program in color, in which Eaton had himself depicted as "Your Happy Planter," jumping from page to page on a golden-shovel pogo stick.

45   On the cultural level, the printed program carried a large reproduction of the "David" statue, with a fig leaf, a Hawaiian lei, and a girl curled around its neck, all illustrating a poem, "The Secret of Hubie's David," which described just how it was decided to add a fig leaf to

Forest Lawn's copy of Michelangelo's "David" in order not to shock "the ladies of L.A."

46   But surely the greatest of all the improvements that Eaton has made on the past is Forest Lawn itself. Here, what might have been just an ordinary "country cemetery" has been parlayed into a solemn institution, profitable and widely imitated, looking like Edgar Guest's idea of Heaven brought to earth, while representing a social level to which all people can aspire after death. And in the future, says Hubert Eaton, "When the place is all filled up, my idea, from a financial standpoint, has always been to make Forest Lawn into a museum and charge admission."

Discussion of Theme

1. Some people say that funerals are for the living rather than the dead. In what way might this be true?
2. Are Eaton's innovations commendable or not?
3. What is Eaton's concept of himself, of cemeteries, of death?
4. Why are the advertisements for Forest Lawn, described in paragraphs 25 and 26, so effective?
5. Has Eaton filled a need in society, or has he created one?

Discussion of Rhetoric

1. Point out the pun in the opening paragraph. Why are there so many puns about the undertaking business?
2. In paragraph 11 what effect does Jacobs achieve by describing the gross physical details in the Hall of the Crucifixion?
3. What is the tone or attitude of this essay? How does Jacobs establish it in the opening paragraphs?
4. The last sentence in paragraph 26 is typical of the many examples of irony to be found in this essay. Find several other examples and explain the purpose or function of the irony in each.
5. Is Jacobs's title an effective one for this essay? What attitude does it help to establish?
6. What is the significance of Eaton's closing remark in paragraph 46? Why did Jacobs choose this statement to end his essay?

Writing Assignments

1. Speculate about the theory that an elaborate funeral and expensive casket alleviate the survivors' guilt feelings toward the dead.
2. As our population grows, space becomes increasingly scarce and, therefore, precious. In this respect, how are we to reconcile the needs of the living with those of the dead?
3. Show the importance of euphemisms in selling insurance or cemetery lots.
4. Has Eaton debased the act of death, or has he served his fellow man by making it less painful?

5. Defend or disprove Eaton's statement (in paragraph 42) concerning college professors.

Library Exploration

1. As a reaction against high-priced funerals, several burial societies have been organized in the United States. What are some of their unique features?
2. Two books receiving widespread acclaim in recent years for their commentary on death and the funeral industry are *The Loved One,* by Evelyn Waugh, and *The American Way of Death,* by Jessica Mitford.

Vocabulary

(2) PROSAIC   commonplace; dull

(3) TENURE   right to hold or keep

(12) STOIC   one unaffected by pleasure or pain

(16) DEMITASSE   half-size coffee cup

(16) PARODIED   imitated with intent to ridicule

(20) VERDANT   lush green

(22) COLUMBARIUM   vault with niches for cremated remains

(25) MANIFEST   evident

(25) OBVIATING   eliminating; doing away with

(32) FORMIDABLE   great; hard to overcome

(40) OSTENSIBLY   apparently; seemingly

(42) CHICANERY   trickery

(42) DEMAGOGUERY   leadership by appeals to emotion and prejudice

(46) PARLAYED   successfully exploited

THE
VOICES
OF
SCIENCE

4

Stuart Chase (1888–   ) is the
author of numerous books and
articles on economics, semantics, and social topics. Born in
New Hampshire, he received his
degree from Harvard. Among
his recent books are "The Most
Probable World" (1968) and
"Danger–Man Talking" (1969).

Many critics of our society,
claiming that its problems are
caused by the effects of science and technology, suggest a
return to "the good old days."
The author of the following
selection maintains that this
philosophy is a retreat. Technology, he says, can provide a
treasure chest of opportunities
to man.

STUART CHASE

Two Cheers
for Technology

1   In contemplating the sorry state of the world today, some observers,
such as the distinguished philosopher and theologian Jacques Ellul,
have come to believe that our troubles are due primarily to science
and technology. Man, they imply, should never have begun the
exploration of the laws governing the material universe. Once formulated, these laws, proceeding on a momentum of their own, will imprison him. "Enclosed within his artificial creation," says Ellul, "man
finds that there is no exit, that he cannot pierce the shell of technology
to find again the ancient milieu to which he was adapted for hundreds
of thousands of years." This would seem to indicate that we did better
in the Stone Age.

2   The Nobel Prize physicist Max Born comes close to agreeing with
this view. "I am haunted by the idea," he declares, "that the break in
human civilization caused by the discovery of the scientific method
may be irreparable."

3   The philosophy of retreat to a simpler era may have had some validity 200 years ago when Rousseau was celebrating the virtues of
Cro-Magnon man, but too much water has gone through the turbines.
The growth curves of science and technology have profoundly
changed the cultural habits of the West and have made deep inroads
on the East—witness Japan.

4   I believe that the way to come to terms with technology today is,
first, to understand it and, then, to encourage its good effects on the
human condition and at the same time try to discourage its bad effects.
I cannot follow the mystique that technology has laws of its own, over
and beyond human intervention.

5   Is it possible to conceive of a civilized society in the 1970s without
electric power, motor vehicles, railroads, airplanes, telephones, television, elevators, flush toilets, central heating, air conditioning, anti-
biotics, vaccines, and antiseptics?

6   Before going any further, it is clear that two definitions are in order.
What is meant by the "human condition"? What is meant by "technology," and what is its relation to "science"?

7   The "human condition" may be defined as a measure of the extent
to which the potential for living is realized under the limitations of the
inborn genes and of the environment of the Earth. Full potential
means adequate food, shelter, clothing, education, and health care,
plus useful and creative work and leisure for every normal baby born.
The slums of Calcutta or Rio, the ghettos of the West, represent a potential close to zero.

8   Alone, the word "technology" implies only a special learned skill
beyond intuitive common sense; hydraulic engineers, for instance, can
make water run uphill. We must descend the semantic abstraction
ladder and ask: Technology for what? For manufacturing a jumbo jet?
A MIRV multiple warhead? A contraceptive pill? An electric razor?
For engineering a trip to the moon? For what?

9   Many people, including a large number of today's college students,
confuse technology with science. "There is a growing feeling in Washington," says *New York Times* science editor Walter Sullivan, "that
efforts to explain science to the young have failed."

10   "Science," or perhaps better "*pure* science," discovers laws of nature and lately some laws of human nature. There is no ulterior motive
in the pursuit of pure science beyond what Veblen once called "idle
curiosity." Einstein was consumed with it. He wanted to know the relation between energy and matter; he wanted to know how the theory
of relativity could be linked to the quantum theory.

11   When a scientific law is established so that all competent observers
agree on its validity, then, in many cases, it may be applied to the satisfaction of various human desires and needs and thus become applied
science, or technology. The pure science of $E=MC^2$ was applied to the
construction of the first atomic bomb—a technological triumph of
dubious benefit to the human condition, except as a warning. However, such knowledge can be applied to the desalting of sea water—a
technological triumph of great utility, as deserts are transformed into
gardens. To condemn technology *in toto* is to forget the gardens, while
to idealize technology is to forget Hiroshima.

12   The transformation of pure science into applied is strikingly illustrated by Raymond Fosdick, sometime head of the Rockefeller Foundation, as he tells in his book *Chronicle of a Generation* of the
184-inch cyclotron financed by the foundation in 1940 for the University of California:

> No one foresaw that this instrument would lead to an atomic bomb or any
> other kind of military weapon. The only motivation behind our assistance
> was to extend the boundaries of knowledge, to stimulate the search for
> truth, in the belief that there is no darkness but ignorance.

13   Consider some of the more notorious and pervading modern technologies. Which of them appear to improve the human condition as
defined and which degrade it? What is the outlook for increasing the
assets and reducing, if not eliminating, the liabilities? To toss the
whole complex into the discard is to rule out not only all high-energy
societies but the way the human mind works, or at least the way many
minds work. Some men want to know *why* — and are off on the course
pioneered by Galileo, Darwin, and Faraday, in pursuit of pure science.
Soon, Edison, Baekeland, and Ford are applying the knowledge
gained. Is there any way to halt idle curiosity? Can we find a method
short of extermination to prevent Homo sapiens — the creature who
thinks — from trying to put dependable knowledge to work?

14   The necessity for caution in evaluation is apparent in the case of the
internal combustion engine — probably the most popular piece of technology ever invented. The automobile has markedly improved the
human condition by providing greater mobility and convenience,
while degrading it with air pollution. How long before the liabilities
overwhelm the assets? Even if the technicians devise a pollution-free
engine, the miseries and tragedies of highway accidents and traffic
jams remain, indeed expand with population and affluence.

15   Where does the balance of a given technology lie now? Where will
it be a decade hence? How does the balance shift from area to area —
high-energy cultures, low-energy cultures, big city, open country?
Under intensive analysis, the balance shifts with time, and with place,
for nearly every item under consideration.

16   There are three major threats to mankind today, all due primarily to
technology: 1) the arms race in nuclear weapons, which, if continued,
can only end in World War III; 2) the accelerating destruction of the
environment; and 3) the population explosion. For easy reference, I
once called these threats "bombs, bulldozers, and babies." The effect
of technology is obvious enough in the first two, but the third requires
a moment's thought. Modern medicine in its control of epidemics, for
instance, has enormously reduced death rates all over the world, in
low-energy societies as well as high. Birth control, however, has not
kept pace with death control, and through the widening gap population pours. At the present rate of growth, there will be twice as many
people in the world by the year 2000. But again we must be careful of
an "all good" or "all bad" evaluation. Modern medicine in one sense
is a great boon, but death control without a compensating birth control is the unquestioned reason for the population explosion that is
rapidly becoming a menace to the human condition.

17   Again, nuclear weapons, by a curious logical paradox, could conceivably become mankind's greatest asset. Robert Oppenheimer once called the atomic bomb "a great peril and a great hope," by which he meant that it made large-scale wars unwinnable — an exercise in mutual suicide. But as diplomacy now stands, the arms race is more of a liability than an asset — particularly when biological and chemical weapons are brought into the equation. I am unaware of anything that can be said in favor of these despicable technologies.

18   The destruction of the environment, which is now on an exponential curve, also seems to be an unmitigated liability to the human condition. There is, however, a small offset. Many of the destructive forces cross national boundaries — industrial smog, oil spills, fallout, pollution of rivers that flow through two or more sovereign states. Only international cooperation can cope with these disasters, and so the demand for a stronger world organization is increased.

19   Bombs, bulldozers, and babies may be the major threats to the human condition today, but they are by no means the only ones for which technology is responsible. Noise pollution, for instance, is an extension of air pollution. Anyone living near a jetport — or even trying to do so — suffers, as does anyone whose home is near a highway infested with heavy-duty trucks. The decibel count goes steadily up in high-energy societies, and more and more people suffer from defective hearing. But we really haven't heard anything yet. Wait until the SSTs smash their fifty-mile corridors of sonic boom from coast to coast, along with smashed windows, crockery, and nervous systems.

20   As agriculture is mechanized by the automated cotton picker and other labor-saving devices, displaced farm workers — black, brown, yellow, and white — lose their livelihoods and descend on the cities, where the ghettos, already overburdened, try to accommodate them. See Harlem in New York, "La Perla" in San Juan, the vast shacktowns of Caracas — see them and weep for the human condition.

21   As the sharecroppers move in — at least in America — the middle class moves out en masse to the suburbs, where the open land is geometrically sliced into subdivisions. The lowing of cattle gives way to the grunt of the bulldozer, and the station wagons pile up at the supermarket. "Spread city," or megalopolis, is rapidly becoming a forbidding place in which to live, for rich as well as poor. Last year, when S. J. Perelman left New York City for good, he exclaimed: "Plants can live on carbon dioxide, but I can't."

22   The international trade in non-nuclear weapons — jet fighters, tanks, machine guns — is now estimated at $5-billion a year. Every mininion in Africa and Asia seems ready to mortgage its future in order to be immediately outfitted with lethal weapons. The big nations, the sellers, in this profitable trade are always glad to clear their stocks of old models.

23   The crime rate is greatly aided by the getaway car, and civilian terror and confusion are aided by anonymous telephone warnings of bombs about to be exploded. The hijacking of airliners, and the consequent holding of passengers as hostages, is something quite new in political terrorism. Its only offset is another demonstration that, in an age of high technology, this is one world or none.

24 Certainly, there are additional liabilities, but those I have indicated are a representative lot—perhaps the most serious ones. Let us turn now to the assets. What has technology done for the good life?

25 The human condition in high-energy societies has been improved by better diets, health care, education, and scientific knowledge of vitamins. Young people are now taller, stronger, and better favored than their parents or grandparents. This is markedly true in Japan. In America, some 40 per cent of all youngsters of college age are in college. When I was a young man, the figure was below 5 per cent.

26 People in high-energy cultures live longer, are more literate, and enjoy more travel and recreation than the generation that preceded them, while the ratio of poor people to total population has declined drastically. No society in history has ever remotely approached the standard of living enjoyed in the United States, defined in either dollars or materials consumed. No society has ever been so well nourished, so well bathed, so well doctored. No civilized society, furthermore, has ever worked such short hours to produce and distribute the necessities of life.

27 Two dark spots in this otherwise bright picture must be noted.

28 America's affluent society does not adequately care for its old people. The elderly have a sharply declining place in the family compared with the grandparents of a simpler age. The average "home for the aged" can hardly be called an asset to the human condition.

29 And secondly, this affluent society is built on an exceedingly shaky foundation of natural resources. Here we connect with the liability of a degenerating environment. The United States with only some 6 per cent of the world's population uses up some 40 per cent of the world's annual production of raw materials. If all the world enjoyed American affluence, there would be about twelve times the current demand for raw materials—an impossible drain on the resources of this planet.

30 Here is an equation that must be faced, probably before the twentieth century has run its course. If the so-called hungry world of Asia, Africa, and Latin America is significantly to increase its living standards, America and other high-energy societies must decrease their consumption of raw materials. This does not mean that the latter must retreat to the economy of scarcity, but it does mean an economy programed for a great reduction in waste, for recycling used materials, for the elimination of planned obsolescence.

31 If the technology of production is really to serve the human condition, it might well have as its goal the concept of "perpetual yield." The lumber barons of the nineteenth century in America operated on a "cut out and get out" program that promised to destroy the forests of the continent. Beginning in Maine, they slashed through New York, Michigan, Wisconsin, Minnesota, and on to the West Coast, leaving behind a desolation where the very soil was burned away. Then came a miracle. The lumber industry, at least some of the larger companies, realized that they were sawing off the limb on which they sat. They halted their wholesale policy of slash and burn, adopted "selective cutting" to keep the forests healthy, and planted millions of young trees. They shifted to a perpetual-yield basis, whereby a forest would be cut no faster than its annual growth.

32   Is this not a sound goal for all economic growth? *Keep the natural resources of the planet on a perpetual-yield basis.* The calculations will change, of course, as technology improves the yield. A fine example is the growing possibility, through intensive research and development, for employing thermonuclear *fusion* as the world's chief energy source. There is very little danger of radiation, and the hydrogen of the seven oceans will form the raw material for the process — good for thousands of years. Coal, oil, natural gas, and hydroelectric developments will no longer be prime sources. Fusion power — probably employing lasers — can be a great asset of technology, indeed, and might be operational within a generation. The rapidly developing new methods for recycling wastes of all kinds, solid and liquid, would also form an important part of the perpetual-yield concept.

33   Labor-saving devices in the field have just about abolished the institution of slavery all over the world, while in the home they have liberated women from a load of grinding toil, at least in high-energy societies.

34   Technology is now making it possible to mine the ocean and is thus opening a vast treasure chest. It has been proposed that the United Nations receive a royalty from these riches as they are developed. No nation, no corporation, no person owns the open oceans and its floor; it belongs to all mankind — with decent respect, or course, to all forms of life within it, and the ecosystems that govern it. Intelligently planned and carefully exploited, it may well be that the raw materials and foodstuffs of the oceans can markedly increase the concept of perpetual yield, and permit a higher ceiling for living standards all round.

35   It is not difficult to make a terrifying indictment of technology. It is not difficult to make a heartening list of benefits. The problem is so complex on one level, and yet, in essence, so simple. Granting the available resources of this planet, how many human beings and their fellow creatures can be supported at a level that makes life worth the living? A dependable evaluation is very difficult. We can be sure, however, that nothing is to be gained by following the prophets of doom back to the Stone Age.

Discussion of Theme

1. According to Chase, how should we come to terms with technology? What is *technology* (as opposed to *science*)?
2. What are the three main threats to mankind, according to the author? In each instance, what was the contribution of technology? How can technology provide the answers?
3. What is a high-energy culture? A low-energy culture? Can you cite examples of each?
4. What is the human condition, as described in this article? How is it related to science and technology?
5. What distinction does Chase make between pure science and applied science?

Discussion of Rhetoric

1. What method does Chase use to support his thesis? Is more than one argumentative device employed?
2. In citing Ellul (paragraph 1) and others who differ with him, is Chase merely setting up "straw men"? Does he state his opponents' views fairly and accurately?
3. What is the significance of the title of this article? Does it tip you off concerning the author's enthusiasm for the subject?
4. How are the first and last paragraphs linked?

Writing Assignments

1. How can the problems of our large cities be solved? Or are they inevitably doomed, despite the wealth and technological knowledge of our nation?
2. Write a response to the question posed in paragraph 5.
3. How might our country "retreat to a simpler era," while maintaining the advantages offered by our technology?
4. Should federal funds for science (grants, contracts, subsidies, and other support) be reduced substantially and diverted to the solution of our domestic problems?

Library Exploration

1. For another view of this subject, read C. P. Snow's essay "The Two Cultures" (on page 345 of this text), and investigate the debate between Snow and F. R. Leavis over the ideas advocated by the former.
2. Three books related to Chase's topic are: *Race to Oblivion*, by Herbert York; *The Technological Society*, by Jacques Ellul; and *Chronicle of a Generation*, by Raymond Fosdick.

Vocabulary

(1) MILIEU   environment; setting

(2) IRREPARABLE   beyond repair

(10) ULTERIOR   hidden

(11) IN TOTO   completely; in its entirety

(14) AFFLUENCE   wealth

(30) OBSOLESCENCE   state of being outmoded

Jacob Bronowski (1908–) is a senior fellow and trustee of the Salk Institute for Biological Studies in San Diego, California. He was educated at the University of Hull, in England, and has served as project head for UNESCO and as director of the National Coal Board in England. Although a mathematician by training, he is known for his work in literature, intellectual history, and the philosophy of science. Among his works are "The Poet's Defence" (1939), and "The Identity of Man" (1965).

This article examines the scientist's responsibility for war and peace, and suggests a new role for science: creating values for modern man.

JACOB BRONOWSKI

Science, the Destroyer or Creator

1 We all know the story of the sorcerer's apprentice; or *Frankenstein* which Mary Shelley wrote in competition with her husband and Byron; or some other story of the same kind out of the macabre invention of the nineteenth century. In these stories, someone who has special powers over nature conjures or creates a stick or a machine to do his work for him; and then finds that he cannot take back the life he has given it. The mindless monster overwhelms him; and what began as an invention to do the housework ends by destroying the master with the house.

2   These stories have become the epitome of our own fears. We have been inventing machines at a growing pace now for about three hundred years. This is a short span even in our recorded history, and it is not a thousandth part of our history as men. In that short moment of time we have found a remarkable insight into the workings of nature. We have used it to make ourselves far more flexible in our adaptation to the outside world than any other animal has ever been. We can survive in climates which even germs find difficult. We can grow our own food and meat. We can travel overland and we can tunnel and swim and fly, all in the one body. More important than any of these, we have come nearest to the dream which Lamarck had, that animals might inherit the skills which their parents learnt. We have discovered the means to record our experience so that others may live it again.

3   The history of other animal species shows that the most successful in struggle for survival have been those which were most adaptable to changes in their world. We have made ourselves by means of our tools beyond all measure more adaptable than any other species, living or extinct; and we continue to do so with gathering speed. Yet today we are afraid of our own shadow in the nine o'clock news; and we wonder whether we shall survive so over-specialised a creature as the Pekinese.

II

4   Everyone likes to blame his sense of defeat on someone else; and for some time scientists have been a favourite scapegoat. I want to look at their responsibility, and for that matter at everybody's, rather more closely. They do have a special responsibility; do not let us argue that out of existence; but it is a complicated one, and it is not the whole responsibility. For example, science obviously is not responsible for the readiness of people, who do not take their private quarrels beyond the stage of insult, to carry their public quarrels to the point of war. Many animals fight for their needs, and some for their mere greeds, to the point of death. Bucks fight for females, and birds fight for their territories. The fighting habits of man are odd because he displays them only in groups. But they were not supplied by scientists. On the contrary, science has helped to end several kinds of group murder, such as witch hunting and the taboos of the early nineteenth century against disinfecting hospitals.

5   Neither is science responsible for the existence of groups which believe themselves to be in competition: for the existence above all of nations. And the threat of war today is always a national threat. Some bone of contention and competition is identified with a national need: Fiume or the Polish corridor or the dignity of the Austrian Empire; and in the end nations are willing to organise and to invite the death of citizens on both sides in order to reach these collective aims. Science did not create the nations; on the contrary, it has helped to soften those strong national idiosyncrasies which it seems necessary to exploit if war is to be made with enthusiasm. And wars are not made by *any* traditional groups: they are made by highly organized societies, they are made by nations. Most of us have seen Yorkshiremen invade Old Trafford, and a bloody nose or two if the day was thirsty. But no

Yorkshireman would have grown pale if he had been told that Lancashire had the atomic bomb.

6   The sense of doom in us today is not a fear of science; it is a fear of war. And the causes of war were not created by science; they do not differ in kind from the known causes of the War of Jenkins' Ear or the War of Roses, which were carried on with only the most modest scientific aids. No, science has not invented war; but it has turned it into a very different thing. The people who distrust it are not wrong. The man in the pub who says "It'll wipe out the world," the woman in the queue who says "It isn't natural"—they do not express themselves very well; but what they are trying to say does make sense. Science has enlarged the mechanism of war, and it has distorted it. It has done this in at least two ways.

III

7 First, science has obviously multiplied the power of the warmakers. The weapons of the moment can kill more people more secretly and more unpleasantly than those of the past. This progress, as for want of another word I must call it—this progress has been going on for some time; and for some time it has been said, of each new weapon, that it is so destructive or so horrible that it will frighten people into their wits, and force the nations to give up war for lack of cannon fodder. This hope has never been fulfilled, and I know no one who takes refuge in it today. The acts of men and women are not dictated by such simple compulsions; and they themselves do not stand in any simple relation to the decisions of the nations which they compose. Grapeshot and TNT and gas have not helped to outlaw war; and I see no sign that the hydrogen bomb or a whiff of bacteria will be more successful in making men wise by compulsion.

8   Secondly, science at the same time has given the nations quite new occasions for falling out. I do not mean such simple objectives as someone else's uranium mine, or a Pacific Island which happens to be knee-deep in organic fertilizer. I do not even mean merely another nation's factories and her skilled population. These are all parts of the surplus above our simple needs which they themselves help to create and which gives our civilization its character. And war in our world battens on this surplus. This is the object of the greed of nations, and this also gives them the leisure to train and the means to arm for war. At bottom, we have remained individually too greedy to distribute our surplus, and collectively too stupid to pile it up in any more useful form than the traditional mountains of arms. Science can claim to have created the surplus in our societies, and we know from the working day and the working diet how greatly it has increased it in the last two hundred years. Science has created the surplus. Now put this year's budget beside the budget of 1750, anywhere in the world, and you will see what we are doing with it.

9 I myself think there is a third dimension which science has added to modern war. It has created war nerves and the war of nerves. I am not thinking about the technical conditions for a war of nerves: the camera man and the radio and the massed display of strength. I am thinking of the climate in which this stage lightning flickers and is made to seem

real. The last twenty years have given us a frightening show of these mental states. There is a division in the mind of each of us, that has become plain, between the man and the brute; and the rift can be opened, the man submerged, with a cynical simplicity, with the meanest tools of envy and frustration, which in my boyhood would have been thought inconceivable in a civilised society. I shall come back to this cleavage in our minds, for it is much more than an item in a list of war crimes. But it is an item. It helps to create the conditions for disaster. And I think that science has contributed to it. Science; the fact that science is there, mysterious, powerful; the fact that most people are impressed by it but ignorant and helpless – all this seems to me to have contributed to the division in our minds. And scientists cannot escape the responsibility for this. They have enjoyed acting the mysterious stranger, the powerful voice without emotion, the expert and the god. They have failed to make themselves comfortable in the talk of people in the street; no one taught them the knack, of course, but they were not keen to learn. And now they find the distance which they enjoyed has turned to distrust, and the awe has turned to fear; and people who are by no means fools really believe that we should be better off without science.

IV

10 These are the indictments which scientists cannot escape. Of course, they are often badly phrased, so that scientists can side-step them with generalities about the common responsibility, and who voted the credits for atomic research anyway; which are perfectly just, but not at all relevant. That is not the heart of the matter; and the people in queues and pubs are humbly groping for the heart. They are not good at saying things and they do not give model answers to interviewers. But when they say "We've forgotten what's right," when they say "We're not fit to handle such things," what is in their minds is perfectly true. Science and society are out of joint. Science has given to no one in particular a power which no one in particular knows how to use. Why do not scientists invent something sensible? Wives say it every time they stub their toe on the waste bin, and husbands say it whenever a fuse blows. Why is it the business of no one in particular to stop fitting science for death and to begin fitting it into our lives? We will agree that warlike science is no more than a by-product of a warlike society. Science has merely provided the means, for good or for bad; and society has seized it for bad. But what are we going to do about it?

11 The first thing to do, it seems to me, is to treat this as a scientific question: by which I mean as a practical and sensible question, which deserves a factual approach and a reasoned answer. Now that I have apologised on behalf of scientists, and this on a scale which some of them will certainly think too ample, let us cut out what usually happens to the argument at this point, the rush of recriminations. The scientists are conscious of their mistakes; and I do not want to discuss the mistakes of non-scientists – although they have made a great many – except those which we all must begin to make good.

12 I have said that a scientific answer must be practical as well as sensible. This really rules out at once the panaceas which also tend to run

the argument into a blind alley at this stage; the panaceas which say summarily "Get rid of them." Naturally, it does not seem to me to be sensible to get rid of scientists; but in any case, it plainly is not practical. And whatever we do with our own scientists, it very plainly is not practical to get rid of the scientists of rival nations; because if there existed the conditions for agreement among nations on this far-reaching scheme, then the conditions for war would already have disappeared. If there existed the conditions for international agreement, say to suspend all scientific research, or to abandon warlike research, or in any other way to forgo science as an instrument of nationalism — if such agreements could be reached, then they would already be superfluous; because the conditions for war would already have disappeared. So, however we might sigh for Samuel Butler's panacea in *Erewhon,* simply to give up all machines, there is no point in talking about it. I believe it would be a disaster for mankind like the coming of the Dark Ages. But there is no point in arguing this. It just is not practical, nationally or internationally.

13   There are no panaceas at all; and we had better face that. There is nothing that we can do overnight, in a week or a month, which can straighten by a laying on of hands the ancient distortion of our society. Do not let us fancy that any one of us out of the blue will concoct that stirring letter to *The Times* which will change the black mood of history — and the instructions to diplomats. Putting scientists in the Cabinet will not do that, and women in the War Office will not, nor will bishops in the Privy Council. There are no panaceas. We are the heirs to a tradition which has left science and society out of step. The man in the street is right: we have never learnt to handle such things. Nothing will do but that we learn. But learning is not done in a year. Our ultimate survival is in our own hands. Our survival while we are learning is a much chancier thing. We had better be realistic about that.

14   Meanwhile we had better settle down to work for our ultimate survival; and we had better start now. We have seen that the diagnosis has turned out to be not very difficult. Science and our social habits are out of step. And the cure is no deeper either. We must learn to match them. And there is no way of learning this unless we learn to understand *both.*

V

15 Of the two, of course, the one which is strange is science. I have already blamed the scientist for that. He has been the monk of our age, timid, thwarted, anxious to be asked to help; and with a secret ambition to play the Grey Eminence. Through the years of childhood poverty he dreamt of this. Scientific skill was a blue door beckoning to him, which would open into the society of dignitaries of state. But the private motives of scientists are not the trend of science. The trend of science is made by the needs of society: navigation before the eighteenth century, manufacture thereafter; and in our age I believe the liberation of personality. Whatever the part which scientists like to act, or for that matter which painters like to dress, science shares the aims of our society just as art does. The difficulties of understanding

either are not fundamental; they are difficulties only of language. To grow familiar with the large ideas of science calls for patience and an effort of attention; and I hope I have shown that it repays them.

16   For two hundred years, these ideas have been applied to technical needs; and they have made our world anew, triumphantly, from top to toe. Our shoes are tanned and stitched, our clothes are spun and dyed and woven, we are lighted and carried and doctored by means which were unknown to neat Mr. Pope at Twickenham in 1740. We may not think it recompenses us for the absence of any Mr. Pope from Twickenham today; we may even hold it responsible. It is certainly not a spiritual achievement. But it has not yet tried to be. It has applied its ideas monotonously to shoe leather and bicycle bells. And it has made a superb job of them. Compare its record in its own field with that of any other ideas of the same age: Burke's ideas of the imagination, or Bentham's on government, or Adam Smith's on political economy. If any ideas have a claim to be called creative, because they have created something, then certainly it is the ideas of science.

17   We may think that all that science has created is comfort; and it certainly has done that—the very word "comfortable" in the modern sense dates from the Industrial Revolution. But have we always stopped to think what science has done not to our mode of living but to our life? We talk about research for death, the threat of war and the number of civilians who get killed. But have we always weighed this against the increase in our own life span? Let us do a small sum. The number of people killed in Great Britain in six years of war by German bombs, flying bombs, and V2's was sixty thousand. They were an average lot of people, which means that on an average they lost half their expectation of life. Quite an easy long division shows that the effect of this in our population of fifty million people was to shorten the average span of life by less than one tenth of one per cent. This is considerably less than a fortnight. Put this on the debit side. And on the credit side, we know that in the last hundred years the average span of life in England has increased by twenty years. That is the price of science, take it or leave it—a fortnight for twenty years of life. And these twenty years have been created by applying to daily life, to clothing and bedding, to hygiene and infection, to birth and death, the simple ideas of science—the fundamental ideas I have been talking about: order, cause, and chance. If any ideas have a claim to be called creative, because they have created life, it is the ideas of science.

VI

18 We have not neglected these ideas altogether in our social organisation. But it is a point I have made several times—we have got hopelessly behind with them. The idea of order is now old enough to have reached at least our filing cabinets. The idea of cause and effect has entered our habits, until it has become the new *a priori* in the making of administrative plans. The difficulty is to dislodge it, now that it is hardening into a scholastic formula. For the idea which has given a new vigour to science in our generation is larger than the machinery of cause and effect. It stipulates no special mechanism between the

present and the future. It is content to predict the future, without insisting that the computation must follow the steps of causal law. I have called this the idea of chance, because its method is statistical, and because it recognises that every prediction carries with it its own measurable uncertainty. A good prediction is one which defines its area of uncertainty; a bad prediction ignores it. And at bottom this is no more than the return to the essentially empirical, the experimental nature of science. Science is a great many things, and I have called them a great many names; but in the end they all return to this: science is the acceptance of what works and the rejection of what does not. That needs more courage than we might think.

19   It needs more courage than we have ever found when we have faced our worldly problems. This is how society has lost touch with science: because it has hesitated to judge itself by the same impersonal code of what works and what does not. We have clung to Adam Smith and Burke, or we have agitated for Plato and Aquinas, through wars and famine, through rising and falling birth-rates, and through libraries of learned argument. And in the end, our eyes have always wandered from the birth-rate to the argument: from the birth-rate to what we have wanted to believe. Here is the crux of what I have been saying. Here is our ultimate hope of saving ourselves from extinction. We must learn to understand that the content of all knowledge is empirical; that its test is whether it works; and we must learn to act on that understanding in the world as well as in the laboratory.

20   This is the message of science: our ideas must be realistic, flexible, unbigoted — they must be human, they must create their own authority. If any ideas have a claim to be called creative, because they have liberated that creative impulse, it is the ideas of science.

VII

21 This is not only a material code. On the contrary, my hope is that it may heal the spiritual cleft which two wars have uncovered. I have seen in my lifetime an abyss open in the human mind: a gulf between the endeavor to be man, and the relish in being brute. The scientist has indeed had a hand in this, and every other specialist too, with his prim detachment and his oracular airs. But of course, the large strain which has opened this fault is social. We have made men live in two halves, a Sunday half and a workday one. We have ordered them to love their neighbour and to turn the other cheek, in a society which has constantly compelled them to shoulder their neighbour aside and to turn their backs. So we have created a savage sense of failure which, as we know now to our cost, can be tapped with an ease which is frightening; and which can thrust up, with explosive force, a symbol to repeat to an unhappy people its most degrading dream.

22   Can science heal that neurotic flaw in us? If science cannot, then nothing can. Let us stop pretending. There is no cure in high moral precepts. We have preached them too long to men who are forced to live how they can: *that* makes the strain which they have not been able to bear. We need an ethic which is moral *and* which works. It is often said that science has destroyed our values and put nothing in their place. What has really happened of course is that science has

shown in harsh relief the division between our values and our world. We have not begun to let science get into our heads; where then was it supposed to create these values? We have used it as a machine without will, the conjured spirit to do the chores. I believe that science can create values: and will create them precisely as literature does, by looking into the human personality; by discovering what divides it and what cements it. That is how great writers have explored man, and this whether they themselves as men have been driven by the anguish in *Gulliver's Travels* or the sympathy in *Moll Flanders*. The insight of science is not different from that of the arts. Science will create values, I believe, and discover virtues, when it looks into man; when it explores what makes him man and not an animal, and what makes his societies human and not animal packs.

23   I believe that we can reach this unity in our culture. . . . Nations in their great ages have not been great in art or science, but in art and science. Rembrandt was the contemporary of Huygens and Spinoza. At that very time, Isaac Newton walked with Dryden and Christopher Wren. We know that ours is a remarkable age of science. It is for us to use it to broaden and to liberate our culture. These are the marks of science: that it is open for all to hear, and all are free to speak their minds in it. They are marks of the world at its best, and the human spirit at its most challenging.

Discussion of Theme

1. In paragraph 7 Bronowski dismisses the argument that nations might be forced to "give up war for lack of cannon fodder. This hope has never been fulfilled, . . ." Is the present resistance to the draft and to wars a sign that the argument has been dismissed prematurely?
2. What support does the author give for his statement that "Science has enlarged the mechanism of war, and it has distorted it"?
3. Who, according to Bronowski, bears the basic responsibility for the weapons used to wage modern warfare? Does he excuse the scientist entirely?
4. According to Bronowski, what are the causes of war?
5. Describe the "spiritual cleft which two wars have uncovered."

Discussion of Rhetoric

1. Why does the author divide the article into sections? Is there different focus on the thesis in each section?
2. What is the relation between the opening anecdote and the central idea of this selection?
3. In what paragraph does Bronowski state his central theme? How does he prepare the reader for his thesis?
4. What is the purpose of the references in paragraphs 5 and 6? In paragraph 23?

5. How does Bronowski avoid alienating his nonscientific reader?
6. In paragraph 7 the author uses the phrase "frighten people into their wits." What is the force of such an alteration of a cliché?

Writing Assignments

1. In the long run, has science done more to support life than to destroy it? Give specific illustrations.
2. Analyze the responsibility of the scientist during war. Does he have the right to refuse to work on the development of weapons?
3. The medieval period is known as the Age of Faith; it has been said that the twentieth century will be known as the Age of Science. State your observations on this idea.
4. The English scientist and novelist C. P. Snow says that our age is breaking up into two cultures — the arts and the sciences. Give some arguments for this view.

Library Exploration

1. What was the SALT conference? What has it accomplished? What nations now possess the H-bomb? Does this increase the possibility of war?
2. Investigate the deliberations that led to the decision to drop the atom bomb in World War II.
3. If you are not familiar with the following references, look them up: Lamarck, Fiume, and the Polish Corridor.

Vocabulary

(1) MACABRE   gruesome
(1) CONJURES   summons as if by magic
(2) EPITOME   embodiment; ideal expression
(3) EXTINCT   died out; vanished (said of a species)
(4) SCAPEGOAT   whipping boy; someone to blame
(5) IDIOSYNCRASIES   peculiarities
(6) QUEUE   waiting line
(6) DISTORTED   twisted; perverted
(8) BATTENS   fattens; grows prosperous
(9) CLEAVAGE   split
(10) INDICTMENTS   accusations; formal charges
(11) RECRIMINATIONS   countercharges
(12) PANACEAS   cure-alls
(13) CONCOCT   devise; fabricate
(15) GREY EMINENCE   a person who exercises power behind the scenes
(16) RECOMPENSES   makes up for; pays back
(17) FORTNIGHT   a period of fourteen nights, or two weeks
(18) A PRIORI   something that is true or false by definition or convention alone
(19) EMPIRICAL   based on observation or experience
(20) UNBIGOTED   unprejudiced
(21) ORACULAR   pronouncing divine wisdom
(22) ETHIC   code of behavior

C. P. Snow (1905–   ) is a distinguished English scientist and novelist. At the beginning of the Second World War he left his teaching post at Cambridge University to administer scientific programs for the British government. Since 1940 he has published eight novels in a series known by the title of the first novel, "Strangers and Brothers."

His general audience probably knows Snow best for his theory that the intellectuals are divided into two distinct "cultures": the literary and the scientific. Here he argues for closing the cultural gap.

C. P. SNOW

The Two Cultures

1   It is about three years since I made a sketch in print of a problem which had been on my mind for some time.[1] It was a problem I could not avoid just because of the circumstances of my life. The only credentials I had to ruminate on the subject at all came through those circumstances, through nothing more than a set of chances. Anyone with similar experience would have seen much the same things and I think made very much the same comments about them. It just happened to be an unusual experience. By training I was a scientist: by vocation I was a writer. That was all. It was a piece of luck, if you like, that arose through coming from a poor home.

2   But my personal history isn't the point now. All that I need say is that I came to Cambridge and did a bit of research here at a time of major scientific activity. I was privileged to have a ringside view of one of the most wonderful creative periods in all physics. And it

---

[1]"The Two Cultures," *New Statesman*, 6 October 1956.

happened through the flukes of war—including meeting W. L. Bragg in the buffet on Kettering station on a very cold morning in 1939, which had a determining influence on my practical life—that I was able, and indeed morally forced, to keep that ringside view ever since. So for thirty years I have had to be in touch with scientists not only out of curiosity, but as part of a working existence. During the same thirty years I was trying to shape the books I wanted to write which in due course took me among writers.

3   There had been plenty of days when I have spent the working hours with scientists and then gone off at night with some literary colleagues. I mean that literally. I have had, of course, intimate friends among both scientists and writers. It was through living among these groups and much more, I think, through moving regularly from one to the other and back again that I got occupied with the problem of what, long before I put it on paper, I christened to myself as the "two cultures." For constantly I felt I was moving among two groups—comparable in intelligence, identical in race, not grossly different in social origin, earning about the same incomes, who had almost ceased to communicate at all, who in intellectual, moral and psychological climate had so little in common that instead of going from Burlington House or South Kensington to Chelsea, one might have crossed an ocean.

4   In fact, one had traveled much further than across an ocean—because after a few thousand Atlantic miles, one found Greenwich Village talking precisely the same language as Chelsea, and both having about as much communication with M.I.T. as though the scientists spoke nothing but Tibetan. For this is not just our problem; owing to some of our educational and social idiosyncrasies, it is slightly exaggerated here; owing to another English social peculiarity it is slightly minimised; by and large this is a problem of the entire West.

5   By this I intend something serious. I am not thinking of the pleasant story of how one of the more convivial Oxford great dons—I have heard the story attributed to A. L. Smith—came over to Cambridge to dine. The date is perhaps the 1890's. I think it must have been at St. John's, or possibly Trinity. Anyway, Smith was sitting at the right hand of the President—or Vice-Master—and he was a man who liked to include all round him in the conversation, although he was not immediately encouraged by the expressions of his neighbours. He addressed some cheerful Oxonian chit-chat at the one opposite to him, and got a grunt. He then tried the man on his own right hand and got another grunt. Then, rather to his surprise, one looked at the other and said, "Do you know what he's talking about?" "I haven't the least idea." At this, even Smith was getting out of his depth. But the President, acting as a social emollient, put him at his ease, by saying, "Oh, those are mathematicians! We never talk to *them*."

6   No, I intend something serious. I believe the intellectual life of the western society is increasingly being split into two polar groups. When I say the intellectual life, I mean to include also a large part of our practical life, because I should be the last person to suggest the two can at the deepest level be distinguished. I shall come back to the

practical life a little later. Two polar groups: at one pole we have the literary intellectuals, who incidentally while no one was looking took to referring to themselves as "intellectuals" as though there were no others. I remember G. H. Hardy once remarking to me in mild puzzlement, some time in the 1930's: "Have you noticed how the word 'intellectual' is used nowadays? There seems to be a new definition which certainly doesn't include Rutherford or Eddington or Dirac or Adrian or me. It does seem rather odd, don't y' know."[2]

7   Literary intellectuals at one pole — at the other scientists, and as the most representative, the physical scientists. Between the two a gulf of mutual incomprehension — sometimes (particularly among the young) hostility and dislike, but most of all lack of understanding. They have a curious distorted image of each other. Their attitudes are so different that, even on the level of emotion, they can't find much common ground. Non-scientists tend to think of scientists as brash and boastful. They hear Mr. T. S. Eliot, who just for these illustrations we can take as an archetypal figure, saying about his attempts to revive verse-drama, that we can hope for very little, but that he would feel content if he and his co-workers could prepare the ground for a new Kyd or a new Greene. That is the one, restricted and constrained, with which literary intellectuals are at home: it is the subdued voice of their culture. Then they hear a much louder voice, that of another archetypal figure, Rutherford, trumpeting: "This is the heroic age of science! This is the Elizabethan age!" Many of us heard that, and a good many other statements beside which that was mild; and we weren't left in any doubt whom Rutherford was casting for the role of Shakespeare. What is hard for the literary intellectuals to understand, imaginatively or intellectually, is that he was absolutely right.

8   And compare "this is the way the world ends, not with a bang but a whimper" — incidentally, one of the least likely scientific prophecies ever made — compare that with Rutherford's famous repartee, "Lucky fellow, Rutherford, always on the crest of the wave." "Well, I made the wave, didn't I?"

9   The non-scientists have a rooted impression that the scientists are shallowly optimistic, unaware of man's condition. On the other hand, the scientists believe that the literary intellectuals are totally lacking in foresight, peculiarly unconcerned with their brother man, in a deep sense anti-intellectual, anxious to restrict both art and thought to the existential moment. And so on. Anyone with a mild talent for invective could produce plenty of this kind of subterranean back-chat. On each side there is some of it which is not entirely baseless. It is all destructive. Much of it rests on misinterpretations which are dangerous. I should like to deal with two of the most profound of these now, one on each side.

10   First, about the scientists' optimism. This is an accusation which has been made so often that it has become a platitude. It has been made

---

[2]This lecture was delivered to a Cambridge audience, and so I used some points of reference which I did not need to explain. G. H. Hardy, 1877–1947, was one of the most distinguished pure mathematicians of his time, and a picturesque figure in Cambridge both as a young don and on his return in 1931 to the Sadleirian Chair of Mathematics.

by some of the acutest nonscientific minds of the day. But it depends upon a confusion between the individual experience and the social experience, between the individual condition of man and his social condition. Most of the scientists I have known well have felt — just as deeply as the non-scientists I have known well — that the individual condition of each of us is tragic. Each of us is alone: sometimes we escape from solitariness, through love or affection or perhaps creative moments, but those triumphs of life are pools of light we make for ourselves while the edge of the road is black; each of us dies alone. Some scientists I have known have had faith in revealed religion. Perhaps with them the sense of the tragic condition is not so strong. I don't know. With most people of deep feeling, however high-spirited and happy they are, sometimes most with those who are happiest and most high-spirited, it seems to be right in the fibres, part of the weight of life. That is as true of the scientists I have known best as of anyone at all.

11   But nearly all of them — and this is where the colour of hope genuinely comes in — would see no reason why, just because the individual condition is tragic, so must the social condition be. Each of us is solitary: each of us dies alone: all right, that's a fate against which we can't struggle — but there is plenty in our condition which is not fate, and against which we are less than human unless we do struggle.

12   Most of our fellow human beings, for instance, are underfed and die before their time. In the crudest terms, *that* is the social condition. There is a moral trap which comes through the insight into man's loneliness: it tempts one to sit back, complacent in one's unique tragedy, and let the others go without a meal.

13   As a group, the scientists fall into that trap less than others. They are inclined to be impatient to see if something can be done: and inclined to think that it can be done, until it's proved otherwise. That is their real optimism, and it's an optimism that the rest of us badly need.

14   In reverse, the same spirit, tough and good and determined to fight it out at the side of their brother man, has made scientists regard the other culture's social attitudes as contemptible. That is too facile: some of them are, but they are a temporary phase and not to be taken as representative.

15   I remember being cross-examined by a scientist of distinction. "Why do most writers take on social opinions which would have been thought distinctly uncivilised and démodé at the time of the Plantagenets? Wasn't that true of most of the famous twentieth-century writers? Yeats, Pound, Wyndham Lewis, nine out of ten of those who have dominated literary sensibility in our time — weren't they not only politically silly, but politically wicked? Didn't the influence of all they represent bring Auschwitz that much nearer?"

16   I thought at the time, and I still think, that the correct answer was not to defend the indefensible. It was no use saying that Yeats, according to friends whose judgment I trust, was a man of singular magnanimity of character, as well as a great poet. It was no use denying the facts, which are broadly true. The honest answer was that there is, in fact, a connection, which literary persons were culpably slow to see, between some kinds of early twentieth-century art and the most im-

becile expressions of anti-social feeling.[3] That was one reason, among many, why some of us turned our backs on the art and tried to hack out a new or different way for ourselves.[4]

17   But though many of those writers dominated literary sensibility for a generation, that is no longer so, or at least to nothing like the same extent. Literature changes more slowly than science. It hasn't the same automatic corrective, and so its misguided periods are longer. But it is ill-considered of scientists to judge writers on the evidence of the period 1914–50.

18   Those are two of the misunderstandings between the two cultures. I should say, since I began to talk about them — the two cultures, that is — I have had some criticism. Most of my scientific acquaintances think that there is something in it, and so do most of the practising artists I know. But I have been argued with by non-scientists of strong down-to-earth interests. Their view is that it is an over-simplification, and that if one is going to talk in these terms there ought to be at least three cultures. They argue that, though they are not scientists themselves, they would share a good deal of the scientific feeling. They would have as little use — perhaps, since they knew more about it, even less use — for the recent literary culture as the scientists themselves. J. H. Plumb, Alan Bullock and some of my American sociological friends have said that they vigorously refuse to be corralled in a cultural box with people they wouldn't be seen dead with, or to be regarded as helping to produce a climate which would not permit of social hope.

19   I respect those arguments. The number 2 is a very dangerous number: that is why the dialectic is a dangerous process. Attempts to divide anything into two ought to be regarded with much suspicion. I have thought a long time about going in for further refinements: but in the end I have decided against. I was searching for something a little more than a dashing metaphor, a good deal less than a cultural map: and for those purposes the two cultures is about right, and subtilising any more would bring more disadvantages than it's worth.

20   At one pole, the scientific culture really is a culture, not only in an intellectual but also in an anthropological sense. That is, its members need not, and of course often do not, always completely understand each other; biologists more often than not will have a pretty hazy idea of contemporary physics; but there are common attitudes, common standards and patterns of behaviour, common approaches and assumptions. This goes surprisingly wide and deep. It cuts across other mental patterns, such as those of religion or politics or class.

21   Statistically, I suppose slightly more scientists are in religious terms unbelievers, compared with the rest of the intellectual world — though there are plenty who are religious, and that seems to be increasingly

[3] I said a little more about this connection in *The Times Literary Supplement,* "Challenge to the Intellect," 15 August 1958. I hope some day to carry the analysis further.

[4] It would be more accurate to say that, for literary reasons, we felt the prevailing literary modes were useless to us. We were, however, reinforced in that feeling when it occurred to us that those prevailing modes went hand in hand with social attitudes either wicked, or absurd, or both.

so among the young. Statistically also, slightly more scientists are on the Left in open politics — though again, plenty always have called themselves conservatives, and that also seems to be more common among the young. Compared with the rest of the intellectual world, considerably more scientists in this country and probably in the U.S. come from poor families.[5] Yet, over a whole range of thought and behaviour, none of that matters very much. In their working, and in much of their emotional life, their attitudes are closer to other scientists than to non-scientists who in religion or politics or class have the same labels as themselves. If I were to risk a piece of shorthand, I should say that naturally they had the future in their bones.

22   They may or may not like it, but they have it. That was as true of the conservatives J. J. Thomson and Lindemann as of the radicals Einstein or Blackett: as true of the Christian A. H. Compton as of the materialist Bernal: of the aristocrats Broglie or Russell as of the proletarian Faraday: of those born rich, like Thomas Merton or Victor Rothschild, as of Rutherford, who was the son of an odd-job handyman. Without thinking about it, they respond alike. That is what a culture means.

23   At the other pole, the spread of attitudes is wider. It is obvious that between the two, as one moves through intellectual society from the physicists to the literary intellectuals, there are all kinds of tones of feeling on the way. But I believe the pole of total incomprehension of science radiates its influences on all the rest. That total incomprehension gives, much more pervasively than we realise, living in it, an unscientific flavour to the whole "traditional" culture, and that unscientific flavour is often, much more than we admit, on the point of turning anti-scientific. The feelings of one pole become the anti-feelings of the other. If the scientists have the future in their bones, then the traditional culture responds by wishing the future did not exist.[6] It is the traditional culture, to an extent remarkably little diminished by the emergence of the scientific one, which manages the western world.

24   This polarisation is sheer loss to us all. To us as people, and to our society. It is at the same time a practical and intellectual and creative loss, and I repeat that it is false to imagine that those three considerations are clearly separable. But for a moment I want to concentrate on the intellectual loss.

25   The degree of incomprehension on both sides is the kind of joke which has gone sour. There are about fifty thousand working scientists in the country and about eighty thousand professional engineers or applied scientists. During the war and in the years since, my colleagues and I have had to interview somewhere between thirty to forty thousand of these — that is, about 25 per cent. The number is large enough to give us a fair sample, though of the men we talked to most would still be under forty. We were able to find out a certain amount of what they read and thought about. I confess that even I,

[5]An analysis of the schools from which Fellows of the Royal Society come tells its own story. The distribution is markedly different from that of, for example, members of the Foreign Service or Queen's Counsel.

[6]Compare George Orwell's *1984,* which is the strongest possible wish that the future should not exist, with J. D. Bernal's *World without War.*

who am fond of them and respect them, was a bit shaken. We hadn't quite expected that the links with the traditional culture should be so tenuous, nothing more than a formal touch of the cap.

26   As one would expect, some of the very best scientists had and have plenty of energy and interest to spare, and we came across several who had read everything that literary people talk about. But that's very rare. Most of the rest, when one tried to probe for what books they had read, would modestly confess, "Well, I've *tried* a bit of Dickens," rather as though Dickens were an extraordinarily esoteric, tangled and dubiously rewarding writer, something like Rainer Maria Rilke. In fact that is exactly how they do regard him: we thought that discovery, that Dickens had been transformed into the type-specimen of literary incomprehensibility, was one of the oddest results of the whole exercise.

27   But of course, in reading him, in reading almost any writer whom we should value, they are just touching their caps to the traditional culture. They have their own culture, intensive, rigorous, and constantly in action. This culture contains a great deal of argument, usually much more rigorous, and almost always at a higher conceptual level, than literary persons' arguments — even though the scientists do cheerfully use words in senses which literary persons don't recognise, the senses are exact ones, and when they talk about "subjective," "objective," "philosophy" or "progressive,"[7] they know what they mean, even though it isn't what one is accustomed to expect.

28   Remember, these are very intelligent men. Their culture is in many ways an exacting and admirable one. It doesn't contain much art, with the exception, an important exception, of music. Verbal exchange, insistent argument. Long-playing records. Colour-photography. The ear, to some extent the eye. Books, very little, though perhaps not many would go so far as one hero, who perhaps I should admit was further down the scientific ladder than the people I've been talking about — who when asked what books he read, replied firmly and confidently: "Books? I prefer to use my books as tools." It was very hard not to let the mind wander — what sort of tool would a book make? Perhaps a hammer? A primitive digging instrument?

29   Of books, though, very little. And of the books which to most literary persons are bread and butter, novels, history, poetry, plays, almost nothing at all. It isn't that they're not interested in the psychological or moral or social life. In the social life, they certainly are, more than most of us. In the moral, they are by and large the soundest group of intellectuals we have; there is a moral component right in the grain of science itself, and almost all scientists form their own judgments of the moral life. In the psychological they have as much interest as most of us, though occasionally I fancy they come to it rather late. It isn't that they lack the interests. It is much more that the whole literature of the traditional culture doesn't seem to them relevant to those interests.

---

[7] *Subjective,* in contemporary technological jargon, means "divided according to subjects." *Objective* means "directed towards an object." *Philosophy* means "general intellectual approach or attitude" (for example, a scientist's "philosophy of guided weapons" might lead him to propose certain kinds of "objective research"). A "progressive" job means one with possibilities of promotion.

They are, of course, dead wrong. As a result, their imaginative understanding is less than it could be. They are self-impoverished.

30   But what about the other side? They are impoverished too — perhaps more seriously, because they are vainer about it. They still like to pretend that the traditional culture is the whole of "culture," as though the natural order didn't exist. As though the exploration of the natural order was of no interest either in its own value or its consequences. As though the scientific edifice of the physical world was not, in its intellectual depth, complexity and articulation, the most beautiful and wonderful collective work of the mind of man. Yet most nonscientists have no conception of that edifice at all. Even if they want to have it, they can't. It is rather as though, over an immense range of intellectual experience, a whole group was tone-deaf. Except that this tone-deafness doesn't come by nature, but by training, or rather the absence of training.

31   As with the tone-deaf, they don't know what they miss. They give a pitying chuckle at the news of scientists who have never read a major work of English literature. They dismiss them as ignorant specialists. Yet their own ignorance and their own specialisation is just as startling. A good many times I have been present at gatherings of people who, by the standards of the traditional culture, are thought highly educated and who have with considerable gusto been expressing their incredulity at the illiteracy of scientists. Once or twice I have been provoked and have asked the company how many of them could describe the Second Law of Thermodynamics. The response was cold: it was also negative. Yet I was asking something which is about the scientific equivalent of: *Have you read a work of Shakespeare's?*

32   I now believe that if I had asked an even simpler question — such as, What do you mean by mass, or acceleration, which is the scientific equivalent of saying, *Can you read?* — not more than one in ten of the highly educated would have felt that I was speaking the same language. So the great edifice of modern physics goes up, and the majority of the cleverest people in the western world have about as much insight into it as their neolithic ancestors would have had.

33   Just one more of those questions, that my non-scientific friends regard as being in the worst of taste. Cambridge is a university where scientists and non-scientists meet every night at dinner.[8] About two years ago, one of the most astonishing experiments in the whole history of science was brought off. I don't mean the sputnik — that was admirable for quite different reasons, as a feat of organisation and a triumphant use of existing knowledge. No, I mean the experiment at Columbia by Yang and Lee. It is an experiment of the greatest beauty and originality, but the result is so startling that one forgets how beautiful the experiment is. It makes us think again about some of the fundamentals of the physical world. Intuition, common sense — they are neatly stood on their heads. The result is usually known as the contradiction of parity. If there were any serious communication between the two cultures, this experiment would have been talked about at

---

[8]Almost all college High Tables contain Fellows in both scientific and non-scientific subjects.

every High Table in Cambridge. Was it? I wasn't here: but I should like to ask the question.

34   There seems then to be no place where the cultures meet. I am not going to waste time saying that this is a pity. It is much worse than that. Soon I shall come to some practical consequences. But at the heart of thought and creation we are letting some of our best chances go by default. The clashing point of two subjects, two disciplines, two cultures — of two galaxies, so far as that goes — ought to produce creative chances. In the history of mental activity that has been where some of the breakthroughs came. The chances are there now. But they are there, as it were, in a vacuum, because those in the two cultures can't talk to each other. It is bizarre how very little of twentieth-century science has been assimilated into twentieth-century art. Now and then one used to find poets conscientiously using scientific expressions, and getting them wrong — there was a time when "refraction" kept cropping up in verse in a mystifying fashion, and when "polarised light" was used as though writers were under the illusion that it was a specially admirable kind of light.

35   Of course, that isn't the way that science could be any good to art. It has got to be assimilated along with, and as part and parcel of, the whole of our mental experience, and used as naturally as the rest.

36   I said earlier that this cultural divide is not just an English phenomenon: it exists all over the western world. But it probably seems at its sharpest in England, for two reasons. One is our fanatical belief in educational specialisation, which is much more deeply ingrained in us than in any country in the world, east or west. The other is our tendency to let our social forms crystallise. This tendency appears to get stronger, not weaker, the more we iron out economic inequalities: and this is specially true in education. It means that once anything like a cultural divide gets established, all the social forces operate to make it not less rigid, but more so.

37   The two cultures were already dangerously separate sixty years ago; but a prime minister like Lord Salisbury could have his own laboratory at Hatfield, and Arthur Balfour had a somewhat more than amateur interest in natural science. John Anderson did some research in organic chemistry in Würzburg before passing first into the Civil Service, and incidentally took a spread of subjects which is now impossible.[9] None of that degree of interchange at the top of the Establishment is likely, or indeed thinkable, now.[10]

38   In fact, the separation between the scientists and non-scientists is much less bridgeable among the young than it was even thirty years ago. Thirty years ago the cultures had long ceased to speak to each other: but at least they managed a kind of frozen smile across the gulf. Now the politeness has gone, and they just make faces. It is not only

[9]He took the examination in 1905.

[10]It is, however, true to say that the compact nature of the managerial layers of English society — the fact that "everyone knows everyone else" — means that scientists and non-scientists do in fact know each other as people more easily than in most countries. It is also true that a good many leading politicians and administrators keep up lively intellectual and artistic interests to a much greater extent, so far as I can judge, than is the case in the U.S. These are both among our assets.

that the young scientists now feel that they are part of a culture on the rise while the other is in retreat. It is also, to be brutal, that the young scientists know that with an indifferent degree they'll get a comfortable job, while their contemporaries and counterparts in English or History will be lucky to earn 60 per cent as much. No young scientist of any talent would feel that he isn't wanted or that his work is ridiculous, as did the hero of *Lucky Jim*, and in fact, some of the disgruntlement of Amis and his associates is the disgruntlement of the underemployed arts graduate.

39   There is only one way out of all this: it is, of course, by rethinking our education. In this country, for the two reasons I have given, that is more difficult than in any other. Nearly everyone will agree that our school education is too specialised. But nearly everyone feels that it is outside the will of man to alter it. Other countries are as dissatisfied with their education as we are, but are not so resigned.

40   The U.S. teach out of proportion more children up to eighteen than we do: they teach them far more widely, but nothing like so rigorously. They know that: they are hoping to take the problem in hand within ten years, though they may not have all that time to spare. The U.S.S.R. also teach out of proportion more children than we do: they also teach far more widely than we do (it is an absurd western myth that their school education is specialised) but much too rigorously.[11] They know that — and they are beating about to get it right. The Scandinavians, in particular the Swedes, who would make a more sensible job of it than any of us, are handicapped by their practical need to devote an inordinate amount of time to foreign languages. But they too are seized of the problem.

41   Are we? Have we crystallised so far that we are no longer flexible at all?

42   Talk to schoolmasters, and they say that our intense specialisation, like nothing else on earth, is dictated by the Oxford and Cambridge scholarship examinations. If that is so, one would have thought it not utterly impracticable to change the Oxford and Cambridge scholarship examinations. Yet one would underestimate the national capacity for the intricate defensive to believe that that was easy. All the lessons of our educational history suggest we are only capable of increasing specialisation, not decreasing it.

43   Somehow we have set ourselves the task of producing a tiny *élite* — far smaller proportionately than in any comparable country — educated in one academic skill. For a hundred and fifty years in Cambridge it was mathematics: then it was mathematics or classics: then natural science was allowed in. But still the choice had to be a single one.

44   It may well be that this process has gone too far to be reversible. I have given reasons why I think it is a disastrous process, for the purpose of a living culture. I am going on to give reasons why I think it is fatal, if we're to perform our practical tasks in the world. But I can think of only one example, in the whole of English educational history,

---

[11] I tried to compare American, Soviet and English education in "New Minds for the New World," *New Statesman*, 6 September 1956.

where our pursuit of specialised mental exercises was resisted with success.

45   It was done here in Cambridge, fifty years ago, when the old order-of-merit in the Mathematical Tripos was abolished. For over a hundred years, the nature of the Tripos had been crystallising. The competition for the top places had got fiercer, and careers hung on them. In most colleges, certainly in my own, if one managed to come out as Senior or Second Wrangler, one was elected a Fellow out of hand. A whole apparatus of coaching had grown up. Men of the quality of Hardy, Littlewood, Russell, Eddington, Jeans, Keynes, went in for two or three years' training for an examination which was intensely competitive and intensely difficult. Most people in Cambridge were very proud of it, with a similar pride to that which almost anyone in England always has for our existing educational institutions, whatever they happen to be. If you study the fly-sheets of the time, you will find the passionate arguments for keeping the examination precisely as it was to all eternity: it was the only way to keep up standards, it was the only fair test of merit, indeed, the only seriously objective test in the world. The arguments, in fact, were almost exactly those which are used today with precisely the same passionate sincerity if anyone suggests that the scholarship examinations might conceivably not be immune from change.

46   In every respect but one, in fact, the old Mathematical Tripos seemed perfect. The one exception, however, appeared to some to be rather important. It was simply — so the young creative mathematicians, such as Hardy and Littlewood, kept saying — that the training had no intellectual merit at all. They went a little further, and said that the Tripos had killed serious mathematics in England stone dead for a hundred years. Well, even in academic controversy, that took some skirting round, and they got their way. But I have an impression that Cambridge was a good deal more flexible between 1850 and 1914 than it has been in our time. If we had had the old Mathematical Tripos firmly planted among us, should we have ever managed to abolish it?

Discussion of Theme

1. Do you believe, as Snow apparently does, that a gulf exists between young scientists and nonscientists in part because the former know "they'll get a comfortable job, while their contemporaries and counterparts in English or History will be lucky to earn 60 percent as much"? Is this a purely British attitude, or does it also exist in America?
2. What charges does Snow bring against scientists? Against literary people?
3. Why should the two cultures understand each other?
4. Does Snow suggest that the gap between the scientist and the literary scholar is a recent phenomenon, or one that dates from earliest times?

Discussion of Rhetoric

1. Note the poetry quoted in the first line of paragraph 8. What does it mean? In what poem do you find it? Why is this particular line so frequently quoted?
2. This essay is developed through comparison and contrast. How does this method determine the organization of the author's ideas?
3. How does Snow establish his authority in the opening paragraphs?
4. What is the purpose of the anecdote in paragraph 5?
5. What kinds of words does Snow use to connect paragraphs 10, 11, 13, and 14?

Writing Assignments

1. In paragraph 15 Snow reports a conversation with a fellow scientist who believes that writers, because of their "uncivilized" social opinions, are responsible for wars. How valid is his argument?
2. What is your concept of an intellectual? Describe the general attributes of such a person, and offer illustrations from either real life or from literature.
3. Give your definition of an educated man (500 words).
4. Examine some of the ways that American education can help close the cultural gap.

Library Exploration

1. An excellent introduction to Snow as a novelist is *The Masters*. Read and report on this or another of his novels.
2. Investigate the controversy between F. R. Leavis, the English literary critic, and Snow.

Vocabulary

(1) RUMINATE reflect
(2) FLUKES chances; strokes of luck
(5) CONVIVIAL sociable; jovial
(5) EMOLLIENT soothing salve
(7) INCOMPREHENSION lack of understanding
(7) ARCHETYPAL model; pattern-setting
(8) REPARTEE clever response
(9) INVECTIVE verbal attack or abuse
(10) PLATITUDE trite remark
(10) ACUTEST sharpest

(12) COMPLACENT smug
(14) FACILE easy; slick
(15) DÉMODÉ out of style
(16) CULPABLY in a manner deserving blame or censure
(19) SUBTILISING refining
(23) PERVASIVELY spread throughout
(26) ESOTERIC understood only by a chosen few
(31) INCREDULITY disbelief
(34) BIZARRE weird; peculiar
(40) INORDINATE excessive; immoderate

The author of over twenty books, Philip Wylie (1902–71) also wrote for films, newspapers, and for "The New Yorker." He was well known for his unrelenting and often controversial attacks on American manners and morals. The book he is perhaps best known for, and which is still widely read, is "A Generation of Vipers," published in 1942.

This article is typical of Wylie's approach to social questions. It is assuredly more than an amusing complaint about supper; it is also a warning about the direction our civilization is taking.

PHILIP WYLIE

Science Has Spoiled My Supper

1 I am a fan for Science. My education is scientific and I have, in one field, contributed a monograph to a scientific journal. Science, to my mind, is applied honesty, the one reliable means we have to find out truth. That is why, when error is committed in the name of Science, I feel the way a man would if his favorite uncle had taken to drink.

2   Over the years, I have come to feel that way about what science has done to food. I agree that America can set as good a table as any nation in the world. I agree that our food is nutritious and that the diet of most of us is well-balanced. What America eats is handsomely packaged; it is usually clean and pure; it is excellently preserved. The only trouble with it is this: year by year it grows less good to eat. It appeals increasingly to the eye. But who eats with his eyes? Almost everything used to taste better when I was a kid. For quite a long time I thought that observation was merely another index of advancing age. But some years ago I married a girl whose mother is an expert cook of the

kind called "old-fashioned." This gifted woman's daughter (my wife) was taught her mother's venerable skills. The mother lives in the country and still plants an old-fashioned garden. She still buys dairy products from the neighbors and, insofar as possible, she uses the same materials her mother and grandmother did — to prepare meals that are superior. They are just as good, in this Year of Grace, as I recall them from my courtship. After eating for a while at the table of my mother-in-law, it is sad to go back to eating with my friends — even the alleged "good cooks" among them. And it is a gruesome experience to have meals at the best big-city restaurants.

3   Take cheese, for instance. Here and there, in big cities, small stores and delicatessens specialize in cheese. At such places, one can buy at least some of the first-rate cheeses that we used to eat — such as those we had with pie and in macaroni. The latter were sharp but not too sharp. They were a little crumbly. We called them American cheeses, or even rat cheese; actually, they were Cheddars. Long ago, this cheese began to be supplanted by a material call "cheese foods." Some cheese foods and "processed" cheese are fairly edible; but not one comes within miles of the old kinds — for flavor.

4   A grocer used to be very fussy about his cheese. Cheddar was made and sold by hundreds of little factories. Representatives of the factories had particular customers, and cheese was prepared by hand to suit the grocers, who knew precisely what their patrons wanted in rat cheese, pie cheese, American and other cheeses. Some liked them sharper; some liked them yellower; some liked anise seeds in cheese, or caraway.

5   What happened? Science — or what is called science — stepped in. The old-fashioned cheeses didn't ship well enough. They crumbled, became moldy, dried out. "Scientific" tests disclosed that a great majority of the people will buy a less-good-tasting cheese if that's all they can get. "Scientific marketing" then took effect. Its motto is "Give the people the least quality they'll stand for." In food, as in many other things, the "scientific marketers" regard quality as secondary so long as they can sell most persons anyhow; what they are after is "durability" or "shippability."

6   It is not possible to make the very best cheese in vast quantities at a low average cost. "Scientific sampling" got in its statistically nasty work. It was found that the largest number of people will buy something that is bland and rather tasteless. Those who prefer a product of a pronounced and individualistic flavor have a variety of preferences. Nobody is altogether pleased by bland foodstuff, in other words; but nobody is very violently put off. The result is that a "reason" has been found for turning out zillions of packages of something that will "do" for nearly all and isn't even imagined to be superlatively good by a single soul!

7   Economics entered. It is possible to turn out in quantity a bland, impersonal, practically imperishable substance more or less resembling, say, cheese — at lower cost than cheese. Chain groceries shut out the independent stores and "standardization" became a principal means of cutting costs.

8   Imitations also came into the cheese business. There are American duplications of most of the celebrated European cheeses, mass-produced and cheaper by far than the imports. They would cause European food-lovers to gag or guffaw — but generally the limitations are all that's available in the supermarkets. People buy them and eat them.

9   Perhaps you don't like cheese — so the fact that decent cheese is hardly ever served in America any more, or used in cooking, doesn't matter to you. Well, take bread. There has been (and still is) something of a hullabaloo about bread. In fact, in the last few years, a few big bakeries have taken to making a fairly good imitation of real bread. It costs much more than what is nowadays called bread, but it is edible. Most persons, however, now eat as "bread" a substance so full of chemicals and so barren of cereals that it approaches a synthetic.

10   Most bakers are interested mainly in how a loaf of bread looks. They are concerned with how little stuff they can put in it — to get how much money. They are deeply interested in using chemicals that will keep the bread from molding, make it seem "fresh" for the longest possible time, and so render it marketable and shippable. They have been at this monkeyshine for a generation. Today a loaf of "bread" looks deceptively real; but it is made from heaven knows what and it resembles, as food, a solidified bubble bath. Some months ago I bought a loaf of the stuff and, experimentally, began pressing it together, like an accordion. With a little effort, I squeezed the whole loaf to a length of about one inch!

11   Yesterday, at the home of my mother-in-law, I ate with country-churned butter and home-canned wild strawberry jam several slices of actual bread, the same thing we used to have every day at home. People who have eaten actual bread will know what I mean. They will know that the material commonly called bread is not even related to real bread, except in name.

12   For years, I couldn't figure out what had happened to vegetables. I knew, of course, that most vegetables, to be enjoyed in their full deliciousness, must be picked fresh and cooked at once. I knew that vegetables cannot be overcooked and remain even edible, in the best sense. They cannot stand on the stove. That set of facts makes it impossible, of course, for any American restaurant — or, indeed, any city-dweller separated from supply by more than a few hours — to have decent fresh vegetables. The Parisians managed by getting their vegetables picked at dawn and rushed in farmers' carts to market, where no middleman or marketman delays produce on its way to the pot.

13   Our vegetables, however, come to us through a long chain of command. There are merchants of several sorts — wholesalers before the retailers, commission men, and so on — with the result that what were once edible products become, in transit, mere wilted leaves and withered tubers.

14   Homes and restaurants do what they can with this stuff — which my mother-in-law would discard on the spot. I have long thought that the famed blindfold test for cigarettes should be applied to city vegetables. For I am sure that if you puréed them and ate them blindfolded, you

couldn't tell the beans from the peas, the turnips from the squash, the Brussels sprouts from the broccoli.

15   It is only lately that I have found how much science has had to do with this reduction of noble victuals to pottage. Here the science of genetics is involved. Agronomists and the like have taken to breeding all sorts of vegetables and fruits—changing their original nature. This sounds wonderful and often is insane. For the scientists have not as a rule taken any interest whatsoever in the taste of the things they've tampered with!

16   What they've done is to develop "improved" strains of things for every purpose but eating. They work out, say, peas that will ripen all at once. The farmer can then harvest his peas and thresh them and be done with them. It is extremely profitable because it is efficient. What matter if such peas taste like boiled paper wads?

17   Geneticists have gone crazy over such "opportunities." They've developed string beans that are straight instead of curved, and all one length. This makes them easier to pack in cans, even if, when eating them, you can't tell them from tender string. Ripening time and identity of size and shape are, nowadays, more important in carrots than the fact that they taste like carrots. Personally, I don't care if they hybridize onions till they are big as your head and come up through the snow; but, in doing so, they are producing onions that only vaguely and feebly remind you of onions. We are getting some varieties, in fact, that have less flavor than the water off last week's leeks. Yet, if people don't eat onions because they taste like onions, what in the name of Luther Burbank do they eat them for?

18   The women's magazines are about one third dedicated to clothes, one third to mild comment on sex, and the other third to recipes and pictures of handsome salads, desserts, and main courses. "Institutes" exist to experiment and tell housewives how to cook attractive meals and how to turn leftovers into works of art. The food thus pictured looks like famous paintings of still life. The only trouble is it's tasteless. It leaves appetite unquenched and merely serves to stave off famine.

19   I wonder if this blandness of our diet doesn't explain why so many of us are overweight and even dangerously so. When things had flavor, we knew what we were eating all the while—and it satisfied us. A teaspoonful of my mother-in-law's wild strawberry jam will not just provide a gastronome's ecstasy: it will entirely satisfy your jam desire. But, of the average tinned or glass-packed strawberry jam, you need half a cupful to get the idea of what you're eating. A slice of my mother-in-law's apple pie will satiate you far better than a whole bakery pie.

20   That thought is worthy of investigation—of genuine scientific investigation. It is merely a hypothesis, so far, and my own. But people—and their ancestors—have been eating according to flavor for upwards of a billion years. The need to satisfy the sense of taste may be innate and important. When food is merely a pretty cascade of viands, with the texture of boiled cardboard and the flavor of library paste, it may be the instinct of *genus homo* to go on eating in the unconscious hope of finally satisfying the ageless craving of the frustrated taste buds. In

the days when good-tasting food was the rule in the American home, obesity wasn't such a national curse.

21 How can you feel you've eaten if you haven't tasted, and fully enjoyed tasting? Why (since science is ever so ready to answer the beck and call of mankind) don't people who want to reduce merely give up eating and get the nourishment they must have in measured doses shot into their arms at hospitals? One ready answer to that question suggests that my theory of overeating is sound: people like to taste! In eating, they try to satisfy that like.

22 The scientific war against deliciousness has been stepped up enormously in the last decade. Some infernal genius found a way to make biscuit batter keep. Housewives began to buy this premixed stuff. It saved work, of course. But any normally intelligent person can learn, in a short period, how to prepare superb baking powder biscuits. I can make better biscuits, myself, than can be made from patent batters. Yet soon after this fiasco became an American staple, it was discovered that a half-baked substitute for all sorts of breads, pastries, rolls, and the like could be mass-manufactured, frozen—and sold for polishing off in the home oven. None of these two-stage creations is as good as even a fair sample of the thing it imitates. A man of taste, who had eaten one of my wife's cinnamon buns, might use the premixed sort to throw at starlings—but not to eat! Cake mixes, too, come ready-prepared—like cement and not much better-tasting compared with true cake.

23 It is, however, "deep-freezing" that has really rung down the curtain on American cookery. Nothing is improved by the process. I have yet to taste a deep-frozen victual that measures up, in flavor, to the fresh, unfrosted original. And most foods, cooked or uncooked, are destroyed in the deep freeze for all people of sense and sensibility. Vegetables with crisp and crackling texture emerge as mush, slippery and stringy as hair nets simmered in Vaseline. The essential oils that make peas peas—and cabbage cabbage—must undergo fission and fusion in freezers. Anyhow, they vanish. Some meats turn to leather. Others to wood pulp. Everything, pretty much, tastes like the mosses of tundra, dug up in midwinter. Even the appearance changes, oftentimes. Handsome comestibles you put down in the summer come out looking very much like the corpses of wooly mammoths recovered from the last Ice Age.

24 Of course, all this scientific "food handling" tends to save money. It certainly preserves food longer. It reduces work at home. But these facts, and especially the last, imply that the first purpose of living is to avoid work—at home, anyhow.

25 Without thinking, we are making an important confession about ourselves as a nation. We are abandoning quality—even, to some extent, the quality of people. The "best" is becoming too good for us. We are suckling ourselves on machine-made mediocrity. It is bad for our souls, our minds, and our digestion. It is the way our wiser and calmer forebears fed, not people, but hogs: as much as possible and as fast as possible, with no standard of quality.

26 The Germans say, *"Mann ist was er isst*—Man is what he eats." If

this be true, the people of the U.S.A. are well on their way to becoming a faceless mob of mediocrities, of robots. And if we apply to other attributes the criteria we apply these days to appetite, that is what would happen! We would not want bright children any more; we'd merely want them to look bright—and get through school fast. We wouldn't be interested in beautiful women—just a good paint job. And we'd be opposed to the most precious quality of man: his individuality, his differentness from the mob.

27   There are some people—sociologists and psychologists among them —who say that is exactly what we Americans are doing, are becoming. Mass man, they say, is on the increase. Conformity, standardization, similarity—all on a cheap and vulgar level—are replacing the great American ideas of colorful liberty and dignified individualism. If this is so, the process may well begin, like most human behavior, in the home—in those homes where a good meal has been replaced by something-to-eat-in-a-hurry. By something not very good to eat, prepared by a mother without very much to do, for a family that doesn't feel it amounts to much anyhow.

28   I call, here, for rebellion.

Discussion of Theme

1. What is meant by "man is what he eats"?
2. Wylie wrote this article in 1954. Are we eating, in the 1970s, more of the sort of foods that Wylie complains about?
3. Does Wylie exaggerate in seeing a connection between standardized foods and a loss of "the great American ideas of colorful liberty and dignified individualism"?
4. Wylie's complaints about his food serve as a springboard for a larger attack. What is this main theme?
5. Do you agree with Wylie that many people are overweight because of the blandness of their diet? The author implies that fewer people were overweight in the past. Is this likely?
6. Wylie's mother-in-law serves an important function in this argument. How would you describe it?

Discussion of Rhetoric

1. Analyze the humor in the phrase "the scientific war against deliciousness." Are there any other examples of witty phrasing?
2. How does the last sentence in paragraph 1 set the tone of this essay?
3. Wylie develops his theme by a series of examples. What are some of them? How does he succeed in introducing each one smoothly?
4. This essay can be divided into three sections: paragraphs 1–18, 19–25, and 26–28. What is the thesis or central idea in each section? How are they linked to form a unified whole?
5. In order to avoid saying simply "it tastes bad," Wylie uses a number

of similes. In paragraph 16, for example, he says that peas taste like "boiled paper wads." Find other similes in the essay. How do they heighten his emphasis?

Writing Assignments

1. If you patronize health-food stores instead of supermarkets, explain your preference for organically grown foods or foods free of artificial supplements and chemical preservatives.
2. Attack Wylie's thesis by showing the benefits of scientific developments in food.
3. Wylie would probably agree with the observation that many products other than food are being produced with emphasis on appearance rather than quality. Describe some of these products.

Library Exploration

1. What are the duties of the Food & Drug Administration? Why is it unable to bring more than a small percentage of violations to court?
2. For a detailed treatment of the techniques used by food processors to make the products mentioned by Wylie more attractive, read Vance Packard's *The Hidden Persuaders*.
3. What actually happens to foods when they are dried or frozen? What structural or chemical changes take place?

Vocabulary

(1) MONOGRAPH   a detailed article on one subject
(2) VENERABLE   ancient and respected
(2) GRUESOME   grisly; ghastly
(6) BLAND   mild; flavorless
(13) IN TRANSIT   on the way
(13) TUBERS   roots
(14) PURÉED   mashed
(15) VICTUALS   foods
(15) POTTAGE   thick soup
(15) AGRONOMISTS   specialists in crop and soil management
(17) HYBRIDIZE   crossbreed
(17) LEEKS   vegetables related to the onion

(18) STAVE OFF   ward off; keep away
(19) GASTRONOME   one who likes good food and drink
(19) TINNED   canned
(19) SATIATE   satisfy; fill
(20) INNATE   inborn
(20) VIANDS   foods
(20) GENUS HOMO   the race of man
(21) BECK   summons
(22) FIASCO   utter and ridiculous failure
(23) TUNDRA   frozen wasteland
(23) COMESTIBLES   edibles; foods

Rachel Carson (1907–65) received a number of awards for her work as a marine biologist and author. She was a rare combination of scientist, writer, and passionate member of the human society. In addition to "The Sea Around Us" (1951), she wrote about the marine world in "Under the Sea Wind" (1952) and "The Edge of the Sea" (1955). Two years before her death she swept into national prominence—and controversy—with her study of insecticides, "Silent Spring" (1962).

This excerpt explains something about the movement of the seas. Despite the technical nature of her subject, Miss Carson's style is lucid and often poetic.

RACHEL CARSON

The Shape of Ancient Seas

Till the slow sea rise and the sheer cliff crumble,
Till terrace and meadow the deep gulfs drink.
Swinburne

1   We live in an age of rising seas. Along all the coasts of the United States a continuing rise of sea level has been perceptible on the tide gauges of the Coast and Geodetic Survey since 1930. For the thousand-mile stretch from Massachusetts to Florida, and on the coast of the Gulf of Mexico, the rise amounted to about a third of a foot between 1930 and 1948. The water is also rising (but more slowly) along the Pacific shores. These records of the tide gauges do not include the transient advances and retreats of the water caused by winds and storms, but signify a steady, continuing advance of the sea upon the land.

2   This evidence of a rising sea is an interesting and even an exciting thing because it is rare that, in the short span of human life, we can actually observe and measure the progress of one of the great earth rhythms. What is happening is nothing new. Over the long span of geologic time, the ocean waters have come in over North America many times and have again retreated into their basins. For the boundary between sea and land is the most fleeting and transitory feature of the earth, and the sea is forever repeating its encroachments upon the continents. It rises and falls like a great tide, sometimes engulfing half a continent in its flood, reluctant in its ebb, moving in a rhythm mysterious and infinitely deliberate.

3   Now once again the ocean is overfull. It is spilling over the rims of its basins. It fills the shallow seas that border the continents, like the Barents, Bering, and China seas. Here and there it has advanced into the interior and lies in such inland seas as Hudson Bay, the St. Lawrence embayment, the Baltic, and the Sunda Sea. On the Atlantic coast of the United States the mouths of many rivers, like the Hudson and the Susquehanna, have been drowned by the advancing flood; the old, submerged channels are hidden under bays like the Chesapeake and the Delaware.

4   The advance noted so clearly on the tide gauges may be part of a long rise that began thousands of years ago—perhaps when the glaciers of the most recent Ice Age began to melt. But it is only within recent decades that there have been instruments to measure it in any part of the world. Even now the gauges are few and scattered, considering the world as a whole. Because of the scarcity of world records, it is not known whether the rise observed in the United States since 1930 is being duplicated on all other continents.

5   Where and when the ocean will halt its present advance and begin again its slow retreat into its basin, no one can say. If the rise over the continent of North America should amount to a hundred feet (and there is more than enough water now frozen in land ice to provide such a rise) most of the Atlantic seaboard, with its cities and towns, would be submerged. The surf would break against the foothills of the Appalachians. The coastal plain of the Gulf of Mexico would lie under water; the lower part of the Mississippi Valley would be submerged.

6   If, however, the rise should be as much as 600 feet, large areas in the eastern half of the continent would disappear under the waters. The Appalachians would become a chain of mountainous islands. The Gulf of Mexico would creep north, finally meeting in mid-continent with the flood that had entered from the Atlantic into the Great Lakes, through the valley of the St. Lawrence. Much of northern Canada would be covered by water from the Arctic Ocean and Hudson Bay.

7   All of this would seem to us extraordinary and catastrophic, but the truth is that North America and most other continents have known even more extensive invasions by the sea than the one we have just imagined. Probably the greatest submergence in the history of the earth took place in the Cretaceous period, about 100 million years ago. Then the ocean waters advanced upon North America from the north, south, and east, finally forming an inland sea about 1000 miles wide that extended from the Arctic to the Gulf of Mexico, and then spread

eastward to cover the coastal plain from the Gulf to New Jersey. At the height of the Cretaceous flood about half of North America was submerged. All over the world the seas rose. They covered most of the British Isles, except for scattered outcroppings of ancient rocks. In southern Europe only the old, rocky highlands stood above the sea, which intruded in long bays and gulfs even into the central highlands of the continent. The ocean moved into Africa and laid down deposits of sandstones; later weathering of these rocks provided the desert sands of the Sahara. From a drowned Sweden, an inland sea flowed across Russia, covered the Caspian Sea, and extended to the Himalayas. Parts of India were submerged, and of Australia, Japan, and Siberia. On the South American continent, the area where later the Andes were to rise was covered by sea.

8   With variations of extent and detail, these events have been repeated again and again. The very ancient Ordovician seas, some 400 million years ago, submerged more than half of North America, leaving only a few large islands marking the borderlands of the continent, and a scattering of smaller ones rising out of the inland sea. The marine transgressions of Devonian and Silurian time were almost as extensive. But each time the pattern of invasion was a little different, and it is doubtful that there is any part of the continent that at some time has not lain at the bottom of one of these shallow seas.

9   You do not have to travel to find the sea, for the traces of its ancient stands are everywhere about. Though you may be a thousand miles inland, you can easily find reminders that will reconstruct for the eye and ear of the mind the processions of its ghostly waves and the roar of its surf, far back in time. So, on a mountain top in Pennsylvania, I have sat on rocks of whitened limestone, fashioned of the shells of billions upon billions of minute sea creatures. Once they had lived and died in an arm of the ocean that overlay this place, and their limy remains had settled to the bottom. There, after eons of time, they had become compacted into rock and the sea had receded; after yet more eons the rock had been uplifted by bucklings of the earth's crust and now it formed the backbone of a long mountain range.

10   Far in the interior of the Florida Everglades I have wondered at the feeling of the sea that came to me — wondered until I realized that here were the same flatness, the same immense spaces, the same dominance of the sky and its moving, changing clouds; wondered until I remembered that the hard rocky floor on which I stood, its flatness interrupted by upthrust masses of jagged coral rock, had been only recently constructed by the busy architects of the coral reefs under a warm sea. Now the rock is thinly covered with grass and water; but everywhere is the feeling that the land has formed only the thinnest veneer over the underlying platform of the sea, that at any moment the process might be reversed and the sea reclaim its own.

11   So in all lands we may sense the former presence of the sea. There are outcroppings of marine limestone in the Himalayas, now at an elevation of 20,000 feet. These rocks are reminders of a warm, clear sea that lay over southern Europe and northern Africa and extended into southwestern Asia. This was some 50 million years ago. Immense numbers of a large protozoan known as nummulites swarmed

in this sea and each, in death, contributed to the building of a thick layer of nummulitic limestone. Eons later, the ancient Egyptians were to carve their Sphinx from a mass of this rock; other deposits of the same stone they quarried to obtain material to build their pyramids.

12   The famous white cliffs of Dover are composed of chalk deposited by the seas of the Cretaceous period, during that great inundation we have spoken of. The chalk extends from Ireland through Denmark and Germany, and forms its thickest beds in south Russia. It consists of shells of those minute sea creatures called foraminifera, the shells being cemented together with a fine-textured deposit of calcium carbonate. In contrast to the foraminiferal ooze that covers large areas of ocean bottom at moderate depths, the chalk seems to be a shallow-water deposit, but it is so pure in texture that the surrounding lands must have been low deserts, from which little material was carried seaward. Grains of windborne quartz sand, which frequently occur in the chalk, support this view. At certain levels the chalk contains nodules of flint. Stone Age men mined the flint for weapons and tools and also used this relic of the Cretaceous sea to light their fires.

13   Many of the natural wonders of the earth owe their existence to the fact that once the sea crept over the land, laid down its deposits of sediments, and then withdrew. There is Mammoth Cave in Kentucky, for example, where one may wander through miles of underground passages and enter rooms with ceilings 250 feet overhead. Caves and passageways have been dissolved by ground water out of an immense thickness of limestone, deposited by a Paleozoic sea. In the same way, the story of Niagara Falls goes back to Silurian time, when a vast embayment of the Arctic Sea crept southward over the continent. Its waters were clear, for the borderlands were low and little sediment or silt was carried into the inland sea. It deposited large beds of the hard rock called dolomite, and in time they formed a long escarpment near the present border between Canada and the United States. Millions of years later, floods of water released from melting glaciers poured over this cliff, cutting away the soft shales that underlay the dolomite, and causing mass after mass of the undercut rock to break away. In this fashion Niagara Falls and its gorge were created.

14   Some of these inland seas were immense and important features of their world, although all of them were shallow compared with the central basin where, since earliest time, the bulk of the ocean waters have resided. Some may have been as much as 600 feet deep, about the same as the depths over the outer edge of the continental shelf. No one knows the pattern of their currents, but often they must have carried the warmth of the tropics into far northern lands. During the Cretaceous period, for example, breadfruit, cinnamon, laurel, and fig trees grew in Greenland. When the continents were reduced to groups of islands there must have been few places that possessed a continental type of climate with its harsh extremes of heat and cold; mild oceanic climates must rather have been the rule.

15   Geologists say that each of the grander divisions of earth history consists of three phases: in the first the continents are high, erosion is active, and the seas are largely confined to their basins; in the second the continents are lowest and the seas have invaded them broadly; in

the third the continents have begun once more to rise. According to the late Charles Schuchert, who devoted much of his distinguished career as a geologist to mapping the ancient seas and lands: "Today we are living in the beginning of a new cycle, when the continents are largest, highest, and scenically grandest. The oceans, however, have begun another invasion upon North America."

16   What brings the ocean out of its deep basins, where it has been contained for eons of time, to invade the lands? Probably there has always been not one alone, but a combination of causes.

17   The mobility of the earth's crust is inseparably linked with the changing relations of sea and land—the warping upward or downward of that surprisingly plastic substance which forms the outer covering of our earth. The crustal movements affect both land and sea bottom but are most marked near the continental margins. They may involve one or both shores of an ocean, one or all coasts of a continent. They proceed in a slow and mysterious cycle, one phase of which may require millions of years for its completion. Each downward movement of the continental crust is accompanied by a slow flooding of the land by the sea, each upward buckling by the retreat of the water.

18   But the movements of the earth's crust are not alone responsible for the invading seas. There are other important causes. Certainly one of them is the displacement of ocean water by land sediments. Every grain of sand or silt carried out by the rivers and deposited at sea displaces a corresponding amount of water. Disintegration of the land and the seaward freighting of its substance have gone on without interruption since the beginning of geologic time. It might be thought that the sea level would have been rising continuously, but the matter is not so simple. As they lose substance the continents tend to rise higher, like a ship relieved of part of its cargo. The ocean floor, to which the sediments are transferred, sags under its load. The exact combination of all these conditions that will result in a rising ocean level is a very complex matter, not easily recognized or predicted.

19   Then there is the growth of the great submarine volcanoes, which build up immense lava cones on the floor of the ocean. Some geologists believe these may have an important effect on the changing level of the sea. The bulk of some of these volcanoes is impressive. Bermuda is one of the smallest, but its volume beneath the surface is about 2500 cubic miles. The Hawaiian chain of volcanic islands extends for nearly 2000 miles across the Pacific and contains several islands of great size; its total displacement of water must be tremendous. Perhaps it is more than coincidence that this chain arose in Cretaceous time, when the greatest flood the world has ever seen advanced upon the continents.

20   For the past million years, all other causes of marine transgressions have been dwarfed by the dominating role of the glaciers. The Pleistocene period was marked by alternating advances and retreats of a great ice sheet. Four times the ice caps formed and grew deep over the land, pressing southward into the valleys and over the plains. And four times the ice melted and shrank and withdrew from the lands it had covered. We live now in the last stages of this fourth with-

drawal. About half the ice formed in the last Pleistocene glaciation remains in the ice caps of Greenland and Antarctica and the scattered glaciers of certain mountains.

21   Each time the ice sheet thickened and expanded with the unmelted snows of winter after winter, its growth meant a corresponding lowering of the ocean level. For directly or indirectly, the moisture that falls on the earth's surface as rain or snow has been withdrawn from the reservoir of the sea. Ordinarily, the withdrawal is a temporary one, the water being returned via the normal runoff of rain and melting snow. But in the glacial period the summers were cool, and the snows of any winter did not melt entirely but were carried over to the succeeding winter, when the new snows found and covered them. So little by little the level of the sea dropped as the glaciers robbed it of its water, and at the climax of each of the major glaciations the oceans all over the world stood at a very low level.

22   Today, if you look in the right places, you will see the evidences of some of these old stands of the sea. Of course the strand marks left by the extreme low levels are now deeply covered by water and may be discovered only indirectly by sounding. But where, in past ages, the water level stood higher than it does today you can find its traces. In Samoa, at the foot of a cliff wall now 15 feet above the present level of the sea, you can find benches cut in the rocks by waves. You will find the same thing on other Pacific islands, and on St. Helena in the South Atlantic, on islands of the Indian Ocean, in the West Indies, and around the Cape of Good Hope.

23   Sea caves in cliffs now high above the battering assault and the flung spray of the waves that cut them are eloquent of the changed relation of sea and land. You will find such caves widely scattered over the world. On the west coast of Norway there is a remarkable, wave-cut tunnel. Out of the hard granite of the island of Torghatten, the pounding surf of a flooding interglacial sea cut a passageway through the island, a distance of about 530 feet, and in so doing removed nearly five million cubic feet of rock. The tunnel now stands 400 feet above the sea. Its elevation is due in part to the elastic, upward rebound of the crust after the melting of the ice.

24   During the other half of the cycle, when the seas sank lower and lower as the glaciers grew in thickness, the world's shorelines were undergoing changes even more far-reaching and dramatic. Every river felt the effect of the lowering sea; its waters were speeded in their course to the ocean and given new strength for the deepening and cutting of its channel. Following the downward-moving shorelines, the rivers extended their courses over the drying sands and muds of what only recently had been the sloping sea bottom. Here the rushing torrents — swollen with melting glacier water — picked up great quantities of loose mud and sand and rolled into the sea as a turgid flood.

25   During one or more of the Pleistocene lowerings of sea level, the floor of the North Sea was drained of its water and for a time became dry land. The rivers of northern Europe and of the British Isles followed the retreating waters seaward. Eventually the Rhine captured

the whole drainage system of the Thames. The Elbe and the Weser became one river. The Seine rolled through what is now the English Channel and cut itself a trough out across the continental shelf — perhaps the same drowned channel now discernible by soundings beyond Lands End.

26   The greatest of all Pleistocene glaciations came rather late in the period — probably only about 200 thousand years ago, and well within the time of man. The tremendous lowering of sea level must have affected the life of Paleolithic man. Certainly he was able, at more than one period, to walk across a wide bridge at Bering Strait, which became dry land when the level of the ocean dropped below this shallow shelf. There were other land bridges, created in the same way. As the ocean receded from the coast of India, a long submarine bank became a shoal, then finally emerged, and primitive man walked across "Adam's Bridge"[1] to the island of Ceylon.

27   Many of the settlements of ancient man must have been located on the seacoast or near the great deltas of the rivers, and relics of his civilization may lie in caves long since covered by the rising ocean. Our meager knowledge of Paleolithic man might be increased by searching along these old drowned shorelines. One archeologist has recommended searching shallow portions of the Adriatic Sea, with "submarine boats casting strong electric lights" or even with glass-bottomed boats and artificial light in the hope of discovering the outlines of shell heaps — the kitchen middens of the early men who once lived here. Professor R. A. Daly has pointed out:

> The last Glacial stage was the Reindeer Age of French history. Men then lived in the famous caves overlooking the channels of the French rivers, and hunted the reindeer which throve on the cool plains of France south of the ice border. The Late-Glacial rise of general sea level was necessarily accompanied by a rise of the river waters downstream. Hence the lowest caves are likely to have been partly or wholly drowned . . . . There the search for more relics of Paleolithic man should be pursued.[2]

28   Some of our Stone Age ancestors must have known the rigors of life near the glaciers. While men as well as plants and animals moved southward before the ice, some must have remained within sight and sound of the great frozen wall. To these the world was a place of storm and blizzard, with bitter winds roaring down out of the blue mountain of ice that dominated the horizon and reached upward into gray skies, all filled with the roaring tumult of the advancing glacier, and with the thunder of moving tons of ice breaking away and plunging into the sea.

29   But those who lived half the earth away, on some sunny coast of the Indian Ocean, walked and hunted on dry land over which the sea, only recently, had rolled deeply. These men knew nothing of the distant glaciers, nor did they understand that they walked and hunted

---

[1] A thirty-mile chain of sandbanks between Ceylon and India, the remainder of an earlier continuous isthmus.

[2] Author's Note: From *The Changing World of the Ice Age*, 1934 edition, Yale University Press, p. 210.

where they did because quantities of ocean water were frozen as ice and snow in a distant land.

30   In any imaginative reconstruction of the world of the Ice Age, we are plagued by one tantalizing uncertainty: how low did the ocean level fall during the period of greatest spread of the glaciers, when unknown quantities of water were frozen in the ice? Was it only a moderate fall of 200 or 300 feet—a change paralleled many times in geologic history in the ebb and flow of the epicontinental seas? Or was it a dramatic drawing down of the ocean by 2000, even 3000 feet?

31   Each of these various levels has been suggested as an actual possibility by one or more geologists. Perhaps it is not surprising that there should be such radical disagreement. It has been only about a century since Louis Agassiz gave the world its first understanding of the moving mountains of ice and their dominating effect on the Pleistocene world. Since then, men in all parts of the earth have been patiently accumulating the facts and reconstructing the events of those four successive advances and retreats of the ice. Only the present generation of scientists, led by such daring thinkers as Daly, have understood that each thickening of the ice sheets meant a corresponding lowering of the ocean, and that with each retreat of the melting ice a returning flood of water raised the sea level.

32   Of this "alternate robbery and restitution" most geologists have taken a conservative view and said that the greatest lowering of the sea level could not have amounted to more than 400 feet, possibly only half as much. Most of those who argue that the drawing down was much greater base their reasoning upon the submarine canyons, those deep gorges cut in the continental slopes. The deeper canyons lie a mile or more below the present level of the sea. Geologists who maintain that at least the upper parts of the canyons were stream-cut say that the sea level must have fallen enough to permit this during the Pleistocene glaciation.

33   This question of the farthest retreat of the sea into its basins must await further searchings into the mysteries of the ocean. We seem on the verge of exciting new discoveries. Now oceanographers and geologists have better instruments than ever before to probe the depths of the sea, to sample its rocks and deeply layered sediments, and to read with greater clarity the dim pages of past history.

34   Meanwhile, the sea ebbs and flows in these grander tides of earth, whose stages are measurable not in hours but in millennia—tides so vast they are invisible and uncomprehended by the senses of man. Their ultimate cause, should it ever be discovered, may be found to be deep within the fiery center of the earth, or it may lie somewhere in the dark spaces of the universe.

Discussion of Theme

1. In this day of vast storage of data it seems curious that there is so little information on the rising level of the oceans. What reasons does Rachel Carson give for this?

2. What evidence does the author give that "in all lands we may sense the former presence of the sea"? How, for example, could a farmer in Nebraska sense the sea?
3. What has modern science contributed to our understanding of the rise and fall of the oceans?

Discussion of Rhetoric

1. Rachel Carson never lost her sense of wonder about the world. Does she arouse a sense of wonder in you? How?
2. Comment on the imagery in paragraph 28. Where else does the author produce pictures with her words?
3. In this essay Miss Carson attempted to present a technical, scientific subject to laymen. Does she succeed? How?
4. Parallel structure is a device used by writers to give sentences greater clarity, force, and rhythm. Find several examples of parallel structure in this essay.
5. Miss Carson cites many familiar names in her opening paragraphs. What is the impact of these names, in view of her subject?
6. What is distinctive about the tone of the writing in paragraphs 5 and 6? What is the effect of this kind of writing? Do you suppose it was intentional? Is it particularly forceful?

Writing Assignments

1. Write a paper in which you attack the dumping of raw sewage and debris into the oceans. How does this practice affect both health and recreation?
2. What philosophical thoughts does this article stimulate in you? Does it make you see man and his world from a new perspective? Do you have a different feeling about the ocean and other natural elements? Does religion enter into your thinking? Write a thoughtful, personal reaction to this article.
3. Describe some aspect of terrestrial evolution that parallels what happened in the oceans over a period of millions of years.

Library Exploration

1. Read the biography of Alexander von Humboldt, after whom the Humboldt Current was named. What features of this current are remarkable?
2. If you enjoyed Miss Carson's essay, you will probably find her books rewarding. *Silent Spring*, for example, points out the dangers of the indiscriminate use of insect and weed killers.

3. Although oceanography is one of the most important sciences today, the average layman still knows relatively little about it. Choose some aspect of the study — such as the coral reefs, ocean currents — and report on the latest findings.

Vocabulary

(1) TRANSIENT temporary; passing

(2) ENCROACHMENTS intrusions

(3) EMBAYMENT bay

(7) SUBMERGENCE covering with water

(9) EONS ages

(10) VENEER coating; layer

(11) PROTOZOAN one-celled animal

(12) NODULES knots; rounded lumps

(13) ESCARPMENT steep slope

(14) BREADFRUIT tropical fruit

(15) EROSION wearing away

(23) INTERGLACIAL formed between two glacial epochs

(24) TURGID swollen

(28) TUMULT violent and noisy commotion

(33) SEDIMENTS materials deposited by water

(34) MILLENNIA thousands of years

George A. W. Boehm (1922–)
is a free-lance writer who spe-
cializes in science reporting. A
native of New York City, he was
educated at Kent School and
Columbia University. He has
written numerous articles in
such publications as "Fortune"
and "Scientific American," and
is the author of "The New World
of Math" (1959), which has been
translated into half a dozen languages.

Does intelligent life exist in
other planetary systems?
Increased interest in flying
saucers, more sophisticated astronomy, and government in-
vestigations have brought new
light to this old question. Mr.
Boehm presents some of the
requirements for such a phenomenon.

GEORGE A. W. BOEHM

Are We Being Hailed from Interstellar Space?

1 More than a century ago, Joseph Johann von Littrow, an astronomer
at the Vienna Observatory, proposed building a geometric array of
bonfires in the Sahara Desert to signal man's presence to the Martians.
The bonfires were never built, but speculation that there was life on
Mars, and possibly on Venus too, persisted until fairly recently. Today
astronomers no longer expect to find intelligent forms of life on the
arid landscape of Mars, beneath the boiling, choking atmosphere of
Venus, or indeed anywhere else in the solar system. But they have
taken on a new hope of finding intelligent beings elsewhere in the
universe.

2   More intently than ever before, scientists are searching for signs that man is not alone; but now, in contrast to von Littrow, they are reconciled to beaming their search trillions of miles beyond the solar system. Although they may achieve no tangible results for many years, never before have they had so much hope for ultimate success.

3   Any contact with life elsewhere might prove shattering to man's ego. Though he has barely entered from the wings, modern, nonphilosophic man fancies that the whole pageant of creation has been staged for his benefit. Unaware of any intellectual rival, he proudly calls himself *Homo sapiens* and regards his intelligence as the acme of evolution. Recently, however, a number of leading scientists have advanced the humbling theory that man is not the only intelligent species in the universe. Elsewhere there may exist thousands of races so superior in intellect that they might look upon man as condescendingly as man regards his domestic animals.

4   A decade ago such speculation was left chiefly to devotees of the sort of fiction that deals with intergalactic warfare and bug-eyed monsters. Most scientists, from what they thought they knew about the origins of Earth and life, supposed that human intelligence (or anything approaching it) was a freak unlikely to have developed more than once in a universe throughout eternity. But in the last few years scientists have gained a better understanding of some of the crucial steps in the evolution from primordial dust and gas to man. They now suspect that a great many places in the Milky Way, our own galaxy of stars, are habitable and, indeed, inhabited.

5   Astronomer Harlow Shapley estimates conservatively that life may exist in the planetary systems of one out of a million stars. Other estimates run as high as one out of four stars. But even on the basis of Shapley's figure, life would be commonplace: in the Milky Way, with more than 100 billion stars, there would be no less than 100,000 inhabited bodies. Throughout the other galaxies that are revealed by powerful telescope there might be literally billions of intelligent races.

6   Now for the first time technology has developed the instruments by which life in outer space might be detected. With the development of radio telescopes and sensitive electronic amplifiers, speculations about other civilizations have taken on a fresh sense of reality. An interstellar radio network, extending hundreds of trillions of miles, is technologically feasible. If intelligent beings do live in the neighborhood of nearby stars, it is theoretically possible to communicate with them, even if their radio transmitters and receivers are no more powerful and sensitive than our own.

7   Man stands to learn a great deal from contact with his remote neighbors. Any civilization that we heard from here on Earth would almost surely be far ahead of us in science and technology. Only since about 1940 has man been able to build radio equipment powerful enough to reach the stars. Thus any beings more than a few years behind us would not be able to communicate with us at all. It is, of course, possible that we would make contact with a civilization that mastered radio just about the time we did. But that would be an incredible coincidence; the twenty-year history of high-power radio represents merely an instant on the time scale of evolution. It is much

more likely that any messages from outer space would come from a people who developed radio at least as far back as the beginning of the Christian era, or perhaps even before man learned to use fire.

8   What such technically mature beings could teach us is anybody's guess. They might be expected to know the secret of taming thermonuclear hydrogen fusion and thus to have in their possession virtually unlimited sources of energy. They might understand the chemistry of life well enough to modify genes and thereby produce living organisms that are tailored to exact specifications. Very likely they would have solved countless scientific problems that our civilization has not yet even encountered.

9   They could immediately convince us of their scientific superiority merely by transmitting for our edification a single nine-digit number like the following: 137.039217. Any terrestrial physicist would recognize the first few figures; this is the "fine structure constant" of atomic physics. A dimensionless number that crops us repeatedly in physics, it represents several basic relationships at the atomic level—e.g., the ratio of the wavelength of light emitted by hydrogen, the simplest atom, to the circumference of the orbit of hydrogen's only electron; or the ratio of the speed of light to the speed of the hydrogen electron; or, in a more involved fashion, the number of uranium atoms needed to sustain a chain reaction. Physicists on Earth know for sure only the first five digits of the fine structure constant, they are not quite sure of the sixth, and they are constantly working to find the seventh. It may yet take them a century or more to calculate or measure the fine structure constant accurately to nine digits.

10   Beyond any such lessons that man might learn from another civilization, the contact would have a profound effect on our society. Says Nobel Prize-winning physicist Edward Purcell of Harvard University: "It's not so important whether we learn anything or whether we just hear 'one, two, three' or some other trivial message. Just knowing we are not alone would change our entire philosophic outlook."

11   This thought worries some people, among them the authors of a recent Brookings Institution report on "Proposed Studies on the Implications of Peaceful Space Activities for Human Affairs" prepared for the National Aeronautics and Space Administration. They note that life elsewhere in the universe could be discovered at any time. They warn that the shock of making contact could lead to the downfall of civilization because "societies sure of their own place in the universe have disintegrated when confronted by a superior society."

12   Purcell himself doesn't see any cause for worry. "The communication would be utterly benign," he says. "We won't be able to threaten one another with objects; persuasion and deceit would be pointless."

13   Behind Purcell's assurance is his conviction that man is unlikely ever to meet his interstellar neighbors face to face, for travel outside of our solar system, he thinks, is physically impossible. According to Purcell's calculations, a space ship would have to accelerate to a speed 99 per cent that of light in order to make a round trip to one of the nearer sunlike stars within the span of a human lifetime. The engine would have to be fantastically big and powerful. The best

imaginable fuel would consist half of anti-matter — that is, a substance consisting of anti-protons, anti-neutrons, and other particles that are, in a sense, inverse to particles that make up ordinary matter. Physicists have observed anti-matter particles only fleetingly, for when anti-matter comes in contact with matter, both are mutually destroyed and converted entirely into energy. A mixture of matter and anti-matter would be the perfectly efficient fuel. Yet to convey a ten-ton payload the engine would need 200,000 tons of each.

14   The fact that no one has the faintest notion of how to isolate and store even an ounce of anti-matter is disheartening enough. But there is a still more serious problem. Even if such a space vehicle could be built, fueled, and launched, its exhaust stream would consist of a billion-billion watts of hard x-rays — enough radiation to doom instantly all life on Earth. Besides, a ship traveling at 99 per cent of the speed of light would collide with swarms of hydrogen atoms that pervade space. The relative speeds of atoms and ship would produce an effect equivalent to the bombardment by a powerful atom smasher. The ten-ton payload would not provide nearly enough shielding to protect passengers from the radiation. "The moral is that we aren't going anywhere, and neither are *they*," Purcell concludes. "Maybe you can get there by magic, but you can't get there by physics."

15   But while the prospect of interstellar travel has been banished, the prospect of interspatial communications has grown brighter. The first step is to select the most likely places to seek out alien civilizations and the best ways of communicating with them. The scientists engaged in this study make two basic philosophic assumptions: the first, that life elsewhere is not radically different from life on Earth; the second, that the evolution of life in other places followed roughly the same course as evolution on Earth. Admittedly these assumptions are bold, but they are the only rational basis we have for theorizing.

16   The consensus is that life can be found only on planets, not on stars. In fact, life, as we conceive of it, can hardly exist in an environment much different from Earth's. Chemistry is presumably pretty much the same throughout the universe; spectroscopic studies of the stars show that their compositions differ only in minor details. It is likely therefore that higher forms of life are limited to the temperature range where water is liquid: between 32° and 212° Fahrenheit. In colder places the life-supporting chemical reactions would take place too slowly for higher plants and animals to evolve. In a hotter climate heat would rupture the delicate chemical bonds between carbon and hydrogen atoms, the principal ingredients of living tissue. It has been suggested that life of a sort could be based on compounds of the element silicon; in this case the temperature limit might be raised by a few hundred degrees. But it is inconceivable that living things, even if made of asbestos, could survive on any star; the coolest stars are close to 3,000°.

17   Astronomers have never actually seen a planet outside the solar system, and up to about twenty years ago they generally believed that planets were extremely rare. According to a theory of Sir James Jeans and others, the solar planets were torn from the sun when it was side-swiped by a passing star. Such near misses could not possibly have

occurred in the Milky Way more than once every few hundred million years.

18   Today, however, astronomers believe that the universe abounds in planets. They have discarded Jeans's theory of planet formation in favor of one that was worked out in some detail about a dozen years ago. According to this theory the solar system originated from a veil of gas and dust, thinner than a wisp of smoke. Slowly at first, then faster and faster, the particles in this tenuous stuff were pulled together by gravity. Eons went by while a dense, swirling cloud took form. From time to time, as the whirlpool of gas contracted, blobs were shed from its rim. Atoms of hydrogen, which made up most of the cloud, were crushed by the pressure of inrushing matter, and they began to fuse, as in an H-bomb but much more slowly. Meanwhile the blobs that had been thrown off solidified and began to spin in orbits around the central mass of nuclear fire. Thus, almost five billion years ago, were born the sun and its planets.

19   The laws of physics provide compelling, though indirect, evidence that much the same thing happened (and is still happening) elsewhere in the Milky Way. All stars are presumably born from rapidly spinning clouds. Yet, except for the largest and hottest, stars generally rotate slowly after taking form. Somehow in the course of evolving the slow stars must have disposed of the energy of spinning. All this energy could not have just disappeared without violating the laws of physics; it must have been transferred to other forms of rotation. Some gas and dust clouds split to form two or three stars, which continue to orbit around one another like circling boxers; sky surveys show that about 40 per cent of stars are twins or triplets. But the rest — the single stars — seem to have dumped their rotational energy into relatively small bodies — namely, planets. If that is the case, at least 50 billion stars in the Milky Way are surrounded by planets, and there may be well over 100 billion potential platforms for life in the galaxy.

20   But only on a small proportion of the planets could intelligent life have evolved. In order for the temperature to be endurable, a planet's orbit has to be just the right size and shape. There are limits also to the size of stars that might support inhabitable planets. Whereas the sun has changed relatively little in the last five billion years and is expected to remain about the same for ten billion more, much larger stars burn out relatively fast. They consume their primary fuel, hydrogen, and start to expand rapidly. They then become "red giants," billowing masses of searing gas that would completely envelop any planets around them. A star twice the mass of the sun, for example, remains stable for only two billion years, which is probably too short a time to permit higher forms of life to evolve. At the other extreme, the smallest stars, about a third the mass of the sun, are relatively cool and quite stable. Some of them will not change for 100 billion years. But the habitable zones around them are very shallow, as astronomer Su-Shu Huang of the National Aeronautics and Space Administration has pointed out. The chance that a planet would be found orbiting at precisely the right distance from a small star is therefore almost nil. So the search for life narrows down to the planets of single stars roughly the size of the sun.

21   Huang believes the size of the planet itself is still another critical factor. If its gravitational pull is much different from that of Earth, it is unlikely to have the kind of atmosphere that living things can breathe. Chemist Harold Urey has theorized that when the solar system was young, the planets were swaddled in blankets of noxious gas consisting mainly of hydrogen, methane (a hydrogen carbon compound), ammonia (a hydrogen nitrogen compound), and water vapor. On Earth this primeval atmosphere underwent a gradual change in the course of some two or three billion years. Ultraviolet light from the sun split some of the water molecules into oxygen and hydrogen, thereby starting a series of chemical reactions that purified the air. The freed oxygen attacked the methane and formed carbon dioxide; the oxygen also released nitrogen from the ammonia. All the time, excess hydrogen, being extremely light, escaped into space; the heavier gases that now make up our atmosphere — oxygen, nitrogen, and carbon dioxide — were held close to Earth by gravity.

22   In contrast, Jupiter, which is 318 times heavier than Earth, has such a strong gravitational pull that hydrogen cannot readily escape. Because a chemical equilibrium has been set up, the atmosphere of this giant planet is still rich in methane and ammonia. Some of the simplest bacteria can exist without air, and they may have evolved on Jupiter. But the atmosphere is unfit for higher forms of life. Mars, on the other hand, is one-tenth as heavy as Earth, and its gravitational attraction is too weak to retain much oxygen or water vapor. The atmosphere of Mars went through the chemical evolution hundreds of millions of years ago, but by now almost all its air seems to have been dissipated. Conceivably, at one stage higher forms of life did exist on Mars. As the air and water were lost, however, they must have died out and been replaced by a succession of simpler plants. Some scientists suspect that lichens may exist on Mars, but evolution in reverse has eliminated the possibility of more complex organisms.

23   Scientists' assumption that there was nothing exceptional about the sequence of events that formed Earth and its atmosphere takes them on to a startling conclusion: given a salubrious climate, life is not only possible, but likely. Some years ago Stanley Miller, one of Urey's students at the University of Chicago, made up a steaming brew that was supposedly a model of Earth's original atmosphere. He then discharged sparks through the vapors to simulate the effect of electrical storms that struck Earth when it was young. After some hours he analyzed the liquid and found traces of surprisingly complex inorganic chemicals, including amino acids, which are fragments of protein.

24   Since then, chemist Melvin Calvin of the University of California has studied specks of organic matter embedded in meteorites. He has found small amounts of compounds that are fragments of nucleotides, which are in turn fragments of deoxyribonucleic acid (DNA), the stuff of heredity-bearing genes. He has also made nucleotide fragments in an experiment similar to Miller's.

25   Calvin now believes he can outline the transition from inanimate matter to life — up to a point. On Earth, the seas were first enriched with chemicals like those created in Miller's experiment. Then in the shuffling of molecules that takes place in solutions of organic chemi-

cals, more complex compounds were formed by chance. These compounds combined with each other and formed still larger molecules. Ultimately chemical evolution led to giant molecules that were capable of reproducing, as are DNA and some other chemicals important to life. With this explanation Calvin describes evolution up to the threshold of life. What happened to breathe the spark of life into the first organisms is still a mystery to science. Nevertheless, Calvin says confidently that life is a "state of matter widely distributed throughout the universe."

26   Chance dominated every stage of evolution from primitive organisms to man, as Darwin and his successors have explained. Each new plant or animal originated as an improbable freak. Yet, on the whole, the course of evolution has been orderly and straightforward, for natural selection has lopped off the mistakes and digressions. In the two billion years or so since life emerged on Earth, a pyramid of life has gradually taken form. More highly organized and adaptable species have been steadily added at the top. And in the last million years man has taken his place at the apex. Given another planet with the physical characteristics of Earth, it can be presumed that biological evolution proceeded in much the same fashion and at about the same pace. If Earth and the life it supports represents a norm, then perhaps half the other habitable planets in the universe have been populated by intelligent beings.

27   Whether all of them are *still* habitable is another question, about which man has reason to be especially curious at this time. It may well be a universal fact that any civilization which has mastered the secret of releasing enormous amounts of energy—as with a hydrogen bomb —is forever in danger of annihilating itself. How long have civilizations elsewhere survived after they have reached this stage? If the life expectancy is only a few hundred years, man has very few living neighbors in the galaxy. The natural tendency toward self-destruction is, of course, imponderable. Astronomer Frank Drake of the National Radio Astronomy Observatory wryly suggests: "We might get a better feeling for the situation if we could first answer the question: 'Is there intelligent life on Earth?'"

28   Scientists are now ready to search nearby regions of the Milky Way for direct evidence of intelligent life. They will use radio telescopes to "listen" for messages, and the chances of success seem reasonably good. Purcell estimates that two 300-foot radio-telescope antennas— one a receiver, the other a transmitter—could communicate over a distance of 500 light-years (3,000 trillion miles). Within that range are some 2,000 sunlike stars that have a good chance of supporting life.

29   Right now no scientist suggests transmitting messages into outer space. In order to send signals, we would have to build a number of costly transmitters—in effect, one large radio telescope for each star we wanted to address—and transmit day in, day out, for a period of years. There might be no positive results within a lifetime, and meanwhile the equipment would be tied up, useless for any other purpose. Listening, on the other hand, is relatively cheap. Adequate radio telescopes are already available, and they can be directed from time to time at particularly promising stars. Purcell feels, "We ought to

plan to listen for at least two centuries before we even consider transmitting."

30   While there is yet no organized program for listening, Drake has already made a preliminary attempt. Last spring, at the N.R.A.O. in Green Bank, West Virginia, he launched Project Ozma (named after the Queen of Oz, the land of fancy created by L. Frank Baum). Using the observatory's radio telescope, Drake spent two months recording radio signals from the direction of two of the nearest stars: Tau Ceti and Epsilon Eridani, each a little more than ten light-years, or 60 trillion miles away. Some 400 hours of listening yielded nothing but a meaningless "hash" of radio noise. But no one had really expected the first Ozma trial to produce positive results. The telescope, an eighty-five-foot dish-shaped antenna, and the amplifiers were not sensitive enough to detect any but the strongest signals beamed directly at Earth. It is entirely possible that the squiggles traced by the instrument's recording pen actually do contain an intelligent message, but the radio noise makes them undecipherable.

31   But the principles employed in Ozma are likely to guide future listening attempts. In planning the project, Drake anticipated a strategy proposed in 1959 by Giuseppe Cocconi and Philip Morrison of Cornell University and enthusiastically endorsed by most other scientists interested in intragalactic communication. It can be summed up as follows: If other civilizations are transmitting in our direction, they want their messages to be readily detected and easily understood. Therefore, like players at charades, they are broadcasting to us as we would broadcast to them, if our positions were reversed. It follows that we should be on the lookout for the kind of messages we would transmit to them.

32   For efficient listening, it is necessary at the outset to make an educated guess about the wave length that outer-space broadcasters would be likeliest to use. Conceivably, they could be transmitting on any part of the electromagnetic spectrum, but scanning the whole spectrum from long-wave radio through infrared, visible, and ultraviolet to x-rays and gamma rays would be an interminable task — like combing a vast forest to find a particular ant. Instead Cocconi and Morrison proposed limiting the search to one branch of a specific tree. They think that any scientifically sophisticated civilization would beam interstellar broadcasts at a frequency of 1,420 megacycles (1,420 million cycles per second). It was on a small portion of the radio band around this frequency that Drake's Project Ozma concentrated.

33   Why 1,420 megacycles? First of all, because this frequency has a special significance for astronomers. Each hydrogen atom emits an infinitesimal amount of energy at this frequency and atomic hydrogen constitutes at least 75 per cent of all the matter in the universe. By measuring the strength of 1,420-megacycle radiation in all directions, radio astronomers have been able to map the distribution of matter in our galaxy. Presumably, other intelligent beings who have mastered radio would also recognize the unique significance of hydrogen and its radiation frequency. Second, our atmosphere — and very likely the atmospheres of other life-bearing planets — is almost perfectly transparent to 1,420-megacycle waves.

34   The next listening project will employ better equipment—i.e., a bigger antenna and more sensitive amplifier. Radio astronomers are confident that if any 1,420-megacycle signals are being sent, they will eventually be detected. The modern radio telescope is a remarkably sensitive receiver. In the decade since radio astronomers started tuning in at the hydrogen frequency, they have got a lot of information about the galaxy, although the total energy collected by all the telescopes has amounted to not quite one erg: slightly less than the energy required to flick the ash from a cigarette.

35   Scientists are reasonably sure that, once they received a recognizable signal, they could understand the message. A signal would have some degree of regularity that would set it apart from cosmic radio noise, which is random and utterly irregular. Deciphering the message would depend more on the cleverness of the sender than on the ingenuity of scientists on Earth. Presumably our partners in communication would be wise enough to employ cryptography in reverse. That is, they would design a code that could easily be broken. And their first messages would include plenty of hints in the form of information that is surely universal among all scientifically minded societies—e.g., numbers and elementary geometry.

36   We would record the signals and study them at our leisure. But in less than ten minutes of transmission the signals should be able to tell us how to project their television pictures on our screen. . . . Once television communication was established, a civilization should be able to describe itself thoroughly and in short order.

37   If powerful radio telescopes failed to pick up signals at 1,420 megacycles, scientists would turn to other parts of the electromagnetic spectrum. Intelligent beings in nearby space might not be transmitting by radio. Our radio communications might seem as crude to them as smoke signals or bonfires on the Sahara do to us. Perhaps some other civilization is even now sending us messages in pulses of light. Earthbound physicists are just now perfecting the "laser," a device that emits a narrow beam of light concentrated at one specific frequency. On some remote planet laser sets might be as commonplace as transistor radios. Or a more advanced technology than ours might have learned how to modulate a beam of neutrinos—weightless, uncharged particles that human physicists are hard put even to detect. If so, they may have to wait more than a century until we learn how to build a neutrino receiver.

38   At least two other long shots might deserve attention. Freeman Dyson, a theoretical physicist at the Institute for Advanced Study, has suggested looking for abnormally strong infrared radiation from stars. He has a hunch that a technologically proficient civilization in need of living space might demolish a spare planet with tools and power we do not yet possess, and reassemble it as a ring surrounding the central star at a comfortable distance for commuting. Such a ring would radiate detectably in the infrared part of the spectrum—specifically, at a wave length of about ten microns if the temperature were suitable for life. Some scientists speculate that in 3,000 years or so man, desperate for elbow-room, might develop the techniques needed to

break pieces from Jupiter and rearrange them as a string of artificial planets along the Earth's orbit.

39 Radio astronomer R. N. Bracewell of Stanford University thinks that we may have already unwittingly received messages from another civilization. He has an idea that space probes may have been put into orbit around Earth by another race. (An unmanned interstellar space probe is conceivable. Since it would not have to complete its mission within a lifetime, it could be dispatched at relatively low speed with a much smaller engine than is required for a manned vehicle.)

40 According to Bracewell, these space probes might try to reveal their presence by repeating back to us radio signals received from Earth. At the same time they might be transmitting back to their home planet an assortment of terrestrial broadcasts. If so, some beings out there have probably formed a strange impression of life on Earth. It has taken many years for our radio broadcasts to be relayed to them. Radio signals travel at the speed of light; thus a planet twenty-five light-years away would just now be receiving earthly broadcasts of circa 1936: the prattlings of Amos and Andy, the crooning of Kate Smith, Gabriel Heatter's voice booming: "There's good news to-night." A few years hence they will hear the sepulchral voice of Raymond Gram Swing, on the eve of World War II. It will be no wonder then if they decide that the end of civilization on Earth is at hand and turn the knob to another planet.

41 Some ancient civilizations, in fact, may have given up on us long ago. "It seems possible to me," says Urey, "that the intelligent life on planets of other stars has been beaming signals to us for the last ten million to hundred million years. And they have simply concluded that there is no one home on Earth; so they have stopped both listening and sending."

42 To establish contact with another planet may require more patience than man possesses. There may be a wait of decades, centuries, or even millenniums before another race decides to beam messages in our direction. If two-way communication is ever set up, men on Earth may have to reconcile themselves to asking questions, knowing they will not live to hear the answers. "But imagine," says Purcell, "that a reply to one of your messages was scheduled to be received forty years from now. What a legacy for your grandchildren."

Discussion of Theme

1. Why does radio astronomer R. N. Bracewell believe that radio signals from our planet would give another civilization a strange impression of life on Earth?
2. Why do scientists believe that if they received a message from interstellar space they could understand it?
3. The author poses a question in his title. Does he answer it?
4. The author suggests that any contact with life in outer space might prove shattering to man's ego. Do you agree? Why? What past discovery in astronomy had a similar result?

Discussion of Rhetoric

1. How does the rhetoric used by science reporters differ from that used by scientists themselves? What special communication skills must a science reporter have?
2. Comment on the effectiveness of a question used as the title of an essay.
3. Boehm has the problem of making incredible distances and periods of time comprehensible to his reader. What techniques does he use? How well does he succeed?
4. What method of development has the author used in organizing his essay? How has this choice determined the arrangement and ordering of his material?

Writing Assignments

1. Write a brief science-fiction story based on the information contained in the article.
2. Speculate on the benefits man might gain from contacting other beings in interstellar space.
3. Write a satiric essay entitled "Is There Intelligent Life on Earth?" in which you view man as he might appear to a visitor from outer space.
4. Boehm quotes a statement to the effect that "societies sure of their own place in the universe have disintegrated when confronted by a superior society." Develop an argument supporting this statement, taking your examples from the history of Western civilization.

Library Exploration

1. What is a quasar?
2. If you are curious about unidentified flying objects, you would enjoy reading the following books: *Report on Unidentified Flying Objects*, by Edward J. Ruppelt, and *Flying Saucers and the U.S. Air Force*, by Lawrence J. Tacker.
3. What is light? Why are distances measured in light-years? Why do all scientists limit theoretical space travel to the speed of light?

Vocabulary

(1) ARID   dry; infertile
(3) ACME   highest point; summit
(3) CONDESCENDINGLY   patronizingly
(4) INTERGALACTIC   between galaxies
(4) PRIMORDIAL   first in time; original
(4) GALAXY   grouping (of stars)
(8) MODIFY   alter; change
(9) EDIFICATION   instruction; improvement

(9) TERRESTRIAL   of the earth

(9) EMITTED   thrown forth; produced

(12) BENIGN   harmless; beneficial

(14) PERVADE   spread throughout

(16) SPECTROSCOPIC   by spectroscope (a device for breaking down light into its component colors)

(18) ABOUNDS IN   is filled with; has lots of

(19) COMPELLING   forceful; overpowering

(20) BILLOWING   surging; swelling

(22) DISSIPATED   wasted

(22) LICHENS   mosslike plants

(23) SALUBRIOUS   healthful; wholesome

(25) THRESHOLD   entrance; beginning point

(26) DIGRESSIONS   departures from the normal

(27) ANNIHILATING   destroying; demolishing

(31) INTRAGALACTIC   within a galaxy

(33) INFINITESIMAL   minute; very small

(35) INGENUITY   cleverness; skill

(35) CRYPTOGRAPHY   handling messages in code

(37) SPECTRUM   white light broken down into its colors (The rainbow is a spectrum.)

(37) MODULATE   regulate; adapt

(39) UNWITTINGLY   unconsciously

(40) SEPULCHRAL   melancholy; gloomy

(42) MILLENNIUMS   thousands of years

THE
ANTIC
MUSE

After graduating from Harvard University, Robert Benchley (1889–1945) became a successful drama critic, magazine writer, and actor. But it was his humor that brought him fame. Casting a friendly yet satiric eye at the foibles of the American middle class, Benchley wrote a dozen books, including "The Treasurer's Report" (1930), "My Ten Years in a Quandary" (1936), and "Inside Benchley" (1942).

The following sample is "pure Benchley"—irreverent, gently satiric, yet containing an implicit commentary on one aspect of American life.

ROBERT BENCHLEY

What College Did to Me

1 My college education was no haphazard affair. My courses were all selected with a very definite aim in view, with a serious purpose in mind—no classes before eleven in the morning or after two-thirty in the afternoon, and nothing on Saturday at all. That was my slogan. On that rock was my education built.

2 As what is known as the Classical Course involved practically no afternoon laboratory work, whereas in the Scientific Course a man's time was never his own until four P.M. anyway, I went in for the classic. But only such classics as allowed for a good sleep in the morning. A man has his health to think of. There is such a thing as being a studying fool.

3 In my days (I was a classmate of the founder of the college) a student could elect to take any courses in the catalogue, provided no two of his choices came at the same hour. The only things he was not supposed to mix were Scotch and gin. This was known as the Elective System. Now I understand that the boys have to have, during the four years, at least three courses beginning with the same letter. This

probably makes it very awkward for those who like to get away of a Friday afternoon for the week-end.

4   Under the Elective System my schedule was somewhat as follows:

Mondays, Wednesdays and Fridays at 1:30:
    Botany 2A (The History of Flowers and Their Meaning)
Tuesdays and Thursdays at 11:00:
    English 26 (The Social Life of the Minor Sixteenth Century Poets)
Mondays, Wednesdays and Fridays at 12:00:
    Music 9 (History and Appreciation of the Clavichord)
Tuesdays and Thursdays at 12:00:
    German 12b (Early Minnesingers—Walter von Vogelweider, Ulric Glannsdorf and Friemann von Stremhofen. Their Songs and Times)
Mondays, Wednesdays and Fridays at 1:30:
    Fine Arts 6 (Doric Columns: Their Uses, History and Various Heights)
Tuesdays and Thursdays at 1:30:
    French 1c (Exceptions to the verb *être*)

5   This was, of course, just one year's work. The next year I followed these courses up with supplementary courses in the history of lace-making, Russian taxation systems before Catharine the Great, North American glacial deposits and Early Renaissance etchers.

6   This gave me a general idea of the progress of civilization and a certain practical knowledge which has stood me in good stead in thousands of ways since my graduation.

7   My system of studying was no less strict. In lecture courses I had my notebooks so arranged that one-half of the page could be devoted to drawings of five-pointed stars (exquisitely shaded), girls' heads, and tick-tack-toe. Some of the drawings in my economics notebook in the course of Early English Trade Winds were the finest things I have ever done. One of them was a whole tree (an oak) with every leaf in perfect detail. Several instructors commented on my work in this field.

8   These notes I would take home after the lecture, together with whatever supplementary reading the course called for. Notes and text-books would then be placed on a table under a strong lamplight. Next came the sharpening of pencils, which would take perhaps fifteen minutes. I had some of the best sharpened pencils in college. These I placed on the table beside the notes and books.

9   At this point it was necessary to light a pipe, which involved going to the table where the tobacco was. As it so happened, on the same table was a poker hand, all dealt, lying in front of a vacant chair. Four other chairs were oddly enough occupied by students, also preparing to study. It therefore resolved itself into something of a seminar, or group conference, on the courses under discussion. For example, the first student would say:
    "I can't open."
    The second student would perhaps say the same thing.
    The third student would say: 'I'll open for fifty cents."
    And the seminar would be on.

10   At the end of the seminar, I would go back to my desk, pile the notes and books on top of each other, put the light out, and go to bed, tired

but happy in the realization that I had not only spent the evening busily but had helped put four of my friends through college.

11   An inventory of stock acquired at college discloses the following bits of culture and erudition which have nestled in my mind after all these years.

12   THINGS I LEARNED FRESHMAN YEAR

1. Charlemagne either died or was born or did something with the Holy Roman Empire in 800.
2. By placing one paper bag inside another paper bag you can carry home a milk shake in it.
3. There is a double l in the middle of "parallel."
4. Powder rubbed on the chin will take the place of a shave if the room isn't very light.
5. French nouns ending in "aison" are feminine.
6. Almost everything you need to know about a subject is in the encyclopedia.
7. A tasty sandwich can be made by spreading peanut butter on raisin bread.
8. A floating body displaces its own weight in the liquid in which it floats.
9. A sock with a hole in the toe can be worn inside out with comparative comfort.
10. The chances are against filling an inside straight.
11. There is a law in economics called *The Law of Diminishing Returns*, which means that after a certain margin is reached returns begin to diminish. This may not be correctly stated, but there *is* a law by that name.
12. You begin tuning a mandolin with A and tune the other strings from that.

13   SOPHOMORE YEAR

1. A good imitation of measles rash can be effected by stabbing the forearm with a stiff whiskbroom.
2. Queen Elizabeth was not above suspicion.
3. In Spanish you pronounce z like th.
4. Nine-tenths of the girls in a girls' college are not pretty.
5. You can sleep undetected in a lecture course by resting the head on the hand as if shading the eyes.
6. Weakness in drawing technique can be hidden by using a wash instead of black and white line.
7. Quite a respectable bun can be acquired by smoking three or four pipefuls of strong tobacco when you have no food in your stomach.
8. The ancient Phœnicians were really Jews, and got as far north as England where they operated tin mines.
9. You can get dressed much quicker in the morning if the night before when you go to bed you take off your trousers and underdrawers at once, leaving the latter inside the former.

14   JUNIOR YEAR

1. Emerson left his pastorate because he had some argument about communion.
2. All women are untrustworthy.
3. Pushing your arms back as far as they will go fifty times each day increases your chest measurement.
4. Marcus Aurelius had a son who turned out to be a bad boy.

5. Eight hours of sleep are not necessary.
6. Heraclitus believed that fire was the basis of all life.
7. A good way to keep your trousers pressed is to hang them from the bureau drawer.
9. The Republicans believe in a centralized government, the Democrats in a decentralized one.
10. It is not necessarily effeminate to drink tea.

15   SENIOR YEAR

1. A dinner coat looks better than full dress.
2. There is as yet no law determining what constitutes trespass in an airplane.
3. Six hours of sleep are not necessary.
4. Bicarbonate of soda taken before retiring makes you feel better the next day.
5. You needn't be fully dressed if you wear a cap and gown to a nine-o'clock recitation.
6. Theater tickets may be charged.
7. Flowers may be charged.
8. May is the shortest month in the year.

16   The foregoing outline of my education is true enough in its way, and is what people like to think about a college course. It has become quite the cynical thing to admit laughingly that college did one no good. It is part of the American Credo that all the college student learns is to catch punts and dance. I had to write something like that to satisfy the editors. As a matter of fact, I learned a great deal in college and have those four years to thank for whatever I know today.

17   (The above note was written to satisfy those of my instructors and financial backers who may read this. As a matter of fact, the original outline is true, and I had to look up the date about Charlemagne at that.)

Discussion of Theme

1. In what ways has college changed since this essay was written?
2. Are there courses taught at your college that bear any resemblance to the courses Benchley lists in paragraphs 4 and 5?
3. What is Benchley criticizing about college besides the elective system?
4. Does this selection strike you as being humorous? In what way? How might it have been regarded differently forty years ago?
5. Does this essay make you wonder how Benchley succeeded in graduating from Harvard?

Discussion of Rhetoric

1. In paragraph 9 would the humor have the same impact if the author eliminated "As it so happened" and "oddly enough"? What do these phrases add to the humor?

2. After proclaiming that his college education "was no haphazard affair" (paragraph 1), Benchley proceeds to demonstrate the opposite with humorous results. Find other examples of this technique.
3. What is the chief principle of organization used in this essay?
4. How would you describe the level of language in this essay?

Writing Assignments

1. Using Benchley's style and format, write your own inventory of what you learned in each of your high school years.
2. Comment on the elective system in your college.
3. Write an analysis of Benchley's humor.
4. What are some of the important things learned outside the classroom in college?

Library Exploration

Some of Robert Benchley's best-known essays and articles have been collected in *The Benchley Roundup* (1954), an anthology edited by the humorist's son Nathaniel.

Vocabulary

(1) HAPHAZARD casual; random

(4) CLAVICHORD early piano-like instrument

(11) INVENTORY itemized list

(11) ERUDITION learning

(11) NESTLED remained (as in a nest)

James Thurber (1894–1961), a native of Ohio, was one of the major American humorists of this century. For over thirty years he contributed stories, essays, and cartoons to "The New Yorker." Some of his best known collections are "My Life and Hard Times" (1933), "The Thurber Carnival" (1945), and "Alarms and Diversions" (1957). He was co-author with Elliot Nugent of "The Male Animal" (1940), a highly successful play.

The following essay exemplifies Thurber's definition of humor: "a kind of emotional chaos told about calmly and quietly in retrospect."

JAMES THURBER

University Days

1 I passed all the other courses that I took at my university, but I could never pass botany. This was because all botany students had to spend several hours a week in a laboratory looking through a microscope at plant cells, and I could never see through a microscope. I never once saw a cell through a microscope. This used to enrage my instructor. He would wander around the laboratory pleased with the progress all the students were making in drawing the involved and, so I am told, interesting structure of flower cells, until he came to me. I would just be standing there. "I can't see anything," I would say. He would begin patiently enough, explaining how anybody can see through a microscope, but he would always end up in a fury, claiming that I could *too* see through a microscope but just pretended that I couldn't. "It takes away from the beauty of flowers anyway," I used to tell him. "We are not concerned with beauty in this course," he would say. "We are concerned solely with what I may call the *mechanics* of flars." "Well," I'd say, "I can't see anything." "Try it just once again," he'd say, and I would put my eye to the microscope and see nothing at all, except now and again, a nebulous milky substance—a phenomenon of maladjustment. You were supposed to see a vivid, restless clockwork of

sharply defined plant cells. "I see what looks like a lot of milk," I would tell him. This, he claimed, was the result of my not having adjusted the microscope properly; so he would readjust it for me, or rather, for himself. And I would look again and see milk.

2   I finally took a deferred pass, as they called it, and waited a year and tried again. (You had to pass one of the biological sciences or you couldn't graduate.) The professor had come back from vacation brown as a berry, bright-eyed, and eager to explain cell-structure again to his classes. "Well," he said to me, cheerily, when we met in the laboratory hour of the semester, "We're going to see cells this time, aren't we?" "Yes, sir," I said. Students to right of me and to left of me and in front of me were seeing cells; what's more, they were quietly drawing pictures of them in their notebooks. Of course, I didn't see anything.

3   "We'll try it," the professor said to me grimly, "with every adjustment of the microscope known to man. As God is my witness, I'll arrange this glass so that you can see cells through it or I'll give up teaching. In twenty-two years of botany, I—" He cut off abruptly for he was beginning to quiver all over, like Lionel Barrymore, and he genuinely wished to hold onto his temper; his scenes with me had taken a great deal out of him.

4   So we tried it with every adjustment of the microscope known to man. With only one of them did I see anything but blackness or the familiar lacteal opacity, and that time I saw, to my pleasure and amazement, a variegated constellation of flecks, specks, and dots. These I hastily drew. The instructor, noting my activity, came back from an adjoining desk, a smile on his lips and his eyebrows high in hope. He looked at my cell drawing. "What's that?" he demanded, with a hint of a squeal in his voice. "That's what I saw," I said. "You didn't, you didn't, you *did*n't!" he screamed, losing control of his temper instantly, and he bent over and squinted into the microscope. His head snapped up. "That's your eye!" he shouted. "You fixed the lens so that it reflects! You've drawn your eye!"

5   Another course that I didn't like, but somehow managed to pass, was economics. I went to that class straight from the botany class, which didn't help me any in understanding either subject. I used to get them mixed up. But not as mixed up as another student in my economics class who came there direct from a physics laboratory. He was a tackle on the football team, named Bolenciecwcz. At that time Ohio State University had one of the best football teams in the country, and Bolenciecwcz was one of its outstanding stars. In order to be eligible to play it was necessary for him to keep up in his studies, a very difficult matter, for while he was not dumber than an ox he was not any smarter. Most of his professors were lenient and helped him along. None gave him more hints, in answering questions, or asked him simpler ones than the economics professor, a thin, timid man named Bassum. One day when we were on the subject of transportation and distribution, it came Bolenciecwcz's turn to answer a question. "Name one means of transportation." the professor said to him. No light came into the big tackle's eyes. "Just any means of transportation," said the professor. Bolenciecwcz sat staring at him. "That is," pursued the professor, "any medium, agency, or method of going from one place

to another." Bolenciecwcz had the look of a man who is being led into a trap. "You may choose among steam, horsedrawn, or electrically propelled vehicles," said the instructor. "I might suggest the one which we commonly take in making long journeys across land." There was a profound silence in which everybody stirred uneasily, including Bolenciecwcz and Mr. Bassum. Mr. Bassum abruptly broke this silence in an amazing manner. "Choo-choo-choo," he said, in a low voice, and turned instantly scarlet. He glanced appealingly around the room. All of us, of course, shared Mr. Bassum's desire that Bolenciecwcz should stay abreast of the class in economics, for the Illinois game, one of the hardest and most important of the season, was only a week off. "Toot, toot, tootoooooooot!" some student with a deep voice moaned, and we all looked encouragingly at Bolenciecwcz. Somebody else gave a fine imitation of a locomotive letting off steam. Mr. Bassum himself rounded off the little show. "Ding, dong, ding, dong," he said, hopefully. Bolenchiecwcz was staring at the floor now, trying to think, his great brow furrowed, his huge hands rubbing together, his face red.

6   "How did you come to college this year, Mr. Bolenciecwcz?" asked the professor. "*Chuff*a chuffa, *chuff*a chuffa."

7   "M'father sent me," said the football player.

8   "What on?" asked Bassum.

9   "I git an 'lowance," said the tackle, in a low, husky voice, obviously embarrassed.

10   "No, no," said Bassum. "Name a means of transportation. What did you *ride* here on?"

11   "Train," said Bolenciecwcz.

12   "Quite right," said the professor. "Now, Mr. Nugent, will you tell us—"

13   If I went through anguish in botany and economics—for different reasons—gymnasium work was even worse. I don't even like to think about it. They wouldn't let you play games or join in the exercises with your glasses on and I couldn't see with mine off. I bumped into professors, horizontal bars, agricultural students, and swinging iron rings. Not being able to see, I could take it but I couldn't dish it out. Also, in order to pass gymnasium (and you had to pass it to graduate) you had to learn to swim if you didn't know how. I didn't like the swimming pool, I didn't like swimming, and I didn't like the swimming instructor, and after all these years I still don't. I never swam but I passed my gym work anyway, by having another student give my gymnasium number (978) and swim across the pool in my place. He was a quiet, amiable blond youth, number 473, and he would have seen through a microscope for me if we could have got away with it, but we couldn't get away with it. Another thing I didn't like about gymnasium work was that they made you strip the day you registered. It is impossible for me to be happy when I am stripped and being asked a lot of questions. Still, I did better than a lanky agricultural student who was crossexamined just before I was. They asked each student which college he was in—that is, whether Arts, Engineering, Commerce, or Agriculture. "What college are you in?" the instructor

snapped at the youth in front of me: "Ohio State University," he said promptly.

14   It wasn't that agricultural student but it was another a whole lot like him who decided to take up journalism, possibly on the grounds that when farming went to hell he could fall back on newspaper work. He didn't realize, of course, that that would be very much like falling back full-length on a kit of carpenter's tools. Haskins didn't seem cut out for journalism, being too embarrassed to talk to anybody and unable to use a typewriter, but the editor of the college paper assigned him to the cow barns, the sheep house, the horse pavilion, and the animal husbandry department generally. This was a genuinely big "beat," for it took up five times as much ground and got ten times as great a legislative appropriation as the College of Liberal Arts. The agricultural student knew animals, but nevertheless his stories were dull and colorlessly written. He took all afternoon on each of them, because he had to hunt for each letter on the typewriter. Once in a while he had to ask somebody to help him hunt. "C" and "L," in particular, were hard letters for him to find. His editor finally got pretty much annoyed at the farmer-journalist because his pieces were so uninteresting. "See here, Haskins," he snapped at him one day, "why is it we never have anything hot from you on the horse pavilion? Here we have two hundred head of horses on this campus — more than any other university in the Western Conference except Purdue — and yet you never get any real low-down on them. Now shoot over to the horse barns and dig up something lively." Haskins shambled out and came back in about an hour; he said he had something. "Well, start it off snappily," said the editor. "Something people will read." Haskins set to work and in a couple of hours brought a sheet of typewritten paper to the desk; it was a two-hundred-word story about some disease that had broken out among the horses. Its opening sentence was simple but arresting. It read: "Who has noticed the sores on the tops of the horses in the animal husbandry building?"

15   Ohio State was a land grant university and therefore two years of military drill was compulsory. We drilled with old Springfield rifles and studied the tactics of the Civil War even though the World War was going on at the time. At 11 o'clock each morning thousands of freshmen and sophomores used to deploy over the campus, moodily creeping up on the old chemistry building. It was good training for the kind of warfare that was waged at Shiloh but it had no connection with what was going on in Europe. Some people used to think there was German money behind it, but they didn't dare say so or they would have been thrown in jail as German spies. It was a period of muddy thought and marked, I believe, the decline of higher education in the Middle West.

16   As a soldier I was never any good at all. Most of the cadets were glumly indifferent soldiers, but I was no good at all. Once General Littlefield, who was commandant of the cadet corps, popped up in front of me during regimental drill and snapped, "You are the main trouble with this university!" I think he meant that my type was the main trouble with the university but he may have meant me individ-

ually. I was mediocre at drill, certainly—that is, until my senior year. By that time I had drilled longer than anybody else in the Western Conference, having failed at military at the end of each preceding year so that I had to do it all over again. I was the only senior still in uniform. The uniform which, when new, had made me look like an interurban railway conductor, now that it had become faded and too tight, made me look like Bert Williams in his bell-boy act. This had a definitely bad effect on my morale. Even so, I had become by sheer practice little short of wonderful at squad manoeuvres.

17   One day General Littlefield picked our company out of the whole regiment and tried to get it mixed up by putting it through one movement after another as fast as we could execute them: squads right, squads left, squads on right into line, squads right about, squads left front into line, etc. In about three minutes one hundred and nine men were marching in one direction and I was marching away from them at an angle of forty-five degrees, all alone. "Company, halt!" shouted General Littlefield. "That man is the only man who has it right!" I was made a corporal for my achievement.

18   The next day General Littlefield summoned me to his office. He was swatting flies when I went in. I was silent and he was silent too, for a long time. I don't think he remembered me or why he had sent for me, but he didn't want to admit it. He swatted some more flies, keeping his eyes on them narrowly before he let go with the swatter. "Button up your coat!" he snapped. Looking back on it now I can see that he meant me although he was looking at a fly, but I just stood there. Another fly came to rest on a paper in front of the general and began rubbing its hind legs together. The general lifted the swatter cautiously. I moved restlessly and the fly flew away. "You startled him!" barked General Littlefield, looking at me severely. I said I was sorry. "That won't help the situation!" snapped the General, with cold military logic. I didn't see what I could do except offer to chase some more flies toward his desk, but I didn't say anything. He stared out the window at the faraway figures of co-eds crossing the campus toward the library. Finally, he told me I could go. So I went. He either didn't know which cadet I was or else he forgot what he wanted to see me about. It may have been that he wished to apologize for having called me the main trouble with the university; or maybe he had decided to compliment me on my brilliant drilling of the day before and then at the last minute decided not to. I don't know. I don't think about it much any more.

Discussion of Theme

1. Does the portrait of the dumb athlete, personified by Bolenciecwcz, hold true today? Has there ever been any truth in it?
2. Can you explain the apparent contradiction between Thurber's difficulties in college and his later success as a writer? Do many people who in later years do well in their chosen field have difficulties in college? Why might this be the case?

Discussion of Rhetoric

1. This essay has neither an introduction nor a conclusion. Does this mar its effectiveness? Why?
2. The organization of this piece is deceptive. What gives it unity?
3. Thurber often uses periodic sentences; for example, the first, second, and fifth sentences of paragraph 1. In each, the key idea is delayed until the last part of the sentence. What makes this effective? Find several other examples.

Writing Assignments

1. Humor can be benign or malevolent. In a sample of the former, describe a teacher you had last year.
2. Give a straightforward description of your experiences in one of your more difficult classes. Examine your own efforts, as well as the nature of the class.
3. Defend or attack the physical-education requirement that most colleges have.

Library Exploration

1. Read a few essays from Thurber's books and trace his use of the modified cliché—how he makes new, effective use of worn phrases.
2. Make a report on Thurber's life and how his own afflictions served his writing in many ways.

Vocabulary

(1) NEBULOUS   indistinct; vague
(1) PHENOMENON   extraordinary feat
(2) DEFERRED   postponed
(4) LACTEAL   milky
(4) OPACITY   the quality or state of being opaque, that is, not transparent or translucent
(4) VARIEGATED   of many colors or varieties
(5) LENIENT   soft; indulgent
(13) ANGUISH   distress
(15) COMPULSORY   obligatory; required
(15) DEPLOY   spread out
(16) MEDIOCRE   ordinary

Steve Allen (1921–) is probably best known for his television and radio roles as announcer, talk-show host, and comedian. Perhaps few of his fans realize that he has written several books and more than two thousand songs. He has long been active in political, social, and environmental reform in this country.

What is humor? What is its purpose? Has it changed in recent years? A famous comedian and student of laughter gives his views.

STEVE ALLEN

The Uses of Comedy

1   If we do not know what humor is, that may be because we do not know what man is. To serious scholars of humor I recommend Arthur Koestler's book, *The Act of Creation,* particularly the section in which he analyzes the phenomenon of laughter, which of course is not the same thing as humor.

2   Dogmatism is out when analyzing humor because humor appears in such a variety of forms. Whatever we say about humor, we are in trouble if we begin a sentence with "humor is," or "all humor," or "humor always." All Humor isn't anything. It isn't even always funny, because what is funny is a matter of personal opinion. Consider your ten favorite comedians or humorists, or your unfavorite comedians or humorists, for that matter. You immediately perceive that they are funny, or unfunny, for different reasons. We laughed at W. C. Fields for reasons quite different from the reasons we laugh at Groucho Marx, and, in turn, each of those reasons is different from why we laugh at Charlie Chaplin or Bill Cosby.

3   Perhaps all humor should be innocent, warmhearted, playful, affectionate, but in fact it is not. We have humor in incongruity. We have humor of the insult. And a great deal of humor falls off the tree unpicked and unwilled.

4   If we cannot define humor in a completely satisfactory way, we can say what some of its functions are. Since comedy is in some way about tragedy, one of its functions is to alleviate the pain we would be constantly suffering were we to concentrate on the tragedy that characterizes life on this planet.

5   Humor is a social lubricant that helps us get over some of the bad spots.

6   Humor is a humanizing agent. We will accept almost any allegation of our deficiencies — cosmetic, intellectual, virtuous — save one, the charge that we have no sense of humor.

7   I suspect that even in a totally mechanized, dehumanized, and authoritarian society humor does not disappear. The all-powerful state with its censorship weapons is not able to prevent the appearance of humor in the streets. I suspect that in Russia there is humor but not much laughter. I remember visiting a huge public park in Moscow on a very beautiful sunny afternoon. The park was crowded but the thing that impressed me immediately and forcibly was that nobody was laughing. Maybe Russians are simply a more somber people than Italians or Eskimos.

8   Tragedy plus time can equal comedy. There was no laughter when the first plane was hijacked by an armed passenger, but two or three weeks later hijacking jokes began to appear on comedy shows and in *New Yorker* cartoons. It seems that the most tragic events can later become the subject matter of humor.

9   An even unhappier thought is the spectacle of audience hilarity in the ancient Roman arena at the sight of Christians being tortured and killed. There is perhaps that ugly reality at the center of all of us which a few thousand years of civilization may have softened and diminished somewhat.

10   While historically Jews, Irish, and Negroes have produced a great deal of our humor, it cannot be only their tragic experiences that account for the humor and the development of their humorous resources. All races have had a tragic background. Man has had a tragic background. But, then, why aren't the Swedes very funny? Why doesn't anybody ever laugh with Orientals the way we laugh with Jews, or Irishmen, or Negroes?

11   Another question: If the dirty joke, the sex-oriented joke, comes out of situations where men are deprived of normal sexual outlets, how can we account for the increase in dirty jokes today when there is also an apparent increase in sexual activity?

12   A further puzzle: Why, when there is a leftward swing of the pendulum in American humor, cannot the right manage a counter-swing? The right loathes the new humor of the left for obvious reasons: left humor attacks persons and institutions that conservatives hold most dear. But why can't the conservatives produce a counter-humor? One cannot imagine a right-wing Lenny Bruce or Mort Sahl.

13   And the youth culture, which is artistically quite vigorous, does not seem to be making much of a contribution to formal, marketable humor. I can only weakly guess at the reason for this — perhaps the older generation, being more straitlaced and repressed, and having lived through more years of tragedy than have the young, needs the

release that humor offers. Young people, without that experience, hang loose and swing; they are more relaxed and have less need for that kind of formal, entertaining humor.

14   One of the great differences between the humor of today and that of fifty years ago is that today humor for the most part is performed whereas the earlier humor was meant to be read. The humorists of the nineteen-twenties saw themselves as continuing the great tradition of Mark Twain, Artemus Ward, Josh Billings. The literary humorists included Irvin S. Cobb, Stephen Leacock, Robert Benchley, Frank Sullivan, S. J. Perelman, Ring Lardner, James Thurber. But with the advent of radio, and then television, and the rise of the popular comedian, those who might have become humorists in their own right took to writing "comedy material" for the entertainers, and humor became more and more mass-production assembly-line jokes. So today more comedy is being written and more comedians are standing up in front of audiences and making them laugh than ever before. Whether it is as good as the comedy or humor of an earlier day is another matter.

Discussion of Theme

1. Why is it difficult to agree on a definition of humor? Are there any common elements in the humor of today's leading comics?
2. In what sense is humor a humanizing agent, as Allen claims?
3. How do tragedy and comedy differ? What does the appeal of each say about human nature?
4. Why do many people enjoy dirty jokes?
5. Reread paragraph 13. Do you agree with Allen's estimate of today's youth?

Discussion of Rhetoric

1. Although Allen says it is difficult—if not impossible—to define humor, he attempts to do so. What method of definition does he use?
2. How is this essay organized? Does it fall into clear-cut divisions?
3. Describe the level and tone of Allen's diction. Is it appropriate to his topic?
4. Does the author state his thesis directly or imply it? Locate his thesis, or state it in your own words.

Writing Assignments

1. Define one of the following terms: *comedy, tragedy, humor.*
2. Analyze the humor (and the appeal to today's youth) of the comics of earlier days; for example, Charlie Chaplin, W. C. Fields, Laurel and Hardy, and the Marx Brothers.
3. Take a look at the state of humor in our society. What is considered funny? Why?

Library Exploration

For an expanded presentation of Steve Allen's ideas, read one of his books: *Letter to a Conservative* (1965); *The Ground is Our Table* (1966); and *Not All Your Laughter, Not All Your Tears* (1969).

Vocabulary

(2) DOGMATISM   unfounded positiveness in matters of opinion

(3) INCONGRUITY   inappropriateness

(6) ALLEGATION   claim or charge

Milton Mayer (1908–ㅤ) has had a varied career as newspaperman, magazine writer, professor, and consultant to the Center for the Study of Democratic Institutions. Educated at the University of Chicago (and a native of that city), he has authored several books, including "They Thought They Were Free: The Germans, 1933-45" (1955); and "The Art of the Impossible: A Study of the Czech Resistance" (1969).

What has happened to our ability to laugh at ourselves? How can one account for the grimness and the savagery underlying much of our humor today? A student of contemporary American society offers some insights.

MILTON MAYER

Hollow Men, Hollow Laughs

1 The light fantastic has gone out all over America. No more people like my Old Man to ask the railroad depot ticket agent for a ticket to Springfield and when the agent says, "Ohio, Missouri, Massachusetts, or Illinois?" to say, "Whichever is cheapest." No more ticket agent. No more depot. No more railroad. Up and away.

2 ㅤUp and away up tight, and nobody up tighter than the dreary young enemies of Dreary Dick. I got into a plane in Cleveland last spring — the same Cleveland where Gene Debs once said, "A man can't live sober in a world like this" — and a collegiate drab took the seat next to me and tried to get her suitcase under it and couldn't. She turned to me and said "What will they do?" "Call out the National Guard," I said. "That's not funny," she said.

3 ㅤThat's not funny.

4 ㅤWhat is any more?

5   This side-splitting, skull-splitting society deserves its comeuppance
for taking the joy out of the lives of its young. Gone the sweet smiling
candor of the hippie who, when the judge said, "Take those stupid
beads off," said, "As soon as you take that stupid robe off, your honor."
Gone the hippie who cadged a dime from a straight and put it in the
parking meter and lay down to sleep in one piece of street rented from
one city for one hour. Gone the saturnine social commentary of the
hippie buttons: "Jesus Saves Green Stamps," "I Am a Human Being
—Do not Fold, Staple, or Mutilate," "Support Mental Health or I'll
Kill You," "Kill a Commie for Christ," "God Is a Teeny-Bopper,"
"Smoking Is Safer Than Breathing," "Help Stamp Out Thinking."

6   Gone the goofy good time they were having—was it only two or
three years ago? Moping mum the merrymen of the Hashbury now.
Gone the garlands, come the rocks. Gone the V sign, come the fist.
Gone the curbside communion, come the confrontation. Gone the
tinkling temple bells, come the pigstickers. Gone, all gone, and come
all the sullen young men (and the furious young ladies demanding
liberation from electric dishwashers and tossing their brassieres to the
winds in protest against their being sex objects). That is not funny.
What is?

7   It isn't only power that is never funny, but the struggle for power,
the struggle to increase it, and the mortal struggle to hold on to it. Who
wants power wants trouble. Who has power has trouble. Trouble isn't
funny. Revolution isn't funny—Lenin is purest pain—and the Counter-
Revolution of Declining Expectations isn't funny. The barricades
aren't funny. And, though the Beatific Vision might be an improvement on Martha Mitchell, the end of the world isn't funny, and the
young alone are intrepid enough to face it (and intrepidity isn't funny).

8   There are only True Believers standing eyeball to eyeball to eyeball now, massively reacting to their massive meaningless apothegms
like "All Power to the People," or "Love It or Leave It," with Pav-
lovian inexorability; members all of what Peter Viereck calls the Sali-
vation Army. The central element of True Belief is its unrelieved
earnestness, the hallmark of the Vision in all its standard and revised
forms. Marx is no jollier than Mark; ponderous Protestants (Oh! Wittenberg!) preaching the unglad tidings of great joylessness to an ex-
cruciated world whose only relief is the *Reader's Digest.*

9   Man is not only an animal, and a rational animal. He (being an
animal) is a laughable and (being rational) a risible animal. If he isn't
grotesque, his posturing ludicrous, his capers contradictory, there is
nothing to be discovered in him. There are more chuckles in the
tragedy of Hamlet than in all the triumphs of Socialist Realism, more
realism in the chin of Philip IV as Velasquez saw it than in the ten
tallest statues of Spiro Agnew. If man was ever going to be good for a
giggle or two, it ought to be now, when he has come apart at the seams
and John Kennedy turns out to have contemplated the advisability
of assassinating a head of state. But no—that's not funny.

10   What's funny? What ever was?

11   Men who are reduced to extremity and know it—such men are
humorous, and no others. Negroes are humorous; not blacks. Jews are
humorous; not Israelis. Czech Communists are humorous; not Rus-

sian Communists. The reason they are humorous is that they have nothing else to lose and nothing else to live by. Humor is man's survival kit. If all Hitler ever wanted to do was destroy the world's joy, he had only to do what he did and put an end to the Jewish jokes (yes, of the Jews' own "anti-Semitic" jokes) that rejoiced the world so salubriously (and so harmlessly to the Jews). End of Moran and Mack, the Two Black Crows. End of the *Lumpenbourgeois'* Moran and Mack, Amos 'n' Andy. If my Old Man had not listened to Amos 'n' Andy, he would have been much more of a bigot than he was.

12   A last look at Dreary Dick's nomination of G. Harrold Carswell to the Supreme Court. One of the counts charged against G. Harrold Carswell was a joke he once told about a "Nigra" who was asked if he was from Indo-China and said, "Nope — I's from outdawh Gawgia." A cornball joke, but a harmless joke; and Carswell's deadly, deadly enemies took it as evidence that he was a racist (as I don't doubt he was). Ridden out of town, as he should have been on his demerits, by a country that could not take a joke.

13   What such a country can take is entertainment. Never have so many provided so much entertainment for so many who laugh themselves silly enough to buy the product that produces the laugh for the sake of selling the product. But what has laughter — which can be evoked by the flagellation of a corpse like Mussolini's — got to do with humor? Laugh, and the joyless world laughs with you; smile unseen and unheard, and you smile alone. The country's smartest entertainer, S. J. Perelman, announces his departure into exile in a far land, and he is all bitterness; others he can entertain, but not himself. The worst thing that ever happened was television, which does our enjoying for us.

14   I suppose I am subject here to the charge of mixing two separate, or at least separable, phenomena. Enjoying oneself is one thing, humor another. But whatever further and loftier (or lower) purpose humor may have, its immediate purpose is pleasuring. If I do not have the capacity to pleasure myself, am I not still profited by other men's capacity to pleasure me? But then I must be pleasurable. I must be capable of being diverted from the doldrum which incapacitates me from doing my own enjoying, and unless I am, the immediate purpose of humor is frustrated. My thesis here is that we are losing our capability of being diverted from our daymare. The hollow man laughs a hollow laugh.

15   A culture which can take round-the-clock entertainment and get up every morning more morose than it was the day before can only be humored; it cannot be humorous. It cannot enjoy itself but only others' enjoyment — or others' representation of enjoyment; humor thrice removed. It is not having, but watching, a good time. This is the vicarious life. As we all know, the vicarious life is not worth living.

16   Tell me it isn't all that bad. Tell me that the landscape still jumps with Dickenses and Clemenses and Wildes and Gilberts and Dooleys and Cohens on the Telephone and Chaplins and Brothers Marx and Fieldses. Tell me that it jumps, not with reflexive pandemonium, but with the music of square pegs in round spheres.

17   Tell me that I shall live to see another *Beggar on Horseback,* hear another Englishman say, "Some say that life is the thing, but I prefer

books." Tell me that Aristophanes and Rabelais without the raunch would be a drag and that Cervantes is a period piece. Tell me that *Twelfth Night,* if it weren't Shakespeare, wouldn't double me up, that I'm confusing fashions in humor with humor itself, and that we are as readily diverted as grandpa and a lot readier than Cotton Mather. Tell me that a clever divil like Swift—and what a bad time *he* had—can always get a sadistic rise out of people and that one or two comedians a generation (or a century) have always been par for the course in any case. Tell me that it is pleasant to read anything but the squibs at the bottom of the page in *The New Yorker* or that our columnists and commentators sparkle.

18   Or tell me that is is about time we took ourselves seriously and that he who can't live sober in a world like this is the butt of a very bad joke.

Discussion of Theme

1. According to Mayer, what has happened to humor among today's youth? Do you agree? Explain.
2. What are True Believers? Why do they lack a sense of humor? What is Mayer's estimate of them? Can you think of any public figures who are True Believers?
3. What is humor, according to the author? Do standards of humor shift, or are they fairly stable from one generation to the next?
4. Explain the meaning of paragraph 18. What is the "very bad joke"?

Discussion of Rhetoric

1. What tone is established in the opening paragraphs of this selection? Is it appropriate? Does Mayer depart from it? Where?
2. What is the rhetorical effect of the one-sentence paragraphs in this article (paragraphs 3, 4, and 10)? In each instance, what is the author trying to do?
3. Comment on the sentence structure of paragraph 6. What is the cumulative effect of the repetition?
4. Mayer uses a number of references and allusions to further his thesis. In paragraph 8, for example, note the third sentence: "Marx is no jollier than Mark; ponderous Protestants (Oh! Wittenberg!)." Explain the references in this sentence and in several others.
5. For what kind of audience is Mayer writing—a general audience or a highly educated, literate one? Explain your answer.

Writing Assignments

1. Develop the following statement from paragraph 15 into a theme: "As we all know, the vicarious life is not worth living."
2. If you disagree with Mayer's contention that young people today are humorless, present your views in a theme.

3. Select several comedians or actors who usually play comedy roles, and analyze what it is that makes them funny.

Library Exploration

1. Investigate some of the psychological and literary theories that attempt to explain comedy and laughter.
2. *A Subtreasury of American Humor,* edited by E. B. White and Katherine S. White, provides a panorama of humor from early days to the present.
3. Read (or listen to) the humor of Mort Sahl and Lenny Bruce. Analyze their appeal.

Vocabulary

(7) INTREPID fearless

(8) APOTHEGMS short sayings

(8) INEXORABILITY the quality of being unyielding or unalterable

(9) RISIBLE capable of laughter

(11) SALUBRIOUSLY beneficially

RELIGION AND PHILOSOPHY: DIVERSE VIEWS

Loren Eiseley (1907–   ) is one of America's most distinguished anthropologists. Born in Nebraska, he received degrees from the University of Nebraska and the University of Pennsylvania, where he is now professor of anthropology and the history of science. The possessor of a distinct and readable literary style, he has gained a wide audience from his books, articles, and poetry. Among his books are "The Mind as Nature" (1962) and "The Unexpected Universe" (1969).

Significant truths are sometimes revealed to us by a hidden teacher, according to Professor Eiseley. His own casual encounter with a spider – described in the following article – led to a profound insight.

LOREN EISELEY

The Hidden Teacher

Sometimes the best teacher teaches only once to a single child or to a grownup past hope.
—ANONYMOUS

1 The putting of formidable riddles did not arise with today's philosophers. In fact, there is a sense in which the experimental method of science might be said merely to have widened the area of man's homelessness. Over two thousand years ago, a man named Job, crouching in the Judean desert, was moved to challenge what he felt to be the injustice of his God. The voice in the whirlwind, in turn, volleyed pitiless questions upon the supplicant—questions that have, in truth, precisely the ring of modern science. For the Lord asked of Job by

whose wisdom the hawk soars, and who had fathered the rain, or entered the storehouses of the snow.

2　A youth standing by, one Elihu, also played a role in this drama, for he ventured diffidently to his protesting elder that it was not true that God failed to manifest Himself. He may speak in one way or another, though men do not perceive it. In consequence of this remark perhaps it would be well, whatever our individual beliefs, to consider what may be called the hidden teacher, lest we become too much concerned with the formalities of only one aspect of the education by which we learn.

3　We think we learn from teachers, and we sometimes do. But the teachers are not always to be found in school or in great laboratories. Sometimes what we learn depends upon our own powers of insight. Moreover, our teachers may be hidden, even the greatest teacher. And it was the young man Elihu who observed that if the old are not always wise, neither can the teacher's way be ordered by the young whom he would teach.

4　For example, I once received an unexpected lesson from a spider.

5　It happened far away on a rainy morning in the West. I had come up a long gulch looking for fossils, and there, just at eye level, lurked a huge yellow-and-black orb spider, whose web was moored to the tall spears of buffalo grass at the edge of the arroyo. It was her universe, and her senses did not extend beyond the lines and spokes of the great wheel she inhabited. Her extended claws could feel every vibration throughout that delicate structure. She knew the tug of wind, the fall of a raindrop, the flutter of a trapped moth's wing. Down one spoke of the web ran a stout ribbon of gassamer on which she could hurry out to investigate her prey.

6　Curious, I took a pencil from my pocket and touched a strand of the web. Immediately there was a response. The web, plucked by its menacing occupant, began to vibrate until it was a blur. Anything that had brushed claw or wing against that amazing snare would be thoroughly entrapped. As the vibrations slowed, I could see the owner fingering her guidelines for signs of struggle. A pencil point was an intrusion into this universe for which no precedent existed. Spider was circumscribed by spider ideas; its universe was spider universe. All outside was irrational, extraneous, at best, raw material for spider. As I proceeded on my way along the gully, like a vast impossible shadow, I realized that in the world of spider I did not exist.

7　Moreover, I considered, as I tramped along, that to the phagocytes, the white blood cells, clambering even now with some kind of elementary intelligence amid the thin pipes and tubing of my body — creatures without whose ministrations I could not exist — the conscious "I" of which I was aware had no significance to these amoeboid beings. I was, instead, a kind of chemical web that brought meaningful messages to them, a natural environment seemingly immortal if they could have thought about it, since generations of them had lived and perished, and would continue to so live and die, in that odd fabric which contained my intelligence — a misty light that was beginning to seem floating and tenuous even to me.

8   I began to see that among the many universes in which the world of living creatures existed, some were large, some small, but that all, including man's, were in some way limited or finite. We were creatures of many different dimensions passing through each other's lives like ghosts through doors.

9   In the years since, my mind has many times returned to that far moment of my encounter with the orb spider. A message has arisen only now from the misty shreds of that webbed universe. What was it that had so troubled me about the incident? Was it that spidery indifference to the human triumph?

10   If so, that triumph was very real and could not be denied. I saw, had many times seen, both mentally and in the seams of exposed strata, the long backward stretch of time whose recovery is one of the great feats of modern science. I saw the drifting cells of the early seas from which all life, including our own, has arisen. The salt of those ancient seas is in our blood, its lime is in our bones. Every time we walk along a beach some ancient urge disturbs us so that we find ourselves shedding shoes and garments, or scavenging among seaweed and whitened timbers like the homesick refugees of a long war.

11   And war it has been indeed—the long war of life against its inhospitable environment, a war that has lasted for perhaps three billion years. It began with strange chemicals seething under a sky lacking in oxygen; it was waged through long ages until the first green plants learned to harness the light of the nearest star, our sun. The human brain, so frail, so perishable, so full of inexhaustible dreams and hungers, burns by the power of the leaf.

12   The hurrying blood cells charged with oxygen carry more of that element to the human brain than to any other part of the body. A few moments' loss of vital air and the phenomenon we know as consciousness goes down into the black night of inorganic things. The human body is a magical vessel, but its life is linked with an element it cannot produce. Only the green plant knows the secret of transforming the light that comes to us across the far reaches of space. There is no better illustration of the intricacy of man's relationship with other living things.

13   The student of fossil life would be forced to tell us that if we take the past into consideration the vast majority of earth's creatures—perhaps over ninety per cent—have vanished. Forms that flourished for a far longer time than man has existed upon earth have become either extinct or so transformed that their descendants are scarcely recognizable. The specialized perish with the environment that created them, the tooth of the tiger fails at last, the lances of men strike down the last mammoth.

14   In three billion years of slow change and groping effort only one living creature has succeeded in escaping the trap of specialization that has led in time to so much death and wasted endeavor. It is man, but the word should be uttered softly, for his story is not yet done.

15   With the rise of the human brain, with the appearance of a creature whose upright body enabled two limbs to be freed for the exploration and manipulation of his environment, there had at last emerged a

creature with a specialization — the brain — that, paradoxically, offered escape from specialization. Many animals driven into the nooks and crannies of nature have achieved momentary survival only at the cost of later extinction.

16   Was it this that troubled me and brought my mind back to a tiny universe among the grass-blades, a spider's universe concerned with spider thought?

17   Perhaps.

18   The mind that once visualized animals on a cave wall is now engaged in a vast ramification of itself through time and space. Man has broken through the boundaries that control all other life. I saw, at last, the reason for my recollection of that great spider on the arroyo's rim, fingering its universe against the sky.

19   The spider was a symbol of man in miniature. The wheel of the web brought the analogy home clearly. Man, too, lies at the heart of a web, a web extending through the starry reaches of sidereal space, as well as backward into the dark realm of prehistory. His great eye upon Mount Palomar looks into a distance of millions of light-years, his radio ear hears the whisper of even more remote galaxies, he peers through the electron microscope upon the minute particles of his own being. It is a web no creature of earth has ever spun before. Like the orb spider, man lies at the heart of it, listening. Knowledge has given him the memory of earth's history beyond the time of his emergence. Like the spider's claw, a part of him touches a world he will never enter in the flesh. Even now, one can see him reaching forward into time with new machines, computing, analyzing, until elements of the shadowy future will also compose part of the invisible web he fingers.

20   Yet still my spider lingers in memory against the sunset sky. Spider thoughts in a spider universe — sensitive to raindrop and moth flutter, nothing beyond, nothing allowed for the unexpected, the inserted pencil from the world outside.

21   Is man at heart any different from the spider, I wonder: man thoughts, as limited as spider thoughts, contemplating now the nearest star with the threat of bringing with him the fungus rot from earth, wars, violence, the burden of a population he refuses to control, cherishing again his dream of the Adamic Eden he had pursued and lost in the green forests of America. Now it beckons again like a mirage from beyond the moon. Let man spin his web, I thought further; it is his nature. But I considered also the work of the phagocytes swarming in the rivers of my body, the unresting cells in their mortal universe. What is it we are a part of that we do not see, as the spider was not gifted to discern my face, or my little probe into her world?

22   We are too content with our sensory extensions, with the fulfillment of that ice age mind that began its journey amidst the cold of vast tundras and that pauses only briefly before its leap into space. It is no longer enough to see as a man sees — even to the ends of the universe. It is not enough to hold nuclear energy in one's hand like a spear, as a man would hold it, or to see the lightning, or times past, or time to come, as a man would see it. If we continue to do this, the great brain — the human brain — will be only a new version of the old trap, and nature is full of traps for the beast that cannot learn.

23   It is not sufficient any longer to listen at the end of a wire to the rustlings of galaxies; it is not enough even to examine the great coil of DNA in which is coded the very alphabet of life. These are our extended perceptions. But beyond lies the great darkness of the ultimate Dreamer, who dreamed the light and the galaxies. Before act was, or substance existed, imagination grew in the dark. Man partakes of that ultimate wonder and creativeness. As we turn from the galaxies to the swarming cells of our own being, which toil for something, some entity beyond their grasp, let us remember man, the self-fabricator who came across an ice age to look into the mirrors and the magic of science. Surely he did not come to see himself or his wild visage only. He came because he is at heart a listener and a searcher for some transcendent realm beyond himself. This he has worshiped by many names, even in the dismal caves of his beginning. Man, the self-fabricator, is so by reason of gifts he had no part in devising — and so he searches as the single living cell in the beginning must have sought the ghostly creature it was to serve.

Discussion of Theme

1. In what way has "the experimental method of science . . . widened the area of man's homelessness"?
2. In what sense can a teacher be "hidden"? What does this imply about the learning process?
3. How does Eiseley show the relationship of man with other life?
4. According to the author, what characteristics have helped man to survive? Is he certain of man's continuing survival?
5. Explain the anecdote concerning the spider. What was the unexpected lesson (paragraph 4)?

Discussion of Rhetoric

1. How does Eiseley relate the anecdote of Job to his thesis?
2. The author uses analogies to explain or illustrate his central idea. Examine carefully one or two of these, and determine whether they help to clarify his thesis.
3. Note the author's use of specific details in various passages. Find such a passage and examine Eiseley's skillful use of diction and "picture-making."
4. How does this selection differ from most scientific writing? How does it resemble poetry?

Writing Assignments

1. Develop the following statement: "Sometimes the best teacher teaches only once to a single child or to a grownup past hope."
2. Select an experience from your own life that was comparable in

significance to that of Eiseley's with the spider. Describe the experience, showing what you learned from it.

3. In a paper, apply Eiseley's ideas on teachers and learning to higher education today. What reforms or changes would you propose?

Library Exploration

1. *The Unexpected Universe* (1969), from which this selection was taken, contains a fuller treatment of the miracle of man and his world.
2. Investigate one of the following: carbon 14; DNA; fossils; radio telescopes; electron microscopes.

Vocabulary

(1) SUPPLICANT   one who makes a request humbly and earnestly

(5) ARROYO   a small steep gulch

(5) GOSSAMER   something light, delicate, or tenuous

(6) CIRCUMSCRIBED   encircled

(6) EXTRANEOUS   external; foreign

(7) MINISTRATIONS   aid; assistance

(7) TENUOUS   slight; unsubstantial

(23) VISAGE   face

(23) TRANSCENDENT   going beyond the universe or material existence

Albert Camus (1913–59) was born and educated in Algiers, then under French rule. He was himself a rebel, a member of the French Resistance in World War II and, like so many of his comrades, a contributor to the intellectualism of postwar France. He was an associate of Jean-Paul Sartre but did not claim to be an existentialist. His serious writing began after the war in Europe, and his main ideas can be found in "The Stranger" (1946), "The Plague" (1948), and "The Myth of Sisyphus" (1955). He also wrote a considerable number of plays and short stories. He was awarded the Nobel Prize in Literature in 1957.

In this selection Camus defines the rebel and analyzes some of the philosophical ideas of rebellion.

ALBERT CAMUS

What Is a Rebel?

1   What is a rebel? A man who says no: but whose refusal does not imply a renunciation. He is also a man who says yes as soon as he begins to think for himself. A slave who has taken orders all his life, suddenly decides that he cannot obey some new command. What does he mean by saying "no"?

2   He means, for instance, that "this has been going on too long," "so far but no farther," "you are going too far," or again "There are certain limits beyond which you shall not go." In other words, his "no" affirms the existence of a borderline. You find the same conception in the rebel's opinion that the other person is "exaggerating," that he is exerting his authority beyond a limit where he infringes on the right of

others. He rebels because he categorically refuses to submit to conditions that he considers intolerable and also because he is confusedly convinced that his position is justified, or rather, because in his own mind he thinks that he "has the right to. . . ." Rebellion cannot exist without the feeling that somewhere, in some way, you are justified. It is in this way that the rebel slave says yes and no at the same time. He affirms that there are limits and also that he suspects—and wishes to preserve—the existence of certain things beyond those limits. He stubbornly insists that there are certain things in him which "are worth while . . ." and which must be taken into consideration.

3   In every act of rebellion, the man concerned experiences not only a feeling of revulsion at the infringement of his rights but also a complete and spontaneous loyalty to certain aspects of himself. Thus he implicitly brings into play a standard of values so far from being false that he is willing to preserve them at all costs. Up to this point he has, at least, kept quiet and, in despair, has accepted a condition to which he submits even though he considers it unjust. To keep quiet is to allow yourself to believe that you have no opinions, that you want nothing, and in certain cases it amounts to really wanting nothing. Despair, like Absurdism, prefers to consider everything in general and nothing in particular. Silence expresses this attitude very satisfactorily. But from the moment that the rebel finds his voice—even though he has nothing to say but no—he begins to consider things in particular. In the etymological sense, the rebel is a turn-coat. He acted under the lash of his master's whip. Suddenly he turns and faces him. He chooses what is preferable to what is not. Not every value leads to rebellion, but every rebellion tacitly invokes a value. Or is it really a question of values?

4   An awakening of conscience, no matter how confused it may be, develops from any act of rebellion and is represented by the sudden realization that something exists with which the rebel can identify himself—even if only for a moment. Up to now this identification was never fully realized. Previous to his insurrection, the slave accepted all the demands made upon him. He even very often took orders, without reacting against them, which were considerably more offensive to him than the one at which he balked. He was patient and though, perhaps, he protested inwardly, he was obviously more careful of his own immediate interests—in that he kept quiet—than aware of his own rights. But with loss of patience—with impatience—begins a reaction which can extend to everything that he accepted up to this moment, and which is almost retroactive. Immediately the slave refuses to obey the humiliating orders of his master, he rejects the condition of slavery. The act of rebellion carries him beyond the point he reached by simply refusing. He exceeds the bounds that he established for his antagonist and demands that he should now be treated as an equal. What was, originally, an obstinate resistance on the part of the rebel, becomes the rebel personified. He proceeds to put self-respect above everything else and proclaims that it is preferable to life itself. It becomes, for him, the supreme blessing. Having previously been willing to compromise, the slave suddenly adopts an

attitude of All or Nothing. Knowledge is born and conscience awakened.

5   But it is obvious that the knowledge he gains is of an "All" that is still rather obscure and of a "Nothing" that proclaims the possibility of sacrificing the rebel to this "All." The rebel himself wants to be "All" — to identify himself completely with this blessing of which he has suddenly become aware and of which he wishes to be recognized and proclaimed as the incarnation — or "Nothing" which means to be completely destroyed by the power that governs him. As a last resort he is willing to accept the final defeat, which is death, rather than be deprived of the last sacrament which he would call, for example, freedom. Better to die on one's feet than to live on one's knees.

6   Values, according to the best authorities, "usually represent a transition from facts to rights, from what is desired to what is desirable (usually through the medium of what is generally considered desirable)." The transition from facts to rights is manifest, as we have seen, in the act of rebellion, as is the transition from "this is how things should be" to "this is how I want things to be," and still more, perhaps, the conception of the submission of the individual to the common good. The appearance of the conception of "All or Nothing" demonstrates that rebellion, contrary to present opinion and despite the fact that it springs from everything that is most strictly individualistic in man, undermines the very conception of the individual. If an individual actually consents to die, and, when the occasion arises, accepts death as a consequence of his rebellion, he demonstrates that he is willing to sacrifice himself for the sake of a common good which he considers more important than his own destiny. If he prefers the risk of death to a denial of the rights that he defends, it is because he considers that the latter are more important than he is. He acts, therefore, in the name of certain values which are still indeterminate but which he feels are common to himself and to all men. We see that the affirmation implicit in each act of revolt is extended to something which transcends the individual insofar as it removes him from his supposed solitude and supplies him with a reason to act. But it is worth noting that the conception of values as pre-existent to any kind of action runs counter to the purely historical schools of philosophy in which values are established (if they are ever established) by action itself. An analysis of rebellion leads us to the suspicion that, contrary to the postulates of contemporary thought, a human nature does exist, as the Greeks believed. Why rebel if there is nothing worth preserving in oneself? The slave asserts himself for the sake of everyone in the world when he comes to the conclusion that a command has infringed on something inside him that does not belong to him alone, but which he has in common with other men — even with the man who insults and oppresses him.

7   Two observations will support this argument. First we can see that an act of rebellion is not, essentially, an egotistic act. Undoubtedly it can have egotistic aims. But you can rebel equally well against a lie as against oppression. Furthermore the rebel — at the moment of his greatest impetus and no matter what his aims — keeps nothing in re-

serve and commits himself completely. Undoubtedly he demands respect for himself, but only insofar as he identifies himself with humanity in general.

8   Then we note that revolt does not occur only amongst the oppressed but that it can also break out at the mere spectacle of oppression of which someone else is the victim. In such cases there is a feeling of identification with other individuals. And it must be made clear that it is not a question of psychological identification — a mere subterfuge by which the individual contrives to feel that it is he who has been oppressed. It can even happen that we cannot countenance other people being insulted in a manner that we ourselves have accepted without rebelling. The suicides of the Russian terrorists in Siberia, as a protest against their comrades being whipped, is a case in point. Nor is it a question of a community of interests. Injustices done to men whom we consider enemies can, actually, be profoundly repugnant to us. Our reaction is only an identification of destinies and a choice of sides. Therefore the individual is not, in himself, an embodiment of the values he wishes to defend. It needs at least all humanity to comprise them. When he rebels, a man identifies himself with other men and, from this point of view, human solidarity is metaphysical. But for the moment we are only dealing with the kind of solidarity that is born in chains.

9   It would be possible for us to define the positive aspect of the values implicit in every act of rebellion by comparing them to a completely negative conception like that of resentment as defined by Scheler. Actually, rebellion is more than an act of revenge, in the strongest sense of the word. Resentment is very well defined by Scheler as an auto-intoxication — the evil secretion, in a sealed vessel, of prolonged impotence. Rebellion, on the other hand, removes the seal and allows the whole being to come into play. It liberates stagnant waters and turns them into a raging torrent. Scheler himself emphasizes the passive aspect of resentment, and remarks on the prominent position it occupies in the psychology of women whose main preoccupations are desire and possession. The mainspring of revolt, on the other hand, is the principle of superabundant activity and energy. Scheler is also right in saying that resentment is always highly flavored with envy. But we envy what we do not possess while the rebel defends what he has. He does not only claim some benefit which he does not possess or of which he was deprived. His aim is to claim recognition for something which he has and which has already been recognized by him, in almost every case, as more important than anything of which he could be envious. Rebellion is not realistic. According to Scheler, resentment always turns into either unscrupulous ambition or bitterness, depending on whether it flourishes in a weak mind or a strong one. But in both cases it is always a question of wanting to be something other than what one is. Resentment is always resentment against oneself. The rebel, on the other hand, from his very first step, refuses to allow anyone to touch what he is. He is fighting for the integrity of one part of his being. At first he does not try to conquer, but simply to impose.

10   Finally, it would seem that resentment takes a delight, in advance, in the pain that it would like the object of its envy to feel. Nietzsche and Scheler are right in seeing an excellent illustration of this feeling in the passage where Tertullian informs his readers that one of the greatest sources of happiness in heaven will be the spectacle of the Roman emperors consumed in the fires of hell. This kind of happiness is also experienced by all the decent people who go to watch executions. The rebel, on principle, persistently refuses to be humiliated without asking that others should be. He will even accept pain provided that his integrity is respected.

11   It is hard to understand why Scheler absolutely identifies the spirit of revolt with resentment. His critique of resentment as a part of humanitarianism (which he considers as the non-Christian form of human love) could perhaps be applied to certain vague forms of humanitarian idealism, or to certain techniques of terror. But it is false in so far as a man's rebellion against his condition is concerned and equally false about the impulse that enlists individuals in the defense of a dignity common to all men. Scheler wants to prove that humanitarian feelings are always accompanied by misanthropy. Humanity is loved in general in order to avoid loving anybody in particular. In some cases this is correct and it is easier to understand Scheler when we realize that for him humanitarianism is represented by Bentham and Rousseau. But man's love for man can be born of other things than an arithmetic calculation of interests or a theoretical confidence in human nature. Despite what the utilitarians say, there exists, for example, the type of logic, embodied by Dostoievski in Ivan Karamazov, that begins with an act of rebellion and ends in metaphysical insurrection. Scheler is aware of this and sums up the conception in the following manner: "There is not enough love in the world to be able to squander it on anything else but the human race." Even if this proposition were true, the profound despair that it implies would merit any other reaction but contempt. Actually, it misinterprets the tortured nature of Karamozov's rebellion. Ivan's drama, on the contrary, arises from the fact that there is too much love without an object. The existence of God being denied, love becomes redundant and then he decides to lavish it on the human race as a generous act of complicity.

12   Nevertheless, in the act of revolt as we have envisaged it up to now, we do not choose an abstract ideal through lack of feeling or for sterile reasons of revenge. We demand that that part of man which cannot be confined to the realm of ideas should be taken into consideration — the passionate side of his nature that serves no other purpose but to help him to live. Does that imply that no act of rebellion is motivated by resentment? No, and we know this from the bitter experience of centuries. But we must consider the idea of revolt in its widest sense — and in its widest sense it goes far beyond resentment. When Heathcliff, in *Wuthering Heights,* says that he puts his love above God and would willingly go to Hell in order to be reunited with the woman he loves, he is prompted not only by his youth and his humiliation but by the consuming experience of a whole lifetime. The same emotion causes Eckart, in a surprising fit of heresy, to say that he prefers Hell

with Jesus to Heaven without Him. This is the very essence of love. Contrary to what Scheler thinks, it would be impossible to over-emphasize the passionate affirmation that underlies the fact of revolt and which distinguishes it from resentment. Rebellion, though apparently negative since it creates nothing, is profoundly positive in that it reveals the part of man which must always be defended.

13   But finally, are not rebellion and the values that it calls into play, interdependent? Reasons for rebellion seem, in fact, to change with the times. It is obvious that a Hindu pariah, an Inca warrior, a primitive native of Central Africa and a member of one of the first Christian communities had quite different conceptions about rebellion. We could even assert, with considerable assurance, that the idea of rebellion has no meaning in those actual cases. However, a Greek slave, a serf, a condottiere of the Renaissance, a Parisian bourgeois during the Regency, and a Russian intellectual at the beginning of the nineteenth century would undoubtedly agree that rebellion is legitimate, even if they differed about the reasons. In other words, the problem of rebellion only seems to assume a precise meaning within the confines of Western thought. It is possible to be even more explicit by saying, like Scheler, that the spirit of rebellion finds few means of expression in societies where inequalities are very great (the Hindu caste system) or, again, in those where there is absolute equality (certain primitive societies). The spirit of revolt can only exist in a society where a theoretic equality conceals great factual inequalities. The problem of revolt, therefore, has no meaning outside our Occidental society. It would be tempting to say that it was relative to the development of individualism if the preceding remarks had not put us on guard against this conclusion.

14   On the basis of the evidence, the only conclusion we can draw from Scheler's remark is that, thanks to the theory of political freedom, there is, in the very heart of our society, an extension of the conception of the rights of man and a corresponding dissatisfaction caused by the application of this theory of freedom. Actual freedom has not increased in proportion to man's awareness of it. We can only deduce, from this observation, that rebellion is the act of an educated man who is aware of his rights. But we cannot say that it is only a question of individual rights. Because of the sense of solidarity that we have already pointed out, it would rather seem that what is at stake is humanity's gradually increasing awareness of itself as it pursues its adventurous course. In fact, for the Inca and the pariah the problem of revolt never arises, because for them it has been solved by tradition before they had time to raise it—the answer being that tradition is sacrosanct. If, in the sacrosanct world, the problem of revolt does not arise, it is because no real problems are to be found in it—all the answers having been given simultaneously. Metaphysic is replaced by myth. But before man accepts the sacrosanct and in order for him to be able to accept it—or before he escapes from it and in order for him to be able to escape from it—there is always a period of soul-searching and revolt. The rebel is a man who is on the point of accepting or rejecting the sacrosanct and determined on creating a human situa-

tion where all the answers are human or, rather, formulated in terms of reason. From this moment every question, every word, is an act of rebellion, while in the sacrosanct world every word is an act of grace. It would be possible to demonstrate in this manner that only two possible worlds can exist for the human mind, the sacrosanct (or, to speak in Christian terms, the world of Grace)[1] or the rebel world. The disappearance of the one is equivalent to the appearance of the other, and this appearance can take place in disconcerting forms. There again we find the attitude of *All or Nothing*. The pressing aspect of the problem of rebellion depends only on the fact that nowadays whole societies have wanted to re-examine their position in regard to the sacrosanct. We live in an unsacrosanct period. Insurrection is certainly not the sum-total of human experience. But the controversial aspect of contemporary history compels us to say that rebellion is one of man's essential dimensions. It is our historical reality. Unless we ignore reality, we must find out values in it. Is it possible to find a rule of conduct outside the realm of religion and of absolute values? That is the question raised by revolt.

15   We have already noted the confused standard of values that are called into play by incipient revolt. Now we must inquire if these values are to be found in contemporary forms of rebellious thought and action and, if they do exist, we must specify their content. But, before going any farther, let us note that the basis of these values is rebellion itself. Man's solidarity is founded upon rebellion, and rebellion can only be justified by this solidarity. We then have authority to say that any type of rebellion which claims the right to deny or destroy this solidarity simultaneously loses the right to be called rebellion and actually becomes an accomplice to murder. In the same way, this solidarity, except in so far as religion is concerned, only comes to life on the level of rebellion. And so the real drama of revolutionary thought is revealed. In order to exist, man must rebel, but rebellion must respect the limits that it discovers in itself—limits where minds meet, and in meeting, begin to exist. Revolutionary thought, therefore, cannot dispense with memory: it is in a perpetual state of tension. In contemplating the results of an act of rebellion, we shall have to say, each time, whether it remains faithful to its first noble promise or whether, through lassitude or folly, it forgets its purpose and plunges into a mire of tyranny or servitude.

16   Meanwhile, we can sum up the initial progress that the spirit of rebellion accomplishes in a process of thought that is already convinced of the absurdity and apparent sterility of the world. In absurdist experience suffering is individual. But from the moment that a movement of rebellion begins, suffering is seen as a collective experience— as the experience of everyone. Therefore the first step for a mind overwhelmed by the strangeness of things is to realize that this feeling of strangeness is shared with all men and that the entire human race

---

[1] There is, of course, an act of metaphysical rebellion at the beginning of Christianity, but the resurrection of Christ and the annunciation of the Kingdom of Heaven interpreted as a promise of eternal life are the answers that render it futile.

suffers from the division between itself and the rest of the world. The unhappiness experienced by a single man becomes collective unhappiness. In our daily trials, rebellion plays the same role as does the "cogito" in the category of thought: it is the first clue. But this clue lures the individual from his solitude. Rebellion is the common ground on which every man bases his first values. I *rebel*—therefore we *exist*.

Discussion of Theme

1. Could Camus's observations in paragraph 4 apply to blacks in contemporary society?
2. Camus says that "reasons for rebellion seem to change with the times." Are there, nevertheless, basic principles underlying rebellion through the ages?
3. Do you derive comfort from Camus's theory that suffering is not solitary but is experienced in common with the entire human race?
4. Do you agree with the last sentence in paragraph 12? Explain.
5. Is it accurate to say that the rebel is actually asserting himself on behalf of all men?

Discussion of Rhetoric

1. How appropriate is Scheler's analogy, paragraph 9?
2. Would Camus's references to Scheler be more meaningful if he identified the man?
3. Is Camus's approach primarily objective or subjective? Support your view with evidence from the selection.
4. Is this piece a definition, or does it attempt to be persuasive as well?

Writing Assignments

1. What have you submitted to that you considered unjust? Do you intend to go on doing so?
2. Analyze the statement, "I rebel—therefore we exist."
3. Describe an act of rebellion in your life that you feel was necessary.

Library Exploration

1. Report on the work of Scheler, who is mentioned several times in this selection.
2. Report on one of Camus's novels.

Vocabulary

(2) INFRINGES   trespasses on; violates

(2) CATEGORICALLY   absolutely; positively

(3) REVULSION   strong aversion

(3) ETYMOLOGICAL   pertaining to the evolution of words

(3) TACITLY   implicitly, that is, implied but not actually spoken or expressed

(4) INSURRECTION   uprising; rebellion

(4) RETROACTIVE   affecting previous events

(4) ANTAGONIST   opponent; adversary

(6) POSTULATES   basic principles; axioms

(7) EGOISTIC   affecting only oneself

(7) IMPETUS   driving force; impulse

(8) SUBTERFUGE   evasion; deception

(8) CONTRIVES   manages

(8) REPUGNANT   revolting; nauseating

(8) METAPHYSICAL   beyond the physical

(9) UNSCRUPULOUS   without principles

(11) MISANTHROPY   dislike of people

(11) REDUNDANT   unnecessarily repetitious

(11) COMPLICITY   partnership or involvement in wrong-doing or evil

(12) ENVISAGED   visualized; seen

(13) PARIAH   member of the lowest caste in India; outcast

(13) CONDOTTIERE   mercenary; hired soldier

(14) SACROSANCT   sacred; untouchable

(15) INCIPIENT   just beginning

(15) LASSITUDE   lethargy; torpor

(15) MIRE   swamp; thick mud

Gordon E. Bigelow (1919–)
received his Ph.D. from Johns
Hopkins University and has
been a professor of English at
the University of Kentucky and
the University of Florida. He is
the coauthor of "The U.S.A.:
Readings in English as a Second Language" (1960) and contributes articles to scholarly
journals including "College English," from which the following
is taken.

In defining six general characteristics of existentialism, Bigelow discusses the similarities
between the "godly" and "ungodly" existentialists.

GORDON E. BIGELOW

A Primer of Existentialism

1 For some years I fought the word by irritably looking the other way
whenever I stumbled across it, hoping that like dadaism and some of
the other "isms" of the French *avant garde* it would go away if I
ignored it. But existentialism was apparently more than the picture it
evoked of uncombed beards, smoky basement cafes, and French
beatniks regaling one another between sips of absinthe with brilliant
variations on the theme of despair. It turned out to be of major importance to literature and the arts, to philosophy and theology, and of increasing importance to the social sciences. To learn more about it, I
read several of the self-styled introductions to the subject, with the
baffled sensation of a man who reads a critical introduction to a novel
only to find that he must read the novel before he can understand the
introduction. Therefore, I should like to provide here something most
discussions of existentialism take for granted, a simple statement of
its basic characteristics. This is a reckless thing to do because there are
several kinds of existentialism and what one says of one kind may not
be true of another, but there is an area of agreement, and it is this common ground that I should like to set forth here. We should not run into

trouble so long as we understand from the outset that the six major themes outlined below will apply in varying degrees to particular existentialists. A reader should be able to go from here to the existentialists themselves, to the more specialized critiques of them, or be able to recognize an existentialist theme or coloration in literature when he sees it.

2   A word first about the kinds of existentialism. Like transcendentalism of the last century, there are almost as many varieties of this *ism* as there are individual writers to whom the word is applied (not all of them claim it). But without being facetious we might group them into two main kinds, the *ungodly* and the *godly*. To take the ungodly or atheistic first, we would list as the chief spokesmen among many others Jean-Paul Sartre, Albert Camus, and Simone de Beauvoir. Several of this important group of French writers had rigorous and significant experience in the Resistance during the Nazi occupation of France in World War II. Out of the despair which came with the collapse of their nation during those terrible years they found unexpected strength in the single indomitable human spirit, which even under severe torture could maintain the spirit of resistance, the unextinguishable ability to say "No." From the irreducible core in the human spirit, they erected after the war a philosophy which was a twentieth-century variation of the philosophy of Descartes. But instead of saying "I think, therefore I am," they said "I can say No, therefore I exist." As we shall presently see, the use of the word "exist" is of prime significance. This group is chiefly responsible for giving existentialism its status in the popular mind as a literary-philosophical cult.

3   Of the godly or theistic existentialists we should mention first a mid-nineteenth-century Danish writer, Soren Kierkegaard; two contemporary French Roman Catholics, Gabriel Marcel and Jacques Maritain; two Protestant theologians, Paul Tillich and Nicholas Berdyaev; and Martin Buber, an important contemporary Jewish theologian. Taken together, their writings constitute one of the most significant developments in modern theology. Behind both groups of existentialists stand other important figures, chiefly philosophers, who exert powerful influence upon the movement — Blaise Pascal, Friedrich Nietzsche, Henri Bergson, Martin Heidegger, Karl Jaspers, among others. Several literary figures, notably Tolstoy and Dostoievski, are frequently cited because existentialist attitudes and themes are prominent in their writings. The electic nature of this movement should already be sufficiently clear and the danger of applying too rigidly to any particular figure the general characteristics of the movement which I now make bold to describe:

4   1. EXISTENCE BEFORE ESSENCE. Existentialism gets its name from an insistence that human life is understandable only in terms of an individual man's existence, his particular experience of life. It says that a man *lives* (has existence) rather than *is* (has being or essence), and that every man's experience of life is unique, radically different from everyone else's and can be understood truly only in terms of his involvement in life or commitment to it. It strenuously shuns that view which assumes an ideal of Man or Mankind, a universal of human nature of which each man is only one example. It eschews the question

of Greek philosophy, *"What is mankind?"* which suggests that man can be defined if he is ranged in his proper place in the order of nature; it asks instead the question of Job and St. Augustine, *"Who am I?"* with its suggestion of the uniqueness and mystery of each human life and its emphasis upon the subjective or personal rather than the objective or impersonal. From the outside a man appears to be just another natural creature; from the inside he is an entire universe, the center of infinity. The existentialist insists upon this latter radically subjective view, and from this grows much of the rest of existentialism.

5   2. REASON IS IMPOTENT TO DEAL WITH THE DEPTHS OF HUMAN LIFE. There are two parts to this proposition — first, that human reason is relatively weak and imperfect, and second, that there are dark places in human life which are "nonreason" and to which reason scarcely penetrates. Since Plato, Western civilization has usually assumed a separation of reason from the rest of the human psyche, and has glorified reason as suited to command the nonrational part. The classic statement of this separation appears in the *Phaedrus,* where Plato describes the psyche in the myth of the chariot which is drawn by the white steeds of the emotions and the black unruly steeds of the appetites. The driver of the chariot is Reason who holds the reins which control the horses and the whip to subdue the surging black steeds of passion. Only the driver, the rational nature, is given human form; the rest of the psyche, the nonrational part, is given a lower, animal form. This separation and exaltation of reason is carried further in the allegory of the cave in *The Republic.* You recall the sombre picture of human life with which the story begins: men are chained in the dark in a cave, with their backs to a flickering firelight, able to see only uncertain shadows moving on the wall before them, able to hear only confused echoes of sounds. One of the men, breaking free from his chains, is able to turn and look upon the objects themselves and the light which casts the shadows; even, at last, he is able to work his way entirely out of the cave into the sunlight beyond. All this he is able to do through his reason; he escapes from the bondage of error, from time and change, from death itself, into the realm of changeless eternal ideas or Truth, and the lower nature which had chained him in darkness is left behind.

6   Existentialism in our time, and this is one of its most important characteristics, insists upon reuniting the "lower" or irrational parts of the psyche with the "higher." It insists that man must be taken in his wholeness and not in some divided state, that whole man contains not only intellect but also anxiety, guilt, and the will to power — which modify and sometimes overwhelm the reason. A man seen in this light is fundamentally ambiguous, if not mysterious, full of contradictions and tensions which cannot be dissolved simply by taking thought. "Human life," said Berdyaev, "is permeated by underground streams." One is reminded of D. H. Lawrence's outburst against Franklin and his rational attempt to achieve moral perfection: "The Perfectability of Man! . . . The perfectability of which man? I am many men. Which of them are you going to perfect? I am not a mechanical contrivance. . . . It's a queer thing is a man's soul. It is the whole of him. Which means it is the unknown as well as the known. . . . The soul

of man is a dark vast forest, with wild life in it." The emphasis in existentialism is not on idea but upon the thinker who has the idea. It accepts not only his power of thought, but his contingency and fallibility, his frailty, his body, blood, and bones, and above all his death. Kierkegaard emphasized the distinction between *subjective* truth (what a person *is*) and *objective* truth (what the person *knows*), and said that we encounter the true self not in the detachment of thought but in the involvement and agony of choice and in the pathos of commitment to our choice. This distrust of rational systems helps to explain why many existential writers in their own expression are paradoxical or prophetic or gnomic, why their works often belong more to literature than to philosophy.

7   3. ALIENATION OR ESTRANGEMENT. One major result of the dissociation of reason from the rest of the psyche has been the growth of science, which has become one of the hallmarks of Western civilization, and an ever-increasing rational ordering of men in society. As the existentialists view them, the main forces of history since the Renaissance have progressively separated man from concrete earthy existence, have forced him to live at ever higher levels of abstraction, have collectivized individual man out of existence, have driven God from the heavens, or what is the same thing, from the hearts of men. They are convinced that modern man lives in a four-fold condition of alienation: from God, from nature, from other men, from his own true self.

8   The estrangement from God is most shockingly expressed by Nietzsche's anguished cry, "God is dead," a cry which has continuously echoed through the writings of the existentialists, particularly the French. This theme of spiritual barrenness is a commonplace in literature of this century, from Eliot's "Hollow Man" to the novels of Dos Passos, Hemingway, and Faulkner. It often appears in writers not commonly associated with the existentialists as in this remarkable passage from *A Story-Teller's Story,* where Sherwood Anderson describes his own awakening to his spiritual emptiness. He tells of walking alone late at night along a moonlit road when,

> I had suddenly an odd, and to my own seeming, a ridiculous desire to abase myself before something not human and so stepping into the moonlit road, I knelt in the dust. Having no God, the gods having been taken from me by the life about me, as a personal God has been taken from all modern men by a force within that man himself does not understand but that is called the intellect, I kept smiling at the figure I cut in my own eyes as I knelt in the road. . . .
> There was no God in the sky, no God in myself, no conviction in myself that I had the power to believe in a God, and so I merely knelt in the dust in silence and no words came to my lips.

In another passage Anderson wondered if the giving of itself by an entire generation to mechanical things was not really making all men impotent, if the desire for a greater navy, a greater army, taller public buildings, was not a sign of growing impotence. He felt that Puritanism and the industrialism which was its offspring had sterilized modern life, and proposed that men return to a healthful animal vigor by renewed contact with simple things of the earth, among them untrammeled sexual expression. One is reminded of the unkempt and delectable raffishness of Steinbeck's *Cannery Row* or of D. H. Lawrence's quasi-religious doctrine of sex, "blood-consciousness" and the "divine otherness" of animal existence.

9   Man's estrangement from nature has been a major theme in literature at least since Rousseau and the Romantic movement, and can hardly be said to be the property of existentialists. But this group nevertheless adds its own insistence that one of modern man's most urgent dangers is that he builds ever higher the brick and steel walls of technology which shut him away from a health-giving life according to "nature." Their treatment of this theme is most commonly expressed as part of a broader insistence that modern man needs to shun abstraction and return to "concreteness" or "wholeness."

10   A third estrangement has occurred at the social level and its sign is a growing dismay at man's helplessness before the great machine-like colossus of industrialized society. This is another major theme of Western literature, and here again, though they hardly discovered the danger or began the protest, the existentialists in our time renew the protest against any pattern or force which would stifle the unique and spontaneous in individual life. The crowding of men into cities, the subdivision of labor which submerges the man in his economic function, the burgeoning of centralized government, the growth of advertising, propaganda, and mass media of entertainment and communication—all the things which force men into Riesman's "Lonely Crowd"—these same things drive men asunder by destroying their individuality and making them live on the surface of life, content to deal with things rather than people. "Exteriorization," says Berdyaev, "is the source of slavery, whereas freedom is interiorization. Slavery always indicates alienation, the ejection of human nature into the external." This kind of alienation is exemplified by Zero, in Elmer Rice's play "The Adding Machine." Zero's twenty-five years as a bookkeeper in a department store have dried up his humanity, making him incapable of love, of friendship, of any deeply felt, freely expressed emotion. Such estrangement is often given as the reason for man's inhumanity to man, the explanation for injustice in modern society. In Camus' short novel, aptly called *The Stranger,* a young man is convicted by a court of murder. This is a homicide which he has actually committed under extenuating circumstances. But the court never listens to any of the relevant evidence, seems never to hear anything that pertains to the crime itself; it convicts the young man on wholly irrelevant grounds—because he had behaved in an unconventional way at his mother's funeral the day before the homicide. In this book one feels the same dream-like distortion of reality as in the trial scene in *Alice in Wonderland*, a suffocating sense of being enclosed by events which are irrational or absurd but also inexorable. Most disturbing of all is the young man's aloneness, the impermeable membrane of estrangement which surrounds him and prevents anyone else from penetrating to his experience of life or sympathizing with it.

11   The fourth kind of alienation, man's estrangement from his own true self, especially as his nature is distorted by an exaltation of reason, is another theme having an extensive history as a major part of the Romantic revolt. Of the many writers who treat the theme, Hawthorne

comes particularly close to the emphasis of contemporary existentialists. His Ethan Brand, Dr. Rappaccini, and Roger Chillingworth are
a recurrent figure who represents the dislocation in human nature
which results when an overdeveloped or misapplied intellect severs
"the magnetic chain of human sympathy." Hawthorne is thoroughly
existential in his concern for the sanctity of the individual human soul,
as well as in his preoccupation with sin and the dark side of human
nature, which must be seen in part as his attempt to build back some
fullness to the flattened image of man bequeathed to him by the Enlightenment. Whitman was trying to do this when he added flesh and
bone and a sexual nature to the spiritualized image of man he inherited from Emerson, though his image remains diffused and attenuated by the same cosmic optimism. Many of the nineteenth-century
depictions of man represent him as a figure of power or of potential
power, sometimes as daimonic, like Melville's Ahab, but after World
War I the power is gone; man is not merely distorted or truncated, he
is hollow, powerless, faceless. At the time when his command over
natural forces seems to be unlimited, man is pictured as weak, ridden
with nameless dread. This brings us to another of the major themes of
existentialism.

12   4. "FEAR AND TREMBLING," ANXIETY. At Stockholm when he accepted the Nobel Prize, William Faulkner said that "Our tragedy
today is a general and universal physical fear so long sustained by now
that we can even bear it. There are no longer problems of the spirit.
There is only one question: When will I be blown up?" The optimistic
vision of the Enlightenment which saw man, through reason and its
extensions in science, conquering all nature and solving all social and
political problems in a continuous upward spiral of Progress, cracked
open like a melon on the rock of World War I. The theories which held
such high hopes died in that sickening and unimaginable butchery.
Here was a concrete fact of human nature and society which the
theories could not contain. The Great Depression and World War II
deepened the sense of dismay which the loss of these ideals brought,
but only with the atomic bomb did this become an unbearable terror,
a threat of instant annihilation which confronted all men, even those
most insulated by the thick crust of material goods and services. Now
the most unthinking person could sense that each advance in mechanical technique carried not only a chromium and plush promise of comfort but a threat as well.

13   Sartre, following Kierkegaard, speaks of another kind of anxiety
which oppresses modern man—"the anguish of Abraham"—the
necessity which is laid upon him to make moral choices on his own
responsibility. A military officer in wartime knows the agony of choice
which forces him to sacrifice part of his army to preserve the rest, as
does a man in high political office, who must make decisions affecting
the lives of millions. The existentialists claim that each of us must
make moral decisions in our own lives which involve the same anguish.
Kierkegaard finds that this necessity is one thing which makes each
life unique, which makes it impossible to speculate or generalize about
human life, because each man's case is irretrievably his own, something in which he is personally and passionately involved. His book

Fear and Trembling is an elaborate and fascinating commentary on the Old Testament story of Abraham, who was commanded by God to sacrifice his beloved son Isaac. Abraham thus becomes the emblem of man who must make a harrowing choice, in this case between love for his son and love for God, between the universal moral law which says categorically, "thou shalt not kill," and the unique inner demand of his religious faith. Abraham's decision, which is to violate the abstract and collective moral law, has to be made not in arrogance but in fear and trembling, one of the inferences being that sometimes one must make an exception to the general law because he is (existentially) an exception, a concrete being whose existence can never be completely subsumed under any universal.

14   5. THE ENCOUNTER WITH NOTHINGNESS. For the man alienated from God, from nature, from his fellow man and from himself, what is left at last but Nothingness? The testimony of the existentialists is that this is where modern man now finds himself, not on the highway of upward Progress toward a radiant Utopia but on the brink of a catastrophic precipice, below which yawns the absolute void, an uncompromised black Nothingness. In one sense this is Eliot's Wasteland inhabited by his Hollow Man, who is

> Shape without form, shade without color
> Paralyzed force, gesture without motion.

This is what moves E. A. Robinson's Richard Cory, the man who is everything that might make us wish that we were in his place, to go home one calm summer night and put a bullet through his head.

15   One of the most convincing statements of the encounter with Nothingness is made by Leo Tolstoy in "My Confession." He tells how in good health, in the prime of life, when he had everything that a man could desire — wealth, fame, aristocratic social position, a beautiful wife and children, a brilliant mind and great artistic talent in the height of their powers — he nevertheless was seized with a growing uneasiness, a nameless discontent which he could not shake or alleviate. His experience was like that of a man who falls sick, with symptoms which he disregards as insignificant; but the symptoms return again and again until they merge into a continuous suffering. And the patient suddenly is confronted with the overwhelming fact that what he took for mere indisposition is more important to him than anything else on earth, that it is death! "I felt the ground on which I stood was crumbling, that there was nothing for me to stand on, that what I had been living for was nothing, that I had no reason for living. . . . To stop was impossible, to go back was impossible; and it was impossible to shut my eyes so as to see that there was nothing before me but suffering and actual death, absolute annihilation." This is the "Sickness Unto Death" of Kierkegaard, the despair in which one wishes to die but cannot. Hemingway's short story, "A Clean, Well-Lighted Place," gives an unforgettable expression of this theme. At the end of the story, the old waiter climbs into bed late at night saying to himself, "What did he fear? It was not fear or dread. It was nothing which he knew too well. It was all a nothing and a man was nothing too. . . . Nada y pues nada, y nada y pues nada." And then because he has

experienced the death of God he goes on to recite the Lord's Prayer in blasphemous despair: "Our Nothing who are in Nothing, nothing be thy nothing. . . ." This is stark, even for Hemingway, but the old waiter does no more than name the void felt by most people in the early Hemingway novels, a hunger they seek to assuage with alcohol, sex, and violence in an aimless progress from bar to bed to bull-ring. It goes without saying that much of the despair and pessimism in other contemporary authors springs from a similar sense of the void in modern life.

16   6. FREEDOM. Sooner or later, as a theme that includes all the others, the existentialist writings bear upon freedom. The themes we have outlined above describe either some loss of man's freedom or some threat to it, and all existentialists of whatever sort are concerned to enlarge the range of human freedom.

17   For the avowed atheists like Sartre freedom means human autonomy. In a purposeless universe man is *condemned* to freedom because he is the only creature who is "self-surpassing," who can become something other than he is. Precisely because there is no God to give purpose to the universe, each man must accept individual responsibility for his own becoming, a burden made heavier by the fact that in choosing for himself he chooses for all men "the image of man as he ought to be." A man *is* the sum total of the acts that make up his life — no more, no less — and though the coward has made himself cowardly, it is always possible for him to change and make himself heroic. In Sartre's novel, *The Age of Reason,* one of the least likable of the characters, almost overwhelmed by despair and self-disgust at his homosexual tendencies, is on the point of solving his problem by mutilating himself with a razor, when in an effort of will he throws the instrument down, and we are given to understand that from this moment he will have mastery over his aberrant drive. Thus in the daily course of ordinary life must men shape their becoming in Sartre's world.

18   The religious existentialists interpret man's freedom differently. They use much the same language as Sartre, develop the same themes concerning the predicament of man, but always include God as a radical factor. They stress the man of faith rather than the man of will. They interpret man's existential condition as a state of alienation from his essential nature which is God-like, the problem of his life being to heal the chasm between the two, that is, to find salvation. The mystery and ambiguity of man's existence they attribute to his being the intersection of two realms. "Man bears within himself," writes Berdyaev, "the image which is both the image of man and the image of God, and is the image of man as far as the image of God is actualized." Tillich describes salvation as "the act in which the cleavage between the essential being and the existential situation is overcome." Freedom here, as for Sartre, involves an acceptance of responsibility for choice and a *commitment* to one's choice. This is the meaning of faith, a faith like Abraham's, the commitment which is an agonizing sacrifice of one's own desire and will and dearest treasure to God's will.

19   A final word. Just as one should not expect to find in a particular writer all of the characteristics of existentialism as we have described

them, he should also be aware that some of the most striking expressions of existentialism in literature and the arts come to us by indirection, often through symbols or through innovations in conventional form. Take the preoccupation of contemporary writers with time. In *The Sound and the Fury,* Faulkner both collapses and expands normal clock time, or by juxtapositions of past and present blurs time into a single amorphous pool. He does this by using various forms of "stream of consciousness" or other techniques which see life in terms of unique, subjective experience—that is, existentially. The conventional view of externalized life, a rational orderly progression cut into uniform segments by the hands of a clock, he rejects in favor of a view which sees life as opaque, ambiguous, and irrational—that is, as the existentialist sees it. Graham Greene does something like this in *The Power and the Glory.* He creates a scene isolated in time and cut off from the rest of the world, steamy and suffocating as if a bell jar had been placed over it. Through this atmosphere fetid with impending death and human suffering, stumbles the whiskey priest, lonely and confused, pursued by a police lieutenant who has experienced the void and death of God.

20   Such expressions in literature do not mean necessarily that the authors are conscious existentialist theorizers, or even that they know the writings of such theorizers. Faulkner may never have read Heidegger—or St. Augustine—both of whom attempt to demonstrate that time is more within a man and subject to his unique experience of it than it is outside him. But it is legitimate to call Faulkner's views of time and life "existential" in this novel because in recent years existentialist theorizers have given such views a local habitation and a name. One of the attractions, and one of the dangers, of existential themes is that they become like Sir Thomas Browne's quincunx: once one begins to look for them, he sees them everywhere. But if one applies restraint and discrimination, he will find that they illuminate much of contemporary literature and sometimes the literature of the past as well.

Discussion of Theme

1. Can a concept like existentialism be adequately defined?
2. Do you believe that each man's life is unique?
3. Do you view man as alienated from his fellows?
4. Is modern man more beset by anxiety and anguish than nineteenth-century man? How is the analogy concerning the anguish of Abraham meaningful to us?

Discussion of Rhetoric

1. What does Bigelow state as his purpose for writing the article? Has he succeeded?
2. Bigelow is apparently not an existentialist. What tone does he adopt toward the philosophy? How does he achieve it?

3. Find the thesis in paragraph 1 and show how it is developed throughout the selection.
4. Of what value are the numbered subheadings in this essay?

Writing Assignments

1. If you disagree that "reason is impotent to deal with the depths of human life," present an argument to refute this position.
2. In recent years the statement "I don't (or didn't) want to get involved" has been offered as a reason for standing by and allowing unjust acts — sometimes even murder — to be committed. Does man have a moral obligation to the rest of humanity? What are the results of people's failure to become involved? Discuss this in terms of one social issue or several.
3. Interpret the existentialist belief that a man creates himself by taking action.

Library Exploration

1. *The Existential Imagination,* edited by Frederick R. Karl and Leo Hamalian, is an anthology of stories and selections (from Shakespeare to Beckett) that exemplifies and illustrates existentialism in literature.
2. *Waiting for Godot*, by Samuel Beckett, is the classic existentialist drama.
3. Jean-Paul Sartre's *The Flies* is an existentialist version of the Oresteian story.
4. Report on one of the following: Jean-Paul Sartre, Albert Camus, Paul Tillich, or Soren Kierkegaard. Pay particular attention to the factors that contributed to his becoming an existentialist.

Vocabulary

(1) AVANT GARDE   the few who lead
(2) FACETIOUS   jocular; flippant
(2) INDOMITABLE   unconquerable
(3) ECLECTIC   composed of elements drawn from many sources
(6) AMBIGUOUS   of doubtful or uncertain nature
(6) CONTINGENCY   dependence on something else
(6) FALLIBILITY   tendency to err

(6) PATHOS   sadness; sorrow
(6) PARADOXICAL   apparently contradictory
(6) GNOMIC   characterized by short pithy statements of general truth
(8) IMPOTENT   lacking in power, strength, or vigor
(8) UNTRAMMELED   unhindered; free
(8) DELECTABLE   delightful; tasty
(10) BURGEONING   rapid growth
(10) INEXORABLE   unalterable

(10) IMPERMEABLE   impenetrable; not permitting passage
(11) RECURRENT   returning again and again
(11) ATTENUATED   weakened; lessened
(11) DAIMONIC   driven by an inner spirit; possessed
(11) TRUNCATED   cut down in size
(13) IRRETRIEVABLY   beyond recall
(13) SUBSUMED   classified within a larger category
(14) PRECIPICE   steep cliff; crag
(15) ALLEVIATE   relieve; lighten
(17) ABERRANT   abnormal
(19) AMORPHOUS   shapeless; vague
(19) FETID   stinking
(20) QUINCUNX   arrangement in a square of five objects, one at each corner and one in the middle

Plato (428–348), Socrates's most famous pupil, founded a philosophical school, the Academy, in 387 B.C. in Athens, where he lectured and wrote. He is considered by many the most important Western philosopher. Among his significant works are "The Republic," "Symposium," and "Timaeus."

This is a concise statement of Plato's unending argument for the triumph of reason over doubt and ignorance.

PLATO

The Allegory of the Cave

1 And now, I said, let me show in a figure how far our nature is enlightened or unenlightened: Behold! human beings living in an underground den, which has a mouth open toward the light and reaching all along the den; here they have been from their childhood, and have their legs and necks chained so that they cannot move, and can only see before them, being prevented by the chains from turning around their heads. Above and behind them a fire is blazing at a distance; and between the fire and the prisoners there is a raised way; and you will see, if you look, a low wall built along the way, like a screen which marionette players have in front of them, over which they show the puppets.

2 I see.

3 And do you see, I said, men passing along the wall carrying all sorts of vessels, and statues and figures of animals made of wood and stone and various materials, which appear over the wall? Some of them are talking, others silent.

4 You have shown me a strange image, and they are strange prisoners.

5 Like ourselves, I replied; and they see only their own shadows, or the shadows of one another, which the fire throws on the opposite wall of the cave?

6 True, he said; how could they see anything but the shadows if they were never allowed to move their heads?

7   And of the objects which are being carried in like manner they would only see the shadows?

8   Yes, he said.

9   And if they were able to converse with one another, would they not suppose that they were naming what was actually before them?[1]

10   Very true.

11   And suppose further that the prison had an echo which came from the other side, would they not be sure to fancy when one of the passers-by spoke that the voice which they heard came from the passing shadow?

12   No question, he replied.

13   To them, I said, the truth would be literally nothing but the shadows of the images.

14   That is certain.

15   And now look again, and see what will naturally follow if the prisoners are released and disabused of their error. At first, when any of them is liberated and compelled suddenly to stand up and turn his neck round and walk and look toward the light, he will suffer sharp pains; the glare will distress him, and he will be unable to see the realities of which in his former state he had seen the shadows; and then conceive some one saying to him, that what he saw before was an illusion, but that now, when he is approaching nearer to being and his eye is turned toward more real existence, he has a clearer vision—what will be his reply? And you may further imagine that his instructor is pointing to the objects as they pass and requiring him to name them—will he not be perplexed? Will he not fancy that the shadows which he formerly saw are truer than the objects which are now shown to him?

16   Far truer.

17   And if he is compelled to look straight at the light, will he not have a pain in his eyes which will make him turn away to take refuge in the objects of vision which he can see, and which he will conceive to be in reality clearer than the things which are now being shown to him?

18   True, he said.

19   And suppose once more, that he is reluctantly dragged up a steep and rugged ascent, and held fast until he is forced into the presence of the sun himself, is he not likely to be pained and irritated? When he approaches the light his eyes will be dazzled, and he will not be able to see anything at all of what are now called realities.

20   Not all in a moment, he said.

21   He will require to grow accustomed to the sight of the upper world. And first he will see the shadows best, next the reflections of men and other objects in the water, and then the objects themselves; then he will gaze upon the light of the moon and the stars and the spangled heaven; and he will see the sky and the stars by night better than the sun or the light of the sun by day?

22   Certainly.

_____

[1] The text is uncertain. Probably the meaning is that in naming the shadows before them the prisoners suppose they see the real things.

23   Last of all he will be able to see the sun, and not mere reflections of him in the water, but he will see him in his own proper place, and not in another; and he will contemplate him as he is.

24   Certainly.

25   He will then proceed to argue that this is he who gives the season and the years, and is the guardian of all that is in the visible world, and in a certain way the cause of all things which he and his fellows have been accustomed to behold?

26   Clearly, he said, he would first see the sun and then reason about him.

27   And when he remembered his old habitation, and the wisdom of the den and his fellow-prisoners, do you not suppose that he would felicitate himself on the change, and pity them?

28   Certainly, he would.

29   And if they were in the habit of conferring honours among themselves on those who were the quickest to observe the passing shadows and to remark which of them went before, and which followed after, and which were together; and who were therefore best able to draw conclusions as to the future, do you think that he would care for such honours and glories, or envy the possessors of them? Would he not say with Homer,

> Better to be the poor servant of a poor master,

and to endure anything, rather than think as they do and live after their manner?

30   Yes, he said, I think that he would rather suffer anything than entertain these false notions and live in this miserable manner.

31   Imagine once more, I said, such a one coming suddenly out of the sun to be replaced in his old situation; would he not be certain to have his eyes full of darkness?

32   To be sure, he said.

33   And if there were a contest, and he had to compete in measuring the shadows with the prisoners who had never moved out of the den, while his sight was still weak, and before his eyes had become steady (and the time which would be needed to acquire this new habit of sight might be very considerable), would he not be ridiculous? Men would say of him that up he went and down he came without his eyes; and that it was better not even to think of ascending; and if any one tried to loose another and lead him up to the light, let them only catch the offender, and they would put him to death.

34   No question, he said.

35   This entire allegory, I said, you may now append, dear Glaucon, to the previous argument; the prison-house is the world of sight, the light of the fire is the sun, and you will not misapprehend me if you interpret the journey upward to be the ascent of the soul into the intellectual world according to my poor belief, which at your desire, I have expressed — whether rightly or wrongly God knows. But, whether true or false, my opinion is that in the world of knowledge the idea of good appears last of all, and is seen only with effort; and, when seen, is also inferred to be the universal author of all things beautiful and right,

parent of light and of the lord of light in this visible world, and the immediate source of reason and truth in the intellectual; and that this is the power upon which he who would act rationally either in public or private life must have his eye fixed.

Discussion of Theme

1. What is meant by "the truth shall make you free"? Do you believe this?
2. Plato says that "he who would act rationally either in public or private life" must be truthful. By Plato's standard, do many of our public personages act rationally? Have standards of rational behavior changed through the years?
3. Why is the concept of truth so difficult to grasp? Why do men in all stations of life attempt to define it?
4. In what areas of his existence is man still in a cave?
5. Explain the allegory of the cave in your own words.

Discussion of Rhetoric

1. Does an allegory actually make it easier or more difficult to grasp an abstraction?
2. Would you understand the allegory without paragraph 35?
3. Plato is painstaking in his development of the allegory. Is this necessary? Would it have been improved if he had condensed it somewhat?
4. What are the strengths and weaknesses of allegory, particularly this one?
5. Glaucon doesn't contribute much. Would straight exposition have been more effective here than dialogue form?

Writing Assignments

1. Plato's allegory suggests the brainwashing of political prisoners. How is brainwashing accomplished? Do societies, in effect, brainwash their citizens? To what extent and by what means?
2. Write an allegory dramatizing a specific condition of man—for example, his anxiety or his humility.
3. Analyze the appeal of Plato to modern thinkers.
4. Suggest what you think Plato would have us stress in our colleges today.
5. Write an imaginary Platonic dialogue in which you deal with one of the following topics—love and marriage, war, friendship, the good life.

Library Exploration

1. You might be interested in Plato's most famous pupil, Aristotle, who differed with Plato in many significant respects.
2. Investigate the use of the dialogue and the criticisms of this form of dialect.

Vocabulary

(1) MARIONETTE   puppet
(15) DISABUSED   set free from error or mistakes in reasoning

(27) FELICITATE   congratulate

Rufus M. Jones (1863–1948)
was a professor of philosophy
at Haverford College for thirty
years. He was born in Maine and
educated at Haverford, the University of Heidelberg, and Harvard. He wrote voluminously on
the Quakers and their religion.
Among his works are "Practical
Christianity" (1899), "A Service
of Love in Wartime" (1920), and
"A Call to What Is Vital" (1948).

As nearly as words can convey
it, this is a description of what a
mystical experience accomplishes.

RUFUS M. JONES

The Mystic's Experience of God

1 According to those who have been there, the experience that we call
mystical is charged with the conviction of real, direct contact and commerce with God. It is the almost universal testimony of those who are
mystics that they find God through their experience. John Tauler says
that in his best moments of "devout prayer and the uplifting of the
mind to God," he experiences "the pure presence of God" in his own
soul; but he adds that all he can tell others about the experience is "as
poor and unlike it as the point of a needle is to the heavens above us."

2 There are many different degrees of intensity, concentration, and
conviction in the experiences of different individual mystics, and also
in the various experiences of the same individual from time to time.
There has been a tendency in most studies of mysticism to regard the
state of ecstasy as *par excellence* mystical experience. That is, however, a grave mistake. The calmer, more meditative, less emotional,
less ecstatic experiences of God possess greater constructive value for
life and character than do ecstatic experiences which presuppose a
peculiar psychical frame and disposition. The seasoned Quaker, in the

corporate hush and stillness of a silent meeting, is far removed from ecstasy, but he is not the less convinced that he is meeting with God.

3   The more normal, expansive mystical experiences come apparently when the personal self is at its best. Its power and capacities are raised to an unusual unity and fused together. The whole being, with its ac- cumulated submerged life, *finds itself*. The process of preparing for any high achievement is a severe and laborious one; but nothing seems easier in the moment of success than is the accomplishment for which the life has been prepared. There comes to be formed within the person what Aristotle called "a dexterity of soul," so that the per- son does with ease what he has become skilled to do. A mystic of the fourteenth century stated the principle in these words: "It is my aim to be to the Eternal God what a man's hand is to a man."

4   There are many human experiences which carry a man up to levels where he has not usually been before, and where he finds himself possessed of insight and energies that he had hardly suspected were his until that moment. One leaps to his full height when the right inner spring is reached. We are quite familiar with the way in which instinc- tive tendencies in us, and emotions both egoistic and social, become organized under a group of ideas and ideals into a single system, which we call a sentiment, such as love, or patriotism, or devotion to truth. It forms slowly, and one hardly realizes that it has formed until some occasion unexpectedly brings it into full operation and we find ourselves able with perfect ease to overcome the most powerful in- hibitory and opposing instincts and habits, which until then had us- ually controlled us. Literary and artistic geniuses supply us with many instances in which, in a sudden flash, the crude material at hand is shot through with vision, and the complicated plot of a drama, the full significance of a character, or the complete glory of a statue stands revealed, as if, to use R. L. Stevenson's illustration, a jinni had brought it on a golden tray as a gift from another world. Abraham Lincoln, striking off in a few intense minutes his Gettysburg address, as beau- tiful in style and perfect in form as anything in human literature, is as good an illustration as we need of the way in which a highly organized person, by a kindling flash, has at his hand all the moral and spiritual gains of a lifetime.

5   We come now to the central question of our consideration: Do mystical experiences settle anything? Are they purely subjective and one-sided, or do they prove to have objective reference and so to be two-sided? Do they take the experiment across the chasm that sepa- rates "self" from "other"?

6   The most striking effect of such experience is not new fact-knowl- edge, not new items of empirical information, but new moral energy, heightened conviction, increased caloric quality, enlarged spiritual vision, an unusual radiant power of life. In short, the whole personality, in the case of the constructive mystics, appears to be raised to a new level of life and to have gained from somewhere many calories of life- feeding, spiritual substance, We are quite familiar with the way in which adrenalin suddenly flushes into the physical system and adds a new and incalculable power to brain and muscle. Under its stimulus a man can carry out a piano when the house is on fire. May not, perhaps,

some energy, from some Source with which our spirits are allied, flush our inner being with forces and powers by which we can be fortified to stand the universe and more than stand it?

7   I believe that mystical experiences do, in the long run, expand our knowledge of God, and do succeed in verifying themselves. Mysticism is a sort of spiritual protoplasm which underlies, as a basic substance, much that is best in religion, in ethics, and in life itself. It has generally been the mystic, the prophet, the seer, who have spotted out new ways forward in the jungle of our world or lifted our race to new spiritual levels. Their experiences have in some way equipped them for unusual tasks, have given supplies of energy to them which their neighbors did not have, and have apparently brought them into vital correspondence with dimensions and regions of reality that others miss. The proof that they have found God, or at least a domain of spiritual reality, is to be seen rather in the moral and spiritual fruits which test out and verify the experience.

8   Consciousness of beauty or of truth or of goodness baffles analysis as much as consciousness of God does. These values have no objective standing ground in current psychology. They are not things in the world of space. They submit to no adequate causal explanation. They have their ground of being in some other kind of world than that of the mechanical order, a world composed of quantitative masses of matter in motion. These experiences of value, which are as real for experience as stone walls are, make very clear the fact that there are depths and capacities in the nature of the normal human mind which we do not usually recognize, and of which we have scant and imperfect accounts in our textbooks. Our minds taken in their full range, in other words, have some sort of contact and relationship with an eternal nature of things far deeper than atoms and molecules.

9   Only very slowly and gradually has the race learned, through finite symbols and temporal forms, to interpret beauty and truth and goodness, which, in their essence, are as ineffable and indescribable as is the mystic's experience of God. Plato often speaks as if he had high moments of experience when he rose to the naked vision of beauty — beauty "alone, separate, and eternal," as he says. But, as a matter of fact, however exalted heavenly and enduring beauty may be in its essence, we know *what it is* only as it appears in fair forms of objects, of body, of soul, of actions; in harmonious blending of sounds or colors; in well-ordered or happily combined groupings of many aspects in one unity, which is as it ought to be. Truth and moral goodness always transcend our attainments, and we sometimes feel that the very end and goal of life is the pursuit of that truth or that goodness which eye hath not seen nor ear heard. But whatever truth we do attain, or whatever goodness we do achieve, is always concrete. Truth is just this one more added fact that resists all attempt to doubt it. Goodness is just this simple everyday deed that reveals a heroic spirit and a brave venture of faith in the midst of difficulties.

10   So, too, the mystic knowledge of God is not some esoteric communication, supplied through trance or ecstasy; it is an intuitive personal touch with God, felt to be the essentially real, the bursting forth of an

intense love for Him, which heightens all the capacities and activities of life, followed by the slow laboratory effects which verify it. "All I could never be" now *is*. It seems possible to stand the universe — even to do something toward the transformation of it. And if the experience does not prove that the soul has found God, it at least does this: it makes the soul feel that proofs of God are wholly unnecessary.

Discussion of Theme

1. After reading the essay, are you persuaded that there is a thing such as a mystical experience? Why (not)?
2. Do you think that the "literary and artistic geniuses" referred to in paragraph 4 may have been exaggerating the ease with which "crude material" was transformed? What might have accounted for the supposed transformation?
3. What practical value does the author believe a mystical experience has for an individual?
4. Do you receive the impression that Jones has undergone what he conceives of as a mystical experience? If so, why do you think this?
5. Can one's faith change physical events?
6. How do you regard the claims of users of hallucinatory drugs concerning their mystical experiences?

Discussion of Rhetoric

1. To what extent are Jones's views based on metaphysical claims? Does he use evaluative statements to support his belief?
2. What figurative language is embodied in the final sentence of paragraph 3?
3. The author raises a question in paragraph 6 but does not answer it. V. hy?
4. Would paragraph 7 be stronger if the author had used examples?
5. Note the use of analogy in paragraph 7. Find other examples.

Writing Assignments

1. Agree or disagree with Jones's statement that "It has generally been the mystic, the prophet, the seer, who have spotted out new ways forward in the jungle of our world or lifted our age to new spiritual levels." Illustrate with specific individuals.
2. Explain: "[W]hatever truth we do attain or whatever goodness we do achieve is always concrete."
3. Define *mysticism*.
4. Analyze a personal experience that might be labeled mystical.

Library Exploration

1. For an account of religious mysticism, read the biographies of St. John of the Cross and St. Theresa of Avila.
2. For a modern view of mysticism, read C. S. Lewis and Paul Tillich.

Vocabulary

(2) ECSTASY   rapturous delight

(2) PSYCHICAL   beyond physical knowledge

(3) EXPANSIVE   broad; comprehensive

(4) EGOISTIC   relating to self-interest

(4) INHIBITORY   restraining

(6) INCALCULABLE   immeasurable

(9) INEFFABLE   inexpressible

(9) TRANSCEND   go above and beyond

(10) ESOTERIC   understood only by a chosen few

(10) INTUITIVE   perceived without conscious reasoning

Clive Staples Lewis (1898–1963) was a professor at Oxford, a scholar in medieval and Renaissance English literature, and a writer of novels, religious works, and children's books. "The Screwtape Letters," published in book form in 1942, is one of literature's most famous examples of sustained irony.

Screwtape, Lewis's personification of a devil, writes to his ignorant nephew Wormwood, who is in training to become a devil himself.

C. S. LEWIS

Screwtape Letters 8 and 9

8
My dear Wormwood,

1 So you "have great hopes that the patient's religious phase is dying away," have you? I always thought the Training College had gone to pieces since they put old Slubgob at the head of it, and now I am sure. Has no one ever told you about the law of Undulation?

2 Humans are amphibians — half spirit and half animal. (The Enemy's determination to produce such a revolting hybrid was one of the things that determined Our Father to withdraw his support from Him.) As spirits they belong to the eternal world, but as animals they inhabit time. This means that while their spirit can be directed to an eternal object, their bodies, passions, and imaginations are in continual change, for to be in time means to change. Their nearest approach to constancy, therefore, is undulation — the repeated return to a level from which they repeatedly fall back, a series of troughs and peaks. If you had watched your patient carefully you would have seen this undulation in every department of his life — his interest in his work, his affection for his friends, his physical appetites, all go up and down. As long as he lives on earth periods of emotional and bodily richness and liveliness will alternate with periods of numbness and poverty. The

dryness and dullness through which your patient is now going are not, as you fondly suppose, your workmanship; they are merely a natural phenomenon which will do us no good unless you make a good use of it.

3   To decide what the best use of it is, you must ask what use the Enemy wants to make of it, and then do the opposite. Now it may surprise you to learn that in His efforts to get permanent possession of a soul, He relies on the troughs even more than on the peaks; some of His special favourites have gone through longer and deeper troughs than anyone else. The reason is this. To us a human is primarily food; our aim is the absorption of its will into ours, the increase of our own area of selfhood at its expense. But the obedience which the Enemy demands of men is quite a different thing. One must face the fact that all the talk about His love for men, and His service being perfect freedom, is not (as one would gladly believe) mere propaganda, but an appalling truth. He really *does* want to fill the universe with a lot of loathsome little replicas of Himself — creatures whose life, on its miniature scale, will be qualitatively like His own, not because He has absorbed them but because their wills freely conform to His. We want cattle who can finally become food; He wants servants who can finally become sons. We want to suck in, He wants to give out. We are empty and would be filled; He is full and flows over. Our war aim is a world in which Our Father Below has drawn all other beings into himself: the Enemy wants a world full of beings united to Him but still distinct.

4   And that is where the troughs come in. You must have often wondered why the Enemy does not make more use of His power to be sensibly present to human souls in any degree He chooses and at any moment. But you now see that the Irresistible and the Indisputable are the two weapons which the very nature of His scheme forbids Him to use. Merely to over-ride a human will (as His felt presence in any but the faintest and most mitigated degree would certainly do) would be for Him useless. He cannot ravish. He can only woo. For His ignoble idea is to eat the cake and have it; the creatures are to be one with Him, but yet themselves; merely to cancel them, or assimilate them, will not serve. He is prepared to do a little over-riding at the beginning. He will set them off with communications of His presence which, though faint, seem great to them, with emotional sweetness, and easy conquest over temptation. But He never allows this state of affairs to last long. Sooner or later He withdraws, if not in fact, at least from their conscious experience, all those supports and incentives. He leaves the creature to stand up on its own legs — to carry out from the will alone duties which have lost all relish. It is during such trough periods, much more than during the peak periods, that it is growing into the sort of creature He wants it to be. Hence the prayers offered in the state of dryness are those which please Him best. We can drag our patients along by continual tempting, because we design them only for the table, and the more their will is interfered with the better. He cannot "tempt" to virtue as we do to vice. He wants them to learn to walk and must therefore take away His hand; and if only the will to walk is really here He is pleased even with their stumbles. Do not be deceived, Wormwood. Our case is never more in danger than

when a human, no longer desiring, but still intending, to do our Enemy's will, looks round upon a universe from which every trace of Him seems to have vanished, and asks why he has been forsaken, and still obeys.

5   But of course the troughs afford opportunities to our side also. Next week I will give you some hints on how to exploit them,

Your affectionate uncle
Screwtape

9
My dear Wormwood,

6 I hope my last letter has convinced you that the trough of dullness or "dryness" through which your patient is going at present will not, of itself, give you his soul, but needs to be properly exploited. What forms the exploitation should take I will now consider.

7   In the first place I have always found that the Trough periods of the human undulation provide excellent opportunity for all sensual temptations, particularly those of sex. This may surprise you, because, of course, there is more physical energy, and therefore more potential appetite, at the Peak periods; but you must remember that the powers of resistance are then also at their highest. The health and spirits which you want to use in reproducing lust can also, alas, be very easily used for work or play or thought or innocuous merriment. The attack has a much better chance of success when the man's whole inner world is drab and cold and empty. And it is also to be noted that the Trough sexuality is subtly different in quality from that of the Peak— much less likely to lead to the milk and water phenomenon which the humans call "being in love," much more easily drawn into perversions, much less contaminated by those generous and imaginative and even spiritual concomitants which often render human sexuality so disappointing. It is the same with other desires of the flesh. You are much more likely to make your man a sound drunkard by pressing drink on him as an anodyne when he is dull and weary than by encouraging him to use it as a means of merriment among his friends when he is happy and expansive. Never forget that when we are dealing with any pleasure in its healthy and normal and satisfying form, we are, in a sense, on the enemy's ground. I know we have won many a soul through pleasure. All the same, it is His invention, not ours. He made the pleasures: all our research so far has not enabled us to produce one. All we can do is to encourage the humans to take the pleasures which our Enemy has produced, at times, or in ways, or in degrees, which He has forbidden. Hence we always try to work away from the natural condition of any pleasure to that in which it is least natural, least redolent of its Maker, and least pleasurable. An ever increasing craving for an ever diminishing pleasure is the formula. It is more certain; and it's better *style*. To get the man's soul and give him *nothing* in return—that is what really gladdens Our Father's heart. And the troughs are the time for beginning the process.

8   But there is an even better way of exploiting the Trough; I mean through the patient's own thoughts about it. As always, the first step

is to keep knowledge out of his mind. Do not let him suspect the law of undulation. Let him assume that the first ardours of his conversion might have been expected to last, and ought to have lasted, forever, and that his present dryness is an equally permanent condition. Having once got this misconception well fixed in his head, you may then proceed in various ways. It all depends on whether your man is of the desponding type who can be tempted to despair, or of the wishful-thinking type who can be assured that all is well. The former type is getting rare among the humans. If your patient should happen to belong to it, everything is easy. You have only got to keep him out of the way of experienced Christians (an easy task now-a-days), to direct his attention to the appropriate passages in scripture, and then set him to work on the desperate design of recovering his old feelings by sheer will-power, and the game is ours. If he is of the more hopeful type your job is to make him acquiesce in the present low temperature of his spirit and gradually become content with it, persuading himself that it is not so low after all. In a week or two you will be making him doubt whether the first days of his Christianity were not, perhaps, a little excessive. Talk to him about "moderation in all things." If you can once get him to the point of thinking that "religion is all very well up to a point," you can feel quite happy about his soul. A moderated religion is as good for us as no religion at all — and more amusing.

9   Another possibility is that of direct attack on his faith. When you have caused him to assume that the trough is permanent, can you not persuade him that "his religious phase" is just going to die away like all his previous phases? Of course there is no conceivable way of getting by reason from the proposition "I am losing interest in this" to the proposition "This is false." But, as I said before, it is jargon, not reason, you must rely on. The mere word *phase* will very likely do the trick. I assume that the creature has been through several of them before — they all have — and that he feels superior and patronising to the ones he has emerged from, not because he has really criticized them but simply because they are in the past. (You keep him well fed on hazy ideas of Progress and Development and the Historical Point of View, I trust, and give him lots of modern Biographies to read? The people in them are always emerging from Phases, aren't they?)

10   You see the idea? Keep his mind off the plain antithesis between True and False. Nice shadowy expressions — "It was a phase" — "I've been through that" — and don't forget the blessed word "Adolescent,"

Your affectionate uncle
Screwtape

Discussion of Theme

1. Does Lewis's version of the devil and of his relationship with God differ basically, or only in details, from the conventional version?
2. Can you enjoy these letters whether or not you have an interest in theological questions?

3. What is Lewis's meaning in the final sentence of paragraph 5? How would the concept be changed if "and still obeys" were left out? Why is this important?
4. Do you agree with Lewis's opinion of when it is easiest to cause a man to succumb to "sensual temptations"? Could the opposite be true just as often?

Discussion of Rhetoric

1. What is Lewis's purpose in capitalizing certain words? Does he overdo this?
2. Why are letters frequently a more effective way than essays to express personal beliefs?
3. Why does he say, "It is jargon, not reason, you must rely on"?
4. Find examples of irony in Letter 9.

Writing Assignments

1. If you disagree with the views expressed in these letters, write a letter to Screwtape explaining your own views on the matter.
2. Considering the Screwtape Letters in light of modern social attitudes, are the religious views Lewis expressed outmoded? Specify which and explain why.
3. Assume the same position as Screwtape and write some advice to a nephew about conformity.

Library Exploration

1. One of Lewis's most popular books on this theme is *Mere Christianity* (1952).
2. Another unusual treatment of the theme of heaven and hell is *Heavenly Discourse,* by Charles Erskine Scott Wood (1927).

Vocabulary

(1) UNDULATION   wavelike movement
(2) AMPHIBIANS   animals who live part of their life in water, part on land
(2) HYBRID   product of cross-
(2) PHENOMENON   observable fact or event
(4) MITIGATED   moderated
(4) INCENTIVES   inducements
(6) EXPLOITED   used for one's own advantage

(7) INNOCUOUS   harmless; ineffective
(7) CONCOMITANTS   accompanying things
(7) ANODYNE   pain reliever
(7) REDOLENT   reeking; smelling
(8) ARDOURS   enthusiasms
(8) ACQUIESCE   accept passively
(10) ANTITHESIS   opposite; contrast

John C. Bennett (1902–   ), Canadian-born president of Union Theological Seminary, is a leading Protestant theologian. He was educated at Oxford and at Union and has taught religion at several colleges and universities. Among his many books are "Social Salvation" (1935), "Christian Ethics and Social Policy" (1946), and "Christians and the State" (1958). He edited "Nuclear Weapons and the Conflict of Conscience" (1962).

In the current debate on the death of God some theologians have countered with reaffirmations of their faith. Here is what one prominent Christian thinker sees as indications that God is still very much alive.

JOHN C. BENNETT

In Defense of God

1   This Easter [1966] many Christians are puzzled and some are deeply disturbed by strange voices within the church proclaiming, "God is dead."

2   I do not think we should exaggerate the importance of this movement. But it would be unwise to ignore the conditions—and the doubts—that have attracted listeners and followers.

3   Some people seem to feel that the theologians who belong to the "death of God" school of thought are merely atheists who have blundered into the church, but this is not true. These men are spokesmen for a faith, however inadequate that faith may seem to those who do not share it. They mean to be Christian, to be loyal followers of Jesus.

4   Statements by two spokesmen, which appeared in *The Christian Century,* will indicate the broad outlines of this new doctrine:

5   "Theology itself is coming to confess that ours is a time in which God is dead," Thomas J. J. Altizer has written. And then he tells what this startling sentence means: "First we must acknowledge that we are not simply saying that modern man is incapable of believing in God, or that modern culture is an idolatrous flight from the presence of God, or even that we exist in a time in which God has chosen to be silent. . . . A theological statement that proclaims the death of God must mean that God is not present in the Word of faith. . . . He is truly absent, he is not simply hidden from view, and therefore he is truly dead."

6   Altizer's thought is extremely complicated and confusing. In place of the God of traditional theology, he has substituted a world view more akin to Buddhist mysticism than to a secularist atheism, and influenced by aspects of Christian teaching about Word and Spirit. The world he portrays is unlike that pictured by others who believe in a godless universe.

7   William Hamilton emphasizes the conviction shared by the leaders of this new theology that the death of God does not mean the end of Christianity, but actually points to a great emphasis on Jesus as the Lord and center of history.

8   "I insist that the time of the death of God is also the time of obedience to Jesus," he says. "This entails a claim that the New Testament Jesus can in fact be known, that a figure of sufficient clarity is available to us so that discipleship to him — to his life, his words and his death — is a possible center for Christian faith and life."

9   Hamilton does not find the new faith bleak and forbidding. He seems to be convinced that its tenets will remove a burden from the shoulders of many Christians who have felt similar doubts, but have not felt free to proclaim them:

10   "The death of God, obedience to Jesus and a new optimism — these are three of the themes I see emerging in the new radical movement in theology today. This movement involves a very small group which is not likely to be influential, but it is buoyant and full of spirit, for it is really excited by the direction in which it is having to move. And at its most euphoric, it really is convinced that it can work out a new way for men to be Christian in the kind of world we live in today."

11   The third theologian generally associated with this school is Paul M. van Buren. He is a more restrained and systematic thinker than the others. He does not emphasize the death of God, but develops a theology that, while centered in Jesus and the Resurrection, has no place for the word "God." For him, this word is too ambiguous to use, and he regards the usual Christian affirmations about God the Father as vetoed by the latest word in philosophy.

12   These three theologians have dramatized a crisis of belief present both inside and outside the church. They have, I believe, blurted out ideas quite widely held, even though they are not ordinarily fully acknowledged. When Hamilton asserts, "We are not talking about the absence of the experience of God, but about the experience of the absence of God," are not those words a confession that might be made by many of our most thoughtful contemporaries?

13   The great theologian Dietrich Bonhoeffer, who provided stimulus for this frank rejection of the presence of God, would himself have been horrified by the use now made of a few paragraphs in his writings. Bonhoeffer wrote about the world that had "come of age" and said, "It is becoming evident that everything gets along without God, and just as well as before. As in the scientific field, so in human affairs generally, what we call 'God' is being more and more edged out of life, losing more and more ground."

14   Even though he wrote from a Nazi prison at a time of historical catastrophe, Bonhoeffer did not revise his idea that man had come of age and that it was not necessary to invoke God to fill gaps in knowledge or to provide support in crises in personal life or in history. But I think that Bonhoeffer's theological self-denying ordinance is now being carried too far. He believed passionately that God as revealed in Christ was at the center of this world of men who had come of age. All that he says needs to be understood in the light of such words as these: "The God who makes us live in this world without using Him as a working hypothesis is the God before whom we are ever standing. Before God and with Him we live without God. God allows himself to be edged out of the world and onto the Cross."

15   There is a baffling paradox here, but it would be false to Bonhoeffer to break the paradox and leave us with a suffering Jesus apart from the God of the world.

16   Many of the questions these thinkers raise I can understand. However, the thought of each of them falls apart as a version of Christianity. The main problem is suggested by the title which *The Christian Century* gave to a review by Hamilton of a book by van Buren: "There is no God and Jesus is His Son"—an echo of a familiar characterization of Santayana's thought. The double cry: "God is dead. Long live Jesus" is more than a paradox. If there is no God, Jesus cannot be the guide for our ultimate beliefs.

17   There are at least three factors in our experience that cause sensitive and honest men to doubt the existence of God or to proclaim the absence of God. In some form, these factors have appeared in many times and places, but they now press upon us more than ever.

18   The first is that God seems to be crowded out of the world most of us experience. We see everywhere many agents at work that are not God, and naturally, most of us ask for signs of His activity.

19   If, however, we are among those who believe all visible agents are God at work, how can the word "God" have meaning of its own? Or, if we try to make a distinction between what God does and what is done by other agents, how can we tell one from the other?

20   The growth of scientific knowledge of nature and human behavior and the historical understanding of the context of events and the web of technological culture all seem to narrow the possible area of any distinctively *divine* action. To some people, this area appears to have vanished altogether. As Altizer puts it: "Surely it is not possible for any responsible person to think that we can any longer know or experience God in nature, in history, in the economic or political arenas, in the laboratory, or in anything which is genuinely modern, whether in

thought or in experience. Wherever we turn in our experience, we experience the eclipse or the silence of God."

21   A second difficulty is the conflict between our recognition of the vast evil in the world in contrast to the Biblical vision of the love of God. In Camus's *The Plague,* a character cries: "I refuse to love a scheme of things in which children are put to torture." We have seen a new universe of horror in which masses of people are victims of gas chambers or bombs. The catastrophes of a nation, a civilization, a generation are perhaps the greatest obstacle to faith in God.

22   Evil and suffering have completely different effects upon different people. For some, they destroy faith in God. For others, they destroy the substitutes for faith in God, and thus lead people into a deeper awareness of God's presence. The Christian community has the Cross, an instrument of torture and punishment, as its central symbol. But unless there are signs of resurrection somewhere in the same context, unless we see some hope that so stark an evil will be overcome, evil and suffering may easily lead to atheism. How can we live so close to the possibility of the annihilation of humanity and observe the apparent frustration of divine purposes? It is not surprising that atheism flourishes in the face of the possibility of such an end of human history, an end caused less by depravity than by the absurd actions of the "righteous."

23   There is a third ground for atheism, and that is a need that some men have felt to emancipate themselves from a God who may seem to threaten their freedom and their dignity. How can man be a free being if he lives under the sovereignty of the God of theism?

24   Does not God overwhelm man by his power? This is a major *motif* in contemporary atheism. The revolt of Karl Marx against God — as he understood the Christian teaching about Him — was basically a revolt in behalf of the humanity of man. This was based upon a profound misunderstanding of God as revealed in Christ, but it was a misunderstanding for which Christians were partly responsible.

25   One reason for the appearance of this new Christian atheism at this juncture in the life of Protestantism is that it follows after a powerful theological movement that affirmed the God of revelation and discarded all intimations of God apart from revelation. For some decades, an absolutely Christocentric approach to God won the minds of many Christian thinkers, including van Buren and Hamilton. The way from God to man and from man to God through Christ alone seemed clear for a time to some theologians, and then this faith lost the power to convince many of them. The negative judgments of philosophers about the arguments for God had confirmed the negative judgments of theologians.

26   I believe that there is a way of reopening the whole question. We must begin by accepting the view that there are no proofs of God and that there is no metaphysical system that can, on its own, provide the basis for belief. We must also recognize the precariousness of the absolutely independent and unsupported revelation of God that comes only through the person of Jesus Christ.

27   Instead, we may say that while there are no proofs of God, there are

intimations that the world of our experience is not self-sufficient without Him. There are pointers to God that will not of themselves convince the unbeliever, but may at least prepare the way for the vision of God made possible by revelation. What are they?

28   The world of our experience is neither a monotonous succession of disconnected sights and sounds nor is it without structures of moral and aesthetic values. The memories and imaginations of men grasp ideas and visions endlessly, and there is at least a partial organization of the ideas and visions of large communities of men.

29   What is the relationship of this organized world of experience to the cosmos as a whole and to all of the vistas of time and space that it reveals? Is our world merely an island of meaning in a sea of meaninglessness so far as value is concerned? Or do we in our experience touch something that is universal, something that gives unifying meaning to the totality of existence?

30   "It is remarkable . . . that men communicate with each other, form lasting and profound friendships, sometimes sacrifice themselves for one another, respect other persons quite differently from things, value creativity, build universities, and are incurably attracted by the ideal of fidelity to understanding," Michael Novak writes. "These facts are odd if the world of which these intelligent subjects are a part is so radically absurd. It seems that in an absurd world there would be neither fruitfulness nor honor in being faithful to understanding. If the real is absurd, man's nobility doubles the absurdity by his failing to grasp the irrelevance of nobility and honesty. If man can make nobility and honesty relevant, the real is not quite as absurd as it seems."

31   When I imagine the possible temporal end of this world, perhaps through some cosmic accident or nuclear annihilation, I ask: Would there remain *anywhere* any awareness that this world had ever existed? Perhaps on other planets there are other worlds of meaning, but what has taken place in our history is not known to them. Given the catastrophe that I project, we are left, if there is no God, with no memory anywhere that human history, with all of its greatness and its misery, its goodness and its depravity, had ever taken place. To me, the test of the credibility of atheism is to be able to live with this prospect, to be able to believe that this world of our experience is an island that may be lost forever, remembered by none. This may be the case, but to believe it taxes my credulity more than faith in God.

32   Harvey Cox, who must not be confused with the death of God theologians, though his thought has contributed to the current ferment on this subject, supports this position. He says: "Despite the efforts of some modern theologians to sidestep it, whether God exists or not is a desperately serious issue. . . . It is the question the Spanish philosopher Miguel Unamuno rightly felt overshadows all other questions man asks: 'Is man alone in the universe or not?'"

33   A second intimation is the sense of absolute obligation that we sometimes experience. This is no mere holdover from a Puritan conscience, for it has an ancient history. Wherever men have felt that it was better, as Plato said, to suffer injustice than to do injustice, prophetic spirits were willing to die rather than to say "yes" falsely to the powers of the world. Much of the moral experience of men can be explained as the

result of the necessities of social survival pressing upon the individual. But it is not possible in this way to explain the conscience of the individual who chooses to oppose the society that surrounds him at cost to himself. In the prophetic tradition, to seek justice has been to know God.

34   A third intimation of God comes from man's impulse to worship, to give himself in devotion and in sacrifice to something beyond himself. There is a logic of worship that reveals itself historically as men find themselves making idols. Today, there is a conflict of opinion between those who say that all men have gods of some kind, gods that become false religious absolutes unless they are overcome by the true God, and those who say that modern men who have come of age can now dispense with all deities, that modern men need no religious devotion of any kind.

35   I think the assumption that all men have a god of some kind is probably false; there are those who are genuinely neutral and detached. But surely, in the case of most men, passionate loyalties involving political fanaticism are likely to fill any vacuum created by atheism. Marxist atheism left room for the Communists' worship of state, party, ideology, program and future utopian goal. Already there are signs in some Communist societies that this is eroding. It may be followed by disillusionment and detachment from ideological commitment. The vacuum that remains may be filled by an absolute scientism, a fervent nationalism. There is also the possibility that as they lose their idols, men will find God again. The God of righteousness and love, who transcends in His being and purpose every human ideal and community and power and scheme of salvation, may deflate the idols and dispel the demons. Worship may be restored to its proper object, and thus sustain and liberate man.

36   The fourth intimation of God is the actual experience of healing, of what may be called grace in the midst of our common experience. Persons in deepest need, victims of estrangement, may actually find themselves blessed by a healing power. As Paul Tillich has said, they may find themselves recipients of grace without knowing what this power is or whence the grace comes. This experience does not provide a proof that any idea of God is true. It is no more than a hint of something that transcends our closed systems of thought and expectation.

37   I try to avoid all false claims for what can be inferred from these intimations of God. I do not regard them as a "natural theology" or a "philosophy of religion" that proves God exists. Much of the religious scepticism that opens the door to atheism in our time stems from a valid rejection of false claims. But that need not leave us in a world with no signs that point to God.

38   The signs I have presented make more sense if there is truth in the full revelation of God that has come to us through the Bible — especially through the life and death and resurrection of Jesus, allowing for much freedom of interpretation of what such words as "resurrection" mean. If this revelation is the bearer of truth, many more of the pieces of our life fit together than if this is not the case.

39   The vision of God as the transcendent Creator who in love identifies himself with His finite and sinful creatures is anything but obvious. It

must be revealed to be believed, but once revealed, it may remain a norm for the divine that has its own persuasive power. Christians see God in this way most clearly in Christ. But there are intimations of this understanding of God in the Old Testament. Is there not a gospel before the Gospel in the words of Isaiah: "For thus says the high and lofty One who inhabits eternity: I dwell in the high and holy place, and also with him who is of a contrite and humble spirit."

40   Often, radical critics make the doctrine of the Trinity one of their major targets. While it is easy to show the inadequacy of all formulations of this doctrine, the doctrine itself has been the way in which two aspects of God have been held together in Christian thought. The God who is the ultimate being is the same God who is *with us*. The critics are right in saying that the threeness of God is less clear than the contrast between the first person of the Trinity on the one hand and the second and third persons on the other. But arguments on this issue should be regarded as marginal. The great affirmation that has been expressed through this doctrine, and that may be expressed in simpler terms, is the faith that the transcendent Creator and Lord of all worlds is *with* His creatures. The ultimate or the holy is joined with love. How this can be is indeed a mystery, but it is better to live with this mystery than it is to cast it aside for a clearer and simpler model of the divine being. Is it not possible that when once we have had this vision of the union of the divine greatness and the divine humility, any other model of greatness may seem less great?

41   The God we encounter in the Bible respects the freedom of man. He is no arbitrary despot whose power prevents men from being themselves. Indeed, God is strangely patient with man. He seeks to persuade rather than to compel. It is true that one of the instruments of His persuasion is the judgment that men bring upon themselves when they persist in resisting Him, but they remain free to resist Him. Today, men, though they may have come of age in some respects, play recklessly with the means of their own annihilation.

42   One of the themes of Christian theology that needs great emphasis today, as the death of God is proclaimed partly to make room for man to be himself, is the reaffirmation of a Christian humanism. All teaching about God that by implication denies the freedom of man or downgrades him, and especially all teaching about God that downgrades some men, leaving them a less than human role, must be renounced. Often in the past, God has been seen as the great preserver of the status quo, which was organized for the benefit of the few at the expense of the many. But today, God is with the revolutionary efforts to raise the many to a position of human dignity and hope.

43   A great theologian of our time, Karl Barth, has often been accused of exalting God at the expense of man. In his earlier thought, he seemed to level all men down because of their sin. But in recent decades, he has leveled all men up because of Christ—whether they had had a conscious relationship to Christ or not. Barth says: "It is thought that the grace of God will be magnified if man is represented as a blotted or at best an empty page. . . . This representation cannot be sustained. Man cannot be depicted as a blotted or empty page." He goes on to chide the church for addressing man as though he were not

human, and he says: "He will rightly defend himself against what he is told. He will not be convicted of sin if he is uncharitably and falsely addressed concerning his humanity."

44 God does not threaten the humanity of man. On the contrary, the humanity of man can be threatened if the final word is that he is alone, that he is unknown to any being other than his fellows, that he is responsible to no authority above the state or the other powers of the world that claim his allegiance. The deepest source of his freedom may still be that he knows that he must "obey God rather than men."

Discussion of Theme

1. Why do you suppose people are so fascinated by the subject of whether or not there is a God?
2. Explain the difference between "the absence of the experience of God" and "the experience of the absence of God." Are you intimate with either?
3. If you believe in God, what do you consider the best evidence of his existence? If you don't, how do you answer Bennett?
4. Do you think that believers such as Altizer and Hamilton add to serious dialogue on the subject of God's existence?
5. Is the sense of absolute obligation a universal experience? Explain your answer.

Discussion of Rhetoric

1. Why does Bennett capitalize God, but not godless?
2. What tone does the author use in discussing theologians who disagree with him?
3. Are Bennett's arguments familiar ones that have been enlivened by commanding rhetoric, or does he introduce fresh reasoning to a much debated subject? If both, specify examples of each.
4. Notice the way Bennett deals first with the con argument and then with the pro argument. What effect has this on the organization of the essay?
5. One reason for the short paragraphs is the fact that the essay first appeared in Look magazine. Should paragraphs be this short for a book? Why?
6. In paragraph 22 the author repeats an idea introduced in paragraph 21. Is this a good transition?

Writing Assignments

1. Describe an experience that either strengthened or weakened (or possibly destroyed) your faith in God.
2. Explain your concept of God.
3. Can religion answer the needs of an individual who has used drugs as a means of solace in our society?

4. Has there been more harm than good done in the name of God?
5. Describe the most important religious decision you ever made.
6. Defend or attack one of Bennett's intimations of the existence of God.

Library Exploration

1. Look up reports on the Dead Sea scrolls and see if any of the information contained in the scrolls is relevant to Bennett's thesis.
2. Check on Bonhoeffer and see if you think he would have been "horrified" at the interpretations Altizer and others are making of his writings.

Vocabulary

(6) SECULARIST worldly; irreligious

(9) TENETS basic principles

(10) EUPHORIC elated

(11) AMBIGUOUS vague; unclear

(22) ANNIHILATION destruction; wiping out

(23) EMANCIPATE free

(23) SOVEREIGNTY power; authority

(24) MOTIF repeated theme

(25) INTIMATIONS hints

(25) CHRISTOCENTRIC Christ-centered

(26) PRECARIOUSNESS riskiness

(29) COSMOS universe

(31) CREDIBILITY believability

THE
LIVELY
ARTS

7

Edmund Carpenter, professor
of anthropology at Fordham
University, has written studies
of the effects of modern technology on man.

To an extent unrealized by most
of us, we become what we behold. Our technology, Carpenter insists, has sculpted
our bodies, programmed our
senses, and modified sexual
differences among us.

EDMUND CARPENTER

They Became What
They Beheld

THE ISLANDER

1   "We don't know who discovered water, but we're certain it wasn't
a fish." *John Culkin.*
2   It's the outsider who sees the environment. The islander sees the
outline of the distant mainland. When he goes ashore, he commands,
for he alone sees form and process.
3   Yeats, Joyce, Shaw, from Ireland; Eliot, from Missouri; Pound from
Idaho, were the innovators of 20th Century English. Beaverbrook,
from the Maritimes; Luce, from a missionary family in China; Thomson, from the Ontario bush, became the giants of 20th Century publishing. Detachment and perspective permit pattern recognition.
4   "In the histories of most peoples, there occur long lapses during
which they lie creatively fallow. Western European man was late by a
millenium or so in adding anything to ancient culture; the Jews
between the Dispersion and their emergence from the ghettos did
nothing that a historian of art and thought could not cover in a long
footnote. When they re-entered the world, the Jews, as though seeing
for the first time the structure to whose piecemeal growth they had
contributed almost nothing, produced within a century a series of epic
innovators—Karl Marx, Sigmund Freud, Albert Einstein—and scores
of hardly less original minds (Kafka, for example). The re-emergence

of the Islamic peoples, when complete, may give us the same kind of constellation." *A. J. Liebling.*

HAIR

5 Chief Long-hair, a Crow Indian, wound his hair with a strap and folded it into a container, which he carried under his arm. It was his sacred medicine and about ten feet long. As this long tress grew, he bound it at intervals with balls of pitch, and on rare occasions released it while galloping on horseback.

6 Taking a scalp meant acquiring an enemy's power.

7 Samson's great strength resided in his hair, but Delilah shaved off his seven shaggy locks, unshorn from childhood, thus robbing him of his supernatural strength and rendering him impotent.

8 In the East Indies, a criminal under torture persisted in denying his guilt until the court ordered his hair cut, at which point he immediately confessed. "One man," recounts *Golden Bough*'s James Frazer, "who was tried for murder, endured without flinching the utmost ingenuity of his torturers till he saw the surgeon standing with a pair of shears. On asking what this was for and being told it was to cut his hair, he begged they would not do it, and made a clean breast."

9 In most preliterate societies, ordinary consciousness is associated with the heart and chest, but the early "Indo-Europeans," according to Onians, "believed that the head contained a different factor, the procreative life-soul or spirit, which survives death, and the seed of new life." Among the reasons for thus honoring the head, he cites the analogy with the flower of fruit, seed pod, at the top or end of a plant; association of sexual experience with sensations and appearances in the head; relating the hair of the head, especially the beard, to pubic hair and to sexual power generally; and, finally, the association of life and strength with the cerebrospinal fluid and with the seed that seemed to flow from, and be part of, the latter.

10 Among the Norse, the hair of thralls was cut short. Among Arabs, what distinguished a freeman was the lock on his forehead, the slave's forehead being shaved. Many religious groups shaved their heads as a symbol of submission.

11 Jews, shorn and naked, entered gas chambers silently. Military inductees are first shorn: In one swift cut, self-identity is muted. Following the trial of the Chicago Seven, the prison warden cut the hair of the prisoners, then exhibited their pictures to a cheering Republican club. French women who slept with German soldiers were punished by having their heads shaved.

12 With literacy, breath, body odors and hair were dissociated from the self, which was sharply delimited. Short hair was required, especially of business and military men: The artist was exempt but never fully approved. Today, the tendency toward long hair is more than social weaponry; it reflects a new self-concept much closer to tribal beliefs. On the surface, the issue seems embarrassingly minor to generate such intense conflict; but in fact its premises are so basic, its emotional roots so deep, that identity itself is challenged.

TELEPHONE

13 "'Hello, Central. Give me Dr. Jazz.'" *Jelly Roll Morton.*

14 The telephone is said to be the only thing that can interrupt that most precious of all moments.

15 Aimee Semple McPherson was buried with a live telephone in her coffin.

16 I once observed a man walking alone past a public phone that rang just as he passed. He hesitated and then, after the second ring, answered it. The call couldn't possibly have been for him.

17 I called various public phones on streets and in terminals and, when someone answered, as almost invariably someone did, I asked why he had. Most said, "Because it rang."

18 On September 6, 1949, a psychotic veteran, Howard B. Unruh, in a mad rampage on the streets of Camden, New Jersey, killed 13 people and then returned home. Emergency police crews, bringing up machine guns, shotguns and tear-gas bombs, opened fire. At this point, an editor on the Camden Evening Courier looked up Unruh's name in the telephone directory and called him, Unruh stopped firing and answered.

19 "Hello."
"This Howard?"
"Yes . . . ."
"Why are you killing people?"

20 "I don't know. I can't answer that yet. I'll have to talk to you later. I'm too busy now."

IGNORING OLD AUDIENCES, CREATING NEW

21 Today's revolutionary movement began with an inspired use of the newly invented LP record. Black humorists, denied access to mass radio audiences, created LP audiences. Though some of these were large, they possessed a sense of intimacy, even conspiracy, totally lacking in radio audiences. When Mort Sahl and others later turned to TV, black humor died. Sahl attributed this to political changes, but I wonder if another factor wasn't involved: Restricting information makes it highly explosive, while widely disseminating information neutralizes its effects.

THEY BECAME WHAT THEY BEHELD

22 "Oh, what a beautiful baby!"

23 That's nothing," replied the mother, "you should see his photograph."

24 All people imitate their creations. Javanese dancers imitate the jerky movements of Javanese puppets. Jazz singers imitate instruments: "I never sing anything I can't play," says Louis Armstrong, "and I never play anything I can't sing."

25 Victorians moved like steam engines: The *grande dame* coming

through an archway (her bustle a coal car) looked like a locomotive emerging from a tunnel.

26   Today's fashions imitate our principal creations, which are electronic. Women imitate light bulbs or TV sets: Their clothes flow; their hair is luminous. They radiate. They can be turned on or off.

27   Illumination comes from within. It has no visible source. It's not dependent upon outside energy. Today's women are cordless.

28   "Is it on?" asked a three-year-old holding a ballpoint pen.

29   Psychologists were recently called to aid a boy who couldn't move or speak unless an electric cord, attached to his body, was plugged in.

30   California hippie: "One couple I know rarely speak but share the same rhythms with tambourines and drums, as well as with their breathing. These rhythms are the same as the ones their electric fan and refrigerator make."

31   Rural children dream of lambs and bunnies; urban children dream of cars and trains. But acidheads have visions of electronic instruments and especially under the influence of "electric drugs," identify with TV sets.

32   "Daddy, are we live or on tape?" *Five-year-old boy.*

33   "It took me a long time to discover that the key thing in acting is honesty. Once you know how to fake that, you've got it made." *Actor in "Peyton Place."*

MATING MEDIA

34 In the 1968 elections, the McCarthy campaign staff was approached with a suggestion for crossing media. In the United States, no law prohibits the mating of radio and TV. In Southern California, for example, Spanish-speaking sports fans watch the picture on TV but listen to a Spanish-speaking sports broadcaster on radio. So it was proposed that the New York–New Jersey area be offered a night of radio sound and TV picture. Five commentators were to provide the audio: John Culkin, Jean Shepherd, Marshall McLuhan, myself and Tony Schwartz, who originated the idea and had a sound studio equipped to handle the project. A bank of small TV sets would offer simultaneous coverage of all principal TV stations in the area; each would be kept on its particular channel. From these the commentators would select programs shown on a master TV set and would direct their comments toward these programs. The plan was to announce in the New York–New Jersey newspapers that at seven P.M. on a certain night, a local radio station would provide that evening's TV audio. For example, the audio for a TV cigarette commercial would be one minute of coughing via radio. If there was a laugh show, it would be pointed out that the laugh tracks were copyrighted in 1935 and that most of the people one heard laughing had been dead for some time. Then listeners would be asked to turn to a channel showing Walter Cronkite, at which point they would hear a taped "countdown," first in English, followed by an A-blast; then in Russian, then Chinese, each followed by blasts and more blasts and in the end by only a child's cry. Finally, and this was the point of the whole project, listeners would be

encouraged to turn to a channel with Hubert Humphrey speaking. Instead of his speech, however, they would hear—on radio—the four letters he wrote to his draft board, gaining exemption from duty in World War Two—one letter citing two lectures he had delivered to an R.O.T.C. class, while in the background would be played Hitler's ranting, bombs and screams: then Humphrey's pro-Vietnam-war speeches—"a glorious adventure and great fun, isn't it?"—while in the background, the explosions and screams continued.

35   The McCarthy team, mostly literary men, saw something profoundly immoral in the suggestion. New forms always seem immoral or chaotic, since they are unconsciously judged by reference to consecrated forms. But a curious contradiction arises: New forms are condemned, but the information they disseminate is believed, while the old and valued aren't even seen.

SERVICE ENVIRONMENTS

36 The moment any service exceeds what any single individual can control, that service is environmental. When environmental services exceed the reach of the greatest private wealth, the society is communistic. In this sense, the United States has been communistic for some time, more fully than any other country. Only a bookkeeping smoke screen conceals this fact. America reached this state via technology, not propaganda or revolution.

37   Television is part of the only environment today's children have ever known. To punish a child by forbidding him to watch TV is as nonsensical as depriving him of heat.

38   To try to restrict this service environment to white adults or to regard its benefits as products of private labor is equally nonsensical. The unemployed Negro youth who demands admission into this environment understands its nature far better than the middle-class white who strives to exclude him.

39   The unskilled-uneducated-unemployed of 1830 London lacked even minimal resources to participate in the service environment. They lacked not only the penny to mail a letter, they lacked the literacy to write it. They lived in the midst of a service environment but could not participate in it. Their admission into it was the reform movement of that day. Today we face a similar challenge: expanding membership in the service environment.

40   Electronic media have made all the arts environmental. Everyone can avail himself of cultural riches beyond what any millionaire has ever known. Today no serious scholar limits himself to Morgan Library when the entire New York Public Library is open daily and paperbacks are everywhere at hand. No art lover restricts himself to Mellon's collection. LPs and magnetic tapes make environmental all recorded music from all times: Music, like a wild bird's song, now belongs to the environment.

41   Today in the United States there are no longer any significant areas of private wealth. The multibillion-dollar service environment of electric information is free for all. Knowledge industries are the only sig-

nificant ones now. Education, news, transportation, entertainment, medicine, arts, telephone are all environmental.

MEDIA AS CODIFIERS

42 "When [Robert] Kennedy's body was brought back to New York from Los Angeles, one of us was at the airport to see it arrive. Standing with a groub of reporters, he noticed that they almost all watched the event on a specially rigged television screen. The actual coffin was passing behind their backs scarcely any farther away than the small-screen version. On these occasions, the tenuous connections between journalism, written or visual, and the real texture of events usually ruptures completely." *"An American Melodrama," by three British journalists.*

43   By "the real texture" is presumably meant the initial sensory experience devoid of all resonances and reflections. But why, on this occasion, the "connection" between that event and its image on TV was said to be "ruptured" escapes me. Any medium abstracts from the given and codifies in terms of that medium's grammar. It converts "given reality" into experienced reality. This is one of its functions. Without such structuring and classifying there could be no meaningful experience. The "real" is in no sense immediately given to us. What is given is too complex, too ambiguous, too raw. It must first be cooked. Instincts aid lower animals in selecting and responding to stimuli. Man has culture. Culture is his means of selecting — structuring — classifying reality, and media are his principal tools for this end.

44   We regard it as "natural" to think in verbal categories, but not in TV categories, yet language is as much a technology as TV.

45   In TV studios, idle employees watch programs on monitors, though the live shows are just as close. Billy Graham reports more converts from closed-circuit TV than from among those watching him live.

46   In New Guinea, when a village leader is ignored by his people, the Papuan government sometimes records his speech on tape, then releases it on radio, to be heard by now-respectful villagers, played to them by the village leader himself, probably on his own radio.

47   In the highlands of New Guinea, I saw men with photographs of themselves mounted on their foreheads, in front of their head feathers. Friends greeted them by examining the photographs.

EMPTINESS

48 Convinced that Americans fear emptiness more than fines, a justice of the peace in Battle Creek, Michigan, devised a remarkable sentence; he forced traffic violators to sit alone in empty rooms for three to five hours. Outraged citizens made him abandon this punishment, which was regarded as unnecessarily cruel.

49   When we have a free day, we look forward to how we will fill it. A person who is unemployed must explain: He is ill, retired, seeking work. To do nothing is indefensible. Millionaires expect their children to work during school vacations. Welfare workers are made uneasy by

Indians sitting in front of gas stations, and when we come upon an idle child, we say, "What, doing nothing? Do something!"

50   Literate man regards silence as empty of value. He calls radio silence "dead air" and condemns any cocktail party marked by long silences. Silence at concerts is usually interrupted by applause from someone who mistakenly thinks the piece is over. A Gilbert Stuart portrait of George Washington, its background unfinished, sells for far less than an identical portrait with background complete.

51   Dorothy Lee writes: "In Western thought — and I speak here of the view of the unsophisticated — space is empty and to be occupied with matter; time is empty and to be filled with activity. In both primitive and civilized non-Western cultures, on the other hand, free space and time have being and integrity. It was this conception of *nothingness* as *somethingness* that enabled the philosophers of India to perceive the integrity of nonbeing, to name the free space and give us the zero."

52   Writing of the Bedouin tribesmen, T. E. Lawrence tells how one of them took him through a deserted palace where each room had a different scent, and then called, "Come and smell the very sweetest scent of all," and led him to a gaping window, where the empty wind of the desert went throbbing past. "This," he told him, "is the best; it has no taste."

SENSORY PROGRAMMING

53 Isolating one sense from all others calls for enormous training and self-control and is probably never fully achieved. Test this yourself: Run water into the bath while switching the light on and off: The sound appears louder in the darkness.

54   A child learns to separate the senses when he learns, in class, to read silently. His legs twist; he bites his tongue; but by an enormous effort he learns to fragment his senses, to turn on one at a time and keep the others in neutral. And so he is indoctrinated into that literate world where readers seek silent solitude, concertgoers close their eyes and museum guards warn, "Don't touch!"

55   But all this is history. Today's students mix homework with radio and hi-fi, even TV and telephone, and experience little difficulty correlating such data, or at least having them coexist. California students get into their wrap-around sports cars (a form of clothing), kick off their sandals so they can feel the freeway coming up through the car, travel at 70 miles an hour with signs flashing past and the oncoming traffic passing at 140 mph; top down; sun and wind in their faces; radio on and every fourth telephone pole in sync with the beat; sharing breakfast with a coed: total sensory involvement. Then they enter class, turn off all senses, put on a tribal face and go numb.

REDISCOVERY OF THE BODY

56 Literate man valued the delimited, controlling self, which he equated with the rational mind. He portrayed this "I" as detached from the body and emotions and in control of both. He said, "*I* lift *my* foot,"

with the "I" controlling *me* and *my*. He excluded passions from the "I"; these lay below: I *lost* my temper, *fell* in love, *delved* into my unconscious, but I *exercised* my reason.

57   Early analysts were called "alienists." Alienation begins when one feels revulsion with one's body, and fears the sensate world. Trudie Shoop, the dancer, helped schizophrenics rediscover themselves by reteaching them the earliest movements of the child.

58   The story is told of a group of Jews, with downcast eyes, entering gas chambers. One girl, a dancer, was ordered by a guard to dance for his amusement. Naked, shorn of her hair, she had no identity. But as she danced, she rediscovered herself in the dance, in her body. This gave her the courage to act: In a magnificent gesture, she attacked her tormentor.

59   If you manipulate people, you must first control their environment. Pavlov couldn't make dogs salivate on signal until he put them in artificial, controlled environments. Literate man was easily manipulated. He lived in a centrally heated, air-conditioned, canned-food world, cut off from personal sensations. He was ashamed of his body. He avoided nudity, was obsessed by toilet etiquette, made sex a sin and gluttony close to it. He became aware of his body only in sports and sex, and sometimes not even then.

60   Today's youths have rediscovered the body. They rebel against controlled environments; they create personal sensory environments.

61   Sharp differences between sexes, which marked the past, today disappear. Sex is cooled down. Men and women dress more alike. They share hair styles. Men wear jewelry. They're interested in lotions, hair dyes, cosmetics. This disturbs older people, who keep saying, "You can't tell the difference," and guffaw. Obviously, that difference must have meant a great deal to them or they wouldn't be so hung up on this stale joke.

62   It's a difference that's meaningless to the young. Young men and women today share a common sensate world. Their feelings about themselves and about this world are much alike. They can talk together. Sex polarization at social gatherings—so "men can talk, women visit"—is meaningless to the young.

63   "And everybilly lived alove with everybiddy else."

VIOLENCE AND THE QUEST FOR IDENTITY

64 William James once wrote that no more fiendish torture could be devised than when you speak, no one answers; when you wave, no one turns; but everyone simply cuts you dead. Soon, he said, there wells up within you such hostility you attack those who ignore you and, if that fails to bring recognition, you turn your hostility inward, upon yourself, to prove you really do exist.

65   Violence offers immediate public recognition. This is especially true for "invisibles," who thereby become—instantly—very visible. In 1967, when armed Black Panthers entered the California Legislative Assembly, pandemonium occurred. Even the threat of violence is a powerful force in any quest for identity.

66   Detribalizing the African slave robbed him of all identity, creating great misery of psychic alienation. Racism brainwashed him of his past, leaving him "Wandering between two worlds, one dead/The other powerless to be born." He became an invisible stranger in a strange land.

67   Though an estimated one third of the post–Civil War American cowboys were black, on screen they all turned white. The black was erased from history, unseen in advertisements and admitted to radio and film only in comic form. He made his first appearance on TV.

68   Today's invisibles demand visible membership in a society that has hitherto ignored them. They want to participate in society from the inside and they want that society to be reconstituted to allow membership for all. Above all, they want to be acknowledged *publicly,* on their own terms.

69   Electronic media make possible this reconstitution of society. But this also leads to a corresponding loss of identity among those whose identity was defined by the old society. This upheaval generates great pain and identity loss. As man is tribally metamorphosed by electronic media, people scurry around frantically in search of their former identities and, in the process, they unleash tremendous violence.

BODY AS SCULPTURE

70   "In the native world," writes Alan Lomax, "painting lives on the body, sculpture is something you use or worship, architecture you do yourself, and literature you recite or dance."

71   Grooming and dress are primary arts. Few activities involve more effort. Yet people rarely think of themselves as sculptors or painters, no matter how much effort they devote to making themselves into living art.

72   In the electronic environment, everyone is constantly bombarded by light images emanating from the cathode tube — Joyce's *Charge of the Light Brigade* — playing on us, going inside us, making us all *Lord of the Flies,* engulfed by flickering images.

73   Asked what she had on when posing for calendar shots, Marilyn Monroe replied, "The radio."

74   We wear our media; they are our new clothes. TV clothes our bodies tattoo style. It writes on our skins. It clothes us in information. It programs us. Nudity ceases to have meaning. How natural that we would now write ads and headlines on nudes.

PUTTING ON THE DOG

75   Pets don't come in breeds or races; they come in styles. Styles match owners. Pet psychoanalysts counsel both pet and owner, on the assumption they share psychic problems.

76   "We train you to train your dog."

77   A pet cemetery in Washington, D.C., guarantees that pets owned by Negroes aren't acceptable.

SENSATE WORLD OF NATIVES

78 When natives talk about their world, they speak about how things smell, taste, feel, sound; toes gripping roots along a slippery bank; peppery food burning the rectum; "He became aware of gentle heat playing on his right cheek and a fine smoke teasing his nostrils, while on the left he heard an odd gurgling sound."

79 "It is pleasant," said a Vedda, "for us to feel the rain beating over our shoulders, and good to go out and dig yams, and come home wet, and see the fire burning in the cave, and sit around it."

80 An Eskimo woman, Uvanuk, delighting in the joy of simply being moved by nature, sang:

> The great sea
> Has sent me adrift,
> It moves me
> As the wind in a great river.
>
> Earth and the great weather
> Move me,
> Have carried me away
> And move my inward parts with joy

81 The phrase translated "moves me" also means "to be in a natural state"; to be moved by nature is to be in nature, to belong there. Emotions are expressed as physical responses: anger, *loosening bowels;* fear, *tightening sinews;* joy, *floating viscera.* Man is small, no more than a weed moved endlessly by the current, but intensely aware of forces acting upon him and delighting in even the most trivial.

82 Toothless Kuilasar, an elderly Eskimo, told of starvation, of children born and husbands lost, of new lands and faces, and concluded, "How happy I have been! How good life has been to me!" She hadn't conquered life, nor been rewarded by it, but life had acted upon her, spoken through her, and this was joy.

Discussion of Theme

1. According to Carpenter, what effect has literacy had on human sensibility and self-concept in Western cultures?
2. Are the examples cited in paragraphs 22-33 a genuine trend, or are they merely isolated and bizarre instances?
3. Carpenter makes a number of "probes" or striking statements — for example, that the United States is communistic. Do you agree? Find other similarly provoking statements.
4. In what ways does man's environment control him? What has been youth's response to this tendency?
5. Why does our society have a preoccupation with keeping busy with work? What might Carpenter's explanation be?

Discussion of Rhetoric

1. Is the thesis of this article stated explicitly, or is it implied? If the later, state the thesis in your own words.
2. What is the chief method of paragraph development used by Carpenter? Is it overworked?
3. Do the vast asides, anecdotes, and allusions create confusion in the reader's mind, or do they help him to follow the central idea?
4. How does Carpenter's essay exemplify his thesis?
5. Explain the purpose of the final paragraph with respect to the rest of the article.

Writing Assignments

1. Apply Carpenter's concepts of the "islander" and the "mainlander" (paragraph 2) to an experience of your own.
2. Analyze the "de-polarization" taking place between the sexes in our society. (Consider, for example, hair and dress styles.)
3. If you disagree with Carpenter, write a refutation.

Library Exploration

For an extended treatment of these ideas, read the works of Marshall McLuhan, as well as others by Carpenter.

Vocabulary

(3) INNOVATORS those who make changes

(10) THRALLS slaves

(42) TENUOUS slight; unsubstantial

(43) CODIFIES arranges systematically

(62) SENSATE perceived by the senses

(65) PANDEMONIUM uproar; chaos

(69) METAMORPHOSED transformed

Marya Mannes (1904–   ), a native of New York currently on the staff of "The Reporter," has written for "Vogue," "Glamour," and other leading publications. She is a popular lecturer; a novelist ("They," 1968); a poetess ("Subverse," 1959); and an essayist ("The New York I Know," 1961).

In this pointed essay, Mrs. Mannes charges that critics who fail to uphold standards in the arts have contributed to their decline. She urges the layman to assume his own responsibility in maintaining such standards.

MARYA MANNES

How Do You Know It's Good?

1 Suppose there were no critics to tell us how to react to a picture, a play, or a new composition of music. Suppose we wandered innocent as the dawn into an art exhibition of unsigned paintings. By what standards, by what values would we decide whether they were good or bad, talented or untalented, successes or failures? How can we ever know that what we think is right?

2   For the last fifteen or twenty years the fashion in criticism or appreciation of the arts has been to deny the existence of any valid criteria and to make the words "good" or "bad" irrelevant, immaterial, and inapplicable. There is no such thing, we are told, as a set of standards, first acquired through experience and knowledge and later imposed on the subject under discussion. This has been a popular approach, for it relieves the critic of the responsibility of judgment and the public of the necessity of knowledge. It pleases those resentful of disciplines, it flatters the empty-minded by calling them open-minded, it comforts the confused. Under the banner of democracy and the kind of equality which our forefathers did *not* mean, it says, in effect, "Who are you to tell us what is good or bad?" This is the same cry used so long and so

effectively by the producers of mass media who insist that it is the public, not they, who decides what it wants to hear and see, and that for a critic to say that *this* program is bad and *this* program is good is purely a reflection of personal taste. Nobody recently has expressed this philosophy more succinctly than Dr. Frank Stanton, the highly intelligent president of CBS television. At a hearing before the Federal Communications Commission, this phrase escaped him under questioning: "One man's mediocrity is another man's good program."

3   There is no better way of saying "No values are absolute." There is another important aspect to this philosophy of *laissez faire*: It is the fear, in all observers of all forms of art, of guessing wrong. This fear is well come by, for who has not heard of the contemporary outcries against artists who later were called great? Every age has its arbiters who do not grow with their times, who cannot tell evolution from revolution or the difference between frivolous faddism, amateurish experimentation, and profound and necessary change. Who wants to be caught *flagrante delicto* with an error of judgment as serious as this? It is far safer, and certainly easier, to look at a picture or a play or a poem and to say "This is hard to understand, but it may be good," or simply to welcome it as a new form. The word "new"—in our country especially—has magical connotations. What is new must be good; what is old is probably bad, and if a critic can describe the new in language that nobody can understand, he's safer still. If he has mastered the art of saying nothing with exquisite complexity, nobody can quote him later as saying anything.

4   But all these, I maintain, are forms of abdication from the responsibility of judgment. In creating, the artist commits himself; in appreciating, you have a commitment of your own. For after all, it is the audience which makes the arts. A climate of appreciation is essential to its flowering, and the higher the expectations of the public, the better the performance of the artist. Conversely, only a public ill-served by its critics could have accepted as art and as literature so much in these last years that has been neither. If anything goes, everything goes; and at the bottom of the junkpile lie the discarded standards too.

5   But what are these standards? How do you get them? How do you know they're the right ones? How can you make a clear pattern out of so many intangibles, including that greatest one, the very private I?

6   Well for one thing, it's fairly obvious that the more you read and see and hear, the more equipped you'll be to practice that art of association which is at the basis of all understanding and judgment. The more you live and the more you look, the more aware you are of a consistent pattern—as universal as the stars, as the tides, as breathing, as night and day—underlying everything. I would call this pattern and this rhythm an order. Not order—*an* order. Within it exists an incredible diversity of forms. Without it lies chaos. I would further call this order—this incredible diversity held within one pattern—health. And I would call chaos—the wild cells of destruction—sickness. It is in the end up to you to distinguish between the diversity that is health and the chaos that is sickness, and you can't do this without a process of association that can link a bar of Mozart with the corner of a Vermeer painting, or a Stravinsky score with a Picasso abstraction; or that can

relate an aggressive act with a Franz Kline painting and a fit of coughing with a John Cage composition.

7   There is no accident in the fact that certain expressions of art live for all time and that others die with the moment, and although you may not always define the reasons, you can ask the questions. What does an artist say that is timeless; how does he say it? How much is fashion, how much is merely reflection? Why is Sir Walter Scott so hard to read now, and Jane Austin not? Why is baroque right for one age and too effulgent for another?

8   Can a standard of craftsmanship apply to art of all ages, or does each have its own, and different, definitions? You may have been aware, inadvertently, that craftsmanship has become a dirty word these years because, again, it implies standard — something done well or done badly. The result of this convenient avoidance is a plenitude of actors who can't project their voices, singers who can't phrase their songs, poets who can't communicate emotion, and writers who have no vocabulary — not to speak of painters who can't draw. The dogma now is that craftsmanship gets in the way of expression. You can do better if you don't know *how* you do it, let alone *what* you're doing.

9   I think it is time you helped reverse this trend by trying to rediscover craft: the command of the chosen instrument, whether it is a brush, a word, or a voice. When you begin to detect the difference between freedom and sloppiness, between serious experimentation and ego-therapy, between skill and slickness, between strength and violence, you are on your way to separating the sheep from the goats, a form of segregation denied us for quite a while. All you need to restore it is a small bundle of standards and a Geiger counter that detects fraud, and we might begin our tour of the arts in an area where both are urgently needed: contemporary painting.

10   I don't know what's worse: to have to look at acres of bad art to find the little good, or to read what the critics say about it all. In no other field of expression has so much double-talk flourished, so much confusion prevailed, and so much nonsense been circulated: further evidence of the close interdependence between the arts and the critical climate they inhabit. It will be my pleasure to share with you some of this double-talk so typical of our times.

11   Item one: preface for a catalogue of an abstract painter:

12   "Time-bound meditation experiencing a life; sincere with plastic piety at the threshold of hallowed arcana; a striving for pure ideation giving shape to inner drive; formalized patterns where neural balances reach a fiction." End of quote. Know what this artist paints like now?

13   Item two: a review in the *Art News*:

14   ". . . a weird and disparate assortment of material, but the monstrosity which bloomed into his most recent cancer of aggregations is present in some form everywhere. . . ." Then, later, "A gluttony of things and processes terminated by a glorious constipation."

15   Item three, same magazine, review of an artist who welds automobile fragments into abstract shapes:

16   "Each fragment . . . is made an extreme of human exasperation, torn at and fought all the way, and has its rightness of form as if by accident. *Any technique that requires order or discipline would just*

be the human ego. No, these must be egoless, uncontrolled, unde-signed and different enough to give you a bang—fifty miles an hour around a telephone pole. . . ."

17 "Any technique that requires order or discipline would just be the human ego." What does he mean—"just be"? What are they really talking about? Is this journalism? Is it criticism? Or is it that other convenient abdication from standards of performance and judgment practiced by so many artists and critics that they, like certain writers who deal only in sickness and depravity, "reflect the chaos about them"? Again, whose chaos? Whose depravity?

18 I had always thought that the prime function of art was to create order *out* of chaos—again, not the order of neatness or rigidity or convention or artifice, but the order of clarity by which one will and one vision could draw the essential truth out of apparent confusion. I still do. It is not enough to use parts of a car to convey the brutality of the machine. This is as slavishly representative, and just as easy, as arranging dried flowers under glass to convey nature.

19 Speaking of which, i.e., the use of real materials (burlap, old gloves, bottletops) in lieu of pigment, this is what one critic had to say about an exhibition of Assemblage at the Museum of Modern Art last year:

20 "Spotted throughout the show are indisputable works of art, accounting for a quarter or even half of the total display. But the remainder are works of non-art, anti-art, and art substitutes that are the aesthetic counterparts of the social deficiencies that land people in the clink on charges of vagrancy. These aesthetic bankrupts . . . have no legitimate ideological roof over their heads and not the price of a square intellectual meal, much less a spiritual sandwich, in their pockets."

21 I quote these words of John Canaday of *The New York Times* as an example of the kind of criticism which puts responsibility to an intelligent public above popularity with an intellectual coterie. Canaday has the courage to say what he thinks and the capacity to say it clearly: two qualities notably absent from his profession.

22 Next to art, I would say that appreciation and evaluation in the field of music is the most difficult. For it is rarely possible to judge a new composition at one hearing only. What seems confusing or fragmented at first might well become clear and organic a third time. Or it might not. The only salvation here for the listener is, again, an instinct born of experience and association which allows him to separate intent from accident, design from experimentation, and pretense from conviction. Much of contemporary music is, like its sister art, merely a reflection of the composer's own fragmentation: an absorption in self and symbols at the expense of communication with others. The artist, in short, says to the public: If you don't understand this, it's because you're dumb. I maintain that you are not. You may have to go part way or even halfway to meet the artist, but if you must go the whole way, it's his fault, not yours. Hold fast to that. And remember it too when you read new poetry, that estranged sister of music.

23 "A multitude of causes, unknown to former times, are now acting with a combined force to blunt the discriminating powers of the mind, and, unfitting it for all voluntary exertion, to reduce it to a state of al-

most savage torpor. The most effective of these causes are the great national events which are daily taking place and the increasing accumulation of men in cities, where the uniformity of their occupations produces a craving for extraordinary incident, which the rapid communication of intelligence hourly gratifies. To this tendency of life and manners, the literature and theatrical exhibitions of the country have conformed themselves."

24   This startlingly applicable comment was written in the year 1800 by William Wordsworth in the preface to his "Lyrical Ballads"; and it has been cited by Edwin Muir in his recently published book, "The Estate of Poetry." Muir states that poetry's effective range and influence have diminished alarmingly in the modern world. He believes in the inherent and indestructible qualities of the human mind and the great and permanent objects that act upon it, and suggests that the audience will increase when "poetry loses what obscurity is left in it by attempting greater themes, for great themes have to be stated clearly." If you keep that firmly in mind and resist, in Muir's words, "the vast dissemination of secondary objects that isolate us from the natural world," you have gone a long way toward equipping yourself for the examination of any work of art.

25   When you come to theatre, in this extremely hasty tour of the arts, you can approach it on two different levels. You can bring to it anticipation and innocence, giving yourself up, as it were, to the life on the stage and reacting to it emotionally, if the play is good, or listlessly, if the play is boring; a part of the audience organism that expresses its favor by silence or laughter and its disfavor by coughing and rustling. Or you can bring to it certain critical faculties that may heighten, rather than diminish, your enjoyment.

26   You can ask yourselves whether the actors are truly in their parts or merely projecting themselves; whether the scenery helps or hurts the mood; whether the playwright is honest with himself, his characters, and you. Somewhere along the line you can learn to distinguish between the true creative act and the false arbitrary gesture; between fresh observation and stale cliché; between the avant-garde play that is pretentious drivel and the avant-garde play that finds new ways to say old truths.

27   Purpose and craftsmanship — end and means — these are the keys to your judgment in all the arts. What is this painter trying to say when he slashes a broad band of black across a white canvas and lets the edges dribble down? Is it a statement of violence? Is it a self-portrait? If it is one of these, has he made you believe it? Or is this a gesture of the ego or a form of therapy? If it shocks you, what does it shock you into?

28   And what of this tight little painting of bright flowers in a vase? Is the painter saying anything new about flowers? Is it different from a million other canvases of flowers? Has it any life, any meaning, beyond its statement? Is there any pleasure in its forms or texture? The question is not whether a thing is abstract or representational, whether it is "modern" or conventional. The question, inexorably, is whether it is good. And this is a decision which only you, on the basis of instinct, experience, and association, can make for yourself. It takes indepen-

dence and courage. It involves, moreover, the risk of wrong decision and the humility, after the passage of time, of recognizing it as such. As we grow and change and learn, our attitudes can change too, and what we once thought obscure or "difficult" can later emerge as coherent and illuminating. Entrenched prejudices, obdurate opinions are as sterile as no opinions at all.

29   Yet standards there are, timeless as the universe itself. And when you have committed yourself to them, you have acquired a passport to that elusive but immutable realm of truth. Keep it with you in the forests of bewilderment. And never be afraid to speak up.

Discussion of Theme

1. Why does Mrs. Mannes believe that "good" and "bad" as criteria for art have become unpopular with both critics and public?
2. There is a psychological concept known as "prestige suggestion," which means that the uninformed are apt to be impressed and, consequently, influenced by the opinions or the work of individuals they have learned to accept as experts. To what extent do you believe that prestige suggestion operates in the arts today?
3. Perhaps you have heard the statement, "I don't know anything about art, but I know what I like." Why do you suppose artists and critics object to this?
4. If art is an attempt to communicate a private view, do you believe that too many modern artists restrict their communication to an increasingly limited audience?
5. What does the author mean by "experience and association" in paragraph 22?

Discussion of Rhetoric

1. Can you make any sense out of the critics' comments quoted in paragraphs 12-16 and 20? Did you have difficulty interpreting them?
2. Can you think of anything to be said in favor of the use of jargon? Is it a deliberate attempt to exclude persons outside the field?
3. Mrs. Mannes employs several striking metaphors. Find them in the essay.
4. How does Mrs. Mannes get the reader interested in her essay in the first paragraph?
5. The author begins with a discussion of what she is against or at least what she disapproves of. Is this effective?

Writing Assignments

1. Mrs. Mannes says that "the prime function of art is to create order out of chaos." What do *you* believe is the prime function of art?

2. Some people—critics included—believe that much contemporary art is a deliberate hoax, perpetrated on the public to boost the artist's ego. What is your opinion of this theory?

3. Has your taste in either art, music, or literature changed from what it was, say, four years ago? In what way? How do you account for the difference?

4. Describe your reactions to a piece of modern symphonic music.

Library Exploration

1. Read Aristotle's *Poetics,* the classical Greek view of the arts.
2. Compile a series of reviews of the same event—an art show, a concert, a play—and illustrate the points of agreement and difference.

Vocabulary

(2) CRITERIA   standards

(2) IRRELEVANT   not relating to the subject

(2) IMMATERIAL   unimportant

(2) SUCCINCTLY   tersely; concisely

(3) LAISSEZ FAIRE   without interference

(3) ARBITERS   persons with absolute power of deciding

(3) FLAGRANTE DELICTO   in the very act

(4) ABDICATION   resigning one's authority

(7) EFFULGENT   splendid; flashy

(8) INADVERTENTLY   unintentionally

(8) PLENITUDE   wealth

(12) PIETY   religious devotion

(12) ARCANA   mysterious knowledge

(12) IDEATION   formation of ideas

(12) NEURAL   relating to nerves

(14) DISPARATE   essentially unlike

(14) GLUTTONY   hoggish eating

(18) ARTIFICE   trickery; ingenious device or expedient

(20) AESTHETIC   appreciative of or sensitive to the beautiful

(21) COTERIE   exclusive group of persons with a common interest or purpose

(23) TORPOR   sloth; laziness

(26) ARBITRARY   selected at random and without reason

(26) AVANT-GARDE   vanguard; forefront

(26) PRETENTIOUS   showy; pretending to importance

(28) INEXORABLY   unalterably

(28) COHERENT   logically consistent

(28) OBDURATE   extremely stubborn

(29) ELUSIVE   evasive; hard to grasp

(29) IMMUTABLE   unchangeable; unvarying

Irving L. Horowitz (1929–)
has taught philosophy, sociology, and anthropology in South
America and England, as well as
at various universities in the
United States. He is currently
professor of sociology at Rut-
gers University. Educated at
City College of New York, Bran-
deis University, and the University of Buenos Aires, he has
written "The Worlds of Development: The Theory and Practice
of International Stratification"
(1966), "The Rise and Fall of
Project Camelot" (1967), and
numerous articles.

Like jazz before it, rock music
has become so specialized that
only the sophisticated can enjoy
it. The result, according to
Horowitz, is that rock is suffering from the same symptoms as
jazz, and it is now going through
its death throes.

IRVING L. HOROWITZ

Rock on the Rocks, or Bubblegum, Anybody?

1 A year ago there were three AM radio stations in New York City that
played only rock music. Now there is one. Four years ago dozens of
discotheques and clubs featured rock music in New York. Now most of
them are out of business.

2   Rock 'n' roll is dying. It is now going through the terminal symptoms
that jazz went through in the '40s and early '50s. And it will die the
same way jazz did—by growing up, by being transformed.

3   Jazz picked up most of its fans during its dance stage. Post-World-War-I flappers and Post-World-War-II beboppers crowded into ballrooms across the country to hear the new music and dance the night away to toe-tapping rhythms.

It's got a good beat. You can dance to it.

4   RAPPORT. For many years there was a close mutual appreciation between performer and audience. But as the art form matured, so did the musicians. They came to know much more about jazz than their audiences did. The fans knew nothing of the notation system, complex rhythms, time signatures. They just wanted to hear *Caravan* or *One O'Clock Jump.* A professional distance began to develop between artist and listener — some musicians looked on their audiences with contempt and took few pains to conceal it.

5   Distance from the general audience was reinforced by the appearance in the late '30s of a new type of fan. In the slang of the day these jazz followers were known as alligators. Like the groupies of the late '60s, they didn't dance — they stood in front of the bandstand all night and listened. Alligators understood. They knew the music. They knew the instruments and the soloists and they appreciated what they heard.

6   In this context many musicians came to define their own worth not in terms of the mass audience and the hit record, but in terms of peer approval. If the guys in the band and a few sophisticated fans appreciated what one was doing musically, then he was a success — and the rest of the audience be damned. Before they would play, the Modern Jazz Quartet and the Charlie Mingus Quartet often made outrageous demands for concert-hall levels of silence in their audiences. The jazz musician came to expect a nonemotional response to emotion. In some sense this is what the rock culture was originally in rebellion against.

7   The transition from get-up-and-dance music to sit-down-and-listen music took several years, but it was discernible in many later jazz bands — Cab Calloway's and Duke Ellington's, for example — and in the swing orchestras of Harry James and Benny Goodman.

8   PACKAGE. Finally, jazz moved from the dance floor to the concert hall. Norman Granz, the Bill Graham of his day, collected the biggest stars into one-nighter packages — Jazz at the Philharmonic — that toured the largest auditoriums in the country. These packaged performances stifled the creativity of many brilliant musicians, but there was big money in them. As Granz's malignant concerts spread through the land, jazz began to die.

9   The big bands acknowledged their mass audiences and, when pressed, they would play their familiar, danceable hits. But to maintain their self-esteem and professional integrity many artists sought other outlets. Small groups began to develop within the larger bands. The big band was for mass appeal — the small group was for displaying musical expertise and for building personal satisfaction. From Artie Shaw's orchestra came the Gramercy Five, and from Benny Goodman's big outfit came the Benny Goodman Trio. Instead of dancing,

audiences were expected to sit and listen to Teddy Wilson's educated
piano or to the cascading vibes of Lionel Hampton.

10   Thelonious Monk and Dizzy Gillespie achieved results similar to
those of Bartok and Stravinsky — by innovating and creatively extending their traditions. The soloist became king, and Charlie Parker and,
later, John Coltrane were canonized.

11   As the musicians grew older, so did their fans. Young, unsophisticated ears didn't know enough about the music to appreciate a good
tenor-sax solo by Lester Young or Ben Webster. Artists became intra-
professional. Financial success ceased to be a criterion for musical
esteem. The musicians who did reach mass audiences had by definition "sold out," and their sounds were disdained — they were "commercial" and "Tin-Pan Alley." And then came rock 'n' roll.

It's got a good beat. You can dance to it.

12   The emphasis again was mass appeal. There were few intrapro-
fessional standards, so an artist's worth was defined in the simplest,
most obvious way — in terms of how many records he could sell. The
focus was on the 45 r.p.m. single, and the Top 40 list was updated
every week.

13   Every music reflects the society in which it flourished. In the Renaissance new needs for humanistic expression gave birth to tonal
music which rejected the previous ecclesiastical doxology of the Medieval period. The ideals of freedom in the French Revolution gave
rise to the chromatics and the gradual development from the sonata to
the cyclical form of the Romantic Movement. Jazz itself, inherently an
interracial music, represented a mixture of polyphonic African rhythms
and modes with the tonal homophony of the European colonizers.

14   And rock music, a child of the technological age, reflects its parent-
age in every aspect. Each year amplifiers and preamplifiers get more
sophisticated and more powerful, speaker systems get larger and
louder, and new electronic gimmicks alter the sound or become part
of it (feedback, cross-phasing, fuzz tones, wah-wah).

15   The contemporary recording process is so complex that a new group
cannot make an album without sophisticated knowledge of electronics — mikeing, mixing and mastering. Since *Sergeant Pepper,* the
multi-track tape recorder has taken over. Voices and instruments are
cut onto separate tracks so that the producer can make the piano
louder than the bass on one chorus, or add echo to one voice but not
another. Six months later, if he feels like it he can add a background of
violins or cricket chirps.

16   Electronic experimentation has taken rock artists away from their
roots — the song and the beat. To hear the Beatles as a group one must
return to *Revolver,* vintage 1966.

17   Today's young take all the gadgetry for granted — they are not alienated by technological innovation, nor are they particularly impressed.
Jazz musicians, on the other hand — especially followers of Gillespie
and Monk — tend to resist technological innovation. Some, like Fred-
die Hubbard and Ornette Coleman, openly state their opposition to

electronic music. They tend to think that any device not to be found in a 19th-Century symphony orchestra is by definition not a musical instrument.

18   HIT. As rock has matured it has gone through many of the self-conscious changes that marked the rise and fall of jazz. In the first place musicians have changed their definition of success. The hit single is no longer necessary. A group can have a successful album without the support of a Top-40 single (for example, Jefferson Airplane, Jimi Hendrix, Country Joe and the Fish). And if an artist is respected by his fellow musicians, finds approval from a devoted circle of sophisticated fans, and is certified by a semiprofessional publication like *Rolling Stone,* he can maintain high self-esteem even while remaining relatively unknown (for example, Van Dyke Parks, Randy Newman, Captain Beefheart).

19   Some artists at their pinnacles — Bob Dylan, for example — have turned their backs on their audiences and retreated into seclusion. They may need to do this to preserve their sanity, but the effect is to increase the separation between artist and audience. The Beatles swore off personal appearances in 1966; Dylan retired to his Woodstock home after his motorcycle accident in 1966 and has made few public appearances since then; Elvis retreated from public appearances and holed up in his Tennessee mansion for nine years before his recent comeback at the International Hotel in Las Vegas.

20   Rock music has just entered the sit-and-listen stage. Even five years ago one could see the young dancing wildly to the ominpresent beat at San Francisco's Fillmore Auditorium. Now the fans don't dance — they sit, they concentrate, they get close to the stage so they can watch the guitarist move his fingers. They know rock music; they know the electric guitar; and they can tell immediately whether their favorite soloist is in peak improvisational form.

21   SUPER-GROUPS. Just as the stars of yesterday's big bands sought professional recognition and creative opportunities by splitting off to form their own trios and quartets, the most talented musicians today look to each other for support in super-groups.

22   Many rock musicians have begun to look down on the mass audience. The leader of a top English group said after a recent U.S. tour that American audiences are indiscriminately appreciative — they applaud and yell for more, whether the performance is inspired or inept. This instills in the rock artist the same disrespect and contempt for the audience that the jazz musician felt when he finally gave in to a half-dozen requests for *Tico Tico.* Frank Zappa, on the first dissolution of the Mothers of Invention, complained that most audiences "wouldn't know music if it came up and bit 'em on the ass."

23   Rock is dying because it has matured and its fans have become self-selective. They sit intently and listen to complex guitar arrangements and improvisations. Eric Clapton, Mike Bloomfield and Frank Zappa are being hailed as the greatest guitarists and rock musicians of our age. Their fans are devoted, musically sophisticated, and old. Young teenagers find it very difficult to follow this improvisational music because they do not have background experience with rock. Their ears

are not yet equipped to understand or appreciate complexity and innovation. Innovation is a break with tradition, and a 13-year-old has
no tradition by which he can judge the improvisational forms being
explored by many rock musicians.

24   BUBBLEGUM. Young teen-agers don't like to sit and listen anyway.
They want to move. And so they turn to the simpler, more danceable
music that has come to be known as *bubblegum.*

It's got a good beat. You can dance to it.

25   To the disbelief and dismay of rock fans, bubblegum music has
scored tremendous financial successes. *Sugar, Sugar* sold six million
copies, making it the fifth largest-selling record in history. It is the
Archies, Tommy Roe and Bobby Sherman who get the golden records
— not Traffic, not Leon Russell, and not Delaney and Bonnie.

26   Rock fans speak of bubblegum in a tone usually reserved for words
like *excreta.* They look down on the 1910 Fruitgum Company with the
same distaste that their parents reserved for Chuck Berry and Danny
and the Juniors: *How can you listen to that garbage over and over?
It's so simple, so repetitious, so childish.* Is this observation any more
true of *Sugar, Sugar* than it was of *At the Hop?*

27   Different types of music appeal to different types of persons, yet
there are always artists at the interface who want to reconcile the generations. Thus, in the mid-'50s white artists came out with cover versions of black rhythm-and-blues songs. In the early '60s rock songs
became legitimate when they were set to the schmaltzy arrangements
of Percy Faith, Ray Conniff, and the Hollyridge Strings. These albums
catered to the older audience. The younger generation snickered as
they would at a 50-year-old housewife who wore a miniskirt and head-
band. Staying young beyond one's chronology is a complex and often
painful undertaking. As Jefferson Airplane explains: "One generation
got old/One generation got soul."

28   Today there are fewer gap-bridging acts. This is partly because
groups are providing their own nostalgic ties with older musical styles.
A Mantovani version isn't needed any more — one can get lush, syrupy
strings on the Beatles' last album, *Let It Be;* and on *Self Portrait,* Bob
Dylan provides his own undercover versions of *Blue Moon* and *I Forgot More Than You'll Ever Know About Love.*

29   VOLTAGE. In the search for new identity and innovation it was inevitable that rock would reiterate jazz. New bands don't feature just
the electric guitar — trumpets, flutes, violins and other traditional instruments are accepted in the contemporary rock band, as long as they are
electric. Many recent bands (Blood, Sweat and Tears, Chicago, and
Cold Blood, for example) are highly reminiscent in their instrumenta-
tion of such earlier groups as Miles Davis' Tentet in the late '40s. And
the loud, brassy arrangements are direct descendants of Count Basie.
A promising new group, Ten Wheel Drive, provides a mixture of Big
Mama Thornton blues and a tenor sax reminiscent of Coltrane, all set
to tight arrangements that remind one of The Jazz Messengers with
Art Blakey and Horace Silver.

30   Other rock artists are reviving traditional jazz forms—on piano, Leon Russell sounds like Jelly Roll Morton, and Janis Joplin was certainly the best jazz singer since Ma Rainey and Bessie Smith.

31   With other artists—Miles Davis, Don Ellis and Gary Burton, for example—the cross-fertilization between musical forms is so complete that classification becomes meaningless, or at least tedious.

32   TRACKS. Other events in the evolution of jazz give hints of the future development of rock. For a brief period jazz found acceptance as background music in movies (*East of Eden, The Man with the Golden Arm*), and later served a similar function on action TV shows (*Peter Gunn, Richard Diamond*). Similarly, rock has recently found its way onto the sound tracks of dramatic movies (*Easy Rider, Zabriskie Point*), and we can expect that soon TV shows will feature rock 'n' roll theme music. After the extended stay of The Who at the Metropolitan Opera, anything can happen.

33   The musical statements that rock will make in its final years can only be guessed at. Innovation in style and song is essential in recent rock music—any group that fails to innovate does not attract a mass audience. No modern artist becomes popular on someone else's songs, unless he has arranged unique interpretations (e.g., Janis Joplin, Joe Cocker).

34   When any music reaches the sit-and-listen phase, it becomes a different music—jazz becomes *modern* jazz, rock becomes *hard* or *acid* rock. The music fails to pick up a new, young audience and it begins to die. Perhaps 20 years from now we will look back on Woodstock as the beginning of the end—similar to Benny Goodman's famous Paramount Theater and Carnegie Hall engagements of 1938. It may have marked the crystallization of the sit-and-listen phase, and therefore the imminent death of rock 'n' roll.

35   Perhaps 15 years from now there will be a bubblegum revival, the Archies will be likened to Bill Haley and the Comets, and Bobby Sherman will be called the musical genius of his time who broke away from tradition and forged the new music.

36   Sociological speculations are many and fascinating. But when some new musical form sweeps the mass audience out from under the aging bubblegum musicians, the young fans will have a clear and classic reason for liking the new music:

It's got a good beat. You can dance to it.

Discussion of Theme

1. According to Horowitz why did jazz lose its place in the forefront of American music? Who was to blame?
2. What did rock 'n' roll offer as a contrast to jazz? Are its musical standards different? How is the audience's role different?
3. How does acid rock reflect the technology of our era? What basic aspect of music has it destroyed?
4. What is bubblegum music? What is its fate?

Discussion of Rhetoric

1. Is Horowitz writing this article for jazz fans, rock fans, or for the musically uninformed? How do you know?
2. Locate several instances of the author's use of jargon. Does it add to or hinder your enjoyment of the article?
3. Does Horowitz betray his own attitude toward one of the styles of music he is analyzing, or is his tone impartial?
4. What developmental device does the author use throughout the article? Is it appropriate?
5. How effective is the conclusion? Explain.

Writing Assignments

1. If you disagree with Horowitz's argument, write a rebuttal.
2. If you believe that musical taste and standards have declined, present your views.
3. Describe your favorite rock group, and explain why you like them.
4. Develop the following title into a theme: "My Favorite Symphony (or composer)."

Library Exploration

1. Who were Bartok and Stravinsky? What innovations did they intro-duce to classical music?
2. Select a historical period—the Renaissance or the eighteenth cen-tury, for example—and study its music.
3. Several articles have been written about the Woodstock festival and other similar gatherings. Report on some of these studies.

Vocabulary

(4) RAPPORT   sympathetic or harmonious relation
(6) PEER   an equal
(8) MALIGNANT   deadly
(11) CRITERION   a standard of judgment
(13) ECCLESIASTICAL   pertain-ing to the church

(13) CYCLICAL FORM   musical composition consisting of several movements
(20) OMNIPRESENT   present everywhere

Clement Greenberg (1909–), a well-known art critic, has been an editor for such publications as the "Nation," "Commentary," and "Partisan Review." A collection of essays in 1961, "Art and Culture," was a popular critical work.

In this defense of "modernist art in general, or abstract art in particular," Greenberg admits that abstract art has been attacked as being pathological, but he shows that "no hard-and-fast line separates it from representational art. . . ."

CLEMENT GREENBERG

The Case for Abstract Art

1   Many people say that the kind of art our age produces is one of the major symptoms of what's wrong with the age. The disintegration and, finally, the disappearance of recognizable images in painting and sculpture, like the obscurity in advanced literature, are supposed to reflect a disintegration of values in society itself. Some people go further and say that abstract, nonrepresentational art is pathological art, crazy art, and that those who practice it and those who admire and buy it are either sick or silly. The kindest critics are those who say it's all a joke, a hoax, and a fad, and that modernist art in general, or abstract art in particular, will soon pass. This sort of thing is heard or read pretty constantly, but in some years more often than others.

2   There seems to be a certain rhythm in the advance in popularity of modernist art, and a certain rhythm in the counterattacks which try to stem it. More or less the same works or arguments are used in all the polemics, but the targets usually change. Once it was the impressionists who were a scandal, next it was Van Gogh and Cézanne, then it was Matisse, then it was cubism and Picasso, after that Mondrian, and now it is Jackson Pollock. The fact that Pollock was an American shows, in a backhanded way, how important American art has lately become.

3   Some of the same people who attack modernist art in general, or abstract art in particular, happen also to complain that our age has lost those habits of disinterested contemplation, and that capacity for enjoying things as ends in themselves and for their own sake, which former ages are supposed to have cultivated. This idea has been advanced often enough to convert it into a cliché. I hate to give assent to a cliché, for it is almost always an oversimplification, but I have to make an exception in this case. While I strongly doubt that disinterested contemplation was as unalloyed or as popular in ages past as is supposed, I do tend to agree that we could do with more of it in this time, and especially in this country.

4   I think a poor life is lived by anyone who doesn't regularly take time out to stand and gaze, or sit and listen, or touch, or smell, or brood, without any further end in mind, simply for the satisfaction gotten from that which is gazed at, listened to, touched, smelled or brooded upon. We all know, however, that the climate of Western life, and particularly of American life, is not conducive to this kind of thing; we are all too busy making a living. This is another cliché, of course. And still a third cliché says that we should learn from Oriental society how to give more of ourselves to the life of the spirit, to contemplation and meditation, and to the appreciation of what is satisfying or beautiful in its own sole right. This last is not only a cliché, but a fallacy, since most Orientals are even more preoccupied than we are with making a living. I hope that I myself am not making a gross and reductive simplification when I say that so much of Oriental contemplative and aesthetic discipline strikes me as a technique for keeping one's eyes averted from ugliness and misery.

5   Every civilization and every tradition of culture seem to possess capacities for self-cure and self-correction that go into operation automatically, unbidden. If the given tradition goes too far in one direction it will usually try to right itself by going equally far in the opposite one. There is no question but that our Western civilization, especially in its American variant, devotes more mental energy than any other to the production of material things and services; and that, more than any other, it puts stress on interested, purposeful activity in general. This is reflected in our art, which, as has been frequently observed, put such great emphasis on movement and development and resolution, on beginnings, middles, and endings — that is, on dynamics. Compare Western music with any other kind, or look at Western literature, for that matter, with its relatively great concern with plot and overall structure and its relatively small concern with tropes and figures and ornamental elaborations; think of how slow-moving Chinese and Japanese poetry is by comparison with ours, and how much it delights in static situations; and how uncertain the narrational logic of non-Western fiction tends to be. Think of how encrusted and convoluted Arabic poetry is by contrast even with our most euphuistic lyrical verse. And as for non-Western music, does it not almost always, and literally, strike us as more monotonous than ours?

6   Well, how does Western art compensate for, correct, or at least qualify its emphasis on the dynamic — an emphasis that may or may not be excessive? And how does Western life itself compensate for, correct, or

at least qualify its obsession with material production and purposeful activity? I shall not here attempt to answer the latter question. But in the realm of art an answer is beginning to emerge of its own accord, and the shape of part of that answer is abstract art.

7   Abstract decoration is almost universal, and Chinese and Japanese calligraphy is quasi-abstract — abstract to the extent that few occidentals can read the characters of Chinese or Japanese writing. But only in the West, and only in the last fifty years, have such things as abstract pictures and free-standing pieces of abstract sculpture appeared. What makes the big difference between these and abstract decoration is that they are, exactly, pictures and free-standing sculpture — solo works of art meant to be looked at for their own sake and with full attention, and not as the adjuncts, incidental aspects, or settings of things other than themselves. These abstract pictures and pieces of sculpture challenge our capacity for disinterested contemplation in a way that is more concentrated and, I daresay, more conscious than anything else I know of in art. Music is an essentially abstract art, but even at its most rarefied and abstract, whether it's Bach's or the middle-period Schoenberg's music, it does not offer this challenge in quite the same way or degree. Music tends from a beginning through a middle toward an ending. We wait to see how it "comes out" — which is what we also do with literature. Of course, the *total* experience of literature and music is completely disinterested, but it becomes that only at a further remove. While undergoing the experience we are caught up and expectant as well as detached — disinterested and at the same time interested in a way resembling that in which we are interested in how things turn out in real life. I exaggerate to make my point — aesthetic experience *has* to be disinterested, and when it is genuine it always is, even when bad works of art are involved — but the distinctions I've made and those I've still to make are valid nevertheless.

8   With representational painting it is something like what it is with literature. This has been said before, many times before, but usually in order to criticize representational painting in what I think is a wrong-headed when not downright silly way. What I mean when I say, in this context, that representational painting is like literature, is that it tends to involve us in the interested as well as the disinterested by presenting us with the images of things that are inconceivable outside time and action. This goes even for landscapes and flower pieces and still lifes. It is not simply that we sometimes tend to confuse the attractiveness of the things represented in a picture with the quality of the picture itself. And it is not only that attractiveness as such has nothing to do with the abiding success of a work of art. What is more fundamental is that the meaning — as distinct from the attractiveness — of what is represented becomes truly inseparable from the representation itself. That Rembrandt confined impasto — thick paint, that is — to his highlights, and that in his later portraits especially these coincide with the ridges of the noses of his subjects is important to the artistic effect of these portraits. And that the effectiveness of the impasto, as impasto — as an abstract element of technique — coincides with its

effectiveness as a means of showing just how a nose looks under a certain kind of light is also genuinely important. And that the lifelike delineation of the nose contributes to the evocation of the personality of the individual to whom the nose belongs is likewise important. And the manner and degree of insight into that individual's personality which Rembrandt exhibits in his portrait is important too. None of these factors can be, or ought to be, separated from the legitimate effect of the portrait as a picture pure and simple.

9   But once we have to do with personalities and lifelikeness we have to do with things from which we cannot keep as secure a distance for the sake of disinterestedness as we can, say, from abstract decoration. As it happens, the whole tendency of our Western painting, up until the later stages of impressionism, was to make distance and detachment on the part of the spectator as insecure as possible. It laid more of a stress than any other tradition on creating a sculpture-like, or photographic, illusion of the third dimension, on thrusting images at the eye with a lifelikeness that brought them as close as possible to their originals. Because of their sculptural vividness, Western paintings tend to be far less quiet, far more agitated and active — in short, far more explicitly dynamic — than most non-Western paintings do. And they involve the spectator to a much greater extent in the practical and actual aspects of the things they depict and represent.

10   We begin to wonder what we think of the people shown in Rembrandt's portraits, *as* people; whether or not we would like to walk through the terrain shown in a Corot landscape; about the life stories of the burghers we see in a Steen painting; we react in a less than disinterested way to the attractiveness of the models, real or ideal, of the personages in a Renaissance painting. And once we begin to do this we begin to participate in the work of art in a so-to-speak practical way. In itself this participation may not be improper, but it does become so when it begins to shut out all other factors. This it has done and does, all too often. Even though the connoisseurs have usually been able in the long run to prefer the picture of a dwarf by Velasquez to that of a pretty girl by Howard Chandler Christy, the enjoyment of pictorial and sculptural art in our society has tended, on every other level than that of professional connoisseurship, to be excessively "literary," and to center too much on merely technical feats of copying.

11   But, as I've said, every tradition of culture tends to try to correct one extreme by going to its opposite. And when our Western tradition of painting came up at last with reservations about its forthright naturalism, these quickly took the form of an equally forthright antinaturalism. These reservations started with late impressionism, and have now culminated in abstract art. I don't at all wish to be understood as saying that it all happened because some artist or artists decided it was time to curb the excesses of realistic painting, and that the main historical significance of abstract art lies in its function as an antidote to these. Nor do I wish to be understood as assuming that realistic or naturalistic art inherently needs, or ever needed, such a thing as an antidote. The motivations, conscious and unconscious, of the first modernist artists, and of present modernists as well, were and are

quite different. Impressionism itself started as an effort to push naturalism further than ever before. And all through the history of art—not
only in recent times—consequences have escaped intentions.

12 It is on a different, and more impersonal and far more general level
of meaning and history that our culture has generated abstract art as
an antidote. On that level this seemingly new kind of art has emerged
as an epitome of almost everything that disinterested contemplation
requires, and as both a challenge and a reproof to a society that ex-
aggerates, not the necessity, but the intrinsic value of purposeful and
interested activity. Abstract art comes, on this level, as a relief, an
archexample of something that does not have to mean, or be useful
for, anything other than itself. And it seems fitting, too, that abstract
art should at present flourish most in this country. If American society
is indeed given over as no other society has been to purposeful
activity and material production, then it is right that it should be reminded, in extreme terms, of the essential nature of disinterested
activity.

13 Abstract art does this in very literal and also very imaginative ways.
First, it does not exhibit the illusion or semblance of things we are already familiar with in real life; it gives us no imaginary space through
which to walk with the mind's eye; no imaginary objects to desire or
not desire; no imaginary people to like or dislike. We are left alone with
shapes and colors. These may or may not remind us of real things; but
if they do, they usually do so incidentally or accidentally—on our own
responsibility as it were; and the genuine enjoyment of an abstract
picture does not ordinarily depend on such resemblances.

14 Second, pictorial art in its highest definition is static; it tries to overcome movement in space or time. This is not to say that the eye does
not wander over a painted surface, and thus travel in both space and
time. When a picture presents us with an illusion of real space, there
is all the more inducement for the eye to do such wandering. But
ideally the whole of a picture should be taken in at a glance; its unity
should be immediately evident, and the supreme quality of a picture,
the highest measure of its power to move and control the visual
imagination, should reside in its unity. And this is something to be
grasped only in an individual instant of time. No expectancy is involved in the true and pertinent experience of a painting; a picture,
I repeat, does not "come out" the way a story, or a poem, or a piece
of music does. It's all there at once, like a sudden revelation. This "at-
onceness" an abstract picture usually drives home to us with greater
singleness and clarity than a representational painting does. And to
apprehend this "at-onceness" demands a freedom of mind and untrammeledness of eye that constitute "at-onceness" in their own right.
Those who have grown capable of experiencing this know what I
mean. You are summoned and gathered into one point in the continuum of duration. The picture does this to you, willy-nilly, regardless
of whatever else is on your mind; a mere glance at it creates the attitude required for its appreciation, like a stimulus that elicits an automatic response. You become all attention, which means that you
become, for the moment, selfless and in a sense entirely identified
with the object of your attention.

15   The "at-onceness" which a picture or a piece of sculpture enforces
on you is not, however, single or isolated. It can be repeated in a succession of instants, in each one remaining an "at-onceness," an instant
all by itself. For the cultivated eye, the picture repeats its instantaneous unity like a mouth repeating a single word.

16   This pinpointing of the attention, this complete liberation and concentration of it, offers what is largely a new experience to most people
in our sort of society. And it is, I think, a hunger for this particular kind
of experience that helps account for the growing popularity of abstract
art in this country: for the way it is taking over in the art schools, the
galleries, and the museums. The fact that fad and fashion are also
involved does not invalidate what I say. I know that abstract art of the
latest variety — that originating with painters like Pollock and Georges
Mathieu — has gotten associated with progressive jazz and its cultists;
but what of it? That Wagner's music became associated with German
ultranationalism, and that Wagner was Hitler's favorite composer, still
doesn't detract from its sheer quality of music. That the present vogue
for folk music started, back in the 1930s, among the Communists
doesn't make our liking for it any the less genuine, or take anything
away from folk music itself. Nor does the fact that so much gibberish
gets talked and written about abstract art compromise it, just as the
gibberish in which art criticism in general abounds, and abounds
increasingly, doesn't compromise art in general.

17   One point, however, I want to make glaringly clear. Abstract art is
not a special kind of art; no hard-and-fast line separates it from representational art; it is only the latest phase in the development of
Western art as a whole, and almost every "technical" device of abstract painting is already to be found in the realistic painting that
preceded it. Nor is it a superior kind of art. I still know of nothing in
abstract painting, aside perhaps from some of the near-abstract cubist
works that Picasso, Braque and Léger executed between 1910 and
1914, which matches the highest achievements of the old masters.
Abstract painting may be a purer, more quintessential form of pictorial
art than the representational kind, but this does not of itself confer
quality upon an abstract picture. The ratio of bad abstract painting to
good is actually much greater than the ratio of bad to good representational painting. Nonetheless, the very best painting, the major painting, of our age is almost exclusively abstract. Only on the middle and
lower levels of quality, on the levels below the first-rate — which is, of
course, where most of the art that gets produced places itself — only
there is the better painting preponderantly representational.

18   On the plane of culture in general, the special, unique value of abstract art, I repeat, lies in the high degree of detached contemplativeness that its appreciation requires. Contemplativeness is demanded in
greater or lesser degree for the appreciation of every kind of art, but
abstract art tends to present this requirement in quintessential form,
at its purest, least diluted, most immediate. If abstract art — as does
happen nowadays — should chance to be the first kind of pictorial art
we learn to appreciate, the chances are that when we go to other kinds
of pictorial art — to the old masters, say, and I hope we all do go to the
old masters eventually — we shall find ourselves all the better able to

enjoy them. That is, we shall be able to experience them with less intrusion of irrelevancies, therefore more fully and more intensely.

19   The old masters stand or fall, their pictures succeed or fail, on the same ultimate basis as do those of Mondrian or any other abstract artist. The abstract formal unity of a picture by Titian is more important to its quality than what the picture images. To return to what I said about Rembrandt's portraits, the whatness of what is imaged is not unimportant — far from it — and cannot be separated, really, from the formal qualities that result from the way it is imaged. But it is a fact, in my experience, that representational paintings are essentially and most fully appreciated when the identities of what they represent are only secondarily present to our consciousness. Baudelaire said he could grasp the quality of a painting by Delacroix when he was still too far away from it to make out the images it contained, when it was still only a blur of colors. I think it was really on this kind of evidence that critics and connoisseurs, though they were almost always unaware of it, discriminated between the good and the bad in the past. Put to it, they more or less unconsciously dismissed from their minds the connotations of Rubens' nudes when assessing and experiencing the final worth of his art. They may have remained aware of the pinkness as a *nude* pinkness, but it was a pinkness and a nudity devoid of most of their usual associations.

20   Abstract paintings do not confront us with such problems. Or at least the frequenting of abstract art can train us to relegate them automatically to their proper place; and in doing this we refine our eyes for the appreciation of non-abstract art. That has been my own experience. That it is still relatively rare can be explained perhaps by the fact that most people continue to come to painting through academic art — the kind of art they see in ads and in magazines — and when and if they discover abstract art it comes as such an overwhelming experience that they tend to forget everything produced before. This is to be deplored, but it does not negate the value, actual or potential, of abstract art as an introduction to the fine arts in general, and as an introduction, too, to habits of disinterested contemplation. In this respect, the value of abstract art will, I hope, prove far greater in the future than it has yet. Not only can it confirm instead of subverting tradition; it can teach us, by example, how valuable so much in life can be made without being invested with ulterior meanings. How many people I know who have hung abstract pictures on their walls and found themselves gazing at them endlessly, and then exclaiming, "I don't know what there is in that painting, but I can't take my eyes off it." This kind of bewilderment is salutary. It does us good not to be able to explain, either to ourselves or to others, what we enjoy or love; it expands our capacity for experience.

Discussion of Theme

1. Greenberg says that abstract art does not confront us with the problems presented by realistic art. What problems is he talking about?

Does abstract art confront us with other problems? If so, what?
2. Do you agree with Greenberg that appreciating abstract art can actually increase our understanding of traditional art? Or would it work the other way around?
3. Perhaps you and your friends have denounced abstract art as a joke, a hoax, or a fad. Does this essay properly answer this charge?
4. What are impressionism and cubism?
5. Why is the *total* experience of literature and music completely disinterested? See paragraph 7.

Discussion of Rhetoric

1. Greenberg refers several times to clichés. What is the difference between a simple truth and a cliché?
2. Is the simile in paragraph 15 appropriate? Does it create a mental image that is at odds with what Greenberg may be trying to convey about abstract art?
3. What technique does Greenberg use to draw us into his essay? Is this used simply to make us agree with him?
4. What is the effect on the piece as a whole of using such awkward combinations as *lifelikeness, connoisseurship, archexample, untrammeledness, at-onceness, contemplativeness, whatness?*

Writing Assignments

1. If you enjoy abstract art, but for reasons different from those that Greenberg presents, explain how you look at modern art and what you see in it.
2. Discuss the difference between art and literature as propaganda and as purely artistic or intellectual vehicles.
3. Explain why you admire a particular work of art—a painting, or a sculpture, or a collage.
4. Frequently there is great beauty either in a "found object," such as a piece of twisted metal in a weathered board, or in many natural objects. If you have been struck by the beauty in an object that was not conceived as art, describe it and explain what it is that gives you pleasure in it.

Library Exploration

1. To learn more about the difficulties faced by artists in their own lifetime, read a biography of Rembrandt or Van Gogh.
2. Fernand Léger's famous painting *Nude Descending a Staircase* provoked an intense reaction when it first appeared. Read about the furor that it aroused; then look at the picture and try to determine why the public became so enraged.

Vocabulary

(1) PATHOLOGICAL sick; diseased

(2) POLEMICS disputes; tirades

(3) DISINTERESTED objective; unbiased

(3) UNALLOYED pure; unmixed

(4) CONDUCIVE contributive; helpful

(4) REDUCTIVE tending to diminish

(5) CONVOLUTED twisted; intertwined

(5) EUPHUISTIC high-flown; affected

(7) CALLIGRAPHY handwriting

(10) CONNOISSEURS those with expert knowledge and discrimination

(11) CULMINATED resulted in; reached

(11) ANTIDOTE remedy

(12) EPITOME typical or ideal representation

(12) ARCHEXAMPLE chief example

(14) UNTRAMMELEDNESS freedom

(14) CONTINUUM unbroken whole

(17) QUINTESSENTIAL perfect; ultimate

(17) PREPONDERANTLY primarily

(20) RELEGATE consign

(20) DEPLORED lamented

(20) SUBVERTING undermining; corrupting

(20) ULTERIOR undisclosed; more remote

(20) SALUTARY beneficial

Aaron Copland (1900–), born in Brooklyn, is one of the nation's leading composers and music authorities. He studied piano and composition with Ricardo Vines and Nadia Boulanger. He has written music for films, ballets, plays, and operas, and has conducted his own symphonic works throughout the world. Among his books are "What to Listen for in Music" (1939), "Music and Imagination" (1952), and "Copland on Music" (1960).

In order to discuss listening to music, the author tackles his subject on three separate planes, beginning with simple enjoyment.

AARON COPLAND

What to Listen for in Music

1 We all listen to music according to our separate capacities. But, for the sake of analysis, the whole listening process may become clearer if we break it up into its component parts, so to speak. In a certain sense we all listen to music on three separate planes. For lack of a better terminology, one might name these: (1) the sensuous plane, (2) the expressive plane, (3) the sheerly musical plane. The only advantage to be gained from mechanically splitting up the listening process into these hypothetical planes is the clearer view to be had of the way in which we listen.

2   The simplest way of listening to music is to listen for the sheer pleasure of the musical sound itself. That is the sensuous plane. It is the plane on which we hear music without thinking, without considering it in any way. One turns on the radio while doing something else and absentmindedly bathes in the sound. A kind of brainless but attractive state of mind is engendered by the mere sound appeal of the music.

3   You may be sitting in a room reading this book. Imagine one note
struck on the piano. Immediately that one note is enough to change
the atmosphere of the room—proving that the sound element in music
is a powerful and mysterious agent, which it would be foolish to deride
or belittle.

4   The surprising thing is that many people who consider themselves
qualified music lovers abuse that plane in listening. They go to concerts in order to lose themselves. They use music as a consolation or
an escape. They enter an ideal world where one doesn't have to think
of the realities of everyday life. Of course they aren't thinking about
the music either. Music allows them to leave it, and they go off to a
place to dream, dreaming because of and apropos of the music yet
never quite listening to it.

5   Yes, the sound appeal of music is a potent and primitive force, but
you must not allow it to usurp a disproportionate share of your interest.
The sensuous plane is an important one in music, a very important
one, but it does not constitute the whole story.

6   There is no need to digress further on the sensuous plane. Its appeal
to every normal human being is self-evident. There is, however, such
a thing as becoming more sensitive to the different kinds of sound
stuff as used by various composers. For all composers do not use that
sound stuff in the same way. Don't get the idea that the value of music
is commensurate with its sensuous appeal or that the loveliest sounding music is made by the greatest composer. If that were so, Ravel
would be a greater creator than Beethoven. The point is that the
sound element varies with each composer, that his usage of sound
forms an integral part of his style and must be taken into account
when listening. The reader can see, therefore, that a more conscious
approach is valuable even on this primary plane of music listening.

7   The second plane on which music exists is what I have called the
expressive one. Here, immediately, we tread on controversial ground.
Composers have a way of shying away from any discussion of music's
expressive side. Did not Stravinsky himself proclaim that his music
was an "object," a "thing," with a life of its own, and with no other
meaning than its own purely musical existence? This intransigent
attitude of Stravinsky's may be due to the fact that so many people
have tried to read different meanings into so many pieces. Heaven
knows it is difficult enough to say precisely what it is that a piece of
music means, to say it definitely, to say it finally so that everyone is
satisfied with your explanation. But that should not lead one to the
other extreme of denying to music the right to be "expressive."

8   My own belief is that all music has an expressive power, some more
and some less, but that all music has a certain meaning behind the
notes and that that meaning behind the notes constitutes, after all,
what the piece is saying, what the piece is about. This whole problem
can be stated quite simply by asking, "Is there a meaning to music?"
My answer to that would be, "Yes." And "Can you state in so many
words what the meaning is?" My answer to that would be, "No."
Therein lies the difficulty.

9   Simple-minded souls will never be satisfied with the answer to the

second of these questions. They always want to have a meaning, and the more concrete it is the better they like it. The more the music reminds them of a train, a storm, a funeral, or any other familiar conception the more expressive it appears to be to them. This popular idea of music's meaning—stimulated and abetted by the usual run of musical commentator—should be discouraged wherever and whenever it is met. One timid lady once confessed to me that she suspected something seriously lacking in her appreciation of music because of her inability to connect it with anything definite. That is getting the whole thing backward, of course.

10   Still, the question remains, How close should the intelligent music lover wish to come to pinning a definite meaning to any particular work? No closer than a general concept, I should say. Music expresses, at different moments, serenity or exuberance, regret or triumph, fury or delight. It expresses each of these moods, and many others, in a numberless variety of subtle shadings and differences. It may even express a state of meaning for which there exists no adequate word in any language. In that case, musicians often like to say that it has only a purely musical meaning. They sometimes go farther and say that *all* music has only a purely musical meaning. What they really mean is that no appropriate word can be found to express the music's meaning and that, even if it could, they do not feel the need of finding it.

11   But whatever the professional musician may hold, most musical novices still search for specific words with which to pin down their musical reactions. That is why they always find Tschaikovsky easier to "understand" than Beethoven. In the first place, it is easier to pin a meaning-word on a Tschaikovsky piece than on a Beethoven one. Much easier. Moreover, with the Russian composer, every time you come back to a piece of his it almost always says the same thing to you, whereas with Beethoven it is often quite difficult to put your finger right on what he is saying. And any musician will tell you that that is why Beethoven is the greater composer. Because music which always says the same thing to you will necessarily soon become dull music, but music whose meaning is slightly different with each hearing has a greater chance of remaining alive.

12   Listen, if you can, to the forty-eight fugue themes of Bach's *Well-Tempered Clavichord*. Listen to each theme, one after another. You will soon realize that each theme mirrors a different world of feeling. You will also soon realize that the more beautiful a theme seems to you the harder it is to find any word that will describe it to your complete satisfaction. Yes, you will certainly know whether it is a gay theme or a sad one. You will be able, in other words, in your own mind, to draw a frame of emotional feeling around your theme. Now study the sad one a little closer. Try to pin down the exact quality of its sadness. Is it pessimistically sad or resignedly sad; is it fatefully sad or smilingly sad?

13   Let us suppose that you are fortunate and can describe to your own satisfaction in so many words the exact meaning of your chosen theme. There is still no guarantee that anyone else will be satisfied. Nor need they be. The important thing is that each one feel for himself the spe-

cific expressive quality of a theme or, similarly, an entire piece of music. And if it is a great work of art, don't expect it to mean exactly the same thing to you each time you return to it.

14   Themes or pieces need not express only one emotion, of course. Take such a theme as the first main one of the *Ninth Symphony,* for example. It is clearly made up of different elements. It does not say only one thing. Yet anyone hearing it immediately gets a feeling of strength, a feeling of power. It isn't a power that comes simply because the theme is played loudly. It is a power inherent in the theme itself. The extraordinary strength and vigor of the theme results in the listener's receiving an impression that a forceful statement has been made. But one should never try to boil it down to "the fateful hammer of life," etc. That is where the trouble begins. The musician, in his exasperation, says it means nothing but the notes themselves, whereas the nonprofessional is only too anxious to hang on to any explanation that gives him the illusion of getting closer to the music's meaning.

15   Now, perhaps, the reader will know better what I mean when I say that music does have an expressive meaning but that we cannot say in so many words what that meaning is.

16   The third plane on which music exists is the sheerly musical plane. Besides the pleasurable sound of music and the expressive feeling that it gives off, music does exist in terms of the notes themselves and of their manipulation. Most listeners are not sufficiently conscious of this third plane. . . .

17   Professional musicians, on the other hand, are, if anything, too conscious of the mere notes themselves. They often fall into the error of becoming so engrossed with their arpeggios and staccatos that they forget the deeper aspects of the music they are performing. But from the layman's standpoint, it is not so much a matter of getting over bad habits on the sheerly musical plane as of increasing one's awareness of what is going on, in so far as the notes are concerned.

18   When the man in the street listens to the "notes themselves" with any degree of concentration, he is most likely to make some mention of the melody. Either he hears a pretty melody or he does not, and he generally lets it go at that. Rhythm is likely to gain his attention next, particularly if it seems exciting. But harmony and tone color are generally taken for granted, if they are thought of consciously at all. As for music's having a definite form of some kind, that idea seems never to have occurred to him.

19   It is very important for all of us to become more alive to music on its sheerly musical plane. After all, an actual musical material is being used. The intelligent listener must be prepared to increase his awareness of the musical material and what happens to it. He must hear the melodies, the rhythms, the harmonies, the tone colors in a more conscious fashion. But above all he must, in order to follow the line of the composer's thought, know something of the principles of musical form. Listening to all of these elements is listening on the sheerly musical plane.

20   Let me repeat that I have split up mechanically the three separate planes on which we listen merely for the sake of greater clarity. Actually, we never listen to one or the other of these planes. What we do

is to correlate them—listening in all three ways at the same time. It takes no mental effort, for we do it instinctively.

21   Perhaps an analogy with what happens to us when we visit the theater will make this instinctive correlation clearer. In the theater, you are aware of the actors and actresses, costumes and sets, sounds and movements. All these give one the sense that the theater is a pleasant place to be in. They constitute the sensuous plane in our theatrical reactions.

22   The expressive plane in the theater would be derived from the feeling that you get from what is happening on the stage. You are moved to pity, excitement, or gaiety. It is this general feeling, generated aside from the particular words being spoken, a certain emotional something which exists on the stage, that is analogous to the expressive quality in music.

23   The plot and plot development is equivalent to our sheerly musical plane. The playwright creates and develops a character in just the same way that a composer creates and develops a theme. According to the degree of your awareness of the way in which the artist in either field handles his material will you become a more intelligent listener.

24   It is easy enough to see that the theatergoer never is conscious of any of these elements separately. He is aware of them all at the same time. The same is true of music listening. We simultaneously and without thinking listen on all three planes.

25   In a sense, the ideal listener is both inside and outside the music at the same moment, judging it and enjoying it, wishing it would go one way and watching it go another—almost like the composer at the moment he composes it; because in order to write his music, the composer must also be inside and outside his music, carried away by it and yet coldly critical of it. A subjective and objective attitude is implied in both creating and listening to music.

26   What the reader should strive for, then, is a more *active* kind of listening. Whether you listen to Mozart or Duke Ellington, you can deepen your understanding of music only by being a more conscious and aware listener—not someone who is just listening, but someone who is listening *for* something.

Discussion of Theme

1. What are the three separate planes on which we all listen to music? Does one of these dominate your listening habits? Which of these planes does Copland consider the simplest?
2. What is "expressive power" in music? Does all music express a certain meaning? Should it?
3. In what way does Copland compare Beethoven with Tschaikovsky? Which of the two composers do you prefer? Why?
4. Why does the author believe that it is important for the layman to "become more alive to music on its sheerly musical plane"? What shortcoming does he say that professional musicians have in relation to the notes themselves?

Discussion of Rhetoric

1. Copland relies heavily on the use of one sort of sentence structure. What is it? Would greater variety have improved his essay?
2. The author is sparing in his use of transitional devices. What quality does this lend his essay?
3. Although he is dealing with abstractions, Copland tries to make his discussion specific. Is he successful?
4. With what paragraph does the conclusion of the essay begin?

Writing Assignments

1. Copland is discussing classical music. Do his comments about planes apply to popular music as well? Illustrate with reference to specific musical compositions.
2. Apply the three planes of listening to a musical experience of your own.
3. Discuss some subject like drama or painting in terms of what you consider its divisions or parts.
4. Define good music.

Library Exploration

1. Describe the historical steps in a major musical development such as progressive jazz.
2. Report on the background and development of an opera by Copland.

Vocabulary

(1) SENSUOUS   appealing to the senses

(4) APROPOS OF   with regard to

(5) POTENT   powerful

(5) USURP   take over

(6) COMMENSURATE   equal in measure

(6) INTEGRAL   intrinsic; essential to completeness

(7) INTRANSIGENT   unyielding

(9) ABETTED   encouraged

(12) PESSIMISTICALLY   darkly; despairingly

(17) ARPEGGIOS   notes of a chord

(17) STACCATOS   notes played sharply and abruptly

(21) ANALOGY   comparison

The authors of the following brief articles have had an unrivaled impact on film making. Ingmar Bergman (1918–), the Swedish stage and film producer, is perhaps best known for "Wild Strawberries" and "The Seventh Seal." Alain Robbe-Grillet (1922–), a native of France, is the author of several novels; he is best known in the United States, however, as the writer of the film script for "Last Year at Marienbad." Michelangelo Antonioni (1929–) was a film critic and maker of documentary films in his native Italy before he achieved fame with "Blow-up."

In the following selections three master craftsmen examine some aspects of the art of film making. Bergman reminds us that the producer is basically a conjurer. Robbe-Grillet tells us that a film is the product of collaboration between the director and his scriptwriter. Finally, Antonioni reminds us that the camera is the vehicle by which the writer's and producer's ideas are transmitted.

The Filmic Arts: A Symposium

THE CONJURER'S ART   Ingmar Bergman

1 When I was ten years old I received my first, rattling film projector, with its chimney and lamp. I found it both mystifying and fascinating. The first film I had was nine feet long and brown in color. It showed a

girl lying asleep in a meadow, who woke up and stretched out her arms, then disappeared to the right. That was all there was to it. The film was a great success and was projected every night until it broke and could not be mended any more.

2   This little rickety machine was my first conjuring set. And even today I remind myself with childish excitement that I am really a conjurer, since cinematography is based on deception of the human eye. I have worked it out that if I see a film which has a running time of one hour, I sit through twenty-seven minutes of complete darkness — the blankness between frames. When I show a film I am guilty of deceit. I use an apparatus which is constructed to take advantage of a certain human weakness, an apparatus with which I can sway my audience in a highly emotional manner — make them laugh, scream with fright, smile, believe in fairy stories, become indignant, feel shocked, charmed, deeply moved or perhaps yawn with boredom. Thus I am either an impostor or, when the audience is willing to be taken in, a conjurer. I perform conjuring tricks with [an] apparatus so expensive and so wonderful that any entertainer in history would have given anything to have it.

STORY AND SCRIPT   Alain Robbe-Grillet

1   The collaboration between a director and his script writer can take a wide variety of forms. One might almost say that there are as many different methods of work as there are films. Yet the one that seems most frequent in the traditional commercial cinema involves a more or less radical separation of scenario and image, story and style; in short, "content" and "form."

2   For instance, the author describes a conversation between two characters, providing the words they speak and a few details about the setting; if he is more precise, he specifies their gestures or facial expressions, but it is always the director who subsequently decides how the episode will be photographed, if the characters will be seen from a distance or if their faces will fill the whole screen, what movements the camera will make, how the scene will be cut, etc. Yet the scene as the audience sees it will assume quite different, sometimes even contradictory meanings, depending on whether the characters are looking toward the camera or away from it, or whether the shots cut back and forth between their faces in rapid succession. The camera may also concentrate on something entirely different during their conversation, perhaps merely the setting around them: the walls of the room they are in, the streets where they are walking, the waves that break in front of them. At its extreme, this method produces a scene whose words and gestures are quite ordinary and unmemorable, compared to the forms and movement of the image, which alone has any importance, which alone appears to have a meaning.

3   This is precisely what makes the cinema an art: it creates a reality with forms. It is in its form that we must look for its true content. The same is true of any work of art, of a novel, for instance: the choice of a narrative style, of a grammatical tense, of a rhythm of phrasing, of a vocabulary carries more weight than the actual story. What novelist worthy of the name would be satisfied to hand his story over to a "phraseologist" who would write out the final version of the text for the reader? The initial idea for a novel involves both the story and its style; often the latter actually comes first in the author's mind, as a painter may conceive of a canvas entirely in terms of vertical lines before deciding to depict a skyscraper group.

4   And no doubt the same is true for a film: conceiving of a screen story, it seems to me, would mean already conceiving of it in images, with all the detail this involves, not only with regard to gestures and settings, but to the camera's position and movement, as well as to the sequence of shots in editing. Alain Resnais and I were able to collaborate only because we saw the film in the same way from the start; and not just in the same general way, but exactly, in the construction of the least detail as in its total architecture. What I wrote might have been what was already in his mind; what he added during the shooting was what I might have written.

IMAGE   Michelangelo Antonioni

1   It is in this spirit that I try to shoot the scenes of my films. I do not read what I am about to shoot each morning — I know the scenario by heart; thus I do not need to study it every morning at my desk. When I arrive at the studio, I ask everyone to leave for a quarter of an hour or twenty minutes, the time required to try out the camera movements, to soak myself in them, to run through the sequence from a technical point of view. I do not shoot several times over, I do not change. I have no doubts about the position of the camera. Obviously, there are problems I set myself, but I resolve them at the beginning and then do not change afterwards.

2   Naturally I cannot work out camera movements at my desk. I have to think about them at the studio. . . . I always use a dolly, even when I am going to shoot an important scene (besides, I prefer vertical rather than horizontal movements). I follow the characters with the movements I have already worked out, and I correct them later if need be. I compose my scenes from behind the camera. Certain directors — for instance, René Clair — work in a different way. I do not say that theirs is not a legitimate system, but I cannot understand how they manage to shoot from little designs and plans they have drawn on paper ahead of time. I feel that the composition is a plastic, figurative element which ought to be seen in its exact dimensions.

Discussion of Theme

1. Which of these authors is most subjective and personal in his discussion of film making?
2. Explain Bergman's statement that he is "either an imposter or a conjurer." Would you agree?
3. According to Robbe-Grillet, what is the contribution of the director to a film?
4. In what way is cinema an art? A craft?

Discussion of Rhetoric

1. Which writer avoids, for the most part, emotional, evocative, or connotative language?
2. What is the purpose of Bergman's anecdote about his first film projector? How does he relate it to his central thesis?
3. "Story and Script" contains a number of transitional phrases that give the selection unity and coherence. Find several of these and determine the function of each.

Writing Assignments

1. Write a review (not merely a plot summary) of a movie that you have seen recently.
2. Should the film be regarded as an art form, or merely a technical product?
3. Develop the following title into a theme: "Movies Are Getting Better (or Worse)."

Library Exploration

For a further treatment of these writers' veiws, read one or more of the following: *Four Screenplays of Ingmar Bergman* (1960), by Ingmar Bergman; *Last Year at Marienbad* (1962), by Alain Robbe-Grillet; and *The World of Film: Michelangelo Antonioni* (1963), by Pierre Leprohon.

John Steinbeck (1902–68), winner of the Nobel Prize in Literature, was born in Salinas, California, and educated at Stanford University. His first successful novel was "Tortilla Flat" (1935). This was followed by "Of Mice and Men" (1937), "The Grapes of Wrath" (1939), "Cannery Row" (1945), and "The Winter of Our Discontent" (1961). The Swedish Academy, which administers the Nobel Prize, stated: "His sympathies always go out to the oppressed, the misfits, and the distressed."

This essay presents, in a humorous vein, a serious comment on the stereotypes that American television often relies on.

JOHN STEINBECK

How to Tell Good Guys from Bad Guys

1 Television has crept upon us so gradually in America that we have not yet become aware of the extent of its impact for good or bad. I myself do not look at it very often except for its coverage of sporting events, news, and politics. Indeed, I get most of my impressions of the medium from my young sons.

2   Whether for good or bad, television has taken the place of the sugar-tit, soothing syrups, and the mild narcotics parents in other days used to reduce their children to semiconsciousness and consequently to seminoisiness. In the past, a harassed parent would say, "Go sit in a chair!" or "Go outside and play!" or "If you don't stop that noise, I'm going to beat your dear little brains out!" The present-day parent suggests, "Why don't you go look at television?" From that moment the screams, shouts, revolver shots, and crashes of motor accidents come

from the loudspeaker, not from the child. For some reason, this is presumed to be more relaxing to the parent. The effect on the child has yet to be determined.

3   I have observed the physical symptoms of television-looking on children as well as on adults. The mouth grows slack and the lips hang open; the eyes take on a hypnotized or doped look; the nose runs rather more than usual; the backbone turns to water and the fingers slowly and methodically pick the designs of brocade furniture. Such is the appearance of semiconsciousness that one wonders how much of the "message" of television is getting through to the brain. This wonder is further strengthened by the fact that a television-looker will look at anything at all and for hours. Recently I came into a room to find my eight-year-old son Catbird sprawled in a chair, idiot slackness on his face, with the doped eyes of an opium smoker. On the television screen stood a young woman of mammary distinction with ice-cream hair listening to a man in thick glasses and a doctor's smock.

4   "What's happening?" I asked.

5   Catbird answered in the monotone of the sleeptalker which is known as television voice, "She is asking if she should dye her hair."

6   "What is the doctor's reaction?"

7   "If she uses Trutone it's all right," said Catbird. "But if she uses ordinary or adulterated products, her hair will split and lose its golden natural sheen. The big economy size is two dollars and ninety-eight cents if you act now," said Catbird.

8   You see, something was getting through to him. He looked punch-drunk, but he was absorbing. I did not feel it fair to interject a fact I have observed—that natural golden sheen does not exist in nature. But I did think of my friend Elia Kazan's cry of despair, and although it is a digression I shall put it down.

9   We were having dinner in a lovely little restaurant in California. At the table next to us were six beautiful, young, well-dressed American girls of the age and appearance of magazine advertisements. There was only one difficulty with their perfection. You couldn't tell them apart. Kazan, who is a primitive of a species once known as men, regarded the little beauties with distaste, and finally in more sorrow than anger cried, "It's years since I've seen or smelled a dame! It's all products, Golden Glint, l'Eau d'Eau, Butisan, Elyn's puff-adder cream—I remember I used to like how women smelled. Nowadays it's all products!"

10   End of digression.

11   Just when the parent becomes convinced that his child's brain is rotting away from television, he is jerked up in another direction. Catbird has corrected me in the Museum of Natural History when I directed his attention to the mounted skeleton of a tyrannosaur. He said it was a brontosaurus but observed kindly that many people made the same error. He argued with his ten-year-old brother about the relative cleanness of the line in Praxiteles and Phidias. He knows the weight a llama will bear before lying down in protest, and his knowledge of entomology is embarrassing to a parent who likes to impart information to his children. And these things he also got from television. I knew that he was picking up masses of unrelated and probably worth-

less information from television, incidentally the kind of information I also like best, but I did not know that television was preparing him in criticism and politics, and that is what this piece is really about.

12 I will have to go back a bit in preparation. When television in America first began to be a threat to the motion-picture industry, that industry fought back by refusing to allow its films to be shown on the home screens. One never saw new pictures, but there were whole blocks of the films called Westerns which were owned by independents and these were released to the television stations. The result is that at nearly any time of the day or night you can find a Western being shown on some television station. It is not only the children who see them. All of America sees them. They are a typically American conception, the cowboy picture. The story never varies and the conventions are savagely adhered to. The hero never kisses a girl. He loves his horse and he stands for right and justice. Any change in the story or the conventions would be taken as an outrage. Out of these films folk heroes have grown up—Hopalong Cassidy, the Lone Ranger, Roy Rogers, and Gene Autry. These are more than great men. They are symbols of courage, purity, simplicity, honesty, and right. You must understand that nearly every American is drenched in the tradition of the Western, which is, of course, the celebration of a whole pattern of American life that never existed. It is also as set in its form as the *commedia dell'arte*.

13 End of preparation.

14 One afternoon, hearing gunfire from the room where our television set is installed, I went in with that losing intention of fraternizing with my son for a little while. There sat Catbird with the cretinous expression I have learned to recognize. A Western was in progress.

15 "What's going on?" I asked.

16 He looked at me in wonder. "What do you mean, what's going on? Don't you know?"

17 "Well, no. Tell me!"

18 He was kind to me. Explained as though I were the child.

19 "Well, the Bad Guy is trying to steal Her father's ranch. But the Good Guy won't let him. Bullet figured out the plot."

20 "Who is Bullet?"

21 "Why, the Good Guy's horse." He didn't add "You dope," but his tone implied it.

22 "Now wait," I said, "which one is the Good Guy?"

23 "The one with the white hat."

24 "Then the one with the black hat is the Bad Guy?"

25 "Anybody knows that," said Catbird.

26 For a time I watched the picture, and I realized that I had been ignoring a part of our life that everybody knows. I was interested in the characterizations. The girl, known as Her or She, was a blonde, very pretty but completely unvoluptuous because these are Family Pictures. Sometimes she wore a simple gingham dress and sometimes a leather skirt and boots, but always she had a bit of a bow in her hair and her face was untroubled with emotion or, one might almost say, intelligence. This also is part of the convention. She is a symbol, and any acting would get her thrown out of the picture by popular acclaim.

27   The Good Guy not only wore a white hat but light-colored clothes, shining boots, tight riding pants, and a shirt embroidered with scrolls and flowers. In my young days I used to work with cattle, and our costume was blue jeans, a leather jacket, and boots with run-over heels. The cleaning bill alone of this gorgeous screen cowboy would have been four times what our pay was in a year.

28   The Good Guy had very little change of facial expression. He went through his fantastic set of adventures with no show of emotion. This is another convention and proves that he is very brave and very pure. He is also scrubbed and has an immaculate shave.

29   I turned my attention to the Bad Guy. He wore a black hat and dark clothing, but his clothing was definitely not only unclean but unpressed. He had a stubble of beard but the greatest contrast was in his face. His was not an immobile face. He leered, he sneered, he had a nasty laugh. He bullied and shouted. He looked evil. While he did not swear, because this is a Family Picture, he said things like "Wall dog it" and "You rat" and "I'll cut your ears and eat 'em," which would indicate that his language was not only coarse but might, off screen, be vulgar. He was, in a word, a Bad Guy. I found a certain interest in the Bad Guy which was lacking in the Good Guy.

30   "Which one do you like the best?" I asked.

31   Catbird removed his anaesthetized eyes from the screen. "What do you mean?"

32   "Do you like the Good Guy or the Bad Guy?"

33   He signed at my ignorance and looked back at the screen. "Are you kidding?" he asked. "The Good Guy, of course."

34   Now a new character began to emerge. He puzzled me because he wore a gray hat. I felt a little embarrassed about asking my son, the expert, but I gathered my courage. "Catbird," I asked shyly, "what kind of a guy is that, the one in the gray hat?"

35   He was sweet to me than. I think until that moment he had not understood the abysmal extent of my ignorance. "He's the In-Between Guy," Catbird explained kindly. "If he starts bad he ends good and if he starts good he ends bad."

36   "What's this one going to do?"

37   "See how he's sneering and needs a shave?" my son asked.

38   "Yes."

39   "Well, the picture's just started, so that guy is going to end good and help the Good Guy get Her father's ranch back."

40   "How can you be sure?" I said.

41   Catbird gave me a cold look. "He's got on a gray hat, hasn't he? Now don't talk. It's about time for the chase."

42   There it was, not only a tight, true criticism of a whole art form but to a certain extent of life itself. I was deeply impressed because this simple explanation seemed to mean something to me more profound than television or Westerns.

43   Several nights later I told that Catbird criticism to a friend who is a producer. He has produced many successful musical comedies. My friend has an uncanny perception for the public mind and also for its likes and dislikes. You have to have if you produce musical shows. He listened and nodded and didn't think it was a cute child story. He said,

"It's not kid stuff at all. There's a whole generation in this country that makes its judgments pretty much on that basis."

44 "Give me an example," I asked.

45 "I'll have to think about it," he said.

46 Well, that was in March. Soon afterward my wife and I went to Spain and then to Paris and rented a little house. As soon as school was out in New York, my boys flew over to join us in Paris.

47 In July, my producer friend dropped in to see us. He was going to take an English show to New York, and he had been in London making arrangements.

48 He told us all of the happenings at home, the gossip and the new jokes and the new songs. Finally I asked him about the McCarthy hearings. "Was it as great a show as we heard?" I asked.

49 "I couldn't let it alone," he said. "I never saw anything like it. I wonder whether those people knew how they were putting themselves on the screen."

50 "Well, what do you think will happen?"

51 "In my opinion, McCarthy is finished," he said and then he grinned. "I base my opinion on your story about Catbird and the Westerns."

52 "I don't follow you."

53 "Have you ever seen McCarthy on television?"

54 "Sure."

55 "Just remember," said my friend. "He sneers. He bullies, he has a nasty laugh and he always looks as though he needs a shave. The only thing he lacks is a black hat. McCarthy is the Bad Guy. Everybody who saw him has got it pegged. He's the Bad Guy and people don't like the Bad Guy. I may be wrong but that's what I think. He's finished."

56 The next morning at breakfast I watched Catbird put butter and two kinds of jam and a little honey on a croissant, then eat the treacherous thing, then lick the jam from the inside of his elbow to his fingers. He took a peach from the basket in the center of the table.

57 "Catbird," I asked, "did you see any of the McCarthy stuff on television?"

58 "Sure," he said.

59 "Was he a Good Guy or a Bad Guy?" I asked.

60 "Bad Guy," said Catbird, and he bit into the peach.

61 And, do you know, I suspect it is just that simple.

Discussion of Theme

1. In real life, do we tend to stereotype people as good guys or bad guys on the basis of overly simple, worthless clues?
2. Does television make it easier for political candidates to masquerade as good guys, with the help of make-up, props, camera angles, carefully controlled questions and situations?
3. A young executive trainee was recently quoted in a newspaper story as saying that he didn't watch as much TV as he used to because, since there was less violence in the programs, "it doesn't

seem as realistic as it did before." What is your opinion of this criticism?
4. What is Steinbeck's criticism of television?
5. What makes the viewer identify with a character in a television program?

Discussion of Rhetoric

1. Steinbeck describes (paragraph 3) the appearance of children watching TV. From then on, how does he reinforce this description? Cite specific examples.
2. The essay opens on a somewhat formal tone. It uses relatively long sentences and fairly abstract diction. What is the effect of such a beginning?
3. This formal tone is soon abandoned in favor of a more intimate and personal approach through the use of shorter sentences, humor, and slang. Why?
4. What functions do the flashbacks and digressions serve? Why are they frequently used in narrative writing?

Writing Assignments

1. Defend your pleasure in watching simple-minded TV programs that make absolutely no intellectual demands on the viewer.
2. Is violence on TV a healthy release for children's tensions and hostilities, or does it make cruelty more acceptable?
3. Is television affecting America's speech habits? If so, how?
4. Write an essay on the unsung heroes of television.

Library Exploration

1. Report on one of the studies that have analyzed the effects of television viewing on children.
2. How are television surveys conducted?

Vocabulary

(2) HARASSED   tormented
(3) BROCADE   a fabric with raised patterns or designs
(3) MAMMARY   bosomy
(5) MONOTONE   single tone
(7) ADULTERATED   contaminated
(11) TYRANNOSAUR   two-footed, flesh-eating dinosaur
(11) BRONTOSAURUS   four-footed, probably herbivorous dinosaur
(11) ENTOMOLOGY   study of insects

(14) FRATERNIZING   associating in a brotherly manner
(14) CRETINOUS   idiotic
(28) IMMACULATE   perfectly clean
(29) IMMOBILE   motionless
(35) ABYSMAL   bottomless
(43) UNCANNY   so far beyond the normal as to seem supernatural
(56) CROISSANT   crescent-shaped French roll

Nicholas Johnson (1934–   ) is
an FCC commissioner and the
author of "How to Talk Back to
Your Television Set." A graduate of the University of Texas
law school, Johnson served as
law clerk to Supreme Court Justice Hugo Black before entering
government service.

As Johnson reminds us, it is not
very smart to ignore the most
significant force in our society.
He gives us some advice: Alert
yourself to the medium. Determine what is worth communicating. Get thinkers together with
creators. Team with professionals and make a program
yourself. In other words, make
television deliver.

NICHOLAS JOHNSON

What Do We Do About Television?

1   Television is more than just another great public resource — like air
and water — ruined by private greed and public inattention. It is the
greatest communications mechanism ever designed and operated by
man. It pumps into the human brain an unending stream of information, opinion, moral values, and esthetic taste. It cannot be a neutral
influence. Every minute of television programing — commercials,
entertainment, news — teaches us something.

2   Most Americans tell pollsters that television constitutes their principal source of information. Many of our senior citizens are tied to their
television sets for intellectual stimulation. And children now spend
more time learning from television than from church and school combined. By the time they enter first grade they will have received more
hours of instruction from television networks than they will later receive from college professors while earning a bachelor's degree.
Whether they like it or not, the television networks are playing the
roles of teacher, preacher, parent, public official, doctor, psychiatrist,

family counselor, and friend for tens of millions of Americans each day of their lives.

3   TV programing can be creative, educational, uplifting, and refreshing without being tedious. But the current television product that drains away lifetimes of leisure energy is none of these. It leaves its addicts waterlogged. Only rarely does it contribute anything meaningful to their lives. No wonder so many Americans express to me a deep-seated hostility toward television. Too many realize, perhaps unconsciously but certainly with utter disgust, that television is itself a drug, constantly offering the allure of a satisfying fulfillment for otherwise empty and meaningless lives that it seldom, if ever, delivers. Well, what do we do about it? Here are a few suggestions:

4   STEP ONE: *Turn on.* I don't mean rush to your sets and turn the on-knob. What I do mean is that we had all better "turn on" to television — wake up to the fact that it is no longer intellectually smart to ignore it. Everything we do, or are, or worry about is affected by television. How and when issues are resolved in this country — the Indochina War, air pollution, race relations — depends as much as anything else on how (and whether) they're treated by the television networks in "entertainment" as well as news and public affairs programing.

5   Dr. S. I. Hayakawa has said that man is no more conscious of communication than a fish would be conscious of the waters of the sea. The analogy is apt. A tidal wave of television programing has covered our land during the past twenty years. The vast majority of Americans have begun to breathe through gills. Yet, we have scarcely noticed the change, let alone wondered what it is doing to us. A few examples may start us thinking.

6   The entire medical profession, as well as the federal government, had little impact upon cigarette consumption in this country until a single young man, John Banzhaf, convinced the Federal Communications Commission that its Fairness Doctrine required TV and radio stations to broadcast $100-million worth of "anti-smoking commercials." Cigarette consumption has now declined for one of the few times in history.

7   What the American people think about government and politics in general — as well as a favorite candidate in particular — is almost exclusively influenced by television. The candidates and their advertising agencies, which invest 75 per cent or more of their campaign funds in broadcast time, believe this: to the tune of $58-million in 1968.

8   There's been a lot ot talk recently about malnutrition in America. Yet, people could let their television sets run for twenty-four hours a day and never discover that diets of starch and soda pop can be fatal.

9   If people lack rudimentary information about jobs, community services for the poor, alcoholism, and so forth, it is because occasional tidbits of information of this kind in soap operas, game shows, commercials, and prime-time series are either inaccurate or missing.

10   In short, whatever your job or interests may be, the odds are very good that you could multiply your effectiveness tremendously by "turning on" to the impact of television on your activities and on our society as a whole — an impact that exceeds that of any other existing institution.

11   STEP TWO: *Tune in.* There are people all over the country with something vitally important to say: the people who knew "cyclamates" were dangerous decades ago, the people who warned us against the Vietnam War in the early Sixties, the people who sounded the alarm against industrial pollution when the word "smog" hadn't been invented. Why didn't we hear their warnings over the broadcast media?

12   In part it is the media's fault, the product of "corporate censorship." But in large part it's the fault of the very people with something to say who never stopped to consider how they might best say it. They simply haven't "tuned in" to television.

13   Obviously, I'm not suggesting you run out and buy up the nearest network. What I am suggesting is that we stop thinking that television programing somehow materializes out of thin air, or that it's manufactured by hidden forces or anonymous men. It is not. There is a new generation coming along that is substantially less frightened by a 16mm camera than by a pencil. You may be a part of it. Even those of us who are not, however, had better tune in to television ourselves.

14   Here is an example of someone who *did*. Last summer, CBS aired an hour-long show on Japan, assisted in large part by former Ambassador Edwin Reischauer. No one, including Ambassador Reischauer and CBS, would claim the show perfectly packaged all that Americans want or need to know about our 100 million neighbors across the Pacific. But many who watched felt it was one of the finest bits of educational entertainment about Japan ever offered to the American people by a commercial network.

15   Ambassador Reischauer has spent his lifetime studying Japan, yet his was not an easy assignment. An hour is not very long for a man who is used to writing books and teaching forty-five-hour semester courses, and there were those who wanted to turn the show into an hour-long geisha party. He could have refused to do the show at all, or walked away from the project when it seemed to be getting out of control. But he didn't. And as a result, the nation, the CBS network, and Mr. Reischauer all benefited. (And the show was honored by an Emmy award.)

16   There are other Ed Reischauers in this country: men who don't know much about "television," but who know more than anyone else about a subject that is important and potentially entertaining. If these men can team their knowledge with the professional television talent of others (and a network's financial commitment), they can make a television program happen. Not only ought they to accept such assignments when asked, I would urge them to come forward and volunteer their assistance to the networks and their local station managers (or to the local cable television system, many of which have been ordered by the FCC to begin local program origination by January 1971). Of course, these offers won't always, or even often, be accepted—for many reasons. But sooner or later the dialogue has to begin.

17   There are many ways you can contribute to a television program without knowing anything about lighting or electronics. Broadcasters in many large communities (especially those with universities) are cashing in on local expertise for quick background when an important news story breaks, occasional on-camera interviews, suggestions for

news items or entire shows, participation as panel members or even hosts, writers for programs, citizen advisory committees, and so forth. Everyone benefits. The broadcaster puts out higher-quality programing, the community builds greater citizen involvement and identification, and the television audience profits.

18   Whoever you are, whatever you're doing, ask yourself this simple question: What do I know or what do I have to communicate that others need to know or might find interesting? If you're a Department of Health, Education and Welfare official charged with communicating vital information about malnutrition to the poor, you might be better off putting your information into the plot-line of a daytime television soap opera than spending a lifetime writing pamphlets. If you're a law enforcement officer and want to inform people how to secure their homes against illegal entry, you might do better by talking to the writers and producers of *Dragnet, I Spy,* or *Mission: Impossible* than by making slide presentations.

19   STEP THREE: *Drop out.* The next step is to throw away most of what you've learned about communication. Don't make the mistake of writing "TV essays" — sitting in front of a camera reading, or saying, what might otherwise have been expressed in print. "Talking heads" make for poor television communication, as educational and commercial television professionals are discovering. Intellectuals and other thinking creative people first have to "drop out" of the traditional modes of communicating thoughts, and learn to swim through the new medium of television.

20   Marshall McLuhan has made much of this clear. If the print medium is linear, television is not. McLuhan's message is as simple as one in a Chinese fortune cookie: "One picture worth thousand words" — particularly when the picture is in color and motion, is accompanied by sound (words and music), and is not tied to an orderly time sequence.

21   Mason Williams, multitalented one-time writer for the Smothers Brothers, is one of the few to see this new dimension in communication. He describes one of his techniques as "verbal snapshots" — short bursts of thought, or poetry, or sound that penetrate the mind in an instant, then linger. Here are some that happen to be about television itself: "I am qualified to criticize television because I have two eyes and a mind, which is one more eye and one more mind than television has." "Television doesn't have a job; it just goofs off all day." "Television is doing to your mind what industry is doing to the land. Some people already think like New York City looks." No one "snapshot" gives the whole picture. But read in rapid succession, they leave a vivid and highly distinctive after-image.

22   Others have dropped out of the older communications techniques and have adapted to the new media. Those students who are seen on television — sitting in, protesting, assembling — are developing a new medium of communication: the demonstration. Denied traditional access to the network news shows and panel discussions, students in this country now communicate with the American people via loud, "newsworthy," media-attractive aggregations of sound and color and people. Demonstrations are happenings, and the news media — like

moths to a flame—run to cover them. Yippie Abbie Hoffman sees this clearer than most:

> So what the hell are we doing, you ask? We are dynamiting brain cells. We are putting people through changes. . . . We are theater in the streets: total and committed. We aim to involve people and use . . . any weapon (prop) we can find. All is relevant, only "the play's the thing." . . . The media is the message. Use it! No fund raising, no full-page ads in *The New York Times*, no press releases. Just do your thing; the press eats it up. Media is free. *Make news.*

23   Dr. Martin Luther King told us very much the same thing. "Lacking sufficient access to television, publications, and broad forums, Negroes have had to write their most persuasive essays with the blunt pen of marching ranks."

24   Mason Williams, Abbie Hoffman, Dr. Martin Luther King, and many others have set the stage for the new communicators, the new media experts. All dropped out of the traditional communications bag of speeches, roundtable discussions, panels, symposia, and filmed essays. And they reached the people.

25   STEP FOUR: *Make the legal scene.* Shakespeare's Henry VI threatened: "The first thing we do, let's kill all the lawyers." Good advice in the fifteenth century perhaps. But bad advice today. We need lawyers. And they can help you improve television.

26   Examples are legion. The United Church of Christ successfully fought *two* legal appeals to the United States Court of Appeals for the District of Columbia, one establishing the right of local citizens groups to participate in FCC proceedings, and one revoking the license of WLBT-TV in Jackson, Mississippi, for systematic segregationist practices. In Media, Pennsylvania, nineteen local organizations hired a Washington lawyer to protest radio station WXUR's alleged policy of broadcasting primarily right-wing political programing. In Los Angeles, a group of local businessmen challenged the license of KHJ-TV, and the FCC's hearing examiner awarded them the channel. There are dozens of other examples of the imaginative use of rusty old legal remedies to improve the contribution of television to our national life.

27   For all their drawbacks, lawyers understand what I call "the law of effective reform"; that is, to get reform from legal institutions (Congress, courts, agencies), one must assert, first, the factual basis for the grievance; second, the specific legal principle involved (Constitutional provision, statute, regulation, judicial or agency decision); and third, the precise remedy sought (legislation, fine, license revocation). Turn on a lawyer, and you'll turn on an awful lot of legal energy, talent, and skill. You will be astonished at just how much legal power you actually have over a seemingly intractable Establishment.

28   STEP FIVE: *Try do-it-yourself justice.* Find out what you can do without a lawyer. You ought to know, for example, that every three years *all* the radio and television station licenses come up for renewal in your state. You ought to know when that date is. It is an "election day" of sorts, and you have a right and obligation to "vote." Not surprisingly, many individuals have never even been told there's an election.

29   Learn something about the grand design of communications in this country. For example, no one "owns" a radio or television station in the sense that you can own a home or the corner drugstore. It's more like leasing public land to graze sheep, or obtaining a contract to build a stretch of highway for the state. Congress has provided that the airwaves are public property. The user must be licensed, and, in the case of commercial broadcasters, that license term is for three years. There is no "right" to have the license renewed. It is renewed only if past performance, and promises of future performance, are found by the FCC to serve "the public interest." In making this finding, the views of local individuals and groups are, of course, given great weight. In extreme cases, license revocation or license renewal contest proceedings may be instituted by local groups.

30   You should understand the basic policy underlying the Communications Act of 1934, which set up the FCC and gave it its regulatory powers. "Spectrum space" (radio and television frequencies) in this country is limited. It must be shared by taxicabs, police cars, the Defense Department, and other business users. In many ways it would be more efficient to have a small number of extremely high-powered stations blanket the country, leaving the remaining spectrum space for other users. But Congress felt in 1934 that it was essential for the new technology of radio to serve needs, tastes, and interests at the local level — to provide community identification, cohesion, and outlets for local talent and expression. For this reason, roughly 95 per cent of the most valuable spectrum space has been handed out to some 7,500 radio and television stations in communities throughout the country. Unfortunately, the theory is not working. Most programing consists of nationally distributed records, movies, newswire copy, commercials, and network shows. Most stations broadcast very little in the way of locally oriented community service. It's up to you to make them change.

31   You have only to exercise your imagination to improve the programing service of your local station. Student groups, civic luncheon clubs, unions, PTAs, the League of Women Voters, and so forth are in an ideal position to accomplish change. They can contact national organizations, write for literature, and generally inform themselves of their broadcasting rights. Members can monitor what is now broadcast and draw up statements of programing standards, indicating what they would like to see with as much specificity as possible. They can set up Citizens Television Advisory Councils to issue reports on broadcaster's performance. They can send delegations to visit with local managers and owners. They can, when negotiation fails, take whatever legal steps are necessary with the FCC. They can complain to sponsors, networks, and local television stations when they find commercials excessively loud or obnoxious. If you think this is dreamy, pie-in-the-sky thinking, look what local groups have done during the past year.

32   Texarkana was given national attention last year when a large magazine reported that the city's population of rats was virtually taking over the city. Of lesser notoriety, but perhaps of greater long-run significance, was an agreement hammered out between a citizens group and

KTAL-TV, the local television station. In January 1969, the Texarkana Junior Chamber of Commerce and twelve local unincorporated associations—with the assistance of the Office of Communications of the United Church of Christ—filed complaints with the FCC, and alleged that KTAL-TV had failed to survey the needs of its community, had systematically refused to serve the tastes, needs, and desires of Texarkana's 26 per cent Negro population, and had maintained no color origination equipment in its Texarkana studio (although it had such equipment in the wealthier community of Shreveport, Louisiana). But they didn't stop there. Armed with the threat of a license renewal hearing, they went directly to the station's management and hammered out *an agreement* in which the station promised it would make a number of reforms, or forfeit its license. Among other provisions, KTAL-TV promised to recruit and train a staff broadly representative of all minority groups in the community: employ a minimum of two full-time Negro reporters; set up a toll-free telephone line for news and public service announcements and inquiries; present discussion programs of controversial issues, including both black and white participants; publicize the rights of the poor to obtain needed services; regularly televise announcements of the public's rights and periodically consult with all substantial groups in the community regarding their programing tastes and needs.

33   The seeds of citizen participation sown in Texarkana have since come to fruition elsewhere. Just recently five citizens groups negotiated agreements with twenty-two stations in Atlanta, Georgia, and similar attempts have been made in Shreveport, Louisiana; Sandersville, Georgia; Mobile, Alabama; and Jackson, Mississippi.

34   In Washington, D.C., last summer a group of students under the supervision of the Institute for Policy Studies undertook a massive systematic review of the license applications of all television stations in the area of Washington, D.C., Virginia, West Virginia, and Maryland. They used a number of "performance charts" by which they evaluated and ranked the stations in amounts of news broadcast, news employees hired, commercials, public service announcements, and other factors. The result was a book that may become a working model for the comparative evaluation of television stations' performances. (IPS, *Television Today: The End of Communication and the Death of Community,* $10 from the Institute for Policy Studies, 1540 New Hampshire Ave., N.W., Washington, D.C.) Citizens groups all over the country can easily follow their example.

35   I have felt for some time that it would be useful to have detailed reviews and periodic reports about the implications of specific television commercials and entertainment shows by groups of professional psychiatrists, child psychologists, educators, doctors, ministers, social scientists, and so forth. They could pick a show in the evening—any show—and discuss its esthetic quality, its accuracy, and its potential national impact upon moral values, constructive opinion, mental health, and so forth. It would be especially exciting if this critical analysis could be shown on television. Such professional comment would be bound to have some impact upon the networks' performance. (Last year's *Violence Commission Report* did.) It would be a

high service indeed to our nation, with rewards as well for the professional groups and individuals involved — including the broadcasting industry. It is not without precedent. The BBC formerly aired a critique of evening shows following prime-time entertainment. It would be refreshing to have a television producer's sense of status and satisfaction depend more upon the enthusiasm of the critics and audience than upon the number of cans of "feminine deodorant spray" he can sell.

36   These examples are only the beginning. Television could become our most exciting medium if the creative people in this country would use a fraction of their talent to figure out ways of improving it.

37   STEP SIX: *Get high (with a little help from your friends).* Have you ever made a film, or produced a TV documentary, or written a radio script? That's a real high. But if you're like me, you'll need help — lots of it — from your friends. If you've got something to say, find someone who's expert in communication: high school or college film-makers, drama students, off-time TV reporters, or local CATV outlets with program origination equipment. Bring the thinkers in the community together with the media creators. CBS did it with Ed Reischauer and its one-hour special on Japan. You can do it, too. Get others interested in television. (A free pamphlet, "Clearing the Air," has just been published by Media Ithaca, Department of Sociology, Cornell University, Ithaca, New York 14850. It explains how average citizens can obtain free air time over radio, television, and CATV.)

38   STEP SEVEN: *Expand your media mind.* Everyone can work for policies that increase the number of radio and television outlets, and provide individuals with access to existing outlets to express their talent or point of view. Those outlets are already numerous. There are now nearly ten times as many radio and television stations as there were thirty-five years ago. There are many more AM radio stations, including the "daytime only" stations. There is the new FM radio service. There is VHF television. And, since Congress passed the all-channel receiver law in 1962, UHF television (channels 14–83) has come alive. There are educational radio and television stations all over the country. There are "listener-supported" community radio stations (such as the Pacifica stations in New York, Los Angeles, Houston, and Berkeley). This increase in outlets has necessarily broadened the diversity of programing. However, since the system is virtually all "commercial" broadcasting, this diversity too often means simply that there are now five stations to play the "top forty" records in your city instead of two. In the past couple years, however, educational broadcasting has gained in strength with the Public Broadcasting Corporation (potentially America's answer to the BBC). Owners of groups of profitable television stations (such as Westinghouse and Metromedia) have begun syndicating more shows — some of which subsequently get picked up by the networks.

39   Cable television (CATV) offers a potentially unlimited number of channels. (The present over-the-air system is physically limited to from five to ten television stations even in the largest communities.) Twelve-channel cable systems are quite common, twenty-channel

systems are being installed, and more channels will undoubtedly come in the future. Your telephone, for example, is a "100-million-channel receiver" in that it can call, or be called by, any one of 100 million other instruments in this country.

40 Cable television offers greater diversity among commercial television programs—at the moment, mostly movies, sports, and reruns—but it can also offer another advantage: public access. The FCC has indicated that cable systems should be encouraged and perhaps ultimately required to offer channels for lease to any person willing to pay the going rate. In the *Red Lion* case last year, the Supreme Court upheld the FCC's fairness doctrine and, noting the monopolistic position most broadcasters hold, suggested that "free speech" rights belong principally to the audience and those who wish to use the station, not the station owner. This concept—which might raise administrative problems for single stations—is easily adaptable to cable television.

41 If someone wants to place a show on a single over-the-air broadcast station, some other (generally more profitable) program must be canceled. A cable system, by contrast, can theoretically carry an unlimited number of programs at the same time. We therefore have the opportunity to require cable systems to carry whatever programs are offered on a leased-channel basis (sustained either by advertising or by subscription fee). Time might even be made available free to organizations, young film-makers, and others who could not afford the leasing fee and do not advertise or profit from their programing. Now is the time to guarantee such rights for your community. City councils all across the nation are in the process of drafting the terms for cable television franchises. If your community is at present considering a cable television ordinance, it is your opportunity to work for free and common-carrier "citizens' access" to the cables that will one day connect your home with the rest of the world.

42 Television is here to stay. It's the single most significant force in our society. It is now long past time that the professional and intellectual community—indeed, anyone who reads magazines and cares where this country is going—turn on to television.

Discussion of Theme

1. According to Johnson, why is it no longer smart to boast, "I never watch TV"?
2. What examples does he cite of the pervasive influence of TV on our lives? Can you think of others?
3. What is "the public interest"? How should television stations serve it? In general, do they?
4. What answers does Johnson give to the question asked in his title? Can you add to his list? Is he realistic?
5. Is Johnson too severe in his description of television today?
6. Are advertisers entitled to exercise editorial control over programs they pay for? Explain.

Discussion of Rhetoric

1. What paragraphs constitute the introduction to this selection? The conclusion?
2. How effectively is this selection organized? Are there sections or paragraphs that could be moved about without damaging its unity?
3. How convincing is Johnson's thesis? How does he develop it? Does he appeal to the emotions and use connotative language, or does he supply evidence?

Writing Assignments

1. Select one of the steps recommended by Johnson (paragraphs 4–38) and explain how you would implement it in your community.
2. Following the example of Mason Williams in paragraph 21, write a series of "verbal snapshots" on one of your favorite subjects.
3. Is television, on the whole, a dangerous force in American politics; or are its effects chiefly beneficial? Present your views in a theme.
4. Write to a network, a citizens' organization, or the FCC, presenting your views on television.
5. Write a theme using the following title: "Television Is Getting Better (or Worse)."

Library Exploration

1. Investigate the findings of various groups—including the 1970 Presidential Commission on Violence Report with respect to the effect of TV on behavior.
2. Find out what the duties of the FCC are.

Vocabulary

(3) TEDIOUS   tiresome
(9) RUDIMENTARY   elementary
(22) AGGREGATIONS   groups; gatherings
(24) SYMPOSIA   meetings or conferences for discussion of a subject
(26) LEGION   many
(27) REVOCATION   recalling; talking back

(30) COHESION   sticking together
(35) ESTHETIC   appreciative of or sensitive to the beautiful
(38) DIVERSITY   variation; difference
(41) SUSTAINED   supported

Karl Shapiro (1913–   ), former editor of "Poetry" magazine, has won the Pulitzer Prize for his poetry. Currently professor of English at the University of California at Davis, he has been acclaimed as one of America's greatest poets of the century. Among his books are "Selected Poems," "To Abolish Children," and "White-Haired Lover," all published in 1968.

In the following article a poet who also teaches college undergraduates denounces today's students as a generation of illiterates. They prefer "sweepings and swill," rather than works of genuine literary merit.

KARL SHAPIRO

Student Illiteracy

1   I am no Jeremiah and will leave the ranting to others. But as a teacher of reading and writing, as a reader and writer myself, I wish to report to you my version of the degeneration of the literary intelligence and its attendant confusions everywhere in our lives.

2   When a professor at a venerable university has his life's work destroyed by student vandals, society may well begin to tremble.

3   Who would have thought, at least since the defeat of Hitler, that American professors would begin to remove their notes and files from their offices and take them home; that they would begin to remove their best or their irreplaceable volumes; that libraries would begin the reduplication of indices as a safety measure; that specially trained police and guards and firemen would replace the old innocuous campus cop.

4   I apologize for invoking these commonplaces, and yet who, except Lewis Carroll perhaps, would have dreamed of students acquiring the power to fire faculties, presidents and chancellors, to determine curricula, and worst of all, to force personal political opinion and dogma upon the teaching community at large, and upon society itself.

5　　My experience is relatively unusual, and I believe I have a perspective upon the degenerative process in literature which should be shared.

6　　For example, I have been engaged in creative writing programs for 20-odd years, virtually from the beginning of this kind of teaching. These programs have corroded steadily and today have reached the point of futility. Students in such programs today, according to my experience all over the United States, can no longer spell, can no longer construct a simple English sentence, much less a paragraph, and cannot speak.

7　　We have the most inarticulate generation of college students in our history, and this may well account for their mass outbreaks of violence. They have no more intelligent way to express themselves.

8　　But what is really distressing is that this generation cannot and does not read. I am speaking of university students in what are supposed to be our best universities. Their illiteracy is staggering.

9　　But of course they say they read. They may slam the professor's anthology on the floor but they will go to a bookshop to buy the innumerable paperback best sellers of their generation, which are almost always trashy rewrites of current sociological or philosophical fads.

10　　The kitsch-camp-op-pop-absurdist-revolutionary sweepings and swill with which they fill their wordless minds are what they bring to class.

11　　They do not want to read; they want to "experience." They do not want to learn; they want to "feel." They have become almost impossible to teach.

12　　As far as I can tell the high school has now reached the level of the grade school; the college is at high school level; the graduate school at college level; and whatever reading and writing is being done is being done by professors, the people who are taking their libraries home.

13　　It appears the modern student enters the university with a contempt for the university, a contempt for society, a contempt for literature, and a contempt for himself. Where did he learn this? Not from school; not from the library. I don't think so.

14　　He learned it from what the new illiterates call the media: TV, radio, newspaper, phonograph, rock festival, magazine and paperback bookstore. He learned it from what the new illiterates call counter culture; he learned it from his contemporaries and the exploiters of cults.

15　　For the first time in history the illiterates have a literature of their own. Armed to the teeth with this quasi-literature, it is little wonder they slam textbooks on the floor and stomp to their cars, barefooted.

16　　I will now introduce the hero, or anti-hero, if you like. He is a real person, and all the information I am going to give you is true and accurate, except for his name. I have changed his name not for any legalistic reason but because I feel humiliated to have to bring up his name at all. Here then is Dylan MacGoon.

17　　I first heard of Dylan MacGoon as I was checking out of a hotel in Milwaukee. The girl behind the desk, who must have seen in the local paper that I was lecturing on poetry, asked me what I thought of the poetry of Dylan MacGoon. Who? I said.

18   That was just about a year ago but in the ensuing months the name began to come at me from all directions. In one university where I gave a poetry reading I was challenged by a student from the audience who wanted to know what I thought of MacGoon. I had seen some of his verses by then and answered that I didn't think anything of them; they were not even trash.

19   I then began to see big ads about MacGoon's three new books, one of which had been commissioned, no less, by one of the largest and most respected publishing houses in New York. What bothered me was that the publisher was my publisher, a company that had printed Robinson Jeffers, all the works of W. H. Auden, Stephen Spender, myself, and many others.

20   How could this be? I tried to put it out of my head. MacGoon however, would not go away.

21   One day I saw him interviewed by a top news commentator, the kind of reporter who is assigned only to prime ministers and field marshals. Mr. MacGoon, said the commentator in tones of authentic awe, you are the foremost best-selling poet in the United States (I think he said the world). And then the commentator asked about MacGoon's creative regimen.

22   MacGoon tried to answer as best he could (language is not his strong point) and succeeded, between the awe of the commentator and his own honest dissimulations, in presenting the image of the poet. His millions of readers and listeners, all under 19, I hope, must have been gladdened.

23   I went to the little public library in the little town I live in, hoping against hope that there would be no MacGoon. There was. Still, I said to myself, the library is next door to a high school, and MacGoon is better for the kids than marijuana. Then again, maybe he isn't.

24   In a desperate attempt to exorcise MacGoon, I finally succumbed to the public prints and reviewed one of his three best sellers in a weekly New York book review. The remarks, in part, went more or less as follows:

25   The downhill speed of American poetry in the last decade has been breathtaking, for those who watch the sport. Poetry plunged out of the classics, out of the modern masters, out of all standards, and plopped into the playpen.

26   There we are entertained with the carnival of the Naughties and the Uglies, who have their own magazines and publishing houses, and the love-torn alienates, nihilists, disaffiliates who croon or "rock" their way into the legitimate publishing establishment. MacGoon falls into the latter category.

27   What hidden message have we here? Is the Beatleization of American poetry becoming a reality? Are the negative values on the rise in poetry also? Will the bilge work its way up to the library and the graduate school and to the art of writing itself? The answer to all these questions is a dismal groan.

28   Publishers, even those who formerly prided themselves on the qual-

ity of their publications, are now miring in the dismal swamp of the adolescent revolution. They seem to drool at the sight of a rock festival, which attracts a quarter to a half million of the new humanoids. They cannot resist the temptation. They seek out MacGoon and pay his overhead.

29   The aftermath of my critique was typical. There were letters and telephone calls and a dressing down from a reporter in Los Angeles who called to ask me to explain myself. He had been assigned to interview MacGoon. The crooner, it seems, had also read my diatribe. When asked what he thought of it he answered: Who cares what he thinks?

30   And the weekly book review dropped me.

31   There are many MacGoons in the country, as well as in Liverpool, the chief ones being Dylan, Leonard Cohen, our hero, and so on. In one of the more literate anarchist magazines I notice a serious explanation of a poem(?) written by a poet (?) named Buffy Sainte-Marie.

32   Buffy's lines, "Little wheel spin and spin/Big wheel turn around and around," which resemble the speech of the mental defective and are the norm of the new poetry, are explicated thus: "In Buffy's song the medieval and Elizabethan image of the microcosm mirroring the macrocosm becomes saturated with historical and political content."

33   We are experiencing a literary breakdown which is unlike anything I know of in the history of letters. It is something new and something to be reckoned with. We have reached the level of mindlessness at which students and the literate public can no longer distinguish between poetry and gibberish.

34   When critics and university students can no longer tell the difference between rock lyrics and the songs of Shakespeare, teaching is no longer possible; standards of good and inferior disappear; discrimination dies: and the true artist goes into hiding.

35   We are in the time that Yeats predicted, and everyone is quoting his famous lines: "The best lack all conviction, while the worst/Are full of passionate intensity."

Discussion of Theme

1. What is taking place in our colleges that reminds Shapiro of the days of Hitler? Is he serious or merely exaggerating?
2. How does he relate violence to the writing skills of college students?
3. What is his opinion of the books that he says students are reading? Can you identify any of those alluded to in paragraph 10? Who is Dylan MacGoon?
4. At what level are today's poets and publishers aiming, according to Shapiro? Do you agree? Is his criticism of students and modern writers justified?

Discussion of Rhetoric

1. Describe the tone of this article. What contributes to it?
2. What was Shapiro's purpose: to irritate his reader, or to "convert" him? How do you know?
3. Is Shapiro's argument weakened by his failure to document his case with examples, details, or other evidence?
4. What is irony? Sarcasm? Does Shapiro employ either in his article?
5. Shapiro says he will "leave the ranting to others." Does he?

Writing Assignments

1. If you would like to defend one of the writers attacked by Shapiro, do so in a paper that clearly states your arguments.
2. Is there a generation gap? If so, is it unique? Is it desirable? What are its origins?
3. Select one of the modern poets mentioned in paragraph 31. If you agree with Shapiro's opinion of the poet, write an analysis of his style, showing why he is inferior.
4. If you disagree with the author of this selection, write a rebuttal.

Library Exploration

1. Read the poetry of Rod McKuen. See if Shapiro's remarks are valid when applied to his work.
2. Select for further study one of the writers mentioned by Shapiro.

Vocabulary

(2) VENERABLE   worthy of reverence, usually because of age

(4) DOGMA   a system of principles or beliefs

(7) INARTICULATE   incapable of speaking clearly, coherently, or effectively

(22) DISSIMULATIONS   false pretenses

(26) NIHILISTS   those who believe that existence is senseless or useless

(32) MICROCOSM   the world in miniature

(32) MACROCOSM   the world; universe

Harold Taylor (1914–   ), a Canadian by birth who is now an American citizen, received degrees from the universities of Toronto and London. He began his teaching career at the University of Wisconsin; in 1945 he became the nation's youngest college president with his appointment to Sarah Lawrence College. In 1959 he returned to teaching and writing. His views on education, communism, and democracy have been published in "On Education and Freedom" (1954).

Taylor's essay is a plea for the restoration of the personal element in modern life and in modern education. Although written in 1960, it has a particular urgency today in view of the swollen enrollments and the continuing student unrest on many campuses.

HAROLD TAYLOR

The Private World of the Man with a Book

1   The temptation of the educator is to explain and describe, to organize a body of knowledge for the student, leaving the student with nothing to do. I have never been able to understand why educators do this so often especially where books are concerned. Much of the time they force their students to read the wrong books at the wrong time, and

insist that they read them in the wrong way. That is, they lecture to the students about what is in the books, reduce the content to a series of points that can be remembered, and if there are discussions, arrange them to deal with the points.

2   Schools and colleges thus empty books of their true meaning, and addict their students to habits of thought that often last for the rest of their lives. Everything must be reduced to a summary, ideas are topic sentences, to read is to prepare for a distant test. This is why so many people do not know how to read. They have been taught to turn books into abstractions.

3   This goes against everything we know about what it means to read a book in real life, life, that is to say, which is uncorrupted by educational purpose. There is only one way to read a book, to give yourself up to it, alone, without instruction as to what you should be finding in it, without the necessity of making it into a series of points, but enjoying it, coming to know in personal terms what is in the mind of the writer. Only after that should there be discussion, criticism, comment by the educators. Otherwise education becomes too much like another kind of real life, the kind in which nobody reads the book, everyone reads the reviews, and everyone talks as if he knew the book.

4   The difficulty is that something happens to educators, and to other people, when they think or talk about education. They draw themselves to their full height and make large statements. They seem not to think that what applies to human experience in general may also apply to experience in schools and colleges. They assume that there is something peculiar about education which demands that unless a book is read out of a sense of duty, as a piece of "material" to be "covered," in order for the reader to become "educated," it is not serving the cause of education.

5   Yet most of the most important experiences that truly educate cannot be arranged ahead of time with any precision. All the educator can do is to surround the student with a rich variety of intellectual and personal experience chosen with a view to quickening his mind and emotions into action. The ends are achieved by indirect means — something said in private conversation one day in the street, a remark by a teacher in the middle of a discussion, a book picked up in someone's room. When George Saintsbury was once asked how to interest the young in good literature, he replied, "Leave books around."

6   I grew up in a city that was culturally sterile, in a college whose curriculum lacked intellectual vitality. There were no little magazines, no experimental theatres, no dance groups, no philosophical movements, no strong views held, no centers of new effort. Those of us who were happy to know about Auden, Spender, MacNeice, Isherwood, Malraux, Faulkner, Hemingway, Melville, James, Dostoevsky, Tolstoy, Dewey, or Marx were quite rare, and we pursued our illicit reading without benefit of curriculum or librarians.

7   We read and talked in our rooms, in the newspaper office, in drugstores, and found the writers who meant most to us in little bookstores and reading rooms, where one person speaks of a book to another, where the books have been left around. In this way we learned what

it was like to become so involved with an idea that sleep was impossible, or, to put it more broadly, to possess an intellectual life of our own. We did the educational things required of us, because that was what the educators wanted. We did them well, won prizes for them. But our real lives were elsewhere.

8   From that day to this I have never been able to understand why educators do not seize upon this truth and make it the center of their educational plans, make one life of the double lives which students lead. The heart of education, where books are concerned, is to get the student alone with a book, in a right state of mind.

9   Students are made to read more than they can ever enjoy, too l.ttle of too many things, in a way calculated to destroy personal involvement with the writer. The brighter the student, the more he is asked to read, until he develops prodigious skill in reading quickly and cleverly, for purposes of taking examinations and talking in discussions. Students are always reading to deadlines, in order to return books to the library, in order to answer questions and prove only that they have covered the ground. The educational system thus becomes a barrier to the creation by the student of a body of knowledge of his own.

10   True learning is not a matter of the formal organization of knowledge of books. It is a series of personal experiences. The written word makes public a state of mind; it transfers from private to public expression a set of ideas and facts that might otherwise remain unknown. For the writer, it is more than communication. It is the revelation, to oneself as writer, of things that have been hidden, now forced into expression.

11   On the other side, the side of the reader, it is the revelation of one person to another, a personal communication in an impersonal world. The reader in his true role is a private person, learning what another private person has to tell him. He may be seated in a library with a thousand others, but his way of knowing is by taking to himself the writer whose book he is reading. The teacher exists to get his students ready to read for and by themselves.

12   I would mark down as one of the physical barriers to the free flow of knowledge in the university and the American community, the absence of a sufficient number of intimate little bookshops and reading rooms where the librarian or the owner who loves books and knows what is in them has assembled a spread of inviting titles to capture the affection and involvement of the reader who comes as a welcome guest.

13   We will not have the atmosphere for learning or the true content of learning until we have teachers who themselves haunt the bookshops and who think of librarians as friends and companions in the pursuit of ideas rather than as clerks and custodians of book collections. Nor will we have the atmosphere for learning in our colleges and in our libraries unless we have librarians who work directly with teachers and students because they want to, and because they too are involved in the intellectual life of their own time.

14   My plea is for the restoration of the personal element in modern life and in modern education at a time when everything is pushing us into collective states of mind, when intellectuals huddle together in com-

mittees that issue reports in anonymous prose, when so many people are willing to strip themselves of their personal qualities in order to become clusters of approved characteristics.

15   It is a time when everybody talks and nobody listens. Instead, people exchange statements which each thinks will raise himself in the estimate of the other. Had we in the United States in recent months been listening to intelligent private persons in Cuba, Japan, Korea, Turkey, and elsewhere in Asian countries, we would have known that their best thinking and their deepest motivations were not of a kind that could respond to the policies which our government had designed for them and so innocently applied.

16   Most communications to the world by governments are calculated efforts at raising the level of impersonality and at concealment of the reality with which they are concerned. This habit of concealment in public speech has crept into private discourse and is seen, for example, in the loss of the old-fashioned habit of writing personal letters which are so honestly personal that they are not intended for eventual publication.

17   At another level, it has meant no longer asking our students for private essays each week which can give their teachers an understanding of who the student is and what are his honest thoughts, what are his weaknesses and inadequacies, what are his strengths, his needs, his hopes. Instead we seek for ways in which he can provide answers to questions he would never dream of asking, answers that merely reflect the demands we make upon him for information on topics of our choosing.

18   In the United States we justify our impersonality and lack of sensitivity to students by referring to the growing size of the student body, the excess of numbers of students who thus cannot be dealt with in personal ways, and we turn to technology for more devices to do the teaching for us. This is surely sensible where mechanical tasks, like keeping records, can be done mechanically, where films and television can bring the immediacy of the outside world into the school and college, or in cases where information is to be conveyed quickly and effectively.

19   But as far as the deeper aims of education are concerned, the problem is not how to distribute more information to larger numbers of students. That, as we have seen, is fairly easy to solve. You put more students into the same classes and pump the material in.

20   The question is: What intellectual, personal, and moral qualities are we developing in our students? What are they learning to care about? What are they doing with their lives?

21   It is as if we were deliberately turning back from the real problems, and keeping ourselves busy while we hope they will go away. We are asking not to know our students by what they say in writing or in speech, but to know whether or not they possess correct information as revealed in mechanical tests that can be graded like eggs, by nonhuman means.

22   What has happened is that many of the concepts of an American public-relations culture and the mass media have been transferred from the realm of business and industry into education, and the uni-

versity has been organized not as a place where student talent is nurtured but as a bureaucracy for the dissemination of information. It has its own organization man, its own managerial class, its own habits of the market place by which the man with the largest amount of published academic prose commands the highest salary and receives the ultimate reward of the university — not to have to teach. With the combination of speeded-up sabbaticals, foundation grants, and continuous leaves of absence, the criterion of highest prestige for the university scholar will soon be that he is excused even from residence at the university and will be paid simply for the privilege of listing his name in the faculty roster. In the meantime, there are students.

23   We must teach these students and citizens the necessity of withdrawal into their own thoughts as a preparation for independent thinking and independent action. They must learn to feel their own emotions, not those that are considered culturally appropriate by the educatiqnal authorities or politically correct by their government. This is why the question of what books should be in the curriculum is one that should be decided, not by committees, but by teachers who themselves can enter into the experience of the young and feel with them the impulses of their own time, by teachers who know the responses the young are making to their own society.

24   Each generation has its own truth, its own private world, its own way of knowing, and we who are educators would be wise to listen to them for the knowledge they can bring. The young have the supreme advantage of not having been here before; they are not yet settled, they have almost no history and they can consider the world freshly (that is, they can and do when they talk to each other), and they test and retest the ideas that are old and known and reputable. They reject some, they revive and re-create others.

25   The comradeship of the young both sustains them in their own image of themselves and gives them the emotional sustenance they need for the independence of their lives. They live apart from us, they hold themselves back, and from the untouchable center of their personal lives they look distantly at our existence and our knowledge as items possessed by beings on a different planet. They are not what they seem to the professor who merely looks at their faces before him. He cannot be certain even of their attention, since they have learned how to occupy a classroom and look attentive while they take their minds elsewhere. He cannot be sure of their respect, since they have learned how to be quiet and how to act respectfully. The silence of the present generation has been in many ways deceptive, and it is false to assume that the silence has meant either consent or lack of creative and critical thought. They have played the system but have not been convinced of its claim to be believed in.

26   They are not to be presented with the familiar lists of the Great Books with an air of authority vested in the educators and the curriculum-makers. The students must be asked to determine for themselves which books are great, which ideas are viable, which values are compelling. To do otherwise is to use the familiar brand-name approach as a form of intellectual propaganda, like saluting the flag or bowing to royalty. It is to take the young through an educational tour

of the museums of literature, to inspire a dutiful and pious attitude to authors rather than an attitude of expectancy and involvement.

27 If our aim is to create a vivid sense of awareness of the joy in learning and the satisfaction of intellectual mastery, we must trust the student to come away from his experience with the authors we ask him to read with ideas and convictions of his own. From the point of view of the student, every idea is inert until it comes alive in his consciousness. But first he must learn to read in personal terms, to invest himself in the reading, to bring something of his own to the book. If the books in his education are ill-chosen, or chosen chiefly on the basis of scholarly correctness, the student can bring almost nothing of himself to the enterprise, because what the author is saying corresponds to nothing in his lived experience. In order to learn how to expand that experience in imagination, to make links to the past and to cultures alien to his own, he must first learn how to come close to books and ideas themselves, he must have an experience with the immediacy of ideas. This involves a different way of choosing books for his education, and usually a sequence different from conventional chronology or historical periods.

28 If he reads, for example, in order to be able to tell an eighteenth-century rationalist from a nineteenth-century romantic, he may very well not be able to tell more than this, nor be able to enter into the experience of the writer whose work he is studying. Or he may simply be able to say to himself that he has read the best representatives of all the great periods in cultural history.

29 Whenever we take a writer out of his natural element, that is, treat him as other than a human being who is writing what he knows, we run the risk of destroying his value to the reader by making him represent a category of thought to which he has been assigned after the fact, usually after his death. In graduate schools, this unnatural treatment of writers leads to the continual preoccupation with tracing influences, classifying authors into categories, and otherwise drawing attention away from the writer himself. The writer must be allowed to stand on his own feet. Indeed, his greatness is established by the fact that he continues to stand on his own feet from generation to generation, and that he is perpetually rediscovered for himself and for what he has to say.

30 The student who is being educated is in fact discovering his own self and learning how to relate it to other selves. At its best, education is a series of private conversations in which all sham, pretense, and intellectual hypocrisy or name-dropping is stripped away and the student is free to respond with honesty to the intellectual and personal situation in which he finds himself. This is why it is so important to keep the student's situation as free of educational formalities as possible, to insist upon some version of the tutorial system, to resist all efforts to build an impersonal administrative machine in place of a fascinating intellectual community, to assure that the student and the teacher are known to each other and that the student may thus benefit by the fact that his individuality is known, recognized, and respected.

31 For it is finally in the individual response of one person to another — whether through books or in person — that the heart of the matter rests.

Discussion of Theme

1. Why are condensations of novels unsatisfactory? What is missing?
2. In paragraph 25 Taylor refers to "the silence of the present generation." The college students of the 1950s were, in fact, called The Silent Generation. How do today's young people compare with those of that era with respect to voicing their beliefs?
3. Is it a good idea to read at least a brief biography of an author before studying his writing?
4. Can all books be read as Taylor recommends in paragraph 3?
5. What would Taylor say about the value of the outlines, digests, and summaries used by many college students?
6. What implications do paragraphs 15 and 16 have for our foreign policy?
7. Reread the last two sentences in paragraph 25. In the light of recent student activity, has Taylor been proved right?

Discussion of Rhetoric

1. What is the connotation of *uncorrupted* in paragraph 3?
2. What is Taylor's definition of true learning? How does it compare with yours?
3. What is the "truth" mentioned by Taylor in paragraph 8? Has he previously defined it, or merely hinted at it?
4. Where does Taylor state his thesis? Does he believe that it will be readily accepted? How does he prepare the reader for it?
5. Comment on the tone and attitude implied in the last sentence of paragraph 22. What is he *really* saying about the importance of students?

Writing Assignments

1. Do you have a favorite bookshop? Write a paper in which you tell why you like it. Describe its appearance, and its atmosphere, its proprietor — whatever contributes to making it special.
2. Compare the books you select for leisure-time reading with those you read for college courses. Be specific about titles, authors, genre.
3. Compare two of your high-school or college courses: the most stimulating and the most boring. What contributed to your reaction in each case: for example, the instructor, subject matter, required reading, other students, amount of discussion permitted in classroom?
4. What do you, personally, gain from discussing a book in class instead of reading it entirely on your own?
5. What books would you have every freshman read? Defend your choices.

Library Exploration

Read: *Strawberry Statement; Getting Straight.*

Vocabulary

(9) PRODIGIOUS   remarkable; enormous

(16) DISCOURSE   conversation

(22) DISSEMINATION   spreading

(22) SABBATICALS   leaves granted to teachers

(22) CRITERION   standard

(25) SUSTENANCE   support

(26) VIABLE   able to develop or grow

(27) INERT   inactive; lifeless

(27) CHRONOLOGY   time sequence

John Ciardi (1916–) is poetry editor of "Saturday Review." He was born in Boston and educated at Tufts University and the University of Michigan. He left his university teaching post "because I found my own papers more interesting to work on than those of my students, and because I thought of a tax problem as more interesting than planned poverty." He is the author of many volumes of poetry, including "Homeward to America" (1940), "From Time to Time" (1951), "How Does a Poem Mean?" (1959), and "You Read to Me, I'll Read to You" (1962).

What is the proper perspective of words like "reality," "humanity," and "poetry"? Ciardi says that poetry "teaches the man an enlargement of his own sense of possibility."

JOHN CIARDI

...an ulcer, gentlemen, is an unwritten poem

1   The poet in our times is a figure of estrangement and he knows it. He not only knows it, he has grown used to the fact and does not much mind it. The truth seems to be, for that matter, that the poet — outside those Golden Ages of folk-poetry now long gone — never did reach more than a few special people in any culture.

2   In the past, however, poets have managed to persuade themselves that they were some sort of social force. Elizabethan poets liked to claim that their sonnets conferred immortality on the ladies they wrote

about. The seventeenth-century satirists were especially fond of the idea that by "holding folly up to ridicule" they purified the intellect of their age. More recently Shelley found it possible to assert that "Poets are the unacknowledged legislators of the world." And even within the last twenty-five years, the social poets of the thirties may be cited as having seriously believed that their poems of social protest had a measurable effect on the government of nations.

3   Stephen Spender, looking back on the mood of poetry in the thirties from the vantage point of 1950, summarized the poet's then-sense of himself as very much a warrior of the practical world:

> It was still possible then to think of a poem as a palpable, overt, and effective anti-fascist action. Every poetic assertion of the dignity of the individual seemed to be a bullet fired in the war against human repression.

4   I know of no sane poet today who persuades himself that the action of his art and imagination has any significant consequence in the practical reality of Dow-Jones averages, election returns, and state-of-the-nation. Wherever the practical world may be, Auden has defined the position of poetry in our time:

> For poetry makes nothing happen: it survives
> In the valley of its saying where executives
> Would never want to tamper; it flows south
> From ranches of isolation and the busy griefs,
> Raw towns that we believe and die in; it survives,
> A way of happening, a mouth.

5   But now — perhaps to prove that poets are no prophets — the executives have wanted to tamper. Under the auspices of the College English Association a group of leading business executives have been meeting regularly with writers and teachers of the liberal arts; and from their problems in the practical world of business management, they seem to be asking seriously what meeting there can be between the arts and the practicalities of industry.

6   The answer to these questions may well be that the poets and the practical men would be mutually happier in leaving one another strictly alone, the poets on their ranches of isolation practising a way of happening, and the practical men in their cities of numbered and lettered glass doors busily pushing the buttons of the world.

7   For the gap that divides the poet from the practical man is real. Nor will it be measurably closed by pointing out that some men have functioned with distinction in both the poetical and the practical imagination. There was a director of public works named Chaucer, there was a bricklayer named Ben Jonson, there was a good soldier named Richard Lovelace — one could compile endlessly. But all that such a list would prove is that some men are ambidextrous: it would not eliminate the distinction between the right hand and the left.

8   A poem is a kind of human behavior. Plowing a field, running a chemical experiment, and analyzing the character of a job-applicant are also kinds of human behavior. The poem may, of course, be about any one of these human actions; but when the poem deals with them, it does so in nonpractical ways. The poet who writes about plowing a

field may find significance in the *idea* of plowing, or he may describe plowing so richly that the riches of the description become a self-pleasing idea in themselves. He does not, however, turn physical soil, plant an actual crop, and take it to the literal human diet by way of a negotiable cash market. In the same way, the poet may create a powerfully penetrating picture of the character of the man the business executive is interviewing for a job. But when the poet has finished his analysis, he has no need to make a payroll decision and to assign the man to a specific job in a specific department.

9   Poetry and practicality are in fact two different worlds with two different orders of experience and of imagination. The poet enters his world as an *as if*: he writes *as if* he were plowing a field, *as if* he were conducting a chemical experiment, *as if* he were analyzing a real man seated before him. He is free with a stroke of the pen to change the lineaments of the world he has imagined. The work-sheets of a poem by Karl Shapiro contain a monumental example of this freedom to *as if* at will.

10   Setting out to describe the (*as if*) dome of darkness that settles over a city at night, he writes in his first draft: "Under the fatherly dome of the universe and the town." Now "fatherly dome" cannot fail to imply a theological universe in the mind of God the Father. For reasons that need not be examined here, Shapiro, in his second draft, rephrased the idea "Under the dome of zero." Simply by changing one central word, Shapiro swung the universe itself from the theological concept of "father" to the scientific concept of "zero." And the poem continued to follow itself as if the process of reversing thirty centuries of human attitudes in a single word amounted to nothing whatever.

11   The practical man has no such large freedom. He enters a world called *is*. When he is at work, he *is* plowing a field, he *is* assembling chemical apparatus, he *is* interviewing an actual man whose name appears on the census listings and who *is* offering his services in return for real and taxable wages.

12   It is only natural, moreover, that men who give their attention to either of these two worlds should not be especially well disposed to the other. Poets tend to think very little of stockbrokers, and stockbrokers tend to think even less—if at all—of poets. And the fact is that some of the best poetry of our times has been written on what may be called an inverted sense of reality, an order of imagination that asserts openly or by implication that what the practical men do is meaningless and that only the *as if* of the vicarious imagination has a place in the final mind of man. So Wallace Stevens, in a poem significantly titled "Holiday in Reality," lists a series of things seen and says of them: "These are real only if I make them so," and concludes:

> Intangible arrows quiver and stick in the skin
> And I taste at the root of the tongue the unreal
> Of what is real.

13   It may be very much to the point that Wallace Stevens, in another part of his imagination, is a vice-president of the Hartford Accident

and Indemnity Company and a specialist in claims on surety bonds. Obviously, however, Wallace Stevens cannot look into his surety bond claims and send in a report that "These are real only if I make them so." That difference between the world of practical solutions and the world of the vicarious imagination must not be blinked away.

14   What must be borne in mind, rather, is the fact that no sane human being is exclusively a practical man. The plant manager may be the most mechanically efficient of calculators during his waking hours; and still his dreams or his nightmares will be human and impractical. What is his order of reality and of business efficiency when he first holds his newborn child? Or when, as some men must in time, he stands by his child's grave? What is his order of reality when he steps out of a late conference and finds a hurricane shaking the earth? Or his wife is ill and the telephone rings: In one ear he hears his assistant howling that the sub-contractor sent the wrong parts and that a rush order is delayed, while with the other he hears the doctor close the bedroom door and start down the stairs to tell him his wife will or will not recover. Which of these realities is more real than the other to live to?

15   The poem does not care and cannot care what happens to that rush order. The poem is of the humanity of the man. And despite the tendency . . . [to admire] only those men who "do things" and to scorn "dreamers," the fact is that no man can be wholly practical or wholly impractical, and that the humanity of any man's life requires some, at least, of both orders of the imagination.

16   There is no poetry for the practical man. There is poetry only for the mankind of the man who spends a certain amount of his life turning the mechanical wheel. But let him spend too much of his life at the mechanics of practicality and either he must become something less than a man, or his very mechanical efficiency will become impaired by the frustrations stored up in his irrational human personality. An ulcer, gentlemen, is an unkissed imagination taking its revenge for having been jilted. It is an unwritten poem, a neglected music, an unpainted watercolor, an undanced dance. It is declaration from the mankind of the man that a clear spring of joy has not been tapped, and that it must break through, muddily, on its own.

17   Poetry is one of the forms of joy, the most articulate, the most expanding, and, therefore, the most fulfilling form. It is no separation from the world; it is the mankind of the world, the most human language of man's uncertain romance with the universe.

18   Despite the slanders of high-minded schoolmarms and even of some of the poets themselves, poetry is not a moral thing. It is a life thing. It is like hunger, or sex-drive, or the pleasure of stretching one's muscles. It exists. It is of the liveness of the man. Because the man is various, it may be mixed in him with the moral or the amoral, with the lofty or the coarse, with the sententious or the foppish, with the brilliant or the trivial. But where the living gift of poetry is real, it survives all added characteristics. Whatever the situation of the poet's learning, morals, or psychic base, the stomach wrinkles, the glands secrete, the consciousness evolves, and the gift, if there is gift

in the man, answers to the rhythm of its own living. As natively as a child sways to music, as blindly as a mouth sucks, as darkly as the hand of the sleeping man reaches to touch the woman and rests resolved and assured when it has found her—just so the human being needs the motion and repose that a good poem is. And just so, the man who has not been estranged from himself by busy motions, not only needs, but knows he needs, these fulfillments.

19   The moralist to the contrary, the impulse to poetry is a play impulse. It will not do to call it anything more high-sounding than that. It is necessary, rather, to see that poetic play is of the very fiber of life and that it runs equally through child's prattle, the designer's pleasure in finding and following the shape of his idea, and the substance of all religious ritual.

20   Form, whether in rhythm (time) or in mass (space) is inseparable from our perception of the world. To respond to form and to take the inevitable next step, which is to re-imagine it, is inseparable from the act of sentience a human life is.

21   That act of imagination and of re-imagination is not easy. It is better than easy: it is joyous. It is what Robert Frost called "the pleasure of taking pains." Taking pains is inseparable from human satisfaction. Every game ever developed by mankind is a way of inventing a difficulty for the sake of overcoming it. The lines a child draws for hopscotch, the rules chess players agree upon, the hurdles a track man puts in his way, are deliberately selected ways of making things hard for oneself. It would be easier to play hopscotch without the lines, but it would be no fun.

22   Poets throughout history have been men who played their life's game against form. However painful the overt subject of the good poem, the dance of the form has been the same life-dance for joy. Keats' sonnet, "On First Looking into Chapman's Homer," is a poem on a happy subject. His sonnet, "When I have fears that I may cease to be," is overtly addressed to his unhappy certainty of his impending death. Keats even concludes his brooding with a statement that nothing in the world matters:

> —then on the shore
> Of the wide world I stand alone, and think
> Till love and fame to nothingness do sink.

But though love and fame and world and time might sink to nothing, the rhymes still fall carefully into place, the meter is kept, the images follow, and the form completes itself in an open performance of the joy and the significance of making the poem well. Even in writing of his death the poet dances his life. Whatever the subject of the poem may seem to be, its true subject is the play of form which asserts, shapes, and fulfills the need of the man. Keats thinking about his death was a tragic man. Keats finding the form of his imagination that could best express and hold his feelings about his death was a joyous man.

23   Now, if we ask what sort of human behavior a poem is, we may answer, "It is this dance." The practical-minded man may still object

that the dance accomplishes nothing: Keats was not spared his death, and nothing in the act of giving shape to his dark thoughts had any effect on the reality of his tubercular lung. True, the poem moved nothing in the physical world. But equally true—even more true— in the act of writing Keats became more alive to himself. And whatever may or may not be measured in foot-pounds, that which gives life to life is a human good.

24   But there is more than the basic dance of joy in the human action of Keats' poem. In essence, Keats has found an act of joy wherewith to express the fact of loss. "Grief brought to numbers cannot be so fierce." All life is attended by losses: an action that can convert those very losses to joys must certainly seem an indispensable human resource.

25   And the more sensitively alive a man is, the more certainly his life must scar him. But it is only the *is*-reality that scars. In the act of re-imagining that reality and of capturing it into the *as-if* of poetic form, the poem releases the mind from the bonds of body and situation. Because the poet is free to *as-if* as many realities as he likes, he can, by that much, see his life as part of all other realities. He can imagine himself from outside himself. And he can imagine himself into the mind and feeling of other men. He is ready to acquire both sympathy and understanding.

26   In shorter terms than these there is no good poetry. And no man who lives his life in shorter terms than these is sufficiently alive. The poet is a man at play, but in Robert Frost's phrase, "the work is play for mortal stakes." However sternly the moralist may frown at this emphasis on the play function of poetry, the supreme statements of man's passion on the planet have been made by those men who were most alive to this play.

27   For in the pursuit of form, one not only finds but enlarges himself. "Endure a change of imagination," says the good poem. It is a long thing to be a man. And it is nothing a man may accomplish unaided. Poetry, by storing the world's best imagination, not only transmits experiences from the past of the race, but teaches the man an enlargement of his own sense of possibility.

28   Imagine, for example, a Greek musician of the Golden Age stumbling out of a time machine into the presence of one of our great symphony orchestras just as Toscanini led it into a Beethoven symphony. However passionately that Greek had devoted himself to his lyre and his harp, he never could have imagined the possibility of such music even as he responds to it and is filled by it. It is unlikely in fact that he could begin to understand the music. When we listen to a symphony, we listen with part of the heritage of the race, with the history that has evolved the tradition of that music, and the imaginary Greek would be missing that memory. As in time, however, he acquired that memory, he would certainly be filled with new possibilities, possibilities he could never have imagined unaided.

29   In a very real sense, all of us are that Greek. Left to ourselves we could not hope to have accomplished enough of the imagination of the race to sense our own possibilities and our own humanity. The presence of a true work of art is always an expansion of the human sense.

30   None of these extensions of the human being, to be sure, are useful in tightening a bolt or in adding a column of figures. A man especially sensitive to this life-play may in fact be too variable in his imagination for mechanical and mathematical accuracy. But to define the practical man in terms as mechanical as bolts and adding machines is to define practically no man at all. What is more practical in world and time than a good human being? Let there be good men and the machine will not want.

Discussion of Theme

1. Why does Ciardi believe that poets and practical men should remain aloof from one another?
2. Are you satisfied with Ciardi's explanation (paragraph 7) of why some poets were also men of practical accomplishments? Does the information about these particular poets destroy Ciardi's argument that poets are basically different from nonpoets?
3. Explain the reasoning Ciardi uses to develop the thought expressed in his title. Do you agree with him?
4. Does Ciardi believe that practical men are inferior to creative ones? Does he want to regard them as insensitive?
5. What does it mean for a man to be "estranged," as Ciardi uses the term?

Discussion of Rhetoric

1. What is Ciardi's definition of a poem? Does he define it in more ways than one?
2. Do you find that some of what Ciardi says is not easily grasped or immediately clear to you? What sentences or phrases require extra thought?
3. Which portions of the article do you consider poetic? What contributes to this quality?
4. What purposes do the first seven paragraphs serve? Why does the author wait until paragraph 8 to define a poem?
5. How effective is Ciardi's frequent use of *but* and *and* to begin sentences?

Writing Assignments

1. If you believe that Ciardi overrates the significance of poetry for mankind, write a paper in which you explain why you feel as you do.
2. Ciardi says that the poet "never did reach more than a few special people in any culture." Explore possible reasons for this.

3. Can the lyrics of today's popular songs be regarded as true poetry? If you believe they can, explain why they communicate effectively with young people, whereas "real poetry" often fails.
4. Using Ciardi's informal diction, write a paper on the contributions of painters, sculptors, or musicians.
5. Use the idea in paragraph 28 of a Greek musician stepping into the twentieth century as the basis for a creative theme.

Library Exploration

1. You might be interested in some further advice on poetry by Ciardi. Check the *Saturday Review* poetry section.
2. Read some selections in *The Poem Itself*, by Stanley Burshaw, and report on suggestions made for understanding poetry.

Vocabulary

(1) ESTRANGEMENT separation; alienation

(2) SATIRISTS writers who use wit or irony to expose vice and folly

(3) PALPABLE capable of being touched or felt

(3) OVERT open to view; not concealed

(7) AMBIDEXTROUS able to use both hands equally well

(8) NEGOTIABLE convertible into cash or equivalent value

(9) LINEAMENTS features; outlines

(12) VICARIOUS experienced through imagined participation in someone else's experience

(12) INTANGIBLE immaterial; not capable of being touched

(18) SENTENTIOUS given to excessive moralizing

(18) FOPPISH vain; affected

(18) REPOSE rest

(20) SENTIENCE awareness

Robert Penn Warren (1905–)
was educated at Vanderbilt,
the University of California,
Yale, and Oxford. He is a poet,
essayist, short-story writer,
and novelist as well as a major
American literary critic. Among
his many novels are "All the
King's Men" (1946), "Circus in
the Attic" (1948), "World Enough
and Time" (1950), and "The
Cave" (1959).

A person who reads fiction demands a story, an imagined
situation, yet he is in reality
looking for a meaning to life itself.

ROBERT PENN WARREN

Why Do We Read Fiction?

1 Why do we read fiction? The answer is simple. We read it because we like it. And we like it because fiction, as an image of life, stimulates and gratifies our interest in life. But whatever interests may be appealed to by fiction, the special and immediate interest that takes us to fiction is always our interest in a story.

2 A story is not merely an image of life, but of life in motion — specifically, the presentation of individual characters moving through their particular experiences to some end that we may accept as meaningful. And the experience that is characteristically presented in a story is that of facing a problem, a conflict. To put it bluntly: No conflict, no story.

3 It is no wonder that conflict should be at the center of fiction, for conflict is at the center of life. But why should we, who have the constant and often painful experience of conflict in life and who yearn for inner peace and harmonious relation with the outer world, turn to fiction, which is the image of conflict? The fact is that our attitude toward conflict is ambivalent. If we do find a totally satisfactory adjustment in life, we tend to sink into the drowse of the accustomed.

Only when our surroundings—or we ourselves—become problematic again do we wake up and feel that surge of energy which is life. And life more abundantly lived is what we seek.

4   So we, at the same time that we yearn for peace, yearn for the problematic. The adventurer, the sportsman, the gambler, the child playing hide-and-seek, the teenage boys choosing up sides for a game of sandlot baseball, the old grad cheering in the stadium—we all, in fact, seek out or create problematic situations of greater or lesser intensity. Such situations give us a sense of heightened energy, of life. And fiction, too, gives us that heightened awareness of life, with all the fresh, uninhibited opportunity to vent the rich emotional charge— tears, laughter, tenderness, sympathy, hate, love, and irony—that is stored up in us and short-circuited in the drowse of the accustomed. Furthermore, this heightened awareness can be more fully relished now, because what in actuality would be the threat of the problematic is here tamed to mere imagination, and because some kind of resolution of the problem is, owing to the very nature of fiction, promised.

5   The story promises us a resolution, and we wait in suspense to learn how things will come out. We are in suspense, not only about what will happen, but even more about what the event will mean. We are in suspense about the story in fiction because we are in suspense about another story far closer and more important to us—the story of our own life as we live it. We do not know how that story of our own life is going to come out. We do not know what it will mean. So, in that deepest suspense of life, which will be shadowed in the suspense we feel about the story in fiction, we turn to fiction for some slight hint about the story in the life we live. The relation of our life to the fictional life is what, in a fundamental sense, takes us to fiction.

6   Even when we read, as we say, to "escape," we seek to escape not from life but to life, to a life more satisfying than our own drab version. Fiction gives us an image of life—sometimes of a life we actually have and like to dwell on, but often and poignantly of one we have had but do not have now, or one we have never had and can never have. The ardent fisherman, when his rheumatism keeps him housebound, reads stories from *Field and Stream*. The baseball fan reads *You Know Me, Al*, by Ring Lardner. The little co-ed, worrying about her snub nose and her low mark in Sociology 2, dreams of being a debutante out of F. Scott Fitzgerald; and the thin-chested freshman, still troubled by acne, dreams of being a granite-jawed Neanderthal out of Mickey Spillane. When the Parthians in 53 B.C. beat Crassus, they found in the baggage of Roman officers some very juicy items called *Milesian Tales*, by a certain Aristides of Miletus; and I have a friend who in A.D. 1944, supplemented his income as a GI by reading aloud *Forever Amber*, by a certain Kathleen Winsor, to buddies who found that the struggle over three-syllable words somewhat impaired their dedication to that improbable daydream.

7   And that is what, for all of us, fiction, in one sense, is—a daydream. It is, in other words, an imaginative enactment. In it we find, in imagination, not only the pleasure of recognizing the world we know and of reliving our past, but also the pleasure of entering worlds we do not know and of experimenting with experiences which we deeply

crave but which the limitations of life, the fear of consequences, or the severity of our principles forbid us to do. Fiction can give us this pleasure without any painful consequences, for there is no price tag on the magic world of imaginative enactment. But fiction does not give us only what we want; more importantly, it may give us things we hadn't even known we wanted.

8   In this sense then, fiction painlessly makes up for the defects of reality. Long ago Francis Bacon said that poetry—which, in his meaning, would include our fiction—is "agreeable to the spirit of man" because it affords "a greater grandeur of things, a more perfect order, and a more beautiful variety" than can "anywhere be found in nature. . . ." More recently we find Freud putting it that the "meagre satisfactions" that man "can extract from reality leave him starving," and John Dewey saying that art "was born of need, lack, deprivation, incompleteness." But philosophers aside, we all know entirely too well how much we resemble poor Walter Mitty.

9   If fiction is—as it clearly is for some readers—merely a fantasy to redeem the liabilities of our private fate, it is flight from reality and therefore the enemy of growth, of the life process. But is it necessarily this? Let us look at the matter in another way.

10   The daydream which is fiction differs from the ordinary daydream in being publicly available. This fact leads to consequences. In the private daydream you remain yourself—though nobler, stronger, more fortunate, more beautiful than in life. But when the little freshman settles cozily with his thriller by Mickey Spillane, he finds that the granite-jawed hero is not named Slim Willett, after all—as poor Slim, with his thin chest, longs for it to be. And Slim's college instructor, settling down to *For Whom the Bell Tolls*, finds sadly that this other college instructor who is the hero of the famous tale of sleeping bags, bridge demolition, tragic love and lonely valor, is named Robert Jordan.

11   In other words, to enter into that publicly available daydream which fiction is, you have to accept the fact that the name of the hero will never be your own; you will have to surrender something of your own identity to him, have to let it be absorbed in him. But since that kind of daydream is not exquisitely custom-cut to the exact measure of your secret longings, the identification can never be complete. In fact, only a very naïve reader tries to make it thrillingly complete. The more sophisticated reader plays a deep double game with himself; one part of him is identified with a character—or with several in turn—while another part holds aloof to respond, interpret and judge. How often have we heard some sentimental old lady say of a book: "I just loved the heroine—I mean I just went through everything with her and I knew exactly how she felt. Then when she died I just cried." The sweet old lady, even if she isn't very sophisticated, is instinctively playing the double game too: She identifies herself with the heroine, but she survives the heroine's death to shed the delicious tears. So even the old lady knows how to make the most of what we shall call her role-taking. She knows that doubleness, in the very act of identification, is of the essence of role-taking: There is the taker of the role

and there is the role taken. And fiction is, in imaginative enactment, a role-taking.

12   For some people—those who fancy themselves hardheaded and realistic—the business of role-taking is as reprehensible as indulgence in a daydream. But in trying to understand our appetite for fiction, we can see that the process of role-taking not only stems from but also affirms the life process. It is an essential part of growth.

13   Role-taking is, for instance, at the very center of children's play. This is the beginning of the child's long process of adaptation to others, for only by feeling himself into another person's skin can the child predict behavior; and the stakes in the game are high, for only thus does he learn whether to expect the kiss or the cuff. In this process of role-taking we find, too, the roots of many of the massive intellectual structures we later rear—most obviously psychology and ethics, for it is only by role-taking that the child comes to know, to know "inwardly" in the only way that finally counts, that other people really exist and are, in fact, persons with needs, hopes, fears and even rights. So the role-taking of fiction, at the same time that it gratifies our deep need to extend and enrich our own experience, continues this long discipline in human sympathy. And this discipline in sympathy, through the imaginative enactment of role-taking, gratifies another need deep in us: our yearning to enter and feel at ease in the human community.

14   Play when we are children, and fiction when we are grown up, lead us, through role-taking, to an awareness of others. But all along the way role-taking leads us, by the same token, to an awareness of ourselves; it leads us, in fact, to the creation of the self. For the individual is not born with a self. He is born as a mysterious bundle of possibilities which, bit by bit, in a long process of trial and error, he sorts out until he gets some sort of unifying self, the ringmaster self, the official self.

15   The official self emerges, but the soul, as Plato long ago put it, remains full of "ten thousand opposites occurring at the same time," and modern psychology has said nothing to contradict him. All our submerged selves, the old desires and possibilities, are lurking deep in us, sleepless and eager to have another go. There is knife-fighting in the inner dark. The fact that most of the time we are not aware of trouble does not mean that trouble is any the less present and significant; and fiction, most often in subtly disguised forms, liberatingly reenacts for us such inner conflict. We feel the pleasure of liberation even when we cannot specify the source of the pleasure.

16   Fiction brings up from their dark oubliettes our shadowy, deprived selves and gives them an airing in, as it were, the prison yard. They get a chance to participate, each according to his nature, in the life which fiction presents. When in Thackeray's *Vanity Fair* the girl Becky Sharp, leaving school for good, tosses her copy of Doctor Johnson's *Dictionary* out of the carriage, something in our own heart leaps gaily up, just as something rejoices at her later sexual and pecuniary adventures in Victorian society, and suffers, against all our sense of moral justice, when she comes a cropper. When Holden

Caulfield, of Salinger's *Catcher in the Rye*, undertakes his gallant and absurd little crusade against the "phony" in our world, our own nighdoused idealism flares up again, for the moment without embarrassment. When in Faulkner's *Light in August* Percy Grimm pulls the trigger of the black, blunt-nosed automatic and puts that tight, pretty little pattern of slugs in the top of the overturned table behind which Joe Christmas cowers, our trigger finger tenses, even while, at the same time, with a strange joy of release and justice satisfied, we feel those same slugs in our heart. When we read Dostoevski's *Crime and Punishment*, something in our nature participates in the bloody deed, and later, something else in us experiences, with the murderer Raskolnikov, the bliss of repentance and reconciliation.

17   For among our deprived selves we must confront the redeemed as well as the damned, the saintly as well as the wicked; and strangely enough, either confrontation may be both humbling and strengthening. In having some awareness of the complexity of self we are better-prepared to deal with that self. As a matter of fact, our entering into the fictional process helps to redefine this dominant self — even, as it were, to recreate, on a sounder basis — sounder because better understood — that dominant self, the official "I." As Henri Bergson says, fiction "brings us back into our own presence" — the presence in which we must make our final terms with life and death.

18   The knowledge in such confrontations does not come to us with intellectual labels. We don't say, "Gosh, I've got 15 per cent of sadism in me" — or 13 percent of unsuspected human charity. No, the knowledge comes as an enactment; and as imaginative enactment, to use our old phrase, it comes as knowledge. It comes, rather, as a heightened sense of being, as the conflict in the story evokes the conflict in ourselves, evokes it with some hopeful sense of meaningful resolution, and with, therefore, an exhilarating sense of freedom.

19   Part of this sense of freedom derives, to repeat ourselves, from the mere fact that in imagination we are getting off scot-free with something which we, or society, would never permit in real life; from the fact that our paradoxical relation to experience presented in fiction — our involvement and noninvolvement at the same time — gives a glorious feeling of mastery over the game of life. But there is something more important that contributes to this sense of freedom, the expansion and release that knowledge always brings; and in fiction we are permitted to know in the deepest way, by imaginative participation, things we would otherwise never know — including ourselves. We are free from the Garden curse: We may eat of the Tree of Knowledge, and no angel with flaming sword will appear.

20   But in the process of imaginative enactment we have, in another way, that sense of freedom that comes from knowledge. The image that fiction presents is purged of the distractions, confusions and accidents of ordinary life. We can now gaze at the inner logic of things — of a personality, of the consequences of an act or a thought, of a social or historical situation, of a lived life. One of our deepest cravings is to find logic in experience, but in real life how little of our experience comes to us in such a manageable form!

21   We have all observed how a person who has had a profound shock needs to tell the story of the event over and over again, every detail. By telling it he objectifies it, disentagling himself, as it were, from the more intolerable effects. This objectifying depends, partly at least, on the fact that the telling is a way of groping for the logic of the event, an attempt to make the experience intellectually manageable. If a child — or a man — who is in a state of blind outrage at his fate can come to understand that the fate which had seemed random and gratuitous is really the result of his own previous behavior or is part of the general pattern of life, his emotional response is modified by that intellectual comprehension. What is intellectually manageable is, then, more likely to be emotionally manageable.

22   This fiction is a "telling" in which we as readers participate and is, therefore, an image of the process by which experience is made manageable. In this process experience is foreshortened, is taken out of the ruck of time, is put into an ideal time where we can scrutinize it, is given an interpretation. In other words, fiction shows, as we have said, a logical structure which implies a meaning. By showing a logical structure, it relieves us, for the moment at least, of what we sometimes feel as the greatest and most mysterious threat of life — the threat of the imminent but "unknowable," of the urgent but "unsayable." Insofar as a piece of fiction is original and not merely a conventional repetition of the known and predictable, it is a movement through the "unknowable" toward the "knowable" — the imaginatively knowable. It says the "unsayable."

23   This leads us, as a sort of aside, to the notion that fiction sometimes seems to be, for the individual or for society, prophetic. Now looking back we can clearly see how Melville, Dostoevski, James, Proust, Conrad and Kafka tried to deal with some of the tensions and problems which have become characteristic of our time. In this sense they foretold our world — and even more importantly, forefelt it. They even forefelt us.

24   Or let us remember that F. Scott Fitzgerald and Hemingway did not merely report a period, they predicted it in that they sensed a new mode of behavior and feeling. Fiction, by seizing on certain elements in its time and imaginatively pursuing them with the unswerving logic of projected enactment, may prophesy the next age. We know this from looking back on fiction of the past. More urgently we turn to fiction of our own time to help us envisage the time to come and our relation to it.

25   But let us turn to more specific instances of that inner logic which fiction may reveal. In *An American Tragedy* Dreiser shows us in what subtle and pitiful ways the materialism of America and the worship of what William James called the "bitch-goddess Success" can corrupt an ordinary young man and bring him to the death cell. In *Madame Bovary* Flaubert shows us the logic by which Emma's yearning for color and meaning in life leads to the moment when she gulps the poison. In both novels we sense this logic more deeply because we, as we have seen, are involved, are accomplices. We, too, worship the bitch-goddess — as did Dreiser. We, too, have yearnings like Emma's,

and we remember that Flaubert said that he himself was Emma Bovary.

26   We see the logic of the enacted process, and we also see the logic of the end. Not only do we have now, as readers, the freedom that leads to a knowledge of the springs of action; we have also the more difficult freedom that permits us to contemplate the consequences of action and the judgment that may be passed on it. For judgment, even punishment, is the end of the logic we perceive. In our own personal lives, as we well know from our endless secret monologues of extenuation and alibi, we long to escape from judgment; but here, where the price tag is only that of imaginative involvement, we can accept judgment. We are reconciled to the terrible necessity of judgment—upon our surrogate self in the story, our whipping boy and scapegoat. We find a moral freedom in this fact that we recognize a principle of justice, with also perhaps some gratification of the paradoxical desire to suffer.

27   It may be objected here that we speak as though all stories were stories of crime and punishment. No, but all stories, from the gayest farce to the grimmest tragedy, are stories of action and consequence —which amounts to the same thing. All stories, as we have said, are based on conflict; and the resolution of the fictional conflict is, in its implications, a judgment too, a judgment of values. In the end some shift of values has taken place. Some new awareness has dawned, some new possibility of attitude has been envisaged.

28   Not that the new value is necessarily "new" in a literal sense. The point, to come back to an old point, is that the reader has, by imaginative enactment, lived through the process by which the values become valuable. What might have been merely an abstraction has become vital, has been lived, and is, therefore, "new"—new because newly experienced. We can now rest in the value as experienced; we are reconciled in it, and that is what counts.

29   It is what counts, for in the successful piece of fiction, a comic novel by Peter de Vries or a gut-tearing work like Tolstoy's *War and Peace*, we feel, in the end, some sense of reconciliation with the world and with ourselves. And this process of moving through conflict to reconciliation is an echo of our own life process. The life process, as we know it from babyhood on, from our early relations with our parents on to our adult relation with the world, is a long process of conflict and reconciliation. This process of enriching and deepening experience is a pattern of oscillation—a pattern resembling that of the lovers' quarrel: When lovers quarrel, each asserts his special ego against that of the beloved and then in the moment of making up finds more keenly than before the joy of losing the self in the love of another. So in fiction we enter imaginatively a situation of difficulty and estrangement—a problematic situation that, as we said earlier, sharpens our awareness of life—and move through it to a reconciliation which seems fresh and sweet.

30   Reconciliation—that is what we all, in some depth of being, want. All religion, all philosophy, all psychiatry, all ethics involve this human fact. And so does fiction. If fiction begins in daydream, if it springs from the cramp of the world, if it relieves us from the burden of being

ourselves, it ends, if it is good fiction and we are good readers, by returning us to the world and to ourselves. It reconciles us with reality.

31   Let us pause to take stock. Thus far what we have said sounds as though fiction were a combination of opium addiction, religious conversion without tears, a home course in philosophy and the poor man's psychoanalysis. But it is not; it is fiction.

32   It is only itself, and that *itself* is not, in the end, a mere substitute for for anything else. It is an art—an image of experience formed in accordance with its own laws of imaginative enactment, laws which, as we have seen, conform to our deep needs. It is an "illusion of life" projected through language, and the language is that of some individual man projecting his own feeling of life.

33   The story, in the fictional sense, is not something that exists of and by itself, out in the world like a stone or a tree. The materials of stories —certain events or characters, for example—may exist out in the world, but they are not fictionally meaningful to us until a human mind has shaped them. We are, in other words, like the princess in one of Hans Christian Andersen's tales; she refuses her suitor when she discovers that the bird with a ravishing song which he has offered as a token of love is only a real bird after all. We, like the princess, want an artificial bird—an artificial bird with a real song. So we go to fiction because it is a *created* thing.

34   Because it is created by a man, it draws us, as human beings, by its human significance. To begin with, it is an utterance, in words. No words, no story. This seems a fact so obvious, and so trivial, as not to be worth the saying, but it is of fundamental importance in the appeal fiction has for us. We are creatures of words, and if we did not have words we would have no inner life. Only because we have words can we envisage and think about experience. We find our human nature through words. So in one sense we may say that insofar as the language of the story enters into the expressive whole of the story we find the deep satisfaction, conscious or unconscious, of a fulfillment of our very nature.

35   As an example of the relation of words, of style, to the expressive whole which is fiction, let us take Hemingway. We readily see how the stripped, laconic, monosyllabic style relates to the tight-lipped, stoical ethic, the cult of self-discipline, the physicality and the anti-intellectualism and the other such elements that enter into his characteristic view of the world. Imagine Henry James writing Hemingway's story *The Killers*. The complicated sentence structure of James, the deliberate and subtle rhythms, the careful parentheses—all these things express the delicate intellectual, social and aesthetic discriminations with which James concerned himself. But what in the Lord's name would they have to do with the shocking blankness of the moment when the gangsters enter the lunchroom, in their tight-buttoned identical blue overcoats, with gloves on their hands so as to leave no fingerprints when they kill the Swede?

36   The style of a writer represents his stance toward experience, toward the subject of his story; and it is also the very flesh of our experience of the story, for it is the flesh of our experience as we read. Only through his use of words does the story come to us. As with language, so with

the other aspects of a work of fiction. Everything there—the proportioning of plot, the relations among the characters, the logic of motivation, the speed or retardation of the movement—is formed by a human mind into what it is, into what, if the fiction is successful, is an expressive whole, a speaking pattern, a form. And in recognizing and participating in this form, we find a gratification, though often an unconscious one, as fundamental as any we have mentioned.

37   We get a hint of the fundamental nature of this gratification in the fact that among primitive peoples decorative patterns are developed long before the first attempts to portray the objects of nature, even those things on which the life of the tribe depended. The pattern images a rhythm of life and intensifies the tribesman's sense of life.

38   Or we find a similar piece of evidence in psychological studies made of the response of children to comic books. "It is not the details of development," the researchers tell us, "but rather the general aura which the child finds fascinating." What the child wants is the formula of the accelerating buildup of tension followed by the glorious release when the righteous Superman appears just in the nick of time. What the child wants, then, is a certain "shape" of experience. Is his want, at base, different from our own?

39   At base, no. But if the child is satisfied by a nearly abstract pattern for the feeings of tenderness and release, we demand much more. We, too, in the build and shape of experience, catch the echo of the basic rhythm of our life. But we know that the world is infinitely more complicated than the child thinks. We, unlike the child, must scrutinize the details of development, the contents of life and of fiction. So the shaping of experience to satisfy us must add to the simplicity that satisfies the child something of the variety, roughness, difficulty, subtlety and delight which belongs to the actual business of life and our response to it. We want the factual richness of life absorbed into the pattern so that content and form are indistinguishable in one expressive flowering in the process that John Dewey says takes "life and experience in all its uncertainties, mystery, doubt and half-knowledge and turns that experience upon itself to deepen and intensify its own qualities." Only then will it satisfy our deepest need—the need of feeling our life to be, in itself, significant.

Discussion of Theme

1. What does Warren say is the difference between our own daydreams and fiction? What is "the double game" that we play when we read?
2. How does role-taking as we read fiction lead us to an awareness of others? How does it enable us to understand ourselves better?
3. Do you believe that people can learn more about life and about other people by reading nonfiction instead of fiction?
4. Why do you read fiction? Is conflict really the center of life?
5. How can something made up from the imagination be a serious comment on the actual world?

Discussion of Rhetoric

1. Is the author dealing in stereotypes in paragraphs 6 and 10? Is this deliberate or only incidental to his purpose? Does "little freshman" (paragraph 10) imply a patronizing attitude on Warren's part? Why does he describe students in this way?
2. What is Warren's definition of a story?
3. What is the implication of "prison yard" in the first sentence of paragraph 16? Do you regard this as appropriate?
4. Explain the allusion in the final sentence of paragraph 19.
5. This is a well-organized essay; the opening of almost every paragraph is an example of good transition. Find several examples and comment on how Warren connects paragraphs.

Writing Assignments

1. What novel(s) have you read that clarified the meaning of your own life for you? How did the book(s) accomplish this?
2. If you enjoy daydreaming, describe some of your daydreams. What useful purpose do daydreams serve? What harm can excessive daydreaming do?
3. If you believe that people can learn more from films than from novels, explain your reasons.

Library Exploration

1. Read James Thurber's *The Secret Life of Walter Mitty.*
2. Read and report on one of Warren's novels.

Vocabulary

(3) AMBIVALENT having contradictory attitudes toward a person, object, or action
(3) DROWSE doze
(6) POIGNANTLY touchingly
(6) ARDENT passionate
(12) REPREHENSIBLE deserving of rebuke
(12) INDULGENCE yielding to a desire
(16) OUBLIETTES dungeons with only a trapdoor in the ceiling
(16) COMES A CROPPER falls headlong; fails disastrously
(16) NIGH-DOUSED nearly quenched
(18) CONFRONTATIONS encounters

(19) PARADOXICAL contradictory
(21) GRATUITOUS uncalled for (often unwanted)
(22) RUCK jumble
(22) IMMINENT about to happen
(26) EXTENUATION partial justification
(26) SURROGATE substitute
(29) OSCILLATION swinging back and forth
(35) LACONIC sparing of words
(35) STOICAL showing indifference to pleasure or pain
(36) RETARDATION slowing down
(38) AURA atmosphere

OTHER PEOPLES,
OTHER PLACES

Eugene Burdick (1918–65) successfully combined two careers: professor of political theory at the University of California at Berkeley, and author and co-author of several best-selling novels. After receiving degrees from Stanford and Oxford universities, Burdick served in the U.S. Navy during World War II, earning the Navy-Marine Corps Cross. He was the author of television plays, motion picture scripts, and magazine articles. He received greatest acclaim, however, for "The Ugly American" (with William Lederer, 1958), and "Fail-Safe" (with Harvey Wheeler, 1962).

Burdick's essay, taken from "The Blue of Capricorn" (1961), will serve as an antidote to those who have a romanticized or idealized version of Polynesia.

EUGENE BURDICK

The Polynesian

1 There is one fragment of the Pacific the American believes he knows well: Polynesia. He may not be quite certain of Sumatra and Mindanao or the difference between a *prau* and a gin pahit, but Polynesia he knows. This is the South Seas, Paradise, the Sunny Isles. It is a place of soft winds, surfboards and outriggers, the pink bulk of the Royal Hawaiian Hotel, the scent of flowers. It is a place where beachcombers, defiantly drunken but still white and superior, watch their *vahines* swim in the waves. In some haunting subtle way a vision of Polynesia creeps into the knowledge of all Americans, a vision flawless and jeweled. In Polynesia the defects of America are magically eliminated. The place is warm and sunny. It glows.

2 My first hint of Polynesia came when I was fourteen. I went to a carnival in Los Angeles which had a side show called South Sea

Mysteries. A deeply tanned girl, wearing a grass skirt made of red cellophane, a flashy artificial lei around her neck and a sequined bra, stepped out through a canvas flap. On the canvas behind the girl were painted brilliant green coconut trees and a circle of nipa huts. As the barker began to talk the girl did the hula. I was mesmerized. I had never seen anything so softly carnal.

3   "Step right in and see the ancient love dance of the old Hawaiian chiefs," the barker chanted. "There was a time when the eyes of commoners were torn out if they saw this dance, and you can see it it for exactly two bits."

4   My attention swung back to the girl. As a hidden phonograph played "My Little Grass Shack," her hands formed a shack, fish swimming, a moon rising, lovers embracing. She was very good, although I did not know it at the time. Her head was level, her feet never left the floor, her haunches undulated. She was erotic but restrained. She gave the impression of being virginal, but also wanton, which was exactly her purpose. I ignored the fact that her tan began to dissolve under the harsh Los Angeles sun and ran down her face in brown drops.

5   That day I was hooked by the South Seas or Polynesia or whatever the barker and the girl and the cheap tent stood for. I had a neat, precise and colorful vision of what it was like. There would be tiny clean islands, ringed with white sand and blue surf, and the air would be warm. In this vision the people were somewhat vague, but they would be lithe, brown, carefree, and they would dance. I didn't know then that millions of other Americans were experiencing exactly the same emotion, as the hula craze and movies like *Bird of Paradise* and a few score Hawaiian bands spread the vision broad and wide.

6   A cold and ununderstanding world kept me from leaving at once for the South Seas, so I turned to the library. The vision grew deeper. In Melville's *Typee* I read for the first time of Fayaway, who became the model for endless South Sea heroines: abandonedly voluptuous, a skin "the color of *cafe au lait*," a magnificent figure, a slightly fey and doomed look about the eyes, possessed of a deep tribal wisdom that shone through her eyes. In all the books, this beautiful stereotype gave herself willingly to the white man although she knew it would end in tragedy.

7   Lord Byron, something of a connoisseur of women and of love, wrote a book called *The Island* and made it clear that natural passions could have full expression in these exotic islands. Diderot, the famous French encyclopedist, wrote a rhapsodic book on Polynesia and argued that the "natural" life was far superior to "civilization." I needed no persuading. I plowed through novels, scientific treatises, biographies of missionaries, good writing and bad writing. It was all like diamond dust against a dull jewel: it ground my vision to a lapidary brightness.

8   Later I was to learn that Melville knew more about whales than about women, that Byron had never been to the South Seas, that Diderot had blantantly fictionalized the voyages of Bougainville. I was also to encounter the numerous works of the professional, nerve-

less, hard-eyed debunkers of Polynesia. None of this made any difference to me, nor, apparently, does it make any difference to most others who go to Polynesia. The rebuffs, the savage letdowns, the hard surprises are many, but seldom is the original vision altered. Indeed, in a strange way, the foreigner's vision of Polynesia has come to transform the reality of the place.

9   Of the hard knocks and surprises which the innocent may expect in Polynesia, first is the low-pressure shock of its simple vastness. Spread out a Mercator map and draw a triangle with Hawaii, Easter Island and New Zealand at the three points. The sides will measure 4500 and 4500 and 4800 miles. Polynesia means many islands, but they are tiny fragments scattered through this Pacific immensity. All the islands of southwest Polynesia, taken together whose archipelagoes like the Marquesas and the Australs and the Cooks, have less land area than the single island of Hawaii.

10   This is one of the great empty spaces of the world. The huge sea plains stretch away endlessly, identical, heaving, changing color but not shape. The heat is solid and uncompromising. When you come upon an island, an unbelievable lost speck, you ache for it to be beautiful. It usually is although not always in the languorous white sand and coral reef tradition. On Nukuhiva in the Marquesas, for example, there are sheer cliffs at the water's edge which rise over a thousand feet and there are also canyons with walls so steep that one must go by sea from valley to valley. Moorea is beautiful in a monumental, craggy, cold-blue manner. And there are some atolls which are bare and ugly . . . but not many. The high islands are a surprise to the Western eye, but a pleasant one.

11   Once ashore you will have a job finding a pure-blooded Polynesian. When you do it will be a shock, especially if it is a woman. She has a short jaw: her body is squat and turns to fat rather early. If she is a fa'a Samoa type her feet will be big, callused and tough. It is true that her hair is black and lustrous and her skin is close enough to café au lait so that she can sunburn, but her body is designed for work, not for dancing. There is something solid, down to earth, almost utilitarian about the Polynesian woman and the tiare behind her ear and the limpidity of her eyes cannot disguise it.

12   You are suddenly aware that you have seen this woman before — in the pictures of Gauguin. He was ruthlessly realistic. The heavy-jawed, squat, bent women of his pictures are not a trick of Impressionism, they are simple reality. The kind of lithe, slim Fayaway beauty is very rare among pure Polynesians.

13   There is another subtly disturbing thing about Polynesian anatomy. I discovered it when I approached a Marquesan reef on which a group of men and women were searching for shellfish. The sun, as always in the tropics, went down abruptly but there was a moment of intense purple light. The figures on the reef turned black — and sexless. I could not tell women from men.

14   Later I learned this was a common experience among newcomers to Polynesia. There is a softness of line, a blurring of body distinctions. Both sexes have the same long swimmer's muscles, both walk in the

same way, there is an absence of the vigorous gestures we ascribe to males, and the women do not develop the protective mannerisms we associate with femininity.

15   This is not to imply that Polynesian women lack beauty. Their beauty is of a different kind: a blending of gait and proud bearing, an aura of autonomy, lips that can form into a pout or the most spontaneous of laughs, a body which somehow does not value sleekness but promises almost too much competence in love-making. Gauguin put it well when writing of one of his models and lovers: "She was not at all handsome according to our aesthetic rules. She was beautiful."

16   There is one word which, in all of its shades and meanings, catches the sense of the Old Way Polynesia and much of the Polynesia now conquered by The Beach. It is the word "simple." There is a great simplicity in the lust of Polynesians for gambling and the cunning with which they can make a gamble of almost anything. They do not gamble as Chinese or Americans gamble; they gamble with a wild plunging abandon, with no sense of probability or odds. Win or lose, they give the same grin. There is also simplicity in the quite unconscious cruelty which Polynesians display toward animals. They will run a horse to a lathering death. A dog with a fishhook caught in its foot will be an object of laughter. I do not recall ever having seen a Polynesian pet a dog or give it food. The dog scavenges for itself.

17   At the same time you can spend weeks in a crowded Polynesian village and not hear a child cry. When it does the closest woman will instantly sweep it up and comfort it. In many dialects the word for "mother" covers almost every female relative and the child will be treated by any of these women with the warmness that we reserve only for our own children.

18   In all of Polynesia there is almost no artistic inventiveness. Rather there is a simple repetition of old designs. Tapa cloths, pandanus mats and seashell necklaces are often done in beautiful patterns, but the patterns are ancient, the outgrowth of timeless trial and error. When asked to invent, to create, to experiment in color, the Polynesian is uncomprehending. When given the choice between a magnificiently muted tapa cloth and a garnish Manchester calico the Polynesian will take the calico and explain his choice: "I like the red. It is prettier. The tapa is dull." This is simplicity itself.

19   The only working artist I know of in Polynesia is Agnes Teepee, the vahine of Don Carlos García-Palacios, a Chilean of the most exquisite sensitivities. Agnes paints big bold abstract paintings which are usually suggestive of tropical plants or the reef or the underwater life. Other Tahitians study her work with the most profound boredom until they can spot something in the painting which is recognizable . . . a sea anemone, a tiare, the eye of a shark. Then they will walk away satisfied. They seem quite incapable of understanding an abstract notion. They are literal minded in an almost rigid sense.

20   There is also a vast simplicity in the way the Polynesian regards youth. The Westerner looks back on youth with a terrible urge to recapture it, to possess it, to imitate it. The Polynesian regards youth more kindly, more benignly. I have never heard a Polynesian express the desire to be young again. He folds gracefully into each phase of

life knowing it is inevitable. He remembers youth not as something lost but something he once enjoyed. An ancient will look at Polynesian youth with the languid tolerant eyes of a lion regarding a litter of frisking cubs. They arouse no envy, no curiosity, no puritanical impulse to inhibit or reform.

21   This simplicity extends to the sex act and explains a basic misunderstanding between the Westerner and the Polynesian. To the Westerner, sex is a dramatic, committing, involving, often frightening thing. For the Polynesian it is a simple matter; as simple as eating or swim- or a prayer or an argument. It need not have consequences. It can be an isolated moment of pleasure. The moment remains discrete, holding no potential of guilt, no web of obligations, no need to murmur love words.

22   Bengt Danielsson, who has lived in Polynesia for many years, states that a casual meeting between a Tahitian boy or girl always leads to intercourse. Only two conditions need exist: a bit of privacy and sure knowledge that the boy and girl are not related. In fa'a Polynesia adolescents often spent their nights together in a separate building where the older children gave sexual instructions to the younger. The language of young children when translated literally would make the brain of even the most progressive parent reel. But the sexual words and phrases are used with no desire to shock and never as swear words. The missionaries have ended the common sex huts but have made almost no inroads into the casualness with which sex is treated.

23   There are some exceptions. In a few Polynesian societies virginity is highly prized and in the fa'a days it was always assumed that female aristocrats would marry as virgins. The deflowering was done publicly by one of the older chiefs from the bridegroom's clan. If blood did not flow the girl's father would smash in her head with a club. Today this kind of behavior is not expected of aristocrats.

24   There are still islands on which the wedding is celebrated by allowing all of the male guests that desire it to have intercourse with the bride. Many a popular bride comes through such an experience half dead from fatigue and takes weeks to recover.

25   One day my wife was sitting on a beach outside of Papeete while I was skin diving. A net fisherman, a big attractive man of about twenty-five, was working the water close to the shore. Perhaps my wife looked lonely. In any case she was alone. The fisherman walked over and said hello to her in French.

26   "Would you like to make love?" he asked, without any introductory remarks and in a very gentle voice. "I know a place just behind these trees."

27   My wife explained that she was waiting for me to come in from skin diving. He looked out toward the reef and then back at my wife.

28   "He may be out there for hours," he said simply.

29   My wife still declined. He was not the least offended. He pointed out the private place beyond the trees in case we should like to use it. Then he went back to his fishing.

30   During the nineteenth century a whole literature developed around the dewy-eyed and innocent South Seas maiden who was seduced by the white man and then abandoned to a life of misery and regret.

This was based on a misreading of Polynesian character. First, the girl was not abandoned; she had the family, the tribe, the island to return to. Secondly, she did not put as much into the affair as the white man imagined—she could not, it was a psychological impossibility. Sex does not mean this to the Polynesian. Thirdly, there was no misery to the situation as such. An individual white *tane* (man) might be miserable to live with but his Polynesian vahine could not be made miserable simply because she had lived with him. Once over, the affair continued only in the tortured imagination of the white man.

31   The girl can be rapt and devoted to a lover, her simplicity and dignity can even be exciting. But what disconcerts the Westerner is to learn that he may well be one of a series of lovers, that he has not bitten deep into her soul, that she does not and cannot see him as the "only" man.

32   After a time this knowledge, so directly counter to our puritanical, high-pitched and intense attitude toward sex, can make white men miserable. They long to make the relationship more tense and involved. For the Polynesian woman this is impossible. She does not know how to become involved and desperate. The act of love-making in Polynesia is much different from the elaborate love-making of Europe and America. There is very little kissing or caressing, very little concern for a simultaneous climax. It is what the Polynesians call "Maori love" as opposed to the white man's form of love. It is quick, silent and often brutal. At the climax a Polynesian couple will often scratch one another's faces and during one of the day-long feasts called *tamaaraa* a particularly attractive girl may go into the bushes with fifteen or twenty men and have welts on her face for days afterwards. The substitute for what white marriage counselors call "foreplay" is the dance. It is the most directly sexual dance in the world. There is no disguising its intention nor its effect. It is meant to be provocative and stimulating and it is.

33   Another facet of the Polynesian simplicity is recklessness. For example, every time a tidal wave strikes the Hawaiian Islands a number of lives are lost unnecessarily. The tidal wave is always preceeded by a powerful outward suck of the ocean which leaves reefs and harbor floors suddenly exposed, fish flopping widly, sandbars steaming in the sun. The Hawaiians cannot resist flocking out onto the reefs, laughing wildly, grabbing for free fish—although they know that in a few moments a wall of water will come sweeping in. When the horizon suddenly tilts skyward and a gray line rises suddenly, they turn and scramble for the beach, roaring with laughter. The silent inexorable rush of the vast wave always traps a few, but despite the keening and wailing for the lost ones, no one thinks of staying away when the next tidal wave comes.

34   Simplicity also embodies a thin red thread of cruelty, childlike indifference to pain in others. Polynesia is no exception. When Captain Cook's death was avenged by a savage bombardment of a Hawaiian town, the native girls on board clapped their hands with delight, shouted *maitai*—"very fine"—enjoyed the pyrotechnic display which was destroying their friends and families.

35   In fa'a Samoa, chiefs often ticked off a subject to be buried alive at the base of each corner post of a new royal residence. Records indicate that the victims grinned up wolfishly as the pole came crashing down on them, and that their families roared wildly and went on with the festivities. Prisoners were often bound tightly with tinder-dry coconut fronds and then set alight, and the whole village watched as the human torch ran desperately for the sea. If he made it, fine; if he did not, the first step in preparing the body for a feast had been taken.

36   In most of Polynesia, The Beach has won a solid victory over the Old Way. Indeed, the victory was won long ago and today it is almost impossible to find a pure Polynesian or an undiluted practice of the Old Way. In some islands the Old Way has virtually vanished, but somehow, in a way which is not clear to anyone, the flavor of the South Seas still comes through. Nowhere is the mystery more puzzling than in Honolulu. By any act of sympathetic interpretation it is not an especially attractive place. The outskirts are ringed with junkyards, used-car lots, small factories and warehouses. The center of the city is badly planned, crowded, noisy, spangled with neon lights. Tract housing crawls hideously up the green mountains and disappears into the perpetual fogs of the Pali. The hotels of Waikiki are international style — tall, sleek, concrete. Enormously tall and enormously profitable, they age quickly in the soft climate, but they will be there forever. The visitor could be in Miami or Dallas or Los Angeles. But somehow the magic of the place still works, and thousands of tourists return to the mainland with the glazed eyes of those who have seen Paradise. Nothing that land developers and commercial bad taste do can destroy two things: the trade winds and the Pacific. The place may be conventional and ordinary, but the soft warm wind and the sparkling sea are there. Apparently they are enough.

37   The "outer islands" of Hawaii, such as Maui and Kauai, and the Big Island are infinitely more attractive than Honolulu, but most tourists stay riveted to Waikiki. Eventually they will move to the outer islands, but right now they are content to gaze mesmerized at the rhythmic sweep of the waves, drink exotic mixtures of rum and fresh pineapple and floating orchids and enjoy the trades. Nowhere is the vision of Polynesia more distorted, stifled and lacquered. But enough is still there to satisfy the American urge to "see the South Seas."

38   Once the traveler leaves Honolulu and moves southward to the Marquesas or Tuamotus or Tahiti or Samoa, the victory of The Beach is less visible, but it is still substantial. There are no slick intercontinental hotels, but there are tin roofs among the coconut thatch. It is true that the most desired import is canned meat (followed by flour, sugar, tobacco and piece goods), but one can still eat a magnificent Old Way meal of broiled fish, a curry of shrimp and octopus and sea snail, breadfruit and a dessert of cool juicy fruits picked from nearby trees. Beachcombers are few and far between, but in Quinn's Bar in Tahiti, for a few francs, you can take a picture of Emile Gauguin, the fat and idle son of Paul Gauguin. It is true that many nipa huts will have a foot-operated Singer sewing machine and an old Victor phonograph, but they will also have the softly beautiful pandanus mats. You will also

see jeep springs used as coconut scrapers and watch native skin divers come up from the depths wearing American diving goggles. But push deeper into the bush, or sail to an island that is the least bit isolated, and at once the lacquer is gone. The mark of The Beach is there, but it is still blurred, still faint.

39   In many ways The Beach has made the reality of Polynesia more like a vision. Take the matter of feminine beauty. As the Polynesian began to intermarry with Chinese, Australians, Portuguese, Americans, Japanese and others, an odd change occurred. The pudgy, squat, waist-less girl began to be replaced by a mestizo of more elegant features, a molded jaw, slimmer legs and slighter build. Today throughout Polynesia there is an amazing incidence of girls who possess the beauty invented by Melville's imagination. The fevered men who went to the South Seas inspired by the nineteenth-century vision were probably disappointed, but their visits guaranteed that future generations of Polynesian women would look hauntingly like Fayaway.

40   The vision which the white man took to Polynesia also worked won-ders with the hula. In cold fact the hula of the Old Way was a shambling, dreary, and very boring dance which went on for hours, a low-grade folk dance performed to the beat of sticks on hollow logs. Even the missionaries found little to remark in it except its tedium. At the same time Polynesia had a courtship dance which was brutal, direct and highly erotic. It was danced infrequently, but few who witnessed it forgot it.

41   It was the genius or the curse or the bland ignorance of The Beach that it modified both these dances and blended them. The result is the modern Hawaiian hula, softly sexual but not violent. It is danced to steel guitars and ukuleles and almost any other kind of instrument. It is, by any standard, a great improvement over the original version, and perhaps more important, it is infinitely more compatible with the soft languorous version of the South Seas. But be prepared for the fact that outside of Hawaii the Hawaiian hula is regarded as a joke. In the Tuamotus and Marquesas and Tahiti the hula is danced the old way. The only time the tamed Hawaiian version is danced is to satirize it. The waving graceful hand motions of the Hawaiian hula will send a group of Polynesians into gales of laughter.

42   Some aspects of Polynesian life are so deeply rooted that The Beach has not affected them at all. One is always aware, for example, that these are an oceanic people. For Westerners the ocean has an ageless thin edge of danger to it. One sees this in the doleful faces of the wives of Portuguese fishermen and the resignation of seamen shipping out of San Francisco. For us the sea is stern, possessed of Calvinistic finality.

43   The Polynesian regards the ocean differently. He loves it. He knows it can be dangerous, but the danger is Olympian, capricious, zestful. A man has a chance against it. The Polynesians will tease the sea, take enormous chances, challenge it to the very edge of impudence.

44   Even the Hawaiians, who have received the fiercest onslaught of softening Western ways, still possess this calculated recklessness. One place they show it is at Makapuu Beach on the windward side of Oahu. The entrance to the beach is flanked by signs which say, "Dan-

ger. Heavy Under-Tow. Off-Limits to Service Personnel." On storm days the wave trains come in with an awesome, towering regularity. They are gray and low at the horizon, but rise to enormous heights as the bottom shoals and turn a bitter green before they dissolve into smoky water. The crash of water is so solid that, standing on the beach, you can feel it as a tiny shock in your teeth.

45   I went body-surfing at Makapuu with two Hawaiian friends and it was not until we were past the surf line and treading water and waiting for a "big one" that I realized what they intended. Body-surfing is a much more intricate art than surfboarding, because you must catch the wave at exactly the right point, arch your shoulders exactly right, and if you know the art, shoot in to the beach with your body out well in front of the wave. Once mastered, it is not particularly dangerous. But what my companions proposed to do was to ride the storm waves directly toward an outcropping of rock and coral against which the waves shattered themselves into the maddest spume I had ever seen. The trick, they patiently explained, was to duck out of the wave just before it hit the rocks, dive deep to escape the turbulence and swim underwater back toward the surf line. It called for exquisite timing.

46   They demonstrated for me a few times. Just as the wave was about to shatter on the rocks I saw their feet flash into the air, their bottoms rolled forward and they disappeared. A half-minute later their heads popped to the surface just beyond the churning white water.

47   I could not do it. Technically I understood what had to be done, and I have surfed a good deal. But I did not view the ocean as they did. What they were doing struck me as a kind of insanity. To launch oneself at forty miles an hour, in the grip of a huge wave, directly at a wall of hard rock and coral was beyond my Westernized capacity. In the end I took the long safe glide into the sandy beach.

48   The Polynesian, on the other hand, has a highly developed skill at sliding neatly by those parts of white culture which bore, stifle or restrain him. He has only the slightest interest in politics. The Malay can become rigid with nationalistic excitement. Polynesians, with the exception of the Maoris, let politics alone. Nor does the Polynesian, merely because he goes to church, really accept the ethical stiffness and content of Western religion. He can understand a chief punishing someone for adultery as a *crime,* as something necessary to maintain a minimum of order. But he cannot see adultery as *sin.* The difference is important. All Polynesian gods are Olympic gods: puckish, capable of mistakes, possessed of human qualities, forgiving, occasionally drunk. The only part of Christian religion which Polynesians understand thoroughly are the Ten Commandments, because they sound very much like Ten Tabus.

49   This shrewd and protective selection of white attitudes is nowhere more obvious than at the movies. I once spent several nights at a hot, tin-roofed, overcrowded theater in Samoa. Each night I saw the same film. So did everyone else in the village. The place steamed with heat, and insects flew like crazy motes up and down the flickering light from the projector. The movie was an ancient Western with a classic cast of good guys, bad guys, fair damsels and wicked Indians.

50   The audience ignored every scene except those that involved shooting, drinking or kissing. In a long dull scene they called on the local Don Juan to tell of his latest exploits. He was reluctant, but he was persuaded. He stood in the aisle and did a bawdy hula and recited his prowess. I was later told that he delicately left out the names of his amours, but the audience gleefully chanted them out. In mid-gesture an Indian appeared on the screen and the Samoan buck dropped into his seat like a man shot. Every eye swung back to the movie, the sound of the insects rose in the silence. At the end of the film, when the cowboy hero kissed his girl modestly on the cheek, the entire audience rose and chanted out a piece of Samoan advice which described in explicit detail what a man should do with a girl in such circumstances.

51   Other audiences in the Pacific will sit frozen in their seats, absorbing every scene, never laughing, enraptured by the study of a life that might be theirs in the future. The air is dense with thought, with a sense of desire. They leave with a sigh. In Polynesia the audience is irreverent, bawdy, Hogarthian, and there is not the slightest indication of desire for "the American way of life."

52   The currents of Western thought are swirling over the vast sun-drenched Pacific. In some places they have dissolved the Old Way forever. In other places they have made only the slightest impression. But wherever The Beach makes itself felt, it is also subtly transformed, softened by the climate and the vast distances. One has the dim, but sure, knowledge that the capacity of the Pacific to resist is nearly infinite, like the reaches of its water.

E. B. White (1899–   ) is best known through the collections of his familiar essays. After his graduation from Cornell University, White began his career as a reporter; he later became contributing editor to "The New Yorker" and "Harper's." He is the author of "Is Sex Necessary?" (with James Thurber, 1929), "One Man's Meat" (1942), and "The Second Tree from the Corner" (1953), as well as children's stories ("Stuart Little" and "Charlotte's Web") and numerous essays.

At first reading, this is a nostalgic description of childhood vacations; yet the reader is left with the uneasy feeling that it is more than just that.

E. B. WHITE

Once More to the Lake

AUGUST, 1941

1 One summer, along about 1904, my father rented a camp on a lake in Maine and took us all there for the month of August. We all got ringworm from some kittens and had to rub Pond's Extract on our arms and legs night and morning, and my father rolled over in a canoe with all his clothes on; but outside of that the vacation was a success and from then on none of us ever thought there was any place in the world like that lake in Maine. We returned summer after summer — always on August first for one month. I have since become a salt-water man, but sometimes in summer there are days when the restlessness of the tides and the fearful cold of the sea water and the incessant wind which blows across the afternoon and into the evening make me wish for the placidity of a lake in the woods. A few weeks ago this feeling got so

strong I bought myself a couple of bass hooks and a spinner and returned to the lake where we used to go, for a week's fishing and to revisit old haunts.

2 I took along my son, who had never had any fresh water up his nose and who had seen lily pads only from train windows. On the journey over to the lake I began to wonder what it would be like. I wondered how time would have marred this unique, this holy spot—the coves and streams, the hills that the sun set behind, the camps and the paths behind the camps. I was sure that the tarred road would have found it out and I wondered in what other ways it would be desolated. It is strange how much you can remember about places like that once you allow your mind to return into the grooves which lead back. You remember one thing, and that suddenly reminds you of another thing. I guess I remember clearest of all the early mornings, when the lake was cool and motionless, remembered how the bedroom smelled of the lumber it was made of and of the wet woods whose scent entered through the screen. The partitions in the camp were thin and did not extend clear to the top of the rooms, and as I was always the first up I would dress softly so as not to wake the others and sneak out into the sweet outdoors and start out in the canoe, keeping close along the shore in the long shadows of the pines. I remembered being very careful never to rub my paddle against the thwart for fear of disturbing the stillness of the cathedral.

3 The lake had never been what you would call a wild lake. There were cottages sprinkled around the shores, and it was in farming country although the shores of the lake were quite heavily wooded. Some of the cottages were owned by nearby farmers, and you would live at the shore and eat your meals at the farmhouse. That's what our family did. But although it wasn't wild, it was a fairly large and undisturbed lake and there were places in it which, to a child at least, seemed infinitely remote and primeval.

4 I was right about the tar: it led to within half a mile of the shore. But when I got back there, with my boy, and we settled into a camp near a farmhouse and into the kind of summertime I had known, I could tell that it was going to be pretty much the same as it had been before—I knew it, lying in bed the first morning, smelling the bedroom, and hearing the boy sneak quietly out and go off along the shore in a boat. I began to sustain the illusion that he was I, and therefore, by simple transposition, that I was my father. This sensation persisted, kept cropping up all the time we were there. It was not an entirely new feeling, but in this setting it grew much stronger. I seemed to be living a dual existence. I would be in the middle of some simple act, I would be picking up a bait box or laying down a table fork, or I would be saying something, and suddenly it would be not I but my father who was saying the words or making the gesture. It gave me a creepy sensation.

5 We went fishing the first morning. I felt the same damp moss covering the worms in the bait can, and saw the dragonfly alight on the tip of my rod as it hovered a few inches from the surface of the water. It was the arrival of this fly that convinced me beyond any doubt that everything was as it always had been, that the years were a mirage and there had been no years. The small waves were the same, chuck-

ing the rowboat under the chin as we fished at anchor, and the boat was the same boat, the same color green and the ribs broken in the same places, and under the floorboards the same fresh-water leavings and debris—the dead helgramite, the wisps of moss, the rusty discarded fishhook, the dried blood from yesterday's catch. We started silently at the tips of our rods, at the dragonflies that came and went. I lowered the tip of mine into the water, tentatively, pensively dislodging the fly, which darted two feet away, poised, darted two feet back, and came to rest again a little farther up the rod. There had been no years between the ducking of this dragonfly and the other one—the one that was part of memory. I looked at the boy, who was silently watching his fly, and it was my hands that held his rod, my eyes watching. I felt dizzy and didn't know which rod I was at the end of.

6   We caught two bass, hauling them in briskly as though they were mackerel, pulling them over the side of the boat in a businesslike manner without any landing net, and stunning them with a blow on the back of the head. When we got back for a swim before lunch, the lake was exactly where we had left it, the same number of inches from the dock, and there was only the merest suggestion of a breeze. This seemed an utterly enchanted sea, this lake you could leave to its own devices for a few hours and come back to, and find that it had not stirred, this constant and trustworthy body of water. In the shallows, the dark, water-soaked sticks and twigs, smooth and old, were undulating in clusters on the bottom against the clean ribbed sand, and the track of the mussel was plain. A school of minnows swam by, each minnow with its small individual shadow, doubling the attendance, so clear and sharp in the sunlight. Some of the other campers were in swimming, along the shore, one of them with a cake of soap, and the water felt thin and clear and unsubstantial. Over the years there had been this person with the cake of soap, this cultist, and here he was. There had been no years.

7   Up to the farmhouse to dinner through the teeming, dusty field, the road under our sneakers was only a two-track road. The middle track was missing, the one with the marks of the hooves and the splotches of dried, flaky manure. There had always been three tracks to choose from in choosing which track to walk in; now the choice was narrowed down to two. For a moment I missed terribly the middle alternative. But the way led past the tennis court, and something about the way it lay there in the sun reassured me; the tape had loosened along the backline, the alleys were green with plantains and other weeds, and the net (installed in June and removed in September) sagged in the dry noon, and the whole place steamed with midday heat and hunger and emptiness. There was a choice of pie for dessert, and one was blueberry and one was apple, and the waitresses were the same country girls, there having been no passage of time, only the illusion of it as in a dropped curtain—the waitresses were still fifteen; their hair had been washed, that was the only difference—they had been to the movies and seen the pretty girls with the clean hair.

8   Summertime, oh summertime, pattern of life indelible, the fade-proof lake, the woods unshatterable, the pasture with the sweet-fern and the juniper forever and ever, summer without end; this was the

background, and the life along the shore was the design, the cottages with their innocent and tranquil design, their tiny docks with the flag-pole and the American flag floating against the white clouds in the blue sky, the little paths over the roots of the trees leading from camp to camp and the paths leading back to the outhouses and the can of lime for sprinkling, and at the souvenir counters at the store the minia-ture birch-bark canoes and the post cards that showed things looking a little better than they looked. This was the American family at play, escaping the city heat, wondering whether the newcomers in the camp at the head of the cove were "common" or "nice," wondering whether it was true that the people who drove up for Sunday dinner at the farmhouse were turned away because there wasn't enough chicken.

9   It seemed to me, as I kept remembering all this, that those times and those summers had been infinitely precious and worth saving. There had been jollity and peace and goodness. The arriving (at the beginning of August) had been so big a business in itself, at the rail-way station the farm wagon drawn up, the first smell of the pine-laden air, the first glimpse of the smiling farmer, and the great importance of the trunks and your father's enormous authority in such matters, and the feel of the wagon under you for the long ten-mile haul, and at the top of the last long hill catching the first view of the lake after eleven months of not seeing this cherished body of water. The shouts and cries of the other campers when they saw you, and the trunks to be unpacked, to give up their rich burden. (Arriving was less exciting nowadays, when you sneaked up in your car and parked it under a tree near the camp and took out the bags and in five minutes it was all over, no fuss, no loud wonderful fuss about trunks.)

10   Peace and goodness and jollity. The only thing that was wrong now, really, was the sound of the place, an unfamiliar nervous sound of the outboard motors. This was the note that jarred, the one thing that would sometimes break the illusion and set the years moving. In those other summertimes, all the motors were inboard; and when they were at a little distance, the noise they made was a sedative, an ingredient of summer sleep. They were one-cylinder and two-cylinder engines, and some were make-and-break and some were jump-spark, but they all made a sleepy sound across the lake. The one-lungers throbbed and fluttered, and the twin-cylinder ones purred and purred, and that was a quiet sound too. But now the campers all had outboards. In the daytime, in the hot mornings, these motors made a petulant, irritable sound; at night, in the still evening when the afterglow lit the water, they whined about one's ears like mosquitoes. My boy loved our rented outboard, and his great desire was to achieve singlehanded mastery over it, and authority, and he soon learned the trick of choking it a little (but not too much), and the adjustment of the needle valve. Watching him I would remember the things you could do with the old one-cylinder engine with the heavy flywheel, how you could have it eating out of your hand if you got really close to it spiritually. Motor boats in those days didn't have clutches, and you made a landing by shutting off the motor at the proper time and coasting in with a dead rudder. But there was a way of reversing them, if you learned the trick, by cutting the switch and putting it on again exactly on the final dying

revolution of the flywheel, so that it would kick back against compression and begin reversing. Approaching a dock in a strong following breeze it was difficult to slow up sufficiently by the ordinary coasting method, and if a boy felt he had complete mastery over his motor, he was tempted to keep it running beyond its time and then reverse it a few feet from the dock. It took a cool nerve, because if you threw the switch a twentieth of a second too soon you would catch the flywheel when it still had speed enough to go up past center, and the boat would leap ahead, charging bull-fashion at the dock.

11   We had a good week at camp. The bass were biting well and the sun shone endlessly, day after day. We would be tired at night and lie down in the accumulated heat of the little bedrooms after the long hot day and the breeze would stir almost imperceptibly outside and the smell of the swamp drift in through the rusty screens. Sleep would come easily and in the morning the red squirrel would be on the roof, tapping out his gay routine. I kept remembering everything, lying in the bed in the morning—the small steamboat that had a long rounded stern like the lip of a Ubangi, and how quietly she ran on the moonlight sails, when the older boys played their mandolins and the girls sang and we ate doughnuts dipped in sugar, and how sweet the music was on the water in the shining night, and what it had felt like to think about girls then. After breakfast we would go up to the store and the things were in the same place—the minnows in a bottle, the plugs and spinners disarranged and pawed over by the youngsters from the boys' camp, the fig newtons and the Beeman's gum. Outside, the road was tarred and cars stood in front of the store. Inside, all was just as it had always been, except there was more Coca Cola and not so much Moxie and root beer and birch beer and sarsaparilla. We would walk out with a bottle of pop apiece and sometimes the pop would backfire up our noses and hurt. We explored the streams, quietly, where the turtles slid off the sunny logs and dug their way into the soft bottom; and we lay on the town wharf and fed worms to the tame bass. Everywhere we went I had trouble making out which was I, the one walking at my side, the one walking in my pants.

12   One afternoon while we were there at that lake a thunderstorm came up. It was like the revival of an old melodrama that I had seen long ago with childish awe. The second-act climax of the drama of the electrical disturbance over a lake in America had not changed in any important respect. This was the big scene, still the big scene. The whole thing was so familiar, the first feeling of oppression and heat and a general air around camp of not wanting to go very far away. In mid-afternoon (it was all the same) a curious darkening of the sky, and a lull in everything that had made life tick; and then the way the boats suddenly swung the other way at their moorings with the coming of a breeze out of the new quarter, and the premonitory rumble. Then the kettle drum, then the snare, then the bass drum and cymbals, then crackling light against the dark, and the gods grinning and licking their chops in the hills. Afterward the calm, the rain steadily rustling in the calm lake, the return of light and hope and spirits, and the campers running out in joy and relief to go swimming in the rain, their bright cries perpetuating the deathless joke about how they were getting

simply drenched, and the children screaming with delight at the new sensation of bathing in the rain, and the joke about getting drenched linking the generations in a strong indestructible chain. And the comedian who waded in carrying an umbrella.

13   When the others went swimming my son said he was going in too. He pulled his dripping trunks from the line where they had hung all through the shower, and wrung them out. Languidly, and with no thought of going in, I watched him, his hard little body, skinny and bare, saw him wince slightly as he pulled up around his vitals the small, soggy, icy garment. As he buckled the swollen belt suddenly my groin felt the chill of death.

D. H. Lawrence (1885–1930) has been called the great high priest of sex in contemporary English literature. Such a judgment is unfair, however, and stems chiefly from his authorship of "Lady Chatterley's Lover," which caused a sensation when it appeared in 1928. Born in Nottingham of lower-class parents, Lawrence taught school for several years upon graduation from college. His novels express his conviction that a new world should be created in which men could live unhampered by notions of racial or religious superiority. His most signficant novels, in addition to "Lady Chatterley's Lover," are "Sons and Lovers" (1913), "Women in Love" (1921), and "The Plumed Serpent" (1926).

It is market day in a Mexican village. Notice that the tempo and tone of the writing match the leisurely pace of the Indians as they plod to the marketplace.

D. H. Lawrence

Market Day

1 This is the last Saturday before Christmas. The next year will be momentous, one feels. This year is nearly gone. Dawn was windy, shaking the leaves, and the rising sun shone under a gap of yellow cloud. But at once it touched the yellow flowers that rise above the *patio* wall, and the swaying, glowing magenta of the bougainvillea, and the fierce red outbursts of the poinsettia. The poinsettia is very splendid, the flowers very big, and of a sure stainless red. They call them Noche Buenas, flowers of Christmas Eve. These tufts throw out their scarlet sharply, like red birds ruffling in the wind of dawn as if going to bathe,

all their feathers alert. This for Christmas, instead of holly-berries. Christmas seems to need a red herald.

2 The Yucca is tall, higher than the house. It is, too, in flower, hanging an arm's-length of soft creamy bells, like a yard-long grape-cluster of foam. And the waxy bells break on their stems in the wind, fall noiselessly from the long creamy bunch, that hardly sways.

3 The coffee-berries are turning red. The hibiscus flowers, rose-coloured, sway at the tips of the thin branches, in rosettes of soft red.

4 In the second *patio,* there is a tall tree of the flimsy acacia sort. Above itself it puts up whitish fingers of flowers, naked on the blue sky. And in the wind these fingers of flowers in the bare blue sky sway with the reeling, roundward motion of tree-tips in a wind.

5 A restless morning, with clouds lower down, moving also with a larger roundward motion. Everything moving. Best to go out in motion too, the slow roundward motion like the hawks.

6 Everything seems slowly to circle and hover toward a central point, the clouds, the mountains round the valley, the dust that rises, the big, beautiful white-barred hawks, *gabilanes,* and even the snow-white flakes of flowers upon the dim palo blanco tree. Even the organ cactus, rising in stock-straight clumps, and the candelabrum cactus, seem to be slowly wheeling and pivoting upon a centre, close upon it.

7 Strange that we should think in straight lines, when there are none, and talk of straight courses, when every course, sooner or later, is seen to be making the sweep round, swooping upon the centre. When space is curved, and the cosmos is sphere within sphere, and the way from any one point to any other point is round the bend of the inevitable, that turns as the tips of the broad wings of the hawk turn upward, leaning upon the air like the invisible half of the ellipse. If I have a way to go, it will be round the swoop of a bend impinging centripetal toward the centre. The straight course is hacked out in rounds, against the will of the world.

8 Yet the dust advances like a ghost along the road, down the valley plain. The dry turf of the valley-bed gleams like soft skin, sunlit and pinkish ochre, spreading wide between the mountains that seem to emit their own darkness, a dark-blue vapor translucent, sombering them from the humped crests downward. The many-pleated, noiseless mountains of Mexico.

9 And away on the footslope lie the white specks of Huayapa, among its lake of trees. It is Saturday, and the white dots of men are threading down the trail over the bare humps to the plain, following the dark twinkle-movement of asses, the dark nodding of the woman's head as she rides between the baskets. Saturday and marketday, and morning, so the white specks of men, like sea-gulls on plough-land, come ebbing like sparks from the palo blanco, over the fawn undulating of the valley slope.

10 They are dressed in snow-white cotton, and they lift their knees in the Indian trot, following the ass where the woman sits perched between the huge baskets, her child tight in the rebozo, at the brown breast. And girls in long, full, soiled cotton skirts running, trotting, ebbing along after the twinkle-movement of the ass. Down they come

in families, in clusters, in solitary ones, threading with ebbing, running, barefoot movement noiseless toward the town, that blows the bubbles of its church-domes above the stagnant green of trees, away under the opposite fawn-skin hills.

11   But down the valley middle comes the big road, almost straight. You will know it by the tall walking of the dust, that hastens also toward the town, overtaking, overpassing everybody. Overpassing all the dark little figures and the white specks that thread tinily, in a sort of under-world, to the town.

12   From the valley villages and from the mountains the peasants and the Indians are coming in with supplies, the road is like a pilgrimage, with the dust in greatest haste, dashing for town. Dark-eared asses and running men, running women, running girls, running lads, twinkling donkeys ambling on fine little feet, under twin great baskets with tomatoes and gourds, twin great nets of bubble-shaped jars, twin bundles of neat-cut faggots of wood, neat as bunches of cigarettes, and twin net-sacks of charcoal. Donkeys, mules, on they come, great pannier baskets making a rhythm under the perched woman, great bundles bouncing against the sides of the slim-footed animals. A baby donkey trotting naked after its piled-up dam, a white, sandal-footed man following with the silent Indian haste, and a girl running again on light feet.

13   Onward, on a strange current of haste. And slowly rowing among the foot-travel, the ox-wagons rolling solid wheels below the high net of the body. Slow oxen, with heads pressed down nosing to the earth, swaying, swaying their great horns as a snake sways itself, the shovel-shaped collar of solid wood pressing down on their necks like a scoop. On, on between the burnt-up turf and the solid, monumental green of the organ cactus. Past the rocks and the floating palo blanco flowers, past the towsled dust of the mesquite bushes. While the dust once more, in a greater haste than anyone, comes tall and rapid down the road, overpowering and obscuring all the little people, as in a cataclysm.

14   They are mostly small people, of the Zapotec race: small men with lifted chests and quick, lifted knees, advancing with heavy energy in the midst of dust. And quiet, small, round-headed women running barefoot, tightening their blue rebozos round their shoulders, so often with a baby in the fold. The white cotton clothes of the men so white that their faces are invisible places of darkness under their big hats. Clothed darkness, faces of night, quickly, silently, with inexhaustible energy advancing to the town.

15   And many of the Serranos, the Indians from the hills, wearing their little conical black felt hats, seem capped with night, above the straight white shoulders. Some have come far, walking all yesterday in their little black hats and black-sheathed sandals. Tomorrow they will walk back. And their eyes will be just the same, black and bright and wild, in the dark faces. They have no goal, any more than the hawks in the air, and no course to run, any more than the clouds.

16   The market is a huge roofed-in place. Most extraordinary is the noise that comes out, as you pass along the adjacent street. It is a huge

noise, yet you may never notice it. It sounds as if all the ghosts in the world were talking to one another, in ghost-voices, within the darkness of the market structure. It is a noise something like rain, or banana leaves in a wind. The market, full of Indians, dark-faced, silent-footed, hush-spoken, but pressing in in countless numbers. The queer hissing murmurs of the Zapotec *idioma,* among the sounds of Spanish, the quiet, aside-voices of the Mixtecas.

17 To buy and to sell, but above all, to commingle. In the old world, men make themselves two great excuses for coming together to a centre, and commingling freely in a mixed, unsuspicious host. Market and religion. These alone bring men, unarmed, together since time began. A little load of firewood, a woven blanket, a few eggs and to-matoes are excuse enough for men, women, and children to cross the foot-weary miles of valley and mountain, To buy, to sell, to barter, to exchange. To exchange, above all things, human contact.

18 That is why they like you to bargain, even if it's only the difference of a centavo. Round the centre of the covered market, where there is a basin of water, are the flowers: red, white, pink roses in heaps, many-coloured little carnations, poppies, bits of larkspur, lemon and orange marigolds, buds of madonna lilies, pansies, a few forget-me-nots. They don't bring the tropical flowers. Only the lilies come wild from the hills, and the mauve red orchids.

19 "How much this bunch of cherry-pie heliotrope?"
20 "Fifteen centavos."
21 "Ten."
22 "Fifteen."
23 You put back the cherry-pie, and depart. But the woman is quite content. The contact, so short even, brisked her up.
24 "Pinks?"
25 "The red ones, Señorita? Thirty centavos."
26 "No. I don't want red ones. The mixed."
27 "Ah!" The woman seizes a handful of little carnations of all colours, carefully puts them together. "Look Señorita! No more?"
28 "No, no more. How much?"
29 "The same. Thirty centavos."
30 "It is much."
31 "No, Señorita, it is not much. Look at this little bunch. It is eight centavos." — Displays a scrappy little bunch. "Come then, twenty-five."
32 "No! Twenty-two."
33 "Look!" She gathers up three or four more flowers, and claps them to the bunch. "Two *reales,* Señorita."
34 It is a bargain. Off you go with multicoloured pinks, and the woman has had one more moment of contact, with a stranger, a perfect stranger. An intermingling of voices, a threading together of different wills. It is life. The centavos are an excuse.

Alexander H. Leighton (1908–
), professor of social psychiatry at Cornell University and
author of several articles and
textbooks in that field, received
his training at Princeton, Cambridge, and Johns Hopkins universities. He has done fieldwork
in anthropology among the
Navaho Indians and the Eskimos of Alaska.

The pain and horror of "that
day" at Hiroshima are re-cre-
ated by Leighton, who visited
Japan as a research leader of
the United States Strategic
Bombing Survey of Japan.

ALEXANDER H. LEIGHTON

That Day at Hiroshima

1   We approached Hiroshima a little after daybreak on a winter day, driving in a jeep below a leaden sky and in the face of a cold, wet wind. On either side of the road, black felt fields were turning green under winter wheat. Here and there peasants worked, swinging spades or grubbing in mud and water with blue hands. Some in black split-toed shoes left tracks like cloven hoofs. To the north, looming close over the level land, mountains thrust heavy summits of pine darkly against the overcast. To the south and far away, the bay lay in dull brightness under fitful rain.

2   "Hiroshima," said the driver, a GI from a Kansas farm, who had been through the city many times, "don't look no different from any other bombed town. You soon get used to it. You'll see little old mud walls right in the middle of town that wasn't knocked down. They been exaggerating about that bomb."

3   Within a few miles the fields along the road were replaced by houses and shops that looked worn and dull yet intact. On the road itself people straggled to work, some on bicycles, most of them on foot—

tattered and bandy-legged old men, girls with red cheeks and bright eyes, ancient women under towering bundles, middle-aged men looking stiff in Western business suits. In one place there were several Koreans together, the women easily distinguished from the Japanese by their white blouses and the full skirts that swung as they strode. At a bus stop a crowd stood waiting in a line long enough to fill a train. Half a mile farther on we passed the bus, small, battered, and gray, standing half obliterated by the cloud of smoke that came from the charcoal burner at the back while the driver stood working at its machinery.

4   Children of all ages waved, laughed, and shouted at us as had the children in other parts of Japan.

5   "Haro-goodabye! Haro-goodabye!"

6   "Jeepu! Jeeeepu!"

7   Like the children of Hamelin to the piper, they came rushing, at the sound of our approach, from doorways and alleyways and from behind houses, to line up by the road and cheer. One little fellow of about six threw himself into the air, his little body twisting and feet kicking in a fit of glee.

8   The adults gazed at us with solemn eyes or looked straight ahead. They were more subdued than those I had seen elsewhere in Japan. The children seemed different, possessed by some common animation denied their elders—an animation which impelled them toward the occupation forces, toward the strong and the new.

9   Presently a two-story trade school appeared, with boards instead of window glass, and then a factory in the same condition. Soon there were shops and houses all along the way with windows missing. A house came into view with its roof pressed down, tiles scattered, and walls bulging outward. A shop with no front, like an open mouth, showed its contents, public and private, clear to the rear window.

10   The road turned to the Ota River, where the tide was running out and boats lay heaved over on the beach. A bridge ended suddenly like a headless neck. Now every house and shop was damaged and lay with only one end or a corner standing.

11   Then all the buildings ceased and we came as if from a forest out on a plain, as if from tumult into silence. Imagine a city dump with its smells of wet ashes, mold, and things rotting, but that runs from your feet almost to the limits of vision. As is often the case with level and desolate places on the earth, the sky seemed close above it. The predominant colors were red and yellow, crumbles of stone, bricks, red earth, and rust. Low walls made rectangles that marked where houses had stood, like sites of prehistoric villages. Here and there in the middle distance, a few large buildings stood about, buttes in the rubble of the plain.

12   "You see them?" said the driver, as if it were a triumph for his side. "The bomb didn't knock *them* down."

13   Running like ruler lines through the waste were black roads surprisingly dotted with people, some on foot and some in carts of all sizes drawn by man, woman, horse, or cow. Clothing was old and tattered and of every combination from full European to full Japanese. People looked as if they had grabbed what they could from a rummage sale.

14   Occasionally, blending like protective coloration with the rubble were shacks built out of fragments of boards and iron. Around them were vegetable gardens, for the most part full of *daikon,* Japanese radish. A few more pretentious sheds were going up, shining bright yellow with new boards.

15   We slowed down to go around a piece of cornice that lay partly across the road like a glacial boulder, and from somewhere in a band of children who cheered and called to us came the gift of a tangerine that landed on the floor of the jeep. Wondering at them, I picked it up and put it in my pocket.

16   When crossing a bridge, we could see down through the swiftly running water to stone and shells on the bottom. This clearness gave a feeling of odd contrast to the disorder of the land. We passed a number of trees burned black but still holding up some leafless branches as if in perpetual winter.

17   The drive ended at a large building that was still standing, a former bank, now a police headquarters, where I had an appointment with the chief to arrange for office space and guides. The driver said, as he got out, "This is it."

II

18 One hears it said that, after all, Japanese cities were really a collection of tinderboxes, while American urban centers are made of stronger stuff. In Hiroshima there were many buildings of types common in the United States and some, prepared against earthquakes, far stronger. The engineers of the U.S. Strategic Bombing Survey concluded from their examination that "the overwhelming bulk of buildings in American cities would not stand up against an atomic bomb bursting at a mile or a mile and a half from them." To this must be added the realization that the bomb dropped at Hiroshima will be considered primitive by future standards.

19   The bank building which housed the police headquarters was a well-made structure of stone, three stories high. Through an imposing entrance my interpreter and I went past tall and solid metal doors that were bent inward like cardboard and no longer usable. The lobby was large and high, but dark because it had no window glass and the openings were boarded up to keep out the wind. Through poor light there loomed the white face of a clock up on one wall, its hands pointing to 8:10 — the time it had stopped on August 6.

20   In the years when that clock had been going, Hiroshima had been a city, at first unknown to Europe and America, then a source of immigrants to the United States, and finally an enemy port. It lay on a delta between the seven mouths of the Ota and was traversed by canals and an ancient highway that connected Kyoto in the east with Shimonoseki in the west. Close around the city stood mountains covered with red pine, while before it stretched the bay, indented with headlands and spread with islands, in places narrow and steep like a fjord. In shallows near the shore, rows of poles stood as if in a bean patch, set in the sea to anchor oysters and to catch edible seaweed passing in the tide. In deeper water, fishing boats with hawkish prows

and planked with red pine were tending nets. A few fishermen used cormorants to make their catch.

21   Hiroshima had expanses of park, residences, gardens, orange and persimmon trees. Since there had been much traveling back and forth by relatives of immigrants to California, the influence of the United States was marked, On main streets there were movies and restaurants with facades that would have fitted into shopping districts of Bakersfield or San Diego.

22   But Hiroshima was also ancient. Its feudal castle raised a five-story keep that could be seen a long distance over the level land of the delta. There were three large temples and many smaller ones and the tombs of the Asano family and of the wife and son of the leader of the Forty-seven Ronin, Oishi-Yoshio. There were also Christian churches, whose bells mingled with the temple gongs and the honking of auto horns and the rattling of trolleys.

23   The people of the city had earned their living by buying and selling farm produce and fish, by making mountain pines into boats for the fishing fleet of the Inland Sea, by meat packing, rubber processing, and oil refining, by making textiles from the cocoons of wild silkworms, by brewing rice and grape wine, by manufacturing paper umbrellas, needles, *tabi* socks, small arms, metal castings, and by working in utilities and services such as electricity, transportation, schools, and hospitals.

24   During the war there was an increase of industrialization, and plants grew up, chiefly in the outskirts.

25   There was a famous gay district with little streets along which a person walking in the night could hear laughter, the twang of the *samisen,* and geishas singing.

26   The university had been an active cultural center but also stressed athletics, particularly swimming. There were sometimes mass aquatic exercises when hundreds of students would swim for miles, strung out in the bay in a long line with boats attending.

27   Although not a fortified town, Hiroshima was a major military command station, supply depot, and staging area because of its protected position and because of Ujina Harbor with access to the Pacific, the Sea of Japan, and the East China Sea. More than a third of the city's land was taken up with military installations, and from the harbor troopships left for Korea, Manchuria, China, and the southern regions. However, toward the end of hostilities, most of the shipping had ceased because of sinkings in the Inland Sea.

28   The population of Hiroshima was given as well over 300,000 before war, but this was reduced by evacuation, before the atomic bomb fell, probably to about 245,000. It is still not certain how many the bomb killed, but the best estimate is from 70,000 to 80,000.

III

29 About seven o'clock on the morning of August 6 there was an air-raid warning and three planes were reported in the vicinity. No one was much disturbed. For a long time B-29's flying over in small numbers had been a common sight. At some future date, Hiroshima might

suffer an incendiary raid from masses of planes such as had devastated other Japanese cities. With this possibility in mind there had been evacuations, and firebreaks were being prepared. But on this particular morning there could be no disaster from just three planes.

30   By 7:30 the "all clear" had sounded and people were thinking again of the day's plans, looking forward to their affairs and engagements of the morning and afternoon. The castle keep stood in the sun. Children bathed in the river. Farmers labored in the fields and fishermen on the water. City stores and factories got under way with their businesses.

31   In the heart of the city near the buildings of the Prefectural Government and at the intersection of the business streets, everybody had stopped and stood in a crowd gazing up at three parachutes floating down through the blue air.

32   The bomb exploded several hundred feet above their heads.

33   The people for miles around Hiroshima, in the fields, in the mountains, and on the bay, saw a light that was brilliant even in the sun, and felt heat. A countrywoman was going out to her farm when suddenly, "I saw a light reflected on the mountain and then a streak just like lightning came."

34   A town official was crossing a bridge on his bicycle about ten miles from the heart of the city when he felt the right side of his face seared, and thinking that he had sunstroke, he jumped to the ground.

35   A woman who was washing dishes noticed that she felt "very warm on the side of my face next the wall. I looked out the window toward the city and saw something like a sun in bright color."

36   At a slower pace, after the flash, came the sound of the explosion, which some people have no recollection of hearing, while others described it as an earth-shaking roar, like thunder or a big wind. A black smoky mass, lit up with color, ascended into the sky and impressed beholders with its beauty. Red, gold, blue, orange, and many other shades mingled with the black.

37   Nearer to the city and at its edges, the explosion made a more direct and individual impact on people. Almost everyone thought that an ordinary bomb had landed very close to him, and only later realized the extent of the damage.

38   A man who was oiling the machinery in a factory saw the lights go out and thought that something must be wrong with the electricity. "But when the roof started crumbling down, I was in a daze, wondering what was happening. Then I noticed my hands and feet were bleeding. I don't know how I hurt myself."

39   Another, who was putting points on needles, was knocked unconscious, and when he came to, found "all my surroundings burned to the ground and flames raging here and there. I ran home for my family without knowing I was burned around my head. When I arrived home, our house was devastated and destroyed by flames. I ran to the neighbors and inquired about my family and learned that they had all been taken to safety across the river."

40   An invalid who was drinking tea said, "The tin roof sidings came swirling into my room and everything was black. Rubble and glass and everything you can think of was blasted into my house."

41   Said a woman, "I was in the back of the house doing the washing. All of a sudden, the bomb exploded. My clothes were burned off and I received burns on my legs, arms, and back. The skin was just hanging loose. The first thing I did was run in the air-raid shelter and lie there exhausted. Then I thought of my baby in the house and ran back to it. The whole house was knocked down and was burning. My mother and father came crawling out of the debris, their faces and arms just black. I heard the baby crying, and crawled in and dug it out from under the burning embers. It was pretty badly burned. My mother carried it to the shelter."

42   In the heart of the city death prevailed and few were left to tell us about it. That part of the picture has to be reconstructed, as in archeology, from the remains.

43   The crowd that stood gazing upward at the parachutes went down withered and black, like a burned-out patch of weeds. Flames shot out of the castle keep. Trolleys bulging with passengers stopped, and all died at once, leaving burned figures still standing supporting each other and fingers fused to the straps. The military at their barracks and offices were wiped out. So too were factories full of workers, including students from schools, volunteers from neighboring towns working on the firebreaks, children scavenging for wood, the Mayor's staff, and the units for air-raid precaution, fire, welfare, and relief. The larger war industries, since they were on the fringe of the city, were for the most part not seriously damaged. Most of the personnel in the Prefectural Government offices were killed, though the Governor himself happened to be in Tokyo. In hospitals and clinics, patients, doctors, and nurses all died together, as did the priests and pastors of the temples and the churches. Of 1780 nurses, 1654 were killed, and 90 per cent of the doctors in Hiroshima were casualties.

44   People who were in buildings that sheltered them from the instantaneous effects that accompanied the flash were moments later decapitated or cut to ribbons by flying glass. Others were crushed as walls and floors gave way even in buildings that maintained their outer shells erect. In the thousands of houses that fell, people were pinned below the wreckage, not killed in many cases, but held there till the fire that swept the city caught up with them and put an end to their screams.

45   A police chief said that he was in his back yard when the bomb went off. He was knocked down and a concrete wall fell over him, but he was able to dig himself out and go at once toward the police station in the bank. "When I arrived at the office, I found ten policemen, some severely wounded. These were evacuated to a place of safety where they could get aid. We tried to clean up the glass from the windows, but fire was spreading and a hot southerly wind was blowing. We used a hose with water from a hydrant and also formed a bucket brigade. At noon the water in the hydrants gave out, but in this building we were lucky because we could pump water from a well. We carried buckets up from the basement to the roof and threw water down over the building. People on the road were fainting from the heat and we threw water on them too and carried them into the one room in the building that had not been affected by the bomb. We applied oil and

ointment to those who had burns.

46 "About 1:00 P.M. we began to apply first aid to the people outside, since the fire seemed under control as far as this building was concerned. A doctor came to help. He himself was wounded in one leg. By night this place was covered by a mass of people. One doctor applied all the first aid."

47 A doctor who was at a military hospital outside Hiroshima said that about an hour after the bomb went off, "many, many people came rushing to my clinic. They were rushing in all directions of the compass from the city. Many were stretcher cases. Some had their hair burned off, were injured in the back, had broken legs, arms, and thighs. The majority of the cases were those injured from glass; many had glass imbedded in the body. Next to the glass injuries, the most frequent were those who had their faces and hands burned, and also the chest and back. Most of the people arrived barefooted; many had their clothes burned off. Women were wearing men's clothing and men were wearing women's. They had put on anything they could pick up along the way.

48 "On the first day about 250 came, who were so injured they had to stay in the hospital, and we also attended about 500 others. Of all of these about 100 died."

49 A talkative man in a newspaper office said that the most severely burned people looked like red shrimps. Some had "skin which still burned sagging from the face and body with a reddish-white skin underneath showing."

50 A reporter who was outside the city at the time of the explosion, but came in immediately afterward, noticed among the dead a mother with a baby held tightly in her arms. He saw several women running around nude, red from burns, and without hair. Many people climbed into the water tanks kept for putting out fires and there died. "The most pathetic cases were the small children looking for their parents. There was one child of about eleven with a four-year-old on his back, looking, looking for his mother in vain."

51 Shortly after the bomb fell, there was a high wind, or "fire storm" engendered by the heat, that tore up trees and, whirling over the river, made water spouts. In some areas rain fell.

52 The severly burned woman who had been washing when the bomb fell said that she went down to the river, where "there were many people just dripping from their burns. Many of them were so badly burned that you could see the meat. By this time it was raining pretty badly. I could not walk or lie down or do anything. Water poured into the shelter and I received water blisters as well as blisters from the burns. It rained a lot right after the bomb."

53 Although the fire burned for days, the major destruction did not take very long. A fisherman out on the bay said, "I saw suddenly a flash of light. I thought something burned my face. I hid in the boat face down. When I looked up later, Hiroshima was completely burned."

IV

54 Hiroshima, of course, never had been prepared for a disaster of the magnitude which overtook it, but in addition the organized sources of

aid that did exist were decimated along with everything else. As a result, rescue had to come from surrounding areas, and soon trucks and trains were picking up the wounded, while hospitals, schools, temples, assembly halls, and tents were preparing to receive them. However, the suburbs and surrounding areas were overwhelmed by the rush of immediate survivors out of the bombed region and so, for about a day, help did not penetrate far into the city. This, together with the fact that survivors who were physically uninjured were stunned and bewildered, resulted in great numbers of the wounded dying from lack of aid.

55   The vice-mayor of a neighboring town that began receiving the wounded about 11:30 in the morning said, "Everybody looked alike. The eyes appeared to be a mass of melted flesh. The lips were split up and also looked like a mass of molten flesh. Only the nose appeared the same as before. The death scene was awful. The patient would turn blue and when we touched the body the skin would stick to our hands."

56   Those who ventured into Hiroshima were greeted by sights they were reluctant to describe. A businessman reported: "The bodies of half-dead people lay on the roadside, on the bridges, in the water, in the gardens, and everywhere. It was a sight no one wants to see. Practically all of these people were nude. Their color was brownish blackish and some of their bodies were dripping. There was a fellow whose head was half burned so that I thought he was wearing a hat." Another man said, "The bodies of the dead were so burned that we could not distinguish men from women."

57   In the public parks great numbers of both wounded and dead were congregated. There were cries for aid and cries for water and there were places where unidentifiable shapes merely stirred.

58   In the late afternoon, aid began to come farther into the city from the outer edges. Rice balls and other food were brought. From their mission up the valley a number of Jesuits came, and one of them, Father Siemes, gave a vivid and careful description of what he had seen, when he was later interviewed by members of the Bombing Survey in Tokyo. He said, "Beneath the wreckage of the houses along the way many had been trapped and they screamed to be rescued from the oncoming flames. They had to be left to their fate."

59   On a bridge, he encountered a procession of soldiers "dragging themselves along with the help of staves or carried by their less severely injured comrades. Abandoned on the bridge there stood with sunken heads a number of horses with large burns on their flanks.

60   "Fukai, the secretary of the mission, was completely out of his mind. He did not want to leave the house when the fires were burning closer, and explained that he did not want to survive the destruction of his fatherland." He had to be carried away by force.

61   After dark, the priests helped pull from the river two children who suffered chills and then died. There was a sand-spit in the river, covered with wounded, who cried for help and who were afraid that the rising tide would drown them. After midnight, "only occasionally did we hear calls for help."

62 Many patients were brought to an open field right behind Hiroshima station, and tents were set up for them. Doctors came in from the neighboring prefectures and from near-by towns such as Yamaguchi, Okayama, and Shimane. The Army also took part in relief measures, and all available military facilities and units were mobilized to that end.

63 A fisherman who came to Hiroshima to see what had happened said, "I cannot describe the situation in words, it was so pitiful. To see so many people dead was a terrible sight. Their clothes were shredded and their bodies puffed up, some with tongues hanging out. They were dead in all shapes."

64 As late as the second day the priests noted that among cadavers there were still many wounded alive. "Frightfully injured forms beckoned to us and then collapsed."

65 They carried some to the hospitals, but "we could not move everybody who lay exposed to the sun." It did not make much difference, anyway, for in the hospitals there was little that could be done. They just lay in the corridors, row on row, and died.

66 A businessman came into Hiroshima on the third day. "I went to my brother's house in the suburbs and found that all were wounded but none killed. They were stunned and could hardly speak. The next day, one of the four children died. She got black and blue in the face, just as if you had mashed your finger, and died fifteen minutes after that. In another half hour, her sister did the same thing and she died also."

67 The wife of a soldier who had been with the Hiroshima troops said, "My husband was a soldier and so he was to die, but when it actually happened, I wondered why we did not all go with him. They called me and I went to see. I was to find him in the heap, but I decided against looking at the bodies. I want to remember him as he was— big and healthy, not some horribly charred body. If I saw that, it would remain forever in my eyes."

68 A police chief told how the dead were collected and burned. "Many could not be identified. In cases where it was possible, the corpses or the ashes were given to the immediate family. Mostly, the cremation was done by the police or the soldiers, and the identified ashes were given to the family. The ashes of those not identified were turned over to the City Hall. There still are boxes in the City Hall. Occasionally even now one is identified, or is supposed to be identified, and is claimed."

69 The destroyed heart of Hiroshima consisted of 4.7 square miles, and the best estimates indicate that the mortality rate was 15,000 to the square mile. For many days funeral processions moved along the roads and through the towns and villages all around Hiroshima. The winds were pervaded by the smell of death and cremation. At night the skies were lit with the flames of funeral pyres.

V

70 Very few of the people we interviewed at Hiroshima attempted to make a play for sympathy or to make us feel guilty. The general manner was one which might be interpreted as due either to lingering

apathy and absence of feeling consequent on shock, or to reserve which masked hate. It was probably a mixture of both, in varying degrees in different people. But on the surface everyone appeared willing to cooperate and oblige.

71   An official of a near-by small town thought that "if America had such a weapon, there was no use to go on. Many high school students in Hiroshima who were wounded in the raid spoke incoherently on their deathbeds saying, 'Please avenge that raid for us somehow.' However, most of the people felt that since it was war, it was just *shikata ga nai*, could not be helped. But we were unified in the idea that we had to win the war."

72   A newspaper reporter said that after the bomb fell, some felt that this was the end, while others wanted to go on regardless. "Those who had actually experienced the bomb were the ones who wanted to quit, while those who had not, wanted to go on."

73   The wife of a soldier killed in the blast said, "Though many are resentful against America, I feel no animosity. It was an understood war and the use of weapons was fair. I only wonder why they didn't let the people know about this bomb and give us a chance, before bombing us, to give up."

74   A police chief believed that the general reaction among the people was one of surprise and a feeling that "we have taken the worst beating, we have been the goats." He said, "They felt that America had done a terrible thing and were very bitter, but after the surrender they turned on the Japanese military. They felt they had been fooled, and wondered if the military knew that the bomb was coming and why they did not take steps. The bomb made no difference in the fighting spirit of the people: it drew them together and made them more cooperative. My eldest son was killed, but I felt that it was destiny that ruled. When I see people who got away without any injury, I feel a little pang of envy naturally, but I don't feel bitter toward them."

75   Poking in the ruins one day, I came on the stone figure of a dog, one of that grinning type derived from China which commonly guards the entrances to temples. It was tilted on its pedestal but undamaged, and the grin gleamed out as if it were hailing me. Its rakish air and its look of fiendish satisfaction with all that lay around drew me on to inspect it more closely. It was then apparent that the look was not directed at me, but out somewhere beyond. It was, of course, only a piece of stone, and it displayed no particular artistic merit; yet in looking at it I felt that I was a clod, while it had a higher, sentient wisdom locked within.

76   The look and the feeling it inspired were familiar and I groped to remember where I had seen it before other than on temple dogs. The eyes were creased in a fashion that did not exactly connotate mirth, and the lips were drawn far back in a smile that seemed to blend bitterness, glee, and compassion. The word "sardonic" came to mind, and this led to recognition and a realization of terrible appropriateness.

77   All who have acquaintance with the dead know the curious smile that may creep over the human face as *rigor mortis* sets in, a smile of special quality called by doctors *risus sardonicus*. The dog had this

look, and it seemed to me probable that some ancient Oriental sculptor, in seeking an expression for temple guardians that would drive off evil spirits, had taken this death grin as his model, and thus it had come down through hundreds of years to this beast looking out on Hiroshima.

78   Many a soldier has seen this face looking up at him from the field of battle, before he himself was wearing it, and many a priest and doctor has found himself alone with it in a darkened room. As with the dog, at first the look seems at you, and then beyond you, as if there lay at last behind it knowledge of the huge joke of life which the rest of us feel vaguely but cannot comprehend. And there is that tinge of compassion that is as dreadful as it is unknowable.

79   As I continued to study this stone face, it began to appear that the grin was not directed at the waste and the destruction around, at the red and yellow and the smells, any more than it was at me. It was not so much a face looking at Hiroshima as it was the face of Hiroshima. The carved eyes gazed beyond the rubble, beyond the gardens of radishes and fields of winter wheat, beyond the toiling adults and the rippling children with their tangerines and shouts of "Haro-good-abye!" surging up with new life like flowers and weeds spreading over devastation, beyond the mountains with red pines in the blue sky, beyond all these, over the whole broad shoulder of the world to where, in cities and towns, watches on wrists and clocks on towers still ticked and moved. The face seemed to be smiling and waiting for the harvest of the wind that had been sown.

80   There was one woman in Hiroshima who said, "If there are such things as ghosts, why don't they haunt the Americans?"

81   Perhaps they do.

Glossary of Rhetorical Terms

The definitions of rhetorical terms in this glossary are designed to be brief and concise rather than detailed and comprehensive. The *Guide to Rhetoric*, which follows the glossary, provides page and paragraph references to various rhetorical devices used in the text.

Allegory a fictional representation of truths or generalizations about human nature. For instance, good and evil may be represented symbolically by persons or animals in a fable.

Allusion a hint or indirect reference to a person, object, or action.

Analogy a comparison of two things or situations that are not exactly alike but still resemble each other in some particulars. Analogy is often used for argument or explanation.

Analysis the technique of dividing a topic into basic parts or divisions to show their relationships and functions.

Argumentation traditionally, one of the four basic kinds of discourse. (The others are *Description*, *Exposition*, and *Narration*.) The purpose of argumentation is to convince the reader of the truth or relevance of the author's position, to persuade him to adopt that point of view, or take the action recommended. The means used are objective evidence and logic.

Balanced Sentence a balanced sentence is one in which similar or opposing thoughts are arranged in parallel structure. See also *Parallelism*.

Beginnings a good beginning does two things: it introduces the subject to be discussed and it catches the reader's interest. Some ways to begin your essays: start with a statement of fact, a short sentence that will startle the reader, an anecdote related to the topic, or a question.

Cause and Effect a common method of development that examines events and their causes.

Chronological Order a method of development commonly used in narrative writing in which events are presented in the order in which they happen in time.

Classification a grouping of persons, objects, or ideas into categories on the basis of similarities or common qualities.

Cliché an overworked or trite expression or phrase.

Coherence a paragraph or an essay has coherence when its various parts (sentences in the first case, paragraphs in the second) fit together to form an integrated whole. See also *Unity*.

Comparison and Contrast a method of paragraph and theme development in which the similarities and differences between two or more objects or ideas are pointed out.

Connotation and Denotation the denotation of a word is its literal dictionary meaning; its connotation is the meaning it conveys because of the context in which it is used or the particular associations it has for the reader.

Contrast See *Comparison and Contrast.*

Deduction a method of reasoning in which the conclusion follows necessarily from the premises presented. The pattern of development proceeds from the general to the specific. See also *Induction.*

Definition in logic, placing a term in a general class and then showing how it differs from others within that class. In rhetoric, definition is a method of development in which the meaning of a term is shown by various techniques; for example, by description, by example, by synonyms, by origin or history, or by comparison or contrast.

Denotation See *Connotation and Denotation.*

Description traditionally, one of the four basic kinds of discourse. (The others are *Argumentation, Exposition,* and *Narration.*) Description conveys a sensory impression of a person, object, or feeling.

Diction in rhetoric, diction refers to choice of words in speaking or writing. The skillful writer chooses words that are clear, effective, and appropriate.

Endings your themes should not merely stop; they should end with an effective conclusion. Some ways to end your essay: summarize your major ideas; conclude with a restatement of your thesis; draw a logical conclusion from the facts you have presented.

Exemplification the use of examples to explain or clarify a subject. Examples may be used either as evidence to support the author's thesis or as illustrations in a deductive pattern.

Exposition traditionally, one of the four basic kinds of discourse. (See also *Argumentation, Description,* and *Narration.*) The purpose of exposition is to inform, illustrate, or explain.

Figurative Language language that goes beyond the literal meaning of the words or phrases. See also *Hyperbole, Litotes, Metaphor, Metonymy, Oxymoron, Personification,* and *Simile.*

Hyperbole the use of extravagent exaggeration for emphasis or intensification (a figure of speech).

Idiom an expression in a language that either does not conform to conventional rules of grammar or has a meaning that cannot be derived from the literal meaning of the words involved. Such common expressions as "to strike a bargain" and "to catch a cold" are idioms. (As idioms wear, they often turn into clichés.)

Imagery language that conveys sensory impressions. In writing, images tell us about the sounds, smells, tastes, and sights of life.

Induction a method of reasoning in which a conclusion is reached by observing a number of specific examples. The pattern of development proceeds from the specific to the general. See also *Deduction.*

Irony   the expression of a meaning that is different from, and sometimes the exact opposite of, the literal meaning of the words themselves. In other words, irony says one thing and means another.

Litotes, or Understatement   a figure of speech that affirms an idea by denying its opposite. For example: This is no small change you have suggested.

Loose Sentence   a sentence with the main idea or statement at the beginning and subordinate statements following.

Metaphor   strictly speaking, a figure of speech that implies a likeness between two otherwise unlike objects; for example, "Tommy wolfed down his dinner." (Compare *Simile*.)

Metonymy and Synecdoche   metonymy is the use of one name for something closely related to it, as when we say "the White House [actually, a representative of the executive branch of the government] announced the appointment of a new Secretary of the Interior this morning." Synecdoche is the use of the part to signify the whole, or vice versa. ("He asked for the girl's hand in marriage.") Some authorities make a distinction between these two figures of speech; others use metonymy to cover both.

Mood   the dominant emotional state or feeling of a literary work.

Narration   the recounting of action over a period of time. Narration is one of the four basic kinds of discourse. (The others are *Argumentation*, *Description*, and *Exposition*.)

Onomatopoeia   words whose names are derived from the sounds they describe: for example, "the boom of the cannon; the buzzing of the bees."

Oxymoron   a paradoxical combination of seemingly contradictory words in one figure of speech. For example: "friendly enemy," "eloquent silence," "mournful optimist."

Paradox   a statement that seems to contradict itself; as a rhetorical device, paradox can be used to attract attention or to create emphasis.

Parallelism   the arrangement of syntactically similar words, phrases, or clauses in equal or parallel structures.

Parody   a literary work that closely imitates the style of another work or author for purposes of humor or ridicule.

Periodic sentence   a sentence whose main elements and ideas are placed at the end rather than the beginning.

Personification   a figure of speech in which human feelings or characteristics are ascribed to nonhuman creatures, objects, or abstract ideas.

Rhetoric   the study of the principles of composition. Included in the study of rhetoric are such matters as usage, coherence, unity, logic, persuasion, appropriateness to the occasion.

Rhetorical Question   a question to which no answer is expected or required. This device is used by writers to dramatize a situation or to make a comment.

Satire   any use of derisive wit to attack human follies or vices by making them appear ridiculous or contemptible.

Sentence Variety variation in the length and structure of sentences. There are certain pitfalls to overcome: a series of short, choppy sentences; rambling, directionless long ones; a series of sentences that begin with the subject only, rather than with an occasional modifier; a series of periodic sentences whose main ideas are buried and therefore lack emphasis.

Simile a figure of speech in which two essentially unlike things are explicitly compared; usually introduced by *like, as,* or *than.* (Compare *Metaphor.*)

Slang the nonstandard vocabulary of a given culture or subculture, often characterized by raciness and spontaneity. Some slang words are colorful or specific and eventually become respectable; others are trite, flat, and vague in meaning.

Style the distinctive characteristics or qualities of a writer's work.

Support in argumentative writing, evidence furnished to prove the author's thesis. Support often consists of observation, personal experience, or reliable authority.

Symbolism a device in which one thing is used to represent another because of association, resemblance, or convention. The moon, for example, is often used as a symbol for romance, distance, or the unattainable.

Synecdoche See *Metonymy.*

Syntax the arrangement of words into phrases and sentences. This term is generally used in commenting on the structure of a literary work.

Thesis the central topic or idea in a composition; the sentence containing such a statement.

Tone the author's attitude toward his topic or his audience as reflected in his writing. Tone can vary from neutral or objective to pompous, sentimental, arrogant, cynical, ironic, or sarcastic. It is determined by diction and by selection and arrangement of facts.

Transition ways in which an author moves from one topic — or aspect of a topic — to another. Transition is usually accomplished by recognizable linguistic devices such as repetition of words and phrases, restatement of sentences, or indirect references. In a great deal of contemporary writing, mechanical devices such as stars, subheads, or a series of periods are used to show transitions.

Understatement See *Litotes.*

Unity the development of one subject or theme at a time. A paragraph or composition that has unity contains only those sentences and ideas that develop its central or guiding purpose. See also *Coherence.*

Usage the actual way in which a language or its elements are used or pronounced. Usage is concerned with the differences between standard and nonstandard, formal and informal, English. See also *Diction.*

Guide to Rhetoric

In the process of analyzing the essays in this text, we annotated each one, marking certain paragraphs for strong and good use of various rhetorical devices. We thought that this information might be helpful to others who are studying the essays from a rhetorical point of view. The following list is by no means exhaustive, but it does offer specific examples of effective usage of eighteen rhetorical principles and devices.

23456/987654321